Frommer's®

New York City

My New York City

by Brian Silverman

NEW YORKERS ARE GREAT COMPLAINERS. WE LIKE TO BITCH AND MOAN. And this is a good thing. Our grumbling keeps us on our toes.

We're also initially suspicious of the new—of invasions to our beloved landscape. When the twin towers of the World Trade Center were constructed, many of us saw them as a blight on the city's famous skyline. Compared with treasures like the Empire State Building and the Chrysler Building, they were abominations. Generations later, we mourn their loss not just because of the lives that went down with them, but because they'd become part of our spiritual landscape, symbols of our sheer brashness, our restless energy, our drive.

What makes New York a true original, however, is not one building or museum but the sum of it all, including the people. Las Vegas can create an instant New York on the Strip, but it's a fantasy—you need New Yorkers to make New York. The city, and the spirit it embodies, just cannot be duplicated. I have no complaints about that.

Here are some of the places I like to go back to over and over. You won't want to miss them either.

© Eric Kamp/Index Stock

CENTRAL PARK (left) I'm very fortunate to live with my family near Central Park. It's like having our own personal nature preserve—except that we share it with thousands of others. Central Park is one of the best places in the city for people-watching, especially during summer. The parade of bikers, joggers, roller-bladers, and strollers is a source of endless amusement. And the park has so many routes I never get never bored. Pictured here is the Mall, with its wide walkway and overarching elms.

THE ROSE CENTER FOR EARTH AND SPACE (above) City icons don't develop overnight. But as soon as this giant glass cube opened 5 years ago, it was an instant hit. Inside, a four-story-high planetarium offers one of the most technologically advanced sky shows on the planet. This futuristic structure, draped in the largest suspended glass curtain wall in the U.S., is the perfect complement to the dusty dinosaurs inside the American Museum of Natural History, the building both share.

SUBWAY MUSICIANS (left) Most of us who live in New York spend a good deal of time taking the subways. It's the fastest and cheapest way to get around and not as complicated as it might seem. Rushing like rats through the stations to make connections, we're cheered on by sounds of music, even if we stop only long enough to drop a quarter in a cup. What makes the beat so special is that you never know when or where you'll hear it, or what it might be. Here, a jazz duo has found an impromptu stage to show off their stuff.

CENTRAL PARK RESERVOIR (below) Also known as the Jacqueline Kennedy Onassis Reservoir, this is my favorite place for a jog. I'm not alone: The 1½-mile jogging track around the reservoir is packed with joggers in the morning and after work. What makes it so special are the views. As you circle east you see the stately apartment buildings of Fifth Avenue. From the north end you can see the Manhattan skyline to the south. The view west reveals the majestic Art Deco apartment buildings that line Central Park West.

GRAND CENTRAL STATION (above) No, it's not a planetarium, it's the "sky ceiling" in the main concourse of the magnificently restored Grand Central Station. The ceiling, lit greenish-blue, depicts the constellations of the winter sky above New York. Be careful staring up; you might get trampled by one of the thousands of commuters who rush through here each day. Grand Central is a pleasure even if you're not catching a train—you could spend hours shopping at the upscale food market, visiting the New York Transit Museum Store, noshing on the dining concourse, or slurping oysters at the landmark Oyster Bar.

LOUIS ARMSTRONG'S BATHROOM (right) This mirrored bathroom happens to be in the former house of jazz great Louis Armstrong. Armstrong could have lived anywhere, but he chose an unassuming house in the blue-collar neighborhood of Corona, Queens. Now a museum, the house has been preserved exactly as it was when his wife passed away in 1983.

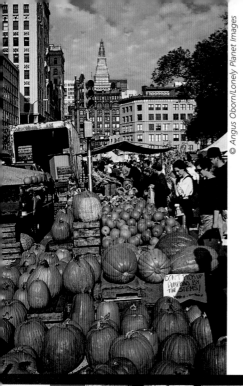

A FOODIE'S TOWN I admit it, I love food, and New York has tremendous variety. Other city greenmarkets are more convenient to my home, but none matches this one in **UNION SQUARE (left)**, not only for the scene but for the variety. The best time to visit is in the summer and fall, when the produce—apples, lettuces, corn, you name it—from local farms is bountiful. The dominant color on a brisk fall day? Pumpkin orange. When I want the best Southern fried chicken in the city, I head to the **M&G DINER (bottom left)** on 125th Street. Waiting on line for smoked fish at **ZABAR'S (upper right)** on a Sunday morning is an Upper West Side tradition. I love walking in Chinatown, where everything is right out on the street, from bootleg DVDs to boxes of ginseng. But what I love best about Chinatown are the countless restaurants, the vegetable markets, and the **FISH MARKETS (bottom right)**, where the catch is so fresh it's still flapping on ice.

FLATIRON BUILDING (left) This architectural icon is one of the most recognizable structures in the world. It was built in 1902 to fill the awkward triangular property created by the intersection of Broadway and Fifth Avenue. Fronted with limestone and terra cotta, it measures just 6 feet across at its narrow end. It's a beauty to look at, but don't bother going inside; I've been there many times (my wife had an office there), and it's not worth the interminable wait for the outdated elevators.

YANKEE STADIUM (below) Rome may have its Colosseum, but New York has Yankee Stadium. There is no more famous sports arena in America than "The House that Ruth Built." You may be from Boston or Chicago and hate the Yankees, but don't hold that against Yankee Stadium. If you're here in the off-season, you can still go for a tour and wander amid the ghosts of all-time greats like Ruth, Gehrig, DiMaggio, and Mantle.

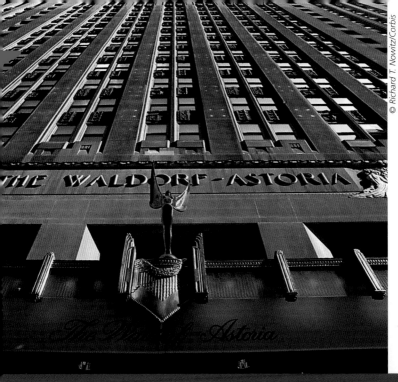

WALDORF-ASTORIA (above) I'm a sucker for old-time, early-20th-century New York hotels. Thankfully, quite a few of these "grande dames" are still around. The Waldorf, comprising one square block and 1,000 rooms, just might be the grandest of them all. This is where kings stay when they come to town; where the president lays his head; and where Secret Service agents of all nationalities are a regular sight. The Waldorf also has fine shops, three restaurants, and four bars.

MUSEUM OF MODERN ART (right) The old MoMA was indistinguishable among the faceless towers on 53rd Street. Following a $425-million renovation, MoMA is now as close to a work of art as a museum can be—it's stunning both inside and out. Anyone who claims a love of modern art has to come here to enjoy one of the greatest collections of 20th-century art in the world.

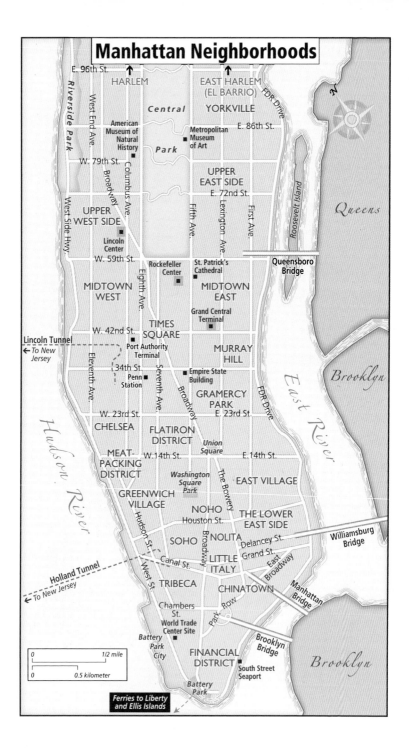

Manhattan Neighborhoods

E. 96th St.

HARLEM

EAST HARLEM
(EL BARRIO)

YORKVILLE

Central

Riverside Park

West End Ave.

American Museum of Natural History

Park

Metropolitan Museum of Art

E. 86th St.

UPPER EAST SIDE

E. 72nd St.

W. 79th St.

Broadway

Columbus Ave.

West Side Hwy.

UPPER WEST SIDE

Lincoln Center

Fifth Ave.

Lexington Ave.

First Ave.

Roosevelt Island

Queens

W. 59th St.

Rockefeller Center

St. Patrick's Cathedral

Queensboro Bridge

Eighth Ave.

MIDTOWN WEST

MIDTOWN EAST

Grand Central Terminal

East River

Brooklyn

TIMES SQUARE

W. 42nd St.

Lincoln Tunnel
← To New Jersey

Port Authority Terminal

MURRAY HILL

Eleventh Ave.

34th St.
Penn Station

Seventh Ave.

Empire State Building

Broadway

GRAMERCY PARK

FDR Drive

W. 23rd St.

E. 23rd St.

Hudson River

CHELSEA

FLATIRON DISTRICT

Union Square

MEAT-PACKING DISTRICT

W. 14th St.

E. 14th St.

Washington Square Park

EAST VILLAGE

GREENWICH VILLAGE

The Bowery

NOHO

Houston St.

THE LOWER EAST SIDE

Hudson St.

SOHO

Broadway

NOLITA

Delancey St.

Williamsburg Bridge

Canal St.

West St.

LITTLE ITALY

Grand St.

East Broadway

Holland Tunnel
← To New Jersey

TRIBECA

CHINATOWN

Manhattan Bridge

Park Row

Chambers St.

World Trade Center Site

0 ——— 1/2 mile
0 ——— 0.5 kilometer

Battery Park City

Brooklyn Bridge

Brooklyn

FINANCIAL DISTRICT

South Street Seaport

Battery Park

Ferries to Liberty and Ellis Islands

Central Park

🛈 Information
Ⓜ Subway stop

Downtown Attractions

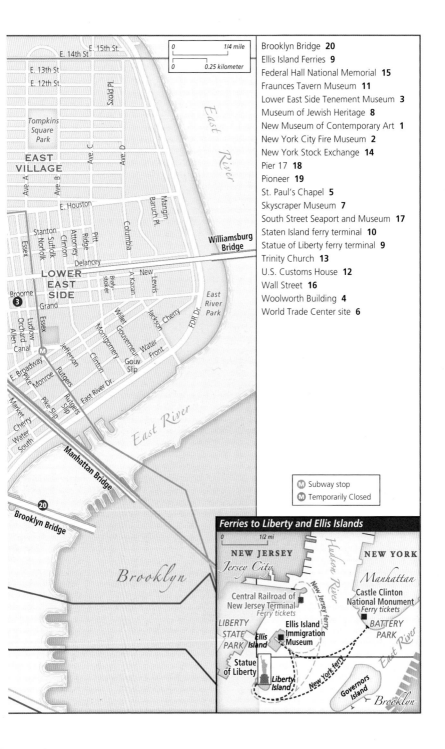

Brooklyn Bridge **20**
Ellis Island Ferries **9**
Federal Hall National Memorial **15**
Fraunces Tavern Museum **11**
Lower East Side Tenement Museum **3**
Museum of Jewish Heritage **8**
New Museum of Contemporary Art **1**
New York City Fire Museum **2**
New York Stock Exchange **14**
Pier 17 **18**
Pioneer **19**
St. Paul's Chapel **5**
Skyscraper Museum **7**
South Street Seaport and Museum **17**
Staten Island ferry terminal **10**
Statue of Liberty ferry terminal **9**
Trinity Church **13**
U.S. Customs House **12**
Wall Street **16**
Woolworth Building **4**
World Trade Center site **6**

Ⓜ Subway stop
Ⓜ Temporarily Closed

Ferries to Liberty and Ellis Islands

Midtown Attractions

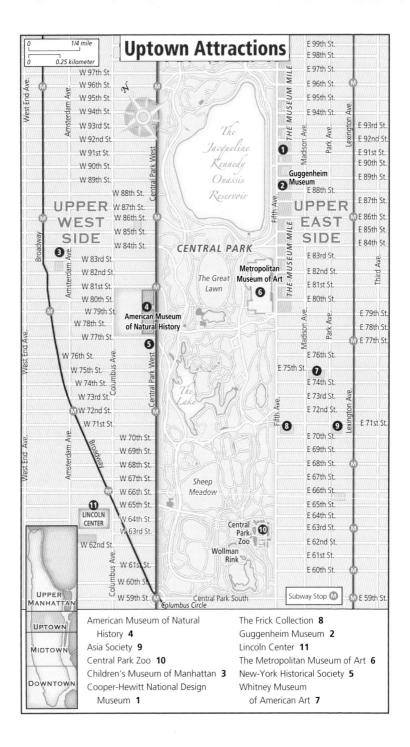

Uptown Attractions

0 — 1/4 mile
0 — 0.25 kilometer

W 97th St.
W 96th St.
W 95th St.
W 94th St.
W 93rd St.
W 92nd St.
W 91st St.
W 90th St.
W 89th St.
W 88th St.
W 87th St.
W 86th St.
W 85th St.
W 84th St.
W 83rd St.
W 82nd St.
W 81st St.
W 80th St.
W 79th St.
W 78th St.
W 77th St.
W 76th St.
W 75th St.
W 74th St.
W 73rd St.
W 72nd St.
W 71st St.
W 70th St.
W 69th St.
W 68th St.
W 67th St.
W 66th St.
W 65th St.
W 64th St.
W 63rd St.
W 62nd St.
W 61st St.
W 60th St.
W 59th St.

West End Ave.
Amsterdam Ave.
Broadway
Columbus Ave.
Central Park West

UPPER WEST SIDE

3

American Museum of Natural History **4**

5

11 LINCOLN CENTER

E 99th St.
E 98th St.
E 97th St.
E 96th St.
E 95th St.
E 94th St.
E 93rd St.
E 92nd St.
E 91st St.
E 90th St.
E 89th St.
E 88th St.
E 87th St.
E 86th St.
E 85th St.
E 84th St.
E 83rd St.
E 82nd St.
E 81st St.
E 80th St.
E 79th St.
E 78th St.
E 77th St.
E 76th St.
E 75th St
E 74th St.
E 73rd St.
E 72nd St.
E 71st St.
E 70th St.
E 69th St.
E 68th St.
E 67th St.
E 66th St.
E 65th St.
E 64th St.
E 63rd St.
E 62nd St.
E 61st St.
E 60th St.
E 59th St.

THE MUSEUM MILE

Madison Ave.
Park Ave.
Lexington Ave.
Fifth Ave.
Third Ave.

1

Guggenheim Museum **2**

UPPER EAST SIDE

CENTRAL PARK

The Jacqueline Kennedy Onassis Reservoir

The Great Lawn

Metropolitan Museum of Art **6**

The Lake

Sheep Meadow

Central Park Zoo **10**

Wollman Rink

7

8

9

Central Park South
Columbus Circle

Subway Stop Ⓜ

UPPER MANHATTAN
UPTOWN
MIDTOWN
DOWNTOWN

American Museum of Natural
   History **4**
Asia Society **9**
Central Park Zoo **10**
Children's Museum of Manhattan **3**
Cooper-Hewitt National Design
   Museum **1**

The Frick Collection **8**
Guggenheim Museum **2**
Lincoln Center **11**
The Metropolitan Museum of Art **6**
New-York Historical Society **5**
Whitney Museum
   of American Art **7**

Frommer's®

New York City
2009

by Brian Silverman

Here's what the critics say about Frommer's:

"Amazingly easy to use. Very portable, very complete."
—*Booklist*

"Detailed, accurate, and easy-to-read information for all price ranges."
—*Glamour Magazine*

"Hotel information is close to encyclopedic."
—*Des Moines Sunday Register*

"Frommer's Guides have a way of giving you a real feel for a place."
—*Knight Ridder Newspapers*

WILEY
Wiley Publishing, Inc.

About the Author

Brian Silverman is a freelance writer whose work has been published in *Saveur, The New Yorker, Caribbean Travel & Life, Islands,* and *Four Seasons.* Among the many topics he writes about are food, travel, sports, and music. He is the author of numerous books including *Going, Going, Gone: The History, Lore, and Mystique of the Home Run,* and the *Twentieth Century Treasury of Sports.* For Frommer's, he has written Complete, Portable, and Budget guides to New York City, as well as *New York City For Dummies.* He lives in Manhattan with his wife and children.

Published by:

Wiley Publishing, Inc.

111 River St.
Hoboken, NJ 07030-5774

ISBN 978-0-470-28562-6

Editor: Kathleen Warnock
Production Editor: M. Faunette Johnston
Cartographer: Andrew Murphy
Photo Editor: Richard Fox
Production by Wiley Indianapolis Composition Services

Front cover photo: Rockefeller Center, building Art Deco facade
Back cover photo: Central Park, Great Lawn

For information on our other products and services or to obtain technical support, please contact our Customer Care Department within the U.S. at 800/762-2974, outside the U.S. at 317/572-3993 or fax 317/572-4002.

Contents

4 New York City Neighborhoods & Suggested Itineraries   69

5 Where to Stay   97

6 Where to Dine   142

(7) Exploring New York City   219

(8) Shopping   300

(9) New York City After Dark   338

List of Maps

Acknowledgments

My editor, Kathleen Warnock, with her guidance and support, helps make working on this book a pleasure rather than a chore and for that I am very thankful. I'd also like to thank Gail Eisenberg for her tireless fact checking of this very fact-filled book.

An Invitation to the Reader

In researching this book, we discovered many wonderful places—hotels, restaurants, shops, and more. We're sure you'll find others. Please tell us about them, so we can share the information with your fellow travelers in upcoming editions. If you were disappointed with a recommendation, we'd love to know that, too. Please write to:

Frommer's New York City 2009
Wiley Publishing, Inc. • 111 River St. • Hoboken, NJ 07030-5774

An Additional Note

Please be advised that travel information is subject to change at any time—and this is especially true of prices. We therefore suggest that you write or call ahead for confirmation when making your travel plans. The authors, editors, and publisher cannot be held responsible for the experiences of readers while traveling. Your safety is important to us, however, so we encourage you to stay alert and be aware of your surroundings. Keep a close eye on cameras, purses, and wallets, all favorite targets of thieves and pickpockets.

Other Great Guides for Your Trip:

Frommer's New York City Day by Day
New York City For Dummies
Pauline Frommer's New York City
Frommer's New York City with Kids
Suzy Gershman's Born to Shop New York
Frommer's NYC Free & Dirt Cheap
Frommer's 24 Great Walks in New York
Frommer's Portable New York City

Frommer's Star Ratings, Icons & Abbreviations

Every hotel, restaurant, and attraction listing in this guide has been ranked for quality, value, service, amenities, and special features using a **star-rating system.** In country, state, and regional guides, we also rate towns and regions to help you narrow down your choices and budget your time accordingly. Hotels and restaurants are rated on a scale of zero (recommended) to three stars (exceptional). Attractions, shopping, nightlife, towns, and regions are rated according to the following scale: zero stars (recommended), one star (highly recommended), two stars (very highly recommended), and three stars (must-see).

In addition to the star-rating system, we also use **seven feature icons** that point you to the great deals, in-the-know advice, and unique experiences that separate travelers from tourists. Throughout the book, look for:

Finds	Special finds—those places only insiders know about
Fun Fact	Fun facts—details that make travelers more informed and their trips more fun
Kids	Best bets for kids and advice for the whole family
Moments	Special moments—those experiences that memories are made of
Overrated	Places or experiences not worth your time or money
Tips	Insider tips—great ways to save time and money
Value	Great values—where to get the best deals

The following **abbreviations** are used for credit cards:

AE	American Express	DISC	Discover	V	Visa
DC	Diners Club	MC	MasterCard		

Frommers.com

Now that you have this guidebook to help you plan a great trip, visit our website at **www.frommers.com** for additional travel information on more than 4,000 destinations. We update features regularly to give you instant access to the most current trip-planning information available. At Frommers.com, you'll find scoops on the best airfares, lodging rates, and car rental bargains. You can even book your travel online through our reliable travel booking partners. Other popular features include:

- Online updates of our most popular guidebooks
- Vacation sweepstakes and contest giveaways
- Newsletters highlighting the hottest travel trends
- Podcasts, interactive maps, and up-to-the-minute events listings
- Opinionated blog entries by Arthur Frommer himself
- Online travel message boards with featured travel discussions

What's New in New York City

The year 2008 was a year of transition for some of the city's major icons, some of which are leaving us for good, some of which are returning with face-lifts. It was the last year for both **Yankee Stadium** and **Shea Stadium,** the former certainly an icon, the latter an icon mostly for Mets' fans but also the place where the Beatles played a historic concert. Both teams will have new stadiums in 2009, the Yankees in "new" **Yankee Stadium** adjacent to the old one, and the Mets at newly named **Citi Field,** also adjacent to Shea. (So Mets fans, you'll still be able to watch your games to the sound of jet engines from planes at LaGuardia.)

The venerable bastion of high-class lodging, the **Plaza Hotel** (© **888/240-7775;** www.fairmont.com/thePlaza), now 100 years old, reopened in early 2008 after a 2-year, $400 million lobby-to-roof renovation. Much of the hotel has been converted into condos, but there are 282 hotel rooms that, now, are some of the most spacious in the city (and possibly the most expensive).

After 2 years in dry dock and an $8 million renovation, the WWII aircraft carrier **USS Intrepid** will make its way back home to Pier 86 at West 46th Street, the **Intrepid Sea, Air & Space Museum** (© 212/245-0072; www.intrepidmuseum. org), for a grand reopening on Veteran's Day, November 11, 2008.

The ongoing 100-plus year, work-in-progress known as the **Cathedral of St. John the Divine** (© 212/316-7490; www.stjohndivine.org), at 112th and Amsterdam Avenue, reached a milestone when scaffolding was removed from the southwest tower in late 2007, revealing more of the cathedral's majestic beauty.

What would Fifth Avenue be without **Gucci**? In 2008, Gucci opened its flagship store at 725 Fifth Ave. (© **212/826-2600;** www.gucci.com/us), a few blocks north of the old one. The new store features 46,000 square feet over three floors with floor-to-ceiling windows.

The best way to get around in New York is and has always been the subways. We mourned the loss of the much-loved subway token when it was phased out, but cannot argue with the convenience of the **MetroCard** and especially the Unlimited MetroCard. But fares of the unlimited MetroCard increased in 2008, with a 1-day pass now $7.50, 7-day pass $25, 14-day pass $47, and a 30-day pass $81.

Below you will find much more of what's new in New York.

ACCOMMODATIONS Besides the renovation at the Plaza, the **Pierre,** another "grande dame" hotel off Fifth Avenue is undergoing major work. Owned and managed by Taj Hotels, Resorts and Palaces, all the rooms and public spaces will be renovated to the tune of $100 million and are expected to reopen in early 2009.

The **Jumeirah Essex House** (© 212/247-0300; www.jumeirahessexhouse. com), with its beacon of a sign overlooking Central Park from Central Park South, has also reopened after a 15-month renovation.

A number of hotels were set to open downtown in 2008–09, though at press time, more than one was pushing its expected occupancy date back, so we may be talking about their grand openings in *next* year's "What's New." Breaking ground in uncharted territory in 2007 was the **Bowery Hotel** (✆ **212/505-9100;** www.theboweryhotel.com), which opened to tremendous hype, much of it well deserved.

The Bowery's owners are also upgrading the landmarked 1907 Jane Street Hotel, a popular, cheap fleabag, into a nicer (but still relatively cheap) "micro hotel for for young travelers with more style than money." As the **Jane** (113 Jane St., ✆ **212/924-6700;** www.thejanenyc.com), it will offer rooms for as low as $99 with shared bathrooms starting in late summer 2008.

Moving into the Meatpacking District hotel scene will be the New York branch of the **Standard,** at 848 Washington St. (✆ **212/645-4646;** www.standardhotels.com). After making it big in Miami and Los Angeles, hotelier Andre Balazs of The Mercer and Hotel QT, are headed to the Big Apple with a debut scheduled for the summer of 2008.

The neighborhoods of downtown continue to rise up, and I mean that literally. Contributing to that ascension are a slew of even more hotels scheduled to open by the end of 2008 or early in 2009, including Robert DeNiro's TriBeCa-located **Greenwich Hotel** at 375 Greenwich St. (✆ **212/475-4756;** www.thegreenwich hotel.com), which was set to open in the late spring of 2008; and hotelier Jason Pomeranc's (60 Thompson) Lower East Side venture **Allen Street Hotel.** For 2010, at 99 Church St., developer Larry Silverstein plans to build an 80-story **Four Seasons** hotel and condominium tower that will make it the tallest residential building in Manhattan.

Back in midtown, in hotel-deprived Hell's Kitchen, Kimpton Hotels (70 Park Ave.) will open the 222-room **Vu Hotel** at 653 Eleventh Avenue, at 48th Street (✆ **212/757-0088;** www.vuhotel.com). At press time, the hotel was scheduled to open in the summer of 2008.

RESTAURANTS   The restaurant trend of 2007 was market-fresh cuisine, with new restaurants such as **Park Avenue Winter,** 100 E. 63rd St. (p. 209; ✆ **212/644-1900;** www.parkavenuenyc.com), specializing in what is fresh at the moment and changing its name, menu, and look seasonally. In winter, it's called Park Avenue Winter, in spring, Park Avenue Spring . . . you get the picture.

Another trend was to showcase top chefs in hotel restaurants. In 2006–07, it was the emergence of **Gordon Ramsay at the London** and Joël Robuchon with **L'Atelier de Joël Robuchon** in the Four Seasons Hotel. In 2007–08, chef Alain Ducasse took over the space that formerly housed Lespinasse, in the St. Regis Hotel, and opened **Adour Alain Ducasse,** 2 E. 55th St. (✆ **212/710-2277;** www.adour-stregis.com); Kerry Heffernan, the much-lauded head chef at 11 Madison Park, was granted prime space in the renovated Jumeirah Essex House to open **South Gate,** 154 Central Park South (p. 183; ✆ **212/484-5120;** www.154southgate.com); and Laurent Tourendel, the chef/restaurateur of the BLT empire, claimed the space formerly occupied by Atelier as home to his newest venture, **BLT Market,** 1430 Sixth Ave. (p. 179; ✆ **212/521-6125;** www.bltmarket.com). And since the reopening of the Plaza Hotel, chef Didier Virot, formerly of Aix has taken over the menu at the hotel's legendary restaurant **Palm Court.**

Close to Lincoln Center, famed chef Daniel Boulud opened his fourth New York restaurant, **Bar Boulud,** 1900

Broadway (© 212/595-0303; www. barboulud.com), putting his own spin on another trend, the wine bar.

The red meat palaces continue to sprout in New York and the biggest in 2007–08 in both size and hype was Stephen Hanson's **Primehouse,** 381 Park Ave. S. (p. 175; © 212/824-2600; www. brguestrestaurants.com).

Manhattan got its first mechanical bull when **Johnny Utah's,** 25 W. 51st St. (p. 184; © 212/265-UTAH; www. johnnyutahs.com), opened in a space near Rockefeller Center.

There's no bull at **Hill Country,** 30 W. 26th St. (p. 176; © 212/255-4544; www.hillcountryny.com), the big, two-level replication of a Texas meat market/roadhouse in the Flatiron district. But what's lacking in mechanical bull is made up for in barbecued beef brisket and enormous beef ribs. Across the East River, in Williamsburg, Brooklyn, a slightly more intimate smokehouse, with the year's best name—**Fette Sau** (Fat Pig)—and even better barbecued pork belly, opened at 354 Metropolitan Ave. (p. 214; © 718/963-3404).

ATTRACTIONS The **New Museum of Contemporary Art** moved into its new home, which resembles an oddly stacked column of boxes, at 235 Bowery (p. 251; © 212/219-1222; www.new museum.org). Whatever you think of the design, its exhibits rival the edginess of its look. And that's a good thing.

And, more than 15 years after the bones of Africans were discovered in lower Manhattan during a construction dig, the **African Burial Ground Memorial** was unveiled at 290 Broadway (© 212/637-2019; www.nps.gov/afbg) to commemorate this sacred site.

In September 2008, the **Museum of Arts and Design** (formerly the American Craft Museum; © 212/956-3535; www.madmuseum.org) will reopen in its new home at 2 Columbus Circle, more than doubling the gallery space.

The **Sports Museum of America,** 26 Broadway (© 212/747-0900; www. sportsmuseum.com), opened in spring 2008, featuring interactive exhibits and sports memorabilia on loan from various Halls of Fame. It's also the new home of the Heisman Trophy and the Billie Jean King International Women's Sports Center (which you can see for a whopping $27 admission fee).

AFTER DARK The massive performing arts complex known as **Lincoln Center** is turning 50 in 2009, and marking the anniversary with wholesale renovations that will add new performing spaces, a restaurant, and visitor center. One venue, **Alice Tully Hall,** will be closed for renovations through February 2009. For information on the renovations and temporary closures, visit **www. lincolncenter.org**.

1

The Best of the Big Apple

We all have our personal tastes; what we like to listen to in terms of music, what kind of food we enjoy, what we relate to in art and architecture. Personal taste is a subjective matter; and I only pay attention to raves, whether they are for a restaurant, artist, musician, or film, if they are universal. If everyone likes it, it has to be good. Well, not always. Anyway, I've compiled, below, my personal favorites we can call the "best of" in many areas from experiences to restaurants. You may not agree, but that's what makes these "best of" lists fun. Just don't take them too seriously.

1 Most Unforgettable New York City Experiences

- **Sailing to the Statue of Liberty,** on Liberty Island in New York Harbor: If you have time to do only one thing on your visit to New York, sail to the Lady in the harbor. No other monument embodies the nation's—and the world's—notion of political freedom and economic potential more than Lady Liberty. It is also the ultimate symbol of New York, the personification of the city's vast diversity and tolerance. See p. 238.

- **Visiting the Empire State Building Observatory at Dusk:** Like the Statue of Liberty, the Empire State Building, once again the tallest building in New York, is one of the city's definitive icons. Arrive at dusk and watch the lights of the city come on. It's pure magic. See p. 231.

- **Walking the Brooklyn Bridge:** Manhattan has five major bridges connecting the island to other shores, and the most historic and fascinating is the Brooklyn Bridge. For a close-up look at what was a marvel of civic engineering when it was built in 1883, and a true New York experience, walk across from Manhattan to Brooklyn. See p. 230.

- **Jogging around the Central Park Reservoir:** Okay, you don't even have to jog it. You can walk the jogging path around the Jacqueline Kennedy Onassis Reservoir and take in the beauty of Central Park, the views of Central Park West, Fifth Avenue, and especially the skyline of midtown Manhattan. See p. 264.

- **Sunday Morning in New York:** This might not sound so unforgettable, but to experience the city minus the noise and activity is something special. I've noticed quite a few tourists, usually jet-lagged Europeans, wandering the parks and streets early Sunday mornings.

- **Walking 125th Street:** Take a walk across this famous Harlem boulevard, and your senses will be overwhelmed with the music, the variety of stores, the restaurants, the stalls selling everything from homemade CDs to bean pies, and the street prophets and musicians. The energy is relentless.

New York Metropolitan Area

- **Traveling underground:** Don't be afraid of the subways. Go underground, MetroCard in hand, and use the fastest means of transport in the city. On the way, you might see music, art, even history in many of the city's refurbished stations.

2 New York's Best Events & Seasons

- **Best Parade: West Indian–American Day Carnival and Parade.** Held on Eastern Parkway in Brooklyn, this is the biggest parade in New York. The music (calypso, soca, reggae, and Latin), the costumes, and the Caribbean food make this unforgettable. If you're lucky enough to be in town on Labor Day, don't miss it. See p. 36.
- **Best Season in New York: Christmas.** Come see the Christmas trees on Park Avenue, the big snowflake on 57th and Fifth, the trees at Rockefeller Center and Lincoln Center, the menorah at Grand Army Plaza at Fifth and 59th Street, the decorations in department store windows, restaurants, and hotels. And even though the crowds, especially around Midtown and Rockefeller Center, might bring out the Scrooge in you, the atmosphere is almost always festive and like no other time of year.
- **Best Time of Year to Come to New York: Summer.** Most people prefer the temperate days of fall to visit New York, and that's when the city is most crowded. But my personal favorite season is summer, when the streets are empty, restaurants and shows are easier to get into, and free outdoor cultural events abound.
- **Best Day to Come to New York: New Year's Day.** The holidays are over; you've had enough festivity— see above—and you've wisely skipped the insanity of New Year's Eve and arisen fresh and (relatively) sober. Get out on the town early; you'll have the city practically to yourself.

3 New York's Best Museums

- **Best Overall Museum: American Museum of Natural History.** You can spend your entire visit to New York at this 4-square-block museum; there is that much to see. From the famed dinosaur halls to the Hall of Ocean Life, the Museum of Natural History houses the world's greatest natural science collection. See p. 229.
- **Best Art Museum: Metropolitan Museum of Art.** Not just the best art museum in New York, but the best in North America. The number of masterworks is mind-boggling. See p. 233.
- **Best-Looking Museum: Museum of Modern Art.** Though the sight of the Guggenheim is the most memorable, and the New Museum of Contemporary Art is oddly attractive, MoMA's $450-million renovation makes it the coolest-looking museum, inside and out, in town. See p. 235.
- **Best New York Museum about New York: Museum of the City of New York.** Start here and get a feel of what the city is like—from past to present. There are always fascinating exhibits. See p. 250.
- **Best Home Posing as a Museum: The Louis Armstrong House Museum.** This unassuming house in Queens was Satchmo's home for almost 30 years and it's been preserved almost exactly as it was when he died in 1971. See p. 295.

4 Best New York City Structures

- **Best Historic Building: Grand Central Terminal.** Despite all the steel-and-glass skyscrapers, there are still many historic marvels standing, and the best is this Beaux Arts gem. This railroad station, built in 1913, was restored in the 1990s to recapture its brilliance. See p. 233.
- **Best Skyscraper: The Chrysler Building.** There is no observation deck, but this Art Deco masterpiece is best viewed from outside or from other observation decks, such as the Empire State Building's. See p. 257.
- **Most Impressive Place of Worship: Cathedral of St. John the Divine.** Construction began on the world's largest Gothic cathedral in 1892 and it's still going on. But this is one structure that benefits from being a work in progress. See p. 261.

5 Best Parks in New York City

- **Best Park: Central Park.** One of the world's greatest urban refuges—a center of calm and tranquillity among the noise and bustle that is Manhattan. See p. 264.
- **Runners-Up for Best Park: Riverside Park.** This 4-mile-long park along the Hudson River is a welcome alternative to the sometimes-over-crowded Central Park.

  Battery Park. At the island's southern tip, walk the promenade and marvel at the harbor with Lady Liberty standing sentinel. See p. 270.

6 Best Places in New York to Take the Kids

- **Central Park:** With its lovely carousel, a zoo, two ice-skating rinks, and numerous playgrounds and ball fields, Central Park is a children's wonderland. See p. 264.
- **Bronx Zoo Wildlife Conservation Park:** This is one of the great zoos in the world—and you don't have to be a kid to love it. See p. 284.
- **New York Hall of Science:** This Queens' museum, in Flushing Meadows–Corona Park, has hands-on exhibits that thrill children from preschool and up. And after the museum, the park offers a carousel, zoo, and boat and bike rentals. See p. 283.
- **Coney Island:** It's not a theme park (yet!), just an old-fashioned amusement park on the beach. There's also the nearby Aquarium and Nathan's Hot Dogs for nourishment. What more could anyone, much less a kid, want? See p. 290.

7 Best Places to Stroll in New York

- **The Upper West Side:** With museums, parks, some old buildings and brownstones, inexpensive restaurants, and a residential feel, this is my favorite neighborhood to stroll.
- **Greenwich Village:** With its historic streets, hidden cafes, cozy restaurants, and eccentric characters, Greenwich Village is a constant, but pleasant, barrage on the senses.
- **Chinatown:** With the relentless activity and crowded sidewalks, Chinatown might not seem like ideal strolling territory, but it's so colorful, it's worth braving the mobs.

- **Brooklyn Heights:** A designated historic district, on your stroll you will be awed by the pristine condition of 19th-century row houses and mansions. But best of all is the view of Manhattan from Brooklyn Heights' famous promenade.

8 Best Things to Do for Free (or Almost) in New York

- **Ride the Staten Island Ferry:** The Staten Island Ferry is used daily by thousands of commuters. Ride it for a great view of the Statue of Liberty, Ellis Island, New York Harbor, and the lower Manhattan skyline. You can't beat the price: free. See p. 237.
- **Attend a Gospel Service:** All around New York, you'll find Sunday gospel services, but for some special soul-stirring, head to Harlem and the **Abyssinian Baptist Church** or Brooklyn and the **Brooklyn Tabernacle.** Services are free, but when the basket is passed, don't be stingy. See p. 261 and 290.
- **Visit Free Museums:** Believe it or not, there are museums in New York that don't charge admission. Two of my favorites are the **National Museum of the American Indian** and the **Federal Hall National Memorial.** See p. 251 and 260.
- **Take in a Game at the West 4th Street Basketball Courts:** Located on West 4th Street and Sixth Avenue. I don't know what's more entertaining: the moves on the court or the inventive trash talk accompanying the games.

9 Best Offbeat New York Experiences

- **Visit the Little Italy of the Bronx:** With the demise of Little Italy in Manhattan, the area around Arthur Avenue, known as the Little Italy of the Bronx, is the place for old-fashioned Italian charm, food, and ambience.
- **Museum of Sex:** How many cities can claim their own Museum of Sex? Not too many! We got your Museum of Sex right here . . . but you must be 18 or older to enter. See p. 247.
- **Roosevelt Island Tram:** Impress your family and friends with a spectacular view of the skyline from the Roosevelt Island Tram. During the 4-minute ride, you will be treated to a gorgeous vista down the East River, with views of the United Nations and the Queensboro, Williamsburg, Manhattan, and Brooklyn bridges. See p. 238.
- **Bike Along the Hudson River:** If walking is not enough exercise for you, a good alternative is to rent a bike and ride the length of Manhattan via the work-in-progress **Hudson River Park.** As of this writing, you can bike from Battery Park to Fort Tryon Park, near the George Washington Bridge. There are detours along the way, which occasionally take you off the paths. For bike-rental info, see p. 268.
- **Take a Food Tour:** You'll find lots of groups that offer tours centered around food, and it's a fantastic way to learn about a neighborhood. What could be better than seeing Brooklyn by way of its pizzerias, or exploring Harlem by sampling African, Caribbean, Latin-American, and soul foods along the way?
- **Ride the International Express:** The no. 7 train is sometimes known as the "International Express." Take it through the borough of Queens, and you will pass one ethnic neighborhood after another, from Indian to Thai, from Peruvian to Columbian, from Chinese to Korean.

10 Best Way to Spend a Day in a Borough Other Than Manhattan

- **In the Bronx:** Spend the morning at the **Bronx Zoo Wildlife Conservation Park** (p. 284) or the **New York Botanical Garden** (p. 286), and then head to **Arthur Avenue,** the Little Italy of the Bronx (see "Best Offbeat New York Experiences," above), for an authentic Italian feast.

- **In Brooklyn:** You can take a look at what's on at the always exciting **Brooklyn Museum of Art** (p. 288), then get some fresh air with a stroll in nearby, lovely **Prospect Park** (p. 292). Cap it off with a sandwich and a slice of cheesecake at **Junior's** (p. 214), on Flatbush Avenue. Or, head for **Coney Island,** whose face will change forever within the life of this book. Go in the summer, hit the beach, the amusement park, the Aquarium, Nathan's Famous hot dogs, and/or maybe a Cyclones baseball game. It's a schlep, but one you will never forget. See. p. 290.

- **In Queens:** Take the 7 train, the **International Express** (see "Best Offbeat New York Experiences," above), to the **Queens Museum of Art** (p. 296), on the grounds of the 1964 World's Fair, or the **Louis Armstrong House Museum** (p. 295). On your way back, stop for a meal at any of the ethnic restaurants you will find within close proximity of the no. 7 train.

11 Best Splurge Hotels in Manhattan

- **Ritz-Carlton New York, Central Park** (160 Central Park South; 𝄐 **212/308-9100;** www.ritzcarlton. com): The combination of a great location across from Central Park, large well-outfitted rooms, and excellent Ritz-Carlton service is as good as it gets. See p. 115.

- **The Mercer** (147 Mercer St.; 𝄐 **888/918-6060** or 212/966-6060; www.mercerhotel.com): The best of the hip, downtown hotels, the Mercer is in the heart of SoHo. The high-ceilinged, loftlike rooms and suites, some with fireplaces, all with ceiling fans and luxurious bathrooms, are spectacular. See p. 106.

- **The Peninsula-New York** (700 Fifth Ave.; 𝄐 **800/262-9467** or 212/956-2888; http://newyork.peninsula. com): The combination of old-world elegance and 21st-century technology is best realized in this practically perfect hotel. See p. 129.

- **The Ritz-Carlton New York, Battery Park** (2 West St.; 𝄐 **212/344-0800;** www.ritzcarlton.com): For magnificent views of the Harbor and all its treasures, not to mention impeccable service on every level, it's hard to top this Ritz. See p. 101.

- **Gramercy Park Hotel** (2 Lexington Ave.; 𝄐 **212/920-3300;** www. gramercyparkhotel.com): Hotelier Ian Schrager and artist Julian Schnabel took a rundown 1925-built legend and restored it to contemporary grandeur. It feels like you're staying in an eclectic museum, but a very comfortable one. See p. 111.

- **The Carlyle, A Rosewood Hotel** (35 E. 76th St.; 𝄐 **800/227-5737** or 212/744-1600; www.thecarlyle. com): You are in rarefied territory when you stay in The Carlyle. Service is white-gloved and rooms are sumptuous. Many have incredible views of the city and Central Park. And don't forget Café Carlyle for cabaret and Bemelmans Bar for a cocktail. See p. 140.

- **The Lowell** (28 E. 63rd St.; 𝄐 **212/ 838-1400;** www.lowellhotel.com): Although smaller and more intimate than the Carlyle, the Lowell is just as elegant and romantic. Rooms are all unique; many have fireplaces, while some have good-size terraces. See p. 140.

12 Best Moderately Priced Hotels in Manhattan

- **Casablanca Hotel** (147 W. 43rd St.; ℂ **888/922-7225** or 212/869-1212; www.casablancahotel.com): In the Theater District, the Casablanca offers clean, well-outfitted rooms at value rates, as well as nice extras such as complimentary breakfast, bottled water, free high-speed Internet, and a roof deck perfect for a cocktail on a balmy evening. See p. 121.
- **Inn on 23rd Street** (131 W. 23rd St. ℂ **877/387-2323** or 212/463-0330; www.innon23rd.com): You cannot do better than this charming inn for top-notch quality and extras. Rooms are rustic and uniquely designed, but all have up-to-date amenities. Breakfast is complimentary and served in a lovely library. See p. 110.
- **Sofitel New York** (45 W. 44th St.; ℂ **212/354-8844;** www.sofitel. com): This relatively new hotel exudes old-world (French) elegance. And you should be able to score some good weekend packages on the Internet. See p. 120.
- **Hotel Metro** (45 W. 35th St.; ℂ **800/356-3870** or 212/947-2500; www.hotelmetronyc.com): You'll find good deals and lots of extras at this Midtown hotel that's popular with Europeans. See p. 123.

13 Best Hotels for Families

- **Hotel Beacon** (2130 Broadway; ℂ **800/572-4969** or 212/787-1100; www.beaconhotel.com): Not only is this hotel a great deal—you can get good-size suites for much less than in Midtown—the Upper West Side, with its parks, the Museum of Natural History, and fun, inexpensive restaurants, is a great neighborhood for children. See p. 137.
- **Doubletree Guest Suites Times Square** (1568 Broadway; ℂ **800/ 222-TREE** or 212/719-1600; http:// doubletree1.hilton.com): This hotel boasts an entire floor of childproof suites, complete with living rooms for spreading out and kitchenettes for preparing light meals. It's also just a block from kid-friendly chain restaurants and the Toys "R" Us superstore. See p. 117.

14 Best Incentives for Hotel-Hopping

- **Best Hotel Suite: Townhouse Suite in the Kitano New York** (66 Park Ave.; ℂ **212/885-7000;** http:// kitano.com). Each of the three one-bedroom suites in the townhouse that is part of this hotel features a hallway leading to a sunken living room with original art, a state-of-the-art stereo system, and a tea maker with green tea. See p. 131.
- **Best Inexpensive Hotel Restaurant: Burger Joint** in **Le Parker Meridien** (118 W. 57th St.; ℂ **800/543-4300** or 212/245-5000; www.parker meridien.com). Hidden off the lobby, this joint has been discovered by locals, so the lines are long, but worth it. The burgers are fabulous (see "Best Burger," below) and under $6. See p. 194.

- **Best Hotel Bar: Bemelmans Bar,** in the Carlyle (35 E. 76th St.; © **800/ 227-5737** or 212/744-1600; www. thecarlyle.com). Named after illustrator Ludwig Bemelmans, who created the *Madeline* books and painted the mural, this romantic, charming bar features white-gloved service and classic cocktails. For more on Bemelmans, see p. 378.
- **Best Hotel for a Romantic Tryst: Hotel Elysée** (60 E. 54th St.; © **800/ 535-9733** or 212/753-1066; www. elyseehotel.com). This lovely old hotel, a favorite of mid–20th-century writers and actors, is discreetly dwarfed between two mammoth office buildings and is the perfect romantic hideaway in the middle of Manhattan. See p. 130.

- **Best Hotel Renovation: Jumeirah Essex House** (160 Central Park South; © **212/247-0300;** www. jumeirahessexhouse.com). Open since 1931, the Essex House was purchased by the Jumeirah Hotel Group, who spent $90 million on renovations. The money was well spent; the rooms are larger, and state-of-the-art technology melds with the hotel's classy Art Deco look. See p. 118.
- **Best Hotel Swim-Up Bar: Hotel QT** (125 W. 45th St.; © **212/354-2323;** www.hotelqt.com). There is much to like about the Hotel QT, but I love the fact that it has a swimming pool—in the lobby—with a swim-up bar. You can't ask for much more in the middle of Manhattan. See p. 124.

15 The Most Unforgettable Dining Experiences in New York

- **Chanterelle** (2 Harrison St.; © **212/ 966-6960;** www.chanterellenyc.com): You'll be made to feel special here, from the impeccable, personalized service in a simple but lovely room to the exquisitely prepared food. Other restaurants try, but this is how it's supposed to be done. See p. 148.
- **The River Café** (1 Water St., Brooklyn; © **718/522-5200;** www.river cafe.com): At the foot of the Brooklyn Bridge, there is no better dining view of Manhattan. Go at twilight as the lights of downtown begin to flicker on. Though the food at restaurants with views is usually not great, you won't be disappointed by the fare here. See p. 213.

- **Aquavit** (65 E. 55th St.; © **212/307- 7311;** www.aquavit.org): Though its new digs are not nearly as charming as its former town-house setting, the service and the food are as good as ever. See p. 191.
- **Big Wong King** (67 Mott St.; © **212/ 964-0540**): Come here for the true Chinatown experience. You'll share tables with Chinese families, order bowls of *congee* with fried crullers, plates of stir-fried vegetables, and platters of roast pork and duck—all served by brusque no-nonsense waiters. I guarantee it will be unforgettable. See p. 154.

16 Best New Restaurants

- **BLT Market** (1430 Ave. of the Americas; © **212/521-6125;** www. bltmarket.com): The newest in the BLT (Bistro Laurent Tourondel)

restaurant empire calls the Ritz Carlton Central Park home. The farmhouse ambience is a bit of a stretch for the neighborhood, but when it comes to the first-rate quality and freshness of the seasonal menu, I easily can forgive. See p. 179.

- **Ed's Lobster Bar** (222 Lafayette St.; ℭ 212/343-3236; www.lobsterbar nyc.com): This seafood "shack" in NoHo brings the taste of New England downtown, thanks to chef/owner Ed McFarland's talent with seafood. They are cheaper in Maine, but Ed's signature lobster roll rivals pretty much anything you will find on that state's rocky coast. See p. 159.
- **Park Avenue Winter** (100 E. 63rd St.; ℭ 212/644-1900; www.park avenyc.com): This somewhat gim-

micky restaurant serves seasonal fare but changes the complete look of the restaurant each season. The gimmick does not detract from the perfectly matched seasonal food you'll find here, whatever time of year you visit. See p. 209.

- **Fette Sau** (354 Metropolitan Ave., Williamsburg, Brooklyn; ℭ 718/963-3404): Not only does this place have the best name for a barbecue joint (it means "fat pig" in German), but the different cuts of meat, pork belly, rib chops, and so forth, are seasoned and smoked as well as I've had anywhere. See p. 214.

17 Best Bites for All Appetites

- **Best BBQ: RUB** (208 W. 23rd St.; ℭ 212/524-4300; www.rubbbq. net). Co-owner Paul Kirk brings his Kansas City pit prowess to New York, with mouth-watering results. Try the "Baron," a little bit of everything for a big crowd. See p. 171.
- **Best for Breakfast: Good Enough to Eat** (483 Amsterdam Ave.; ℭ 212/496-0163; www.goodenoughtoeat. com). They've been lining up on Amsterdam Avenue every weekend for over 20 years for chef/owner Carrie Levin's bountiful home-cooked breakfasts. But why wait in line? You're on vacation; go during the week. See p. 207.
- **Best for Brunch: Norma's,** at Le Parker Meridien hotel (118 W. 57th St.; ℭ 212/708-7460; www.parker meridien.com). Though I am not a devotee of brunch (see box "Breakfast, Not Brunch," on p. 206), I make an exception for Norma's. Skip the traditional breakfast items and go for creative interpretations such as the asparagus-and-seared-rock-lobster omelet. See p. 185.
- **Best Jewish Deli: Katz's Delicatessen** (205 E. Houston St.;

ℭ 212/254-2246; www.katzdeli. com). This is the choice among those who know their kreplach, knishes, and pastrami. No cutesy sandwiches named for celebrities here, just topnotch Jewish classics. See p. 156.

- **Best Burger: Burger Joint,** at Le Parker Meridien hotel (118 W. 57th St.; ℭ 212/708-7414; www.parker meridien.com). Who woulda thunk that a fancy hotel such as Le Parker Meridien would be the home to a "joint" that serves great burgers at great prices? See p. 194.
- **Best Pizzeria: Patsy's Pizzeria** (2287 First Ave.; ℭ 212/534-9783; www. patsyspizzeriany.com). This great East Harlem pizzeria has been cranking out coal-oven pizza since 1932. You can also order by the slice here, but only do so if the pie is fresh out of the oven. See p. 187.
- **Best Pizza in an Italian Restaurant: La Pizza Fresca Ristorante** (31 E. 20th St.; ℭ 212/598-0141; www. lapizzafresca.com). The Italian menu and wine list is vast, but you won't spend much time on it after you've sampled the restaurant's magnificent, authentic Neapolitan pizzas straight

out of their own wood burning oven. See p. 177.

- **Best 20th-Century Steakhouse: Frankie & Johnnie's** (32 W. 37th St., © 212/997-8940; and 269 W. 45th St., © 212/997-9494; www. frankiesandjohnnies.com). Whether you choose the former speakeasy that is the original location in the Theater District or the newer branch in John Barrymore's former townhouse, your steak, particularly the house sirloin, will remind you why Frankie & Johnnie's has been around since 1926. See p. 181.

- **Best 21st Century Steakhouse: Porter House New York** (10 Columbus Circle; © 212/823-9500; www. porterhousenewyork.com). New steakhouses sprout every year with much hype; this one in the Time Warner Center and helmed by chef Michael Lomonaco distinguished itself far ahead of the pack of new steakhouses. See p. 197.

- **Best Mutton Chop: Keens Steakhouse** (72 W. 36th St.; © 212/947-3636; www.keens.com). Of course, it might be the *only* restaurant in New York that offers a mutton chop, but that's not the only reason to head to Keens. The other "chops" are first-rate, and the rooms—there are several—are like museum pieces without the stuffiness. See p. 181.

- **Best Greek Restaurant: Kefi** (222 W. 79th St.; © 212/873-0200). In the space that formerly held Onera, chef Michael Psilakis has gone from nouveau Greek to traditional, with stunning results. You won't believe basic Greek taverna food could be so good. See. p. 203.

- **Best for Families: Virgil's Real BBQ** (152 W. 44th St.; © 212/921-9494; www.virgilsbbq.com). In Times Square, Virgil's, in a sense, is a theme restaurant, the theme being barbecue, but they do an excellent job of it. It's loud, colorful, and has great options for children. See p. 185.

- **Best Cheap Meal: Gray's Papaya** (2090 Broadway; © 212/799-0243). Though the $3.50 "recession special"— two hot dogs and a fruit drink—is almost a $1 increase from the previous recession, it's still a bargain. But is it any good? Witness the lines out the door every day for lunch. See p. 205.

- **Best Ice Cream: Brooklyn Ice Cream Factory** (Fulton Ferry Landing Pier, Brooklyn; © 718/246-3963). The perfect reward after a brisk walk across the Brooklyn Bridge. Rich homemade ice cream, with a view of the Manhattan skyline; it's a tough combination to beat. See p. 214.

- **Best Bagel: Absolute Bagels** (2788 Broadway; © 212/932-2052). They're not huge like some bagels these days, but they are always hot and baked to perfection. See p. 177.

- **Best Soul Food: Charles' Southern Style Kitchen** (2841 Eighth Ave.; © 877/813-2920 or 212/926-4313). Not only does this Harlem restaurant serve the best soul food in the city, it also offers the best buffet. For $9.95 on weekdays and $12 on weekends, the down-home offerings will tempt you to make any number of visits to the buffet line. See p. 212.

- **Best New/Old Dining Room: Country** (90 Madison Ave.; © 212/889-7100; www.countryinnewyork. com). Designed by architect David Rockwell, the upstairs restaurant in the Carlton Hotel is a marvel, with mosaic tiles, dramatic chandeliers, nooks overlooking the hotel lobby, and, most impressive, a gorgeous Tiffany skylight dome that had been hidden for years and was uncovered during the renovation. See p. 191.

18 Best Shopping in New York

- **Best Store: Saks Fifth Avenue.** Not as overwhelming as other department stores, Saks is consistently good. And don't miss those window displays at Christmas. See p. 312.
- **Best Clothes Store: Barneys.** This store is the pinnacle, with prices to match. See p. 309.
- **Best Shopping Zone: SoHo, NoHo, and Nolita.** All three neighborhoods are within walking distance of one another and feature the newest, trendiest boutiques. See chapter 10.
- **Best Old World Italian Food Store: DiPalo's Dairy.** This 1910-originated store is one of the last vestiges of Old Little Italy, and is still in the DiPalo family. See p. 323.
- **Best Old World Jewish Food Store: Russ & Daughters.** This smoked-fish purveyor has been a mainstay on the Lower East Side since 1914. Like DiPalo's above, the Russ family has been in charge since the beginning. See p. 325.

19 Best Culture & Nightlife in New York

- **Best Performance Space: Carnegie Hall.** One of the world's great performance spaces, with an array of world-class talent on display almost every night. See p. 352.
- **Best Free Cultural Event: Shakespeare in the Park.** Imagine Shakespeare performed by stars, under the stars, in Central Park. No wonder it has become a New York institution. See p. 354.
- **Best Children's Theater: Paper Bag Players.** For children ages 4 to 9, this group performs in the winter and offers tales told in imaginative and original ways. See p. 342.
- **Best Jazz Club: The Village Vanguard.** Acoustics and sightlines aren't great, but you can't do better for good-quality jazz. See p. 364.
- **Best Rock Club: Mercury Lounge.** This venue is intimate but not obscure. The Merc is the best for hard-edged rock 'n' roll. See p. 360.
- **Best Comedy Club: Gotham Comedy Club.** Comfortable and sophisticated, this is where the best come to hone their acts. See p. 368.
- **Best Cocktail: Pegu Club,** 77 W. Houston, 2nd floor. Supreme mixologist Audrey Saunders has opened a club where everything is top label and all juices and mixers are freshly made. See p. 371.
- **Best Pub: Ear Inn.** An old hanger-on in chic SoHo, this old joint continues to survive among the lush lounges that surround it. See p. 369.
- **Best Dive Bar: Subway Inn.** Sure, I know you came to New York to go to a dive bar. Enter the Subway Inn, and it's as if you stepped into a 1940s film noir—minus the cigarette smoke, of course. See p. 377.
- **Best Beer Bar: Spuyten Dyvil.** This Williamsburg, Brooklyn bar is ground zero for local beer geeks. Enjoy a draft at this place, which also features a great jukebox. See p. 381.
- **Best Bar with a View: Rise Bar,** in the Ritz-Carlton Battery Park Hotel. With views of Lady Liberty, the harbor, and lovely sunsets. See p. 372.
- **Best Exclusive Bar: Rose Bar,** in the Gramercy Park Hotel. This magnificent room with its Schnabel originals, incredible sound system, beautiful people, and expensive cocktails is worth groveling to enter. See p. 376.

2

New York City in Depth

Etymologists have done their best to trace the factual origins of the term "Big Apple" to New York City. Some say it had to do with a horse racing reference. The prize for the horse being an apple, and in the 1920's, with so many race tracks in New York, it was referred to as the "Big Apple"—the city that jockeys and trainers aspired to conquer. It was Gotham, the Empire City, the City that Never Sleeps, the Melting Pot, the Capital of the World, a city "so nice, they named it twice." After all, when a place is world-class in finance, culture, and media, it's difficult to sum up your grandeur in one easy name. Though, the Big Apple works pretty well. Also "New York City."

How do eight million people function, live, work, and even thrive on top of each other? It's mind-boggling if you think about it too much. And for those of us who do live here, it's best not to ponder the enormity of it all. We're in too much of a hurry.

But forget the monuments, the glass towers, the arenas and theaters of New York, it is the people who made the city. It's the place to prove yourself; to "make a brand new start of it"; and where "if [you] can make it there, [you can] make it anywhere." And it's the people, and their vast unique contributions who keep the city thriving. Whether they are from Ireland, Italy, West Africa, France, Israel, Pakistan, Mexico, Haiti or Manhattan (Kansas), it's that mix of people and cultures that have always been the most solid foundation of the city.

The variety and diversity that has always been New York's trademark seems to form a collective unifying and feisty spirit that is essential to the city's character. Build a fence around New York and keep people out? Are you kidding me? That would be like sucking the lifeblood from the streets—the city would wither and die! No, here in New York, our arms remain open to the world. It's what has made us great in the past and will continue to do so.

1 New York City Today

We New Yorkers have heard the proud refrain from local politicos many times: how New York is better than ever. The FBI has rated New York as the safest big city in the United States. It's cleaner than it ever was. The number of hotels, restaurants, and clubs keeps growing, and they get better every year. This rebirth has helped bring in an estimated 46 million tourists in 2007 and even more are projected in the next few years. Everything seems rosy.

Why then, are some of us worried about our city? With this boom, those of us who have been here a long time and have seen the changes from a city in need to what it is today, fret that this renaissance is one without character. We worry that with a Starbucks on every corner and new glass-and-steel condos sprouting like mushrooms at the expense of an old favorite bookstore or our local Cuban/Chinese joint, that we are slowly losing our identity—the fear being that we will become like Everycity, U.S.A.

But change is inevitable. "Of the city's five boroughs, Manhattan, in particular, refuses to remain as it was. It is dynamic, not static. What seems permanent when you are 20 is too often a ghost when you are 30" Pete Hamill writes in his book *Downtown: My Manhattan.*

And the longer you live in this town, the more ghosts you will encounter. But New Yorkers adapt . . . sometimes painfully. Hamill explains, "The New York version of nostalgia is not simply about lost buildings or their presence in the youth of the individuals who lived with them. It involves an almost fatalistic acceptance of the permanent presence of loss. Nothing will ever stay the same . . . Irreversible change happens so often in New York that the experience affects character itself. New York toughens its people against sentimentality by allowing the truer emotion of nostalgia. Sentimentality

is always about a lie. Nostalgia is about real things gone."

So though we might mourn loss, we also anticipate and expect change—it's part of our way of life. We know that a restaurant, show, club, or store might be the hottest thing now, but a couple months later, the next one has opened or been discovered and that once hot spot quickly becomes passé.

But some icons and institutions are so entrenched in our daily lives that we could never accept their loss. What would we do without that reassuring sight of the Lady in the Harbor or the gleaming spire of the Empire State Building? Or the perfect pizza? Or a Sunday in Central Park? Or the rumbling of the trains beneath the earth? Or the sounds of jazz from a Village club? So while New York is ever-changing, as long as its core remains the same we might complain a bit, but we aren't going anywhere.

In fact, New York City is predicted to add one million *more* residents by 2030 and must figure out where to put them, how to move them around, and what they'll be doing. The city has embarked on an ambitious, long-term plan (called **PlaNYC 2030**) to improve the rapidly aging infrastructure, find ways to fuel its energy needs more sustainably, and expand the mass transit system to accommodate

New York City Timeline

- **1524** Giovanni da Verrazano sails into New York Harbor.
- **1609** Henry Hudson sails up the Hudson River.
- **1621** The Dutch West India Company begins trading from New York City.
- **1626** The Dutch pay 60 guilders ($24) to the Lenape

Tribe for the island of New Amsterdam.
- **1664** The Dutch surrender New Amsterdam to the British and the island is renamed after the brother of King Charles II, the Duke of York.
- **1765** The Sons of Liberty burn the British Governor in effigy.
- **1776** Independence from England is declared.

- **1789** The first Congress is held at Federal Hall on Wall Street, and George Washington is inaugurated.
- **1792** The first stock exchange is established on Wall Street.
- **1820** New York City is the nation's largest city, with a population of 124,000.
- **1859** Central Park opens.

millions more people, as well as figure out ways to build housing that will keep lower- and middle-income people within its borders.

There's been a movement toward congestion pricing (charging vehicles a high premium to drive in Manhattan during the day), which narrowly was defeated in 2008, but because productivity goes down when traffic jams go up, expect to see a new take on solving the traffic crisis in the next several years. And that's just the tip of the iceberg.

It's a big challenge, but as a city that has come up with ingenious solutions since its birth, you can bet New York will be heading into its 400th birthday with some unique (and showy) ways to figure out what's going to happen in the next half-millennium or so.

2 Looking Back at New York City

COLONIAL DAYS (1524–1776)

The area that became New York City was the home to many Native Americans before Giovanni da Verrazano arrived in 1524. And it wasn't until 1609, when Henry Hudson, while searching for the Northwest Passage, claimed it for the Dutch East India Company, that New York was recognized as a potential, profitable settlement in the New World.

Hudson (the river that separates Manhattan from the mainland is named after him) said of New York, "It is as beautiful a land as one can hope to tread upon." The treading didn't really start until years later, but by 1625, Dutch settlers established a fur trade with the locals and called their colony New Amsterdam. A year later, Peter Minuit of the Dutch West India Company made that famous deal for the island. He bought New Amsterdam from the Lenape Tribe for what has widely been reported as $24.

New Amsterdam became a British colony in the 1670s, and during the Revolutionary War it was occupied by British troops. England controlled New York until 1783, when it withdrew from the city 2 years *after* the end of the American Revolution.

Two years after that, New York was named the first capital of the United States. The first Congress was held at Federal Hall on Wall Street in 1789, and George Washington was inaugurated president. But New York's tenure as the capital didn't last long. A year later, the government headed south to the newly created District of Columbia.

- **1863** The draft riots rage throughout New York; 125 people die, including 11 African-Americans who are lynched by mobs of Irish immigrants.
- **1883** The Brooklyn Bridge opens.
- **1886** The Statue of Liberty is completed.
- **1892** Ellis Island opens; begins processing over a million immigrants yearly.

- **1904** The first subway departs from City Hall.
- **1920** Babe Ruth joins the New York Yankees.
- **1923** Yankee Stadium opens.
- **1929** The stock market crashes.
- **1931** The Empire State Building opens and is the tallest building in the world.
- **1939** The New York World's Fair opens in Flushing Meadows, Queens.

- **1947** The Brooklyn Dodgers sign Jackie Robinson, the first African American to play in the Major Leagues.
- **1957** Elvis Presley performs live in New York on the *Ed Sullivan Show*.
- **1969** The Gay Rights movement begins with the Stonewall Rebellion in Greenwich Village.

continues

A MELTING POT CITY

By 1825, New York City's population swelled to 250,000 and rose again to a half-million by midcentury. The city was a hotbed of Union recruitment during the Civil War; in the 1863 draft riots, Irish immigrants violently protested the draft and lynched 11 African Americans.

With industry booming, the late 19th century was termed the "Gilded Age." New York City was an example of this label in action; millionaires built mansions on Fifth Avenue, while rows of tenements teeming with families (made up of the cheap, mostly immigrant laborers who were employed by the industrial barons) filled the city's districts. In 1880, the city's population boomed to 1.1 million.

More European immigrants poured into the city between 1900 and 1930, arriving at Ellis Island and then fanning out into such neighborhoods as the Lower East Side, Greenwich Village, Little Italy, and Harlem. With the city population in 1930 at seven million and a Depression raging, New York turned to a feisty mayor named Fiorello La Guardia for help. With the assistance of civic planner Robert Moses, who masterminded a huge public works program, the city was remade. Moses did some things well, but his highway, bridge, tunnel, and housing projects ran through (and sometimes destroyed) many vibrant neighborhoods.

POST–WORLD WAR II & TODAY

While most of the country prospered after World War II, New York, with those Moses-built highways and a newly forming car culture, endured an exodus to the suburbs. By 1958, the Dodgers had left Brooklyn and the Giants had left the Polo Grounds in upper Manhattan. This economic slide climaxed in the late 1970s with the city's declaration of bankruptcy.

As Wall Street rallied during the Reagan years of the 1980s, New York's fortunes also improved. In the 1990s, with Rudolph Giuliani—whom they haven't named anything after yet—as the mayor, and then followed by the current mayor, Michael Bloomberg, the city rode a wave of prosperity that left it safer, cleaner, and more populated. The flip side of this boom was that Manhattan became more homogenized. Witness the Disney-fication of Times Square—the ultimate symbol of New York's homogenization—and the growing gap between the rich and poor.

Everything changed on September 11, 2001, when terrorists flew planes into the Twin Towers of the World Trade Center. But New York's grit and verve showed itself once more, as the city immediately began to rebound emotionally from that terrible tragedy. The financial aftermaths

- **1990** David Dinkins becomes the first African-American mayor of New York City.
- **2000** The New York Yankees beat the New York Mets in the first Subway Series in 44 years. New York's population exceeds eight million.
- **2001** Terrorists use hijacked planes to crash into the Twin Towers of the World Trade Center, bringing the towers down and killing over 3,000 people.
- **2003** Smoking is banned in all restaurants and bars.
- **2006** Construction begins on the controversial Freedom Tower, to be built at the site of the World Trade Center.
- **2008** The last season for old Yankee Stadium; version 2.0 opens in 2009.

of the attacks were also short-lived, and the city has experienced an unprece-dented building boom in the first decade of the 21st Century.

3 New York City's Architecture

New York City contains a wealth of architectural styles, from modest row houses to ornate churches to soaring skyscrapers. Constructed over 300 years, these buildings represent the changing tastes of the city's residents from Colonial times to the present. A brief look at the city's most popular styles provides a unique perspective on the city's past, present, and future.

GEORGIAN (1700–76)

This style reflects Renaissance ideas made popular in England, and later in the United States, through the publication of books on 16th-century Italian architects. In the United States, the style was seen as an appropriate expression of the relative prosperity and security of the colonies. It was a sharp contrast to the unadorned Colonial style that preceded it.

St. Paul's Chapel, on Broadway between Vesey and Fulton streets (1764–66, Thomas McBean), the only pre-Revolutionary building remaining in Manhattan, is an almost perfect example of the Georgian style, with a pediment, colossal columns, Palladian window, quoins, and balustrade above the roof line (see illustration). Although it's a 20th-century reconstruction of a formal English house built here in 1719, **Fraunces Tavern,** 54 Pearl St., is another fine example of the style.

St. Paul's Chapel

FEDERAL (1780–1820)

Federal was the first truly American architectural style. Federal was popular with successful merchants throughout the cities and towns of the eastern seaboard. Its connection to the prosperous empires of Rome and Greece was seen as an appropriate reference for the young United States.

In New York, the Federal style was popular for row houses built after the 1811 creation of the city's grid pattern of avenues and streets.

In the **West Village,** near and along Bedford Street between Christopher and Morton streets, are more original Federal-style houses than anywhere else in Manhattan. House nos. 4 through 10 (1825–34) on Grove Street, just off Bedford, present one of the most authentic groups of late Federal–style houses in America.

GREEK REVIVAL (1820–60)

The Greek Revolution in the 1820s, in which Greece won its independence from the Turks, recalled to American intellectuals the democracy of ancient Greece and its elegant architecture, created around 400 B.C. At the same time, the War of 1812

Federal Hall National Memorial

diminished American affection for the British influence, including the still-dominant Federal style. The style was so popular it came to be known as the National Style, and was used for numerous state capitols, as well as the U.S. Capitol in Washington, D.C.

Perhaps the city's finest Greek Revival building is **Federal Hall National Memorial** (1834–42), at 26 Wall St., where George Washington took his presidential oath in 1789 (see illustration). It has a Greek temple front, with Doric columns and a simple pediment, resting on a high base, called a *plinth,* with a steep flight of steps.

GOTHIC REVIVAL (1830–60)

The term *Gothic Revival* refers to a literary and aesthetic movement of the 1830s and 1840s that occurred in England and later in the United States. The revival style was used for everything from timber cottages to stone castles and churches. Some structures had only one or two Gothic features, most commonly a steeply pitched roof or pointed arches, whereas other buildings, usually churches, were accurate copies of English Gothic structures.

Trinity Church, at Broadway and Wall Street (Richard Upjohn, 1846), is one of the most celebrated, authentic Gothic Revival structures in the United States. Here you see all the features of a Gothic church: a steeple, battlements, pointed arches, Gothic tracery, stained-glass windows, *flying buttresses* (an external bracing system for supporting a roof or vault), and medieval sculptures. This was the tallest building in the area until the late 1860s.

ITALIANATE (1840–80)

The architecture of Italy served as the inspiration for this building style. Its adaptability made it immensely popular in the 1850s. In New York, the style was used for urban row houses and commercial buildings. The development of cast iron at this time permitted the mass production of decorative features that few could have afforded in carved stone. This led to the creation of cast-iron districts in nearly every American city, including New York.

New York's **SoHo–Cast Iron Historic District** has 26 blocks jammed with cast-iron facades, many in the Italianate manner. The single richest section is **Greene Street** between Houston and Canal streets. Stroll along here and take in building after building of sculptural facades.

EARLY SKYSCRAPER (1880–1920)

The invention of the skyscraper can be traced directly to the use of cast iron in the 1840s, such as those seen in New York's SoHo. Experimentation with cast and wrought iron eventually allowed buildings to rise higher. (Previously, buildings were restricted by the height supportable by their load-bearing walls.) Important technical innovations—involving safety elevators, electricity, fireproofing, foundations, plumbing, and telecommunications—combined with advances in skeletal construction to create a new building type, the skyscraper. These buildings were spacious, cost-effective, efficient, and quickly erected—in short, the perfect architectural solution for America's growing downtowns.

Solving the technical problems of the skyscraper did not resolve how the building should look.

New York's early skyscrapers relied heavily on historical decoration. A good early example in the Beaux Arts mode is the **American Surety Company,** at 100 Broadway (Bruce Price, 1895). The triangular **Flatiron Building,** at Fifth Avenue and 23rd Street (Daniel H. Burnham & Co., 1902), has strong tripartite divisions and Renaissance Revival detail. And, finally, the later **Woolworth Building** (Cass Gilbert, 1913), on Broadway at Park Place, dubbed the "Cathedral of Commerce," is a neo-Gothic skyscraper with flying buttresses, spires, sculptured gargoyles, and pointed arches.

BEAUX ARTS (1890–1920)

This style takes its name from the Ecole des Beaux-Arts in Paris, where a number of prominent American architects (including **Richard Morris Hunt** [1827–95], **John Mervin Carrère** [1858–1911], and **Thomas Hastings** [1860–1929], to name only a few) received their training, beginning around the mid–19th century. These architects adopted the academic design principles of the Ecole, which emphasized the study of Greek and Roman structures, composition, and symmetry, and the creation of elaborate presentation drawings. Because of the idealized origins and grandiose use of classical forms, the Beaux Arts in America was seen as the ideal style for expressing civic pride.

New York has several exuberant Beaux Arts buildings, exhibiting the style's key features. The **New York Public Library,** at Fifth Avenue and 42nd Street (Carrère & Hastings, 1911), is perhaps the best example. Others of note are **Grand Central Terminal,** at 42nd Street and Park Avenue (Reed & Stem and Warren & Whetmore, 1903–13), and the **U.S. Customs House** (Cass Gilbert, 1907), on Bowling Green between State and Whitehall streets.

INTERNATIONAL STYLE (1920–45)

In 1932, the Museum of Modern Art hosted its first architecture exhibit, titled simply "Modern Architecture." Displays included images of International Style buildings from around the world, many designed by architects from Germany's Bauhaus, a progressive design school. The structures shared a stark simplicity and functionalism, a definite break from historically based, decorative styles.

The International Style was popularized in the U.S. through the teachings and designs of **Ludwig Mies van der Rohe** (1886–1969), a German émigré based in Chicago. Interpretations of the "Miesian" International Style were built in most U.S. cities, including New York, as late as 1980.

Two famous examples of this style are the **Seagram Building,** at 375 Park Ave. (Ludwig Mies van der Rohe, 1958), and **Lever House,** 390 Park Ave., between 53rd and 54th streets (Skidmore, Owings & Merrill, 1952). The latter is credited for popularizing the use of plazas and glass curtain walls.

Another well-known example is the Secretariat building in the **United Nations** complex, at First Avenue and 46th Street (1947–53), designed by an international committee of architects.

ART DECO (1925–40)

Art Deco is a decorative style that took its name from a Paris exposition in 1925. The jazzy style embodied the idea of modernity. One of the first widely accepted styles not based on historic precedents, it influenced all areas of design from jewelry and household goods to cars, trains, and ocean liners.

Art Deco buildings are characterized by a linear, hard edge, or angular composition, often with a vertical emphasis and highlighted with stylized decoration. The New York zoning law of 1916, which required setbacks in buildings above a certain height to ensure that light and air could reach the street, gave the style its distinctive profile.

Despite the effects of the Depression, several major Art Deco structures were built in New York in the 1930s, often providing crucial jobs. **Rockefeller Center** (Raymond Hood, 1932–40), a complex that sprawls from 48th to 50th streets, between Fifth and Sixth avenues, includes 30 Rockefeller Plaza, a tour de force of Art Deco style, with a soaring, vertical shaft and aluminum details. The **Chrysler Building,** Lexington Avenue at 42nd Street (William Van Alen, 1930), is a towering tribute to the automobile (see illustration). The Chrysler's needlelike spire with zigzag patterns in glass and metal is a distinctive feature on the city's skyline. The famous **Empire State Building,** Fifth Avenue at 34th Street (Shreve, Lamb & Harmon, 1931), contains a black- and silver-toned lobby among its many Art Deco features.

Chrysler Building

POSTMODERN (1975–90)

After years of steel-and-glass office towers in the International Style, Postmodernism burst on the scene in the 1970s with the reintroduction of historical precedents in architecture. With many feeling that the office towers of the previous style were too cold, Postmodernists began to incorporate classical details and recognizable forms into their designs—often applied in outrageous proportions.

The **Sony Building,** at 550 Madison Ave. (Philip Johnson/John Burgee, 1984), brings the distinctive shape of a Chippendale cabinet to the New York skyline. The **Morgan Bank Headquarters,** 60 Wall St. (Kevin Roche, John Dinkeloo & Assocs., 1988), resembles a classical column, with modern interpretations of a base, shaft, and capital. The base of the column mirrors the style of the facade of the 19th-century building across the street.

The new building boom at the beginning of the 21st century has brought edifices designed by such modern architectural giants as Frank Gehry, who designed the **IAC Building** on West 18th Street with the look of billowing curtains; and Renzo Piano designed the 52-story headquarters of the *New York Times* at 620 Eighth Ave. at 42nd Street, which opened in November 2007 (and was climbed by not one, but two, "human spiders" on the same day in June 2008!).

4 New York in Popular Culture: Books, Film, TV & Music

BOOKS

For the definitive history of the birth of New York City to the end of the 19th century, there is no better read than the Pulitzer Prize–winning *Gotham: A History of New York City to 1898,* by Edwin R. Burrows and Mike Wallace (Oxford University Press). Another recommended historical look at the growth of New York City, this one told in a breezy narrative tone, is *The Epic of New York City: A Narrative History,* by Edward Robb Ellis (Kodansha).

Luc Sante's *Low Life: Lures and Snares of Old New York* (Vintage Departures) details the bad old days of brothels, drug dens, and gambling saloons in New York in the early 20th century—it's a lively, fascinating read.

One of master biographer Robert Caro's early works, *The Power Broker: Robert Moses and the Fall of New York* (Random House) focuses on how the vision of master dealmaker Robert Moses transformed New York to what it became in the second half of the 20th century.

The 2004-published *Downtown,* by Pete Hamill (Little Brown & Co.), is as concise a history of the area to the south of Times Square as you will find—and told in Hamill's typically breezy and gritty style, while Hamill's 2003 novel, *Forever,* chronicles the 3 centuries of a man who has been given the gift of eternal life as long as he never leaves the island of Manhattan. In *The Great Bridge: The Epic Story of the Building of the Brooklyn Bridge* (Simon & Schuster), author David McCullough devotes his estimable talents to the story of the building of the Brooklyn Bridge.

The companion to the PBS Series (see below) *New York,* by Ric Burns, Lisa Ades, and James Sanders (Knopf), uses lavish photographs and illustrations to show the growth of New York City.

My all-time favorite book about New York is a children's classic called *This Is New York* (Universe Publishing), written and illustrated by M. Sasek in 1960. The book was recently reissued and, with an update added, is as fresh as it was all those years ago.

New York has been fertile fodder for novelists, and the city is often a character in itself. The novels with New York as the backdrop are too numerous to begin to chronicle. Here are some of my personal favorites:

Call it Sleep, by Henry Roth: This 1934 novel tells the story of a poor Jewish boy and his coming to terms with his old-world parents and the modern world of New York around him.

I, the Jury, by Mickey Spillane: This 1947 potboiler, by New York native Spillane, introduces tough-guy detective Mike Hammer as he investigates the dark side of the upper-class of New York.

Last Exit to Brooklyn, by Hubert Selby, Jr.: This 1964 novel takes place in and around what is now the Red Hook/Brooklyn Navy Yard section of Brooklyn, and the portrait is bleak to say the least.

A Rage in Harlem, by Chester Himes: All of the novels in Chester Himes' Coffin Ed Johnson and Gravedigger Jones detective series are vivid looks at Harlem in the 1940s and 1950s, written, amazingly, when Himes was living in Paris.

Time and Again, by Jack Finney: This time-travel fantasy, written in 1970, takes the main character from present day New York to the city in 1882, where Finney gets the period detail perfectly.

The Fortunate Pilgrim, by Mario Puzo: Famous as the author of *The Godfather,* this more literary, semiautobiographical effort about an Italian-American family growing up in Hell's Kitchen is a masterpiece and was sadly dismissed when it was published in 1965.

New York City Playlist

The energy of New York City's streets provides inspiration to songwriters and musicians. New York is probably the most vibrant city for music in the world. From songsmiths crowding such storied places as Tin Pan Alley and the Brill Building, to the folkies wandering Bleecker Street, the styles of music and songs about New York are countless. Everyone has a song that means "New York" to them, so here are *my* top ten New York City songs.

1. **"Autumn in New York":** This 1934 jazz standard has been performed by greats including Ella Fitzgerald, Frank Sinatra, Charlie Parker and Louis Armstrong. My favorite rendition is the one performed by the Modern Jazz Quartet.
2. **"Downtown":** This 1965 mega-hit, performed by Petula Clark, is an early anthem to the thrill of nightlife "downtown." It's as timely today as it was 45 years ago.
3. **"I Guess the Lord Must Be in New York City":** Harry Nilsson wrote this song in 1968 for the movie *Midnight Cowboy,* but the director of that movie, John Schlesinger, used Nilsson's other song "Everybody's Talkin" instead. He really couldn't go wrong with either.
4. **"On Broadway":** This 1963 hit for the Drifters, another theme about making it in New York, has been covered by many, including guitarist George Benson who had a huge hit with it and did not "catch the Greyhound bus for home."
5. **"Spanish Harlem":** This hit for Ben E. King in 1961, from songwriters Jerry Leiber and Phil Spector, had a distinctive Latin beat, evoking the

When the Sacred Ginmill Closes, by Lawrence Block: Block, in his Matt Scudder mystery series, uses New York as a major character. This is my favorite in the series.

The Mambo Kings Play Songs of Love, by Oscar Hijuelos: This story about two Cuban musicians who emigrate to New York, specifically upper Manhattan, in the early 1950s, deservedly won the Pulitzer Prize for fiction in 1990.

FILMS

There are not many places as cinematic as New York City. Filmmakers, like novelists, view the city as a character. The list of movies in which New York plays a crucial role are too many to mention, but here are some of the top New York City movies that are worth renting before you visit.

Possibly the best New York City promotional film is the musical **On the Town** (1948), with Gene Kelly and Frank Sinatra, about three sailors with 24 hours' leave spent exploring Gotham. Shot on location, all the landmarks were captured in beautiful Technicolor.

Woody Allen is a New York filmmaker and shoots almost all his films in the city. One of his best—and a good, but maybe a bit dated, look at neurotic New York— is **Annie Hall** (1977).

Following in Woody Allen's footsteps are director Rob Reiner and writer Nora Ephron, who made **When Harry Met Sally** (1989). It's sort of a poor-man's *Annie Hall* but a gorgeous cinematic tribute to New York. The famous "I'll have what she's having" scene was filmed in **Katz's Delicatessen** (p. 156).

influx of Puerto Ricans to the city at the time. The red rose in Spanish Harlem became a "black" rose when Aretha Franklin covered the song in 1971.

6. **"Summer in the City":** This 1966 hit by the Lovin Spoonful captures the raw grit of a stifling New York summer. It really is "a pity the days can't be like the nights in the summer in the city."

7. **"Take the A Train":** The signature tune by Duke Ellington and lyrics by Billy Strayhorn refer to the A train that runs from Brooklyn, through Manhattan, and up to Harlem. And the A train is *still* the "quickest way to get to Harlem."

8. **"The Message":** "It's like a jungle sometimes . . ." This 1982 hip-hop classic by Grandmaster Flash and the Furious Five masterfully re-creates the urban rage of the time.

9. **Theme from "New York, New York":** Start spreadin' the news: This Kander and Ebb classic was the theme song for the Martin Scorsese movie of the same name. Liza Minnelli sang it in the film, but it's the Frank Sinatra version that has become synonymous with the city and all its challenges.

10. **"Walk on the Wild Side":** Lou Reed's 1972 classic was produced by David Bowie and was a big hit despite its obviously dark and downright perverse undertones. With "A hustle here and a hustle there/New York City is the place where they said. . . ."

"I love this dirty town," says Burt Lancaster in the gritty, crackling *Sweet Smell of Success* (1957). In the beautifully photographed black-and-white movie, Lancaster plays malicious gossip columnist J. J. Hunsecker, and Tony Curtis is perfectly despicable as the groveling publicist Sidney Falco.

It seems like since the beginning of New York time, the city was the place people came to become famous. Joe Buck (Jon Voight) came to New York from Texas to be a big shot in the 1969 Academy Award–winner *Midnight Cowboy,* but it took a third-rate conman, Ratso Rizzo (Dustin Hoffman), to transform Voight into a pathetic male hustler. The movie is a bleak, but realistic look at the timeless New York story.

Another filmmaker identified with New York is Martin Scorsese. He has made many films where New York plays a central role, from *Mean Streets* (1973) to *Gangs of New York* (2002), which was actually filmed in Italy. But the one film in which New York is a character, and not a very flattering one, is *Taxi Driver.* The Academy Award–nominated 1976 movie about an alienated and psychotic taxi driver is tough and bloody, but to see images of seedy Times Square as it was before its recent reincarnation, there is no better film.

Though long, Sergio Leone's *Once Upon A Time in America* (1984), about Jewish gangsters in the first part of the 20th Century, evokes the period masterfully and features stunning New York City locations.

Live *Not* from New York (but about New York)

Some of the best television shows about New York were never filmed in New York, with the exception of some stock footage. Here is my list of the best New York television not filmed in New York.

- *Seinfeld* (1990–98): You couldn't get it any more accurate than this show. It was as if they bottled the New York attitude in so many ways and made sure it was let loose on the set. The show has even spawned location tours in the city led by the real-life Kramer. Not that there's anything wrong with that. He's real, and he's spectacular.

- *All in the Family* (1971–79): Archie Bunker, brilliantly played by Carroll O'Connor, was the quintessential white, blue-collared New York bigot, who lived with his "dingbat" wife, Edith, and daughter and son-in-law ("Meathead") in a small house in Astoria.

- *NYPD Blue* (1993–2005): As long as the show didn't spend too much time outdoors (the California light was a big giveaway), but stayed inside the precinct house, this gritty cop drama, especially in its first few years, was a good, tough look at city detectives, and occasionally, their rear ends.

- *Taxi* (1978–83): The cross-section of taxi drivers, at the time, showed the diversity of the city. Now, however, though still entertaining, it is very dated: You won't see a Checker cab on the street anymore, and you are most likely to be driven by drivers from countries ranging from the West Indies to West Africa to Pakistan. The haunting theme and opening shots of a taxi driving over the Queensboro Bridge remain classics.

- *Welcome Back Kotter* (1975–79): Oh to return to the innocent days of Brooklyn public schools when your only worries were "delinquent" Sweathogs, such as Vinnie Barbarino, Arnold Horshack, a Puerto Rican–Jew named Juan Epstein, and Freddie "Boom Boom" Washington—big afros and all—taught by a wise-cracking teacher named Kotter. John Travolta, of course, is famous for playing another Brooklynite: *Saturday Night Fever*'s Tony Manero.

The fourth largest city in America, Brooklyn, has also been a colorful location. John Travolta's march under the elevated train in Bensonhurst to the tune of the Bee Gee's "Staying Alive" in *Saturday Night Fever* (1977) and Gene Hackman's frenetic and dizzying car chase under the same tracks in *The French Connection* (1971) are two of the best Brooklyn-centric movies.

The best history of New York on video is the Ric Burns documentary *New York: A Documentary Film* (1999), which aired on PBS. The seven-disc, 14-hour DVD (also available on VHS) is a must-see for anyone interested in the evolution of this great city.

TELEVISION

The medium of television was born in New York City in the late 1940s and 1950s. Many early pioneering television programs were filmed in New York, often in front of live audiences. Breaking new ground, programs such as the *Philco Television Playhouse* and *Playhouse 90* featured original dramas by heavyweight writers, including Paddy Chayefsky, Gore Vidal, and Rod Serling; directors such as Sidney Lumet and Arthur Penn; and actors, including Robert Redford, Jack Klugman, and Rod Steiger.

Comedy was a big part of the early days of television and the talent level was impressive: Best among the programs was *Your Show of Shows* (1950–54), which showcased the talents of Sid Caesar, Carl Reiner, and Mel Brooks among others who would improvise and devise sketches in a 90-minute show each week; the show was an inspiration for another New York–based comedy sketch series, *Saturday Night Live.*

The sitcom was also hatched during this period in New York. The best, by far, was the story of the timeless travails of a city bus driver named Ralph Kramden, his wife Alice, and their friends, Ed and Trixie Norton, all who lived in Brooklyn. The ensemble team of Jackie Gleason, Art Carney, Audrey Meadows, and Joyce Randolph, and a very limited set, formed what is now history in *The Honeymooners* (1955–56).

In the 1960s, most television production moved to the West Coast, but a few mainstays remained, such as the *Ed Sullivan Show* and the *Tonight Show with Johnny Carson,* which migrated west in 1972; a few soap operas, including *Guiding Light, As the World Turns,* and *All My Children,* continue to be shot in New York.

While most sitcoms and dramas were produced in Los Angeles, there were a couple of notable exceptions that used New York as their home base, including classic shows *The Odd Couple* (1970–75) and *The Cosby Show* (1984–92).

In the 1990s and up to the present, New York has seen a resurgence of film and television production, including *Law and Order* and all its spinoffs, *Late Show with David Letterman,* the HBO series *Sex and the City, 30 Rock,* the *Daily Show,* and the *Colbert Report.*

3

Planning Your Trip to New York City

One of the few constants about New York City is that things are always changing. If it's not new stadiums for the Yankees and Mets, it's a change in taxi fares. One beloved restaurant closes down . . . and another hot, trendy joint takes its place. Hotels refurbish, reinvent, and get built from the ground up. One season there's a new museum, the next a new governor. You need to keep up with these things!

This entire book is designed to help you plan and enjoy your trip, and this particular chapter focuses on the "ready, set . . ." part before you go. Whether you're a first-time visitor or someone who's been here many times, take a look at the information below. It outlines our best advice for planning your trip, whether you'll be arriving from an international destination (all the better to take advantage of the favorable currency exchange rates) or from down the road.

If you haven't been here in some time, here's a basic reality check: New York City is cleaner and safer than ever before. It's also more expensive.

Bring money. Bring comfortable shoes, because walking is one of the best ways to get around. Bring your appetite, your party clothes, your intellect, and curiosity. Bring your patience and sense of humor. Before you know it, you'll be discussing the finer points of your favorite new ethnic cuisine and navigating the subway like a pro.

For additional help in planning your trip and for more on-the-ground resources in New York City, please turn to the "Fast Facts, Toll-Free Numbers, & Websites," appendix on p. 387.

1 Visitor Information

Before you leave home, your best information source (besides this book, of course) is **NYC & Company,** the organization that fronts the New York Convention & Visitors Bureau (NYCVB), located at 810 Seventh Ave., New York, NY 10019. You can call ✆ **800/NYC-VISIT** to request the *Official NYC Guide* detailing hotels, restaurants, theaters, attractions, events, and more. The guide is free and will arrive in 7 to 10 days. (*Note:* I've received complaints that they sometimes take longer.)

You can find a wealth of free information on the bureau's website, **www.nyc visit.com**. To speak with a live travel counselor, call ✆ **212/484-1222,** which is staffed weekdays from 8:30am to 6pm EST, weekends from 8:30am to 5pm EST.

We include a fold-out map of Manhattan with this book, and you will also need a transit map, which you can get at the Times Square Visitors Center (p. 67) or at most larger subway stations. We also include a map of most of the Manhattan subway lines on the inside back cover of this book.

For visitor-center and information-desk locations once you arrive, see "Visitor Information" in the "Getting Around" section, later this chapter.

FOR U.K. VISITORS The **NYCVB Visitor Information Center** is at 36 Southwark Bridge Rd., London, SE1 9EU (© **020/7202-6367**). You can order the Official NYC Visitor Kit by sending an A5-size self-addressed envelope and 72p postage to the above address. For New York–bound travelers in London, the center also offers free one-on-one travel-planning assistance.

2 Entry Requirements

New regulations issued by the Department of Homeland Security now require every air traveler entering the U.S. to show a passport. As of January 23, 2007, all persons, including U.S. citizens, traveling by air between the United States and Canada, Mexico, Central and South America, the Caribbean, and Bermuda are required to present a valid passport. As of January 31, 2008, U.S. and Canadian citizens entering the U.S. at land and sea ports of entry from within the western hemisphere will need to present a passport for admission to the U.S.

For information on how to obtain a passport (for both U.S. citizens and international visitors), go to "Passports" in the "Fast Facts," appendix (p. 391).

VISAS

The U.S. Department of State has a **Visa Waiver Program (VWP)** allowing citizens of the following countries to enter the United States without a visa for stays of up to 90 days: Andorra, Australia, Austria, Belgium, Brunei, Denmark, Finland, France, Germany, Iceland, Ireland, Italy, Japan, Liechtenstein, Luxembourg, Monaco, the Netherlands, New Zealand, Norway, Portugal, San Marino, Singapore, Slovenia, Spain, Sweden, Switzerland, and the United Kingdom. (**Note:** This list was accurate at press time; for the most up-to-date list of countries in the VWP, consult **www.travel.state. gov/visa**.) Canadian citizens may enter the United States without visas; they will need to show passports (if traveling by air) and proof of residence, however.

Note: Any passport issued on or after October 26, 2006, by a VWP country must be an **e-Passport** for VWP travelers to be eligible to enter the U.S. without a visa. Citizens of these nations also need to present a round-trip air or cruise ticket upon arrival. E-Passports contain computer chips capable of storing biometric information, such as the required digital photograph of the holder. (You can identify an e-Passport by the symbol on the bottom center cover of your passport.) If your passport doesn't have this feature, you can still travel without a visa if it is a valid passport issued before October 26, 2005, and includes a machine-readable zone, or between October 26, 2005, and October 25, 2006, and includes a digital photograph. For more information, go to **www.travel.state.gov/visa**.

Citizens of all other countries must have (1) a valid passport that expires at least 6 months later than the scheduled end of their visit to the U.S., and (2) a tourist visa, which may be obtained without charge from any U.S. consulate.

As of January 2004, many international visitors traveling on visas to the United States will be photographed and fingerprinted on arrival at Customs in airports and on cruise ships in a program created by the Department of Homeland Security called **US-VISIT.** Exempt from the extra scrutiny are visitors entering by land or those (mostly in Europe; see p. 29) that don't require a visa for short-term visits. For more information, go to the Homeland Security website at **www.dhs.gov/ dhspublic**.

Cut to the Front of the Security Line as a Registered Traveler

In 2003, the **Transportation Security Administration (TSA)** (www.tsa.gov) approved a pilot program to help ease the time spent in line for airport security screenings. In exchange for personal information and a fee, persons can be prescreened as registered travelers, granting them a front-of-the-line position when they fly. The program is run through private firms—the largest and most well-known is Steven Brill's **Clear** (www.flyclear.com), and it works like this: travelers complete an online application, providing specific points of personal information including name, addresses for the previous 5 years, birth date, social security number, driver's license number, and a valid credit card (you're not charged the $99 fee until your application is approved). Print out the completed form and take it, along with proper ID, with you to an "enrollment station" (this can be found in over 20 participating airports and in a number of American Express offices around the country). At the enrollment station, a Clear representative will record your biometrics necessary for clearance; in this case, your fingerprints and your irises will be digitally recorded.

Once your application has been screened against no-fly lists, outstanding warrants, and other security measures, you'll be issued a clear plastic card with a computer chip containing your information. Each time you fly through participating airports, go to the Clear Pass station next to the standard TSA screening line. Insert your card into a slot and place your finger on a scanner to read your print—when the information matches up, you're cleared to go to the head of the security line. You'll still have to follow all other security procedures, such as removing your shoes and walking through the x-ray machine, but Clear promises to cut 30 minutes off your wait time at the airport.

Each time I've used my Clear Pass, my travel companions are still waiting to go through security while I'm sitting down, reading, and sipping my overpriced smoothie. Granted, registered traveler programs are not for the infrequent traveler, but for those who fly on a regular basis, it's a perk I'm willing to pay for.

—David A. Lytle, Frommers.com

For specifics on how to get a visa, go to "Visas" in the "Fast Facts," appendix (p. 393).

MEDICAL REQUIREMENTS

Unless you're arriving from an area known to be suffering from an epidemic (particularly cholera or yellow fever), inoculations or vaccinations are not required for entry into the United States.

CUSTOMS
WHAT YOU CAN BRING INTO THE U.S.

Every visitor older than 21 years of age may bring in, free of duty, the following: (1) 1 liter of wine or hard liquor; (2) 200 cigarettes, 100 cigars (but not from Cuba), or 3 pounds of smoking tobacco; and (3) $100 worth of gifts. These exemptions are offered to travelers who spend at least 72 hours in the United States and who have not claimed them within the preceding 6 months. It is forbidden to bring into the country almost any meat products (including canned, fresh, and dried meat products such as bouillon, soup mixes, etc.). Generally, condiments, including vinegars, oils, and spices, coffee, tea, and some cheeses and baked goods are permitted. Avoid rice products, as rice can often harbor insects. Bringing fruits and vegetables is not advised, though not prohibited. Customs will allow produce depending on where you got it and where you're going after you arrive in the U.S. Foreign tourists may carry in or out up to $10,000 in U.S. or foreign currency with no formalities; larger sums must be declared to U.S. Customs on entering or leaving, which includes filing form CM 4790. For details on U.S. Customs and Border Protection, consult your nearest U.S. embassy or consulate, or **U.S. Customs** (www.customs.ustreas.gov).

WHAT YOU CAN TAKE HOME FROM NEW YORK

Canadian Citizens: For a clear summary of Canadian rules, write for the booklet I Declare, issued by the Canada Border Services Agency (© **800/461-9999** in Canada, or 204/983-3500; www.cbsa-asfc.gc.ca).

U.K. Citizens: For information, contact **HM Customs & Excise** at © **0845/010-9000** (from outside the U.K., 020/8929-0152), or consult their website at **www.hmce.gov.uk**.

Australian Citizens: A helpful brochure, available from Australian consulates or Customs offices, is *Know Before You Go.* For more information, call the **Australian Customs Service** at © **1300/363-263,** or log on to **www.customs.gov.au**.

New Zealand Citizens: Most questions are answered in a free pamphlet available at New Zealand consulates and Customs offices: *New Zealand Customs Guide for Travellers, Notice no. 4.* For more information, contact **New Zealand Customs,** The Customhouse, 17–21 Whitmore St., Box 2218, Wellington (© **04/473-6099** or 0800/428-786; www.customs.govt.nz).

3 When to Go

Summer or winter, rain or shine, there's always great stuff going on in New York City, so there's no real "best" time to go.

Culture hounds might come in fall, winter, and early spring, when the theater and performing-arts seasons reach their heights. During summer, many of the top cultural institutions, especially Lincoln Center, offer free, alfresco entertainment. Those who want to see the biggest hits on Broadway usually have the best luck getting tickets in the slower months of January and February.

Gourmands might find it easiest to land the best tables during July and August, when New Yorkers escape the city on weekends. If you prefer to walk every city block to take in the sights, spring and fall usually offer the mildest and most pleasant weather.

New York is a nonstop holiday party from early December through the start of the New Year. Celebrations of the season abound in festive holiday windows and events such as the lighting of the Rockefeller Center tree and the Radio City Christmas Spectacular—not to mention those terrific seasonal sales that make New York a holiday shopping bonanza.

However, keep in mind that hotel prices go sky high (more on that below), and the crowds are almost intolerable. If you'd rather have more of the city to yourself—better chances at restaurant reservations and shows, easier access to museums and other attractions—choose another time of year to visit.

MONEY MATTERS   Hotel prices have gone up the past couple of years and bargains are harder to find. Therefore, if money is a big concern, you might want to follow these rough seasonal guidelines.

Bargain hunters might want to visit in winter, between the first of the year and early April. Sure, you might have to bear some cold weather, but that's when hotels are suffering from the post-holiday blues, and rooms often go for a relative song—a song in this case may mean a room with a private bathroom for as little as $150. AAA cardholders can do even better in many cases (generally a 5%–10% savings if the hotel offers a AAA discount). However, be aware that the occasional convention or event, such as February's annual Fashion Week, can sometimes throw a wrench in your winter savings plans.

Spring and fall are traditionally the busiest and most expensive seasons after holiday time. Don't expect hotels to be handing you deals, but you may be able to negotiate a decent rate.

The city is drawing more families these days, and they usually visit in the summer. Still, the prospect of heat and humidity keeps some people away, making July and the first half of August a cheaper time to visit than later in the year; good hotel deals are often available.

During the Christmas season, expect to pay top dollar for everything. The first 2 weeks of December—the shopping weeks—are the worst when it comes to scoring an affordable hotel room; that's when shoppers from around the world converge on the town to catch the holiday spirit and spend, spend, spend. But Thanksgiving can be a great time to come, believe it or not: Business travelers have gone home, and the holiday shoppers haven't yet arrived. It's a little-known secret that most hotels away from the Thanksgiving Day Parade route have empty rooms, and they're usually willing to make great deals to fill them.

WEATHER   Many consider that long week or 10 days that arrive each summer between mid-July and mid-August, when temperatures can go up to as high as 100°F (38°C) with 90% humidity, as New York's worst weather. Don't get put off by this—summer has its compensations, such as wonderful free open-air concerts and other events, as I've mentioned—but bear it in mind. If you are at all temperature sensitive, your odds of getting comfortable weather are better in June or September.

Another period when you might not like to stroll around the city is during January or February, when temperatures are commonly in the 20s°F (below 0°C) and those concrete canyons turn into wind tunnels. The city looks gorgeous for about a day after a snowfall, but the streets soon become a slushy mess. Again, you never know—temperatures have regularly been in the 30s and mild 40s (single digits Celsius) during the past few global-warmed winters. If you hit the weather jackpot, you could have a bargain bonanza (see "Money Matters," above).

Fall and spring are the best times in New York. From April to June and September to November, temperatures are mild and pleasant, and the light is beautiful. With the leaves changing in Central Park and just the hint of crispness in the air, October is a fabulous time to be here—but expect to pay for the privilege.

If you want to know what to pack just before you go, check the Weather Channel's online 10-day forecast at **www.weather.com**; I like to balance it against CNN's online 5-day forecast at **www.cnn.com/weather**. You can also get the local weather by calling ©️ **212/976-1212.**

New York's Average Temperature & Rainfall

	Jan	Feb	Mar	Apr	May	June	July	Aug	Sept	Oct	Nov	Dec
Daily Temp. (°F)	32	34	42	53	63	72	77	76	68	58	48	37
Daily Temp. (°C)	0	1	6	12	17	22	25	24	20	14	9	3
Days of Precipitation	11	10	11	11	11	10	11	10	8	8	9	10

NEW YORK CITY CALENDAR OF EVENTS

The following information is always subject to change. Confirm before you make plans around a specific event. Call the venue or the NYCVB at 𝄢 212/484-1222, go to www.nycvisit.com, or buy a copy of **Time Out New York** for the latest details.

For an exhaustive list of events beyond those listed here, check **http://events.frommers. com**, where you'll find a searchable, up-to-the-minute roster of what's happening in cities all over the world.

January

New York National Boat Show. Slip on your Top-Siders and head to the **Jacob K. Javits Convention Center** for the boat show, which promises a leviathan fleet of boats and marine products from the world's leading manufacturers. Call 𝄢 212/984-7000 or visit **www.boatshows.com**, **www. nyboatshow.com**, or **www.javitscenter. com**. First or second week in January.

Restaurant Week. Twice a year some of the best restaurants in town offer three-course prix-fixe meals at *almost* afford-able prices. At lunch, the deal is $24.07 (as in 24/7), while dinner is $35. Some restaurants in 2007 included standouts such as Esca, LeCirque, and Union Square Café. Call 𝄢 212/484-1222 for info, or visit **www.nycvisit.com**. Late January.

February

Chinese New Year. Every year, China-town rings in its own New Year (based on a lunar calendar) with 2 weeks of celebrations, including parades with dragon and lion dancers, plus vivid costumes of all kinds. The parade usu-ally winds throughout Chinatown along Mott, Canal, and Bayard streets, and along East Broadway. Call the **NYCVB hot line** at 𝄢 212/484-1222 or the **Asian American Business Development Center** at 𝄢 212/966-0100. Chinese New Year falls on Janu-ary 26 in 2009, and it's the Year of the Ox.

Westminster Kennel Club Dog Show. The ultimate purebred-pooch fest. Some 30,000 dog fanciers from the world over congregate at **Madison Square Garden** for the 133rd "World Series of Dogdom." All 2,500 dogs are American Kennel Club Champions of Record, competing for the Best in Show trophy. Check the website **www.westminsterkennelclub.org** for further info. Tickets are available after January 1 via **Ticketmaster** (𝄢 212/ 307-7171; www.ticketmaster.com). February 9 and 10, 2009.

March

Triple Pier Antiques Show. The city's largest and most comprehensive antiques show takes place over 2 con-secutive weekends, as more than 600 dealers exhibit their treasures, ranging from jewelry to home furnishings, on three piers along the Hudson River between 48th and 51st streets. **Pier 88** features 20th-century modern col-lectibles; **Pier 90** has all manner of Americana, including country rustic, folk art, and Arts and Crafts; and **Pier 92** houses 18th- and 19th-century for-mal European antiques. Call 𝄢 212/ 255-0020 for this year's dates, plus a calendar of additional shows. Usu-ally mid-March, and again in mid-November.

St. Patrick's Day Parade. More than 150,000 marchers join in the world's largest civilian parade, as Fifth Avenue, from 44th to 86th streets, rings with the sounds of bands and bagpipes. The parade usually starts at 11am, but go extra early if you want a good spot. Call ℭ **212/484-1222.** March 17.

Easter Parade. This isn't a traditional parade, *per se*: There are no marching bands, no baton twirlers, and no protesters. Once upon a time, New York's gentry came out to show off their tasteful but discreet toppings. Today, if you were planning to slip on a tasteful little number—say something delicately woven in straw with a simple flower or two that matches your gloves—you will *not* be the grandest lady in this springtime hike along Fifth Avenue, from 48th to 57th streets. It's more about flamboyant exhibitionism, with hats and costumes that get more outrageous every year, and anybody can join in for free. The parade generally runs Easter Sunday from about 10am to 3 or 4pm. Call ℭ **212/484-1222.** April 12, 2009.

April

New York International Auto Show. Here's the irony: You don't need a car in New York, yet this is the largest car show in the U.S. Held at the Javits Center, many concept cars show up that will never roll off the assembly line but are fun to dream about. Call ℭ **800/282-3336** or visit **www.auto showny.com** or **www.javitscenter. com**. Call for dates.

TriBeCa Film Festival. Conceived in 2002 by the unofficial mayor of TriBeCa, Robert De Niro, the festival has grown in popularity and esteem every year. In 2008, the 12-day festival featured over 250 films and included such special events as a Family Festival Street Fair, music performances and art exhibitions, and outdoor "drive-in" films. Call ℭ **212/941-2400** or visit **www.tribecafilmfestival.org**. Last week in April/early May.

May

Bike New York: The Great Five Boro Bike Tour. The largest mass-participation cycling event in the United States attracts about 30,000 cyclists from all over the world. After a 42-mile ride through the five boroughs, finalists are greeted with a traditional New York–style celebration of food and music. Call ℭ **212/932-BIKE** (2453), or visit **www.bikenewyork.org** to register. First or second Sunday in May.

Ninth Avenue International Food Festival. Street fairs are part of the New York landscape each summer, but this is one of the best. You can spend the day sampling Italian sausages, homemade pierogi, spicy curries, and other ethnic dishes. Street musicians, bands, and vendors add to the festive atmosphere stretching along Ninth Avenue from 37th to 57th streets. Call ℭ **212/484-1222.** Early to mid-May.

Fleet Week. About 10,000 Navy and Coast Guard personnel are "at liberty" in New York for the annual Fleet Week at the end of May. Usually from 1 to 4pm daily, you can watch the ships and aircraft carriers as they dock at the piers on the west side of Manhattan, tour them with on-duty personnel, and watch some dramatic exhibitions by the U.S. Marines. Even if you don't take in any of the events, you'll know it's Fleet Week because those 10,000 sailors invade Midtown in their starched white uniforms. It's wonderful—just like *On the Town* come to life. Call ℭ **212/245-0072,** or visit **www.fleetweek.navy.mil** (your best source for a full list of events) or **www.intrepidmuseum.org**. Late May.

June

Belmont Stakes. The third jewel in the Triple Crown is held at **Belmont Park Race Track** in Belmont, Long Island. If a Triple Crown winner is to be named, it will happen here. For information, call ✆ **516/488-6000** or visit **www.nyra.com**. Early June.

Museum Mile Festival. Fifth Avenue, from 82nd to 104th streets, is closed to cars from 6 to 9pm as 20,000-plus strollers enjoy live music, from Broadway tunes to string quartets; street entertainers; and free admission to nine Museum Mile institutions, including the Metropolitan Museum of Art and the Guggenheim. Call ✆ **212/606-2296** or any of the participating institutions for details. Usually the second Tuesday in June.

Parades, parades, parades. During the summer there is a parade for almost every holiday, nationality or ethnicity. June is the month for (among others) the sometimes raucous but very colorful **Puerto Rican Day Parade** and the **Lesbian and Gay Pride Week and March,** where Fifth Avenue goes wild as the LGBT community celebrates with bands, marching groups, floats, and plenty of panache. The parade starts on upper Fifth Avenue around 52nd Street and continues into the Village, where a street festival and a waterfront dance party with fireworks cap the day. Call ✆ **212/807-7433** or check **www.hopinc.org**. Mid- to late June.

SummerStage. A summer-long festival of outdoor performances in **Central Park,** featuring world music, pop, folk, and jazz artists, ranging from Steve Earle to Craig David to Basement Jaxx to the New York Grand Opera to the Chinese Golden Dragon Acrobats. Shows are often free, but some big-name shows (called "fundraisers")

require tickets. Call ✆ **212/360-2756,** or visit **www.summerstage.org**. June through August.

Shakespeare in the Park. The Delacorte Theater in **Central Park** is the setting for first-rate free performances under the stars—including at least one Shakespeare play each season—most often with stars on the stage. For details, see "Park It! Shakespeare, Music & Other Free Fun," in chapter 9. Call ✆ **212/539-8500,** or visit **www.publictheater.org**. June through August.

Restaurant Week. Late June (see "January," above).

July

Independence Day Harbor Festival and 4th of July Fireworks Spectacular. Start the day amid the crowds at the Great July 4th Festival in lower Manhattan, and then catch Macy's fireworks extravaganza (one of the country's most fantastic) over the East River (the best vantage point is from FDR Dr., which closes to traffic several hours before sunset). Call ✆ **212/484-1222** or Macy's Visitor Center at 212/494-3827. July 4.

Lincoln Center Festival 2009. This festival celebrates the best of the performing arts from all over—theater, ballet, contemporary dance, opera, nouveau circus performances, even puppet and media-based art. Recent editions have featured performances by Ornette Coleman, the Royal Opera, the Royal Ballet, and the New York Philharmonic. Schedules are available in mid-March, and tickets go on sale in May or early June. Call ✆ **212/546-2656,** or visit **www.lincolncenter.org**. Throughout July.

Midsummer Night's Swing. Dancing duos head to the **Lincoln Center's Josie Robertson Plaza** for evenings of big-band swing, salsa, and tango under the stars to the sounds of top-flight bands. Dance lessons are offered with purchase of a ticket. Call ℂ **212/875-5766**, or visit **www.lincolncenter.org**. July and August.

Mostly Mozart. World-renowned ensembles and soloists (Alicia de Larrocha and André Watts have performed in the past) are featured at this month-long series at **Avery Fisher Hall.** Schedules are available in mid-April, and tickets go on sale in early May. Call ℂ **212/875-5030** or 212/546-2656 for information, 212/721-6500 to order tickets through Center Charge, or visit **www.lincoln center.org**. Late July through August.

August

Lincoln Center Out of Doors. This series of free music and dance performances is held outdoors on the plazas of **Lincoln Center.** Call ℂ **212/875-5766** or 212/546-2656, or visit **www.lincolncenter.org** for the schedule (usually available in mid-July). Throughout August.

Harlem Week. The world's largest black and Hispanic cultural festival actually spans almost the entire month, to include the Black Film Festival, the Harlem Jazz and Music Festival, and the Taste of Harlem Food Festival. Expect a full slate of music, from gospel to hip-hop, and lots of other festivities. Call ℂ **212/484-1222.** Throughout August.

New York International Fringe Festival. Held in a variety of downtown venues and park spaces for a crowd looking for the next underground hit, this arts festival presents alternative as well as traditional theater, musicals, dance, comedy, and all manner of performance. Hundreds of events are held at all hours over about 10 days. The quality can vary wildly (lots of performers use

Fringe as a workshop to develop their acts and shows), and some performances really push the envelope. Nonetheless, you'd be surprised at how many shows are actually *good*. Call ℂ **888/FRINGE-NYC** or 212/279-4488; to purchase tickets through Ticket Web, ℂ **800/965-4827;** or visit **www.fringe nyc.org**. Late August.

U.S. Open Tennis Championships. The final Grand Slam event of the tennis season is held at the Arthur Ashe Stadium at the USTA National Tennis Center, the largest public tennis center in the world, at **Flushing Meadows Park** in Queens. Tickets go on sale in May or early June. The event sells out immediately because many tickets are held by corporate sponsors who hand them out to customers. (It's worth it to check the list of sponsors to determine if anyone you know has a ticket connection.) You can usually buy scalped tickets outside the complex (an illegal practice, of course), which is next to Shea Stadium. The last few matches of the tournament are the most expensive, but you'll see more tennis early on, when your ticket allows you to wander the outside courts and view several matches. Call ℂ **866/OPEN-TIX** (it's always busy) or 718/760-6200 well in advance; visit **www.us open.org** or **www.usta.com** for information. Two weeks around Labor Day.

September

West Indian–American Day Parade. This annual Brooklyn event is New York's largest and best street celebration. Come for the extravagant costumes, pulsating rhythms (soca, calypso, reggae), bright colors, folklore, food (jerk chicken, oxtail soup, Caribbean soul food), and two million hip-shaking revelers. The route can change from year to year, but it usually runs along Eastern Parkway from Utica

Avenue to Grand Army Plaza (at the gateway to Prospect Park). Call ✆ 718/467-1797, or visit www.wiadca.org. Labor Day.

Broadway on Broadway. This free alfresco afternoon show features the songs and casts from nearly every Broadway show on a stage in the middle of Times Square. Call ✆ 212/768-1560, or visit www.timessquarenyc.org and click on "Events." Sunday in mid-September.

New York Film Festival. Legendary hits *Pulp Fiction* and *Mean Streets* both had their U.S. premieres at the Film Society of Lincoln Center's 2-week festival, a major stop on the film-fest circuit. Schedules in recent years have included advance looks at *No Country for Old Men, Volver,* and *The Queen.* Screenings are held in various Lincoln Center venues; advance tickets are a good bet always, and a necessity for certain events (especially evening and weekend screenings). Call ✆ 212/875-5600 (for recorded information), 212/875-5050 for box office information, or check out www.filmlinc.com. Two weeks from late September to early October.

BAM Next Wave Festival. One of the city's most important cultural events takes place at the **Brooklyn Academy of Music.** The months-long festival showcases experimental new dance, theater, and music by both renowned and lesser-known international artists. Recent performances have included Astor Piazzolla's *Maria de Buenos Aires* (featuring Piazzolla disciple Gidon Kremer), the 25th anniversary of the Kronos Quartet, and choreographer Bill T. Jones's *We Set Out Early . . . Visibility Was Poor* (set to the music of Igor Stravinsky, John Cage, and Peteris Vask). Call ✆ 718/636-4100, or visit www.bam.org. September through December.

October

Feast of St. Francis. Animals from goldfish to elephants are blessed as thousands of *Homo sapiens* look on at the **Cathedral of St. John the Divine.** A magical experience—pets, of course, are welcome. A festive fair follows the blessing and music events. Buy tickets in advance because they can be hard to get. For tickets, call the cathedral's box office at ✆ 212/662-2133, or visit www.stjohndivine.org. First Sunday in October.

Ice-Skating. Show off your skating style in the limelight at the diminutive **Rockefeller Center** rink (✆ 212/332-7654; www.rockefellercenter.com), open from mid-October to mid-March or early April (you'll skate under the magnificent Christmas tree for the month of Dec). In Central Park, try **Wollman Rink,** on the east side of the park between 62nd and 63rd streets (✆ 212/439-6900; www.wollmanskatingrink.com), and **Lasker Rink,** midpark between 106th and 108th streets (✆ 917/492-3857). Both Central Park skating rinks usually close in early April.

The Pond in Bryant Park. The season here is a short one—from October to mid-January—but the skating is free. Call ✆ 866/221-5157 or 212/382-2953, or visit www.thepondatbryantpark.com.

Big Apple Circus. New York City's homegrown, not-for-profit performing-arts circus is a favorite with children and anyone who's young at heart. Big Apple is committed to maintaining the classical circus tradition with sensitivity, and only features animals that have a traditional working relationship with humans. A tent is pitched in **Damrosch Park** at **Lincoln Center.** Call ✆ 800/922-3772, or visit www.bigapplecircus.org. Late October through January.

Greenwich Village Halloween Parade. This is Halloween at its most outrageous. You may have heard Lou Reed singing about it on his classic album *New York*—he wasn't exaggerating. Drag queens and assorted other flamboyant types parade through the Village in wildly creative costumes. The parade route has changed over the years, but most recently it has started after sunset at Spring Street and marched up Sixth Avenue to 23rd Street or Union Square. Call the *Village Voice* Parade hot line at ✆ 212/475-3333, ext. 14044, visit **www.halloween-nyc.com**, or check the papers for the exact route so you can watch—or participate—if you have the threads and the imagination. October 31.

November

New York City Marathon. Some 30,000 runners from around the world participate in the largest U.S. marathon, and more than a million fans cheer them on as they follow a route that touches all five New York boroughs and finishes at Central Park. Call ✆ 212/423-2249 or 212/860-4455, or visit **www.nyrr.org**, where you can find applications. First Sunday in November. November 2, 2008.

The Chocolate Show. This burgeoning 4-day event devoted to chocolate takes place each year about 2 weeks before Thanksgiving and is open to the public. The event is at the Metropolitan Pavilion in Chelsea and features booths representing over 50 of the world's best chocolate makers with tastings, demonstrations, and activities for children. For info, call **866/CHOC-NYC** or 212/889-5112, or visit **www.chocolateshow.com**. November 7 to 9, 2008.

Radio City Music Hall Christmas Spectacular. A rather gaudy extravaganza, but lots of fun, this event stars the Radio City Rockettes and a cast that includes live animals (just try to picture the camels sauntering into the Sixth Ave. entrance!). For information, call ✆ 212/307-1000, or visit **www.radiocity.com**; you can also buy tickets at the box office or via Ticketmaster's **Radio City Hot Line** ((✆ 212/307-1000)), or visit **www.ticketmaster.com**. Throughout November and December.

Triple Pier Antiques Show. The city's largest antiques show takes place over 2 consecutive weekends, usually before Thanksgiving; for details, see "March," above. Call ✆ 212/255-0020, or visit **www.stellashows.com**. November 15 to 16, 2008.

Macy's Thanksgiving Day Parade. The procession from Central Park West and 77th Street and down Broadway to Herald Square at 34th Street continues to be a national tradition. Huge hot-air balloons in the forms of Rocky and Bullwinkle, Snoopy, the Pink Panther, Bart Simpson, and other cartoon favorites are the best part. The night before, you can usually see the big blow-up on Central Park West at 79th Street; call in advance to see if it will be open to the public. Call ✆ 212/484-1222 or Macy's Visitor Center at 212/494-2922. November 27, 2008.

The Nutcracker. Tchaikovsky's holiday favorite is performed by the New York City Ballet at **Lincoln Center.** The annual schedule is available beginning in mid-July, and tickets usually go on sale in early October. Call ✆ 212/870-5570, or go online to **www.nycballet.com**. Late November through early January.

Lighting of the Rockefeller Center Christmas Tree. The annual lighting ceremony is accompanied by ice skaters, singing, entertainment, and a *huge* crowd. The tree stays lit 24/7 until after the New Year. Call ℭ **212/332-6868,** or visit **www.rockefeller center.com.** Late November or early December.

December

Holiday Trimmings. Stroll down festive Fifth Avenue and you'll see a 27-foot sparkling snowflake floating over the intersection outside **Tiffany's,** the **Cartier** building beribboned with red bows, wreaths warming the necks of the **New York Public Library**'s lions, and fanciful figurines in the windows of **Saks Fifth Avenue** and **Lord & Taylor.** Madison Avenue between 55th and 60th streets is also a good bet; **Sony Plaza** usually displays something fabulous, as does **Barney's New York.** Throughout December.

Christmas Traditions. In addition to the **Radio City Music Hall Christmas Spectacular** and the New York City Ballet's staging of *The Nutcracker* (see "November," above), traditional holiday events include *A Christmas Carol* at **The Theater at Madison Square Garden** (ℭ 212/465-6741 or www.the garden.com; for tickets, ℭ 212/307-7171 or www.ticketmaster.com), usually featuring a big name to draw in the crowds. At **Avery Fisher Hall** is the National Chorale's singalong performances of Handel's *Messiah* (ℭ 212/875-5030; www.lincolncenter.org) for a week before Christmas. Don't worry if the only words you know are "Alleluia, Alleluia!"—a lyrics sheet is given to ticket holders. Throughout December.

Lighting of the Hanukkah Menorah. Everything is done on a grand scale in New York, so it's no surprise that the world's largest menorah (32 ft. high) is at Manhattan's **Grand Army Plaza,** Fifth Avenue and 59th Street. Hanukkah celebrations begin at sunset, with the lighting of the first of the giant electric candles. December 21, 2008.

New Year's Eve. The biggest party of all is in **Times Square,** where raucous revelers count down the year's final seconds until the ball drops at midnight at 1 Times Sq. This one, in the cold surrounded by thousands of drunks, is a masochist's delight. Call ℭ **212/768-1560** or 212/484-1222, or visit **www. timessquarenyc.org.** December 31.

Runner's World **Midnight Run.** Enjoy **fireworks** followed by the New York Road Runners Club's annual run in **Central Park,** which is fun for runners and spectators alike; call ℭ **212/860-4455,** or visit **www.nyrr.org.** December 31.

Brooklyn's fireworks celebration. Head to Brooklyn for the city's largest New Year's Eve **fireworks** celebration at Prospect Park. Call ℭ **718/965-8999,** or visit **www.prospectpark.org.** December 31.

New Year's Eve Concert for Peace. The Cathedral of St. John the Divine is known for its annual concert, whose past performers have included the Manhattan School of Music Chamber Sinfonia, Tony Award–winning composer Jason Robert Brown *(Parade),* American soprano Lauren Flanigan, and the Forces of Nature Dance Company. Call ℭ **212/316-7540** for information, 212/662-2133 for tickets, or go online to **www.stjohndivine.org.** December 31.

4 Getting There & Getting Around

GETTING TO NEW YORK CITY
BY PLANE

Three major airports serve New York City: **John F. Kennedy International Airport** (© 718/244-4444) in Queens, about 15 miles (1 hr. driving time) from midtown Manhattan; **LaGuardia Airport** (© 718/533-3400), also in Queens, about 8 miles (30 min.) from Midtown; and **Newark International Airport** (© 973/961-6000) in nearby New Jersey, about 16 miles (45 min.) from Midtown. Information about all three airports is available online at **www.panynj.gov**; click on the "All Airports" tab on the left.

Even though LaGuardia is the closest airport to Manhattan, it has a bad reputation for delays and terminal chaos, in both ticket-desk lines and baggage claim. You may want to use JFK or Newark instead. (JFK has the best reputation for timeliness, such as it is, among New York–area airports.)

Almost every major domestic carrier serves at least one of the New York–area airports; most serve two or all three. Among them **American** (© 800/433-7300; www.aa.com), **Continental** (© 800/525-3273; www.continental.com), **Delta** (© 800/221-1212; www.delta.com), **Northwest** (© 800/225-2525; www.nwa.com), **US Airways** (© 800/428-4322; www.usairways.com), and **United** (© 800/864-8331; www.united.com).

In recent years, there has been rapid growth in the number of start-up, no-frills airlines serving New York (and 2008 brought the demise of some of them, so definitely check and see whether the following are still flying when you are planning your trip). You might check out Atlanta-based **AirTran** (© 800/AIR-TRAN); Denver-based **Frontier** (© 800/432-1359; www.flyfrontier.com), Milwaukee- and Omaha-based **Midwest Airlines** (© 800/452-2022; www.midwestairlines.com), or Detroit-based **Spirit Airlines** (© 800/772-7117; www.spiritair.com). The JFK-based cheap-chic airline **JetBlue** ⊛ (© 800/JETBLUE; www.jetblue.com) has taken New York by storm with its low fares and classy service to cities throughout the nation. The nation's leading discount airline, **Southwest** (© 800/435-9792; www.iflyswa.com), flies into MacArthur (Islip) Airport on Long Island, 50 miles east of Manhattan.

Arriving at the airport

IMMIGRATION & CUSTOMS CLEARANCE International visitors arriving by air, no matter the port of entry, should cultivate patience and resignation before setting foot on U.S. soil. U.S. airports have considerably beefed up security clearances in the years since the terrorist attacks of September 11, and clearing Customs and Immigration can take as long as 2 hours.

⌒Tips **Choosing Your NYC-Area Airport**

It's more convenient to fly into Newark than JFK if your destination is Manhattan, and fares to Newark are often cheaper than those to the other airports. Newark is particularly convenient if your hotel is in Midtown West or downtown. Taxi fare into Manhattan from Newark is roughly equivalent to the fare from JFK—both now have **AirTrains** in place (see "Getting Into Town from the Airport," p. 42), but the AirTrain to Newark from Manhattan is quicker.

Getting into Town from the Airport

Since there's no need to rent a car in New York, you're going to have to figure out how you want to get from the airport to your hotel and back.

For transportation information for all three airports (JFK, LaGuardia, and Newark), call **Air-Ride** (© **800/247-7433**), which offers 24-hour recorded details on bus and shuttle companies and car services registered with the New York and New Jersey Port Authority. Similar information is available at **www.panynj. gov/airports**; click on the airport at which you'll be arriving.

The Port Authority runs staffed Ground Transportation Information counters on the baggage-claim level at each airport where you can get information and book various kinds of transport. Most transportation companies also have courtesy phones near the baggage-claim area.

Generally, travel time between the airports and Midtown by taxi or car is 45 to 60 minutes for JFK, 20 to 35 minutes for LaGuardia, and 35 to 50 minutes for Newark. Always allow extra time, especially during rush hour, peak holiday travel times, and if you're taking a bus.

SUBWAYS & PUBLIC BUSES For the most part, your best bet is to stay away from the MTA when traveling to and from the airport. You might save a few dollars, but subways and buses that currently serve the airports involve multiple transfers, and you'll have to drag your luggage up and down staircases. On some subways, you'd be traveling through undesirable neighborhoods. Spare yourself the drama.

The only exception to this rule is the subway service to and from JFK (to a certain extent), which connects with the new AirTrain (see the box "AirTrains: Newark & JFK—The Very Good & the Not-So-Very Good," below). The subway *can* be

more reliable than taking a car or taxi at the height of rush hour, but *a few words of warning:* This isn't the right option for you if you're bringing more than a single piece of luggage or if you have very young children in tow, since there's a good amount of walking and some stairs involved in the trip, and you'll have nowhere to put all those bags on the subway train. And *do not* use this method if you're traveling to or from the airport after dark or too early in the morning—it's not the safest or fastest way during those times. For additional subway information, see "Getting Around," later in this chapter.

TAXIS Despite significant rate hikes the past few years, taxis are still a quick and convenient way to travel to and from the airports. They're available at designated taxi stands outside the terminals, with uniformed dispatchers on hand during peak hours at JFK and LaGuardia, around the clock at Newark. Follow the GROUND TRANSPORTATION or TAXI signs. There may be a long line, but it generally moves pretty quickly. Fares, whether fixed or metered, do not include bridge and tunnel tolls ($4–$6) or a tip for the cabbie (15%–20% is customary). They do include all passengers in the cab and luggage—never pay more than the metered or flat rate, except for tolls and a tip (8pm–6am a $1 surcharge also applies on New York yellow cabs). Taxis have a limit of four passengers, so if there are more in your group, you'll have to take more than one cab. For more on taxis, see "By Taxi," p. 54.

- **From JFK:** A flat rate of $45 to Manhattan (plus tolls and tip) is charged. The meter will not be turned on and the surcharge will not be added. The flat rate does not apply on trips from Manhattan to the airport.
- **From LaGuardia:** $24 to $28, metered, plus tolls and tip.

AirTrains: Newark & JFK—the Very Good & the Not-So-Very Good

First the very good: A few years back, a new rail link revolutionized the process of connecting by public transportation to the New York-area airport in New Jersey: **AirTrain Newark,** which now connects Newark-Liberty International Airport with Manhattan via a speedy monorail/rail link.

Even though you have to make a connection, the system is fast, pleasant, affordable, and easy to use. Each arrivals terminal at Newark Airport has a station for the AirTrain, so just follow the signs once you collect your bags. All AirTrains head to **Newark International Airport Station,** where you transfer to a **NJ Transit** train. NJ Transit will deliver you to New York Penn Station at 33rd Street and Seventh Avenue, where you can get a cab or transfer to the subway or bus.

The trip from my apartment on Manhattan's Upper West Side to the Newark Alitalia terminal, for example, was under a half-hour and cost me less than $14 ($11.55 for the AirTrain link via Penn Station plus $2 for the subway to get to Penn Station). That's a savings of at least $35, compared to what it would have been if I took a cab, not to mention the time I saved. NJ Transit trains run two to three times an hour during peak travel times (once an hour during early and late hours), and depart from their own lobby/waiting area in Penn Station; you can check the schedules on monitors before you leave the airport terminal, and again at the train station. NJ Transit tickets can be purchased from vending machines at both the air terminal and the train station (no ticket is required to board the AirTrain). The one-way fare is $11.55 (children under 5 ride free). (On your return trip to the airport, the AirTrain is far more predictable, time-wise, than subjecting yourself to the whims of traffic.)

• **From Newark:** The dispatcher for New Jersey taxis gives you a slip of paper with a flat rate ranging from $30 to $38 (toll and tip extra), depending on where you're going in Manhattan, so be precise about your destination. New York yellow cabs aren't permitted to pick up passengers at Newark. The yellow-cab fare from Manhattan to Newark is the meter amount plus $15 and tolls (about $69–$75, perhaps a few dollars more with tip). Jersey taxis aren't permitted to take passengers from Manhattan to Newark.

PRIVATE CAR & LIMOUSINE SERVICES Private car and limousine companies provide convenient 24-hour door-to-door airport transfers for roughly the same cost of a taxi. The advantage they offer over taking a taxi is that you can arrange your pickup in advance and avoid the hassles of the taxi line. Call at least 24 hours in advance (even earlier on holidays), and a driver will meet you near baggage claim (or at your hotel for a return trip). You'll probably be asked to leave a credit card number to guarantee your ride. You'll likely be offered the choice of indoor or curbside pickup; indoor pickup is more expensive but makes it easier to

Note that travelers heading to points beyond the city can also pick up Amtrak and other NJ Transit trains at Newark International Airport Station to their final destinations.

Now the not-so-very good: A few bumpy years after opening in 2003, after years of anticipation and $1.9 billion, AirTrain JFK is beginning to operate more efficiently. Though you can't beat the price—only $7 if you take a subway to the AirTrain, $12 if you take the Long Island Rail Road—you won't save much on time getting to the airport. From midtown Manhattan, the ride can take anywhere from 40 minutes to over an hour, depending on your connections. The connections can be confusing. Only a few subway lines connect with the AirTrain: the A, E, J, and Z; the E, J, Z to Jamaica Station and the Sutphin Blvd.–Archer Ave. Station; and the A to Howard Beach/JFK Airport Station. The MTA is contemplating adding connections to the AirTrain in lower Manhattan sometime in the next decade, there's not much they can do now to speed up the trip.

A word of warning for both AirTrains: If you have mobility issues, mountains of luggage, or a bevy of small children, skip the AirTrain. You'll find it easier to rely on a taxi, car service, or shuttle service that can offer you door-to-door transfers.

For more information on AirTrain Newark, call ✆ **888/EWR-INFO,** or go online to **www.airtrainnewark.com.** For connection details, click on the links on the AirTrain website, or contact **NJ Transit** (✆ **800/626-RIDE;** www.njtransit.com) or **Amtrak** (✆ **800/USA-RAIL;** www.amtrak.com).

For more information on AirTrain JFK, go online to **www.airtrainjfk.com.** For connection details, click on the links on the AirTrain website or the MTA site, **www.mta.nyc.ny.us/mta/airtrain.htm.**

hook up with your driver (who usually waits in baggage claim bearing a sign with your name on it). You can save a few dollars if you arrange for an outside pickup; call the dispatcher as soon as you clear baggage claim and then take your luggage out to the designated waiting area, where you'll wait for the driver to come around, which can take anywhere from 10 minutes to a half-hour. Besides the wait, the other disadvantage of this option is that curbside can be chaos during prime deplaning hours.

Vehicles range from sedans to vans to limousines and tend to be relatively clean and comfortable. Prices vary slightly by company and the size of car reserved, but expect a rate roughly equivalent to taxi fare if you request a basic sedan and have only one stop; toll and tip policies are the same. (*Note:* Car services are not subject to the flat-rate rule that taxis have for rides to and from JFK.) Ask when booking what the fare will be and if you can use your credit card to pay for the ride so there are no surprises at drop-off time. There may be waiting charges tacked on if the driver has to wait an excessive amount of time due to flight delays when picking you up, but the car companies will usually check on your flight to get an accurate landing time.

I've had the best luck with **Carmel** (© **800/922-7635** or 212/666-6666) and **Legends** (© **888/LEGENDS** or 212/888-8884; www.legendslimousine. com); **Allstate** (© **800/453-4099** or 212/333-3333) and **Tel-Aviv** (© **800/222-9888** or 212/777-7777) also have reasonable reputations. (Keep in mind, though, that these services are only as good as the individual drivers—and sometimes there's a lemon in the bunch. If you have a problem, report it immediately to the main office.)

For a bit more luxury and service, the best option I've found is **Luxor Limo** (© **866/990-4111;** www.luxorlimo.com), where the cars are spacious and the drivers as reliable as you will find, and with rates not much higher than the above companies.

These car services are good for rush hour (no ticking meters in rush-hour traffic), but if you're arriving at a quieter time of day, taxis work fine.

PRIVATE BUSES & SHUTTLES

Buses and shuttle services provide a comfortable and less expensive (but usually more time-consuming) option for airport transfers than do taxis and car services.

Super Shuttle serves all three airports; **New York Airport Service** serves JFK and LaGuardia; **Olympia Trails and Express Shuttle USA** serves Newark. These services are my favorite option for getting to and from Newark during peak travel times because the drivers usually take lesser-known streets that make the ride much quicker than if you go with a taxi or car, which will virtually always stick to the traffic-clogged main route.

The familiar blue vans of **Super Shuttle** (© **800/258-3826;** www.supershuttle. com) serve all three area airports, providing door-to-door service to Manhattan and points on Long Island every 15 to 30 minutes around the clock. As with Express Shuttle, you don't need to reserve your airport-to-Manhattan ride; just go to the ground-transportation desk or use the courtesy phone in baggage claim and ask for Super Shuttle. Hotel pickups for your return trip require 24 to 48 hours' notice; you can make your reservations online. Fares run $13 to $22 per person, depending on the airport, with discounts available for additional persons in the same party.

(Tips) **Coping with Jet Lag**

Jetlag is a pitfall of traveling across time zones. If you're flying north–south and you feel sluggish when you touch down, your symptoms will be the result of dehydration and the general stress of air travel. When you travel east–west or vice-versa, your body becomes confused about what time it is, and everything from your digestive system to your brain is knocked for a loop. Traveling east is more difficult on your internal clock than traveling west because most peoples' bodies are more inclined to stay up late than to fall asleep early.

Here are some tips for combating jet lag:

- **Reset your watch** to your destination time before you board the plane.
- **Drink lots of water** before, during, and after your flight. Avoid alcohol.
- **Exercise and sleep well** for a few days before your trip.
- If you have trouble sleeping on planes, **fly eastward on morning flights.**
- **Daylight** is the key to resetting your body clock. At the website for **Outside In** (www.bodyclock.com), you can get a customized plan of when to seek and avoid light.

If You're Flying into MacArthur Airport on Southwest

Southwest Airlines is one of several carriers flying into New York via Long Island's MacArthur Airport, 50 miles east of Manhattan. (The others are Delta, Spirit, Northwest, and US Airways). If you're on one of these flights (because the price was *sooooo* low), here are your options for getting into the city:

Colonial Transportation (© 631/589-3500; www.colonialtransportation. com), Classic Transportation (© 631/567-5100; www.classictrans.com), and Legends (© 888/LEGENDS or 888/888-8884; www.legendslimousine.com) will pick you up at Islip Airport and deliver you to Manhattan via private sedan, but expect to pay about $125 plus tolls and tip for door-to-door service (which kind of defeats the purpose of flying a budget airline). Be sure to arrange for it at least 24 hours in advance.

For a fraction of the cost, you can catch a ride aboard a Hampton Jitney coach (© 631/283-4600; www.hamptonjitney.com) to various drop-off points on Midtown's east side. The cost is $29 per person, plus a minimal taxi fare from the terminal to the Hampton Jitney stop. Hampton Jitney can explain the details and arrange for taxi transport.

Colonial Transportation (© 631/589-3500; www.colonialtransportation.com) also offers regular shuttle service that traverses the 3 miles from the airport to the Ronkonkoma Long Island Rail Road station, where you can pick up an LIRR train to Manhattan. The shuttle fare is $5 per person, $1 for each additional family member accompanying a full-fare customer. From Ronkonkoma, it's about a 1½-hour train ride to Manhattan's Penn Station; the one-way fare is $13 at peak hours, $9.50 off-peak (half-fare for seniors 65 or older and kids 5–11). You can also catch the Suffolk County Transit bus no. S-57 between the airport and the station Monday to Saturday for $1.50. Trains usually leave Ronkonkoma once or twice every hour, depending on the day and time. For more information, call © 718/217-LIRR, or visit www.mta.nyc.ny.us/lirr.

For additional options and the latest information, call © 631/467-3210, or visit www.macarthurairport.com.

New York Airport Service (© 718/875-8200; www.nyairportservice.com) buses travel from JFK and LaGuardia to the Port Authority Bus Terminal (42nd St. and Eighth Ave.), Grand Central Terminal (Park Ave. between 41st and 42nd sts.), and to select Midtown hotels between 27th and 59th streets, plus the Jamaica LIRR Station in Queens, where you can pick up a train for Long Island. Follow the GROUND TRANSPORTATION signs to the curbside pickup, or look for the uniformed agent. Buses depart the airport every 20 to 70 minutes (depending on your departure point and destination) between 6am and midnight. Buses to JFK and LaGuardia depart the Port Authority and Grand Central Terminal on the Park Avenue side every 15 to 30 minutes, depending on the time of day and the day of the week. To request direct shuttle service from your hotel, call the above number at least 24 hours in advance. One-way fare for JFK is $15, $27 round-trip; to LaGuardia it's $12 one-way and $21 round-trip.

Olympia Airport Express (© 800/8-Newark or 212/964-6233; www.coachusa.com/olympia) provides service every 15 to 30 minutes (depending on the time of day) from Newark Airport to Penn Station (the pickup point is the northwest corner of 34th St. and Eighth Ave., and the drop-off point is the southwest corner), the Port Authority Bus Terminal (on 42nd St., between Eighth and Ninth aves.), and Grand Central Terminal (on 41st St., between Park and Lexington aves.). Passengers to and from the Grand Central Terminal location can connect to Olympia's Midtown shuttle vans, which service select Midtown hotels. Call for the exact schedule for your return trip to the airport. The one-way fare runs $13, $22 round-trip; seniors and passengers with disabilities ride for $6.

BY CAR

From the **New Jersey Turnpike** (I-95) and points west, there are three Hudson River crossings to the city's West Side: the **Holland Tunnel** (lower Manhattan), the **Lincoln Tunnel** (Midtown), and the **George Washington Bridge** (upper Manhattan). From **upstate New York,** take the **New York State Thruway** (I-87), which crosses the Hudson River on the Tappan Zee Bridge and becomes the **Major Deegan Expressway** (I-87)

through the Bronx. For the East Side, continue to the Triborough Bridge and then down the FDR Drive. For the West Side, take the Cross Bronx Expressway (I-95) to the Henry Hudson Parkway or the Taconic State Parkway to the Saw Mill River Parkway to the Henry Hudson Parkway south.

From **New England,** the **New England Thruway** (I-95) connects with the **Bruckner Expressway** (I-278), which leads to the Triborough Bridge and the FDR Drive on the East Side. For the West Side, take the Bruckner to the Cross Bronx Expressway (I-95) to the Henry Hudson Parkway south.

Note that you'll have to pay tolls along some of these roads and at most crossings. If your state has an **E-ZPass** program (**www.ezpass.com**), as most states in the Northeast do, your pass will allow you to go through the designated E-ZPass lanes.

Once you arrive in Manhattan, park your car in a garage (expect to pay $20–$45 per day) and leave it there. Don't use your car for traveling within the city. Public transportation, taxis, and walking

---

Getting to the Other Boroughs & the 'Burbs

If you're traveling to a borough other than Manhattan, call **ETS Air Service** (② **718/221-5341**) for shared door-to-door service. For Long Island service, call **Classic Transportation** (② **631/567-5100**; www.classictrans.com) for car service. For service to Westchester County or Connecticut, contact **Connecticut Limousine** (② **800/472-5466** or 203/878-2222; www.ctlimo.com) or **Prime Time Shuttle of Connecticut** (② **866/2-TheAir**; www.primetimeshuttle.com).

If you're traveling to points in New Jersey from Newark Airport, call **Olympic Airporter** (② **800/822-9797** or 732/938-6666; www.olympicairporter.com) for Ocean, Monmouth, Middlesex and Mercer counties, plus Bucks County, Pennsylvania; or **State Shuttle** (② **800/427-3207** or 973/729-0030; www.stateshuttle.com) for destinations throughout New Jersey.

Additionally, **New York Airport Service** express buses (② **718/875-8200**; www.nyairportservice.com) serve the entire New York metropolitan region from JFK and LaGuardia, offering connections to the Long Island Rail Road; the Metro-North Railroad to Westchester County, upstate New York, and Connecticut; and New York's Port Authority terminal, where you can pick up buses to points throughout New Jersey.

Long-Haul Flights: How to Stay Comfortable

- Your choice of airline and airplane will definitely affect your leg room. Find more details about U.S. airlines at **www.seatguru.com**. For international airlines, the research firm Skytrax has posted a list of average seat pitches at **www.airlinequality.com**.

- Emergency exit seats and bulkhead seats typically have the most legroom. Emergency exit seats are usually left unassigned until the day of a flight (to ensure that someone able-bodied fills them); it's worth getting to the ticket counter early to snag one of these spots for a long flight. Many passengers find that bulkhead seating offers more legroom, but remember that bulkhead seats have no storage space on the floor in front of you.

- To have two seats for yourself in a three-seat row, try for an aisle seat in a center section toward the back of coach. If you're traveling with a companion, book an aisle and a window seat. Middle seats are usually booked last, so chances are good you'll end up with three seats to yourselves. And in the event that a third passenger is assigned the middle seat, he or she will probably be more than happy to trade for a window or an aisle.

- To sleep, avoid the last row of any section or the row in front of an emergency exit, as these seats are least likely to recline. Avoid seats near toilet and galley areas. Avoid seats in the back of many jets—these can be narrower than those in the rest of coach. Or reserve a window seat so you can rest your head and avoid being bumped in the aisle.

- Get up, walk around, and stretch every 60 to 90 minutes to keep your blood flowing. This helps avoid **deep vein thrombosis,** or "economy-class syndrome." See the box "Avoiding 'Economy-Class Syndrome,'" later in this chapter.

- Drink water before, during, and after your flight to combat the lack of humidity in airplane cabins. Avoid caffeine and alcohol, which will dehydrate you.

will easily get you where you want to go without the headaches of parking, gridlock, and dodging crazy cabbies.

For listings of the major car rental agencies in New York City, please see the "Toll-Free Numbers & Websites" section in the appendix (p. 394).

BY TRAIN

Amtrak (© **800/USA-RAIL;** www.amtrak.com) runs frequent service to New York City's **Penn Station,** on Seventh Avenue between 31st and 33rd streets, where you can get a taxi, subway, or bus to your hotel. To get the best rates, book early (as much as 6 months in advance) and travel on weekends.

If you're traveling to New York from a city along Amtrak's Northeast Corridor—such as Boston, Philadelphia, Baltimore, or Washington, D.C.—Amtrak may be your best travel bet now that they've rolled out their new high-speed Acela trains. The Acela Express trains cut travel time from D.C. down to 2½ hours, and travel time from Boston to a lightning-quick 3 hours.

GETTING AROUND

Frankly, Manhattan's transportation systems are a marvel. It's simply miraculous that so many people can gather on this little island and move around it. For the most part, you can get where you're going pretty quickly and easily using some combination of subways, buses, and cabs; this section will tell you how to do just that.

But between traffic gridlock and subway delays, sometimes you just can't get there from here—unless you walk. Walking can sometimes be the fastest way to navigate the island. During rush hours, you'll easily beat car traffic while on foot, as taxis and buses stop and groan at gridlocked corners (don't even *try* going crosstown in a cab or bus in Midtown at midday). You'll also see a lot more by walking than you will if you ride beneath the street in the subway or fly by in a cab. So pack your most comfortable shoes and hit the pavement—it's the best, cheapest, and most appealing way to experience the city.

BY SUBWAY

Run by the **Metropolitan Transit Authority,** also known as the MTA, (www.mta. info/nyct/subway), the much-maligned subway system is actually the fastest way to travel around New York, especially during rush hours. Some 4.5 million people a day seem to agree with me, as it's their primary mode of transportation. The subway is quick, inexpensive, relatively safe, and efficient, as well as being a genuine New York experience.

The subway runs 24 hours a day, 7 days a week. The rush-hour crushes are roughly from 8 to 9:30am and from 5 to 6:30pm on weekdays; the rest of the time the trains are much more manageable.

Paying Your Way

The subway fare is $2 (half-price for seniors and those with disabilities), and children under 44 inches tall ride free (up to three per adult).

Tokens are no longer available. People pay with the **MetroCard,** a magnetically encoded card that debits the fare when swiped through the turnstile (or the fare box on any city bus). Once you're in the system, you can transfer freely to any subway line that you can reach without exiting your station. MetroCards also allow

---

Tips **Sidewalks of New York**

What's the primary means New Yorkers use for getting around town? The subway? Buses? Taxis? Nope. **Walking.** They stride across wide, crowded pavements without any regard for traffic lights, weaving through crowds at high speeds, dodging taxis and buses whose drivers are forced to interrupt the normal flow of traffic to avoid flattening them. **Never take your walking cues from the locals.** Wait for walk signals and always use crosswalks—don't cross in the middle of the block. Do otherwise and you could quickly end up as a flattened statistic (or at least get a ticket for jaywalking).

Always pay attention to the traffic flow. Walk as though you're driving, staying to the right. Pay attention to what's happening in the street, even if you have the right of way. At intersections, keep an eye out for drivers who don't yield, turn without looking, or think a yellow traffic light means "Hurry up!" as you cross. Unfortunately, most bicyclists seem to think that the traffic laws don't apply to them; they'll often blithely fly through red lights and dash the wrong way on one-way streets, so be on your guard.

For additional important safety tips, see "Playing It Safe," later in this chapter.

Subway Stops for New York's Top Attractions

MUSEUMS

American Museum of Natural History	**B, C** to 81st Street
The Cloisters	**A** to 190th Street
Ellis Island	**4, 5** to Bowling Green or **N, R** to Whitehall Street 1 to South Ferry
Guggenheim Museum	**4, 5, 6** to 86th Street
Intrepid Sea-Air-Space Museum	**A, C, E** to 42nd Street–Port Authority
Metropolitan Museum of Art	**4, 5, 6** to 86th Street
Museum of Modern Art	**E, V** to Fifth Avenue or B, D, F to 47–50th streets–Rockefeller Center.

HISTORIC BUILDINGS AND ARCHITECTURE

Brooklyn Bridge	**4, 5, 6** to Brooklyn Bridge–City Hall
Chrysler Building	**4, 5, 6, 7, S** to Grand Central–42nd Street
Empire State Building	**B, D, F, V, N, R, Q, W** to 34th Street–Herald Square
Grand Central Terminal	**4, 5, 6, 7, S** to Grand Central–42nd Street
Rockefeller Center	**B, D, F, V** to 47–50th streets–Rockefeller Center
Staten Island Ferry	**1** to South Ferry (first five cars)
United Nations	**4, 5, 6, 7, S** to Grand Central–42nd Street
Yankee Stadium	**4, B, D** to 161st River Avenue–Yankee Stadium

NEIGHBORHOODS

Chinatown	**6, J, M, Z, N, R, Q, W** to Canal Street
Greenwich Village	**A, C, E, B, D, F, V** to West 4th Street
Times Square	**1, 2, 3, 7, N, R, W, S** to 42nd Street–Times Square
Wall Street	**4, 5** to Wall Street or **N, R** to Rector Street

CHURCHES

Cathedral of St. John the Divine	**1** to Cathedral Parkway (110th St.)
St. Patrick's Cathedral	**B, D, F, V** to 47–50th streets–Rockefeller Center or **E, V** to Fifth Avenue–53rd Street

you **free transfers** between the bus and subway within a 2-hour period.

MetroCards can be purchased from staffed token booths, where you can only pay with cash; at the ATM-style vending machines now located in every subway station, which accept cash, credit cards, and debit cards; from a MetroCard merchant, such as most Rite Aid drugstores; Hudson News, at Penn Station and Grand Central Terminal; or at the MTA information desk at the **Times Square**

Information Center, 1560 Broadway, between 46th and 47th streets.

MetroCards come in a few different configurations:

Pay-Per-Ride MetroCards can be used for up to four people by swiping up to four times (bring the entire family). You can put any amount from $4 (two rides) to $80 on your card. Every time you put $7 or more on your Pay-Per-Ride MetroCard, it's automatically credited 15%—that's one free ride for every $15 you spend. You can buy Pay-Per-Ride MetroCards at any subway station; most stations have automated MetroCard vending machines, which allow you to buy MetroCards using your major credit card or debit card. MetroCards are also available from many shops and newsstands around town in $10 and $20 values. You can refill your card at any time until the expiration date on the card, usually about a year from the date of purchase, at any subway station.

Unlimited-Ride MetroCards, which can't be used for more than one person at a time or more frequently than 18-minute intervals, are available in four values: the **daily Fun Pass,** which allows you a day's worth of unlimited subway and bus rides for $7; the **7-Day MetroCard,** for $25; a **14-day MetroCard** for $47; and the **30-Day MetroCard,** for $81.

Seven-, 14- and 30-day Unlimited-Ride MetroCards can be purchased at any subway station or from a MetroCard merchant. Fun Passes, however, cannot be purchased at token booths—you can only buy them at a MetroCard vending machine; from a MetroCard merchant; or at the MTA information desk at the Times Square Information Center. Unlimited-Ride MetroCards go into effect the first time you use them—so if you buy a card on Monday and don't begin to use it until Wednesday, Wednesday is when the clock starts ticking on your MetroCard.

A Fun Pass is good from the first time you use it until 3am the next day, while 7- and 30-day MetroCards run out at midnight on the last day. These Metro-Cards cannot be refilled. (At press time there were strong rumors that the 7-Day Metro Card and 30-Day Metro Card rates were going up).

Tips for using your MetroCard: The MetroCard swiping mechanisms at turnstiles are the source of much grousing among subway riders. If you swipe too fast or too slow, the turnstile will ask you to swipe again. If this happens, ***do not move to a different turnstile,*** or you may end up paying twice. If you've tried repeatedly and really can't make your MetroCard work, tell the token booth

---

Subway Service Interruption Notes

The subway map featured on the inside back cover of this book was as accurate as possible at press time, but service is always subject to change, for reasons ranging from "a sick passenger" to regularly scheduled construction. Your best bet is to contact the **Metropolitan Transit Authority (MTA)** for the latest details; call ✆ **718/330-1234** or visit **www.mta.nyc.ny.us**, where you'll find system updates that are thorough, timely, and clear. (You can also sign up online to receive service advisories by e-mail.) Also read any posters that are taped up on the platform or notices written on the token booth's whiteboard. Once in town, you can stop at the MTA desk at the **Times Square Information Center,** 1560 Broadway, between 46th and 47th streets (where Broadway meets Seventh Ave.) to pick up the latest subway map. (You can also ask for one at any token booth, but they might not always be stocked.)

Tips **Help Mapping Your Subway Route**

If you're not sure how to get, say, from the Museum of Natural History to the Brooklyn Bridge, you might want to visit **www.hopstop.com**. Offering navigation help on several major U.S. subway systems, the useful widget can tell you how to get from one place to the other underground. (It also gives you a comparison for time/cost using a taxi or car service). You can modify your request by specifying "more walking" or "fewer transfers."

---

clerk; chances are good, though, that you'll get the movement down after a couple of uses.

If you're not sure how much money you have left on your MetroCard, or what day it expires, use the station's MetroCard Reader, usually located near the station entrance or the token booth (on buses, the fare box will also provide you with this information).

To locate the nearest MetroCard merchant, or for any other MetroCard questions, call ✆ **800/METROCARD** (out of NYC only) or 212/METROCARD (212/638-7622) Monday through Friday between 7am and 11pm, Saturday and Sunday from 9am to 5pm. Or go online to **www.mta.nyc.ny.us/metrocard**, which can give you a full rundown of MetroCard merchants in the tri-state area.

Using the System

As you can see from the full-color subway map on the inside back cover of this book, the subway system basically mimics the lay of the land aboveground, with most lines in Manhattan running north and south, like the avenues, and a few lines east and west, like the streets.

To go up and down the east side of Manhattan (and to the Bronx and Brooklyn), take the 4, 5, or 6 train.

To travel up and down the West Side (and also to the Bronx and Brooklyn), take the 1, 2, or 3 line; the A, C, E, or F line; or the B or D line.

The N, R, Q, and W lines first cut diagonally across town from east to west and then snake under Seventh Avenue before shooting out to Queens.

The crosstown S line, the Shuttle, runs back and forth between Times Square and Grand Central Terminal. Farther downtown, across 14th Street, the L line works its own crosstown magic.

Lines have assigned colors on subway maps and trains—red for the 1, 2, 3 line; green for the 4, 5, 6 trains; and so on— but nobody ever refers to them by color. Always refer to them by number or letter when asking questions. Within Manhattan, the distinction between different numbered trains that share the same line is usually that some are express and others are local. **Express trains** often skip about three stops for each one that they make; express stops are indicated on subway maps with a white (rather than solid) circle. Local stops are usually about 9 blocks apart.

Directions are almost always indicated using "uptown" (northbound) and "downtown" (southbound), so be sure to know what direction you want to head in. The outsides of some subway entrances are marked UPTOWN ONLY or DOWNTOWN ONLY; read carefully, as it's easy to head in the wrong direction. Once you're on the platform, check the signs overhead to make sure that the train you're waiting for will be traveling in the right direction. If you do make a mistake, it's a good idea to wait for an express station, such as 14th Street or 42nd Street, so you can get off and change to the other direction without paying again.

Tips For More Bus & Subway Information

For additional transit information, call the Metropolitan Transit Authority's **MTA/New York City Transit's Travel Information Center** at ✆ **718/330-1234.** Extensive automated information is available at this number 24 hours a day, and travel agents are on hand to answer your questions and provide directions daily from 6am to 9pm. Customers who don't speak English can call ✆ **718/330-4847.** For online information that's always up-to-the-minute, visit **www.mta. nyc.ny.us.**

To request system maps, call the **Map Request Line** at ✆ **718/330-3322** (although realize that recent service changes may not yet be reflected on printed maps). Riders with disabilities should direct inquiries to ✆ **718/596-8585;** hearing-impaired riders can call ✆ **718/596-8273.** For MetroCard information, call ✆ **212/METROCARD** (638-7622) weekdays from 7am to 11pm, weekends 9am to 5pm, or go online to **www.mta.nyc.ny.us/metrocard.**

You can get bus and subway maps and additional transit information at most information centers (see "Visitor Information" in "Orientation," earlier in this chapter). A particularly helpful MTA transit information desk is located at the **Times Square Information Center,** 1560 Broadway, between 46th and 47th streets, where you can also buy MetroCards. Maps are sometimes available in subway stations (ask at the token booth), but rarely on buses.

The days of graffiti-covered cars are gone, but the stations—and an increasing number of trains—are not as clean as they could be. Trains are air-conditioned (move to the next car if yours isn't), though during the dog days of summer the platforms can be sweltering. In theory, all subway cars have PA systems to allow you to hear the conductor's announcements, but they don't always work well. It's a good idea to move to a car with a working PA system in case sudden service changes are announced that you'll want to know about.

For **subway safety tips,** see "For More Bus & Subway Information," below.

BY BUS

Less expensive than taxis and more pleasant than subways (they provide a mobile sightseeing window on Manhattan), MTA buses are a good transportation option. Their big drawback: They can get stuck in traffic, sometimes making it quicker to walk. They also stop every couple of blocks, rather than the 8 or 9 blocks that local subways traverse between stops. So for long distances, the subway is your best bet; but for short distances or traveling crosstown, try the bus.

Paying Your Way

Like the subway fare, **bus fare** is $2, half-price for seniors and riders with disabilities, and free for children under 44 inches (up to three per adult). The fare is payable with a **MetroCard** or **exact change.** Bus drivers don't make change, and fare boxes don't accept dollar bills or pennies. You can't purchase MetroCards on the bus, so you'll have to have them before you board; for details on where to get them, see "Paying Your Way," under "By Subway," above.

If you pay with a MetroCard, you can transfer to another bus or to the subway for free within 2 hours. If you pay cash, you must request a **free transfer** slip that allows you to change to an intersecting bus route only (transfer points are listed on the transfer paper) within 1 hour of issue. Transfer slips cannot be used to enter the subway.

Using the System

You can't flag a city bus down—you have to meet it at a bus stop. **Bus stops** are located every 2 or 3 blocks on the right-side corner of the street (facing the direction of traffic flow). They're marked by a curb painted yellow and a blue-and-white sign with a bus emblem and the route number or numbers, and usually an ad-bedecked Plexiglass bus shelter. Guide-a-Ride boxes at most stops display a route map and a hysterically optimistic schedule.

Almost every major avenue has its own **bus route.** They run either north or south: downtown on Fifth, uptown on Madison, downtown on Lexington, uptown on Third, and so on. There are **crosstown buses** at strategic locations all around town: 8th Street (eastbound); 9th (westbound); 14th, 23rd, 34th, and 42nd (east- and westbound); 49th (eastbound); 50th (westbound); 57th (east- and westbound); 65th (eastbound across the West Side, through the park, and then north on Madison, continuing east on 68th to York Ave.); 67th (westbound on the East Side to Fifth Ave., and then south on Fifth, continuing west on 66th St., through the park and across the west side to West End Ave.); and 79th, 86th, 96th, 116th, and 125th (east- and westbound). Some bus routes, however, are erratic: The M104, for example, starts at the East River, then turns at Eighth Avenue and goes up Broadway. The buses of the Fifth Avenue line go up Madison or Sixth and follow various routes around the city.

Most routes operate 24 hours a day, but service is infrequent at night. Some say that New York buses have a herding instinct: They arrive only in groups. During rush hour, main routes have "limited" buses, identifiable by the red card in the front window; they stop only at major cross streets.

To make sure that the bus you're boarding goes where you're going, check the map on the sign that's at every bus stop, get your hands on a route map (see "For More Bus & Subway Information," above), or **just ask.** The drivers are helpful, as long as you don't hold up the line too long.

While traveling, look out the window not only to take in the sights but also to keep track of cross streets so you know when to get off. Signal for a stop by pressing the tape strip above and beside the windows and along the metal straps, about 2 blocks before you want to stop. Exit through the pneumatic back doors (not the front door) by pushing on the yellow tape strip; the doors open automatically (pushing on the handles is useless unless you're as buff as Hercules). Most city buses are equipped with wheelchair lifts, making buses the preferable mode of public transportation for wheelchair-bound travelers; for more on this topic,

---

Tips Take a Free Ride

The Alliance for Downtown New York's **Downtown Connection** offers a free bus service that provides easy access to downtown destinations, including Battery Park City, the World Financial Center, and South Street Seaport. The buses, which run daily, every 10 minutes or so, from 10am to 7:30pm, make dozens of stops along a 5-mile route from Chambers Street on the west side to Beekman Street on the east side. For schedules and more information, call the Downtown Connection at ⓒ 212/566-6700, or visit **www.downtownny.com**.

⟨Tips **Taxi-Hailing Tips**

When you're waiting on the street for an available taxi, look at the **medallion light** on the top of the coming cabs. If the light is out, the taxi is in use. When the center part (the number) is lit, the taxi is available—this is when you raise your hand to flag the cab. If all the lights are on, the driver is off-duty. Taxi regulations limit the number of people permitted to take a cab to four, so expect to split up if your group is larger.

---

see "Specialized Travel Resources," on p. 59. Buses also "kneel," lowering down to the curb to make boarding easier.

BY TAXI

If you don't want to deal with public transportation, finding an address that might be a few blocks from the subway station, or sharing your ride with 3.5 million other people, then take a taxi. The biggest advantages are, of course, that cabs can be hailed on any street (provided you find an empty one—often simple, yet at other times nearly impossible) and will take you right to your destination. I find they're best used at night when there's little traffic and when the subway may seem a little daunting. In Midtown at midday, you can usually walk to where you're going more quickly.

Official New York City taxis, licensed by the Taxi and Limousine Commission (TLC), are yellow, with the rates printed on the door and a light with a medallion number on the roof. You can hail a taxi on any street. *Never* accept a ride from any other car except an official city yellow cab (livery cars are not allowed to pick up fares on the street, despite what the driver tells you when he pulls over to see if he can pick up a fare).

The base fare on entering the cab is $2.50. The cost is 40¢ for every ⅕ mile or 40¢ per 60 seconds in stopped or slow-moving traffic (or for waiting time). There's no extra charge for each passenger or for luggage. However, you must pay bridge or tunnel tolls (sometimes the driver will front the toll and add it to your bill at the end; most times, however, you pay the driver before the toll). You'll pay a $1 surcharge between 4 and 8pm and a 50¢ surcharge after 8pm and before 6am. A 15% to 20% tip is customary.

Most taxis are now equipped with a device that allows you to pay by credit card, though some drivers will claim the machine is broken (there is a transaction fee for credit cards that cuts into their income) and ask you to pay in cash. You can choose to either add the tip to the credit card, or tip the driver in cash.

And forget about hopping into the back seat and having some cigar-chomping, all-knowing driver turn and ask, "Where to, Mac?" Nowadays many, if not most, taxi drivers may not have the best grasp of English. If their driving is scaring you, ask them to slow down, stop slamming on the brakes *quite* so hard, and taking off like a rocket when the light turns green. Always wear your seat belt—taxis are required to provide them.

The TLC has posted a **Taxi Rider's Bill of Rights** sticker in every cab. Drivers are required by law to take you anywhere in the five boroughs, to Nassau or Westchester counties, or to Newark Airport. They are supposed to know how to get you to any address in Manhattan and all major points in the outer boroughs. They are also required to provide air-conditioning and turn off the radio on demand, and they cannot smoke while you're in the cab. They are required to be polite.

You are allowed to dictate the route that is taken. It's a good idea to look at a map before you get in a taxi. Taxi drivers have been known to jack up the fare on visitors who don't know better by taking a circuitous route between points A and B. Know enough about where you're going to know that something's wrong if you hop in a cab at Sixth Avenue and 57th Street to go to the Empire State Building (Fifth Ave. and 34th St.), say, and suddenly find yourself on Ninth Avenue.

On the other hand, listen to drivers who propose an alternate route. These guys spend 8 or 10 hours a day on these streets, and they know where the worst traffic is, or where Con Ed has dug up an intersection that should be avoided. A knowledgeable driver will know how to get you to your destination quickly and efficiently.

Another important tip: **Always make sure the meter is turned on at the start of the ride.** You'll see the red LED readout register the initial $2.50 and start calculating the fare as you go. I've witnessed unscrupulous drivers buzzing unsuspecting visitors around the city with the meter off, and then overcharging them at drop-off time.

Always ask for the receipt—it comes in handy if you need to make a complaint or have left something in a cab. In fact, it's a good idea to make a mental note of the driver's four-digit medallion number (usually posted on the divider between the front and back seats) just in case you need it later. You probably won't, but it's a good idea to play it safe.

A taxi driver is obligated to take you to your desired destination. If a taxi driver is on duty but refuses to take you to your desired destination (which happens on occasion when you want to go to an outer borough destination or very far uptown), get the driver's name and medallion number and file a complaint with the Taxi and Limousine Commission.

For all driver complaints, including the one above, and to report lost property, call 🕿 **311** or 212-NEWYORK (outside the metro area). For details on getting to and from the local airports by taxi, see "By Plane," under "Getting There," earlier in this chapter. For further taxi information—including a complete rundown of your rights as a taxi rider—point your Web browser to **www.ci.nyc.ny.us/taxi**.

BY CAR

Forget driving yourself around the city. It's not worth the headache. Traffic is horrendous, and you don't know the rules of the road (written or unwritten) or the arcane alternate-side-of-the-street parking regulations (in fact, precious few New Yorkers do). You don't want to find out the monstrous price of parking violations or live the Kafkaesque nightmare of liberating a vehicle from the tow pound. Not to mention the security risks.

If you do arrive in New York City by car, park it in a garage (expect to pay at least $25–$45 per day) and leave it there for the duration of your stay. (In our hotel chapter, we note if a hotel has a garage, or offers discounted parking, and the rate). If you drive a rental car in, return it as soon as you arrive and rent another when you leave.

Just about all of the major car-rental companies, have multiple Manhattan locations. For listings of the major car rental agencies in New York City, please see the Toll-Free Numbers & Websites appendix (p. 387).

TRAVELING FROM THE CITY TO THE SUBURBS

The **PATH** (🕿 **800/234-7284;** www.panynj.gov/path) system connects cities in New Jersey, including Hoboken and Newark, to Manhattan by subway-style trains. Stops in Manhattan are at the World Trade Center, Christopher and 9th streets, and along Sixth Avenue at 14th, 23rd, and 33rd streets. The fare is $1.75 one way.

New Jersey Transit (© 800/772-2222; www.njtransit.com) operates commuter trains from Penn Station, and buses from the Port Authority at Eighth Avenue and 42nd Street, to points throughout New Jersey.

The **Long Island Rail Road** (© 718/217-LIRR; www.mta.nyc.ny.us/lirr) runs from Penn Station, at Seventh Avenue between 31st and 33rd streets, to Queens (ocean beaches, Shea Stadium, Belmont Park) and points beyond on Long Island, to even better beaches and summer hot spots such as the Hamptons. You can also connect to the Fire Island ferry from the LIRR.

Metro-North Railroad (© 800/METRO-INFO or 212/532-4900; www.mta.nyc.ny.us/mnr) departs from Grand Central Terminal, at 42nd Street and Lexington Avenue, for areas north of the city, including Westchester County, the Hudson Valley, and Connecticut.

5 Money & Costs

MONEY & COSTS

New York City can be one of the most expensive destinations in the United States (though if you're visiting from Europe, where the dollar is taking a beating, you may be pleasantly surprised by the prices).

For international visitors, said dollars are denominated in the following manner: The most common bills are the $1 (a "buck"), $5, $10, and $20 denominations. There are also $2 bills (seldom encountered), $50 bills, and $100 bills (the last two are usually not welcome as payment for small purchases).

Coins come in seven denominations: 1¢ (1 cent, or a penny); 5¢ (5 cents, or a nickel); 10¢ (10 cents, or a dime); 25¢ (25 cents, or a quarter); 50¢ (50 cents, or a half dollar); the gold-colored Sacagawea coin, worth $1; and the rare silver dollar.

It's always advisable to bring money in a variety of forms on a vacation: a mix of cash, credit cards, and even traveler's checks. You should also exchange enough petty cash if you're traveling from another country to cover airport incidentals, tipping, and transportation to your hotel before you leave home, or withdraw money upon arrival at an airport ATM.

You never have to carry too much cash in New York, and while the city's pretty safe, it's best not to overstuff your wallet (although always make sure you have at least $20 in taxi fare on hand).

ATMS

In most Manhattan neighborhoods, you can find a bank with **ATMs** (automated teller machines) every couple of blocks. Many small stores and delis have ATMs with varying fees to withdraw money from your bank account or credit card.

The **Cirrus** (© 800/424-7787; www.mastercard.com) and **PLUS** (© 800/843-7587; www.visa.com) networks span the country; you can find them even in remote regions. Go to your bank card's website to find ATM locations at your destination. Be sure you know your daily withdrawal limit before you depart.

Note: Many banks impose a fee every time you use a card at another bank's ATM, and that fee is often higher for international transactions than for domestic ones (which are creeping up; I've seen a $3 fee at some major bank ATMs). In addition, the bank from which you withdraw cash may charge its own fee. To compare banks' ATM fees within the U.S., use **www.bankrate.com**. Visitors from outside the U.S. should also find out whether their bank assesses a 1% to 3% fee on charges incurred abroad.

Tips **Easy Money**

If you're coming to New York from another country, you'll avoid lines at airport ATMs by exchanging at least some money—just enough to cover airport incidentals and transportation to your hotel—before you leave home.

When you change money, ask for some small bills or loose change. Petty cash will come in handy for tipping and public transportation. Consider keeping the change separate from your larger bills, so that it's readily accessible and you'll be less of a target for theft.

CREDIT CARDS & DEBIT CARDS

Credit cards are the most widely used form of payment in the United States: **Visa** (Barclaycard in Britain), **Master-Card** (EuroCard in Europe, Access in Britain, Chargex in Canada), **American Express, Diners Club,** and **Discover.** They also provide a convenient record of all your expenses, and offer relatively good exchange rates. You can withdraw cash advances from your credit cards at banks or ATMs, but high fees make credit-card cash advances a pricey way to get cash. (Make sure you have your credit card PIN number before you leave home.)

It's highly recommended that you travel with at least one major credit card. You must have a credit card to rent a car, and hotels and airlines usually require a credit card imprint as a deposit against expenses.

ATM cards with major credit card backing, known as **"debit cards,"** are now a commonly acceptable form of payment in most stores and restaurants. Debit cards draw money directly from your checking account. Some stores enable you to receive cash back on your debit-card purchases as well (which can save you money on ATM fees). The same is true at most U.S. post offices.

TRAVELER'S CHECKS

Though credit cards and debit cards are more often used, traveler's checks are still widely accepted and U.S. International visitors should make sure that traveler's checks are denominated in U.S. dollars; foreign-currency checks are often difficult to exchange.

You can buy traveler's checks at most banks. Most are offered in denominations of $20, $50, $100, $500, and sometimes $1,000. Generally, you'll pay a service charge ranging from 1% to 4%.

The most popular traveler's checks are offered by **American Express** (© **800/807-6233;** © **800/221-7282** for card holders—this number accepts collect calls, offers service in several foreign languages, and exempts Amex gold and platinum cardholders from the 1% fee.); **Visa** (© **800/732-1322**)—AAA members can obtain Visa checks for a $9.95 fee (for checks up to $1,500) at most AAA offices or by calling © **866/339-3378;** and **MasterCard** (© **800/223-9920**).

Be sure to keep a copy of the traveler's checks serial numbers separate from your checks in the event that they are stolen or lost. You'll get a refund faster if you know the numbers.

6 Health

STAYING HEALTHY

If you get sick, consider asking your hotel concierge to recommend a local doctor— even his or her own. This will probably yield a better recommendation than any toll-free telephone number would.

Avoiding "Economy-Class Syndrome"

Deep vein thrombosis, or as it's known in the world of flying, "economy-class syndrome," is a blood clot that develops in a deep vein. It's a potentially deadly condition that can be caused by sitting in cramped conditions—such as an airplane cabin—for too long. During a flight (especially a long-haul flight), get up, walk around, and stretch your legs every 60 to 90 minutes to keep your blood flowing. Other preventative measures include frequent flexing of the legs while sitting, drinking lots of water, and avoiding alcohol and sleeping pills. If you have a history of deep vein thrombosis, heart disease, or another condition that puts you at high risk, some experts recommend wearing compression stockings or taking anticoagulants when you fly; always ask your physician about the best course for you. Symptoms of deep vein thrombosis include leg pain or swelling, or even shortness of breath.

There are also several walk-in medical centers, like **DOCS at New York Healthcare,** 55 E. 34th St., between Park and Madison avenues (© **800/673-3627** or 212/252-6001), for non-emergency illnesses. The clinic, affiliated with Beth Israel Medical Center, is open Monday through Thursday from 8am to 8pm, Friday from 8am to 7pm, Saturday from 9am to 3pm, and Sunday from 9am to 2pm.

The **NYU Downtown Hospital** offers physician referrals at © **888/698-3362** or 212/312-5000. You can also try the emergency room at a local hospital. Many hospitals also have walk-in clinics for emergency cases that are not life-threatening; you may not get immediate attention, but you won't pay the high price of an emergency-room visit. We list more hospitals and emergency numbers under the appendix on p. 388.

If you suffer from a chronic illness, consult your doctor before your departure. For such conditions as epilepsy, diabetes, or heart problems, wear a **MedicAlert identification tag** (© **888/633-4298;** www.medicalert.org), which will immediately alert doctors to your condition and give them access to your records through MedicAlert's 24-hour hot line.

Pack **prescription medications** in their original containers in your carry-on luggage. Also bring along copies of your prescriptions in case you lose your pills or run out. Don't forget an extra pair of contact lenses or prescription glasses.

If you have dental problems on the road, a service known as **1-800-DENTIST** (© **800/336-8478**) will provide the name of a local dentist.

We list **additional emergency numbers** in the "Fast Facts" appendix, p. 388.

7 Safety

STAYING SAFE

The FBI consistently rates New York City as one of the safest large cities in the United States, but it is still a large city and crime most definitely exists. Here are a few tips for staying safe in New York:

- Trust your instincts, because they're usually right.

- You'll rarely be hassled, but it's always best to walk with a sense of purpose and self-confidence. Don't stop in the middle of the sidewalk to pull out and peruse your map.

- Anywhere in the city, if you find yourself on a deserted street that feels unsafe, it probably is; leave as quickly as possible.

• If you do find yourself accosted by someone with or without a weapon, remember to keep your anger in check and that the most reasonable response (maddening though it may be) is not to resist.

SUBWAY SAFETY TIPS In general, the subways are safe, especially in Manhattan. There are panhandlers and questionable characters like anywhere else in the city, but subway crime has gone down to 1960s levels. Still, stay alert and trust your instincts. Always keep a hand on your personal belongings.

When using the subway, **don't wait for trains near the edge of the platform** or on extreme ends of a station. During non–rush hours, wait for the train in view of the token-booth clerk or under the yellow DURING OFF HOURS TRAINS STOP HERE signs, and ride in the train operator's or conductor's car (usually in the center of the train; you'll see his or her head stick out of the window when the doors open). Choose crowded cars over empty ones—there's safety in numbers.

Avoid subways late at night, and splurge on a cab after about 10 or 11pm—it's money well spent to avoid a long wait on a deserted platform. Or take the bus.

8 Specialized Travel Resources

TRAVELERS WITH DISABILITIES
Most disabilities shouldn't stop anyone from traveling in the U.S. Thanks to provisions in the Americans with Disabilities Act (ADA), most public places are required to comply with disability-friendly regulations. Almost all public establishments (including hotels, restaurants, museums, and so on, but not including certain National Historic Landmarks), and at least some modes of public transportation provide accessible entrances and other facilities for those with disabilities.

New York is more accessible to travelers with disabilities than ever before. The city's bus system is wheelchair friendly, and most of the major sightseeing attractions are easily accessible. Even so, **always call first** to be sure that the places you want to go to are fully accessible.

Most hotels are ADA-compliant, with suitable rooms for wheelchair-bound travelers as well as those with other disabilities. But before you book, **ask lots of questions based on your needs.**

Many city hotels are in older buildings that have been modified to meet requirements; still, elevators and bathrooms can be on the small side, and other impediments may exist. If you have mobility issues, you'll probably do best to book one of the city's newer hotels, which tend to be more spacious and accommodating. At **www.access-able.com** (see below), you'll find links to New York's best accessible accommodations (click on "World Destinations"). Some Broadway theaters and other performance venues provide total wheelchair accessibility; others provide partial accessibility. Many also offer lower-priced tickets for theatergoers with disabilities and their companions, though you'll need to check individual policies and reserve in advance.

Hospital Audiences, Inc. (© 212/575-7676; www.hospitalaudiences.org) arranges attendance and provides details about accessibility at cultural institutions as well as cultural events adapted for people with disabilities. Services include "Describe!," which allows visually impaired theatergoers to enjoy theater events; and the invaluable **HAI Hot Line** (© 212/575-7676), which offers accessibility information for hotels, restaurants, attractions, cultural venues, and much more. This nonprofit organization also publishes *Access for All,* a guidebook on accessibility, available free-of-charge on the website **www.hospitalaudiences.org**.

Another terrific source for travelers with disabilities who are coming to New York City is **Big Apple Greeter** (© 212/669-8159; www.bigapplegreeter.org). All of its employees are extremely well versed in accessibility issues. They can provide a resource list of city agencies that serve those with disabilities, and they sometimes have special discounts available to theater and music performances. Big Apple Greeter even offers one-to-one tours that pair volunteers with visitors with disabilities; they can even introduce you to the public transportation system if you like. Reserve at least 1 week ahead.

GETTING AROUND Super Shuttle-Express Shuttle USA (© 800/BlueVan or 212/258-3826; www.supershuttle.com) operates minibuses with lifts from Newark airports to Midtown hotels by reservation; arrange pickup 3 or 4 days in advance. **Olympia Trails** (© 877/894-9155; www.coachusa.com/olympia provides service from Newark Airport, with half-price fares for travelers with disabilities (be sure to prepurchase your tickets to guarantee the discount fare, as drivers can't sell discounted tickets). Not all buses are appropriately equipped, so call ahead for the schedule of accessible buses (press "0" to reach a real person).

Taxis are required to carry people who have folding wheelchairs and service dogs. However, don't be surprised if they don't run each other down trying to get to you; even though you shouldn't have to, you may have to wait a bit for a friendly (or fare-desperate) driver to come along.

Public buses are an inexpensive and easy way to get around New York. All buses' back doors are supposed to be equipped with wheelchair lifts (though the city has had complaints that not all are in working order). Buses also "kneel,"

lowering their front steps for people who have difficulty boarding. Passengers with disabilities pay half-price fares ($1). The **subway** isn't fully wheelchair accessible, but a list of about 30 accessible subway stations and a guide to wheelchair-accessible subway itineraries is on the MTA website. Call © **718/596-8585** for bus and subway transit info, or go online to **www.mta.nyc.ny.us/nyct** and click on the wheelchair symbol.

You're better off not trying to rent your own car to get around the city. But if you consider it the best mode of transportation for you, **Wheelchair Getaways** (© 800/642-2042 or 800/344-5005; www.wheelchairgetaways.com) rents specialized vans, with wheelchair lifts and other features for travelers with disabilities, throughout the New York metropolitan area.

Organizations that offer a vast range of resources and assistance to disabled travelers include **MossRehab** (© 800/CALL-MOSS; www.mossresourcenet.org); the **American Foundation for the Blind** (AFB; © 800/232-5463; www.afb.org); and **SATH** (**Society for Accessible Travel & Hospitality;** © 212/447-7284; www.sath.org). **AirAmbulance Card.com** is now partnered with SATH and allows you to preselect top-notch hospitals in case of an emergency.

Access-Able Travel Source (© 303/232-2979; www.access-able.com) offers a database on travel agents from around the world with experience in accessible travel; destination-specific access information; and links to such resources as service animals, equipment rentals, and access guides.

Many travel agencies offer customized tours and itineraries for travelers with disabilities. Among them are **Flying Wheels Travel** (© 507/451-5005; www.flyingwheelstravel.com) and **Accessible Journeys** (© 800/846-4537 or 610/521-0339; www.disabilitytravel.com).

Flying with Disability (www.flying-with-disability.org) is a comprehensive information source on airplane travel. **Avis Rent a Car** (© **888/879-4273**) has an "Avis Access" program that offers services for customers with special travel needs. These include specially outfitted vehicles with swivel seats, spinner knobs, and hand controls; mobility scooter rentals; and accessible bus service. Be sure to reserve well in advance.

Also check out the quarterly magazine *Emerging Horizons* (www.emerging horizons.com), available by subscription ($16.95 year U.S.; $21.95 outside U.S.).

The "Accessible Travel" link at **Mobility-Advisor.com** (www.mobility-advisor.com) offers a variety of travel resources to disabled persons.

British travelers should contact **Holiday Care** (© **0845/124-9971** in UK only; www.holidaycare.org.uk) to access travel information and resources for disabled and elderly people.

For more on organizations that offer resources to disabled travelers, go to **www.frommers.com**.

GLBT TRAVELERS

Gay and lesbian culture is as much a part of New York's basic identity as yellow cabs, high-rises, and Broadway theater. Indeed, in a city with one of the world's largest, loudest, and most powerful GLBT populations, homosexuality is squarely in the mainstream. So city hotels tend to be neutral on the issue, and gay couples shouldn't have a problem. Check out "The Gay & Lesbian Scene," in chapter 9 for nightlife suggestions.

All over Manhattan, but especially in such neighborhoods as the **West Village** (particularly Christopher St., famous the world over as the main drag of New York gay-male life) and **Chelsea** (especially Eighth Ave., from 16th to 23rd sts., and W. 17th to 19th sts., from Fifth to Eighth aves.), shops, services, and restaurants have a lesbian and gay flavor.

The **Oscar Wilde Bookshop,** 15 Christopher St. (© **212/255-8097;** www.oscarwildebooks.com), is the city's best gay and lesbian bookstore and a good source for information on the city's gay community.

The **Lesbian, Gay, Bisexual & Transgender Community Center,** familiarly known as "The Center," is at 208 W. 13th St., between Seventh and Eighth avenues (© **212/620-7310;** www.gaycenter.org). The center is the meeting place for more than 400 lesbian, gay, and bisexual organizations. You can check the online events calendar, which lists hundreds of happenings—lectures, dances, concerts, readings, films—or call for the latest. Their site offers links to gay-friendly hotels and guesthouses in and around New York, plus tons of other information; the staff is also friendly and helpful in person or over the phone.

Other good sources for lesbian and gay events are the two free weekly newspapers, *Gay City News* (www.gaycitynews.com) and the *New York Blade* (www.nyblade.com), and the free magazines *HX* (www.hx.com), *Next* (www.nextmagazine.com), and *GONYC* (www.gomag.com), which is lesbian-oriented. You'll also find lots of information on their websites.

The weekly *Time Out New York* (www.timeoutny.com) boasts a terrific gay and lesbian section. The Center (see above) publishes a monthly guide listing many events (also listed on its website).

In addition, there are lesbian and gay musical events, such as performances by the **New York City Gay Men's Chorus** (© **212/344-1777;** www.nycgmc.org); health programs sponsored by the **Gay Men's Health Crisis** (GMHC; © **800/AIDS-NYC** or Hotline 212/367-1000; www.gmhc.org); the **Gay & Lesbian National Hot Line** (© **888/TheGLNH;** www.glnh.org), offering peer counseling and information on upcoming events; and many other organizations.

The International Gay and Lesbian Travel Association (IGLTA; © 800/448-8550 or 954/776-2626; www.iglta.org) is the trade association for the gay and lesbian travel industry, and offers an online directory of gay- and lesbian-friendly travel businesses and tour operators.

Many agencies offer tours and travel itineraries specifically for gay and lesbian travelers.

Gay.com Travel (© 800/929-2268 or 415/644-8044; www.gay.com/travel or www.outandabout.com) is an online successor to the popular *Out & About* print magazine. It provides regularly updated information about gay-owned, -oriented, and -friendly lodging, dining, sightseeing, nightlife, and shopping establishments in every important destination worldwide. British travelers should click on the "Travel" link at **www.uk.gay.com** for advice and gay-friendly trip ideas.

The Canadian website **GayTraveler** (gaytraveler.ca) offers ideas and advice for gay travel all over the world.

The following travel guides are available at bookstores, or you can order them online: *Spartacus International Gay Guide, 35th Edition* (Bruno Gmünder Verlag; www.spartacusworld.com/gayguide) and the *Damron* guides (www.damron.com), with annual books for gay men and lesbians.

For more gay and lesbian travel resources, visit **www.frommers.com**.

SENIOR TRAVEL

Members of **AARP**, 601 E St. NW, Washington, DC 20049 (© **888/687-2277**; www.aarp.org), get discounts on hotels, airfares, and car rentals. AARP offers members a wide range of benefits, including *AARP: The Magazine* and a newsletter. Anyone over 50 can join.

New York subway and bus fares are half-price ($1) for people 65 and older. Many museums and sights (and some theaters and performance halls) offer discounted admittance and tickets to seniors, so don't be shy about asking. Always bring an ID card, especially if you've kept your youthful glow.

Many hotels offer senior discounts; **Choice Hotels** (which include Comfort Inns, some of my favorite affordable Midtown hotels; see chapter 5, "Where to Stay"), for example, gives 30% off their published rates to anyone over 50, provided you book your room through their nationwide toll-free reservations number (that is, not directly with the hotels or through a travel agent). For a complete list of Choice Hotels, visit **www.hotelchoice.com**.

Many reliable agencies and organizations target the 50-plus market. **Elderhostel** (© **800/454-5768**; www.elderhostel.org) arranges worldwide study programs (including some in New York City) for those ages 55 and over.

Recommended publications offering travel resources and discounts for seniors include: the quarterly magazine *Travel 50 & Beyond* (www.travel50andbeyond.com) and the bestselling paperback *Unbelievably Good Deals and Great Adventures That You Absolutely Can't Get Unless You're Over 50 2005–2006, 16th Edition* (McGraw-Hill), by Joann Rattner Heilman.

Frommers.com offers more information and resources on travel for seniors.

FAMILY TRAVEL

To locate accommodations, restaurants, and attractions that are particularly kid-friendly, refer to the "Kids" icon throughout this guide.

For more extensive recommendations, you might want to purchase a copy of *Frommer's New York City with Kids,* an entire guidebook dedicated to family visits to the Big Apple.

Good bets for the most timely information include the "Weekend" section of Friday's *New York Times,* which has a section dedicated to the week's best kid-friendly activities; the weekly *New York* magazine, which has a full calendar of children's events in its listings section; and *Time Out New York,* which also has a weekly kids section with a bit of an alternative bent. The *Big Apple Parents' Paper* is usually available, for free, at children's stores and other locations in Manhattan; you can also find good information from the folks behind the paper at **www.parentsknow.com**.

The first place to look for **babysitting** is in your hotel (better yet, ask about babysitting when you reserve). Many hotels have babysitting services or will provide you with lists of reliable sitters. If this doesn't pan out, call the **Baby Sitters' Guild** (© 212/682-0227; www.babysitters guild.com). The sitters are licensed, insured, and bonded, and can even take your child on outings.

Recommended family travel websites include **Family Travel Forum** (www. familytravelforum.com), a comprehensive site that offers customized trip planning; **Family Travel Network** (www. familytravelnetwork.com), an online magazine providing travel tips; **Travel-WithYourKids.com** (www.travelwith yourkids.com), a comprehensive site, written by parents for parents, that offers advice for long-distance and international travel with children.

For a list of more family-friendly travel resources, turn to the experts at From-mers.com.

STUDENT TRAVEL

Check out the **International Student Travel Confederation** (**ISTC;** www.istc. org) website for comprehensive travel services information and details on how to get an **International Student Identity Card** (**ISIC**), which qualifies students for substantial savings on rail passes, plane tickets, entrance fees, and more. It also provides students with basic health and life insurance and a 24-hour helpline. The card is valid for a maximum of 18 months.

You can apply for the card online or in person at **STA Travel** (© **800/781-4040** in North America; © 132-782 in Australia; © 0871/2-300-040 in the U.K.; www.statravel.com), the biggest student travel agency in the world; check out the website to locate STA Travel offices worldwide. If you're no longer a student but are still under 26, you can get an **International Youth Travel Card** (**IYTC**) from the same people, which entitles you to some discounts. **Travel CUTS** (© **800/592-2887;** www.travel cuts.com) offers similar services for both Canadians and U.S. residents. Irish students may prefer to turn to **USIT** (© **01/ 602-1904;** www.usit.ie), an Ireland-based specialist in student, youth, and independent travel.

9 Sustainable Tourism

"Green" travel in New York City? That seems like an odd combination, yet there's a lot that New York does that makes it (in some ways) an environmentally-friendly destination, not the least of which is its highly useful (and much-used) mass transit system.

Sustainable tourism is conscientious travel. It means being careful with the environments you explore, and respecting the communities you visit. Two overlapping components of sustainable travel are **ecotourism** and **ethical tourism.** The **International Ecotourism Society**

(TIES) defines ecotourism as responsible travel to natural areas that conserves the environment and improves the well-being of local people. TIES suggests that eco-tourists follow these principles:

- Minimize environmental impact.
- Build environmental and cultural awareness and respect.
- Provide positive experiences for both visitors and hosts.
- Provide direct financial benefits for conservation and for local people.
- Raise sensitivity to host countries' political, environmental, and social climates.

- Support international human rights and labor agreements.

While much of the focus of ecotourism is about reducing impacts on the natural environment, ethical tourism concentrates on ways to preserve and enhance local economies and communities, regardless of location. In New York City? You can embrace ethical tourism by using mass transit, staying at a hotel or B&B that makes an effort to be "green," shopping at a locally-owned store, and eating at a diner, coffee shop, or mom-and-pop eatery instead of at a fast food chain.

It's Easy Being Green

Here are a few simple ways you can help conserve fuel and energy when you travel:

- Each time you take a flight or drive a car, greenhouse gases release into the atmosphere. You can help neutralize this danger to the planet through "carbon offsetting"—paying someone to invest your money in programs that reduce your greenhouse gas emissions by the same amount you've added. Before buying carbon offset credits, make sure that you're using a reputable company, one with a proven program that invests in renewable energy. Reliable carbon offset companies include **Carbonfund** (www.carbonfund.org), **TerraPass** (www.terrapass.org), and **Carbon Neutral** (www.carbonneutral.org).
- Whenever possible, choose nonstop flights; they generally require less fuel than indirect flights that stop and take off again. Try to fly during the day—some scientists estimate that nighttime flights are twice as harmful to the environment. And pack light—each 15 pounds of luggage on a 5,000-mile flight adds up to 50 pounds of carbon dioxide emitted.
- At hotels, request that your sheets and towels not be changed daily. (Many hotels already have programs like this in place.) Turn off the lights and air-conditioner (or heater) when you leave your room.
- Use public transport where possible—trains, buses, and even taxis are more energy-efficient forms of transport than driving. In New York City, it's also the most efficient, cost-effective way to get around Manhattan.

Frommers.com: The Complete Travel Resource

Planning a trip or just returned? Head to **Frommers.com,** voted Best Travel Site by *PC Magazine.* We think you'll find our site indispensable before, during, and after your travels—with expert advice and tips; independent reviews of hotels, restaurants, attractions, and preferred shopping and nightlife venues; vacation giveaways; and an online booking tool. We publish the complete contents of over 135 travel guides in our **Destinations** section, covering over 4,000 places worldwide. Each weekday, we publish original articles that report on **Deals and News** via our free **Frommers.com Newsletters.** What's more, **Arthur Frommer** himself blogs 5 days a week, with cutting opinions about the state of travel in the modern world. We're betting you'll find our **Events** listings an invaluable resource; it's an up-to-the-minute roster of what's happening in cities everywhere—including concerts, festivals, lectures, and more. We've also added weekly **podcasts, interactive maps,** and hundreds of new images across the site. Finally, don't forget to visit our **Message Boards,** where you can join in conversations with thousands of fellow Frommer's travelers and post your trip report once you return.

10 Packages for the Independent Traveler

Package tours are simply a way to buy the airfare, accommodations, and other elements of your trip (such as car rentals, airport transfers, and sometimes even activities) at the same time and often at discounted prices.

One good source of package deals is the airlines themselves. Most major airlines offer air/land packages, including **American Airlines Vacations** (© 800/321-2121; www.aavacations.com), **Delta Vacations** (© 800/654-6559; www.delta vacations.com), **Continental Airlines Vacations** (© 800/301-3800; www.co vacations.com), and **United Vacations** (© 888/854-3899; www.unitedvacations. com). Several big **online travel agencies**—Expedia, Travelocity, Orbitz, and Lastminute.com—also do a brisk business in packages.

Travel packages are also listed in the travel section of your local Sunday newspaper. Or check ads in the national travel magazines such as *Arthur Frommer's Budget Travel Magazine, Travel & Leisure, National Geographic Traveler,* and *Condé Nast Traveler.*

11 Escorted General-Interest Tours

Escorted tours are structured group tours with a group leader. The price usually includes everything from airfare to hotels, meals, tours, admission costs, and local transportation.

If you're not a big-city person, or it's your first time in New York City, you might find your comfort level in an escorted group.

Despite the fact that escorted tours require big deposits and predetermine hotels, restaurants, and itineraries, many people derive security and peace of mind from the structure they offer. Escorted tours let travelers sit back and enjoy the trip without having to drive or worry about details. They take you to the maximum number of sights in the minimum amount of time, with the least amount of hassle. They're particularly convenient for people with limited mobility, and they can be a great way to make new friends.

On the downside, you'll have little opportunity for serendipitous interactions with locals. The tours can be jam-packed with activities, leaving little room for individual sightseeing, whim, or adventure—plus they often focus on the heavily touristed sites, so you miss out on many a lesser-known gem.

For more information on Escorted General-Interest Tours, including questions to ask before booking your trip, see Frommers.com.

12 Staying Connected

TELEPHONES

Generally, hotel surcharges on long-distance and local calls are astronomical, so you're better off using your **cellphone** or a **public pay telephone.** Many convenience stores and drugstores sell **prepaid calling cards** in denominations up to $50; for international visitors these can be the least expensive way to call home. Many public pay phones at airports now accept American Express, MasterCard, and Visa credit cards. **Local calls** made from pay phones cost either 25¢ or 50¢ (no pennies, please).

That said, there aren't as many payphones on the streets of New York City as there used to be because of the prevalence of cellphones, and the ones that are there are often out-of-order.

CELLPHONES

Just because your cellphone works at home doesn't mean it'll work everywhere in the U.S. (thanks to our nation's fragmented cellphone system). It's a good bet that your phone will work in major cities, but take a look at your wireless company's coverage map on its website before heading out. If you need to stay in touch at a destination where you know your phone won't work, **rent** a phone that does from **InTouch USA** (© 800/872-7626; www.intouchglobal.com) or a rental car location, but beware that you'll pay $1 a minute or more for airtime.

If you're not from the U.S., you'll be appalled at the poor reach of the **GSM (Global System for Mobile Communications) wireless network,** which is used

---

Tips Hey, Google, Did You Get My Text Message?

It's bound to happen: The day you leave this guidebook back at the hotel for an unencumbered stroll through the West Village, you'll forget the address of the lunch spot you had earmarked. If you're traveling with a mobile device, send a text message to © 46645 (GOOGL) for a lightning-fast response. For instance, type "pink teacup new york" and within 10 seconds you'll receive a text message with the address and phone number. This nifty trick works in a range of search categories: Look up weather ("weather Philadelphia"), language translations ("translate goodbye in Spanish"), currency conversions ("10 usd in pounds"), movie times ("harry potter 60605"), and more. If your search results are off, be more specific ("the abbey gay bar west hollywood"). For more tips and searches, see **www.google.com/intl/en_us/mobile/sms/**. Regular text-message charges apply.

Where to Check Your E-mail in the City That Never Sleeps

If your hotel doesn't offer free access to its business center or a terminal in the lobby to check your email (and many do), where can you go to check it if you don't have a computer with you?

All branches of the **New York Public Library** (www.nypl.org) feature computers that offer free access to the Internet, electronic databases, library catalogs and Microsoft Office. They are also supposed to offer Wi-Fi, but we've found that having it listed on their Web site and actually having it operative can be two different things.

More free access is available at the **Times Square Visitors Center**, 1560 Broadway, between 46th and 47th streets (© **212/768-1560**; daily 8am–8pm), has computer terminals that you can use to send e-mails courtesy of Yahoo!; you can even send an electronic postcard, with a photo of yourself, home to Mom.

Open 24/7 in the heart of Times Square, **easyInternetcafé** ☆, 234 W. 42nd St., between Seventh and Eighth avenues (© **212/398-0775**; www.easy everything.com/map/nyc1.html), is the first stateside branch of a worldwide chain of Internet cafes. Boasting flatscreen monitors and a super-fast T3 connection, this mammoth place makes accessing the Internet cheap through the economy of scale: Access is available for as little as $1, and the length of time that buck buys you fluctuates depending on the occupancy at the time you log on. This will generally work out to the cheapest Web time you can buy in the city.

CyberCafe (www.cyber-cafe.com)—in Times Square at 250 W. 49th St., between Broadway and Eighth Avenue (© **212/333-4109**)—is more expensive at $6.40 per half-hour, with a half-hour minimum (you're billed $3.20 for every subsequent 15 min.). But their T1 connectivity gives you super-fast access, and they offer a full range of other cyber, copy, fax, and printing services.

FedEx Kinko's (www.kinkos.com) charges 30¢ per minute ($15 per hour) and there are dozens of locations around town. In addition, an increasing number of delis and copy shops frequently stick an INTERNET sign in the window, and you can log on in a unit wedged into a corner next to the ATM for a couple bucks, while you drink your genuine New York City deli coffee.

by much of the rest of the world. Your phone will probably work in most major U.S. cities; it definitely won't work in many rural areas. To see where GSM phones work in the U.S., check out **www. t-mobile.com/coverage**. And you may or may not be able to send SMS (text-messaging) home.

VOICE-OVER INTERNET PROTOCOL (VOIP)

If you have Web access while traveling, consider a broadband-based telephone service (in technical terms, **Voice over Internet protocol,** or **VoIP**) such as Skype (www.skype.com) or Vonage (www.vonage.com), which allow you to make free international calls from your laptop or in a cybercafe. Neither service requires the people you're calling to also have that service (though there are fees if they do not). Check the websites for details.

INTERNET & E-MAIL
WITH YOUR OWN COMPUTER

More and more hotels, resorts, airports, cafes, and retailers are going Wi-Fi (wireless fidelity), becoming "hotspots" that offer free high-speed Wi-Fi access or charge a small fee for usage. Wi-Fi is found in campgrounds and RV parks, and, in some places, even covers entire towns. Most laptops sold today have built-in wireless capability. To find public Wi-Fi hotspots at your destination, go to **www.jiwire.com**; its Hotspot Finder holds the world's largest directory of public wireless hotspots.

For dial-up access, most business-class hotels in the U.S. offer dataports for laptop modems, and a few thousand hotels in the U.S. and Europe now offer free high-speed Internet access.

Wherever you go, bring a **connection kit** of the right power and phone adapters, a spare phone cord, and a spare Ethernet network cable—or find out if your hotel supplies them to guests.

WITHOUT YOUR OWN COMPUTER

Most major airports have **Internet kiosks** or Wi-Fi areas that provide basic Web access for a per-minute, -hour, or -day fee that's usually much higher than cybercafe prices. Check out copy shops such as **Kinko's** (FedEx Kinkos), which offers computer stations with fully loaded software (as well as Wi-Fi).

For help locating cybercafes and other establishments where you can go for Internet access, see the box "Where to Check Your E-mail in the City That Never Sleeps," p. 67.

4

New York City Neighborhoods & Suggested Itineraries

There are a lot of neighborhoods on the (relatively) small island of Manhattan, and more to explore in the other boroughs. Each has its own vibe, and here I'll lay out a thumbnail description of the major parts of town, as well as mentioning how they rank in terms of places to stay, eat, and see the sights.

Once I've given you the lay of the land, I'll give you some itineraries that make the most of your time in New York City, whether you're here for just a day or a bit longer than that.

1 New York City Neighborhoods in Brief

Because they grew up over the course of hundreds of years, Manhattan neighborhoods have multiple, splintered personalities and fluid boundaries. Still, it's relatively easy to agree upon what they stand for in general terms—so if you stop a New Yorker on the street and ask him or her to point you to, say, the Upper West Side or the Flatiron District, they'll know where you want to go. From south to north, here is how I've defined Manhattan's neighborhoods throughout this book.

Downtown

Lower Manhattan: South Street Seaport & the Financial District At one time, this was New York—period. Established by the Dutch in 1625 (hence the city's original name, New Amsterdam), New York's first settlements sprang up on the southern tip of Manhattan island; everything uptown was farm country and wilderness. This is still the best place in the city to search for the past.

Lower Manhattan constitutes everything south of Chambers Street. **Battery Park,** the point of departure for the Statue of Liberty, Ellis Island, and Staten Island, is on the southern tip. The **South Street Seaport,** touristy but still a reminder of times when shipping was the lifeblood of the city, is a bit north on the East Side; it's

south of the Brooklyn Bridge, which stands proudly as the ultimate achievement of New York's 19th-century industrial age.

The rest of the area is considered the **Financial District,** but may be more famous now as **Ground Zero.** Until September 11, 2001, the Financial District was anchored by the **World Trade Center,** with the World Financial Center complex and Battery Park City to the west, and **Wall Street** running crosstown a little south and to the east. Construction has begun on the new complex, but it will be years to complete. What won't take so long to build are the hundreds of new condo developments in the area.

City Hall remains the northern border of the district, abutting Chambers Street (look for City Hall Park on the

Downtown

For those of us who live uptown, lower Manhattan is practically a different planet, but one which has much to offer. The website for the **Alliance for Downtown New York** (www.downtownny.com), updated daily; is a trusty source to keep abreast on new developments and exciting downtown events.

map). Most of the streets around here are narrow concrete canyons, with Broadway serving as the main uptown-downtown artery.

Just about all of the major subway lines congregate here before they either end or head to Brooklyn.

TriBeCa Bordered by the Hudson River to the west, the area north of Chambers Street, west of Broadway, and south of Canal Street is the *Triangle Below Canal* Street, or TriBeCa. Since the 1980s, as SoHo became saturated with chic, the spillover has been transforming TriBeCa into one of the city's more cutting edge, exclusive neighborhoods, where celebrities and families coexist in cast-iron warehouses converted into expensive apartments. Artists' lofts and galleries as well as hip antiques and design shops pepper the area, as do some of the city's best restaurants.

Robert De Niro gave the neighborhood a huge boost when he established the TriBeCa Film Center, and Miramax headquarters gave the area further capitalist-chic cachet. Still, such historic streets as White (especially the Federal-style building at no. 2) and Harrison (the stretch west from Greenwich St.) evoke a bygone, more human-scale New York, as do a few holdout businesses and pubs.

The main uptown-downtown drag is **West Broadway** (2 blocks west of Broadway). Consider the Franklin Street subway station on the 1 line to be your gateway to the action.

Chinatown New York City's most famous ethnic enclave is bursting past its traditional boundaries and has encroached on Little Italy. The former marshlands northeast of City Hall and below Canal Street, from Broadway to the Bowery, are where Chinese immigrants arriving from San Francisco were forced to live in the 1870s. This booming neighborhood is a conglomeration of Asian populations. It offers tasty cheap eats from Szechuan to Hunan to Cantonese to Vietnamese to Thai. Exotic shops offer strange foods, herbs, and souvenirs; bargains on clothing and leather are plentiful. It's a blast to walk down Canal Street, peering into the stores and watching crabs escape from their baskets at the fish markets.

The Canal Street (J, M, Z, N, R, 6, Q, W) station will get you to the heart of the action. The streets are crowded during the day and empty out after around 9pm; they remain quite safe, but the neighborhood is more enjoyable during the bustle.

Little Italy Little Italy, traditionally the area east of Broadway between Houston and north of Canal streets, is a shrinking community, due to the encroachment of thriving Chinatown. It's now limited mainly to **Mulberry Street,** where you'll find most restaurants. With rents going up in the trendy Lower East Side, the chic spots are moving in, further intruding upon the old-world landscape. The best way to reach Little Italy is to walk east from

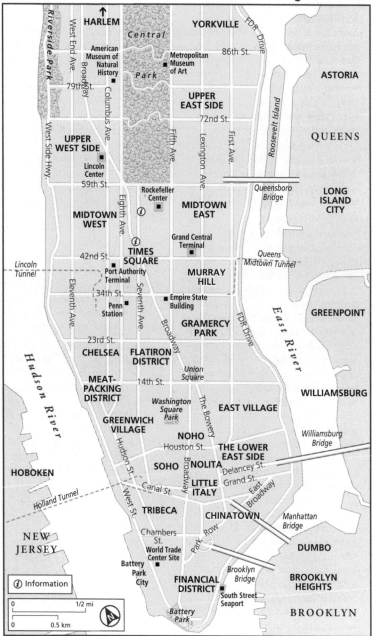

Manhattan Neighborhoods

Visiting the Lower East Side

The **Lower East Side Business Improvement District** operates a neighborhood **visitor center** at 261 Broome St., between Orchard and Allen streets (© **866/ 224-0206** or 212/226-9010), that's open daily from 10am to 4pm. Stop in for an Orchard Street Bargain District shopping and dining guide (which they can also send you in advance), plus other information on this historic yet freshly hip 'hood. You can also find shopping, dining, and nightlife directories online at **www.lowereastsideny.com**.

the Spring Street station (on the no. 6 line) to Mulberry Street; turn south for Little Italy (you can't miss the year-round red, green, and white street decorations).

The Lower East Side The Lower East Side boasts the best of both old and new New York—though the new is eking out what is left of the old. But still, witness the stretch of Houston between Forsyth and Allen streets, where Yonah Shimmel's Knish Shop sits shoulder-to-shoulder with the Sunshine Theater, an arthouse cinema. Some say the Lower East Side has come full circle: Self-important hipsters with Ivy League educations and well-honed senses of entitlement (and trust funds) have come back to the neighborhoods their immigrant grandparents worked to escape.

Of all the successive waves of immigrants and refugees who passed through this densely populated tenement neighborhood from the mid–19th century to the 1920s, Eastern European Jews left the most lasting impression. The Jewish communities, which popped up between Houston and Canal streets east of the Bowery, are now just part of history. The neighborhood has experienced quite a renaissance over the last few years and makes a fascinating stop for both nostalgists and nightlife hounds.

There are some remnants of what was once the largest Jewish population in America along **Orchard Street,** where you'll find great bargain-hunting in its old-world fabric and clothing stores still thriving between the club-clothes boutiques and lounges. Keep in mind these shops close early on Friday afternoon and all day on Saturday (the Jewish Sabbath). The exponentially expanding trendy set can be found in the blocks between Allen and Clinton streets south of Houston and north of Delancey, with more new shops, bars, and restaurants popping up every day.

This area is not well served by the subway system (one cause for its years of decline), so your best bet is to take the F train to Second Avenue (you can get off closer to First) and walk east on Houston; when you see Katz's Deli, you've arrived. You can also reach the LES from the Delancey Street station on the F line, and the Essex Street station on the J, M, and Z lines.

SoHo & Nolita No relation to the London neighborhood of the same name, **SoHo** got its moniker as an abbreviation of "*So*uth of *Ho*uston Street." This fashionable neighborhood extends down to Canal Street, between Sixth Avenue to the west and Lafayette Street (1 block east of Broadway) to the east. It's easily accessible by subway: Take the N or R to the Prince Street station; the C, E, or 6 to Spring Street; or the F, B, D or V train to the Broadway-Lafayette stop.

An industrial zone during the 19th century, SoHo retains the impressive cast-iron architecture of the era, and in many places, cobblestone peeks out from beneath the street's asphalt. In the early 1960s, artists began occupying the drab, deteriorating buildings, turning it into the trendiest neighborhood in the city. SoHo is now a prime example of urban gentrification and a major New York attraction thanks to its restored buildings, fashionable restaurants, and stylish boutiques. On weekends, the cobbled streets and narrow sidewalks are packed with shoppers, with the prime action between Broadway and Sullivan Street north of Grand Street.

Some critics claim that SoHo is a victim of its own popularity—witness the departure of art galleries and boutiques that have fled to TriBeCa and Chelsea as well as the influx of mall-style stores such as J. Crew and Victoria's Secret. Still, SoHo is one of the best shopping neighborhoods in the city, and few are more fun to browse. High-end street peddlers set up along the boutique-lined sidewalks, hawking jewelry, books, and their own art. At night the neighborhood is transformed into a terrific (albeit pricey) dining and barhopping neighborhood.

In recent years SoHo has been crawling east, taking over Mott and Mulberry streets—and Elizabeth Street—north of Kenmare Street, an area now known as **Nolita** for *No*rth of *Li*ttle I*ta*ly. Nolita is becoming known for its hot shopping prospects, which include a number of pricey antiques and home-design stores. Taking the no. 6 train to Spring Street will get you closest by subway, but it's just a short walk east from SoHo proper.

The East Village & NoHo The **East Village,** which extends between 14th Street and Houston Street, from Broadway east to First Avenue and beyond to Alphabet City—Avenues A, B, C, and D—is where you can still find some of the city's real bohemians. Once, flower children tripped along St. Marks Place and listened to music at the Fillmore East; now the East Village is a mix of affordable ethnic and trendy restaurants, clothing designers and kitschy boutiques, some music clubs, and Ukrainian dive bars. Several Off- and Off-Off-Broadway theaters also call this place home.

The gentrification that has swept the city has made a huge impact on the East Village, but there's still a seedy element some won't find appealing—and some will. It's here where you can spend an afternoon at the sparkling new New Museum of Contemporary Art, and then have a drink at the celebrity-magnet bar of the Bowery Hotel, while around the corner you'll see a line of homeless men making their way to a nearby soup kitchen. It's here where yuppies and other ladder-climbing types make their homes alongside old-world Russian immigrants, who have lived in the neighborhood forever, and the drag queens and squatters who settled here in between. The neighborhood still embraces ethnic diversity, with strong elements of its Ukrainian and Irish heritages, while 6th Street, between First and Second avenues, is referred to as Little India.

The East Village isn't very accessible by subway unless you're traveling along 14th Street (the L line will drop you off at Third and First aves.) or take the 4, 5, 6, N, Q, R, or W to 14th Street/Union Square; the N, R, or W to 8th Street; or the 6 to Astor Place and walk east.

Until the 1990's, **Alphabet City** resisted gentrification and remained a haven of drug dealers and other unsavory types—no more. Bolstered by a major real-estate boom, this way-east area of the East Village has blossomed. French bistros and smart shops have popped up on every corner. Nevertheless, the neighborhood can be deserted late at night, since it's generally the province of locals. It's far off the subway lines, so know where you're going if you venture out here.

The southwestern section of the East Village, around Broadway and Lafayette between Bleecker and 4th streets, is called **NoHo** (for *No*rth of *Ho*uston), and has a completely different character. As you might have guessed from its name, this area has developed much more like its neighbor to the south, SoHo. Here you'll find a crop of trendy lounges, stylish restaurants, cutting-edge designers, and upscale antiques shops. NoHo is fun to browse; the Bleecker Street stop on the no. 6 line will land you in the heart of it, and the Broadway-Lafayette stop on the B, D, F, and V lines will drop you at its southern edge.

Greenwich Village Tree-lined streets crisscross and wind, following ancient streams and cow paths. Each block reveals yet another row of Greek Revival town houses, a well-preserved Federal-style house, or a peaceful courtyard or square. This is "the Village," from Broadway west to the Hudson River, bordered by Houston Street to the south and 14th Street to the north. It defies Manhattan's orderly grid system with streets that predate it, virtually every one chockablock with activity, and unless you live here, it may be impossible to master the lay of the land—so be sure to take a map along as you explore.

The Seventh Avenue line (1, 2, 3) is the area's main subway artery, while the West 4th Street station (where the A, C, and E lines meet the B, D, F, and V lines) serves as its central hub.

Nineteenth-century artists such as Mark Twain, Edgar Allan Poe, Henry James, and Winslow Homer first gave the Village its reputation for embracing the unconventional. Groundbreaking artists such as Edward Hopper and Jackson Pollock were drawn in, as were writers such as Eugene O'Neill, E. E. Cummings, and Dylan Thomas. Radical thinkers from John Reed to Upton Sinclair basked in the neighborhood's liberal ethos, and beatniks Allen Ginsberg, Jack Kerouac, and William Burroughs dug the free-swinging atmosphere.

Now, like so many neighborhoods, gentrification and escalating real-estate values have just about pushed out the artistic element, but culture and counterculture still rub shoulders in cafes, renowned jazz clubs, neighborhood bars, Off- and Off-Off- Broadway theaters, and an endless variety of tiny shops and restaurants.

The Village is probably the most chameleonlike of Manhattan's neighborhoods. Some of the highest-priced real estate in the city runs along lower Fifth Avenue, which dead-ends at **Washington Square Park.** Serpentine **Bleecker Street** stretches through most of the neighborhood and is emblematic of the area's historical bent. The anything-goes attitude in the Village has fostered a large gay community, still in evidence around **Christopher Street** and Sheridan Square (including the landmarked Stonewall Bar). The streets west of Seventh Avenue, the **West Village,** boasts some of the city's most charming, historic brownstones. Three colleges—New York University, Parsons School of Design, and the New School for Social Research—keep the area thinking young.

Streets are often crowded with weekend warriors and teenagers, especially on Bleecker, West 4th, 8th, and

Value **Free New York City Tours**

If you'd like to tour a specific neighborhood with an expert guide, call **Big Apple Greeter** (© **212/669-8159;** www.bigapplegreeter.org) at least 3 to 4 weeks ahead of your arrival. To expedite your reservation, go to the website and fill out the form in advance. This nonprofit organization has specially trained volunteers who take visitors around town for a free 2- to 4-hour visit of a particular neighborhood. And they say New York isn't friendly!

surrounding streets, and have been known to become increasingly sketchy west of Seventh Avenue in the very late hours, especially on weekends. Keep an eye on your wallet when navigating the weekend throngs. Washington Square Park was cleaned up a couple of years back, but it's still best to stay out of the area after dark.

Midtown

Chelsea & the Meat-Packing District

Chelsea has come on strong in recent years as a trendy address, especially for the gay urban professionals. A low-rise composite of town houses, tenements, lofts, and factories, the neighborhood comprises roughly the area west of Sixth Avenue from 14th to 30th streets. (Sixth Ave. itself below 23rd St. is considered part of the Flatiron District; see below.) Its main arteries are Seventh and Eighth avenues, and it's primarily served by the C or E and 1 subway lines.

The **Chelsea Piers** sports complex to the far west and a host of shops (both unique boutiques and big names such as Williams-Sonoma), well-priced bistros, and thriving bars along the main drags have contributed to the area's rebirth. Even the Hotel Chelsea—the neighborhood's most famous architectural and literary landmark, where Thomas Wolfe and Arthur Miller wrote, Bob Dylan composed "Sad-Eyed Lady of the Low Land," Viva and Edie Sedgwick of

Andy Warhol fame lived, and Sid Vicious killed Nancy Spungeon—has been renovated. Chelsea is also the home of the Joyce Theater, New York's principal modern dance venue.

One of the most influential trends in Chelsea has been the establishment of far **West Chelsea** (from Ninth Ave. west) and the adjacent **Meat-Packing District** (south of West Chelsea, roughly from 17th St. to Little W. 12th St.) as the style-setting neighborhoods for the 21st century. What SoHo was in the 1960s, this industrial west world (dubbed "the Lower West Side" by *New York* magazine) is today. New restaurants, shopping, and super-hot restaurants pop up daily in the Meat-Packing District, while the area from West 22nd to West 29th streets, between Tenth and Eleventh avenues, is home to numerous dance clubs and the cutting edge of today's New York art scene. This area is still in transition and continually evolving. Like much of Manhattan, sleek glass condo towers are rising and an ambitious "High Line" project, a park along Tenth Avenue—between 33rd Street and 14th Street in the remains of an old elevated railway—is in development. With galleries and bars in converted warehouses and former meat lockers, browsing can be frustrating, and, despite the influx of high-end real estate, the sometimes-desolate streets a tad intimidating.

The Flatiron District, Union Square & Gramercy Park These adjoining and at places overlapping neighborhoods are some of the city's most appealing. Their streets have been rediscovered by New Yorkers and visitors alike, largely thanks to the boom-to-bust dotcom revolution of the late 1990s; the Flatiron District served as its geographical heart and earned the nickname "Silicon Alley" in the process. These neighborhoods boast great shopping and dining opportunities and a central-to-everything location that's hard to beat. A number of impressive new hotels have been added to the mix over the last few years. The commercial spaces are often large, loft-like expanses with witty designs and graceful columns.

The **Flatiron District,** south of 23rd Street to 14th Street, between Broadway and Sixth Avenue, and centered on the historic Flatiron Building on 23rd (so named for its triangular shape) and Park Avenue South, is littered with celebrity-chef run restaurants. Below 23rd Street along Sixth Avenue (once known as the Ladies' Mile shopping district), mass-market discounters such as Filene's Basement, Bed Bath & Beyond, and others have moved in. The shopping gets classier on Fifth Avenue, where you'll find a mix of national names and hip boutiques. Lined with Oriental-carpet dealers and high-end fixture stores, Broadway is becoming the city's home-furnishings alley; its jewel is the justifiably famous ABC Carpet & Home, with eight floors of gorgeous textiles, housewares, and gifts on one side of Broadway, and an equally dazzling display of floor coverings on the other.

Union Square is the hub of the entire area; the N, Q, R, 4, 5, 6, W, and L trains stop here, making it easy to reach from most other city neighborhoods. Long in the shadows of the more bustling (Times and Herald) and high-toned (Washington) city squares, Union Square has experienced a major renaissance. Local businesses joined forces with the city to rid the park of drug dealers a few years back, and now it's a delightful place to spend an afternoon. Union Square is best known as the setting for New York's premier greenmarket every Monday, Wednesday, Friday, and Saturday from 8am to 6pm. In-line skaters take over the market space in the after-work hours. A number of hip restaurants rim the square, as do superstores such as the city's best Barnes & Noble superstore, Whole Foods supermarket, and a Virgin Megastore.

From about 16th to 23rd streets, east from Park Avenue South to about Second Avenue, is the leafy, largely residential district known as **Gramercy Park.** The pity of the Gramercy Park district is that so few can enjoy the park: Built by Samuel Ruggles in the 1830s to attract buyers to the area, it is the only private park in the city and is locked to all but those who live on its perimeter (the rule is that your windows have to overlook the park in order for you to have a key). At the southern endpoint of Lexington Avenue (at 21st St.), it is one of the most peaceful spots in the city. If you know someone who has a magic key, go there.

At the northern edge of the area, fronting the Flatiron Building on 23rd Street and Fifth Avenue, is another of Manhattan's lovely little parks, **Madison Square.** Across from its northeastern corner once stood Stanford White's original Madison Square Garden (in whose roof garden White was murdered in 1906 by possibly deranged, but definitely jealous, millionaire Harry K. Thaw). It's now majestically

Impressions

"I'm opposed to the redevelopment. I think there should be one neighborhood in New York where tourists are afraid to walk."
                                        —Fran Leibowitz, on the "new" Times Square

presided over by the massive New York Life Insurance Building, the masterful New York State Supreme Court, and the Metropolitan Life Insurance Company, whose tower in 1909 was the tallest building in the world at 700 feet.

Times Square & Midtown West Midtown West, the vast area from 34th to 59th streets west of Fifth Avenue to the Hudson River, encompasses several famous names: Madison Square Garden, the Garment District, Rockefeller Center, the Theater District, and Times Square. This is New York's tourism central, where you'll find the bright lights and bustle that draw people from all over. As such, this is the city's biggest hotel neighborhood, with options running the gamut from cheap to chic.

The 1, 2, 3 subway line serves the massive neon-lit station at the heart of Times Square, at 42nd Street between Broadway and Seventh Avenue, while the F, V, B, D line runs up Sixth Avenue to Rockefeller Center. The N, R Q, and W line cuts diagonally across the neighborhood, following the path of Broadway before heading up Seventh Avenue at 42nd Street. The A, C, E line serves the west side, running along Eighth Avenue.

If you know New York but haven't been here in a few years, you'll be quite surprised by the "new" **Times Square.** Longtime New Yorkers like to *kvetch* nostalgic about the glory days of the old peep-show-and-porn-shop Times Square that this cleaned-up, Disneyfied version supplanted. And there

really is not much here to offer the native New Yorker. The revival, however, has been nothing short of an outstanding success for tourism. Grand old theaters have come back to life as Broadway and children's playhouses, and scores of new family-friendly restaurants and shops have opened. Plenty of businesses have moved in— MTV studios overlook Times Square at 1515 Broadway, and *Good Morning America* has its own street-facing studio at Broadway and 44th Street. The neon lights have never been brighter, and Middle America has never been more welcome. Expect dense crowds, though; it's often tough to make your way along the sidewalks.

Most of the great Broadway theaters light up the streets off Times Square, in the west 40s, just east and west of Broadway. At the heart of the **Theater District,** where Broadway meets Seventh Avenue, is the TKTS booth, where crowds line up daily to buy discount tickets for that day's shows.

To the west of the Theater District, in the 40s and 50s between Eighth and Tenth avenues, is **Hell's Kitchen,** an area that is much nicer than its ghoulish name and one of my favorites in the city. The neighborhood resisted gentrification until the mid-1990s but has grown into a charming, less touristy adjunct to the neighboring Theater District. Ninth Avenue, in particular, has blossomed into one of the city's finest dining avenues; just stroll along and you'll have a world of dining to choose from, ranging from American diner to sexy Mediterranean to traditional Thai. Stylish boutiques and bars have also popped up in this area in the last several years. Realtors have tried to rename the area Clinton, but locals have held fast to the Hell's Kitchen moniker with delight. In the last couple of years, it's become one of Manhattan's more popular gay neighborhoods, as rents in first the West Village, then Chelsea, have caused a northward migration.

Unlike Times Square, gorgeous **Rockefeller Center** has needed no renovation. Situated between 46th and 50th streets, from Sixth Avenue east to Fifth, this Art Deco complex contains some of the city's great architectural gems, which house hundreds of offices, a number of NBC studios (including *Saturday Night Live, Late Night with Conan O'Brien,* and the famous glass-walled *Today* show studio at 48th St.), and some pleasing upscale boutiques (attention, shoppers: Saks Fifth Avenue is just on the other side of Fifth). If you can negotiate the crowds, holiday time is a great time to be here, as ice-skaters take over the central plaza and the huge Christmas tree twinkles against the night sky.

Along Seventh Avenue, south of 42nd Street, is the **Garment District,** of little interest to tourists except for its sample sales, where some great new fashions are sold off cheap to serious bargain-hunters willing to scour the racks. That part of town plays host to many small theater companies if you're venturing into the Off-Off-Broadway scene. Other than that, it's a pretty commercial area. Between Seventh and Eighth avenues and 31st and 33rd streets, **Penn Station** sits beneath unsightly behemoth **Madison Square Garden,** where the Rangers, Liberty, and the Knicks play. Taking up all of 34th Street, between Sixth and Seventh avenues, is **Macy's,** the world's largest department store; exit Macy's at the southeast corner and you'll find more famous-label shopping around **Herald Square.** The blocks around 32nd Street just west of Fifth Avenue have developed into a thriving Koreatown, with midprice hotels and bright, bustling Asian restaurants offering some of the best-value stays and eats in Midtown.

Midtown West is also home to some of the city's most revered museums and cultural institutions, including **Carnegie Hall,** the **Museum of Modern Art,** and **Radio City Music Hall,** to name just a few.

Midtown East & Murray Hill Midtown East, the area including Fifth Avenue and everything east from 34th to 59th streets, is the more upscale side of the Midtown map. This side of town is short of subway trains, served primarily by the Lexington Avenue 4, 5, 6 line.

Midtown East is where you'll find the city's finest collection of grand hotels, mostly along Lexington Avenue and near the park at the top of Fifth. The stretch of **Fifth Avenue** from Saks at 49th Street, extending to the 24-hour Apple Store and F.A.O. Schwarz at 59th St., is home to the city's most high-profile haute shopping, including Tiffany & Co. and Bergdorf Goodman, but more midprice names, such as Banana Republic and Liz Claiborne, have moved their stores in over the last few years. The stretch of 57th Street between Fifth and Lexington avenues is also known for high-fashion boutiques (Chanel, Hermès) and high-ticket galleries, but change is underway since names such as Levi's and Niketown squeezed in. You'll find plenty of spillover along **Madison Avenue,** a great strip for shoe shopping in particular.

Manhattan Address Locator

To locate avenue addresses, cancel the last figure, divide by 2, and add (or subtract) the key number below. The answer is the nearest numbered cross street, approximately.

Avenue A:	add 3	11th Avenue:	add 15
Avenue B:	add 3	Amsterdam Avenue:	add 59
Avenue C:	add 3	Columbus Avenue:	add 59
First Avenue:	add 3		or 60
Second Avenue:	add 3	Lexington Avenue:	add 22
Third Avenue:	add 10	Madison Avenue:	add 27
Sixth Avenue:	subtract 12	Park Avenue:	add 34
Eighth Avenue:	add 9	Park Avenue South:	add 8
Ninth Avenue:	add 13	West End Avenue:	add 59
Tenth Avenue:	add 14	York Avenue:	add 4

Note special instructions for finding address locations on the following:

Fifth Avenue

63 to 108:	add 11	776 to 1286:	cancel last figure
109 to 200:	add 13	of house number and subtract 18	
201 to 400:	add 16	(do not divide house number by 2)	
401 to 600:	add 18	1310 to 1494: cancel last figure	
601 to 775:	add 20	of house number. For 1310, sub-	

of house number. For 1310, subtract 20, and for every additional 20 street numbers, increase deduction by 1

Seventh Avenue

1 to 1800:	add 12	above 1800:	add 20

Broadway

Anything from 1 to 754 is south of 8th Street, and hence a named street.

756 to 846:	subtract 29	847 to 953:	subtract 25
above 953:	subtract 31		

Central Park West

Cancel last figure and add 60

Riverside Drive

Cancel last figure and

Up to 567:	add 72	568 and up:	add 78

Magnificent architectural highlights include the recently repolished **Chrysler Building,** with its stylized gargoyles glaring down on passersby; the Beaux Arts tour de force that is **Grand Central Terminal; St. Patrick's Cathedral;** and the glorious **Empire State Building.**

Far east, swank Sutton and Beekman places are enclaves of beautiful town houses, luxury living, and pocket parks that look out over the East River.

Along this river is the **United Nations,** which isn't officially in New York City, or even the United States, but on a parcel of international land belonging to member nations.

Claiming the territory east from Madison Avenue, **Murray Hill** begins somewhere north of 23rd Street (the line between it and Gramercy Park is fuzzy), and is most clearly recognizable north of 30th Street to 42nd Street. This brownstone-lined quarter is largely a quiet residential neighborhood, most notable for its handful of good budget and midprice hotels. The stretch of Lexington Avenue in the high 20s is known as Curry Hill and has usurped the East Village's Little India as the destination for inexpensive, high-quality Indian and Pakistani food.

Uptown

Upper West Side North of 59th Street and encompassing everything west of Central Park, the Upper West Side contains **Lincoln Center,** arguably the world's premier performing-arts venue; the **Time Warner Center** with its upscale shops such as **Hugo Boss, A/X Armani,** and **Sephora; Jazz at Lincoln Center;** the **Mandarin Oriental Hotel;** the gargantuan **Whole Foods Market,** and possibly the most expensive food court in the world, with restaurants such as **Per Se** and **Masa.** The Upper West Side is also the home of the **American Museum of Natural History,** whose Dinosaur Halls and magnificent Rose Center for Earth and Space garner rave reviews. You'll also find a growing number of midprice hotels whose larger-than-Midtown rooms and nice residential location make them some of the best values—and some of my favorite places to stay—in the entire city.

Unlike the more stratified Upper East Side, the Upper West Side is home to an egalitarian mix of middle-class yuppiedom, laid-back wealth (lots of celebs and media types call the grand apartments along Central Park West home), and ethnic families here from before gentrification.

The neighborhood runs all the way up to Harlem, around 125th Street, and encompasses **Morningside Heights,** where you'll find **Columbia University** and the perennial construction project known as the **Cathedral of St. John the Divine.**

But prime Upper West Side—the part you're most likely to explore—is the area running from Columbus Circle at 59th Street into the 80s, between the park and Broadway. North of 59th Street is where Eighth Avenue becomes Central Park West, the eastern border of the neighborhood (and the western border of Central Park); Ninth Avenue becomes Columbus Avenue, lined with attractive boutiques and cafes; and Tenth Avenue becomes Amsterdam Avenue, less charming than Columbus to the east and less trafficked than bustling Broadway (whose highlights are the gourmet megamarts Zabar's and Fairway) to the west; still, Amsterdam has blossomed into quite a happening restaurant and bar strip over the last couple of years. You'll find Lincoln Center in the mid-60s, where Broadway crosscuts Amsterdam.

Two major subway lines service the area: the 1, 2, 3 line runs up Broadway, while the B and C trains run up Central Park West, stopping at the Dakota apartments (where John Lennon was shot and Yoko Ono still lives) at 72nd Street, and at the Museum of Natural History at 81st Street.

Upper East Side North of 59th Street and east of Central Park is some of the city's most expensive residential real estate. This is New York at its most gentrified: Walk along Fifth and Park avenues, especially between 60th and 80th streets, and you're sure to encounter some of the wizened WASPs and Chanel-suited socialites that make up the most rarefied of the city's population. Madison Avenue, from 60th Street well into the 80s, is the moneyed crowd's main shopping strip, recently vaunting ahead of Hong Kong's Causeway Bay to become the most expensive retail real estate *in the world*—so bring your platinum card. You can also use it to stay at one of the neighborhood's luxurious hotels, such as the Carlyle or the Plaza Athénée, or to dine at four-star wonders such as Café Boulud and Daniel.

The main attraction of this neighborhood is **Museum Mile,** the stretch of Fifth Avenue fronting Central Park that's home to no fewer than 10 terrific cultural institutions, including Frank Lloyd Wright's **Guggenheim,** and anchored by the mind-boggling **Metropolitan Museum of Art.** But the elegant rows of landmark town houses are worth a look alone: East 70th Street, from Madison east to Lexington, is one of the world's most charming residential streets. If you want to see where real people live, move east to Third Avenue and beyond; that's where affordable restaurants and active street life start popping up.

A second subway line is under construction, but years away from completion. For now, the Upper East Side is served solely by the crowded Lexington Avenue line (4, 5, 6 trains), so wear your walking shoes (or bring taxi fare) if you're heading up here to explore.

Harlem Harlem has benefited from a dramatic image makeover in the last few years, and with new restaurants, condos, clubs, and stores is becoming a neighborhood in demand.

Harlem is actually several areas. **Harlem proper** stretches from river to river, beginning at 125th Street on the West Side, 96th Street on the East Side, and 110th Street north of Central Park. East of Fifth Avenue, **Spanish Harlem (*El Barrio*)** runs between East 100th and East 125th streets. Harlem proper, in particular, is benefiting greatly from the revitalization that has swept so much of the city, with national-brand retailers moving in, restaurants and hip nightspots opening everywhere, and visitors arriving to tour historic sites related to the golden age of African-American culture, when great bands such as the Count Basie and Duke Ellington orchestras played the Cotton Club and Sugar Cane Club, and literary giants such as Langston Hughes and James Baldwin soaked up the scene.

Some houses date from a time when the area was something of a country retreat, and represent some of the best brownstone mansions in the city. On **Sugar Hill** (from 143rd to 155th sts., between St. Nicholas and Edgecombe aves.) and **Striver's Row** (W. 139th St. between Adam Clayton Powell Jr. and Frederick Douglass blvds.) are a significant number of fine town houses. For cultural visits, there's the Morris-Jumel Mansion, the Schomburg Center, the Studio Museum, and the Apollo Theater.

You'll find 125th a fun place to shop, with its mix of such national chains as Old Navy standing side-by-side with emporiums of hip-hop fashion.

By all means, come see Harlem—it's one of the city's most vital, historic neighborhoods, and no other feels quite so energized right now. Your best bet for seeing all the sights is to take a guided tour (see "Organized Sightseeing Tours," p. 274); if you head up on your own, come in daylight. Don't wander thoughtlessly, especially at night. If you head up after dark to a restaurant or nightspot, be clear and confident about where you're going and stay alert.

Washington Heights & Inwood At the northern tip of Manhattan, Washington Heights (the area from 155th St. to Dyckman St., with adjacent Inwood running to the tip) is home to a large segment of Manhattan's Latino community, plus an increasing number of yuppies who don't mind trading a half-hour subway commute to Midtown for lower rents. **Fort Tryon Park** and **the Cloisters** are the two big reasons for visitors to come up this way. The Cloisters houses the Metropolitan Museum of Art's stunning medieval collection, in a building perched atop a hill, with excellent views across the Hudson to the Palisades. Committed off-the-beaten-path sightseers might also want to visit the **Dyckman Farmhouse,** a historic jewel built in 1783 and the only remaining Dutch Colonial structure in Manhattan.

The Outer Boroughs

Manhattan is just one of the five boroughs that make up the very Big Apple. The others are Brooklyn, the Bronx, Queens, and Staten Island. People who live in the outer boroughs are sometimes (insultingly) referred to by Manhattanites as "B&T" (Bridge & Tunnel), because they have to cross a bridge or go through a tunnel to get to Manhattan.

It's an outmoded attitude, because while Manhattan remains the capital (at least in its own mind) of all that is cool and hip, its rents are too high for most people who aren't independently

wealthy or with very high-paying jobs, so the hipsters may hang in Manhattan, but are more likely to live (and establish scenes in) Brooklyn and Queens, in neighborhoods ranging from Williamsburg to Greenpoint to Astoria to Long Island City. And, they have the best views of Manhattan.

Believe me when I tell you there are a lot of things to see (and great places to eat) in B&T-land, and see if you can find the time to cross the waters and take a look.

Brooklyn Brooklynites are quick to tell you that their borough is the fourth-largest city in the United States. That's because this borough is about pride and attitude. And though it has been over 45 years since the team left, don't even talk about the Dodgers.

Brooklyn is also about neighborhoods and diversity; the borough is a pleasure to explore, though gentrification is creeping into many of the once diverse neighborhoods. Some highlights include New York's first historic district, **Brooklyn Heights,** with its elegant brownstones; the Promenade, with its spectacular view of Manhattan; and the romantic River Cafe. To get to Brooklyn Heights, take the A, C, F to Jay Street; the 2, 3 to Clark Street; or the M (during rush hours), R to Court Street.

One of the first Brooklyn neighborhoods to undergo major gentrification was **DUMBO** (Down Under the Manhattan Bridge Overpass). What was once a scattering of warehouses is now a thriving (far from starving) artist's colony, with those warehouses now converted into expensive lofts, and just about impossible for most artists to afford. The main drag is **Washington Street,** and businesses are beginning to populate the area. It's here where you'll find **Jacques Torres Chocolate,** the **Brooklyn Ice Cream Factory,** and

Grimaldi's Pizza. The best way to get to DUMBO is the F train to York Street or the A or C to High Street.

Brooklyn's now, way-past-hip neighborhood (though the very hippest say it's "over") is **Williamsburg.** In the early 1990s, artists began to flee Manhattan's high rents to live here among the Hispanic and Hasidic communities already there. Now, though, the pioneers have seen their once independent and inexpensive enclave being transformed into Brooklyn's version of SoHo. There are a number of funky, youth-oriented boutiques along the neighborhood's main drag, **Bedford Avenue,** but Williamsburg is also the home of that venerable red-meat institution, **Peter Luger.** The best train to take to get to Williamsburg from Manhattan is the L to Bedford Avenue.

Other emerging neighborhoods are **Carroll Gardens, Cobble Hill,** and **Boerum Hill. Smith Street** cuts through all three and has become a booming restaurant destination. To get to Smith Street, the best train is the F, with stops at either Carroll Street or Bergen Street.

Downtown Brooklyn off Flatbush Avenue is probably best known for **BAM,** the **Brooklyn Academy of Music.** You'll also find a number of department stores and one of the borough's most beloved landmarks, **Junior's,** the diner noted for its cheesecakes. Many subway lines converge in downtown Brooklyn at the Pacific Street/Atlantic Avenue station, including the 2, 3, 4, 5, B, D, M, N, Q, and R, as well as the LIRR commuter railroad (you can catch a train at Penn Station in Manhattan).

Park Slope is probably the heart of Brooklyn; it is here and in nearby Prospect Heights where you find the **Brooklyn Museum,** the **Brooklyn Botanical Gardens,** and **Prospect Park** and the new **Richard Meier** glass condos, symbolic of the change that is enveloping Brooklyn. The 2, 3 trains to Grand Army Plaza will land you close to all of the above.

In its heyday during the early 20th century, **Coney Island** was to New York what South Beach is to Miami. This was where everyone flocked to escape the heat and grime of a New York summer day. Few remnants of Coney Island's past remain, such as the long-defunct parachute ride; but during the summer, you can still ride on one of the best roller coasters anywhere, the famous **Cyclone.** And Astroland, the famous amusement park due to close after the 2007, received a reprieve and will endure at least through the summer of 2008. Coney Island is also the home of the **New York Aquarium** and the minor-league baseball team the Cyclones. To get to Coney Island, take the F or Q to West 8th Street, Brooklyn.

The Bronx Perhaps the most famous destination in the Bronx, and next to Rome's Colosseum may be one of the most celebrated sports arenas in the world, is **Yankee Stadium**—with 2008 to be that marvelous monument's last season. Even if you are a Yankee hater, you will be awed by both the old and the new stadium, a modernized replica of the House that Ruth Built. The 4, B, or D trains all stop there.

The Bronx is also the home of the United States' largest metropolitan animal park, the **Bronx Zoo,** and the **New York Botanical Gardens.** Both are wonders worthy of an excursion. To get to the Bronx Zoo, you can take the 2 train to Pelham Parkway and walk to the Bronxdale entrance of the zoo. To get to the Botanical Gardens, you can take Metro-North from Grand Central Station to the Botanical Gardens station.

While visiting the Bronx Zoo or the Botanical Gardens, stop at the Little Italy of the Bronx, **Arthur Avenue,** for a mouthwatering walk past meat markets, delis, vegetable stands, fish markets, cafes, and restaurants. To get to Arthur Avenue, take the 4, B, or D train to Fordham Road and transfer to the no. 12 bus east, or the no. 2 or 5 train to Pelham Parkway and the no. 12 bus west.

Queens   Queens is the largest borough in New York and it's also the city's most ethnically diverse. There are more languages spoken in this 109 square miles than anywhere else on the planet. All that ethnicity translates into an adventurous eater's paradise. I've dined on Thai, Peruvian, Indian, Guyanese, Greek, Colombian, and Brazilian here, and I've barely scratched the surface. But there's more to Queens than just food.

Astoria, with its large Greek community, is also the home of the **American Museum of the Moving Image,** dedicated to the movies—film, video, and digital. To get there, take the R to Steinway Street or the N/W to 36th Avenue, or the F and V trains to Queensbridge or Queens Plaza.

With former warehouses and factories being converted to expensive condos, **Long Island City,** directly across the river from Manhattan's Upper East Side, is becoming Queens' version of DUMBO. It is also where you will find a number of museums, including the **Noguchi Museum, Socrates Park,** and the **P.S. 1 Contemporary Art Center.** The best train to take to get to Long Island City is the no. 7. The no. 7 train is also known as the International Express, running through one ethnic community after another; get off at just about any spot and you'll see signs in an assortment of languages. The no. 7 train will also take you to Flushing, where you'll find **Shea Stadium,** home of the Mets, though 2008 is to be that stadium's last season as well; the Louis Armstrong Stadium and the Arthur Ashe Stadium at **Flushing Meadow Park,** where the **U.S. Open** is held each September; and the **Queens Museum of Art** on the grounds of the 1964 World's Fair.

Staten Island   Staten Island is the most remote of the boroughs and most enjoyably reached by ferry. There is a suburban feel to the borough, making it a haven for commuters. The free **Staten Island Ferry** gets you to the borough. If you decide to spend time in Staten Island, take in a **Staten Island Yankees** minor-league baseball game. The stadium is within walking distance of the ferry and has lovely views of downtown Manhattan.

2 Suggested New York City Itineraries

I've lived in New York for more than half my life and I still haven't seen it all. That's not because I don't want to, it's just there is so much to see. So it's understandable if you feel a bit overwhelmed by all the options. Seeing the best of New York requires endurance, patience, perseverance, good walking shoes, a $7 daily MetroCard Fun Pass (p. 50), and a subway map. For some attractions—such as the Empire State Building or a Broadway play—you should score tickets *before* you come to New York to avoid long lines or a shutout. Besides your own two feet, the subway will be your best bet to cover the most ground. I also recommend a few bus routes that will not only get you to some of New York's best attractions, but will also act as your own tour bus on which you'll see sights on the way.

THE BEST OF NYC IN 1 DAY

If you want to have any chance of seeing the best of New York in just 1 day, you need to get an early start. You also need a plan of attack. You don't want to waste time zigzagging around the city to various attractions. So I recommend taking on New York by thirds. On the first third, we will concentrate on the best of midtown Manhattan. *Start: Pier 83 on 42nd St.*

---

❶ Circle Line Sightseeing Cruise 🏵🏵

By starting your day on the water on this 2-hour half-island cruise, you'll get a good overview of Manhattan. You'll pass by the Statue of Liberty and Ellis Island; see the lower Manhattan skyline; head up the East River, where you will go under the Brooklyn, Manhattan, and Williamsburg bridges; and view the United Nations and the East Side skyline, including the Empire State and Chrysler buildings. See p. 274.

Afterwards, take the M42 42nd Street crosstown bus to Fifth Avenue, where you'll come to the:

❷ New York Public Library 🏵🏵

You'll recognize this building by the lion sculptures guarding its gates. Step inside for more grandeur, especially the incredible **Main Reading Rooms,** where you might want to take a break and read the paper (if you have time). While you're here, take a look at the library's backyard, **Bryant Park.** If there are tents up, it means you're here during one of the two Fashion Weeks. Or between November and January, **the Pond** ice skating rink will be up. See p. 257.

❸ Grand Central Terminal 🏵🏵

Before stepping into this magnificent working train station, take a look east toward Lexington Avenue and then crane your neck up. You'll see my favorite skyscraper, the **Chrysler Building** 🏵🏵. Okay, now enter Grand Central, where approximately 500,000 commuters dash through daily. I hope it's not rush hour . . . but even if it is, you really won't have to

worry about colliding with a commuter: The building and the stupendous main concourse were constructed so cleverly that despite the perceived chaos, people rarely bump into each other. You'll want to spend hours examining the beautiful detail throughout the terminal, but you don't have hours to spare. A walk through the main concourse and a look at the sky ceiling will be evidence enough. See p. 233.

> ### 4️⃣ GRAND CENTRAL TERMINAL
>
> You're hungry now and the choices in the Grand Central Terminal dining concourse are plentiful and good. Chow down on anything from Indian food to pizza. Or opt for a heartier (and more expensive!) lunch at the legendary **Oyster Bar & Restaurant** or upstairs overlooking the concourse at **Michael Jordan's—The Steakhouse.** See p. 194 and 172.

❺ Empire State Building 🏵🏵🏵

It's an 8-block walk down Fifth Avenue from Grand Central Station to the Empire State Building. Let's hope it's a beautiful day because I want your view from the top of this historic structure, the tallest building in New York, to be pristine. You already have your tickets (don't you?), so you don't have to wait at the ticket booth (see box "Empire State Building Ticket Buying" on p. 232 for details). The elevator will zip you up to the 86th story, where you will get a panoramic view of Manhattan. See p. 231.

The Best of NYC in 1 Day

1 Circle Line Sightseeing Cruise
2 New York Public Library
3 Grand Central Terminal
5 Empire State Building
6 Museum of Modern Art
7 Rockefeller Center
8 Fifth Avenue
9 King Cole Bar
10 Times Square

East River

Upper Manhattan
Uptown
Midtown
Downtown

Subway stop
"Take a Break" stop

Sutton Pl. South Sutton Pl.
Roosevelt Island Tram
Queensboro Bridge

Beckman Place
Mitchell Place
United Nations
Queens-Midtown Tunnel
FDR Drive

First Ave.
Second Ave.
Third Ave.
Lexington Ave.
Park Ave.
Vanderbilt Ave.
Madison Ave.
Fifth Ave.
Sixth Ave. (Ave. of the Americas)
Seventh Ave.
Broadway
Eighth Ave.
Ninth Ave.
Tenth Ave.
Eleventh Ave.
Twelfth Ave.

MIDTOWN EAST
MURRAY HILL
St. Patrick's Cathedral
Grand Central Terminal
New York Public Library
Empire State Bldg.
Rockefeller Center
Bryant Park
TIMES SQUARE
Port Authority
GARMENT DISTRICT
Penn Station/Madison Square Garden
THEATER DISTRICT
MIDTOWN WEST
Restaurant Row
DeWitt Clinton Park
Columbus Circle
CENTRAL PARK
The Pond
Central Park South

E. 62nd St.
E. 61st St.
E. 60th St.
E. 59th St.
E. 58th St.
E. 57th St.
E. 56th St.
E. 55th St.
E. 54th St.
E. 53rd St.
E. 52nd St.
E. 51st St.
E. 50th St.
E. 49th St.
E. 48th St.
E. 47th St.
E. 46th St.
E. 45th St.
E. 44th St.
E. 43rd St.
E. 42nd St.
E. 41st St.
E. 40th St.
E. 39th St.
E. 38th St.
E. 37th St.
E. 36th St.
E. 35th St.
E. 34th St.
E. 33rd St.

W. 62nd St.
W. 61st St.
W. 60th St.
W. 59th St.
W. 58th St.
W. 57th St.
W. 56th St.
W. 55th St.
W. 54th St.
W. 52nd St.
W. 51st St.
W. 50th St.
W. 49th St.
W. 48th St.
W. 47th St.
W. 46th St.
W. 45th St.
W. 44th St.
W. 43rd St.
W. 42nd St.
W. 41st St.
W. 40th St.
W. 39th St.
W. 38th St.
W. 37th St.
W. 36th St.
W. 35th St.
W. 34th St.
W. 33rd St.

Hudson River
Lincoln Tunnel
Javits Convention Center

0 1/4 mi
0 0.25 km

Take the B or D train uptown to Seventh Avenue. Walk east across 53rd Street to the:

❻ Museum of Modern Art 🍿🍿

Yes, the $20 suggested admission is outrageous, but this is New York and you are getting used to outrageous. And you'll forget about the admission charge once you peruse the exhibits in this beautiful museum. Airy and expansive, with sky-lit, open galleries along with smaller, intimate rooms, the museum is one of a kind. See p. 235.

❼ Rockefeller Center 🍿🍿

A short walk from MoMA is the Rockefeller Center complex. If you are here during the Christmas holidays, you'll fight the crowds for a glimpse of the Christmas tree and the skaters in the small rink. If your timing is right, you might be able to squeeze in the 70-minute NBC Studio Tour. If not, you'll see **Radio City Music Hall** 🍿 and **30 Rockefeller Plaza** 🍿. If you did not have advance tickets for the Empire State Building and the line was much too long, take the elevator up 70 floors to **Top of the Rock** 🍿🍿 for, arguably, as good a view as you would have at the Empire State Building. Across the street (Fifth Avenue) you'll see **St. Patrick's Cathedral.** See p. 235.

❽ Fifth Avenue

Is a street an attraction? When it's one of the most famous in the world, it is. Walk north up Fifth Avenue from Rock Center and pass such big-name stores as Saks Fifth Avenue, Henri Bendel, the NBA Store, Tiffany & Co., Cartier, Bergdorf Goodman, FAO Schwarz, and the Apple Store. You'll also see Trump Tower from the popular *Apprentice* TV series. At 59th Street, you'll see the ornate Plaza Hotel, which, after extensive renovations, reopened as a hotel/condo in 2008. Across the street you'll see the southern end of Central Park. See p. 264.

> ### 🍹 KING COLE BAR
> Now would be a good time to rest your legs as well as your senses. Head back down Fifth Avenue a few blocks to the lounge at the St. Regis Hotel. This is where the Bloody Mary was supposedly invented, and it's the perfect place for a late-afternoon or early-evening cocktail. 2 E. 55th St., at Fifth Avenue. ☎ 212/753-4500. See p. 378.

❿ Times Square

You've got tickets for a Broadway show, so before you head into the theater, this is your chance to see what Times Square is all about. The lights are blinding, the crowds are thick, and the noise is infernal, but that's Times Square. There's nowhere like it in the world. But don't linger too long! Broadway curtains rise promptly! See p. 239.

THE BEST OF NYC IN 2 DAYS

On your second day, you'll head downtown and explore the city where it began. You'll wander through streets that are as old as any in New York, and some that are curiously towered by ultramodern, gleaming steel-and-glass skyscrapers. Again, you'll want to get a very early start because there is so much to see and always too little time. ***Start: Subway: 1 to South Ferry or 4 or 5 to Bowling Green.***

❶ Statue of Liberty 🍿🍿🍿

You saw Lady Liberty on your Circle Line half-island tour yesterday, but now you want to get up close and personal with her. Ferries leave from Battery Park every half-hour beginning at 8:30am. On Liberty Island, you can take one of two tours. The Promenade Tour takes visitors through the monument lobby, past the original torch to the Statue of Liberty exhibit for a 20- to 30-minute ranger-guided tour and then outdoors to the lower promenade. The Observatory Tour incorporates the promenade tour and makes a visit to the pedestal observation platform where you can view the statue's interior framework through a new glass ceiling portal. See p. 238.

❷ Ellis Island 👁👁

Your Statue of Liberty ferry ticket also includes a stop at Ellis Island; ferries to Ellis Island leave Liberty Island every half-hour. The Immigration Museum is one of the most touching in the city. Incredible, personal details of the immigrant experience are on display, from personal letters and jewelry to battered valises. You could spend all day, but you don't have time! Wander through the Registry room and you'll hear the echoes of hundreds of different languages of immigrants who came through these doors to a better life. See p. 231.

❸ Wall Street

Back in Manhattan, the walk up to the Financial District is not long. Along the way you'll see structures such as **Castle Clinton National Monument,** the remnants of a fort built in 1808 to defend New York Harbor against the British, and the impressive **U.S. Customs House,** which houses the Museum of the American Indian, part of the Smithsonian Institution. Once on Wall Street, stop for a photo-op at the **Federal Hall National Memorial,** with the statue of George Washington in front, and the **New York Stock Exchange,** across the street. Unfortunately, the exchange is no longer open for tours, but if you are a person of some significance, they might let you ring the opening day's bell. See p. 239.

Take the free Downtown Connection bus that travels from Battery Park to South Street Seaport, with stops along the way including one at Wall Street. See chapter 5 for details.

❹ South Street Seaport

Here the streets are really old—so old they are rough with cobblestones. This is a 17th-century historic district with restored 18th- and 19th-century buildings still standing. The interesting South Street Seaport Museum will fill you in on more of the 11 square blocks of seafaring history. Also part of the seaport complex is Pier 17, a historic barge that now is the home to various stores that you are probably very familiar with. See p. 254.

Take the A or C train at Broadway–Nassau Street toward Brooklyn and get off at High Street, the first stop in Brooklyn.

5️⃣ GRIMALDI'S PIZZERIA

You are now in Brooklyn and probably very hungry. You'll need nourishment for your next adventure, and where better than this famed pizzeria, in the shadow of the Brooklyn Bridge? 19 Old Fulton St., between Front and Water streets. © **718/858-4300.** See p. 186.

❻ Brooklyn Bridge 👁👁👁

You have been well fed, and so now you have the energy to make the approximately half-hour stroll back to Manhattan across one of the greatest suspended bridges in the world. The view of the Manhattan skyline is spectacular—make sure you have plenty of room in the card of your digital camera. See p. 230.

❼ Lower East Side Tenement Museum 👁

When you visited Ellis Island, you learned about the immigrants' struggles to gain entry into this country. Now visit the prototype of a Lower East Side tenement where many of those immigrants lived. The only way to see the museum is by guided tour, which takes place every 40 minutes on weekdays and every half-hour on weekends. See p. 245.

Legend

- ⓂSubway stop
- ⓂClosed indefinitely
- ☕"Take a Break" stop

Map labels

W. 15th St. · W. 14th St. · W. 13th St. · ❿ Union Square ⓫ · E. 15th · E. 14th St. · E. 13th St. · E. 12th St. · E. 11th St.

W. 11th St. · W. 10th St. · W. 9th St. · E. 9th St. Wanamaker Stuyvesant · E. 9th St. · E. 10th St.

Jane St. · W. 12th St. · Bethune St. · Bank · W. 11th St. · Perry · Charles · W. 10th St. · Christopher · Barrow · Morton · Leroy · Clarkson · W. Houston · King · Charlton · Spring · Dominick · Broome

Greenwich Ave. · Waverly Pl. · W. 4th St. · Bleecker · Waverly · ❾ Washington Square Park · Washington · W. 4th Pl. · W. 3rd St.

GREENWICH VILLAGE

University Pl. · Fourth Ave. · Broadway · Astor Pl. · Lafayette

Tompkins Square Park · St Mark's Pl. · E. 7th St. · E. 6th St. · E. 5th St. · E. 4th St. · E. 3rd St. · E. 2nd St.

EAST VILLAGE · Ave. A · Ave. B

Gt. Jones · Bond · Bleecker · NOHO · E. 1st St. · E. Houston

NOLITA · Stanton · Rivington · Delancey · Broome · Canal

Clinton · Attorney · Suffolk · Norfolk · Essex · Ludlow · Orchard · Allen · Eldridge · Jefferson

Prince · SOHO · Spring · Broome · Grand · Kenmare

W. Broadway · Wooster · Greene · Mercer · Crosby · Lafayette

Mott · Mulberry · Elizabeth · Bowery · Chrystie · Forsyth

LITTLE ITALY · Hester · Canal

❼ ❽

Holland Tunnel · Canal · Watts · Desbrosses · Vestry · Laight · Hubert · Beach · N Moore · Franklin · Harrison

TRIBECA · Lispenard · Walker · White · Franklin · Leonard · Worth

Howard · Canal · Centre · Baxter · Mulberry · Bayard

CHINATOWN · Division · E. Broadway · Rutgers · Henry · Madison · Monroe · Cherry · Market · Catherine · Water · South

Manhattan Bridge · Pike · Pike Slip

West St. · Greenwich St. · Hudson St. · Washington · Greenwich St. · Varick · Sixth Ave. · Thompson · Sullivan · MacDougal · La Guardia · Carmine · Downing · Bedford · Grove · Cornelia · Jones · Commerce · 7th Ave. S · Hudson St.

Jay · Thomas · Duane · Reade · Chambers · Warren · Murray · Park Pl. · Barclay · Vesey

City Hall Park · Park Row · Spruce · Beekman Pl. · Frankfort · Robert F. Wagner Pl. · Dover · Peck Slip

Brooklyn Bridge

❻ ❺→

West St. · Greenwich St. · World Trade Center site · Church · Dey · Cortlandt · Liberty · Cedar · Albany · Carlisle · Rector · W. Thames · JP Ward · Battery Pl. · 2nd Pl.

Liberty · Cortlandt · John · Platt · Maiden · Cedar · Pine · Exchange Pl. · ❸ Wall St.

Trinity Pl. · Broadway · Nassau · William · Pearl · Cliff · Gold · Fulton · Ann · Beekman · John · Fletcher · Water · Front · South · John · Pearl · Water · Front · Peck Slip · Beekman · South St. Viaduct

❹

FINANCIAL DISTRICT

Morris · Rector · Exchange Pl. · Beaver · Stone · Water · Broad · Whitehall · Pearl · Bridge · State

New · Bowling Green · Battery Pl. · South · 1st Pl. · South Gardens

Battery Park City · South End Ave.

Battery Park

To Ellis Island · To Liberty Island

East River

Inset (lower left)

MANHATTAN · Hudson River · Map Area

Inset (lower right)

0 · 1/2 mi

NEW JERSEY · Central Railroad of New Jersey Terminal · Ferry tickets

LIBERTY STATE PARK · Ellis Island Immigration Museum · ❷ Ellis Island

Statue of Liberty · ❶ Liberty Island

Hudson River · NEW YORK · MANHATTAN · Castle Clinton National Monument · Ferry tickets · BATTERY PARK · East River · Governors Island

Scale bar

0 · 1/4 mi
0 · 0.25 km

Numbered list

1. Statue of Liberty
2. Ellis Island ferries
3. Wall Street
4. South Street Seaport
5. Grimaldi's Pizza
6. Brooklyn Bridge
7. Lower East Side Tenement Museum
8. Il Laboratorio del Gelato
9. Washington Square Park
10. Union Square Park
11. Pete's Tavern

Tips Here are Some Things *Not* to Do in NYC

New York has so much going for it, the good overwhelms the bad. But there is bad, and I'm not talking about the obvious. I'm talking about experiences that might be perceived as good, but take my word for it: They are not. So, despite what you have heard, the following are a few experiences you can avoid:

New Year's Eve in Times Square: You see it on television every year, and now you're here. This is your chance to be one of the thousands of revelers packed together in the frigid cold to watch the ball drop. *Don't do it!* Despite the happy faces you see on TV, the whole thing is a miserable experience and not worth the forced elation of blowing on a noisemaker at midnight with half a million others. You won't find many New Yorkers here; we know better.

Three-Card Monte: When you see a crowd gathered around a cardboard box with one man flipping cards, madly enticing innocent rubes into his game, while another guy scans the crowd for undercover cops, keep on walking. Don't stop and listen to the dealer's spiel or think you can be the one to beat him at his game. You can't. Buy a lottery ticket instead; your odds are much better.

Horse-Drawn Carriage Rides: Pity those poor beasts of burden. They get dragged out in the heat (though not extreme heat) and cold (though not extreme cold) with a buggy attached just to give passengers the feel of an old-world, romantic buggy ride through Central Park. But the horses look so forlorn, as if it's the last thing they want to do. And they don't even get a cut of the generous take: $40 for a 20-minute ride, $60 for 45 minutes, excluding tip. If you want a slow, leisurely ride through Central Park, minus the ripe and frequent smell of horse poop, consider an alternative called **Manhattan Rickshaw Company** (*©* **212/604-4729**; www.manhattanrickshaw.com). The beast of burden has two legs, and pedals you and a companion in the back of a pedicab, where the rate is negotiable but is usually about $1 per minute with a $15 minimum.

⑧ IL LABORATORIO DEL GELATO
Just across the street from the Lower East Side Tenement Museum is a wonderful ice-cream-and-gelato shop where you can experience a multitude of homemade ice cream and sorbet flavors. Pick up a cone or cup for the walk to the subway. 95 Orchard St., between Broome and Delancey streets. *©* **212/343-9922.**

Take the F or V train at Second Avenue and Houston Street two stops uptown to West 4th Street.

⑨ Washington Square Park
Welcome to the center of Greenwich Village. This neighborhood's bohemian tradition is best represented by this park and the characters in it. On the north end of the park, you'll see a row of elegant late-19th-century town houses and Washington Square Arch, patterned after the Arc de Triomphe in Paris. See p. 272.

Chain Restaurants: Oh yes; they're here, probably to stay—and most likely with more to come. I'm referring to those restaurants with familiar names like Olive Garden, Applebee's, Red Lobster, and Domino's. When you begin to feel the pangs of hunger, ask yourself: Did I come to New York to eat what I can eat in every city or town in this country? Or did I come here to experience what makes New York so unique? Well, that includes the amazing variety of unchained restaurants, from the coffee shops and diners to the bargain-priced ethnic cuisine and higher-end dining experiences. So bypass the old standards, and try something different and exciting. You won't regret it.

The Feast of San Gennaro: At one time this was a genuine Italian feast (see the films *Godfather II* and *Mean Streets* for the Feast in the good old days). Its decline has pretty much coincided with the decline of Little Italy, a neighborhood that is just a shell of what it once was. Now the Feast, held annually for 2 weeks in September, is just an overblown and overcrowded street fair with bad food, cheap red wine, and games of chance you have no chance of winning.

Driving in the City: You have been warned already about driving in the city, but some people are stubborn and just can't give up the so-called freedom of maneuvering a car in heavy traffic, battling yellow cabs, and searching fruitlessly for a legal parking spot. With subways, buses, and your feet, New York has the best and fastest public transportation. A car is a luxury you want no part of.

Waiting on Lines for Breakfast: (And please note, New Yorkers wait *on* line, not *in* line). Sometimes New Yorkers can be masochistic—and silly. They hear about a restaurant that serves a great breakfast, and they begin lining up on weekend mornings to eat. Sometimes they wait for over an hour, standing outside, winter or summer, to order pancakes, omelets, or whatever else the breakfast menu offers. They do this even though many coffee shops and diners are serving patrons the same foods at much less cost and without more than a minute's wait. Now what would you do?

⑩ Union Square Park

About 10 blocks north of Washington Square Park, you'll find this small but welcome bit of park. And if it is a Monday, Wednesday, Friday, or Saturday, you'll be in for a treat because the city's best greenmarket, the **Union Square Greenmarket** 𝘈𝘈, will be buzzing with activity. See p. 272.

⑪ PETE'S TAVERN

A few blocks east of Union Square Park is Pete's Tavern, the city's oldest continually operating establishment. Look familiar? You may have seen it in an episode of *Seinfeld, Sex and the City,* or *Law & Order* or else on the big screen. Stop in for a pint to quench your thirst after that full day of walking. 129 E. 18th St. (at Irving Place). ✆ 212/473-7676. www.petestavern. com. Subway: L, N, R, 4, 5, 6, to 14th St./Union Sq. See p. 370.

THE BEST OF NYC IN 3 DAYS

You've seen a sizable chunk of the best of Manhattan, but there's still plenty left to fill up a day. We haven't even gotten to some of the city's great museums or that urban oasis called Central Park. We'll do all that and maybe even escape to the wilds of the Bronx before the day is done. If the weather's nice, plan on a picnic in Central Park. *Start: B or C to 72nd Street.*

---

❶ The Dakota

We'll start our day in front of this 1884-built apartment building. This was standing when the only thing around it was greenery. The building has a dubious past: It was here where John Lennon lived (and where Yoko Ono still lives) and where he was shot and killed. Across the street in Central Park is **Strawberry Fields** ⊛, named in honor of the former Beatle; fans gather here every year on the anniversary of his death, December 8. See p. 256.

❷ American Museum of Natural History ⊛⊛⊛

Don't try to cover too much ground at this 4-square-block museum; you'll be here all day. Pick a few of the highlights, like the Fossils Halls where the dinosaurs reside, the Hall of Biodiversity, and the Culture Halls. On the 81st Street side of the building, you'll find the **Rose Center for Earth and Space,** where you can marvel at the beauty of the cosmos in the grand Hayden Planetarium. See p. 229.

❸ Central Park ⊛⊛⊛

From the Museum of Natural History, cross the street to Central Park and enter at 81st Street. Follow the path east, and just south of the Delacorte Theater, you'll see Belvedere Castle. Climb to the top and soak in the view of the park. To the north, you'll see the Great Lawn, sight of so many concerts, and beyond that the Jacqueline Kennedy Onassis Reservoir. To the south you'll see the lake with its rowboats (rent one if you have

time) and the skyline of Manhattan. See p. 264.

> ### ❹ A PICNIC IN THE PARK
> If you didn't pack a lunch, stop in the **Zabars** (at 80th and Broadway.), and get your lunch to go. Head to the park and grab a bench, or spread out a blanket and take in the sunshine.

❺ Metropolitan Museum of Art ⊛⊛⊛

Continuing east across Central Park, you'll hit Fifth Avenue and the Met. As with the Museum of Natural History, there is no way you can see all the Met has to offer in one visit, but stop by the Temple of Dendur, a gift from the Egyptian government, and the museum's collection of European paintings—including 37 Monets. There are various free (after the admission charge) museum highlight tours. They last an hour and will give you a pretty good overview of this great museum. See p. 233.

❻ Solomon R. Guggenheim Museum ⊛

Continuing on our minitour of Museum Mile, that stretch of artistic real estate that runs on upper Fifth Avenue, is the Guggenheim. You'll know it when you see it; there's nothing else like this Frank Lloyd Wright–designed museum, and now you have the chance to walk the spiraling rotunda. But get off the rotunda and take a look at some of the permanent

Subway stop
"Take a Break" stop

ST. NICHOLAS PARK

0   1/4 mi
0   0.25 km

HARLEM

E. 125th St.
W. 125th St.

MARCUS GARVEY PARK

THE BRONX

Yankee Stadium

BARNARD COLLEGE
COLUMBIA UNIVERSITY

MORNINGSIDE PARK

E. 116th St.

EAST HARLEM

Map Area

RIVERSIDE PARK

W. 114th St.
W. 113th St.
Cathedral of St. John the Divine

W. 115th St.
W. 114th St.
W. 113th St.
W. 112th St.
W. 111th St.

MANHATTAN

Douglass Circle
Cathedral Pkwy.
W. 109th St.
W. 108th St.
W. 107th St.
W. 106th St.
W. 105th St.
W. 104th St.

Central Park North
Frawley Circle
E. 110th St.
E. 109th St.
E. 108th St.
E. 107th St.

Harlem Meer
Lasker Rink & Pool

W. 103rd St.

The Great Hill

Conservatory Garden
Museum of the City Of New York

The Pool

North Meadow

CENTRAL PARK

East Meadow

W. 97th St.
W. 96th St.
W. 95th St.
W. 94th St.
JOAN OF ARC PARK
W. 93rd St.
Soldiers and Sailors Monument
W. 92nd St.
W. 91st St.
W. 90th St.
W. 89th St.
W. 88th St.
W. 87th St.
W. 86th St.

97th St Transverse Rd.
Tennis Courts

Jacqueline Kennedy Onassis Reservoir

Jewish Museum
Cooper-Hewitt Museum
Guggenheim Museum

E. 96th St.
E. 95th St.
E. 94th St.
E. 93rd St.
E. 92nd St.
E. 91st St.
E. 90th St.
E. 89th St.
E. 88th St.
E. 87th St.
E. 86th St.

86th St Transverse Rd.

UPPER EAST SIDE

Children's Museum
W. 82nd St.
W. 81st St.
W. 80th St.
W. 79th St.

Hayden Planetarium
American Museum of Natural History

GREAT LAWN
Delacorte Theater
Belvedere Lake
Belvedere Castle
Obelisk
79th St Transverse Rd.

Metropolitan Museum Of Art

E. 85th St.
E. 84th St.
E. 83rd St.
E. 82nd St.
E. 81st St.

W. 77th St.
W. 76th St.
W. 75th St.
W. 74th St.
W. 73rd St.
W. 72nd St.

New York Historical Society

The Ramble
The Lake
Boat House

Conservatory Pond

Strawberry Fields

UPPER WEST SIDE

Sheep Meadow
Tavern on the Green
W. 66th St
W. 65th St LINCOLN CENTER

Bandshell
The Mall
East Green
65th St Transverse Rd.
Zoo

❶ The Dakota
❷ American Museum of Natural History
❸❹ Central Park
❺ Metropolitan Museum of Art
❻ Solomon R. Guggenheim Museum
❼ Cathedral of St. John the Divine
❽ M&G Diner
❾ Apollo Theater

collection that includes works by Picasso, Chagall, and Klee. Or wander into the new Kandinsky Gallery for a dose of the master's eye-opening works. See p. 237.

Take the M96 crosstown bus at Fifth Avenue and 97th Street West. Get off at Amsterdam Avenue and 96th Street and transfer to an uptown M11 or M7 bus. Get off at 110th Street.

❼ Cathedral of St. John the Divine 🅰

On the east side of Amsterdam, you will see the world's largest Gothic cathedral. Construction began in 1892 and is still not finished. You can explore the inside of the cathedral on your own or opt for a tour. If you're here at Easter or during the Feast of St. Francis in October, don't miss the blessing of animals—where the creature congregation has been known to include an elephant or camel. See p. 261.

Take the M11 or M7 uptown bus to 125th St.

> ### 🎱 M&G DINER
> This is the place for first-rate soul food. If you're hungry, order the pan-fried chicken. If all you want is a coffee, a slice of home-made carrot cake goes perfectly with it. 383 W. 125th St., at St. Nicholas Avenue. ✆ 212/864-7326. See p. 212.

❾ Apollo Theater 🅰

Walk a few blocks east of the M&G and you will arrive at a city landmark that is as well known as La Scala or the Taj Mahal. And if it's Wednesday, make sure you have tickets, because Amateur Night at the Apollo is an experience not to be missed. There would be no "American Idol" without this Harlem institution. But even if it's not Wednesday, you can tour this historic theater where Bessie Smith, James Brown, Stevie Wonder and so many other greats played. See p. 350.

THE ESSENTIAL NEW YORK EATING ITINERARY

New York has countless restaurants of quality and variety. If you want a sampling of true New York cuisine, follow the "required eating" itinerary below. Whether you jam the stops below into 1, 2 or 3 days, a gargantuan appetite is required. For full reviews of the places listed below, see Chapter 6, "Where to Dine."

❶ Bagels with Lox

Start your food tour at **Barney Green-grass, the Sturgeon King** (541 Amsterdam Avenue; ✆ 212/724-4707), where they have been making that famous combination, bagels and lox, since 1908. If there is anything more satisfying than a fresh, out-of-the-oven bagel with a schmear of cream cheese and a slice of lox, I don't know what it is. This might be one of the most popular breakfast items in New York.

❷ Cuban/Chinese

There used to be dozens of Cuban/Chinese restaurants in Manhattan, most on the Upper West Side. The boom began in the late 1950's after the Cuban revolution

and the beginning of the Castro regime. Chinese-Cubans emigrated to New York and opened up restaurants serving both Cantonese-style Chinese food and traditional Cuban food. A few are left, and my favorite is **Flor de Mayo** (2651 Broadway; ✆ 212/663-5520. Here I can order a big bowl of wonton soup followed by a huge plate of yellow rice and black beans.

❸ Chicken and Waffles

You're out late, maybe listening to jazz at one of Harlem's many clubs, it's getting near dawn, and you can't decide whether you want dinner or breakfast. You can't resist the fried chicken, but waffles sound good, too. So you try both—maple syrup melding with the hot sauce; sweet with

Essential New York Eating

Amy Ruth's (Chicken and Waffles) **3**
Barney Greengrass, the Sturgeon King **1**
Brooklyn Ice Cream Factory **8**
Flor de Mayo (Cuban/Chinese) **2**
Grand Central Oyster Bar **4**
Joe's Pizza **5**
Nathan's Famous (hot dogs) **6**
Peter Luger (steaks) **7**

savory. The birthplace of this dish is said to be Wells Chicken and Waffles in Harlem in 1938. Wells is long gone, but chicken and waffles live on. For the best rendition, go to **Amy Ruth's** (113 W. 116th St.; ☎ **212/280-8779**) for chicken and waffles, as well as grits and fish cakes—another outstanding combo.

❹ The New York Oyster

There was a time when New York was more the Big Oyster than the Big Apple. The local harbor beds overflowed with oysters and the mollusk helped feed the city. You can recall those glory days at the **Grand Central Oyster Bar** in Grand Central Station (☎ **212/490-6650**) where, since 1913, oysters have been the specialty. Order them on the half shell from Long Island, Washington State, Maine, Virginia, or Canada, with the Metro North commuter trains rumbling in the background. It's a true New York eating experience if there ever was one.

❺ A Slice of Pizza

Toss on some red pepper or garlic, and eat it standing up to capture the grease before it stains your clothes. That's the way we've been eating pizza in New York for years. The classic New York slice, however, has been on the decline ever since the chain pizzerias have corrupted the landscape. For the best "slice" head to **Joe's Pizza** (7 Carmine St.; ☎ **212/255-3946**) in the Village, open late, satisfying your cravings.

❻ The Hot Dog

This might be an obvious choice, but I don't think so. You can find carts selling cheap hot dogs throughout the city. You might be tempted to try one just to say you did. And I think you should; it definitely is a New York experience. But even better, take the train out to Coney Island and sample a **Nathan's Famous** dog right on the boardwalk (1310 Surf Ave.; ☎ **718/946-2202**). Maybe it's the salty sea air. Maybe it's the crisp skin of the hot dog, or the way it's perfectly fried. Whatever it is, you won't forget your Nathan's hot dog on Coney Island.

❼ The New York Strip

Some of New York's oldest restaurants are steakhouses, and for good reason. They keep it simple. Some might have sawdust on the floors, others clay pipes on the ceiling, or photos of celebrities on the walls, but that is about as fancy as they get. What they do is serve quality, properly-aged meat cooked to perfection and presented in a no-nonsense, no frills manner. And no one does that better than **Peter Luger** in Williamsburg, Brooklyn (178 Broadway; ☎ **718/387-7400**).

❽ Ice Cream with a View

If you've been able to sample the above essential New York eating experiences into 1, 2 or 3 days, finish your tour off at the **Brooklyn Ice Cream Factory** (1 Water St.; ☎ **718/246-3963**) where the homemade ice cream is absolutely delicious and the view at river's edge of Manhattan, just below the Brooklyn Bridge, is equally stunning.

5

Where to Stay

It's official: Hotel rates in New York are the most expensive in the United States. In 2007, the average price of a hotel room soared to over $300 per night. But it seems that the outrageous hotel rates have not deterred visitors: More than 46 million came to the city that year. So get over any notions that you might find rates comparable to those back home. That said, there are bargains out there at every price level; but a bargain in New York might be a king's ransom in St. Louis.

If you want to spend less than $125 a night, you may have to put up with some inconveniences, such as sharing a hall bathroom with your fellow travelers. (Europeans seem to have an easier time with this than Americans.) If you want a room with standard amenities—such as a private bathroom or a real closet (rather than just a bar screwed to the wall)—plan on spending at least $150 a night. If you do better than that, you've made a fantastic deal.

New York hotel rooms give everybody a new perspective on "small." Space is the city's biggest asset, and getting some will cost you. If you're on a tight budget, don't be surprised if your room isn't much bigger than the bed that's in it and your bathroom has a sink so small you'll have difficulty spitting out your toothpaste without spilling it. Even expensive rooms can be on the small side, lack closet space, or have smallish bathrooms.

PRICE CATEGORIES & RACK RATES The **rates** quoted in the listings below are "rack rates"—the maximum rates that a hotel charges for rooms. I've used these rack rates to divide the hotels into four price categories, ranging from "Very Expensive" to "Inexpensive," for easy reference. But rack rates are only guidelines, and there are often ways around them; see "Tips for Saving on Your Hotel Room," below.

The hotels listed below have provided us with their best rate estimates for 2008, and all quoted rates were correct at press time. Be aware, however, that **rates can change at any time.** Rates are always subject to availability, seasonal, even daily fluctuations, and plain-old rate hikes. It's smart to expect price shifts in both directions in late 2008 and 2009 as hoteliers adjust to new demand patterns.

PET POLICIES I've indicated in the listings below those hotels that accept pets. However, understand that these policies may have limitations, such as weight and breed restrictions; may require a deposit and/or a signed waiver against damages; and may be revoked at any time. Always inquire when booking if you're bringing Fluffy or Spike—*never* just show up with a pet in tow.

TIPS FOR SAVING ON YOUR HOTEL ROOM

In the listings below, I've tried to give you an idea of the kind of deals that may be available at particular hotels: which ones have the best packages, which ones offer AAA and other discounts, which ones allow kids to stay with Mom and Dad for free, and so on. But there's no way of knowing what the offers will be when you're booking, so also consider these general tips:

- **Ask about special rates or other discounts.** Always ask whether a room less expensive than the first one quoted is available, or whether any special rates apply to you. You may qualify for corporate, student, military, senior, or other discounts. Mention membership in AAA, AARP, frequent-flier programs, or trade unions, which may entitle you to special deals. Find out the policy on children—do kids stay free or is there a special rate?

- **Choose your season carefully.** Room rates can vary dramatically—by hundreds of dollars in some cases—depending on what time of year you visit. Winter, from January through March, is best for bargains, with summer (especially July–Aug) second best. Fall is the busiest and most expensive season after Christmas, but November tends to be quiet and rather affordable, as long as you're not booking a parade-route hotel on Thanksgiving weekend. All bets are off at Christmastime—expect to pay top dollar for everything. For more on this subject, see "Money Matters," in "When to Go," in chapter 3.

- **Go uptown or downtown.** The advantages of a Midtown location are overrated, especially when saving money is your object. The subway can whisk you anywhere you want to go in minutes; even if you stay on the Upper West Side, you can be at the ferry launch for the Statue of Liberty in about a half-hour. You'll get the best value for your money by staying outside the Theater District, in the residential neighborhoods where real New Yorkers live, such as Greenwich Village, Chelsea, Murray Hill, or the Upper West Side. These are the neighborhoods where real New Yorkers hang out, too, so you won't want for good eats, nightlife, or Big Apple bustle.

- **Visit over a weekend.** If your trip includes a weekend, you might be able to save big. Business hotels tend to empty out, and rooms that go for $300 or more Monday through Thursday can drop dramatically, as low as $150 or less, once the execs have headed home. These deals are prevalent in the Financial District, but they're often available in tourist-friendly Midtown, too. Also, you'll find that Sunday nights are the least expensive. Check the hotel's website for weekend specials. Or just ask when you call.

- **Shop online.** Hotels often offer "Internet only" deals that can save you 10% to 20% or more over what you'd pay if you booked over the telephone. Also, hotels often advertise all of their available deals on their websites, so you don't have to rely on a reservation agent to fill you in. What's more, some of the discount reservations agencies (see below) have sites that allow you to book online. And consider joining the **Playbill Online Theater Club** (www.playbillclub.com), a free service that offers some excellent members-only rates at select city hotels, in addition to discounts on theater tickets. American Automobile Association members can often score the best discounts by booking at **www.aaa.com**. Travel search sites such as **Microsoft Expedia** (www.expedia.com), **Priceline** (www.priceline.com), **BookIt** (www.bookit.com) and **Travelocity** (www.travelocity.com) offer other discount options. Shop around. And if you have special needs—a quiet room, a room with a view—call the hotel directly and make your needs known after you've booked online.

- **Dial direct.** When booking a room in a chain hotel, you'll often get a better deal by calling the hotel's reservation desk rather than the chain's main number.

- **Make deals with the budget chains.** With a few exceptions, I have not listed budget chains in this chapter. In my opinion, they tend to lack the character and local feel that most independently run hotels have. And it's that feel, I believe, that is so much a part of the travel experience. Still, when you're looking for a deal, they can be a good option. Most hotels—particularly such chains as Comfort Inn and Best Western—are market-sensitive. Because they hate to see rooms sit empty, they'll often negotiate good rates at the last minute and in slow seasons.

  You can also pull out all the stops for discounts at a budget chain, from auto-club membership to senior status. You might be able to take advantage of corporate rates or discounted weekend stays. Most chain hotels let the kids stay with parents for free. Ask for every kind of discount; if you find that you get an unhelpful reservation agent, call back. Of course, there's no guarantee.

  Two chains with franchises in Manhattan include **Best Western** (© 800/780-7234; www.bestwestern.com), though their rack rates for New York hotels are higher than you'd expect, and **Howard Johnson** (© 800/446-4656; www.hojo.com). There's a Best Western at South Street Seaport and at two Midtown locations, and a Howard Johnson on the Lower East Side. Check their websites for all the details.

  At these and other franchised hotels—such as the ones run by **Apple Core Hotels** (www.applecorehotels.com), a management company that handles the **Comfort Inn Midtown,** the **Ramada Inn Eastside,** Manhattan's first **Red Roof** (p. 125), the **Super 8 Hotel Times Square,** and **La Quinta,** 7 W. 32nd St. (© 212/736-1600; www.laquinta.com)—doubles can go for as little as $109. Check with the franchiser if you're not quoted a good advance-booking rate or through the management company's online reservations system; their global 800 and online reservations systems will often garner you a better rate, which might include a promotion—or, at minimum, an "Internet User's Rate" that's 10% lower than the standard.

  A good source for deals is **Choice Hotels** (© 877/424-6423; www.hotelchoice.com), which oversees Comfort Inn, Quality Hotel, and Clarion Hotel chains, all of which have Manhattan branches.

  Another hotel to try is the **Hilton Garden Inn,** 790 Eighth Ave., at 48th Street (© 212/581-7000; www.hiltongardenill.com).

- **Investigate reservations services.** These outfits usually work as consolidators, buying up or reserving rooms in bulk, and then dealing them out to customers at a profit. You can get 10% to 50% off; but remember, these discounts apply to rack rates—inflated prices that people rarely end up paying. You may get a decent rate, but always call the hotel directly to see if you can do better.

Quikbook (© **800/789-9887** or 212/779-7666 outside the U.S.; www. quikbook.com) is the best of the bunch. You might also try the **Hotel Reservations Network,** also known as HotelDiscount!com (© **800/715-7666;** www. hoteldiscount.com).

Note: Never just rely on a reservations service or an online-booking site. Do a little homework; compare the rack rates to the discounted rates being offered to see what kind of deal they're actually offering. If you're being offered a stay in a hotel I haven't recommended, do more research on it, especially if it isn't a reliable chain name such as Holiday Inn or Hyatt. It's not a deal if you end up at a dump.

• **Avoid excess charges and hidden costs.** When you book a room, ask whether the hotel charges for parking. Use your own cellphone, pay phones, or prepaid phone cards instead of dialing direct from hotel phones, which usually have exorbitant rates. And don't be tempted by minibar offerings: Most hotels charge through the nose for water, soda, and snacks. Finally, ask about local taxes and service charges, which can increase the cost of a room by 15% or more. If a hotel insists upon tacking on an "energy surcharge" that wasn't mentioned at check-in, you can often make a case for getting it removed.

• **Buy a money-saving package deal.** A travel package that combines your airfare and your hotel stay for one price may just be the best bargain of all. In some cases, you'll get airfare, accommodations, transportation to and from the airport, plus extras—maybe an afternoon sightseeing tour or restaurant and shopping discount coupons—for less than the hotel alone would have cost had you booked it yourself. For more on this, see "Packages for the Independent Traveler," in chapter 3.

• **Rely on a qualified professional.** Certain hotels give travel agents discounts in exchange for steering business their way, so if you're shy about bargaining, an agent may be better equipped to negotiate discounts for you.

• **Consider B&B accommodations or an apartment.** If Big Apple hotels seem too expensive, or you'd just like something a little more like home, consider renting a room in a genuine New York apartment—or even an entire apartment. These accommodations can range from spartan to splendid, from a hosted bedroom in a private home to an unhosted, fully equipped apartment with multiple bedrooms. No matter what, you can pretty much guarantee that you'll get more for your money than if you book into a regular hotel. However, you need to be rather independent-minded to enjoy this option. For more, see the sidebar "Plenty of Room at the Inn," later in this chapter.

The place to start with is **Manhattan Getaways** (© **212/956-2010;** www. manhattangetaways.com). Judith Glynn maintains a beautifully kept and managed network of bed-and-breakfast rooms (from $110 nightly) and unhosted apartments (from $150) around the city. There's a 3-night minimum stay, and credit cards are accepted. Another decent bet is **A Hospitality Company** (© **800/ 987-1235** or 212/813-2244; www.metro-home.com), which owns and manages 300 apartments around Manhattan starting at $139 a night, or $850 weekly for a basic studio. These are rather sparsely furnished apartments, and the company offers little in the way of service (it took me 5 days to get my TV fixed when I was displaced from my home by renovation), but the apartments are clean and do the trick. There's no minimum stay, and credit cards are accepted. Cleaning services are available for longer stays.

Additional agencies that can book you into a B&B room or a private apartment, with prices starting at $90 nightly, include **Abode Apartment Rentals** (☏ **800/835-8880** or 212/472-2000; www.abodenyc.com); **City Sonnet** (☏ **212/614-3034;** www.citysonnet.com); **Manhattan Lodgings** (☏ **212/677-7616;** www.manhattanlodgings.com); and **New York Habitat** (☏ **212/255-8018;** www.nyhabitat.com). Be sure to get all details in writing and an exact total up front to avoid disappointments.

1 South Street Seaport & the Financial District

VERY EXPENSIVE

Ritz-Carlton New York, Battery Park 🏵🏵🏵   Perfect on almost every level, the only drawback to this Ritz-Carlton is that it's so far downtown. But the location, on the extreme southern tip of Manhattan, is also one of its strengths. Where else can you get, in most rooms anyway, magnificent views of New York Harbor from your bedroom—complete with telescope for close-ups of Lady Liberty? And where else can you have a cocktail in your hotel bar and watch the sun set over the harbor? This modern, Art Deco–influenced high-rise differs from the English-countryside look of most Ritz-Carltons, including its sister hotel on Central Park (p. 115), but that's where the differences end. You'll find the full slate of comforts and services typical of Ritz-Carlton, from Frette-dressed feather beds to the chain's signature Bath Butler, who will draw a scented bath in your own deep soaking tub. If you don't mind the location and the commute to Midtown and beyond, you won't find a more luxurious choice.

2 West St., New York, NY 10004. ☏ 800/241-3333 or 212/344-0800. Fax 212/344-3801. www.ritzcarlton.com. 298 units. $350–$545 double; from $750 suite. Extra person 12 and over $30 (starting from $100 on club level). Check website for promotional weekend packages. AE, DC, DISC, MC, V. Valet parking $60. Subway: 4, 5 to Bowling Green. **Amenities:** Restaurant; lobby lounge (w/outdoor seating) for afternoon tea and cocktails; 14th-floor cocktail bar w/light dining and outdoor seating; state-of-the-art health club w/views; spa treatments; 24-hr. concierge; well-equipped business center w/24-hr. secretarial services; 24-hr. room service; laundry service; dry cleaning; Ritz-Carlton Club Level w/5 food presentations daily; technology butler and bath butler services. *In room:* A/C, TV w/pay movies and video games, Wi-Fi, high-speed Internet, dataport, minibar, fridge, hair dryer, safe, CD player, DVD w/surround sound in suites and Club rooms.

EXPENSIVE/MODERATE

Exchange Hotel 🏵   This cozy hotel is a solid, midpriced choice if you are looking for a downtown location. A short walk from Wall Street, the South Street Seaport, Brooklyn Bridge, and Chinatown, the Exchange Hotel features personalized service and a few perks such as free wireless Internet and a complimentary continental breakfast. Recently renovated in a sleek, contemporary style, standard and deluxe guest rooms are on the small size, but are outfitted nicely with plasma televisions, mini-refrigerators and microwaves. The suites are roomy with a separate living room, black leather furniture and a full-size kitchen. Bathrooms are tight in both the guest rooms and suites and sadly include those very fashionable marble bowl sinks that look good, but don't leave much space of any of your toiletries. That minor complaint aside, the Exchange is a welcome addition to an area much too lacking in lodging.

129 Front St. (btwn Wall and Pine sts.) New York, N.Y. 10005. ☏ 212/742-0003. Fax 212/742-0124. www.exchange hotel.com. 53 units. AE, DC, MC, V. $299–$389; suites $310–$469. Parking $25. Subway: 2, 3 to Wall St. **Amenities:** Lounge; free complimentary continental breakfast; access to nearby fitness club; laundry/valet service. *In room:* A/C, TV/VCR, free Wi-Fi, full-sized kitchens in suites, minifridge, iron/ironing board, safe, microwave.

Wall Street District Hotel by Holiday Inn ⟨R⟩   This is one of lower Manhattan's most technologically advanced hotels. The comfortable queen-bedded rooms are stocked with everything an executive might need, including an 8-foot L-shaped workstation with desk-level inputs, dual-line portable phones, and the kind of office supplies you never bring but always need, such as paper clips and tape. About half the rooms have PCs with Microsoft Word and Office applications and a CD drive. The top floor is dedicated to SMART rooms, which feature Toshiba Satellite laptop computers (with carrying case), fax/printer/copiers, and other upgraded amenities, plus buffet breakfast. Room decor is chain standard, but fresh and comfortable; an easy chair and ottoman expand seating options. The staff prides itself on meeting the needs of its bullish guests, so expect to be well cared for.

15 Gold St. (at Platt St.), New York, NY 10038. ✆ 800/HOLIDAY, 212/232-7800, or 212/232-7700. Fax 212/425-0330. www.holidayinnwsd.com or www.holiday-inn.com. 138 units. $249–$400 double; from $389 suite. Check for discounts galore (AAA, AARP, corporate, government, military), plus deeply discounted weekend rates and other specials. AE, DC, DISC, MC, V. Parking $30. Subway: 2, 3, 4, 5, A, C, J, M, Z to Fulton St./Broadway–Nassau St. **Amenities:** Restaurant; bar; exercise room and access to nearby health club; concierge; self-service business center; 24-hr. room service; delivery from 24-hr. deli; laundry service; dry cleaning; executive-level rooms; CD library. *In room:* A/C, TV w/pay movies/Internet access/Nintendo, high-speed Internet, dataport, minibar, coffeemaker, hair dryer, iron, safe, CD player.

The Wall Street Inn ⟨R⟩ *(Finds)*   This intimate hotel (along with the **Exchange,** p. 101) is one of the preferred choices for those working on the Street. It's also a good choice for visitors who don't want to work. This intimate, seven-story hotel is ideal for those who want a lower Manhattan location without corporate blandness. The lovely early American interiors boast a pleasing freshness. The hotel is warm, comforting, and serene, and the friendly, professional staff offers the kind of personalized service you won't get from a chain. Rooms aren't huge, but the bedding is top-quality and all the conveniences are at hand. Rooms ending in "01" are smallest; seventh-floor rooms are best: the bathrooms have extra counter space and whirlpool tubs.

9 S. William St. (at Broad St.), New York, NY 10004. ✆ 800/747-1500 or 212/747-1500. Fax 212/747-1900. www.thewallstreetinn.com. 46 units. $279–$450 double. Rates include continental breakfast. Ask about corporate, group, and/or deeply discounted weekend rates (as low as $265 at press time). AE, DC, DISC, MC, V. Parking $36 nearby. Subway: 2, 3 to Wall St.; 4, 5 to Bowling Green. **Amenities:** Well-outfitted exercise room w/sauna and steam; concierge; business center; babysitting arranged; laundry service; dry cleaning; common guest kitchen w/microwave; video library. *In room:* A/C, TV/VCR, fax, high-speed Internet, fridge, hair dryer, iron, safe.

2 TriBeCa & Lower East Side

To locate the hotels in this section, see the map on p. 103.

VERY EXPENSIVE

Tribeca Grand Hotel ⟨R⟩   This sister to the **Soho Grand** (p. 106) is set on a triangular plot just south of SoHo; its decidedly retro brick-and-cast-iron exterior blends perfectly with the surrounding neighborhood. Set along open atrium-facing corridors, the streamlined guest rooms boast generous built-in work space (with a Herman Miller Aeron chair) and state-of-the-art technology. But because the rooms face the atrium, noise levels can be a problem, so each room is equipped with a noise-dulling device. The rooms, however, take a back seat to what's below: a dramatic eight-story atrium lobby, with its soaring proportions consumed by the popular **Church Lounge,** an upscale lounge and restaurant.

Downtown Accommodations

The Bowery Hotel **4**
Cosmopolitan Hotel-
TriBeCa **12**
Duane St. Hotel **11**
Exchange Hotel **14**
Holiday Inn
Downtown/SoHo **9**
Hotel Gansevoort **1**
Hotel on Rivington **6**
Larchmont Hotel **2**
The Mercer **5**
Ritz-Carlton New York,
Battery Park **16**
60 Thompson **7**
Soho Grand **8**
Tribeca Grand **10**
Wall Street District Hotel
by Holiday Inn **13**
The Wall Street Inn **15**
Washington Square Hotel **3**

Ⓜ Subway stop
Ⓜ Closed indefinitely

2 Sixth Ave. (at White & Church sts.), New York, NY 10013. © **877/519-6600** or 212/519-6600. Fax 212/519-6700. www.tribecagrand.com. 203 units. From $450 double; from $699 suite. Promotional and Internet-only rates as low as $259 at press time; ask about corporate rates and value-added packages. AE, DC, DISC, MC, V. Parking $45. Subway: 1 to Franklin St.; A, C, E to Canal St. Pets accepted. **Amenities:** Restaurant; lounge; fitness center; 24-hr. concierge; business center w/complete workstations; 24-hr. room service; same-day laundry and dry cleaning; CD libraries; coffee, tea, and cocoa bar on each floor; screening room. *In room:* A/C, TV/VCR w/Internet access, fax/printer/copier, high-speed Internet, dataport, minibar, hair dryer, safe, CD player, iPods (provided by request and based on availability).

EXPENSIVE

The Hotel on Rivington 🎦🎦   The contrast of a gleaming 21-story, glass-tower luxury hotel in the midst of 19th- and early-20th-century Lower East Side tenement buildings is striking, but an accurate representation of what that neighborhood has become. From the floor-to-ceiling windows of your room, surrounded by amenities such as flatscreen TVs, Japanese soaking tubs in the bathrooms, and Tempur-Pedic mattresses, not only do you have incredible, unobstructed city views, but you can look down and spot ancient Lower East Side landmarks such as the sign for the Schapiro Kosher wine factory. You may not be close to the center of Manhattan, but you will be in a location where old-world customs and institutions coexist with the new and the super-cool. Along with the views, three-quarters of the rooms have private terraces, the option of in-room spa services, and heated, tiled floors in the large bathrooms where you can enjoy your view of the city as you bathe—which also means someone with binoculars might just have a view of you, too.

107 Rivington St. (between Ludlow & Essex sts.), New York, NY 10002. © **212/475-2600.** Fax 212/475-5959. www.hotelonrivington.com. 110 units. From $395 double. AE, DC, MC, V. Parking $50. Subway: F to Delancey St. **Amenities:** Restaurant; fitness center; in-room spa services available; concierge; 24-hr. room service; laundry service; dry cleaning. *In room:* A/C, TV, Wi-Fi, dataport, fridge, hair dryer, CD players and JBL On Stage iPod speaker system available.

MODERATE

Duane Street Hotel 🎦 *Finds*   This small, cozy TriBeCa-located hotel opened with minimal fanfare in late 2007. But you don't need hype to sell solid goods and that's what they have here. The rooms are on the small size and designed with IKEA-ish style furnishing, but like the loft apartments in the neighborhood, the walls are hardwood, the ceilings are high and the windows large providing more of a sense of space. Bathrooms are spacious and well-outfitted with showers equipped with rain shower heads. Every room has a good-sized desk and a 32-inch plasma HDTV. Best of all is the personable, extremely helpful staff that seems to enjoy doing the little extras to improve your stay. The Duane Street Hotel is welcome addition to a vibrant neighborhood with limited midpriced hotel options.

130 Duane Street (at Church St.), New York, NY 10013. © **212/964-4600.** Fax 212/964-4800; www.duanestreet hotel.com. 45 units. $259–$799 doubles. AE, DC, DISC, MC, V. Subway: A, C, to Chambers Street. **Amenities:** Restaurant; concierge; business center; off-site fitness center; in-room spa services. *In room:* A/C, TV, free Wi-Fi, hair dryer, safe, CD player.

INEXPENSIVE

Cosmopolitan Hotel–Tribeca 🎦 *Value*   Behind a plain-vanilla TriBeCa awning is one of the best hotel deals in Manhattan for budget travelers who prefer a private bathroom. Everything is strictly budget but nice: The modern IKEA-ish furniture includes a work desk and an armoire (a few rooms have a dresser and hanging rack instead); for a few extra bucks, you can have a love seat, too. Beds are comfy, and

Sleep Tight and . . .

My job as author of this book has many perks. One is to lie on 300-count Frette sheets, sample room service from three-star restaurants, and soak in Jacuzzi tubs in luxury hotels so I can accurately report to you whether that particular hotel is worthy of its astronomical rate. But the job comes with some risks and I encountered a grisly example recently. I had inspected a popular moderate hotel for possible inclusion into this book and was staying at the hotel to see if it lived up to the superficial tour I had previously taken. You learn much more by actually staying a night at a hotel than you do from a tour, and I had problems with the amenities in the room; no chair for example, a very small desk that was shared with a television, and inefficient use of space in the bathroom. Upon checkout, I decided I could not recommend the hotel to my readers.

The next day, after showering, as if exacting revenge on me for my decision and/or reinforcing it, I noticed red, itchy, welt-like blotches on my back and side. And the revelation hit me. I had been bitten by the new scourge of New York: bedbugs. I had read the articles saying that they were making a comeback and were on their way to replacing cockroaches as the number one pest, but I never thought I would become a victim.

Bedbugs apparently travel well, and because of this the hotel industry is particularly vulnerable. They hide in mattresses and are nocturnal, biting while the victim is asleep. They are also very difficult to totally exterminate and require repeat visits from an exterminator; a hotelier's nightmare if there ever was one. The good news is that a bedbug bite does not transmit disease and is more an itchy nuisance than a health hazard.

Bedbugs do not discriminate as to class of hotel; they enjoy lounging in the beds of the best hotels as much as we do. If you are concerned, before you get into bed, check the mattress and the seams in and around the bed frame. You might see their droppings which are tiny blood-tinged specks. I know that's why you came to New York; to search for bedbug droppings.

No hotel would ever broadcast that they have had a bedbug problem, but you might want to check a few travel message boards or websites, including **www.frommers.com, www.tripadvisor.com**, or **www.hotelchatter.com**, to see if anyone has posted a message about bedbugs where you plan to stay. Otherwise, good night and sleep tight!

sheets and towels are of good quality. Rooms are small but make the most of the limited space, and the entire place is pristine. The two-level minilofts have lots of character, but expect to duck on the second level. Management does a great job of keeping everything fresh. The TriBeCa location is safe, super-hip, and subway-convenient. Services are kept at a bare minimum to keep costs down, so you must be a low-maintenance guest to be happy here.

95 W. Broadway (at Chambers St.), New York, NY 10007. ⓒ **888/895-9400** or 212/566-1900. Fax 212/566-6909. www.cosmohotel.com. 105 units. $200–$270 double. AE, DC, MC, V. Subway: 1, 2, 3, A, C to Chambers St. *In room:* A/C, TV, dataport, ceiling fan.

3 SoHo

To locate the hotels in this section, see the map on p. 103.

VERY EXPENSIVE

The Mercer 𝒜𝒜𝒜   One of the first and the best of the downtown, celebrity-crawling, hip and trendy hotels, the Mercer is a place where even those who represent the antithesis of hip (and I'm speaking personally) can feel at home. Though SoHo can be a bit over the top with its high-end boutiques, cutting-edge restaurants, and a constant parade of too serious fashionistas on the streets, it is still an exciting place. And the corner of Mercer and Prince streets, the location of the hotel, is probably the epicenter of SoHo. Still, once inside there is a pronounced calm—from the postmodern library lounge and the relaxed Mizrahi-clad staff, to the huge soundproof loftlike guest rooms; the hotel is a perfect complement to the scene outside your big window. The Mercer is one of the few New York hotels with ceiling fans, and even if you don't need them, they look nice whirring above your extremely comfortable bed. The tile-and-marble bathrooms have a steel cart for storage, and an oversize shower stall or oversize two-person tub (state your preference when booking).

147 Mercer St. (at Prince St.), New York, NY 10012. ℭ 888/918-6060 or 212/966-6060. Fax 212/965-3838. www. mercerhotel.com. 75 units. $600–$700 double; $800–$900 studio; from $1,250 suite. AE, DC, DISC, MC, V. Parking $35 nearby. Subway: N, R to Prince St. **Amenities:** Restaurant; lounge; food and drink service in lobby; free access to nearby Crunch fitness center; 24-hr. concierge; secretarial services; 24-hr. room service; laundry service; dry cleaning; video, DVD, and CD libraries. *In room:* A/C, TV/DVD, Wi-Fi, dataport, minibar, safe, CD player, ceiling fan.

60 Thompson 𝒜   Some hotels have more comfortable rooms, others have better service, but few can match the all-around hipness of SoHo's 60 Thompson. A magnet for downtown celebs, 60 Thompson provides some excellent people-watching opportunities in the **Thom Bar** and the gorgeous rooftop bar, **A60.** The chic, soft-toned accommodations, designed by the same designer who did Giorgio Armani's Central Park West apartment, are spacious but spare, while bathrooms are enormous and luxuriously coated in Italian marble. The hotel has 11 suites including the magnificent Thompson Loft, a duplex penthouse suite with amazing views, four-poster bed, and a fireplace that is a favorite of visiting rock groups.

The Thompson is a smoker-friendly hotel, so ask for a nonsmoking room or bring your ionizer if the smell of stale cigarette smoke bothers you.

60 Thompson St. (btwn Broome and Spring sts.), New York, NY 10012. ℭ 877/431-0400 or 212/431-0400. Fax 212/431-0200. www.thompsonhotels.com. 100 units. From $639 double; from $750 suite. AE, DISC, MC, V. Valet parking $43. Subway: C, E to Spring St. **Amenities:** Restaurant; 2 bars; access to nearby health club; concierge; 24-hr. room service (limited menu 1–7am); nonsmoking rooms. *In room:* A/C, TV, high-speed Internet, minibar, hair dryer, iron, safe, DVD/CD player.

Soho Grand   Even after 12 years, the Soho Grand still retains its cool. The **Grand Bar,** one level above the street and just a few feet from the check-in desk, with its sofas and comfy chairs, was one of the first "lounge bars" in New York and has remained a hot spot. Guest rooms, however, have not quite kept up with the times and could use a makeover; bathrooms are a good size but spare.

Make sure you ask for a nonsmoking room; the hotel attracts a hip, European crowd that enjoys a nicotine fix and the cigarette stench can linger well after the guests have departed. But you choose the Soho Grand more for the name and all that it implies rather than for comfort and service.

310 W. Broadway (at Grand St.), New York, NY 10013. © **212/965-3000.** Fax 212/965-3244 (reservations) or 212/965-3200 (guests). www.sohogrand.com. 363 units. From $454 double; from $5,000 loft suites. Corporate, promotional, and Internet-only rates as low as $259; your travel agent may be able to do even better. AE, DC, DISC, MC, V. Parking $45. Subway: A, C, E, N, R, 1 to Canal St. Pets accepted. **Amenities:** Restaurant; bar and lounge; fitness center; concierge; 24-hr. room service; laundry service; dry cleaning; nonsmoking rooms; butler's pantry w/complimentary coffee, tea, and hot chocolate on every floor. In room: A/C, TV/VCR, dataport, minibar, hair dryer, safe, CD player, iPods.

MODERATE

Holiday Inn Downtown/SoHo

This Holiday Inn is on the northern edge of Chinatown, but its just-off-SoHo location is perfect for hipsters who want access to the chic scene without its high price tag. It's everything you'd expect from this good-value chain: clean, well outfitted, reliable, and comfortable. The guest rooms are standard but have everything you need. Doubles are a good-value bet for small families or sharing friends. You'll find Asian touches throughout the hotel—a nod to the brink-of-Chinatown location—and a well-respected Asian restaurant. Rack rates are high, but it's easy to snag a discount or score a room on the low end with advance booking.

138 Lafayette St. (at Howard St., 1 block north of Canal St.), New York, NY 10013. © **800/HOLIDAY** or 212/966-8898. Fax 212/966-3933. www.hidowntown-nyc.com. 227 units. From $169 double; from $599 executive suite. Extra person $20. Children 18 and under stay free in parent's room. Check for AAA, AARP, government, corporate, and other discounts. AE, DC, DISC, MC, V. Parking $44. Subway: 6, J, M, N, R, Q, W to Canal St. **Amenities:** Restaurant; bar; access to nearby health club; concierge; fax and copy service; room service (6:30am–11pm); laundry service; dry cleaning. In room: A/C, TV w/pay movies, fax (in most junior suites), dataport, coffeemaker, hair dryer, iron, CD player.

4 Greenwich Village, the East Village & the Meat-Packing District

To locate the hotels in this section, see the map on p. 103.

EXPENSIVE

The Bowery Hotel ⨁⨁

Despite the history associated with its name and location, the Bowery Hotel, opened in 2007, is about as far from as a flophouse as you could imagine. Standing alone in the heart of NoHo, the Bowery Hotel, though new, has that burnished, dark wood look inside, most evident in the expansive lobby with a fireplace, comfy velvet draperies and furniture, vintage paneling, Moroccan tiles, and an adjoining outdoor area complete with plush lounge chairs. The rooms, and there are no two the same, are very large and airy by New York standards with high ceilings, ceiling fans, many with huge terraces and all with spectacular views. What the Gansevoort Hotel did for the Meat-Packing District, the Bowery Hotel is doing for the Bowery—making a once desolate area a hip destination.

335 Bowery (at 3rd St.), New York, N.Y. 10003. © **212/505-9100.** Fax 212/505-9700. www.theboweryhotel.com. 135 units. From $525 doubles; from $750 suites. AE, DISC, MC, V. Parking $31 self parking, $45 valet. **Amenities:** Restaurant; bar; concierge; 24-hour room service; laundry and dry cleaning service. In room: A/C, HDTV/DVD, Wi-Fi, minibar, hair dryer, iron, safe, iPod stereo and docking system.

Hotel Gansevoort ⨁⨁

This sleek, 14-floor zinc-colored tower is the symbolic anchor of the white hot Meat Packing district. Despite its potentially excessive trendiness, the Gansevoort offers excellent, personable service. As well, rooms are a good size with comfortable furnishings in soft tones and high-tech amenities such as plasma televisions and wireless Internet. Suites have a living room and separate bedroom and some have small balconies and bay windows. Corner suites offer adjoining guest rooms for families or larger parties. The generous-size bathrooms are done up in

Tips Plenty of Room at the Inn

When you think of accommodations in New York, you usually think big—tall, sturdy, monoliths with hundreds of rooms. You don't think of quaint antiques-laden guesthouses or inns where a home-cooked breakfast is served. But New York is a diverse city and that diversity can be found in its accommodations, too. So if you want an alternative to the quintessential huge New York hotel and would prefer a taste of urban hominess where you might actually meet your innkeeper, here are a few options.

On the steep end of the economic scale, but worth the price if authentic 19th-century Victorian romance is what you are seeking, is the fabulous **Inn at Irving Place** ♠♠. Housed in a 170-year-old townhouse, rates range from $445 to $645 and the rooms are named after late-19th- or early-20th-century New Yorkers, many inspired by the works of Edith Wharton and Henry James. Complimentary breakfast is served in Lady Mendl's parlor, where, if the weather is nippy, you'll find a comforting fire roaring. See p. 114 for a detailed review.

Breakfast prepared by culinary students of the New School is one of the highlights of the **Inn on 23rd Street** ♠♠♠. Each of the inn's 14 rooms, which range from $219 to $359, are distinctly decorated by the personable owners, Annette and Barry Fisherman, with items they've collected from their travels over the years. See p. 110 for a detailed review.

The first home of the Gay Men's Health Crisis, an 1850 brownstone in the heart of Chelsea, is now the charming **Colonial House Inn,** 318 W. 22nd St., between Eighth and Ninth avenues (② **800/689-3779** or 212/243-9669; www.colonialhouseinn.com). This 20-room four-story walk-up caters to a largely gay and lesbian clientele, but everybody is welcome, and straight couples are a common sight. Some rooms have shared bathrooms; deluxe rooms have private bathrooms and some have working fireplaces. There's a roof deck with a clothing-optional area. Breakfast is included in the rates, which range from $110 to $130 for a shared bathroom or $135 to $160 for a deluxe room.

On the increasingly popular yet still residential Upper West Side is the aptly named **Country Inn the City** ♠, 270 W. 77th St., between Broadway

---

ceramic, stainless steel, and marble and are impeccably appointed. In all the guest rooms and throughout the hotel, original art by New York artists is on display. The **G Spa,** a 5,000-square-foot spa and fitness center and the indoor/outdoor O Bar are destinations unto themselves.

By the time you read this, the Meat-Packing District might be "over," but you can be sure the Hotel Gansevoort is here to stay.

18 Ninth Ave. (at 13th St.), New York, NY 10014. ② **877/426-7386** or 212/206-6700. Fax 212/255-5858. www.hotelgansevoort.com. 187 units. From $435 double; from $675 suite. Parking $40. Subway: A, C, E to 14th St. Pet-friendly floors. **Amenities:** Restaurant; rooftop bar and lounge; indoor/outdoor pool; spa and fitness center; concierge; business center; 24-hr. room service; laundry service; dry cleaning; rooftop garden. *In room:* A/C, TV, Wi-Fi, high-speed Internet, dataport, minibar, hair dryer, iron, safe, 2-line telephones, voice mail.

and West End Avenue (© 212/580-4183; www.countryinnthecity.com). This 1891 town house has only four rooms, but all are spacious, quaintly deco-rated, and equipped with full kitchens. Rates range from $210 to $350 and include breakfast items stocked in your refrigerator. But you're on your own in many respects; there is no resident innkeeper and a maid services your room only every few days. Still, if you are the independent sort, the inn's charm makes it an excellent choice.

If you want the genuine New York brownstone experience, go to Harlem. It's anything but a flophouse, but that's what they call **Harlem Flophouse,** 242 W. 123rd St., between Adam Clayton Powell and Frederick Douglass boulevards (© 212/662-0678; www.harlemflophouse.com). Owner Renee Calvo has restored the historic row house to Harlem Renaissance splendor, when the "flophouse" was frequented by top musicians and artists of that era. If you visit in the summer, you just might get invited to one of Calvo's impromptu barbecues. Rates ($100–$175) include free Wi-Fi; for $15 extra you get a full breakfast.

Like Harlem, Brooklyn boasts a number of historic districts with restored brownstones, some of which have been converted to inns. One of the most interesting is **Akwaaba Mansion,** 347 MacDonough St. (© 866/INN-DULJ 718/455-5958; www.akwaaba.com), a restored 1860s Italianate villa in Bed-ford-Stuyvesant, outfitted with Afrocentric elegance. Four suites are avail-able in the 18-room home, each with private bathroom with either a claw-foot or a Jacuzzi tub ($160–$165 double)—including a hearty, South-ern-style breakfast.

The historic neighborhood of Park Slope is the heart of brownstone Brooklyn and home to **Bed & Breakfast on the Park,** 113 Prospect Park West (© 718/499-6115; www.bbnyc.com). In an 1895 Victorian town house across the street from Prospect Park, this inn has two beautifully outfitted units (from $300). A sumptuous breakfast is served in the formal dining room. Six more rooms with private bathrooms are available for guests who are will-ing to splurge.

INEXPENSIVE

Larchmont Hotel *★★ Value*   If you're willing to share a bathroom, it's hard to do better for the money at this wonderful European-style hotel. Each bright guest room is tastefully done in rattan and outfitted with a writing desk, a minilibrary of books, an alarm clock, a wash basin, and a few extras that you normally have to pay a lot more for, such as cotton bathrobes, slippers, and ceiling fans. Every floor has two shared bathrooms (with hair dryers) and a small, simple kitchen. The management is con-stantly renovating, so everything feels clean and fresh. What's more, those looking for a hip downtown base couldn't be better situated, because some of the city's best shop-ping, dining, and sightseeing—plus your choice of subway lines—are just a walk away.

This hotel has devoted followers who recommend it to all their friends, so book *well* in advance (the management suggests 6–7 weeks' lead time).

27 W. 11th St. (btwn Fifth and Sixth aves.), New York, NY 10011. © 212/989-9333. Fax 212/989-9496. www.larchmonthotel.com. 62 units, all with shared bathroom. $80–$99 single; $109–$120 double. Rates include continental breakfast. Children under 13 stay free in parent's room. AE, MC, V. Parking $25 nearby. Subway: A, B, C, D, E, F, V to W. 4th St. (use 8th St. exit); F to 14th St. **Amenities:** Tour desk; room service (10am–6pm); common kitchenette. *In room:* A/C, TV, hair dryer, safe, ceiling fan.

Washington Square Hotel   Popular with a young international crowd, this affordable hotel sits behind a pretty facade facing Washington Square Park (historically Henry James territory, now the midst of New York University) in the heart of Greenwich Village. The lobby is a pleasant place for tea in the afternoon and cocktails in the evening. The rooms are tiny but pleasant. Each comes with a firm bed, a private bathroom, and a small closet with a pint-size safe. It's worth paying a few extra dollars for a south-facing room on a high floor, since the others can be a bit dark. Bathrooms were also renovated, with the addition of granite counters. On-site is a good restaurant and lounge, **North Square Lounge,** which even draws locals with its stylish design, well-priced cocktails and international bistro fare, and Sunday jazz brunch.

103 Waverly Place (btwn Fifth and Sixth aves.), New York, NY 10011. © 800/222-0418 or 212/777-9515. Fax 212/979-8373. www.wshotel.com. 160 units. $156–$175 single; $185–$210 double; $225–$260 quad. Rates include continental breakfast. Inquire about special rates and jazz packages. AE, MC, V. Parking $30 nearby. Subway: A, B, C, D, E, F, V to W. 4th St. (use 3rd St. exit). **Amenities:** Restaurant and lounge; exercise room; laundry service; dry cleaning. *In room:* A/C, TV, high-speed Internet, dataport, hair dryer, iron, safe.

5 Chelsea

To locate the hotels in this section, see the map on p. 112.

MODERATE

Inn on 23rd Street ☆☆☆ *(Finds)*   Behind an unassuming entrance in the middle of bustling 23rd Street is one of New York's true lodging treasures: a real urban bed-and-breakfast with as personal a touch as you will find anywhere. All 14 guest rooms are spacious. Each has a king or queen bed outfitted with a supremely comfy pillow-top mattress and top-quality linens, satellite TV, a large private bathroom with thick Turkish towels, and a roomy closet. Rooms have themes based on how they are designed; there's the Rosewood Room, with '60s built-ins; the elegantly Asian Bamboo Room; and Ken's Cabin, a large, lodgelike room with cushy, well-worn leather furnishings and wonderful Americana relics. The inn features a lovely library where the complimentary breakfast is served, where there is also an honor bar to make yourself a drink for cheaper than you would pay in any hotel in the city, and where wine and cheese are served on Friday and Saturday. The only drawback is that the inn is so comfortable and accommodating, you might be tempted to lounge around all day instead of getting out there and seeing the town.

131 W. 23rd St. (btwn Sixth and Seventh aves.), New York, NY 10011. © 877/387-2323 or 212/463-0330. Fax 212/463-0302. www.innon23rd.com. 14 units. $219–$259 double; $359 suite. Rates include continental breakfast. Extra person $25. Children under 12 stay free in parent's room. AE, DC, DISC, MC, V. Parking $20 nearby. Subway: F, 1 to 23rd St. **Amenities:** Fax and copy service; cozy library w/stereo and VCR. *In room:* A/C, TV, high-speed Internet, dataport, hair dryer, iron.

INEXPENSIVE

Also consider the intimate **Colonial House Inn** (© 800/689-3779 or 212/243-9669). For more information, see the sidebar "Plenty of Room at the Inn," above.

Chelsea Lodge ★★ (Value   In a lovely brownstone on a landmark block in the heart of Chelsea, this small hotel is charming and a terrific value. Impeccable renovations have restored original woodwork to mint condition. The beds are the finest and best outfitted I've seen in this price category. The only place with a similar grown-up sensibility for the same money is Greenwich Village's **Larchmont Hotel** (p. 109), but there, all bathroom facilities are shared; at Chelsea Lodge, each room has its own sink and in-room shower stall, so you only have to share a cute toilet room with your neighbors. The rooms are petite, the open closets are small, and beds are full-size (queens wouldn't cut it). Considering the stylishness, the amenities, and the neighborhood, you'd be hard-pressed to do better for the money. It's best for couples rather than shares. *Tip:* Try to book no. 2A, which is bigger than most, or one of the first-floor rooms, whose high ceilings make them feel more spacious.

318 W. 20th St. (btwn Eighth and Ninth aves.), New York, NY 10011. ⓒ **800/373-1116** or 212/243-4499. Fax 212/243-7852. www.chelsealodge.com. 22 units, all with semiprivate bathroom. $119 single; $129 double. AE, DC, DISC, MC, V. Parking about $27 nearby. Subway: 1 to 18th St.; C, E to 23rd St. *In room:* A/C, TV, Wi-Fi, ceiling fan.

6 Union Square, the Flatiron District & Gramercy Park

To find the hotels described in this section, see p. 112.

VERY EXPENSIVE

Gramercy Park Hotel ★★★   Shuttered for 2 years, this 1925-built legend bordering charming Gramercy Park has been redone stunningly by famed hotelier Ian Schrager. Start with the lobby, with its eclectic mix of art: Julian Schnabel-designed lamps, two 10-foot Italian fireplaces, red velvet curtains, Moroccan tiles, bronze tables, and a magnificent Venetian glass chandelier. What once was a 500-plus room hotel now features only 185 rooms; so, where the former version had tiny rooms, now there is space. More than half of the rooms are suites, some with views overlooking Gramercy Park, and all have mahogany English drinking cabinets where the minibar and DVD player are hidden, some variation of the overstuffed lounge chair, and a portrait of Schnabel's friend, the late Andy Warhol. Beds are velvet-upholstered, tables feature leather tops, and photos by world famous photo-journalists adorn the walls. Bathrooms are large and feature wood-paneled walls. If you choose to leave your room, the hotel's magnificent **Rose Bar** is where you should venture first (p. 376).

2 Lexington Ave (at 21st St), New York, N.Y. 10010. ⓒ **212/920-3300.** Fax 212/673-5890. www.gramercyparkhotel. com. 185 units. From $595 double; from $700 suite. AE, DC, DISC, MC, V. Parking $55. Subway: 6 to 23rd St. **Amenities:** Restaurant; 2 bars, fitness center and spa, 24-hour room service, laundry service; dry cleaning; 24-hour concierge. *In room:* A/C, TV/DVD, Wi-Fi, high-speed Internet, dataport, minibar, hair dryer, safe, CD player, iPod and docking station.

EXPENSIVE

Carlton Hotel on Madison Avenue ★★   This 1904 Beaux Arts hotel was getting worn around the edges when it was rescued by architect David Rockwell and refurbished magnificently a few years ago. The highlight of that $60-million renovation is the grand, sweeping lobby complete with a marble curving staircase and a cathedral-like high ceiling. While the **Roger** (p. 132) a few blocks up, also recently renovated, went for a cool, sleek, modern-tropical look, the Hotel Carlton has tried to recapture the majestic glory of the past blended with New Age nods such as contemporary furnishings in the lobby along with a bubbling, two-story waterfall. Rooms are a generous size and retain that Beaux Arts motif with the addition of modern amenities such

Midtown, Chelsea & Gramercy Park Accommodations

E. 64th St.
E. 63rd St.
E. 62nd St.
E. 61st St.
Roosevelt Island Tram

UPPER EAST SIDE

E. 60th St.
Queensboro Bridge

E. 59th St.
E. 58th St.
E. 57th St.
E. 56th St.
E. 55th St.
E. 54th St.

MIDTOWN EAST

E. 53rd St.
E. 52nd St.
E. 51st St.
E. 50th St.
E. 49th St.
E. 48th St
E. 47th St.
E. 46th St.
E. 45th St.

United Nations

E. 44th St.
E. 43rd St.
E. 42nd St.

Rockefeller Center

Grand Central Terminal

Bryant Park
New York Public Library

E. 41st St.
E. 40th St.
E. 39th St.
E. 38th St.

MURRAY HILL

Queens-Midtown Tunnel

E 37th St. Tunnel Exit
E 36th St.
E. 35th St.
E. 34th St.

Tunnel Entrance

Empire State Bldg.

W 32nd St.
E. 33rd St.
E. 32nd St.
E. 31st St.
E. 30th St.
E. 29th St.
E. 28th St.
E. 27th St.
E. 26th St.
E. 25th St.
E. 24th St.
E. 23rd St.
E. 22nd St.
E. 21st St.
E. 20th St.
E. 19th St.
E. 18th St.
E. 17th St.
E. 16th St.
E. 15th St.
E. 14th St.

Madison Square Park

Peter Cooper Village

Stuyvesant Town

FLATIRON DISTRICT

GRAMERCY PARK

Gramercy Park

Union Square

Novotel New York **4**
The Peninsula-New York **54**
The Plaza **62**
The Regency **64**
Red Roof Inn **30**
Ritz-Carlton New York, Central Park **61**
Rockefeller Center Hotel **52**
The Roger **29**
The Royalton **41**
70 Park Avenue **35**
The Sherry Netherland **63**
Skyline Hotel **8**
Sofitel New York **42**
St. Regis **55**
Thirty Thirty **27**
Travel Inn 15
Trump International Hotel & Tower **1**
W Times Square **10**
W Union Square **20**
Waldorf=Astoria and the Waldorf Towers **48**
The Westin New York at Times Square **14**
Washington Jefferson Hotel **7**

| 0 | 1/4 mi |
| 0 | 0.25 km |

Upper Manhattan

Uptown

Midtown

Downtown

as wireless Internet and iPod clock radios. The marble bathrooms offer plenty of counter space; some rooms have bathtubs while others just have showers.

88 Madison Ave. (btwn 28th and 29th sts.), New York, NY 10016. © **800/601-8500** or 212/532-4100. Fax 212/889-8683. www.carltonhotelny.com. 316 units. $329 standard; from $450 suite. AE, DC, DISC, MC, V. Valet parking $40. Subway: 6 to 28th St./Lexington Ave. **Amenities:** Restaurant; concierge; business center; limited room service; laundry service; dry cleaning. *In room:* A/C, TV, Wi-Fi, iron/ironing board, safe, iPod clock radio.

Hotel Giraffe ⭐⭐   In the increasingly fashionable Madison Park area, this hotel is a real charmer with a calm, intimate feel. Guest rooms are stylish, evoking an urban European character, with high ceilings, velveteen upholstered chairs, and black-and-white photographs from the 1920s and 1930s. All the rooms are good size, with high ceilings, while deluxe rooms and suites feature French doors that lead to small balconies with large windows and remote-controlled blackout shades. Bathrooms are spacious with plenty of marble counter space and glass-paneled doors, and all rooms have marble-topped desks. But what really separates this hotel from so many others are its services: A continental breakfast is included in the rate and served in the hotel's lobby, where coffee, cookies, and tea are available all afternoon, and wine, cheese, and piano music are offered each evening. There is also a lovely rooftop garden.

365 Park Ave. South (at 26th St.), New York, NY 10016. © **877/296-0009** or 212/685-7700. Fax 212/685-7771. www.hotelgiraffe.com. 73 units. $409–$559 from $650 1- or 2-bedroom suite; from $2,500 penthouse suite. Rates include continental breakfast and evening wine and cheese accompanied by piano music. Check website or ask about reduced rates (as low as $299 at press time). AE, DC, MC, V. Parking $28. Subway: 6 to 28th St. **Amenities:** Restaurant; 2 bars; complimentary access to nearby gym; concierge; business services; limited room service; laundry service; dry cleaning; rooftop garden; video and CD libraries. *In room:* A/C, TV/VCR, Wi-Fi, dataport, minibar, hair dryer, iron, safe, CD player.

Inn at Irving Place ⭐⭐   This 170-year-old town house offers antique charm more easily found in the Berkshires than in the heart of what used to be Silicon Alley. All rooms are spacious, with period antique furniture and art, nonworking fireplaces, and big bathrooms with pedestal sinks and brass fixtures, while the junior suites feature small but luxurious sitting areas. The rooms are named for famous 19th-century New Yorkers such as Edith Wharton, O. Henry, and Washington Irving. The Madame Olenska (bonus points if you know who she was) junior suite features a king bed and a window nook overlooking Irving Place where you can curl up with a glass of sherry or a cup of tea. Breakfast in bed, tea served in your room, or in-room massages can all be easily arranged by the inn's helpful staff.

56 Irving Place (btwn 17th and 18th sts.), New York, NY 10003. © **800/685-1447** or 212/533-4600. Fax 212/533-4611. www.innatirving.com. 12 units. From $415 superior suite; from $585 junior suite. Extra person $25. Rates include continental breakfast. 2-night minimum on weekends. AE, DC, MC, V. Parking $25–$30 nearby. Subway: N, R, 4, 5, 6 to 14th St./Union Sq. No children under 12. **Amenities:** 2 restaurants; lounge; access to nearby health club; concierge; 24-hr. room service; in-room massage; laundry service; dry cleaning; video and CD libraries. *In room:* A/C, TV/VCR, dataport, minibar, hair dryer, CD player, laptops and fax machines on request.

W Union Square ⭐   Überarchitect David Rockwell transformed the magnificent 1911 Guardian Life building overlooking leafy Union Square into a new gem, successfully fusing original Beaux Arts detailing with bold, clean-lined modernism and a relaxing, grown-up air. Rooms boast distinctive touches, such as luminous mother-of-pearl counters in the bathrooms. Star chef Todd English's Mediterranean-accented **Olives** restaurant gets raves, and nightclub impresario Rande Gerber's dark and sultry **Underbar** is just downstairs.

201 Park Ave. South (at 17th St.), New York, NY 10003. ☎ **212/253-9119.** Fax 212/253-9229. www.starwood.com. $400–$550 double. Check website for specials. AE, DC, DISC, MC, V. Subway: N, R, W, 4, 5, 6 to Union Sq. **Amenities:** Restaurant; bar; fitness center; concierge; 24-hr. room service; laundry service; valet services; video library. *In room:* A/C, TV/DVD, high-speed Internet, dataport, fridge.

INEXPENSIVE

Gershwin Hotel ⚑ *Kids*   This creative-minded, Warholesque hotel caters to up-and-coming artistic types—and well-established names with an eye for good value—with its bold modern art collection and wild style. The lobby was recently renovated, and along with a new bar, **Gallery at the Gershwin,** much of the original art remains. The standard rooms are clean and bright, with Picasso-style wall murals and Philippe Starck–ish takes on motel furnishings. Superior rooms are best, as they're newly renovated, and well worth the extra $10; all have a queen bed, two twins, or two doubles, plus a newish private bathroom with cute, colorful tile. If you're bringing the brood, two-room suites, or Family Rooms, are a good option. For the *very* low budget traveler, the Gershwin also offers hostel-style accommodations at $33 a night in multibed rooms.

The hotel is more service-oriented than you usually see at this price level, and the staff is professional. At press time, a restaurant was in the works for late in 2008.

7 E. 27th St. (btwn Fifth and Madison aves.), New York, NY 10016. ☎ **212/545-8000.** Fax 212/684-5546. www.gershwinhotel.com. 150 units. $109–$285 double; $239–$385 family room. Extra person $20. Check website for discounts or other value-added packages. For hostel rooms, use this website: www.gershwinhostel.com. AE, MC, V. Parking $25 3 blocks away. Subway: N, R, 6 to 28th St. **Amenities:** Bar; tour desk; babysitting; laundry service; dry cleaning; Internet access. *In room:* A/C, TV, Wi-Fi, dataport, hair dryer, iron.

7 Times Square & Midtown West

To find the hotels described in this section, see p. 112.

VERY EXPENSIVE

Ritz-Carlton New York, Central Park ⚑⚑⚑ *Kids*   There's a lot to like about this hotel—from its location overlooking Central Park to the impeccable and personable service—but what I like best is that this luxury hotel manages to maintain a homey elegance and does not intimidate you with an overabundance of style. Rooms are spacious and decorated in English-country style. Suites are larger than most New York apartments. Rooms facing Central Park come with telescopes, and all have flatscreen TVs with DVD players; the hotel even has a library of Academy Award–winning films for you to borrow. The marble bathrooms are also oversize and feature a choice of bathrobes. For families who can afford the steep prices, the hotel is extremely kid-friendly. Suites have sofa beds, and cribs and rollaway beds can be brought in. Children are given in-room cookies and milk. While the kids are entertained, the older folks can be pampered with facials or massages at the Switzerland-based La Prairie spa or dine at the hotel's restaurant, **BLT Market** (p. 179).

50 Central Park South (at Sixth Ave.), New York, NY 10019. ☎ **212/308-9100.** Fax 212/207-8831. www.ritzcarlton.com. 259 units. $650–$1,295 double; from $995 suite. Package and weekend rates available. AE, DC, DISC, MC, V. Parking $50. Subway: N, R, W to 5th Ave and F to 57th St. Pets under 60 lbs. accepted. **Amenities:** Restaurant; bar; lobby lounge for tea and cocktails; fitness center; La Prairie spa and facial center; concierge; complimentary Bentley limousine service; business center; 24-hr. room service; babysitting; overnight laundry; dry cleaning; technology butler and bath butler services. *In room:* A/C, TV/DVD, high-speed Internet, dataport, minibar, hair dryer, iron, safe, telescopes in rooms w/park view.

EXPENSIVE

Affinia Manhattan ☆ You'll never forget you are in New York when you stay at the Affinia Manhattan. From the large lobby—sort of a mini-version of the Waldorf=Astoria's, where a Grand Central Station–like information booth in its center features a series of televisions with video images of New York landmarks. Furthering the New York theme, "New York Experience" kits are available, free of charge. Though the New York theme is fun, all you really need to do is look out your window, where you just might see the Empire State Building, and you'll know very well what city you are in. All rooms are suites with full kitchens. The room decor here is old-school—no edgy furniture or amenities, but there is plenty of space. Bathrooms are small by comparison but include New York details such as black-and-white tiled floors.

371 Seventh Ave. (at 31st St.), New York, NY 10001. ☎ 212/563-1800. Fax 212/643-8028. www.affinia.com. 526 units (all suites). Rates from $339. Check website for specials and Internet rates, which were as low as $199 at press time. AE, DC, MC, V. Parking $40. Subway: 1, 2, 3 to 34th St. **Amenities:** Restaurant; bar; fitness center; concierge; business center; room service; laundry service; dry cleaning. *In room:* A/C, TV, high-speed Internet, kitchen, hair dryer, iron/ironing board, safe, 2-line cordless phone.

Aka Central Park ☆ In 2007, Aka emerged in New York with four extended-stay residences with hotel-like amenities in locations such as Times Square, Sutton Place, the United Nations-area and Central Park. But, because the Aka properties operate like a combination apartment/hotel; your stay can be as brief as just 1 night. The rooms, all of them spacious studios to two bedrooms, feature full modern kitchens, marble bathrooms, two televisions, and services such as a concierge, fitness center, wireless Internet, and a complimentary weekday breakfast. I found the Central Park location, 1 block from Central Park South, the homiest of the group. It's a very attractive and more calming alternative to the nearby hotel hysteria.

42 W. 58th St. (btwn 5th–6th Aves.) New York, NY, 10019. ☎ 212/753-3500. Fax 646/744-3120; www.stayaka.com. 134 units. Rates from $395. AE, DC, MC, V. Parking $50 per day. Subway: N, R, Q, W to 57th St. **Amenities:** Complimentary breakfast (weekdays), health club and spa services, concierge, business center, room service, laundry service, dry cleaning. *In room:* A/C, 2 TVs, Wi-Fi, full kitchen, hair dryer/ironing board, safe, 2-line cordless phone w/complimentary local telephone services, CD/DVD player.

The Algonquin ☆☆ The atmosphere in this 1902 landmark building is so steeped in writers' lore that you'll feel guilty turning on the television instead of reading the latest issue of the *New Yorker* that's provided in the guest rooms. Rooms can be extremely cramped, but they are equipped with possibly the most comfortable, inviting beds in the city as well as 21st-century technology such as high-speed Internet and flatscreen TVs. If you have a tendency toward claustrophobia, head to the plush lobby, where you can sit in cushy chairs, sip exquisite (and expensive) cocktails, have a snack, or just read or play on your laptop (the lobby is Wi-Fi-equipped). For a special splurge, stay in one of the roomy one-bedroom suites, where all that is missing to get you going on that novel you've been toying with is a manual Smith Corona typewriter.

Meals are served in the recently renovated and celebrated **Round Table Room,** while the fabulous **Oak Room** (p. 365) is one of the city's top cabaret rooms, featuring such esteemed talents as Andrea Marcovicci and Julie Wilson.

59 W. 44th St. (btwn Fifth and Sixth aves.), New York, NY 10036. ☎ 888/304-2047 or 212/840-6800. Fax 212/944-1419. www.algonquinhotel.com. 174 units. $399–$699 double; from $349 suite. Check website or inquire about discounted rates or special package deals. AE, DC, DISC, MC, V. Parking $28 across the street. Subway: B, D, F, V to 42nd St. **Amenities:** 2 restaurants; lounge; bar; exercise room; concierge; limited room service; laundry service; dry cleaning. *In room:* A/C, TV w/pay movies, high-speed Internet, dataport, hair dryer, iron, safe.

The Blakely New York ★★ *(Finds)* The Blakely has a clubby yet modern feel to it and is an excellent small-Midtown-hotel option. The rooms are all generously sized: None are smaller than 300 square feet and, if it matters to you, some have views of the City Center dome across the street. The dark cherry wood furniture helps perpetuate the clubhouse aura that is contrasted, happily, by modern amenities such as flatscreen TVs and wireless Internet in all the rooms. Marble bathrooms are well sized and appointed; bathroom suites have separate tubs and showers. The lobby, though redesigned after the renovation, remains small and can get hectic at times, but the staff is helpful and efficient. Off the lobby is the Italian restaurant **Abboccato** (p. 180.)

136 W. 55th St. (btwn Sixth and Seventh aves.), New York, NY 10019. ✆ 212/245-1800. Fax 212/582-8332. www. blakelynewyork.com. 120 units. $260–$365 double; $585–$695 suite. Check the website for packages and seasonal specials. AE, DISC, MC, V. Parking $33. Subway: N, R to 57th St. **Amenities:** Restaurant; complimentary access to nearby health club; concierge; limited room service. *In room:* A/C, TV, Wi-Fi, minibar, fridge, coffeemaker, iron/ironing board, safe, CD/DVD player, microwave.

Doubletree Guest Suites Times Square ★ *(Kids)* For many, the location of this 43-story Doubletree, in the heart of darkness known as Times Square, where the streets are constantly gridlocked, the neon burns holes into your eye sockets, and the noise level is ear-splitting, might offer a more Vegaslike experience than a true New York one. But at times we all must make sacrifices for our children, and this Doubletree, location and all, is perfect for the kids. From the fresh-baked chocolate-chip cookies served upon arrival, the spacious, affordable suites big enough for two 5-year-olds to play hide-and-seek (as mine did), and the all-day children's room-service menu to the proximity to the gargantuan Toys "R" Us, the TKTS booth, and other kid-friendly Times Square offerings, this Doubletree is hard to beat for families. Bathrooms have two entrances so the kids don't have to traipse through the parent's rooms.

1568 Broadway (at 47th St. & Seventh Ave.), New York, NY 10036. ✆ 800/222-TREE or 212/719-1600. Fax 212/921-5212. www.doubletree.com. 460 units. From $349 suite. Extra person $20. Children under 18 stay free in parent's suite. Ask about senior, corporate, and AAA discounts and special promotions. AE, DC, DISC, MC, V. Parking $35. Subway: N, R to 49th St. **Amenities:** Restaurant; lounge; fitness center; concierge; limited room service; babysitting; laundry service; dry cleaning. *In room:* A/C, 2 TVs w/pay movies and video games, high-speed Internet, dataport, minibar, fridge, wet bar w/coffeemaker, hair dryer, iron, safe, microwave.

Flatotel ★★ *(Kids)* *(Finds)* In the heart of midtown Manhattan and surrounded by Sheratons and other brand name hotels, the Flatotel, (Flat, like an apartment in London combined with hotel amenities) offers something those brands do not: space. All the hotel's sleek, apartmentlike rooms, especially the suites, are large by New York standards and all feature refrigerators and microwaves, while suites have kitchenettes or full kitchens, two flatscreen TVs, and generous desks. The marble bathrooms are spacious and well-equipped. The hotel features 60 one- to three-bedroom family suites with dining areas and full kitchens in each. In some suites on higher floors—the hotel is 47 stories—you have spectacular, river-to-river views. Though the hotel has the appearance of a corporate refuge, with its dark marble and metal tones, its services are personable and more like a boutique than the Midtown monolith it appears to be.

132 West 52nd St (btwn Sixth and Seventh aves.), New York, NY 10019. ✆ 800/FLATOTEL or 212/887-9400. Fax 212/887-9795. www.flatotel.com. 288 units. From $399 doubles; from $549 suites. AE, DC, DISC, MC, V. Parking $30 self parking, $47 valet. Subway: B,D,E to Seventh Ave. **Amenities:** Restaurant; bar; fitness center; business center; concierge; room service; dry cleaning. *In room:* A/C, TV, high-speed Internet, dataport, fridge, microwave, coffee/tea maker, iron/ironing board, hair dryer, safe, CD player.

Hotel Mela   New in 2007, Hotel Mela adds to the hotel-heavy presence on West 44th Street. Advertised as a "luxury boutique" property—the hotel was converted from an office building—and that sleek, contemporary spirit, despite a few antique touches in design, prevails. The hotel has a corporate feel, but with a central location; close to Times Square, Rockefeller Center, Bryant Park and the rest of Midtown makes it an ideal spot for the leisure traveler as well. Rooms, though a bit on the small side, are well equipped with comfortable beds, kings or queens, Egyptian combed cotton linen sheets, 310-count duvet covers, LCD TVs, and free wireless Internet. The bathrooms make the most of space with plenty of shelf room. Service is personable making the Hotel Mela a good, solid addition to those who seek something a bit more intimate in hectic Times Square.

120 W. 44th St. (btwn Broadway and Sixth Ave.), New York, NY, 10036. ℭ **877/452-6352.** Fax 212/704-9680. www.hotelmela.com. 230 units. Doubles from $439 (check the Internet for specials as low as $259 at press time). AE, DC, DISC, MC, V. Parking $45. Subway: B, D, F, V to 42nd St. **Amenities:** Restaurant; bar; fitness center; concierge; 24-hour room service; same day dry cleaning and laundry. *In room:* A/C, TV, Wi-Fi, minibar, hair dryer, safe, CD player.

Jumeirah Essex House 🦋🦋🦋   In 2006, the Dubai-based hotel group Jumeirah took over managing the landmark 76-year old hotel overlooking Central Park, which had become worn around the edges. After a $90-million renovation, the hotel was unveiled, and the results are sparkling. The lobby has been spruced up but retains the Art Deco look with its black-and-white marble floor, white banquettes where afternoon tea is now served, and historic photos of New York lining the corridors. The rooms have been updated with neat wall-to-wall wooden cabinetry, leather-framed mirrors, and window blinds that mirror the leaf patterns you might see across the street in the park. State-of-the art technology, such as "stumble lights" underneath nightstands so your path to a late-night bathroom engagement won't be totally in the dark, has been added as part of the renovations. You won't find tiny rooms here, nor should you; suites are magnificent, especially those overlooking the park.

160 Central Park South, (btwn Sixth and Seventh aves.), New York, NY, 10019. ℭ **888/645-5697** or 212/247-0300. Fax 212/315-1839. www.jumeirahessexhouse.com. 515 units. From $709 doubles; from $959 suites, Valet parking $55. AE, DC, DISC, MC, V. Subway: N, R, W, Q to 57th St. **Amenities:** Restaurant; bar; lobby lounge; afternoon tea; fitness center; spa; concierge; room service; business center; dry cleaning. *In room:* A/C, TV, Wi-Fi, minibar, hair dryer, iron, safe, speaker phones.

Le Parker Meridien 🦋🦋 *Kids*   Not many hotels in New York can rival the attributes of this hotel: Its location on 57th Street, not too far from Times Square and a close walk from Central Park and Fifth Avenue shopping, is practically perfect; the 17,000-square-foot fitness center, called Gravity, features basketball and racquetball courts, a spa, and a rooftop pool; three excellent restaurants, including **Norma's** (p. 185), for breakfast, and the aptly-named **Burger Joint,** rated by many as the best burger in the city; a gorgeous, bustling lobby that also serves as a public space; and elevators with televisions that show *Tom and Jerry* and Charlie Chaplin shorts that are a wonder for the kids. The spacious hotel rooms, though a bit on the IKEA side, have a fun feel to them, with hidden drawers and swirling television platforms, inventively exploiting an economical use of space. Rooms have wood platform beds with feather beds, built-ins that include large work desks, stylish Aeron chairs, free high-speed Internet, and 32-inch flatscreen TVs with VCR, CD, and DVD players. The slate-and-limestone bathrooms are large but unfortunately come with shower only.

118 W. 57th St. (btwn Sixth and Seventh aves.), New York, NY 10019. ℭ **800/543-4300** or 212/245-5000. Fax 212/307-1776. www.parkermeridien.com. 731 units. $600–$800 double; from $780 suite. Extra person $30. Excellent

packages and weekend rates often available (as low as $225 at press time). AE, DC, DISC, MC, V. Parking $45. Subway: F, N, Q, R to 57th St. Pets accepted. **Amenities:** 3 restaurants; rooftop pool; fantastic fitness center and spa; concierge (2 w/Clefs d'Or distinction); weekday morning courtesy car to Wall St.; full-service business center; 24-hr. room service; laundry service; dry cleaning. *In room:* A/C, 32-in. TV w/DVD/CD player, high-speed Internet, dataport, minibar, hair dryer, iron, safe, nightly complimentary shoeshine.

The London NYC *✦*   Its curiously un–New York name aside, the London, formerly the RHIGA Royal Hotel, after a major renovation, is the quintessential New York Midtown hotel. The London NYC features a sleek, airy look. The lobby is high-ceilinged and bright with white marble attended by black-coated, derby-wearing porters. Off the lobby is the blue-gray leather-wrapped **London Bar,** while through a set of closed doors is the hotel's restaurant, **Gordon Ramsay at The London,** helmed by famed chef, Gordon Ramsay. The rooms are spacious, with big windows providing spectacular views of the neighborhood—the hotel, with 54 floors, is one of the New York's tallest. Nice electronic amenities include flatscreen LCD televisions, iHome iPod docking stations, and wireless Internet (inexplicably for a daily charge). The addition of oak-parquet floors gives the hotel's cool feel more of a rustic homey touch. The white-tiled bathrooms have been designed by the bathroom purveyor Waterworks and feature their amenities. The hotel's suites include two televisions, a separate parlor area, some with French doors, and bathrooms with two showerheads.

151 W. 54th St. (btwn Sixth and Seventh aves.) New York, N.Y. 10019. *✆* **866/690-2029** or 212/468-8856. Fax 212/468-8747. www.thelondonnyc.com. 562 units. $499–$1,199 double, AE, DC, MC, V. Parking $55. Subway: B, D, E to Seventh Ave. **Amenities:** Restaurant; bar; fitness center; concierge; 24-hour business center; 24-hour room service; laundry service; dry cleaning. *In room:* A/C, TV, Wi-Fi, minibar, hair dryer, safe, iPod home docking stations.

The Michelangelo *✦✦* *(Finds)*   Owned by the Italian-based Starhotel, this is the group's only U.S. property, and it offers a welcome dose of Italian hospitality in the heart of New York. From the moment you enter the spacious lobby, which is adorned with Italian marble, you feel as if you have departed from the rapid-fire sight-and-sound assault of nearby Times Square. Off the lobby is a lounge where coffee and cappuccino are served all day and a complimentary Italian breakfast of pastries and fruit is offered each morning. The rooms come in various sizes and are decorated in three styles: Art Deco, country French, and neoclassical. I prefer the country French, but whatever the style, the rooms are all of a good size and include marble foyers, Italian fabrics, king beds, and two television sets (one in the bathroom). The bathrooms are well maintained and feature deep whirlpool bathtubs.

152 W. 51st St. (btwn Sixth and Seventh aves.), New York, NY 10019. *✆* **800/237-0990** or 212/765-0505. Fax 212/581-7618. www.michelangelohotel.com. 178 units. From $595 double; from 6555 suite. Rates include Italian breakfast. Visit website for (sometimes substantial) discounts. AE, DC, DISC, MC, V. Parking available 2 blocks away: $29 per day self-park, $40 per day valet. Subway: N, R to 49th St. **Amenities:** Restaurant; lounge; fitness center; concierge; complimentary morning limo service to Wall St.; 24-hr. room service; laundry service; dry cleaning. *In room:* A/C, TV, fax, high-speed Internet, minibar, hair dryer, iron, safe.

The Muse *✦*   The beauty of the Muse is that it is a Times Square hotel that feels like it's miles away, an inspired oasis in the midst of the bustle and noise that is Times Square. In the intimate, mahogany-paneled lobby, you will be personally checked in by a concierge, and brought to your room by a bellman who will familiarize you with the amenities. All the rooms are good sized, with feather beds and custom linens. The bathrooms are sumptuous and well outfitted. Service is solid and anticipatory; you even get your own personalized business cards. My only complaint, and it's not that unusual in New York, was the cacophony of garbage trucks working on 46th Street before sunrise. Try to secure a back room if street noise is an issue.

130 W. 46th St. (btwn Sixth and Seventh aves.), New York, NY 10036. © 877/692-6873 or 212/485-2400. Fax 212/485-2789. www.themusehotel.com. 200 units. $229–$399 double; from $399 suite. AE, DC, DISC, MC, V. Parking $43. Subway: B, D, F, V to 42nd St. Pets accepted. **Amenities:** Restaurant; good fitness room; concierge; business services; limited room service; in-room massage; laundry service; dry cleaning. *In room:* A/C, TV w/pay movies, high-speed Internet, dataport, coffeemaker, hair dryer, iron, safe, CD player.

The Shoreham 🖈 No, it's not on the luxury level of the Peninsula or the St. Regis down the block, but after a multimillion-dollar renovation that spruced up the rooms with organic citrus tones, modernized the lobby, added amenities such as champagne or sparkling water upon check-in and a 24-hour self-service coffee bar, and a charge of about half the price, the Shoreham is a more than worthy, less-expensive alternative to those other hotels down the block. Rooms vary in size and amenities, and though all have been upgraded or totally renovated, it's better to spring for a deluxe or a suite where you will get a bigger bathroom, some with five-head rain showers and Jacuzzis. All rooms have flatscreen high-definition televisions. The hotel offers the little extras that give you value, such as a complimentary shoeshine, *New York Times,* two bottles of Voss water, wireless Internet, and for fashionistas, a complimentary daily copy of *Women's Wear Daily.*

33 W. 55th St. (btwn Fifth and Sixth aves.), New York, NY 10019. © 800/553-3347 or 212/247-6700. Fax 212/765-9741. www.shorehamhotel.com. 174 units. $309–$609 double. Check website for Internet rates and other special deals. AE, MC, V. Parking nearby $45 with in/out privileges. Subway: B, D, E to Seventh Ave. **Amenities:** Restaurant; bar; 24-hr. cappuccino and coffee; fitness club; 24-hr. room service; room spa service; laundry service; dry cleaning; complimentary shoeshine. *In room:* A/C, TV, Wi-Fi, minifridge, hair dryer, iron/ironing board, safe, VCR/DVD/CD player.

Sofitel New York 🖈🖈🖈 *(Finds)* There are many fine hotels on 44th Street between Fifth and Sixth avenues (see the sidebar "Hotel Row," p. 122), but the best, in my estimation, is the soaring Sofitel. Upon entering the hotel and the warm, inviting lobby with check-in tucked off to the side, you wouldn't think you were entering a hotel that is this young, which is one of the reasons why the hotel is so special. The designers have successfully melded modern, new-world amenities with European old-world elegance. The rooms are spacious and ultracomfortable, adorned with art from New York and Paris. The lighting is soft and romantic, the walls and windows soundproof. Suites are extra-special, equipped with king beds, two televisions, and pocket doors separating the bedroom from a sitting room. Bathrooms in all rooms are magnificent, with separate showers and soaking tubs.

45 W. 44th St. (btwn Fifth and Sixth aves.), New York, NY 10036. © 212/354-8844. Fax 212/354-2480. www.sofitel.com. 398 units. $299–$599 double; from $439 suite. 1 child stays free in parent's room. AE, DC, MC, V. Parking $45. Subway: B, D, F, V to 42nd St. Pets accepted. **Amenities:** Restaurant; bar; exercise room; concierge; 24-hr. room service; laundry service; dry cleaning. *In room:* A/C, TV w/pay movies and Internet access, high-speed Internet, dataport, minibar, hair dryer, iron, safe, CD player.

The Westin New York at Times Square The 10-color—mostly copper and blue—glass edifice looks more like a transplant from Miami Beach than something familiar to New York City terrain. And if that isn't enough to distinguish itself, the hotel also boasts a beam of light that rises through an atrium, then up to the top of the 45-story tower and into the already well-illuminated sky of Times Square.

Rooms are spacious, with the Club Rooms and Suites being the biggest, and feature the same amenities, including Westin's Heavenly Bed—a custom Simmons Beautyrest pillow-top mattress set dressed in layer upon layer of fluffy down and crisp white linen—and the signature Heavenly Bath, featuring the luxurious two-head shower. The hotel is located on busy Eighth Avenue, taking up the block between 42nd and 43rd streets; rooms facing 42nd Street and Eighth can be loud. In 2007, the hotel opened a spa and a series of spa rooms featuring massage chairs.

270 W. 43rd St. (at Eighth Ave.), New York, NY 10036. (C) 800/WESTIN-1, 866/837-4183, or 212/201-2700. Fax 212/201-2701. www.westinnewyork.com. 863 units. $349–$599 double; $469–$2,000 suite. AE, DC, DISC, MC, V. Parking $27, $48 valet parking. Subway: A, C, or E to 42nd St. **Amenities:** Restaurant; bar; 2,500-sq.-ft. fitness center and spa ($10 per day, $30 per week); concierge and theater desk; business center; 24-hr. room service; laundry service; dry cleaning; currency exchange; internal access to E Walk, a 200,000-sq.-ft. entertainment-and-retail complex featuring a 13-movie theater. In room: A/C, TV w/pay movies, high-speed Internet, dataport, minibar, hair dryer, safe.

W Times Square ⋒   Take the elevator to the seventh floor to the ultramodern, loungelike lobby to check-in, where the only way to distinguish hotel employees from guests is the tiny "W" pin they wear. Otherwise, everyone is dressed in the dark tones of Kenneth Cole–designed "urban" attire. The lobby bar always seems to be busy—or maybe that's just the lounge music that plays continuously throughout all the hotel's public spaces. Most rooms boast magnificent views of the neon spectacle of Times Square, but double-paned windows keep the rooms surprisingly quiet. Standard rooms are compact but roomy enough, with a big Plexiglas desk, mirrors everywhere (is that good or bad?), a 27-inch TV, and the Westin Heavenly Bed. Bathrooms in the standard rooms are small and a bit clumsy, featuring a semiopen shower stall and a huge sink that takes up what little counter space there is. Suites are similarly designed and will get you an extra bathroom and a flatscreen TV.

1567 Broadway (at 47th St.), New York, NY 10036. (C) 888/625-5144 or 212/930-7400. Fax 212/930-7500. www.whotels.com. 507 units. From $300 double; from $599 suite. AE, DC, DISC, MC, V. Parking $52. Subway: N, R to 49th St. Pets up to 40 lb. accepted. **Amenities:** Restaurant; 2 bars; fitness center and spa; concierge; 24-hr. room service; laundry service; dry cleaning. In room: A/C, TV/DVD/CD player, high-speed Internet, minibar, hair dryer, iron, safe.

MODERATE

Casablanca Hotel ⋒⋒ *(Value)*   Located just off Broadway in the middle of Times Square, the Casablanca Hotel is an oasis in the middle of all that mayhem. Where, in **Rick's Café,** the Casablanca's homey guest lounge, you can sit by a fire, read a paper, check your e-mail, watch television on the gargantuan-size screen, or sip a cappuccino from the serve-yourself cappuccino/espresso machine. Or, if the days or nights are balmy, you can lounge on the rooftop deck or second-floor courtyard. Or you can just retreat to your room. They might not be the biggest around, but they are well outfitted with ceiling fans, free bottles of water, and beautifully tiled bathrooms where, if you wish, you can open the window and let sounds outside remind you where you really are. The Casablanca is an HK Hotels property (The Library, Gansevoort, Elysée, and Giraffe), and like those hotels, service is top-notch. Because of its location, moderate prices, and size (only 48 rooms), the Casablanca is in high demand, so book early.

147 W. 43rd St. (just east of Broadway), New York, NY 10036. (C) 888/922-7225 or 212/869-1212. Fax 212/391-7585. www.casablancahotel.com. 48 units. $249–$299 double; from $399 suite. Rates include continental breakfast, all-day cappuccino, and weekday wine and cheese. Check website for Internet rates and other special deals. AE, DC, MC, V. Parking $25 next door. Subway: N, R, 1, 2, 3 to 42nd St./Times Sq. **Amenities:** Cyber lounge; free access to New York Sports Club; concierge; business center; limited room service; laundry service; dry cleaning; video library. In room: A/C, TV/VCR, dataport, minibar, hair dryer, CD player, ceiling fan.

Hotel Row

There are hundreds of hotels in Manhattan, but most are spread out over a good chunk of real estate. There is, however, 1 block—West 44th Street, between Fifth and Sixth avenues—where the hotels stand practically side by side.

The block has a sophisticated, urbane, and literary feel to it, emanating from the 1902-built **Algonquin** ✯✯ (59 W. 44th St.; p. 116), where the *New Yorker* was born, where Lerner and Loewe wrote *My Fair Lady,* and—most famously—where some of the biggest names in 1920s literati, among them Dorothy Parker, met to trade boozy quips at the celebrated Algonquin Round Table.

Next to the Algonquin, at 55 W. 44th St., sits the 65-room Jeffrey Bilhuber–designed **City Club** (© **212/921-5500**; www.cityclubhotel.com). The structure started out in 1904 as a gentlemen's club and saw many incarnations over the last century, but its latest life, as the ultrafashionable City Club, casts aside the usual style of the New York "boutique" property—cramped and minimalist decor that make a virtue of discomfort. City Club's modernist elements are tempered with traditional touches such as Queen Anne chairs, natural Frette linens, vintage books, chocolate marble, and Hermès bath products you'd be afraid to steal. This haven for mavens of fashion also is the home of one of Daniel Boulud's restaurant's, **db Bistro Moderne** (p. 180).

For many years there was a barbershop adjacent to the lobby of the **Iroquois Hotel,** 49 W. 44th St. (© **212/840-3080**; www.iroquoisny.com), called the Dumont Barbershop and Shoeshine. The shop's principal barber, Louis Fontana, used to notice a young man hanging out on the stoop of the hotel, which, at the time, was a men's residence. When Louie (as he was known by

414 Hotel ✯ *Finds*   Located a block from Times Square and close to exciting Hell's Kitchen, this place offers 37-inch flatscreen TVs in every room, spacious, well-equipped bathrooms; complimentary bottled water, continental breakfast, and Wi-Fi; in-room refrigerators; and a lovely courtyard. It all sounds too good for a budget hotel. But if you want all that and don't want to pay anything close to what hotels offering much less are asking, then you also have to endure the 414's thin walls; if stomping above you is a problem ask for a top floor room, which would mean you would have to walk the four floors: the hotel does not have an elevator. Despite these inconveniences, the 414 Hotel has comfortable, clean rooms and all the perks make it a very good Midtown moderate choice.

414 W. 46th St., (btwn Ninth and Tenth aves.) New York, NY 10036. © **866/414-HOTEL** or 212/399-0006. Fax 212/957-8710. www.hotel414.com. 22 units. $169–$259 double. Subway: A, C, E, 7, 42nd Street. **Amenities:** Complimentary continental breakfast; comp coffee, juice, tea; concierge; dry cleaning (upon request); business services (upon request). *In room:* A/C, TV, Wi-Fi, dataport, fridge, hair dryer, safe.

Hotel 41 ✯ *Finds*   Like the **Casablanca Hotel** (p. 121) a few blocks up, Hotel 41 offers a stylish, comfortable, and moderate alternative to the many gleaming, glittering his regulars) asked the kid why he was hanging around the barbershop, the kid stuttered that he needed a haircut but couldn't afford one; he was an actor looking for work. "Kid, what's your name?" the legend goes. The kid answered, "James Dean." Big-hearted Louis gave him a haircut for free that day. That's a true story and part of the legend of the Iroquois Hotel. The 114-room hotel, after a full renovation some years ago, is now a member of the Small Luxury Hotels of the World and features a suite named after its former most famous resident.

Just next to the Iroquois, at 45 W. 44th St., is the **Sofitel New York** 𝒦𝒦𝒦 (p. 120); from the appearance of the lobby and entrance, you might think you have entered a hotel built in the same era as the others. But take a look from across the street; the glittering curved tower was built less than 6 years ago. Despite its newness, the hotel blends in perfectly on historic Hotel Row.

Closer to Fifth Avenue and on the south side of the block at 12 W. 44th St. is the **Mansfield** 𝒦 (𝒞 **800/255-5167** or 212/277-8700; www.mansfield hotel.com), which was built as a bachelor's residence in 1905 and, in keeping with the block's literary and artistic tradition, was once the home of poet W.B. Yeats's father. The hotel was renovated in 2007, restoring it to its former grandeur.

Finally, and closer to Sixth Avenue, at 44 W. 44th St., is the Philippe Starck–designed **Royalton** (𝒞 **800/697-1791** or 212/869-4400; www.morgan-shotelgroup.com). Though it is also set in an early-20th-century building, the feel is late 1990s, with that minimalist Starck style. The solitary homage to the past is the presence of working fireplaces in 40 of the hotel's 169 rooms. In keeping with the block's artistic tradition, the Royalton is a favorite of music, fashion, and film types.

and more pricey hotels that tower over Times Square. Just seven floors high, the Hotel 41 features minimalist modern decor in the guest rooms. Rooms, for these prices, are of decent size, but what sets the hotel apart are the freebies: high-speed Internet, complimentary continental breakfast, free espresso or cappuccino all day, in-room DVD players with the hotel's DVD library available for viewing, plush bathrobes in the rooms, double-paned windows (a necessity in Times Square), and refrigerators in all rooms. If you plan to stay for more than a few days, try for one of the junior suites or, for a splurge, Penthouse no. 2, which features a large outdoor deck. Service is boutique-friendly, and off the lobby is **Bar 2156** a lively bar/restaurant (where breakfast is served) that draws a local after-work crowd.

206 W. 41st St. (btwn Seventh and Eighth aves.), New York, NY 10036. 𝒞 **212/703-8600.** Fax 212/302-0895. www.hotel41nyc.com. 47 units. $289–$469 double; $609–$999 suite. Check the website for Internet specials. AE, DC, DISC, MC, V. Parking $30. Subway: 1, 2, 3, 7, A, C, E, N, Q, R, S, W to Times Sq. Pets accepted. **Amenities:** Restaurant; bar; access to nearby fitness center; limited room service; continental breakfast; coffee all day. *In room:* A/C, TV/DVD, free high-speed Internet, fridge, hair dryer, safe.

Hotel Metro 𝒦𝒦 𝒦*ids*   The Metro is the choice in Midtown for those who don't want to sacrifice either style or comfort for affordability. This Art Deco–style jewel has larger rooms than you'd expect for the price. They're outfitted with retro furnishings, playful fabrics, fluffy pillows, smallish but beautifully appointed marble bathrooms, and alarm clocks. Only about half the bathrooms have tubs, but the others have shower stalls big enough for two (junior suites have whirlpool tubs). The family room is an ingenious invention: a two-room suite that has a second bedroom in lieu of a sitting area; families on tighter budgets can opt for a roomy double/double.

The comfy, fire-lit library/lounge area off the lobby, where complimentary buffet breakfast is laid out and the coffeepot's on all day, is a popular hangout. Service is attentive; and the rooftop terrace boasts a breathtaking view of the Empire State Building and makes a great place to order up room service from the **Metro Grill.**

45 W. 35th St. (btwn Fifth and Sixth aves.), New York, NY 10001. ℂ 800/356-3870 or 212/947-2500. Fax 212/279-1310. www.hotelmetronyc.com. 179 units. $250–$365 double; $245–$420 triple or quad; $255–$425 family room; $275–$475 suite. Extra person $25. 1 child under 13 stays free in parent's room. Rates include continental breakfast. Check with airlines and other package operators for great-value package deals. AE, DC, MC, V. Parking $20 nearby. Subway: B, D, F, V, N, R to 34th St. **Amenities:** Restaurant; alfresco rooftop bar in summer; good fitness room; salon; limited room service; laundry service; dry cleaning. *In room:* A/C, TV, high-speed Internet, dataport, fridge, hair dryer, iron.

Hotel QT ✦✦ (Value Owned by Andre Balazs, of the **Mercer** (p. 106), Hotel QT offers much of the Mercer's style without the hefty rates. From its enviable Midtown location to its many extras such as a swimming pool in the lobby, steam room and sauna, free high-speed Internet, complimentary continental breakfast, and good-size rooms, including a number with bunk beds, Hotel QT is one of the best moderate options in the Times Square area. Upon entering, you check in at a kiosk/front desk where you pick up periodicals or essentials to stock your minibar. Making your way to the elevators, you might see guests swimming in the lobby pool or having a drink at the pool's swim-up bar, an unusual site in the Big Apple. The rooms are sparse in tone, but the queen- and king-size platform beds are plush and dressed with Egyptian cotton sheets. The biggest drawback is the bathrooms: There are no doors on the bathrooms—sliding doors conceal the shower (none of the rooms have tubs) and the toilet.

125 W. 45th St. (btwn Sixth Ave. and Broadway), New York, NY 10036. ℂ 212/354-2323. Fax 212/302-8585. www.hotelqt.com. 140 units. $199–$350 double. AE, DC, MC, V. Parking nearby $25. Subway: B, D, F, V to 47th–50th St./Rockefeller Center. **Amenities:** Bar; swimming pool; gym; sauna; steam room; complimentary continental breakfast. *In room:* A/C, TV, free Wi-Fi, free high-speed Internet, minifridge, hair dryer, iron/ironing board, safe, CD player, DVD player, 2-line speakerphones w/free local calls.

Novotel New York ✦ (Kids Run expertly by the French company Accor (**Sofitel,** p. 120), this towering hotel on the northern fringe of Times Square, with its bilingual staff and a selection of international newspapers, attracts an international crowd. But domestic visitors shouldn't neglect what is a good moderate option in one of the busiest parts of the city. The vast, sunny lobby on the seventh floor, with open views of Times Square, is the hotel's pride and joy; it is also the location of the underrated **Café Nicole,** where a breakfast buffet is offered. Guest rooms, though pleasant and of a decent size, are more motel-like in decor. Rooms were recently renovated and many have spectacular views of Times Square and/or the Hudson River. All are soundproof. A family-friendly hotel, kids under 16 can stay free in their parent's room and eat free at Café Nicole (with some restrictions).

226 W. 52nd St. (at Broadway), New York, NY 10019. ℂ 212/315-0100. Fax 212/765-5365 www.novotel.com. 480 units. From $209 double. 2 children under 16 eat for free and stay free in parent's room. AE, DC, DISC, MC, V. Parking $30. Subway: B, D, E to Seventh Ave. Pets accepted. **Amenities:** Restaurant; bar; fitness room; concierge; limited room service; dry cleaning. *In room:* A/C, TV, Wi-Fi, high-speed Internet, minibar, hair dryer.

Washington Jefferson Hotel ⊛   This is one of the few affordable hotels in the heart of my favorite Manhattan neighborhood for dining, Hell's Kitchen. The lobby has a warm and welcoming ambience, with a friendly, snappily attired staff and more than a dash of designer style. Snazzy blue-carpeted halls lead to rooms that are *small*— don't say I didn't warn you—but attractively outfitted in a palette of soft grays. Nice touches include platform beds with generous cushioned headboards and fluffy goose-down comforters. The gorgeous limestone-and-slate bathrooms are stylish and rela-tively spacious, although some have showers only. Score 1 of the 18 king rooms if you can; they're roomy and boast a pullout love seat as well as a Jacuzzi tub in the bath-room. The Japanese restaurant in the hotel is just a sample of some of the different ethnic cuisines you will find in the neighborhood.

318 W. 51st St. (btwn Eighth and Ninth aves.), New York, NY 10019. ✆ **888/567-7550** or 212/246-7550. Fax 212/246-7622. www.wjhotel.com. 135 units. $179–$349 double. Ask about special deals. AE, DC, DISC, MC, V. Parking $35 nearby. Subway: C, E to 50th St. **Amenities:** Restaurant; exercise room; limited room service. *In room:* A/C, TV w/pay movies/video games/Internet access, dataport, hair dryer, iron, safe.

INEXPENSIVE

Americana Inn ⊛ *Value*   In the budget-basic category the hotel is professionally run and immaculately kept. Rooms are mostly spacious, with good-size closets, private sinks, and an alarm built into the TV; the beds are the most comfortable I've found at this price. Most rooms come with a double bed or two twins; a few can accommodate three guests in two twin beds and a pullout sofa, or in three twins. One hall bathroom accommodates every three rooms or so; all are spacious and spotless. Every floor has a common kitchenette with microwave, stove, and fridge (BYO cooking utensils, or go plastic). The five-story building has an elevator, and four rooms are accessible for trav-elers with disabilities. The Garment District location is convenient for Midtown sight-seeing and shopping; ask for a back-facing room away from the street noise.

69 W. 38th St. (at Sixth Ave.), New York, NY 10018. ✆ **888/HOTEL-58** or 212/840-6700. Fax 212/840-1830. www.theamericaninn.com 50 units, all with shared bathroom. $110–$150 double. Extra person $20 Check website for specials (winter rates as low as $60 double). AE, MC, V. Parking $30 nearby. Subway: B, D, F, V to 34th St. **Amenities:** Common kitchen. *In room:* A/C, TV, hair dryer (ask reception).

La Quinta Inn Manhattan *Value*   The first and only La Quinta Inn in Manhattan is another excellent Midtown budget choice. Housed in a 1904 Beaux Arts structure on the block known as Little Korea, La Quinta Inn offers standard motel amenities along with motel-like prices. Like the other Apple Core properties, including the Red Roof Inn across the street, service is friendly and a continental breakfast adds to the value. The rooms are basic in motel-room decor and size, but there's nothing wrong with that, especially at these prices. Bathrooms are small but clean and well equipped. There's even a cozy rooftop bar that offers indoor and outdoor seating in the shadow of the majestic Empire State Building. And if you like Korean barbecue and dumplings, you won't have to travel far; the block is packed with some good Korean restaurants.

17 W. 32nd St. (btwn Fifth and Sixth aves.), New York, NY 10001. ✆ **800/551-2303** or 212/736-1600. www.la-quinta-manhattan.com. 181 units. $89–$329 double (usually less than $189). Rates include continental breakfast. Children under 13 stay free in parent's room. AE, DC, DISC, MC, V. Parking $26. Subway: B, D, F, N, R, V to 34th St. **Amenities:** Breakfast room; bar; exercise room; concierge; business center; laundry service; dry cleaning. *In room:* A/C, TV w/pay movies and video games, Wi-Fi, dataport, coffeemaker, iron.

Red Roof Inn ⊛ *Value*   Manhattan's first and only Red Roof Inn offers relief from Midtown's high-priced hotel scene. The hotel occupies a former office building that was gutted and laid out fresh, allowing for more spacious rooms and bathrooms than you'll usually find in this price category. The lobby feels smart, and elevators are quiet and efficient. In-room amenities—including coffeemakers and TVs with on-screen Web access—are better than most competitors', and furnishings are new and comfortable. Wi-Fi is available throughout the property. The location—on a bustling block lined with nice hotels and affordable Korean restaurants, a stone's throw from the Empire State Building and Herald Square—is excellent. Be sure to compare the rates offered by Apple Core Hotel's reservation line (the management company) and those quoted on Red Roof's national reservation line and website, as they can vary significantly. Complimentary continental breakfast adds to the good value.

6 W. 32nd St. (btwn Broadway and Fifth Ave.), New York, NY 10001. ℂ 800/755-3194, 800/RED-ROOF, or 212/643-7100. Fax 212/643-7101. www.applecorehotels.com or www.redroof.com. 171 units. $89–$329 double (usually less than $189). Rates include continental breakfast. Children under 13 stay free in parent's room. AE, DC, DISC, MC, V. Parking $26. Subway: B, D, F, N, R, V to 34th St. **Amenities:** Breakfast room; wine-and-beer lounge; exercise room; concierge; laundry service; dry cleaning. *In room:* A/C, TV w/pay movies and Internet access, Wi-Fi, dataport, fridge, coffeemaker, hair dryer, iron, video games.

Skyline Hotel *(Kids* *(Value*   This fairly-recently renovated motor hotel offers predictable comforts and some uncommon extras—inexpensive storage parking ($10 per day) and a lovely indoor pool—that make it a good value. A pleasant lobby leads to motel-standard rooms that are bigger than most in this price range. There are two room categories: standard, with two twin beds, and deluxe, with either a king bed with sofa or a queen bed. The deluxe with king and sofa is best for families. They boast decent-size closets, small work desks (in most), and double-paned windows that open to let fresh air in and shut out a surprising amount of street noise when closed. Everything is well kept. Another plus for the family is the pool, which has a tiled deck and plush deck chairs, but it's only open limited hours, so call ahead if it matters.

725 Tenth Ave. (at 49th St.), New York, NY 10019. ℂ 800/433-1982 or 212/586-3400. Fax 212/582-4604. www.skylinehotelny.com. 230 units. $209–$389 standard; $219–$409 deluxe. Extra person $20. Children 14 and under stay free in parent's room. Check website or inquire about special rates (as low as $99 at press time). AE, DC, DISC, MC, V. Parking $10 (charge for in/out privileges). Subway: A, C, E to 50th St. Pets accepted with $200 deposit. **Amenities:** Restaurant; bar w/extensive beer list; indoor pool; big-screen TV; Internet access in lobby. *In room:* A/C, TV w/pay movies/video games/high-speed Internet, dataport, hair dryer, iron, safe.

Travel Inn *(Kids* *(Value*   Extras such as a huge outdoor pool and sun deck, a sunny and up-to-date fitness room, and *free* parking (with in and out privileges!) make the Travel Inn another terrific deal, similar to the one offered by the **Skyline Hotel** (see above). Like the Skyline, the Travel Inn may not be loaded with personality, but it does offer the clean, bright regularity of a good chain hotel. Rooms are oversize and comfortably furnished, with extra-firm beds and work desks; even the smallest double is sizable and has a roomy bathroom, and double/doubles make great affordable shares for families. A total renovation over the last couple years has made everything feel like new, even the tiled bathrooms. Though a bit off the track, Off-Broadway theaters and affordable restaurants are at hand, and it's a 10-minute walk to the Theater District.

515 W. 42nd St. (just west of Tenth Ave.), New York, NY 10036. ℂ 888/HOTEL58, 800/869-4630, or 212/695-7171. Fax 212/967-5025. www.thetravelinnhotel.com. 160 units. $105–$250 double. Extra person $10. Children under 16 stay free in parent's room. AAA discounts available; check website for special Internet deals. AE, DC, DISC, MC, V. Free self-parking. Subway: A, C, E to 42nd St./Port Authority. **Amenities:** Coffee shop; terrific outdoor pool w/deck chairs and lifeguard in season; fitness center; Gray Line tour desk; 24-hr. room service. *In room:* A/C, TV, dataport, hair dryer, iron.

Family-Friendly Hotels

Lugging the kids to New York City can be a daunting experience. Finding a hotel that makes that experience (whether in the accommodations or in the amenities), a bit less daunting can be a huge help. Here are some of the city's best accommodations for families:

Doubletree Guest Suites Times Square (Times Sq.; p. 117)   An entire floor of childproof suites, plus a Kids Club for ages 3 to 12.

Flatotel (Midtown West; p. 117)   With one- to three-bedroom suites equipped with full kitchens, this is a great Midtown option for the family.

Gershwin Hotel (Flatiron District; p. 115)   High space-to-dollar ratio with the Family Room, a two-room suite.

Hotel Beacon (Upper West Side; p. 137)   In-room kitchenette, on-site Laundromat, and spacious rooms in a kid-friendly neighborhood—what more do you want?

Hotel Metro (Midtown West; p. 123)   The sitting rooms of the hotel's Family Room suites are smartly converted into second bedrooms.

Le Parker Meridien (Midtown West; p. 118)   Cartoons playing in the elevators, a great swimming pool, a kid-friendly burger joint in the lobby, and spacious rooms and suites.

The Lowell (Upper East Side; p. 140)   Total *luxe*, but with the feel of a residential dwelling. Most units are equipped with a kitchenette or full kitchen.

Novotel New York (Midtown West; p. 124)   Kids under 16 stay free in their parent's room and eat free at the hotel's beautiful Café Nicole.

The Regency (Midtown East; p. 131)   A big welcome by longtime kids' concierge Kaptain Kidz, with goodies for the children upon arrival.

Ritz-Carlton New York, Central Park (Midtown West; p. 115)   You'll pay dearly for it, but kids love the in-room cookies and milk.

Skyline Hotel and **Travel Inn** (Midtown West; p. 126)   Inexpensive ($10) to free parking at the Skyline and Travel Inn, respectively, oversize rooms, and swimming pools (a rarity in affordable hotels).

8 Midtown East & Murray Hill

To find the hotels described in this section, see p. 112.

Also consider the grandest of dames, the **Plaza,** at Fifth Avenue and Central Park South (© **212/759-3000;** www.fairmont.com/thePlaza) which, at press time, was just re-opening. After a $400 million, 2-year renovation, the Plaza, like so many other hotels, is part condo, and part hotel. There are now 282 guest rooms ranging from a roomy 482-square feet guest room to suites of almost 1,500 square feet, some with terraces, and all rooms and suites feature white glove butler service. The world famous **Palm Court** is open once again for high (expensive) tea, and the **Oak Room** and Oak

Bar for cocktails and dinner. New at the Plaza are the lobby's **Champagne Bar** and the **Rose Club** overlooking the lobby and a fitness, club helmed by trainer to the stars, Radu. Rates start at (gulp) $1,000 per night. What would Eloise think?

VERY EXPENSIVE

Affinia Dumont ☾☾   The Affinia Dumont is the perfect choice for fitness-focused guests: when you book a room, you can request a complimentary "Fit Kit" that will be prepared based on your needs for an in-room workout. The hotel also has a terrific fitness spa, complete with the weights, cardio equipment, and massage and skin treatments. But even if you don't want to break a sweat, the hotel features amenities that make it an attractive option. The suites range from studios to two-bedrooms, and all include full kitchens, at least one 27-inch TV, a large desk with an ergonomic chair, the "Affinia Bed," with a custom-designed mattress and four-selection "pillow menu," and a minibar stocked with unusual options, such as health elixirs with such names as Depth Recharger or Virtual Buddha. The hotel is a bit away from the center of Midtown, but still within easy walking distance of Herald Square shopping, the Empire State Building, Madison Square Garden, and Grand Central Station.

150 E. 34th St. (btwn Third and Lexington aves.), New York, NY 10016. ☎ **212/481-7600.** Fax 212/889-8856. www.affinia.com. 241 units. From $350 studio suite; from $450 1-bedroom suite; from $650 2-bedroom suite. AE, DC, MC, V. Valet parking $42. Subway: 6 to 33rd St. **Amenities:** Restaurant; health club and spa; fitness concierge; concierge; limited room service; coin-operated laundry; grocery-shopping service. *In room:* A/C, TV/VCR, high-speed Internet, dataport, full kitchen, minibar, hair dryer, iron, safe (laptop size), Fit Kit.

The Benjamin ☾☾★   From the retro sign and clock on Lexington Avenue to the high-ceilinged marble lobby, when you enter the Benjamin, it's as if you've stepped into the Jazz Era of 1920s New York. But the in-room amenities are most definitely 21st-century high tech. All rooms are airy, but the deluxe studios and one-bedroom suites are extra large. There are even a few one-bedroom suites with terraces. The hotel features "sleep concierge," or *guarantee* a good night's sleep, and a pillow menu with 11 options, including buckwheat and Swedish Memory. I chose the standard down pillow and did not have to exercise the guarantee. If you are a light sleeper, however, book a room off Lexington Avenue, which can get busy most weeknights and mornings. Bathrooms feature Frette robes, TV speakers, and water pressure from the shower head strong enough to make you think you've experienced a deep-tissue massage. The hotel also features a good fitness center and a Wellness Spa.

125 E. 50th St. (at Lexington Ave.), New York, NY 10022. ☎ **888/4-BENJAMIN,** 212/320-8002, or 212/715-2500. Fax 212/715-2525. www.thebenjamin.com. 209 units. From $459 superior double; from $499 deluxe studio; from $559 suite. Call or check website for special weekend-stay offers. AE, DC, DISC, MC, V. Parking $45. Subway: 6 to 51st St.; E, F to Lexington Ave. Pets accepted. **Amenities:** Restaurant; cocktail lounge; state-of-the-art exercise room; full-service spa; concierge; sleep concierge; business services; 24-hr. room service; dry cleaning; valet service. *In room:* A/C, TV w/pay movies/video games/Internet access, fax/copier/printer, high-speed Internet, dataport, kitchenette, minibar, coffeemaker, laptop-size safe, china, microwave.

Four Seasons Hotel New York ☾☾   Designed by überarchitect I. M. Pei, this modernist tower of honey-hued limestone rises 52 stories, making it the city's tallest hotel and providing hundreds of rooms with a view. As soon as you enter the soaring lobby, with its marble floors and backlit onyx ceiling, you'll know this place is special. From the stellar service—only surpassed by the Ritz-Carlton hotels and Trump International—to the fantastic facilities, including a luxurious spa, this is a stunner.

The completely soundproof guest rooms are among the city's largest, averaging 600 square feet (183 sq. meters), and feature massive windows (50% of which boast Central Park views). About two dozen of the priciest rooms also have terraces. The mammoth Florentine marble bathrooms have soaking tubs that fill in 60 seconds, and separate showers with pressure controls.

57 E. 57th St. (btwn Park and Madison aves.), New York, NY 10022. © **800/819-5053,** 800/487-3769, or 212/758-5700. Fax 212/758-5711. www.fourseasons.com. 368 units. $725–$925 double; from $1,550 suite. Extra rollaway bed $50. Check for value-added packages and other deals. AE, DC, DISC, MC, V. Parking $60. Subway: N, R, 4, 5, 6 to 60th St. **Amenities:** Restaurant; bar w/evening entertainment; lobby lounge for afternoon tea and light fare; 5,000-sq.-ft. spa and fitness center w/whirlpool, steam, and sauna; children's program; concierge; business center w/secretarial services; 24-hr. room service; in-room massage; babysitting; laundry service w/1-hr. pressing; dry cleaning. In room: A/C, TV w/pay movies, high-speed Internet, dataport, minibar, hair dryer, safe.

The Peninsula-New York ✹✹✹ Housed in a beauty of a landmark Beaux Arts building, the Peninsula is the perfect combination of old-world charm and modern, state-of-the-art technology. Rooms are huge with plenty of closet and storage space, but best of all is the bedside control panel that allows you to regulate lighting, television, stereo, air-conditioning, and signal the DO NOT DISTURB sign on your door. Even though you really don't have to leave the comfort of your bed, eventually you will need to go to the bathroom, and when you do, you'll not be disappointed. The huge marble bathrooms all have spacious soaking tubs with yet another control panel at your fingertips, including the controls for, in most rooms, a television so you can watch while taking your bubble bath (now that's happy excess). The Peninsula also features one of the best and biggest New York hotel health clubs and spas, the rooftop **Pen-Top Bar,** and a faultless concierge desk.

700 Fifth Ave. (at 55th St.), New York, NY 10019. © **800/262-9467** or 212/956-2888. Fax 212/903-3949. www. peninsula.com. 239 units. $775–$1125 double; from $1,275 suite. Extra person $50. Children under 12 stay free in parent's room. Winter weekend package rates from $585 at press time. AE, DC, DISC, MC, V. Valet parking $55. Subway: E, V to Fifth Ave. Pets accepted. **Amenities:** Restaurant; rooftop bar; library-style lounge for afternoon tea and cocktails; tri-level rooftop health club and spa w/treatment rooms; heated pool; exercise classes; whirlpool; sauna; and sun deck; 24-hr. concierge; business center; 24-hr. room service; in-room massage; babysitting; laundry service; dry cleaning. In room: A/C, TV w/pay movies, fax, Wi-Fi, high-speed Internet, minibar, hair dryer, laptop-size safe, complimentary "water bar" w/5 choices of bottled water.

St. Regis ✹✹✹ When John Jacob Astor built the St. Regis in 1904, he set out to create a hotel that would reflect the elegance and luxury he was used to in hotels in Europe. Over a hundred years later, the St. Regis, now a New York landmark, still reflects that European splendor. This Beaux Arts classic is a marvel: antique furniture, crystal chandeliers, silk wall coverings, and marble floors adorn both the public spaces and the high-ceilinged, airy guest rooms. The suites are particularly ornate, some with French doors, four-poster beds, and decorative fireplaces. The marble bathrooms are spacious and feature separate showers and tubs. In a nod to the future, plasma televisions were recently added in all the rooms, along with LCD screens in the bathrooms. Service is efficiently white-gloved and every guest is assigned a personal, tuxedoed butler, on call 24 hours to answer any reasonable requests. **Afternoon tea** is served daily in the Astor Court and chef Alain Ducasse claimed the former Lespinasse space for his new venture, **Adour.**

2 E. 55th St. (at Fifth Ave.), New York, NY 10022. © **212/753-4500.** Fax 212/787-3447. www.stregis.com. 256 units. $695–$995 double; from $1,150 suite. Check Internet for specials as low as $400 at press time. AE, DC, DISC, MC, V. Parking $55. Subway: E, V to Fifth Ave. **Amenities:** Restaurant; historic bar; tea lounge; fitness center and spa; concierge; 24-hr. room service; babysitting; laundry service; 24-hr. butler service; valet service. In room: A/C, TV, high-speed Internet, minibar, hair dryer, safe, DVD/CD player.

The Sherry-Netherland 🐸🐸🐸 One of New York's classic *grande dame* hotels, this 1927-built beauty, from the marble-and-bronze lobby and the Italian Renaissance–painted paneled elevators, the Sherry is pure old-school luxury. Though it's a big building, only 77 rooms are used for the hotel; the rest are private residential co-ops. Guest rooms vary in decor, but each is grandly proportioned with high ceilings, big bathrooms, and walk-in closets. The rooms are spacious and every one features high-quality furnishings and art. About half are suites with kitchenettes that have a cook-top or microwave, often both. Bathrooms are huge and impeccably designed and outfitted. And with an enviable location at Fifth and 58th, opposite Central Park and adjacent to the Plaza Hotel, most of the rooms have glorious views.

781 Fifth Ave. (at 59th St.), New York, NY 10022. 🕾 877/743-7710 or 212/355-2800. Fax 212/319-4306. www.sherry netherland.com. 77 units. $499–$1,250 double; from $785 1- or 2-bedroom suite. Children stay free in parent's room. AE, DC, DISC, MC, V. Parking $55. Subway: N, R to Fifth Ave. Pets accepted. **Amenities:** Fitness room; concierge; business center; salon; limited room service; in-room massage; babysitting; laundry service; dry cleaning; video library. *In room:* A/C, TV/VCR, fax, free high-speed Internet, fridge w/free soft drinks.

EXPENSIVE

Also consider another all-suite hotel from the Affinia group, this one called **Affinia 50,** 155 E. 50th St., between Third and Lexington avenues (🕾 **212/751-5710;** www. affinia.com).

Dylan Hotel In the landmarked 1903-built Chemist's Club building, the Dylan is a combination of Beaux Arts opulence and modern, sleek Jeffrey Beers–designed interiors. That combination is evident in the lobby with muted colors and glass paneling centered on a magnificent, gilded age, marble staircase. The rooms also reflect that mix with impressive 11-foot ceilings along with high-tech amenities. The marble bathrooms with Italian-porcelain-bowl style sinks look nice, but I find them cumbersome and lacking in shelf space. If you can, check out the Alchemy Suite, the former Chemist Club's mock laboratory with a vaulted ceiling, stained glass windows, and stone doorways; it's most definitely a one-of-a-kind room. The **Benjamin Steakhouse** (p. 173) is the hotel's restaurant and features a 10-foot working fireplace. Though the rates are comparable, the Dylan doesn't offer the services of the **Library Hotel** (across the street) but if you can't get a room there, it's a perfectly acceptable local alternative.

52 E. 41st St, New York, N.Y. 10017 (btwn Park and Madison aves.). 🕾 **212/338-0500.** Fax 212/338-0569. www.dylanhotel.com. 107 units. From $429 double; from $899 suites. Check website for specials. AE, DC, DISC, MC, V. Parking $45. Subway: 4, 5, 6, 7, S to Grand Central Station-42nd St. **Amenities:** Restaurant; fitness center; 24-hour concierge; 24-hour business center; limited room service (breakfast, dinner until 11pm); laundry service; dry cleaning. *In room:* A/C, TV, free Wi-Fi, free high-speed Internet, dataport, minibar, iron/ironing board, safe.

Hotel Elysée 🐸🐸 This romantic gem of a hotel in the heart of Midtown might be easy to miss: It's dwarfed by modern glass towers on either side of it. But that it is so inconspicuous is part of the Elysée's immense romantic appeal. Built in 1926, the hotel has a storied past as the preferred address for artists and writers, including Tennessee Williams, Jimmy Breslin, Maria Callas and Vladimir Horowitz (who donated a Steinway, which still resides in the Piano Suite). The hotel still retains that sexy, discreet feel. Rooms have many quirky features; some have fireplaces, others have kitchens or solariums, and all are decorated in country-French furnishings. Good-size bathrooms are done up in Italian marble and are well outfitted. Off the gorgeous black and white marble-floored lobby is the legendary **Monkey Bar** (p. 379). On the second floor is the Club Room, where a free continental breakfast is offered daily, along with complimentary wine and cheese weekday evenings.

60 E. 54th St. (btwn Park and Madison aves.), New York, NY 10022. ☎ **800/535-9733** or 212/753-1066. Fax 212/ 980-9278. www.elyseehotel.com. 101 units. From $395 double; from $495 suite. Check the website for seasonal specials. Rates include continental breakfast and weekday evening wine and cheese. AE, DC, DISC, MC, V. Parking $30. Subway: E, V to Fifth Ave. **Amenities:** Restaurant; bar; free access to nearby gym; concierge; limited room service; laundry service; dry cleaning. *In room:* A/C, TV/VCR, Wi-Fi, dataport, minibar, hair dryer, iron, safe.

The Kitano New York 🎭🎭🎭 *(Finds*   Owned by the Kitano Group of Japan, this elegant Murray Hill gem offers a unique mix of East and West sensibilities. The marble and mahogany lobby, with its Y-shaped staircase and Botero bronze *Dog,* is one of the most attractive in New York. The hotel was first opened in 1973; in the mid-1990s, along with acquiring an 1896 landmark town house next door, the Kitano was fully renovated. If you're a lucky (and wealthy) individual, you'll get the opportunity to stay in one of three one-bedroom town-house suites, each with sunken living room, bay windows, and original, eclectic art. Or, if your sensibilities are Eastern-oriented, the hotel offers a Tatami suite, with tatami mats, rice paper screens, and a Japanese Tea Ceremony room. Most rooms are not quite that luxurious or unique, but all include tasteful mahogany furniture, soundproof windows, and, for a real taste of Japan, green tea upon arrival; marble bathrooms are large and have heated towel racks and removable shower heads. On the mezzanine-level is a bar, which on Wednesday through Saturday evenings offers the acclaimed **Jazz at the Kitano.**

66 Park Ave. (at 38th St.), New York, NY 10016. ☎ 800/548-2666 or **212/885-7000.** Fax 212/885-7100. www. kitano.com. 149 units. $480–$605 double; from $715 suite. Check website for specials (as low as $239 at press time). AE, DC, DISC, MC, V. Parking $40. Subway: 4, 5, 6, 7, S to Grand Central. **Amenities:** 2 restaurants; bar w/live jazz; access to a nearby health club; concierge; complimentary limo service to Wall St. on weekdays; limited room service; laundry service; dry cleaning. *In room:* A/C, TV, fax, high-speed Internet, dataport, hair dryer, iron, complimentary tea.

The Library Hotel 🎭🎭 *(Finds*   Located 1 block from the New York Public Library, each of the Library Hotel's 10 guest-room floors is dedicated to 1 of the 10 major categories of the Dewey Decimal System. When I visited the hotel, I was appropriately booked into a "Geography and Travel" room. Overall, the hotel has a pleasing, informal feel. Guest rooms, which come in three categories—petite (really small), deluxe, and junior suites—feature mahogany built-ins, generous desks, and immaculate marble bathrooms; all are extremely comfortable. The Library's public spaces—a reading room where weekday wine and cheese and a complimentary daily breakfast are served, a writer's den with a fireplace and flatscreen TV, and a rooftop terrace—all help make the Library a welcome refuge in the heart of the city.

299 Madison Ave. (at 41st St.), New York, NY 10017. ☎ 877/793-7323 or 212/983-4500. Fax 212/499-9099. www.libraryhotel.com. 60 units. $345–$435 double; $525 Love Room or junior suite; $960 2-room family suite. Rates include continental breakfast buffet, all-day snacks, and weekday wine and cheese. Inquire about corporate, promotional, and weekend rates (as low as $329 at press time). AE, DC, MC, V. Parking $30 nearby. Subway: 4, 5, 6, 7, S to 42nd St./Grand Central. **Amenities:** Restaurant; free access to nearby health club; business center; 24-hr. room service; laundry service; dry cleaning; video library of American Film Institute's Top 100 films. *In room:* A/C, TV/VCR, high-speed Internet, dataport, minibar, hair dryer, iron, laptop-size safe, CD player.

The Regency 🎭🎭 *(Kids*   The Regency has long been a haven for celebrities and those who aspire to celebrity status. But even if you aren't on the cover of a magazine, a stay at the Regency might make you feel like a star. The guest rooms are all huge, featuring a king bed or two doubles, a large marble writing desk with an ergonomic chair, and a small eating table. The bathrooms, though not enormous, are equipped with terry-cloth robes and a small television. Suites are typically grandiose, ranging from the 450-square-foot Executive, with two bathrooms and French doors, to the Grand

Suite, with two bedrooms and two marble bathrooms. Despite its elegance, the Regency is a surprisingly good choice for kids. Children under 18 stay free when sharing a room with their parents; rollaway beds are an additional $25 for the stay. Complimentary homemade hot chocolate is served in the lobby in the winter months, replaced by lemonade in the summer. The hotel's restaurant, 540 Park Avenue, is one of the great power-breakfast spots in the city, while **Feinstein's at The Regency** (p. 365) is considered the standard when it comes to cabaret.

540 Park Ave. (at 61st St.), New York, NY 10021. ℰ **800/233-2356** or 212/759-4100. Fax 212/826-5674. www.loews hotels.com. 351 units. $419–$699 double; from $539 suite. Children under 18 stay free in parent's room; additional $25 for rollaway bed. AE, DC, MC, V. Parking $49. Subway: 4, 5, 6, N, R to 59th St. Pets accepted. **Amenities:** 2 restaurants; cabaret; fitness center; children's program; concierge; 24-hr. room service; laundry service; dry cleaning. *In room:* A/C, TV w/VCR, high-speed Internet, dataport, minibar, hair dryer, iron, safe, CD player.

The Roger 𝒢𝒢 The hotel's namesake, Roger Williams, in time abandoned his puritanical roots to become a secular leader. Starting from the welcoming lobby with its odd assortment of mod yet comfortable seating, where small jazz combos entertain 3 nights a week, to the many different varieties of rooms—some small, some generous, some with huge landscaped terraces, others with views of the Empire State building and all with impressive amenities such as quilts, flatscreen TVs, complimentary high-speed and wireless Internet, and good-size marble bathrooms—the Roger is one of the top choices in what is a quiet yet convenient Midtown location. A floating granite staircase leads from the lobby to a mezzanine lounge, where you can have breakfast in the morning and drink cocktails by candlelight at night.

131 Madison Ave. (at E. 31st St.), New York, NY 10016. ℰ **888/448-7788** or 212/448-7000. Fax 212/448-7007. www.hotelrogerwilliams.com. 200 units. From $289 a night at press time. AE, DC, DISC, MC, V. Subway: 6 to 28th St./Lexington Ave. **Amenities:** Lounge; fitness center; concierge; laundry service; dry cleaning; complimentary Wi-Fi; conference suite. *In room:* A/C, flatscreen TV, Wi-Fi, high-speed Internet, minibar, iron/ironing board, safe.

70 Park Avenue 𝒢 Formerly the Doral Park Avenue, this Murray Hill property underwent a complete renovation when the San Francisco-based Kimpton Hotels took it over. Part of the renovation included design by Jeffrey Bilhuber who, with his warm earth tones, has created a homey, residential feel. In keeping with Kimpton's New Age trademark, the hotel encourages environmental awareness (including guest recycling and water-saving programs) and guests get a yoga channel on their TVs.

The lobby is a beauty with a long wooden table that serves as the concierge station and a 14-foot limestone and sandstone fireplace. Guest rooms, though not overly large, are efficiently constructed with an economical use of space: Note the minibar tucked into a dresser and the mahogany armoire that serves as the closet. In the room where I stayed, there were five huge mirrors, which could be a good thing or a bad thing depending on your self-esteem. Bathrooms in standard rooms are a bit tight but well outfitted, while a number of guest rooms offer two-person whirlpool spa tubs.

70 Park Ave. (btwn 37th and 38th sts.), New York, NY 10016. ℰ **877/707-2752** or 212/973-2400. Fax 212/973-2401. www.70parkave.com. 205 units. $325–$525 double; from $1,000 suites. (check website for Internet specials) AE, DC, DISC, MC, V. Valet parking $42. Subway: 4, 5, 6, 7, S to Grand Central. Pets accepted. **Amenities:** Restaurant; bar; complimentary wine reception; access to nearby fitness center; concierge; 24-hr. room service; laundry service. *In room:* A/C, TV, high-speed Internet, dataport, minibar, hair dryer, iron, safe, cordless telephone, DVD/CD player, voice mail.

Waldorf=Astoria and the Waldorf Towers 𝒢𝒢 If you are looking for the epitome of old-school elegance, you can't do better than the Waldorf=Astoria. This massive 1-square-block Art Deco masterpiece is not only a hotel icon, it's a genuine New

York City landmark. Here you'll find a lobby so big and grand, it's reminiscent of Grand Central Station, including having its own signature clock. With over 1,000 rooms, the pace can be hectic, and at times the lines for checking in might remind you of the post office. And what rooms they are; no two the same, yet all are airy, with high ceilings, traditional decor, comfortable linens and beds, and spacious marble bathrooms, along with fax machines and high-speed Internet access. For even more opulence, try a suite in the **Waldorf Towers,** where most rooms are bigger than most New York City apartments.

   Peacock Alley, off the main lobby is also open for breakfast, lunch and dinner, but famous for the sumptuous Sunday brunch.

301 Park Ave. (btwn 49th and 50th sts.), New York, NY 10022. ℭ 800/WALDORF, 800/774-1500, or 212/355-3000. Fax 212/872-7272 (Astoria) or 212/872-4875 (Towers). www.waldorfastoria.com or www.waldorf-towers.com. 1,245 units (180 in the Towers). Waldorf=Astoria $229–$585 double; from $549 suite. Waldorf Towers $549–$959 double; from $799 suite. Extra person $35. Children under 18 stay free in parent's room. Corporate, senior, seasonal, and weekend discounts may be available (as low as $189 at press time), as well as attractive package deals. AE, DC, DISC, MC, V. Parking $55. Subway: 6 to 51st St. **Amenities:** 4 restaurants; 4 bars; 3,000-sq.-ft. fitness center and excellent spa; concierge and theater desk; expansive 24-hr. business center; salon; 24-hr. room service; laundry service; dry cleaning; executive-level rooms. Tower rooms include butler service, Clefs d'Or concierge. *In room:* A/C, TV w/pay movies, high-speed Internet (in executive-level rooms and suites), dataport, minibar, coffeemaker, hair dryer, iron. Waldorf Towers suites include kitchenette or wet bar w/fridge, safe.

MODERATE

Doubletree Metropolitan Hotel *(Value*   With its retro 1960s look, this Doubletree brand hotel features a lobby stocked with mod furniture on which guests can lounge and surf the Internet on their laptops (the public spaces have Wi-Fi). Guest rooms are on the smallish side, and even with the renovations (including LCD televisions), they still have a cookie-cutter, motel feel to them. The beds, however, are like other Doubletree properties, extremely comfortable, guaranteeing the "Sweet Dreams by Doubletree Sleep Experience."

569 Lexington Ave. (at 51st St.), New York, NY 10022. ℭ 800/836-6471, 212/752-7000. Fax 212/758-6311. www.dtnewyork.com. 755 units. Rates $250–$350 single; $300–$450 double. Check website for specials as low as $199. AE, DC, MC, V. Parking $30 nearby. Subway: 6 to 51st St.; E, V to Lexington Ave. **Amenities:** Restaurant; bar; fitness center; concierge; business center; limited room service; barbershop; nail salon. *In room:* A/C, TV, high-speed Internet, hair dryer, iron, safe, 2-line telephone.

INEXPENSIVE

Hotel Grand Union *(Value*   This centrally located hotel is big with budget-minded international travelers. A pleasant white-on-white lobby leads to clean and spacious rooms with nice extras that are uncommon in this price category, such as hair dryers and free HBO. Fluorescent overhead lighting, unattractive colonial-style furniture, and an utter lack of natural light dampen the mood—but considering the roominess, low rates, and central-to-everything location, the Grand Union is a good deal. Room no. 309, a nicely configured quad with two twins and a queen in a separate alcove, is great for families. Most bathrooms have been outfitted in granite or tile; ask for a newly renovated one. The staff is helpful, and there's a pleasant sitting room off the lobby and an adjacent coffee shop for morning coffee or a quick burger.

34 E. 32nd St. (btwn Madison and Park aves.), New York, NY 10016. ℭ 212/683-5890. Fax 212/689-7397. www.hotelgrandunion.com. 95 units. $175–$300 single or double; $215–$325 twin or triple; $255–375 quad. Call or check website for special rates (as low as $90 at press time). AE, DC, DISC, MC, V. Parking $22 nearby. Subway: 6 to 33rd St. **Amenities:** Coffee shop; tour desk; fax service; Wi-Fi. *In room:* A/C, TV, dataport, fridge, hair dryer.

Hotel Pet Peeves

In my research for this book, I spend a lot of (perhaps *too* much) time in hotels trying to weed out the good from the bad. Many think it's a glamorous job: staying at luxury New York hotels, indulging in room service, spa services, and lounging in plush robes while I do my "research." Yet, it is still a *job*, and while I certainly enjoy the fun parts, I have compiled an extensive list of things that bug me about hotels (for more on real bugs, see the sidebar, "Sleep Tight and. . ." earlier in this chapter), little irritants that make me shake my head when they occur. So here is my top ten list of hotel pet peeves, things that you should look out for next time you book a room . . . if you can.

1. **Noisy hallways:** Is it just me and where I'm placed in a hotel that the storage rooms for housekeeping are right next to my room? Or are they on every floor? The opening and closing of doors, chattering of housekeepers, rattling of carts—and it goes on well into the night and begins first thing in the morning.
2. **Temperature control:** I'll be the first to admit that I'm not very technologically savvy, but why can't I ever get the right temperature in any of my rooms? It's always too hot or too cold, no matter what I do.
3. **Smoking rooms:** I always request a nonsmoking room. Why, then, when I check into a room, is there often that stale barroom smell, like a sense memory of the days when smoking was allowed in bars. If a Spanish rock band was staying in your suite before you, an air purifying ionizer should be provided to you at no charge.
4. **An extra charge to use the fitness facilities:** It seems that the hotel's that practice this outrageous policy are the ones whose rates are equally outrageous. We can safely call this greed.
5. **Charging extra for wireless Internet:** See above.

Hotel Thirty Thirty ⚘ (*Value*   Thirty Thirty is just right for bargain-hunting travelers looking for a splash of style with an affordable price tag. The design-conscious tone is set in the loftlike industrial-modern lobby. Rooms are mostly on the smallish side but do the trick for those who intend to spend their days out on the town rather than holed up here. Configurations are split between twin/twins (great for friends), queens, and queen/queens (great for triples, budget-minded quads, or shares that want more spreading-out room). Nice features include cushioned headboards; firm mattresses; two-line phones; nice built-in wardrobes; and spacious, nicely tiled bathrooms. A few larger units have kitchenettes, great if you're staying for a while, as you'll appreciate the extra room and the fridge. There's no room service, but delivery is available from nearby restaurants.

30 E. 30th St. (btwn Madison and Park aves.), New York, NY 10016. ⓒ **800/804-4480** or 212/689-1900. Fax 212/689-0023. www.thirtythirty-nyc.com. 243 units. $249–$349 double; $279–$399 double with kitchenette; $399–$499 quad. Call for last-minute deals, or check website for special promotions (as low as $99 at press time). AE, DC, DISC, MC, V. Parking $30 1 block away. Subway: 6 to 28th St. Pets accepted with advance approval. **Amenities:** Restaurant; concierge; laundry service; dry cleaning. *In room:* A/C, TV, dataport, hair dryer.

6. **Overstuffed minibars:** You bought a beer at a local deli that you would like to drink while watching a game on the enormous HDTV in your room. You want to keep the beer cold, but, no matter how hard you try, you cannot squeeze it into that minibar . . . and if you take something out, sensors that monitor removal of items will record it and charge you, even though you didn't drink it.

7. **Complimentary bottled water, or lack thereof:** Many hotels now provide a bottle or two when you check in, yet, those same culprits who charge for wireless Internet and using the fitness facilities make you take it out of the over-stuffed minibar and charge you $5 for it. (Or they put it by the bed or in the bathroom with a little note that tells you how much it costs).

8. **Lack of bathroom counter space:** Many hotels now feature those big glass or porcelain tub–like sinks, and they look great and are perfect for scooping big handfuls of water onto your face. But when I unpack my toiletries, I would like to keep my toothbrush, toothpaste, shaving cream and razor close to the sink instead of on top of the toilet bowl.

9. **Single-paned windows:** You might get away with them at a beachside resort, but in New York City it is essential to have double- or, better yet, triple-paned windows, especially if your room happens to overlook a busy street.

10. **Showers without shower curtains or shower doors:** I know, designers think a half-pane of Plexiglas is sufficient to keep water from spilling onto the bathroom floor and it looks very hip. Why, then, do I think something is missing when I take a shower? (Well, except for a puddle on the floor. That's there.)

Murray Hill Inn   In a renovated five-story walk-up in a pleasant and quiet residential neighborhood, the Murray Hill Inn is shoestring basic—but there's no arguing with its cleanliness. Rooms are tiny and outfitted with not much more than either one or two beds with motel-standard bedspread and furnishings, a wall rack, a phone, and a small TV; most rooms with shared bathroom also have private sinks (request one when booking). These Euro-style rooms share the in-hall bathrooms that are new and spotless. Some of the doubles have alcoves that can accommodate third travelers on cots if you're on an extra-tight budget. Rooms with private bathrooms are the nicest; most also have pullout sofas that can accommodate an extra traveler or two. Don't expect much in terms of facilities beyond a pleasant (if tiny) lobby, plus a downstairs sitting area with a vending machine, an ATM, and a luggage-storage area.

143 E. 30th St. (btwn Lexington and Third aves.), New York, NY 10016. ℂ **888/996-6376** or 212/545-0879. Fax 212/545-0103. www.murrayhillinn.com. 45 units, 3 with shared bathroom. $99 double with shared bathroom; $129–$159 double with private bathroom; $95–$169 private deluxe. Extra person $15. Children under 12 stay free in parent's room. AE, MC, V. Parking about $25 nearby. Subway: 6 to 28th St. *In room:* A/C, TV, Wi-Fi.

9 Upper West Side

To find the hotels described in this section, see p. 112.

VERY EXPENSIVE

Trump International Hotel & Tower ✦✦✦   From the outside, it's the prototypical, not very attractive Trump creation—a tall, dark monolith, hovering over Columbus Circle and lower Central Park. But go inside and spend a night or two, experience services such as your own "Trump Attaché," a personal concierge who will provide comprehensive services; take advantage of such first-class facilities as the 6,000-square-foot health club with lap pool and a full-service spa; or order room service from the hotel's signature restaurant, the four-star **Jean-Georges.**

Guest rooms are surprisingly understated, with high ceilings and floor-to-ceiling windows, some with incredible views of Central Park and all with telescopes for taking in the view, and marble bathrooms with Jacuzzi tubs. But if that's not enough—it certainly was for me—you also get two complimentary bottles of Trump water, complete with a picture of the Donald on each one. For a hotel this well run, you can forgive the man for his excesses.

1 Central Park West (at 60th St.), New York, NY 10023. ✆ **212/299-1000.** Fax 212/299-1150. www.trumpintl.com. 167 units. From $765 double; from $1,200 1- or 2-bedroom suite. Children stay free in parent's room. Check website for special rates and package deals; also try booking through www.travelweb.com for discounted rates. AE, DC, DISC, MC, V. Parking $48. Subway: A, B, C, D, 1 to 59th St./Columbus Circle. **Amenities:** Restaurant; spa and health club w/steam, sauna, and pool; Clefs d'Or concierge; staffed business center w/secretarial services; 24-hr. room service; in-room massage; babysitting; laundry service; dry cleaning; butler (personal attaché); CD library. *In room:* A/C, TV/VCR w/pay movies and video games, fax/copier/printer, high-speed Internet, dataport, minibar, coffeemaker, hair dryer, iron, laptop-size safe, DVD/CD player.

MODERATE

In addition to the hotels below, also consider the romantic **Country Inn the City** ✦, 270 W. 77th St., between Broadway and West End Avenue (✆ **212/580-4183;** www.countryinnthecity.com), comprised of four self-contained units in a charming 1891 town house (see "Plenty of Room at the Inn," p. 108).

Excelsior Hotel   The elegant Excelsior almost gives the Lucerne (see below) a run for its money. The chic residential location is across from the Museum of Natural History and steps from Central Park. However, the staff doesn't quite live up to the Lucerne's impeccable example. Freshly done in an attractive traditional style, the guest rooms boast high-quality furnishings, commodious closets, two-line phones, thick terry bathrobes, a work desk, and free bottled water. The pretty new bathrooms are most impressive. The two-bedded rooms are large enough to accommodate budget-minded families (a few even have two queens), and suites feature pullout sofas and pants presses. The sunny museum-facing rooms are only worth the extra dough if a park view is really important to you, as all rooms are relatively bright and quiet. On the second floor is a gorgeous library-style lounge with working fireplace, books, games, gorgeous leather seating, writing desks, and a large flatscreen TV with DVD player.

45 W. 81st St. (btwn Columbus Ave. and Central Park West), New York, NY 10024. ✆ **212/362-9200.** Fax 212/580-3972. www.excelsiorhotelny.com. 198 units. $299–$499 double; $399–$699 1-bedroom suite; $499–$899 2-bedroom suite. Extra person $20. Children 12 and under stay free in parent's room. Inquire about seasonal rates and specials (winter rates can go as low as $199 double). AE, DC, DISC, MC, V. Parking $27 nearby. Subway: B, C to 81st St./Museum of Natural History. **Amenities:** Breakfast room w/2 open-air decks and daily breakfast buffet; exercise

room; concierge; laundry service; dry cleaning. *In room:* A/C, TV w/pay movies/video games/Internet access, fax/copier, Wi-Fi, dataport, hair dryer, iron, safe.

Hotel Beacon 🐾🐾 *(Kids) (Value)*   For families, you won't find a better location—or value. Close to Central Park and Riverside Park, the Museum of Natural History and Lincoln Center, and major subway lines, the Beacon's location is ideal. Rooms are generously sized and feature a kitchenette, a roomy closet, and a marble bathroom. Nearly all standard rooms feature two double beds, and they're plenty big enough to sleep a family on a budget. The large one- and two-bedroom suites are some of the best bargains in the city; each has two closets and a pullout sofa in the well-furnished living room. The two-bedrooms have a second bathroom, making them well outfitted enough to house a small army—including my own. There's no room service, but a wealth of good budget dining options that deliver, along with such excellent markets as the aforementioned Fairway, make the Beacon even more of a home away from home.

2130 Broadway (at 75th St.), New York, NY 10023. *©* **800/572-4969** or 212/787-1100. Fax 212/724-0839. www. beaconhotel.com. 236 units. $210–$325 single or double; from $295 1- or 2-bedroom suite. Extra person $15. Children under 17 stay free in parent's room. Check website for special deals (doubles from $145; 1-bedroom suites as low as $195 at press time). AE, DC, DISC, MC, V. Parking $41 1 block away. Subway: 1, 2, 3 to 72nd St. **Amenities:** Coffee shop adjacent; access to health club in the building; concierge; laundry service; dry cleaning; coin-op laundry; fax and copy service; Internet center. *In room:* A/C, TV w/pay movies, kitchenette, hair dryer, iron, laptop-size safe.

The Lucerne 🐾🐾 *(Finds)*   As a longtime resident of the Upper West Side, I can easily say the Lucerne, in a magnificent 1903 landmark building, best captures the feel of that special neighborhood. Service is impeccable, especially for a moderately priced hotel and everything is fresh and immaculate. The rooms are comfortable and big enough for kings, queens, or two doubles, with attractive bathrooms complete with travertine counters. Some of the rooms have views of the Hudson River. The suites are extra-special and include kitchenettes, stocked minifridges, microwaves, and sitting rooms with sofas and extra TVs. The highly-rated **Nice Matin** (p. 203) offers room service for breakfast, lunch, and dinner. But if you don't want to dine there, you can sample some of the neighborhood food at nearby Zabar's or H&H Bagels.

201 W. 79th St. (at Amsterdam Ave.), New York, NY 10024. *©* **800/492-8122** or 212/875-1000. Fax 212/362-7251. www.thelucernehotel.com. 250 units. $280–$440 Superior Queen; $310–$470 Superior Double; $330–$490 Superior King or Deluxe Double; $360–520 Deluxe King; $390–$600 1-bedroom suite. Extra person $20. Children under 16 stay free in parent's room. AAA discounts offered, check website for Internet deals. AE, DC, DISC, MC, V. Parking $29 nearby; valet parking $42. Subway: 1 to 79th St. **Amenities:** Restaurant; fitness center; business center; limited room service; laundry service; dry cleaning. *In room:* A/C, TV w/Nintendo and Internet access, dataport, Wi-Fi, coffeemaker, hair dryer, iron, in-room safe.

INEXPENSIVE

Hotel Belleclaire 🐾   This Beaux Arts hotel boasts a great Upper West Side location and renovated, stylish guest rooms that are larger than most. The accommodations, though simple, do the job, and the management seems intent on pleasing. The rooms have small, freshly tiled bathrooms with tub/shower combos (six have roll-in showers to accommodate travelers with disabilities). Beds have cushioned headboards, and there are nice fabric-covered cubes for modular seating; closets are small. The shared-bathroom units are the same but have in-room sinks and share hall bathrooms at a ratio of three to one. The family suite features two attached, semiprivate bedrooms

Uptown Accommodations

Affinia Gardens **10**

The Carlyle: A Rosewood Hotel **8**

Country Inn the City **5**

Excelsior Hotel **2**

Hotel Beacon **6**

Hotel Belleclaire **4**

Hotel Newton **1**

Hotel Plaza Athénée **19**

The Lowell **12**

The Lucerne **3**

The Regency **11**

Trump International Hotel & Tower **7**

Ⓜ Subway stop

Upper Manhattan

Uptown

Midtown

Downtown

with a bathroom, a minifridge, and a big walk-in closet. This is a decent choice in a first-class residential neighborhood.

250 W. 77th St. (at Broadway), New York, NY 10024. ☎ 877/HOTEL-BC (468-3522) or 212/362-7700. Fax 212/362-1004. www.hotelbelleclaire.com. 189 units, 39 with shared bathroom. $109–$229 double with shared bathroom; $169–$389 double with private bathroom; $299–$489 family suite. Ask about AAA, group, and other discounts. AE, DC, DISC, MC, V. Parking $25 nearby. Subway: 1 to 79th St. **Amenities:** Access to nearby health club; tour desk; laundry service; dry cleaning; fax. *In room:* A/C, TV w/pay movies and games, Wi-Fi, dataport, fridge, hair dryer, iron.

Hotel Newton ⊛ *Value* On the northern extreme of the Upper West Side, the Newton doesn't scream "budget" at every turn. As you enter the pretty lobby, you're greeted by a uniformed staff that's attentive and professional. The rooms are generally large, with good, firm beds, a work desk, and a sizable bathroom, plus roomy closets in most (a few of the cheapest have wall racks only). Some are big enough to accommodate

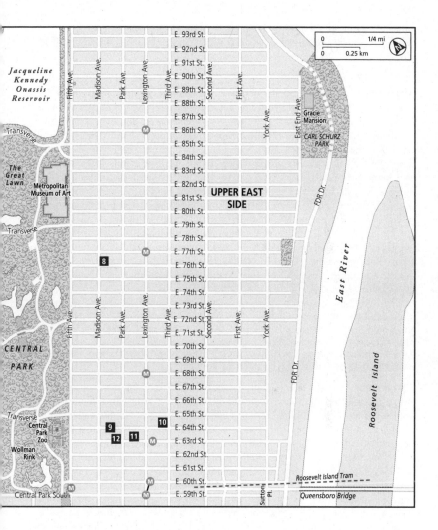

families, with two doubles or two queen beds. The suites feature two queen beds in the bedroom, a sofa in the sitting room, plus niceties such as a microwave, minifridge, and iron, making them well worth the few extra dollars. The bigger rooms and suites have been upgraded with cherry wood furnishings, but even the older laminated furniture is much nicer than I usually see in this price range. The 96th Street express subway stop is just a block away, and the Key West Diner next door is a favorite for huge, cheap breakfasts.

2528 Broadway (btwn 94th and 95th sts.), New York, NY 10025. ℂ **888/HOTEL58** or 212/678-6500. Fax 212/678-6758. www.hotelnewtoncom. 110 units. $95–$175 double or junior suite. Extra person $25. Children under 15 stay free in parent's room. AAA, corporate, senior, and group rates available; check website for special Internet deals. AE, DC, DISC, MC, V. Parking $27 nearby. Subway: 1, 2, 3 to 96th St. **Amenities:** 24-hr. room service. *In room:* A/C, TV, Wi-Fi, hair dryer.

10 Upper East Side

To find the hotels described in this section, see p. 138.

VERY EXPENSIVE

The Carlyle, A Rosewood Hotel ✾✾✾   This 34-story *grande dame* towers over Madison Avenue majestically, perfectly epitomizes the old-world, moneyed neighborhood where it stands. Service is white-glove (literally) and doormen actually wear bowler hats; many celebrities and dignitaries, some with faces obscured by silk scarves, sip tea in the hotel's cozy Gallery. Guest rooms range from singles to seven-room suites, some with terraces and full dining rooms. All have marble bathrooms with whirlpool tubs and all the amenities you'd expect from a hotel of this caliber. The English manor–style decor is luxurious but not excessive, creating the comfortably elegant ambience of an Upper East Side apartment. Many apartments have breathtaking views of either downtown or the West Side and Central Park.

The marble-floored lobby with Piranesi prints and murals is a beauty. . The hotel's supper club **Cafe Carlyle** (p. 365) is the place for first-rate cabaret. Charming **Bemelmans Bar,** named after illustrator Ludwig Bemelmans, who created the Madeline books and painted the mural here (see "Checking into Hotel Bars," in chapter 9), is a great spot for cocktails.

35 E. 76th St. (at Madison Ave.), New York, NY 10021. ✆ **800/227-5737** or 212/744-1600. Fax 212/717-4682. www.thecarlyle.com. 180 units. $650–$950 double; from $950 1- or 2-bedroom suite. AE, DC, DISC, MC, V. Parking $48. Subway: 6 to 77th St. Pets under 25 lbs accepted. **Amenities:** 3 restaurants (including one of the city's best cabaret rooms); tearoom; bar; high-tech fitness room w/sauna, Jacuzzi, and spa services; concierge; 24-hr. room service; laundry service; dry cleaning; video library. *In room:* A/C, TV/VCR, fax/copier/printer, high-speed Internet, pantry kitchenette or full kitchen w/minibar, hair dryer, safe, CD player.

Hotel Plaza Athénée ✾✾✾   This hideaway in New York's most elegant neighborhood (the stretch of Madison Ave. in the 60s) is elegant, luxurious, and oozing with sophistication. With antique furniture, hand-painted murals, and the Italian-marble floor that adorns the lobby, the Plaza Athénée has a European feel. In that tradition, service here is as good as it gets, with personalized check-in and attentive staff at every turn. The rooms come in a variety of shapes and sizes, and are all high-ceilinged and spacious; entrance foyers give them a residential feel. They are designed in rich fabrics and warm colors that help set a tone that makes you want to lounge in your room longer than you should. Many of the suites have terraces large enough to dine on. The Portuguese-marble bathrooms are outfitted with thick robes made for the hotel. The lush, leather-floored lounge is called **Bar Seine** and is a welcome spot for a predinner cocktail. The restaurant, **Arabelle,** receives high praise for its weekend brunch.

37 E. 64th St. (btwn Madison and Park aves.), New York, NY 10021. ✆ **800/447-8800** or 212/734-9100. Fax 212/772-0958. www.plaza-athenee.com. 149 units. $755–$825 double; from $1,620 suite. Check for packages and seasonal specials (as low as $495 at press time). AE, DC, DISC, MC, V. Parking $53. Subway: F to Lexington Ave. **Amenities:** Restaurant; bar; fitness center; Clefs d'Or concierge; business center; 24-hr. room service; laundry service; dry cleaning. *In room:* A/C, TV, fax, high-speed Internet, dataport, minibar, hair dryer, safe.

The Lowell ✾✾✾ *Kids*   The Lowell's style of luxury is best described as elegant, sophisticated 20th-century opulence. It has the feel of a residential dwelling; the lobby is small and clubby with first-rate European, old-world service. The rooms are the real treasures; each unique and all a good size. About two-thirds are suites with kitchenettes or full kitchens; some have terraces and most have working fireplaces. In the rooms you'll also find nice big, cushy armchairs, lots of leather, interesting artwork, and porcelain figurines scattered about. Bathrooms are Italian marble and outfitted with Bulgari amenities. On a quiet, tree-lined street 1 block from Central Park and right in the middle of Madison Avenue shopping, the Lowell's location is ideal for those who want (and can afford) an urban retreat away from the Midtown madness.

28 E. 63rd St. (btwn Madison and Park aves.), New York, NY 10021. ℂ **212/838-1400.** Fax 212/319-4230. www. lowellhotel.com. 70 units. From $735 doubles; from $935 suites. Ask about packages and weekend and seasonal rates. AE, DC, DISC, MC, V. Parking $49. Subway: F to Lexington Ave. Pets under 15 lb. accepted. **Amenities:** 2 restaurants; tearoom; well-outfitted fitness room; 24-hr. concierge; limousine service; secretarial services; 24-hr. room service; babysitting; laundry service; dry cleaning; video library. *In room:* A/C, TV/VCR/DVD, fax/copier, Wi-Fi, dataport, minibar, hair dryer, CD player.

EXPENSIVE

Affinia Gardens 🕸 *(Finds)*   One of the newest members of the Affinia hospitality group (the Benjamin, p. 128, Affinia Dumont, p. 128, Affinia Manhattan, p. 116), this Upper East Side property has a residential feel that is true to the neighborhood. Affinia has transformed the hotel into an oasis of tranquility. Off the lobby is the lounge, appropriately called "Serenity," a 24-hour quiet zone where you can sit in comfort, sip tea, and unwind. If you choose to relax in your room, you can order, free of charge, a "tranquility kit." Or you can just lay back on the very comfortable Affinia bed and snooze to the calming natural sound of the ocean, brook, wind, or forest that come with the clock radio/CD player. This is an all-suite hotel and rooms range from junior suites to two-bedrooms; all are generously sized and come with full kitchens. Bathrooms, proportionally, are on the smallish side but well outfitted. Though it's in a good, highly desirable New York neighborhood, the hotel is a bit out of the way from the center of things. But that can be a plus if tranquility is truly what you seek.

215 E. 64th St. (btwn Second and Third aves.), New York, NY 10021. ℂ **866/AFFINIA** or 212/355-1230. Fax 212/ 758-7858. www.affinia.com. 136 units. Rates from $399, all suites. Check website for specials and Internet rates. Valet parking $32. AE, DC, DISC, MC, V. Subway: 6 to 68th St.–Lexington Ave. Fitness club; small business center; limited room service; coin-operated laundry. *In room:* A/C, TV/DVD, high-speed Internet, dataport, kitchen, iron, safe, CD player/clock radio.

6

Where to Dine

Attention, foodies: Welcome to your mecca. Without a doubt, New York is the best restaurant town in the country, and one of the finest in the world. Other cities might have particular specialties, but no other culinary capital spans the globe as successfully as the Big Apple.

New Yorkers can be fickle. One moment a restaurant is hot, the next it's passé. So, restaurants close with a frequency we wish applied to the arrival of subway trains. Always call ahead.

But there's one thing we all have to face sooner or later: Eating in many of the more high profile restaurants in New York isn't cheap. Wherever you're from, particularly if you hail from the reasonably-priced American heartland, New York's restaurants will seem *expensive.* Yet good value abounds, especially if you're willing to try ethnic cuisine (including types you may not have had before), and venture beyond tourist zones into such neighborhoods as Chinatown, Harlem, Upper Manhattan, the East Village, the upper Upper West Side, and the boroughs. I've included inexpensive restaurants in every neighborhood, including some of the city's best-kept secrets, so you'll know where to get good value for your money no matter where you are in Manhattan.

RESERVATIONS

Reservations are always a good idea in New York, and a necessity for popular restaurants if your party is bigger than two. Do yourself a favor and call ahead as a rule of thumb so you won't be disappointed. If you're booking dinner on a weekend night, it's a good idea to call a few days in advance if you can.

Call *far* ahead for any special meal you don't want to miss—a month in advance is a good idea. Most top places start taking reservations exactly 30 days in advance, so if you want to eat at a hot restaurant at a popular hour—Saturday at 8pm, say, at Chanterelle—be sure to mark your calendar and start dialing 30 days prior at 9am. If you're booking a holiday dinner, call even earlier.

But if you didn't call well ahead and your heart's set on dinner at BLT Market or Buddakan, don't despair. Often, early or late hours—between 5:30 and 6:30pm or after 9pm—are available, especially on weeknights. And try calling the day before or first thing in the morning, when you may be able to take advantage of a last-minute cancellation. Or go for lunch, which is usually much easier to book without lots of advance notice. If you're staying at a hotel with a concierge, don't be afraid to use them—they can often get you into hot spots that you couldn't get into on your own.

But what if they don't *take* reservations? Lots of restaurants, especially at the affordable end of the price continuum, don't take reservations at all. One of the ways they keep prices down is by packing people in as quickly as possible. Thus, the best cheap and midprice restaurants often have a wait. Again, your best bet is to go early. Often you can get in more quickly on a weeknight. Or just go, knowing that you're

---

Tips **Make Reservations on the 'net**

OpenTable (www.opentable.com) allows you to book a reservation—and get an instant confirmation—over the Web at about 150 restaurants throughout Manhattan. You'll also find that an increasing number of restaurants offer online reservations through their own websites.

---

going to have to wait if you head to a popular spot; hunker down with a cocktail at the bar and enjoy the festivities around you.

SMOKING POLICY

You cannot light up in any restaurant in the city. Some restaurants entice smokers with back gardens or patios where smoking is permitted, but otherwise, you'll have to step out to the sidewalk (or "Bloomberg Lounge") for a cigarette. Some restaurants provide benches, chairs, and ashtrays, but it gets mighty cold out there in the winter.

TIPPING

Tipping is easy in New York. The way to do it: Double the 8.375% sales tax and *voilà,* happy waitstaff. In fancier venues, another 5% is appropriate for the captain. If the wine steward helps, hand him or her 10% of the bottle's price.

Leave $1 per item, no matter how small, for the checkroom attendant.

MORE SOURCES FOR SERIOUS FOODIES

Of course, New York has far more fabulous dining than I have room to discuss here—although the listings below are enough to keep you fat and happy for a year, much less the length of a vacation. But if you'd like a wider selection, a few good sources are available online or from your local bookstore.

Your best online sources are the online arm of the weekly *New York* magazine (www. nymag.com), which also features a daily food blog; **New York Today** (www.nytoday. com), the *New York Times's* arts and lifestyle site, where you can access a database of the paper's stellar restaurant reviews; and the *Village Voice* (www.villagevoice.com), especially for the cheap-eats reviews by Robert Sietsema. For a good online source with reader's reviews and menus, try **www.menupages.com**, which has over 6,000 menus online.

Without a doubt, the best online source for the serious foodie is **www. chowhound.com**, a national website with message boards in local areas, including New York, where you can make an inquiry about a certain restaurant, type of food, location, and so on, and within a few hours, you might have five or more informative responses.

The *Zagat Survey,* which has made a name for itself rating restaurants based on extensive diner surveys, maintains a searchable database of city restaurants at **www.zagat.com**, so if you're willing to do your research before you leave home (or if you're toting a laptop), there's no need to acquire a hard copy of the no-frills guide. They do, however, charge a fee to access the online information. At press time, a year's subscription of Zagat online was $24.95 and a 30-day subscription was $4.95.

The slick weekly *Time Out New York* has an "Eat Out" section that always includes listings for *TONY*'s 100 Favorite Restaurants in every issue, as well as coverage of new openings and dining trends. Weekly *New York* magazine also maintains extensive restaurant listings in its listings section at the back of the magazine.

1 Restaurants by Cuisine

AMERICAN

See also "Contemporary American," below.

Artie's New York Delicatessen (Upper West Side, $, p. 190)

Bar Blanc (West Village, $$$, p. 164)

Big Nick's Burger and Pizza Joint ⊛ (Upper West Side, $, p. 205)

Brgr ⊛ (Chelsea, $, p. 194)

Bubby's Pie Company ⊛ (TriBeCa and Brooklyn, $$, p. 152 and 206)

Burger Joint ⊛⊛ (Midtown West, $, p. 194)

City Bakery ⊛ (Flatiron District, $, p. 178)

Clinton St. Baking Company ⊛ (Lower East Side, $, p. 156)

Cookshop ⊛⊛ (Chelsea, $$$, p. 170)

Country ⊛⊛ (Midtown East, $$$, p. 191)

Ed's Lobster Bar ⊛⊛ (NoHo, $$, p. 159)

Good Enough to Eat ⊛ (Upper West Side, $, p. 207)

The Grocery (Brooklyn, $$, p. 215)

Norma's ⊛⊛ (Midtown West, $$, p. 185)

New York Burger Co. (Flatiron District $, p. 194)

The Odeon ⊛ (TriBeCa, $$, p. 153)

P.J. Clarke's ⊛ (Midtown East, Financial District, Upper West Side, $$, p. 194)

Rare Bar & Grill ⊛ (Greenwich Village, Midtown East, $$, p. 195)

Serendipity 3 ⊛ (Upper East Side, $, p. 210)

Shake Shack (Flatiron District, $, p. 195)

Tavern on the Green (Upper West Side, $$$, p. 197)

Telepan ⊛⊛ (Upper West Side, $$$, p. 202)

Walker's (TriBeCa, $, p. 369)

ASIAN FUSION/PAN-ASIAN/PACIFIC RIM

Buddakan ⊛ (Chelsea, $$$, p. 167)

Cendrillon ⊛⊛ (SoHo, $$, p. 158)

Momofuku Noodle Bar ⊛ (East Village, $$, p. 161)

Nyonya ⊛ (Chinatown, $, p. 154)

BARBECUE/SOUTHERN

Blue Smoke (Flatiron District, $$, p. 183)

Daisy May's BBQ (Midtown West, $$, p. 182)

Dinosaur Bar-B-Que (Harlem, $, p. 210)

Fette Sau ⊛⊛ (Williamsburg, Brooklyn, $$, p. 214)

Hill Country ⊛ (Flatiron District, $$, p. 176)

Johnny Utah's ⊛ (Midtown West, $$, p. 184)

Rack & Soul (Upper West Side, $$, p. 183)

RUB ⊛⊛ (Chelsea, $$, p. 171)

The Smoke Joint (Fort Greene, Brooklyn, $$, p. 183)

Virgil's Real BBQ ⊛⊛ (Times Square, $$, p. 185)

BRAZILIAN

Porcao ⊛ (Flatiron District, $$$, p. 175)

BREAKFAST & BRUNCH

Absolute Bagels (Upper West Side, $, p. 177)

Artie's New York Delicatessen (Upper West Side, $, p. 190)

Barney Greengrass, the Sturgeon King (Upper West Side, $, p. 190)

Big Wong King ⊛ (Chinatown, $, p. 154)

Bubby's Pie Company ⊛ (TriBeCa and Brooklyn, $$, p. 152 and 206)

Café Luluc (Brooklyn, $$, p. 215)

Clinton St. Baking Company ௯
(Lower East Side, $, p. 156)
Ess-A-Bagel (Midtown East, $,
p. 177)
Good Enough to Eat ௯ (Upper West
Side, $, p. 207)
Katz's Delicatessen ௯௯ (Lower East
Side, $, p. 156)
Metro Marché ௯ (Times Square, $$,
p. 185)
Murray's Bagels (Greenwich Village,
$, p. 177)
Norma's ௯௯ (Midtown West, $$,
p. 185)
Sylvia's (Harlem, $, p. 212)
Veselka ௯ (East Village, $, p. 164)

CHINESE

Big Wong King ௯ (Chinatown, $,
p. 154)
Little Pepper (Queens, $, p. 218)
New York Noodletown ௯௯ (China-
town, $, p. 154)
Wo Hop (Chinatown, $, p. 162)

CONTEMPORARY AMERICAN

Bar Blanc ௯ (West Village, $$$, p. 164)
BLT Market ௯௯ (Midtown West,
$$$$, p. 179)
Country ௯௯ (Midtown East, $$$,
p. 191)
Ouest ௯௯௯ (Upper West Side, $$$,
p. 202)
Park Avenue Winter ௯௯ (Upper East
Side, $$$, p. 209)
The River Café (Brooklyn, $$$$,
p. 213)
South Gate ௯ (Midtown West, $$$,
p. 183)
Water's Edge ௯௯ (Queens, $$$,
p. 215)

CONTINENTAL

Tavern on the Green (Upper West
Side, $$$, p. 197)

FILIPINO

Cendrillon ௯௯ (SoHo, $$, p. 158)
Ihawan (Queens, $, p. 218)

FRENCH

Café Boulud ௯ (Upper East Side,
$$$, p. 208)
Café des Artistes ௯ (Upper West Side,
$$$$, p. 197)
Capsouto Frères ௯ (TriBeCa, $$$,
p. 150)
Chanterelle ௯௯௯ (TriBeCa, $$$$,
p. 148)
Chez Napolean (Midtown West, $$,
p. 163)
Country ௯௯ (Midtown East, $$$,
p. 191)
Daniel (Upper East Side, $$$$, p. 201)
db Bistro Moderne ௯ (Midtown
West, $$$, p. 180)
Jean-Georges ௯௯௯ (Upper West
Side, $$$$, p. 201)
Landmarc ௯௯ (TriBeCa, Upper West
Side, $$$, p. 150)
Le Bernardin (Midtown West, $$$$,
p. 201)
Marseille ௯ (Midtown West, $$,
p. 184)
Mas ௯௯ (Greenwich Village, $$$,
p. 166)
Metro Marché ௯ (Times Square, $$,
p. 185)
Nice Matin ௯ (Upper West Side, $$,
p. 203)
Nizza ௯௯ (Midtown West, $, p. 188)
Paradou ௯ (Meat-Packing District,
$$$, p. 166)
Sapa ௯௯ (Flatiron District, $$$,
p. 175)

GOURMET SANDWICHES/
DELI/TAKEOUT

Absolute Bagels (Upper West Side, $,
p. 177)
Artie's New York Delicatessen (Upper
West Side, $, p. 190)
Barney Greengrass, the Sturgeon King
(Upper West Side, $, p. 190)
Carnegie Deli (Midtown West, $,
p. 190)
Eisenberg's Coffee Shop (Flatiron
District, $, p. 163)

Ess-A-Bagel (Midtown East, $, p. 177)

Gray's Papaya (Upper West Side, Greenwich Village, $, p. 152)

H&H Bagels (Upper West Side, Midtown West, $, p. 177)

Junior's (Brooklyn, Midtown East, $, p. 194)

Kalustyan's ✿ (Midtown East, $, p. 194)

Katz's Delicatessen ✿✿ (Lower East Side, $, p. 156)

Kossar's Bialys (Lower East Side, $, p. 177)

Murray's Bagels (Greenwich Village, $, p. 177)

Nathan's Famous (Brooklyn, $, p. 152)

2nd Avenue Deli (Midtown East, $, p. 190)

Stage Deli (Midtown West, $, p. 190)

Shorty's ✿ (Midtown West, $, p. 153)

GREEK

Anthos ✿✿ (Midtown West, $$$$, p. 178)

Kefi ✿✿✿ (Upper West Side, $$, p. 203)

Mia Dona ✿✿ (Midtown East, $$$, p. 192)

Molyvos ✿✿ (Midtown West, $$$, p. 180)

Thalassa ✿ (TriBeCa, $$$, p. 151)

Uncle Nick's (Midtown West, $, p. 189)

INDIAN

Bombay Talkie ✿ (Chelsea, $$, p. 171)

Brick Lane Curry House ✿ (East Village, $$, p. 161)

Chola ✿✿ (Midtown East, $$, p. 193)

Dévi ✿✿ (Flatiron District, $$$, p. 174)

Tamarind ✿✿ (Flatiron District, $$$, p. 176)

ITALIAN

Abboccato ✿ (Midtown West, $$$, p. 180)

A Voce ✿✿ (Flatiron District, $$$, p. 173)

Barbetta ✿✿ (Midtown West, $$$, p. 180)

Becco ✿ (Midtown West, $$, p. 184)

Bread ✿ (Nolita, SoHo, $, p. 160)

Bread Tribeca ✿ (TriBeCa, $$, p. 151)

Carmine's ✿ (Upper West Side, Times Square, $$, p. 202)

Celeste ✿✿ (Upper West Side, $, p. 205)

Covo Trattoria & Pizzeria ✿ (Harlem, $, p. 210)

'Cesca ✿✿ (Upper West Side, $$$, p. 197)

Dominick's (Bronx, $$, p. 213)

Ferdinando's Focacceria ✿ (Brooklyn, $, p. 215)

Fiamma Osteria ✿✿ (SoHo, $$$, p. 158)

Frankie and Johnnie's Pine Restaurant (Bronx, $$, p. 213)

Gemma ✿ (East Village, $$$, p. 160)

'inoteca ✿✿ (Lower East Side, $$, p. 156)

La Lunetta (Brooklyn, Flatiron District, $$, p. 215)

Landmarc ✿✿ (TriBeCa, Upper West Side, $$$, p. 150)

La Pizza Fresca Ristorante ✿✿ (Flatiron District, $$, p. 177)

Lupa ✿✿ (SoHo, $$, p. 159)

Mario's Restaurant (Bronx, $$, p. 213)

Mia Dona ✿✿ (Midtown East, $$$, p. 192)

Naples 45 ✿ (Midtown East, $$, p. 193)

Nick's Family-Style Restaurant and Pizzeria ✿ (Upper East Side, $, p. 209)

Nizza ✿✿ (Midtown West, $, p. 188)

Paola's ✿ (Upper East Side, $$$, p. 208)

JAPANESE

Le Miu ✿✿ (East Village, $$$, p. 161)

Masa (Upper West Side, $$$$, p. 201)

Sapporo ✿ (Midtown West, $, p. 189)

JEWISH DELI

Artie's New York Delicatessen (Upper West Side, $, p. 190)

Barney Greengrass, the Sturgeon King (Upper West Side, $, p. 190)

Carnegie Deli (Midtown West, $, p. 190)

Junior's (Brooklyn, Midtown East, $, p. 194)

Katz's Delicatessen *(x(x* (Lower East Side, $, p. 156)

Stage Deli (Midtown West, $, p. 190)

KOREAN

Mandoo Bar *(x* (Midtown West, Greenwich Village, $, p. 188)

LATIN AMERICAN/SPANISH/ SOUTH AMERICAN

El Faro *(x* (Greenwich Village, $$, p. 163)

Flor de Mayo (Upper West Side, $, p. 205)

Rayuela *(x(x* (Lower East Side, $$$, p. 155)

MEDITERRANEAN

A.O.C. Bedford *(x(x* (Greenwich Village, $$$, p. 164)

Landmarc *(x(x* (TriBeCa, Upper West Side, $$$, p. 150)

Savann *(x* (Upper West Side, $$, p. 203)

MEXICAN/TEX-MEX/ SOUTHWESTERN

Noche Mexicana *(x* (Upper West Side, $, p. 207)

Pampano *(x(x* (Midtown East, $$$, p. 192)

MIDDLE EASTERN

Afghan Kebab House (Midtown West, $, p. 188)

Kalustyan's *(x* (Midtown East, $, p. 194)

Zaytoons (Brooklyn, $$, p. 215)

PIZZA

Big Nick's Burger and Pizza Joint *(x* (Upper West Side, $, p. 205)

Covo Trattoria & Pizzeria *(x* (Harlem, $, p. 210)

DiFara Pizza *(x* (Brooklyn, $, p. 186)

Grimaldi's Pizzeria (Brooklyn, $, p. 186)

Joe's Pizza (Greenwich Village, $, p. 153)

John's Pizzeria (Times Square, Greenwich Village, Upper East Side, $, p. 186)

La Pizza Fresca Ristorante *(x(x* (Flatiron District, $$, p. 177)

Lombardi's (Little Italy, $, p. 187)

Naples 45 *(x* (Midtown East, $$, p. 193)

Pala *(x* (Lower East Side, $$, p. 156)

Patsy's Pizzeria *(x(x* (Harlem, $, p. 187)

Totonno's Pizzeria Napolitano (Upper East Side, Brooklyn, $, p. 187)

PORTUGUESE

Pao! *(x* (SoHo, $$, p. 159)

SCANDINAVIAN

Aquavit *(x(x(x* (Midtown East, $$$, p. 191)

SEAFOOD

BLT Fish *(x(x* (Flatiron District, $$$, p. 174)

Ed's Lobster Bar *(x(x* (NoHo, $$, p. 159)

Le Bernardin (Midtown West, $$$$, p. 201)

The Neptune Room *(x* (Upper West Side, $$$, p. 200)

New York Noodletown *(x(x* (Chinatown, $, p. 154)

Oceana *(x(x(x* (Midtown East, $$$, p. 192)

Ocean Grill *(x(x* (Upper West Side, $$$, p. 200)

Oyster Bar & Restaurant *(x* (Midtown East, $$, p. 194)

Vincent's Clam Bar (Little Italy, $$, p. 162)

SOUL FOOD

Amy Ruth's (Harlem, $, p. 212)
Charles' Southern Style Kitchen 𝔊
  (Harlem, $, p. 212)
M&G Diner (Harlem, $, p. 212)
Miss Mamie's Spoonbread Too
  (Harlem, $$, p. 212)
Rack & Soul (Upper West Side, $$,
  p. 183)
Sylvia's (Harlem, $, p. 212)

SPANISH

El Faro 𝔊 (Greenwich Village, $$,
  p. 163)
La Nacional 𝔊𝔊 (Chelsea, $$, p. 171)
Rayuela 𝔊𝔊 (Lower East Side, $$$,
  p. 155)

STEAK

Ben Benson's Steakhouse (Midtown
  West, $$$$, p. 173)
Benjamin Steakhouse 𝔊 (Midtown
  East, $$$$, p. 173)
BLT Steak 𝔊𝔊𝔊 (Midtown East,
  $$$, p. 191)
Bull and Bear (Midtown East, $$$,
  p. 172)
Frankie & Johnnie's 𝔊𝔊 (Midtown
  West, $$$, p. 181)
Harry's Steak and Café 𝔊𝔊 (Financial
  District, $$$, p. 150)
Jackson Avenue Steakhouse 𝔊
  (Queens, $$$, p. 216)
Kobe Club 𝔊 (Midtown West, $$$$,
  p. 179)

Keens Steakhouse 𝔊𝔊𝔊 (Midtown
  West, $$$, p. 181)
Michael Jordan's—The Steak House
  𝔊𝔊 (Midtown East, $$$, p. 172)
Peter Luger Steakhouse 𝔊𝔊 (Brooklyn,
  $$$, p. 213)
Porter House New York 𝔊𝔊 (Upper
  West Side, $$$$, p. 197)
Post House 𝔊𝔊 (Upper East Side,
  $$$, p. 207)
Primehouse 𝔊 (Flatiron District, $$$,
  p. 175)
Quality Meats 𝔊 (Midtown West,
  $$$$, p. 173)
Strip House 𝔊𝔊 (Greenwich Village,
  $$$, p. 166)
Uncle Jack's Steakhouse 𝔊 (Midtown
  West, $$$$, p. 173)

SWISS

Trestle on Tenth 𝔊 (Chelsea, $$$,
  p. 170)

THAI

Arunee Thai (Queens, $, p. 218)
Kittichai 𝔊 (SoHo, $$$, p. 158)
Wondee Siam 𝔊 (Midtown West, $,
  p. 189)

UKRAINIAN

Veselka 𝔊 (East Village, $, p. 164)

VIETNAMESE

Pho Viet Huong 𝔊 (Chinatown, $,
  p. 155)
Sapa 𝔊𝔊 (Flatiron District, $$$,
  p. 175)

2 Financial District, South Street Seaport & TriBeCa

To find the restaurants reviewed below, see the map on p. 149.

VERY EXPENSIVE

Chanterelle 𝔊𝔊𝔊 CONTEMPORARY FRENCH One of New York's best "special occasion" restaurants mainly because, well, they treat you *so* special. The dining room is a charmer with changing daily floral displays and an interesting modern-art collection. Tables are far enough apart to give diners plenty of intimacy, something rare in many New York restaurants these days. Your server will work with you on your choices, pairing items that go best together. The French-themed menu is seasonal and changes every few weeks, but one signature dish appears on almost every menu:

Where to Dine in the Financial District, TriBeCa, Chinatown & Little Italy

Big Wong King **12**
Bread Tribeca **9**
Bubby's Pie **3**
Capsuto Freres **1**
Chanterelle **5**
Chinatown Ice Cream Factory **13**
Harry's Steak & Café **8**
Landmarc **6**
New York Noodletown **14**

Nyonya **10**
Odeon **7**
Pho Viet Huong **16**
Thalassa **4**
Vincent's Clam Bar **11**
Walker's **2**
Wo Hop **15**

a marvelous grilled seafood sausage. Cheese lovers should opt for a cheese course—the presentation and selection can't be beat. The wine list is superlative but expensive. Still, you don't come to Chanterelle on the cheap—you come to celebrate.

2 Harrison St. (at Hudson St.). ℂ 212/966-6960. www.chanterellenyc.com. Reservations recommended well in advance. Fixed-price lunch $42; a la carte lunch $22–$30; 3-course fixed-price dinner $95; tasting menu $125. AE, DISC, MC, V. Mon–Wed 5:30–10:30pm; Mon–Sat noon–2:30pm; Thurs–Sat 5:30–11pm; Sun 5–10pm. Subway: 1 to Franklin St.

EXPENSIVE

Capsouto Frères ✦ FRENCH   In 1980, before the triangle below Canal Street was given the acronym TriBeCa, and before the neighborhood became rife with celebrities and hip restaurants, Capsouto Frères opened. And through TriBeCa's amazing growth and its devastation after 9/11 and subsequent rebirth, Capsouto Frères has not only survived—a feat unto itself—but it has thrived with a loyal following. What accounts for the restaurant's longevity? Is it the simple, home-style French cuisine: the famous soufflés; the spicy *saucisson;* the always reliable sole meunière, steak frites, or cassoulet; the warm, wood-floored, high-ceilinged always-festive dining room; the gregarious and engaging hosts; the *freres* Jacques, Sammy, and Albert? Or is it a combination of all of the above? Whatever it is, it works. Sturdy and reliable Capsouto Frères offers a literal taste of what it was like before Robert De Niro "discovered" TriBeCa.

451 Washington St. (at Watts St.). ℂ 212/966-4900. www.capsoutofreres.com. Reservations recommended. Lunch prix fixe $24; main courses $12–$24; dinner prix fixe $35; main courses $16–$29. AE, DC MC, V. Tues–Fri noon–3:30pm; Sun–Thurs 6–10:30pm; Fri–Sat 6–11pm; brunch Sat–Sun noon–3:30pm. Subway: 1, A, C, E to Canal St.

Harry's Steaks & Café ✦✦ *Finds* STEAKHOUSE   Harry's is a crowd pleaser. It's a steakhouse, with all the accoutrements of your traditional red meat joint; dry-aged beef with hearty sides; it's a cafe, with a bountiful original menu, but equally dense selection, and it's a lively, Wall Street-area bar with a well-stocked spirits and wine selection. When you enter, you'll see the bar and you'll hear the traders celebrating their day's winnings, adjacent to the bar is the large cafe featuring leather banquettes. Down a few steps from the Café is the steakhouse, carved out of an old stone wine cellar. But it doesn't matter where you eat, the kitchen is the same and you can order from either menu. When I visited, I chose to mix and match from both menus. I started with a superb Greek salad topped with white anchovies from the Café menu followed by the grilled triple cut pork chops served on a bed of sauerkraut, accompanied by a Mason jar of fresh apple sauce with a chili pepper embedded in it. The side of escarole with white beans and prosciutto was almost a meal itself. The dry-aged rib steak is as good as you'll find anywhere west of Peter Luger's, but it was the crackling pork shank, from the Café menu, a gargantuan shank on the bone, its skin fried to crackling that stole the show. Just looking at it could send one's cholesterol soaring, but experiencing it is worth the health risk.

1 Hanover Square (at Pearl St.). ℂ 212/785-9200. www.harrysnyc.com. Reservations recommended. Main courses: $13–$43. AE, DC, DISC, MC, V. Café open 7 days; 11:30am–midnight; Steakhouse Mon–Fri 11am–11pm. Subway: 2, 3 to Wall St.

Landmarc ✦✦ *Finds* MEDITERRANEAN/FRENCH/ITALIAN   This cozy, intimate TriBeCa restaurant is too good to be considered just a neighborhood joint. Chef/owner Marc Murphy has put his own distinctive spin on this Italian/French rendition of a bistro. You'll find excellent smoked mozzarella and ricotta fritters alongside escargots bordelaise. It will be up to you to decide whether you imagine yourself in a Tuscan trattoria or a Provençal bistro. Or you can mix and match cuisines. Try the pasta of the day accompanied by mussels with a choice of sauce—Provençal, Dijonnaise, or the comforting blend of shallots, parsley, and white wine. Steaks and chops are cooked over an open fire and the steaks are offered with a variety of sauces; I had the hangar with a shallot bordelaise that complemented the meat perfectly. What keeps the neighbors pouring in, along with the excellent food, are the remarkably affordable wines sold, not by the glass, but by the bottle or half bottle. Desserts are simple, small, and priced that way, with none more than $3. For a special treat or if you've brought the kids, ask for the cotton candy. Now you won't find *that* in a Tuscan trattoria. Landmarc recently added an uptown location, at the Time Warner Center (10 Columbus Circle; ℂ **212/823-6123**).

179 W. Broadway (btwn Leonard and Worth sts.). ℂ **212/343-3883**. www.anvilny.com. Reservations recommended. Main courses $15–$34. AE, DC, DISC, MC, V. Mon–Fri noon–2am; Sat, Sun 9am–4pm and 5:30pm–2am. Subway: 1 to Franklin St.

Thalassa ℱ GREEK   Greek food is best when prepared simply with the freshest ingredients, especially fish, and Thalassa does a remarkable job of living up to that standard. The variety of seafood is staggering: When I visited, the options included fresh langoustines from Scotland, pound-and-a-half shrimp from Mexico, and a number of oyster selections. For starters, the kataifi-pastry-wrapped diver scallops with sheep's milk butter was a revelation, while the octopus, simply grilled with a red-wine vinaigrette, was as good as I've had west of Astoria (the very Greek neighborhood in Queens). The main courses won't disappoint either; the pan-roasted Dover sole was delicately prepared and perfectly seasoned with a touch of olive oil and lemon, while the sea bream with slices of diver scallops on top was exceptional. The knowledgeable sommelier can help you select a Greek wine from the restaurant's cellar, where a number of unusual and good Greek cheeses are also stored. The restaurant is large; tables are spaced well enough apart for intimacy, and service is attentive and pleasant.

179 Franklin St. (btwn Greenwich and Hudson sts.). ℂ **212/941-7661**. www.thalassanyc.com. Reservations recommended. Prix-fixe lunch $24; main courses dinner $28–$42. AE, DC, DISC, MC, V. Mon–Fri noon–3pm and Mon-Thurs 6–11pm; Fri–Sat 6–midnight; Sun 5–10pm. Subway: 1 to Franklin St.

MODERATE
Bread Tribeca ℱ NORTHERN ITALIAN   Bread Tribeca is one of the few restaurants in New York to feature the cuisine of Italy's Liguria region. What is Ligurian cuisine? Seafood is a big part of it; and Bread Tribeca does a good job with its *fritto misto,* a mixture of fried fish (such as calamari, cod, and mussels) and vegetables, and its *zuppa de pesce,* assorted seafood in a saffron-tomato sauce. Homemade pastas are another trademark of Ligurian food; and at Bread Tribeca you'll find *pansotti,* raviolilike dumplings served with a walnut sauce, and fresh *taglierini,* a spaghettilike pasta that's slightly overwhelmed by the dense combination of haricots verts, potatoes, and a surprisingly subtle pesto. A wood-burning oven turns out excellent thin-crust pizzas and roasted meats and, like its sister restaurant (see **Bread,** p. 160), the breads are superb, including a remarkable combination of sardine, tomato, and peperoncini slathered on a baguette. Most of the tables are communal, so if the restaurant is crowded, don't expect intimacy; and the 50-inch television that runs movies (when I was there last, *Chocolat*) is often a distraction, not a complement, to the food. On weekends a deejay spins calming, low-key music to accompany the rustic food.

301 Church St. (at Walker St.). ℂ **212/334-0200**. www.breadtribeca.com. Reservations recommended. Main courses $9–$27 lunch; $14–$27 dinner. AE, DC, DISC, MC, V. Sun–Thurs 11:30am–11pm; Fri–Sat 11:30am–midnight. Subway: A, C, E to Canal St.

Food in a N.Y. Minute

I do my best in this chapter to not mention the fast-food-chain options in the city. There was a time, though it's hard to believe, that McDonald's and Domino's pizza (oops I mentioned their names) were not to be found in New York. They are here now and, sadly, they are here to stay. But you needn't resort to the same options you can find in any town when you need a quick food fix. Here are a few original options you should consider before parting the golden arches.

New York is a hot dog town. You can buy them from street vendors all over the city and doing so is something everyone should experience. But once might be enough. If you want an original New York dog, **Nathan's Famous,** established in 1916, is the best example. There are Nathan's Famous hot dogs all over the city now, but though the hot dogs are the same, they just don't taste as good as the ones served in its original location on the **Coney Island boardwalk** in Brooklyn, 1310 Surf Ave., at Stillwell Avenue (© **718/946-2202**). If a 145-pound Japanese man can eat 53½ hot dogs in 12 minutes, you can certainly handle at least two—including an order of their fantastic crinkle-cut fries.

For the cheapest quick meal, nothing can match **Gray's Papaya.** This 24-hour hot-dog stand is a New York institution. Hot dogs go for 75¢, and the "Recession Special," two hot dogs and a drink, overly sweetened papaya, piña colada, or orange juice, is a whopping $3.50. The hot dogs are delicious, though for your own good, don't be tempted to eat more than two, despite the low prices. There are three Gray's Papaya around the city, but

Bubby's Pie Company ☞ AMERICAN   You might have to wait on line to eat at Bubby's. You might get squeezed in at a table perilously close to another couple. And you might have to talk quite loudly to maintain a conversation with your dining companion. But your level of discomfort will subside as soon as you begin to consume Bubby's comfort food. Whether it is the slow-cooked pulled barbecue pork, the magnificent, lighter-than-air meatloaf, or the buttermilk-fried half chicken, coupled with such sides as collard greens, sautéed spinach, macaroni and cheese, or baked beans, Bubby's dishes define comfort. Take Bubby's advice and save room for the desserts, especially the homemade pies; one taste of the chocolate peanut-butter pie immediately brought on happy childhood flashbacks. Breakfast is big here and lasts well into the middle of the day. On weekends, though, here in trendy TriBeCa, the wait for brunch can be lengthy. Celebrities need comfort, too, and you might spot one or two at Bubby's seeking anonymity and down-home chow. Bubby's also has a branch across the river in the DUMBO neighborhood of Brooklyn.

120 Hudson St. (at N. Moore St.). © **212/219-0666.** www.bubbys.com. Reservations recommended for dinner (not accepted for brunch). Main courses $10–$15 breakfast, brunch, and lunch; $10–$21 dinner. DC, DISC, MC, V. Mon–Thurs 8am–11pm; Fri 8am–midnight; Sat 9am–4:30pm and 6pm–midnight; Sun 9am–10pm. Subway: 1 to Franklin St. Bubby's Brooklyn: 1 Main St. (at Water St.). © **718/222-0666.** Subway: A, C to High St.; F to York St.

the best is the original at the corner of 72nd Street and Broadway, at 2090 Broadway (© 212/799-0243).

Like the hot dog, pizza is also a New York staple. I discuss the best pizza in New York in the box "Pizza, New York–Style," (p. 186), but most of the places mentioned in that box require sitting down and ordering a whole pie. For the quick slice, my personal favorite is **Joe's Pizza,** 7 Carmine St., at Bleecker Street (© 212/255-3946). Joe's offers the epitome of what a slice is supposed to taste like: thin-crusted with the proper balance of sauce, which actually has flavor, and cheese that doesn't taste like something you could bounce off a wall. And because Joe's is so popular, the pizza turns over quickly, almost always guaranteeing a fresh slice. Be prepared to wait in line during busy evening hours and then take your slice outside and eat it like a real New Yorker—standing up.

In Philadelphia, arguments rage over who makes the best cheesesteak. But we are in New York, and of the few Philly-style-cheesesteak establishments, my pick is **Shorty's** ⓕ, formerly known as Tony Luke's, 576 Ninth Ave., between 41st and 42nd streets (© 212/967-3055). On the edge of the Theater District, in the shadow of the Port Authority Bus Terminal, Shorty's location is about as gritty as it gets. But that just adds to the appeal of Shorty's gargantuan sandwiches. The cheesesteak, with your choice of cheese juices— Provolone, American, or Whiz (go for the Whiz, of course)—drenching the fresh Italian roll, is hard to resist, but if you can, order the roast pork Italian: roast pork with peppers, onions, and broccoli rabe. Try squeezing into your seat at the theater after one of *those!*

The Odeon ⓕ AMERICAN BRASSERIE   For over 2 decades, the Odeon has been a symbol of the TriBeCa sensibility; in fact, the restaurant can claim credit for the neighborhood's cachet—it was the first to lure artists, actors, writers, and models to the area below Canal Street before it was given its moniker. Why did they come? They came to drink, schmooze, and enjoy the hearty no-frills brasserie grub such as the country frisée salad with bacon, Roquefort cheese, and pear vinaigrette and the truffled poached egg, *moules frites* (mussels with fries), and sautéed cod. Though the restaurant is not quite the celebrity magnet it was in its heyday of the 1980s, the food, drink, and that inviting, open, Art Deco-ish room has withstood the test of time and has surpassed trendy to claim well-deserved New York establishment status.

145 W. Broadway (at Thomas St.). © 212/233-0507. www.theodeonrestaurant.com Reservations recommended. Main courses $13–$35 at lunch; $19–$35 at dinner (most less than $21); fixed-price lunch $27. AE, DC, DISC, MC, V. Mon–Fri noon–11pm; Sat 10am–midnight; Sun 10am–11pm. Subway: 1, 2, 3 to Chambers St.

INEXPENSIVE

For an inexpensive alternative in TriBeCa, consider the pub **Walker's** (see chapter 9), 16 N. Moore St., at Varick Street (© 212/941-0142), where you can get a good burger and fries for less than $10.

3 Chinatown

To find the restaurants reviewed below, see the map on p. 157.

INEXPENSIVE

Also consider two restaurants that have stood the test of time, **Wo Hop,** 17 Mott St., between Worth and Mosco streets (© **212/962-8617**), and **Vincent's Clam Bar,** 119 Mott St., at Hester Street (© **212/226-8133;** www.originalvincents.com). For more on both, see the box "Old Friends" on p. 162.

Big Wong King ♠ CHINESE/CANTONESE   A couple of years ago, Big Wong was called New Big Wong. This year they want to be called Big Wong King. No matter. They will always be Big Wong and that's a good thing. Why mess with success? For over 30 years, Big Wong has been an institution for workers from the nearby courthouses and Chinese families who come to feast on *congee* (rice porridge) and fried crullers for breakfast (see "Breakfast, Not Brunch," p. 206). They also come for the superb roasted meats, the pork and duck seen hanging in the window, the comforting noodle soups, and the terrific barbecued ribs. This is simple, down-home Cantonese food—lo mein, chow fun, bok choy in oyster sauce—cooked lovingly, and so cheap. If you don't mind sharing a table, and brusque service at best, Big Wong is a must at any time of day.

67 Mott St. (btwn Canal and Bayard sts.). © 212/964-0540. Appetizers $1.50–$5; congee $1.50–$6; soups $3–$5; Cantonese noodles $5.25–$11. No credit cards. Daily 8:30am–9pm. Subway: N, R.

New York Noodletown ♠♠ CHINESE/SEAFOOD   So what if the restaurant has all the ambience of a school cafeteria? I'm wary of an overadorned dining room in Chinatown; the simpler the better. New York Noodletown is simple, but the food is the real thing. Seafood-based noodle soups are spectacular, as is the platter of chopped roast pork. Those two items alone would make me happy. But I'm greedy and wouldn't leave the restaurant without one of its perfectly prepared shrimp dishes, especially the salt-baked shrimp. If your hotel room has a fridge, take the leftovers home—they'll make a great snack the next day. New York Noodletown keeps very long hours, which makes it one of the best late-night bets in the neighborhood, too.

28½ Bowery (at Bayard St.). © 212/349-0923. Reservations accepted. Main courses $4–$15. No credit cards. Daily 9am–3am. Subway: N, R, 6 to Canal St.

Nyonya ♠ *(Finds* ASIAN/MALAYSIAN   You won't find many Malaysian restaurants in New York, but one of the few, and one of the best, is Chinatown's Nyonya. This spacious, bustling restaurant designed like a South Asian tiki hut offers efficient, friendly service, but it's the huge portions of exotic, spicy food that are the real treat.

⌒Tips A Chinatown Sweet Treat

When in Chinatown, after sitting down at a dim sum banquet or a noodle joint, skip the feeble dessert offerings and head to one of my favorite ice cream shops in the city, the **Chinatown Ice Cream Factory** ♠, 65 Bayard St., between Mott and Elizabeth streets (© **212/608-4170;** www.chinatownicecreamfactory.com). The ice cream here features Asian flavors such as almond cookie, litchi, and an incredible green tea.

Coconut milk, curry, and chili-pepper-laden dishes are staples of Malaysian cuisine and the norm at Nyonya. The Malaysian national dish, *roti canai* (an Indian pancake with a curry-chicken dipping sauce), is outstanding. The noodle soups are meals in themselves; *prawn mee* (egg noodles, shredded pork, and large shrimp in a spicy shrimp broth) is sinus-clearing, while the curry spareribs are spectacular. Even the drinks and desserts are exotic, including *sooi pooi* drink (sour plum) and *pulut hitam* (creamy black glutinous rice with coconut milk). But vegetarians beware: There's not much on the menu for you here; most dishes are prepared in either a meat or fish broth.

194 Grand St. (btwn Mulberry and Mott sts.). ✆ 212/334-3669. Appetizers $2.25–$8; noodle soups $4.25–$6; main dishes $5.95–$23. No credit cards. Sun–Thurs 11am–11:30pm; Fri–Sat 11am–midnight. Subway: 6 to Spring St.

Pho Viet Huong 🐸 *Value* VIETNAMESE   Chinatown has its own enclave of Vietnamese restaurants, and the best is Pho Viet Huong. The menu is vast and needs intense perusing, but your waiter will help you pare it down. The Vietnamese know soup, and *pho*, a beef-based soup served with many ingredients, is the most famous, but the hot-and-sour *canh* soup, with either shrimp or fish, is the real deal. The small version is more than enough for two to share while the large is more than enough for a family. The odd pairing of barbecued beef wrapped in grape leaves is another of the restaurant's specialties and should not be missed, while the *bun,* various meats and vegetables served over rice vermicelli, are simple, hearty, and inexpensive. You'll even find Vietnamese sandwiches here: French bread filled with ham, chicken, eggs, lamb, and even pâté. For the daring, there are the frogs' legs, but don't expect what you're used to at your friendly neighborhood French restaurant—these require patience and fortitude. All of the above is best washed down with an icy cold Saigon beer.

73 Mulberry St. (btwn Bayard and Canal sts.). ✆ 212/233-8988. Appetizers $3–$8.50; soups $6–$7; Main courses $10–$25. AE, MC, V. Daily 10:30am–10:30pm. Subway: 6, N, R, Q to Canal St.

4 Lower East Side

EXPENSIVE

Rayuela 🐸🐸 NUEVO LATINO   Rayuela bills it's cuisine as *estilo libre Latino*, translated means "freestyle Latino." So the menu features a hodgepodge of Latino foods; a little Peruvian here, a dash of Mexican there, maybe a dollop of Cuba with a scoop of Spain. I had to admit that the freestyle thing made me nervous; I'm a traditionalist when it comes to ethnic cuisine but once I tasted the corvina ceviche, one of ten ceviches on the menu, my fears were quickly dashed. The classic Peruvian ceviche of king fish marinated in blood-orange juice, lime, cilantro with garlic and onions was refreshingly tart. Like so many restaurants, you can make your meal from various small plates and Rayuela is no exception; the appetizer *of camarones* con chorizo, shrimp in a spicy salsa with fufu, a root vegetable, and thin yucca fries is a worthy nod to the cuisine of the Dominican Republic and a worthy complement to the ceviche. Despite the abundance of small plates, it's hard to ignore Rayuela's entrees, especially the *surena*, an Ecuadorian seafood stew of mussels, clams, shrimp, octopus, and scallops in a broth flavored with coconut and garlic. In the now foodie neighborhood of the Lower East Side, Rayuela offers two levels; a bustling downstairs lounge and small bites scene where a live olive tree grows and more intimate dining on the upstairs level. Whichever floor you eat, Rayuela's food will not disappoint.

165 Allen St., (btwn Rivington and Stanton sts.). ✆ 212/253-8840. www.rayuelanyc.com. Reservations recommended. Ceviches $12–$17; main courses: $22–$31. AE, DC, DISC, MC, V. Sun–Thurs 5:30–11pm; Fri–Sat 5:30pm–midnight; brunch Sat–Sun 10am–5pm. Subway: F, V to Second Avenue.

MODERATE

'inoteca 🎔🎔 *Finds* ITALIAN SMALL PLATES   The Lower East Side was once the home to many Kosher wine factories, but you'll find only Italian wines at cozy 'inoteca. The list is over 250 bottles long, but even better are the exquisitely prepared small plates that complement the wines. Though the Italian-language menu is a challenge, servers are helpful in translating. The panini stand out in their freshness and their delicacy, with the *coppa* (a spicy cured ham) with hot peppers and *rucola* (arugula) being the standout. The *tramezzini,* a crustless sandwich, is nothing like the crustless sandwiches served at high tea. Here, among other things, you can have yours stuffed with tuna and chick peas or with *pollo alla diavola,* spicy shredded pieces of dark-meat chicken. The "Fritto" section includes a wonderful mozzarella *in corroza,* breaded mozzarella stuffed with a juicy anchovy sauce and lightly fried. Whatever you order, don't rush; 'inoteca is a place to go slow, to savor both wine and food.

98 Rivington St. (at Ludlow St.). ✆ 212/614-0473. www.inotecanyc.com. Reservations accepted for parties of 6 or more. Panini $8–$17; *piatti* (small plates) $8–$11. AE, MC, V. Daily noon–3am; brunch Sat–Sun 10am–4pm. Subway: F, J, M, Z to Delancey St.

Pala 🎔 PIZZA   Don't go to Pala expecting your typical New York City pizza. The owners studied how pizza was made in Italy and have done their best to try to replicate it. Apparently, traditional New York City pizza can be tough to digest (the only pizza I have trouble digesting is bad pizza—or eating too much of it), so Pala has concocted a special pizza-making process, including a slow-rising dough that they claim makes their pies easier on the belly. I can attest that consuming practically a whole *zucca* pie (oblong-shaped and topped with sautéed pumpkin, pancetta, and smoked *scamorza* cheese) along with a few slices of a *bufala cruda* (buffalo mozzarella, cherry-tomato sauce, and fresh basil) did no damage to my stomach except for possibly expanding it. I'm sure the glass of sparkling, chilled Lambrusco, a nice complement to the pizza, aided in my digestion, but I must give credit to Pala's scientific approach. There's nothing scientific about the nonpizza items such as the addictive *fiori di zucca* (fried zucchini blossoms stuffed with buffalo mozzarella and anchovies) or the tender, marinated fresh artichokes with lemon, oil, and Parmesan cheese shavings. Pala, which opened in early 2006, is loud and lively, with long, wooden picniclike tables—a welcome addition to the Lower East Side culinary scene.

198 Allen St. (btwn Stanton and Houston sts.). ✆ 212/614-7252. www.pala-ny.com. Pizza $12–$22. AE. Tues–Thurs 4pm–midnight; Fri 4pm–1am; Sat noon–1am; Sun noon–midnight. Subway: F, V to Second Ave.

INEXPENSIVE

Clinton St. Baking Company 🎔 *Finds* AMERICAN   Though they are open all day, breakfast and desserts are the best offerings here. The blueberry pancakes with maple butter and the buttermilk-biscuit egg sandwich are worth braving the morning lines for, while the desserts, all homemade and topped with a scoop or two of ice cream from the Brooklyn Ice Cream Factory, are good any time of day.

4 Clinton St. (at Houston St.). ✆ 646/602-6263. www.clintonstreetbaking. Main courses $8–$14. No credit cards. Mon–Fri 8am–11pm (closed 4–6pm); Sat 10am–11pm; Sun 10am–4pm. Subway: F or V to Second Ave.

Katz's Delicatessen 🎔🎔 *Value* JEWISH DELI   Arguably the city's best Jewish deli. The motto is "There's Nothing More New York Than Katz's," and it's spot-on. Founded in 1888, this cavernous, brightly lit place is suitably Noo Yawk, with dill pickles, Dr. Brown's cream soda, and old-world attitude to spare. Take the ticket they

Where to Dine in SoHo, Nolita, the East Village & on the Lower East Side

Bread **13**
Brick Lane Curry House **4**
Cendrillon **16**
Clinton St. Baking Co. **9**
Ed's Lobster Bar **15**
Fiamma **18**
Gemma **5**
Inoteca **10**
Katz's Delicatessen **8**
Kittichai **17**

Kossar's Bialys **12**
Le Miu **3**
Lombardi's Pizza **14**
Lupa **6**
Momofuku
  Noodle Bar **1**
Pala **7**
Pao! **19**
Rayuela **11**
Veselka **2**

give you when you come in and either head for the cafeteria-style line, or seat your-self in the "waiter service" area. But one word of caution: Katz's has become a serious tourist destination, so if you see a big tour bus parked in front, you might be in for a long wait. (And remember to tip your carver, who gives you a plate with a sample of the succulent pastrami or corned beef as he prepares your sandwich!)

205 E. Houston St. (at Ludlow St.). ⓒ 212/254-2246. www.katzdeli.com. Reservations not accepted. Sandwiches $3–$10; other main courses $5–$18. AE, DC, DISC, MC, V. ($20 minimum). Sun–Tues 8am–10pm; Wed 8am–11pm; Thurs 8am–midnight; Fri–Sat 8am–3am. Subway: F to Second Ave.

5 SoHo & Nolita

To locate the restaurants reviewed below, see the map on p. 157.

EXPENSIVE

Fiamma ⓐ MODERN ITALIAN   From Stephen Hanson (Blue Water Grill, Ruby Foo's, Dos Caminos), the Steven Spielberg of restaurateurs, comes his art-house effort, and this one wins all the awards. A Hanson trademark, the restaurant is beautifully designed, depicting a modern northern-Italian style with mirrors, lustrous red walls, leather chairs, and a glass elevator that can deposit you on any of the four floors. New chef Fabio Trabocchi has installed some fanciful and unique creations to the menu such as spicy grilled calamari with scallops, an onion compote appetizer, and striped bass with fennel, oysters and clams. Some of his creations are on the fussy side, but the flavors always interesting. The Fiamma, under Trabocchi's lead, is now anything but traditional Italian. Dinner is a scene, so don't expect intimacy; but lunch, with a similar menu, is a much more relaxed option.

206 Spring St. (btwn Sixth Ave. and Sullivan St.). ⓒ 212/653-0100. www.brguestrestaurants.com. Reservations rec-ommended. Pasta $22–$26; main courses $29–$44. AE, DISC, MC, V.; Tues–Thurs 6–11pm; Fri 6pm–midnight; Sat 5:30pm–midnight. Subway: C, E to Spring St.

Kittichai ⓐ THAI   The hotel **60 Thompson** (p. 106) and its public spaces are a magnet for people of the beautiful kind, and Kittichai, the restaurant that shares the hotel's address, more than reinforces that reputation. From the Thai-silk-and-wood-covered walls to the model-like servers to the luminous reflecting pool where candles float peacefully in the restaurant's center, everything is pristine at Kittichai. But don't let all that style intimidate you from trying the restaurant's inventive and flavorful food. Kittichai offers Thai tapas and, of these, the fish cakes and the sesame-spiced chicken lollipops stand out. And even a vegetarian might be tempted by the chocolate back-ribs appetizer. For the entrees, I was extremely content with the hearty short ribs in green curry, while the clay-pot prawns with vermicelli and prosciutto (that Thai sta-ple) was like nothing I'd ever had in any other Thai restaurant. Despite the peaceful aura created by the design, Kittichai can reach high decibel levels, so be prepared.

60 Thompson St. (btwn Broome and Spring sts.). ⓒ 212/219-2000. www.kittichairestaurant.com. Reservations rec-ommended. Appetizers $7–$19; main courses $19–$36. Sun–Wed 5:30–11pm; Thurs–Sat 5:30pm–midnight. Subway: C, E to Spring St.

MODERATE

Cendrillon ⓐⓐ *Finds* FILIPINO/ASIAN   In SoHo, whether dining, drinking, or shopping, you must be on guard for excessive pretense. But there is nothing preten-tious about Cendrillon. This is authentic yet innovative Filipino food in a comfort-able setting with exposed brick, a skylight in the main dining room, and cozy booths up front. How authentic? Try a shot of *lambagong,* also known as coconut grappa. It's a potent alcoholic drink distilled from the coconut flower sap and blended with sugar-cane sap, and as far as I know, Cendrillon is the only restaurant in New York to serve this Filipino specialty. The drink will ignite your appetite for the flavors to follow, such as the amazing squash soup with crab dumplings or the fresh *lumpia* with tamarind and peanut sauce (Asian vegetables wrapped in a purple-yam–and-rice wrapper). Cendrillon's chicken adobo (chicken braised in a marinade of vinegar, soy, chilies, and garlic) renders the bird as tender and tasty as you could ever imagine, while Romy's (the chef/owner) spareribs, marinated in rice wine and garlic, rubbed with spices, and cooked in a Chinese smokehouse, are as good as any ribs I've had cooked in a Texas smokehouse. You'll be tempted by just about everything on this menu, but save room for such exotic desserts as the Buko pie, made with coconut and topped with vanilla-bean ice cream, or the *halo halo,* a parfait stuffed with ice creams and sorbets with flavors such as avocado, jackfruit, and purple yam.

45 Mercer St. (btwn Broome and Grand sts.). Ⓒ 212/343-9012. www.cendrillon.com. Main courses $15–$24. AE, DISC, MC, V. Sun 11am–10pm; Tues–Sat 11am–10:00pm. Subway: N/R to Prince St.; 6 to Spring St.; 1, A, C, E to Canal St.

Ed's Lobster Bar ⋆⋆ SEAFOOD

You may be a long way in distance (and price) from a roadside shack in Maine or Cape Cod when dining at Ed's Lobster Bar, but take a seat on the long white marble counter, close your eyes, sink your teeth into Ed's signature lobster roll (prepared cold with mayonnaise) and you might just think that it's the rocky Atlantic coast outside the window rather than bustling Lafayette Street in the middle of NoHo. After you've tried the overstuffed lobster roll, if you still have room, try the oysters, raw or delicately fried. Or the fried Ipswich clams . . . or the steamers . . . or the chowder . . . really there's not much you won't want to try. Thankfully unpretentious, Ed's is straight-ahead New England seafood served in a casual, laid-back dining room and whitewashed bar. They even have paper bibs, homemade pickles, and Belfast Bay lobster ale on tap. What more, really, could you want in a seafood "shack" in downtown New York city?

222 Lafayette St. (btwn Spring and Kenmare sts.). Ⓒ 212/343-3236. www.lobsterbarnyc.com. Main courses: $15–$30. (Lobster and oysters at market price). Tues–Fri noon–3pm; Sat noon–4pm; Sun noon–9pm; Tues–Thurs 5pm–11pm; Fri–Sat 5pm–midnight. Subway: 6 to Spring St.

Lupa ⋆⋆ (Value) ROMAN ITALIAN

This Roman-style *osteria* is always a hot ticket. For one, it's blessed with an impeccable pedigree: One of its owners is Mario Batali, who has built a mini-empire in the Manhattan restaurant world. Second, it offers high-quality food at good value—you can eat well here and not have to max out your credit card. And finally, the food is consistently tasty. Don't expect big portions—that's part of the secret to the good value—but don't worry, you won't starve. The menu is thoughtful and creative, focusing on lusty Roman fare such as ricotta gnocchi with sausage and fennel, or pork saltimbocca. Wines, too, have been thoughtfully chosen, and you can order a bottle from the extensive list or sample one of several varieties that come in a carafe. Here, perhaps more than at any other Batali enterprise, the service hits just the right notes: Servers are warm and supremely knowledgeable. Make a reservation, or go early to snag one of the tables set aside for walk-ins.

170 Thompson St. (btwn Houston and Bleecker sts.). Ⓒ 212/982-5089. www.luparestaurant.com. Reservations recommended. *Primi* $9–$16; *secondi* $16–$20. AE, MC, V. Daily noon–midnight. Subway: A, B, C, D, E, F, Q, to W. 4th St.

Pao! ⋆ PORTUGUESE

New York has multiple restaurants of almost every ethnicity, yet there is a surprising scarcity of Portuguese eateries. Of the few, this cozy, comfortable charmer is the best. Pao!, which translates to "bread," keeps it simple, and the results are pure and authentic. Start with *caldo verde,* traditional Portuguese soup, made with kale, potatoes, and wonderfully smoky *linguica* (Portuguese sausage). The baked-octopus salad, tender and soaked in a garlic/cilantro vinaigrette, rivals any I've had in numerous Greek restaurants, while the cod cakes, another Portuguese standard, are light and not too salty. The combination of pork and seafood might seem odd, but it's common in Portugal; Pao!'s pairing of pork and clams is an acquired taste—one I've happily acquired. Salt cod is to Portugal what hamburgers are to the United States, and I'll take Pao!'s hearty *bacalhau a braz*—salt cod with egg, onion, and straw potatoes—over hamburger most any day. To complement the food, stick with a delicious Portuguese wine, from which there are many to choose. Desserts are egg-based and delicate; the soft pound cake with lemon egg custard filling is heavenly.

322 Spring St. (at Greenwich St.). ⓒ **212/334-5464.** Reservations recommended. AE, DC, MC, V. Lunch $12–$14; dinner $17–$20. Mon–Fri noon–2:30pm; daily 6–11pm. Subway: C, E to Spring St.

INEXPENSIVE

Also consider **Lombardi's Pizza,** 32 Spring St., between Mott and Mulberry streets (ⓒ **212/941-7994;** see "Pizza, New York–Style," p. 186).

Bread ⓡ ITALIAN   The older, smaller sibling of **Bread Tribeca** (p. 151) does bread like no other sandwich shop. The bread comes from Balthazar Bakery down the street, but it's what they do with it that makes this eatery so special. For example, they take a rustic ciabatta loaf, slather it with Sicilian sardines, Thai mayonnaise, tomato, and lettuce, and then turn it over to their panini press. The result is a gooey convergence of flavors that you will attempt to gobble down gracefully. It *will* fall apart, but that's okay; someone will be along shortly with more napkins. Besides the spectacular sardine sandwich, the Italian tuna with mesclun greens and tomatoes in a lemon dressing, and the fontina with grilled zucchini, eggplant, arugula, and tomato in a balsamic vinaigrette are also standouts. Really, there are no losers on the bread side of Bread's menu, which also includes salads, pastas, and "plates." The 32-seat restaurant is in chic Nolita, and if you are lucky, you might even be treated by the sight of a breathtakingly thin model doing her best to keep the contents of one of Bread's sandwiches from staining her designer duds.

20 Spring St. (btwn Mott and Elizabeth sts.). ⓒ **212/334-1015.** Reservations not accepted. Breads $7–$9.50; plates $6–$16. AE, DC, DISC, MC, V. Sun–Thurs 10:30am–midnight; Fri–Sat 10:30am–1am. Subway: 6 to Spring St.

6 The East Village & NoHo

To locate the restaurants reviewed below, see the map on p. 157.

EXPENSIVE

Gemma ⓡ ITALIAN   Following the rustic, slightly worn look of the new-in-2007 Bowery Hotel where it is housed, Gemma features a farmhouse look with an open kitchen, wood-fired oven, hanging slabs of cured Prosciutto di Parma and other meats, and a lively, loud bar. The clientele, like that of the hotel, however, is anything but rustic. Both hotel and restaurant are celebrity and fashion magnets, but don't hold that against either. Thankfully the food doesn't try to live up to the forced sense of style of those who dine there. At Gemma they keep it relatively simple and do try to follow the rustic look with equally rustic food. Staring at those slabs of meat, it's hard to resist trying a platter, along with a sampling of some of the excellent *formaggi.* You could linger with a glass of wine and the meat and cheese, but then you might miss out on some of the other small plates such as crostini with black-olive tapenade or the zucchini flowers, fried and stuffed with ricotta. The pastas are familiar and some better than others; the spaghetti puttanesca was perfectly briny, with capers and anchovies. You can end your meal with the huge Nutella calzone that is Gemma's signature dessert.

335 Bowery (at 3rd St.). ℭ 212/505-9100. Reservations not accepted. Main courses: $21–$39. AE, DC, DISC, MC, V. Sun–Wed 7am–midnight; Thurs–Sat 7am–1am. Subway: B, D, F, V to Broadway-Lafayette St.

Le Miu 🖈🖈 *Finds* JAPANESE   What happens when four celebrated Japanese chefs from various notable restaurants (Nobu 57 and Megu to name two) come together to open their own joint? In some cases, the result could be chaos, but in the case of Le Miu, good things happened. The restaurant, a slim, austere space tucked away on a bustling East Village block, is a refuge for those seeking absolutely fresh, delicately prepared sushi standards along with some interesting innovations. The Le Miu tartar, tuna, yellowtail, and salmon tartar topped with caviar is a welcoming beginning followed by sardine with ginger ceviche. The Saikyo miso marinated black cod in a phyllo jacket and the king crab leg with a curry milk sauce are revelations that I will now have to happily schlep down to the East Village to continue to experience, especially since the prices, for sushi this good, are hard to beat. Le Miu also has an impressive hot- and cold-sake list—the perfect companion to the chef's creations.

107 Ave. A (btwn 6th and 7th sts.). ℭ 212/473-3100. www.lemiusushi.com. Reservations recommended. Prix-fixe $55–$75; main courses $14–$28. AE, DC, MC, V. Sun–Wed 5:30pm–midnight; Thurs–Sat 5:30pm–1am. Subway: F, V to Second Ave.

MODERATE

Momofuku Noodle Bar 🖈 ASIAN   In 2007, this popular East Village noodle slurping destination moved from a tiny space to still small, but manageably sleek confines a few blocks up the street. Now there are a few communal tables along with a slightly larger bar. With the move came an expanded menu. Instead of only noodles, at the practically unclassifiable Momofuku, you will find such items on the menu as fried veal sweetbreads, spicy honeycomb tripe, grilled beef tongue, country ham and hash browns, and grits and shrimp—this in a supposed Asian noodle bar. But despite the seemingly contradictory menu, the Southern-style Asian noodle combo works. Still, unless you have a craving for offal, come to Momofuku for the noodles; the ramen in particular. And in the Momofuku Ramen, a big bowl brimming with rich broth, noodles, shredded smoky pulled pork, and a poached egg (as if the dish needed more heartiness), you actually can get a taste of the South and of Asia all in one bowl. Of the hot items, the roasted brussel sprouts with a kimchee puree, bacon, and carrots is a revelation, while the steamed pork bun is stuffed with a side of pork belly. Service is brisk, but try to get to Momofuku early or for lunch, before the lines begin to form.

171 First Ave. (btwn 10th and 11th sts.) ℭ 212/777-7773. Reservations not accepted. Main courses: $10–$17. AE, DISC, MC, V. Daily noon–4pm; Sun–Thurs 5:30pm–11pm; Fri–Sat 5:30pm–midnight. Subway: L at Third Ave.

MODERATE

Brick Lane Curry House 🖈 *Finds* INDIAN   The vibrancy of the traditional Indian restaurants, seemingly interconnected on the block of East 6th Street known as "Little India," has diminished over the years, but this relatively new addition has added some welcome vigor. The food is so good at Brick Lane that they don't even need the requisite sitar players to draw in customers. But beware: They don't compromise on

Moments Old Friends

New York has many restaurants that are considered institutions; places that have been around forever and are known throughout the world. When you think of classic New York restaurants that have survived for decades, you might think of the **Carnegie Deli** (see the box "The New York Deli News," p. 190), the **Grand Central Oyster Bar** (p. 194), or the **Peter Luger Steakhouse** (p. 213). But there are countless lesser-known restaurants that can also be considered New York institutions. You may not have heard of them, but those of us who live here know about them. The menus remain pretty much the same; not succumbing to the ever-changing food trends, the service is usually old-school; turnover is low, and your waiter will probably recognize you from your last visit, which might have been a year or two earlier. At these places, it's not about the quality of the food, which will most likely not be four-star, it's more about the familiar. And there is always something comforting about the familiar.

I first experienced Chinatown's **Wo Hop**, 17 Mott St., between Worth and Mosco streets (✆ **212/962-8617**), established in 1938, when I was in college. Of course it had to be cheap, and you couldn't find a cheaper restaurant in New York. It was open 24 hours—I have fond memories of dining late at night and then ascending the stairs from the subterranean restaurant to witness a sunny dawn; portions were huge and the food was dense. Time has stood still at Wo Hop, and though the prices have gone up, it's still one of the cheapest eateries in the city, still open 24 hours, and still dishing out huge portions of dense food. Here you'll find those Chinese-American classics you might remember from your youth: egg drop soup, chow mein, egg foo young, and subgum (bonus points to anyone who knows what "subgum" means) vegetables. And though most of the food here is heavily battered and swimming in corn-starch-thickened "brown" sauces, either oyster or black bean, there is no denying Wo Hop's comfort level.

At around the same time I discovered Wop Hop, I was introduced to **Vincent's Clam Bar,** 119 Mott St., at Hester Street (✆ **212/226-8133**; www.originalvincents.com), a few blocks up in Little Italy. At the time, there was still a remnant of what Little Italy used to be that is now gone. But Vincent's has been around since 1904, and though, like the rest of Little Italy, there is a touristy, theme-restaurant atmosphere to it, where else can you actually still order that old Italian-American favorite, scungilli? Like the shrinking Italian presence in Little Italy, scungilli (sliced conch) has practically disappeared from the menus of Italian restaurants. Here they pile it so

their spice. In fact, they might just have the hottest dish to be found in the city. It's a curry called "*phaal*" that requires a verbal disclaimer by the customer to not hold the restaurant liable for any physical or emotional damage incurred from eating it. If you are able to finish it, the restaurant promises a bottle of beer on the house. But there is no need to blister your intestines: The other, less hazardous, curries will bring on a good enough sweat, including the excellent Madras and the tangy Goan. Brick Lane's high on top of your linguine that if you are able to eat it all, you just might begin to understand why its demand has dwindled. Vincent's tomato sauce is unique and tastes exactly how I remember it from my first visit; rich and tomato-paste-thickened. It comes in three flavors: sweet, medium, and hot. But beware: The hot is fiery, and the best way to experience it is with a semistale biscuit and as an accompaniment to fried seafood.

I admit, I'm a relative newcomer to **El Faro** ⋆, 823 Greenwich St., at Horatio Street (✆ **212/929-8210;** www.elfaronyc.com), the oldest Spanish restaurant in New York, which will celebrate its 82nd birthday in 2009. But one visit and you will feel like you are a regular and longtime friend of the Lurgis family, who have owned the restaurant since 1959. Maybe you'll get to sit in what was writer James Baldwin's favorite corner table—the restaurant is mentioned in his biography—or one of the tables off the bar, possibly the one where a resident ghost is rumored to occasionally sit. The menu features dishes brought from Spain that are now familiar, such as *paella a la Valenciana,* shrimp *al ajillo,* and *mariscada* (mixed seafood) with green sauce. All this is complemented with El Faro's potent signature sangria, also known as "truth serum."

We all know how hard it is to make it on Broadway and to make it as a pretheater restaurant and survive for almost 50 years is a significant feat. But that's what **Chez Napolean,** 365 W. 50th St, between 8th and 9th Avenues (✆ **212/265-6980;** www.cheznapolean.com) has done. Located in the shadow of Worldwide Plaza, the Bruno family, led by matriarch "grandmere" Marguerite, have run Chez Napolean since 1960, serving traditional gallic cuisine. The presentation and preparation of the restaurant's *coq au vin* and the *beauf bourguignon* remain today exactly as it was before Marguerite was a "grandmere."

People ask me for recommendations for a "real deal" diner in New York. My answer is always: **Eisenberg's Coffee Shop,** 174 Fifth Ave., at 22nd Street (✆ **212/675-5096**). This old-world luncheonette has been dishing up the same eggs/bacon/burgers/sandwiches since 1929, at pretty much the same prices—adjusted slightly for inflation, of course. The waiters and cooks seemingly have been working at Eisenberg's since the Eisenhower era. More likely than not, you'll be greeted with a growled "Hiya, sweetheart," or a gravelly "What'll it be, love?" If a tuna sandwich were on a "Best of" list, Eisenberg's version would win. Feel a little run down? A bowl of Eisenberg's matzo-ball soup will perk you up. Or sit at the counter and order an egg cream with real, from-the-bottle, seltzer.

signature *boti* rolls (chicken tikka served in fresh-baked bread) are special, while the *rassam* soup of the day, a thin, clear soup that changes daily, will help clear your sinuses even before you touch a curry. There are also a number of vegan items.

306–308 E. 6th St. (btwn First and Second aves.). ✆ 212/979-2900. www.bricklanecurryhouse.com. Reservations recommended. Appetizers $6–$10; curries $12–$19. AE, DC, DISC, MC, V. Sun–Thurs 1–11pm; Fri–Sat 1pm–1am. Subway: 6 to Astor Place.

INEXPENSIVE

Veselka ⚅ UKRAINIAN DINER   Whenever the craving hits for hearty eastern European fare at old-world prices, Veselka fits the bill with fluffy and light (if that's possible) pierogi (small doughy envelopes filled with potatoes, cheese, or sauerkraut), *kasha varnishkes* (cracked buckwheat and noodles with mushroom sauce), stuffed cabbage, grilled Polish kielbasa, freshly made potato pancakes, and such classic soups as a sublime borscht. Breakfast is special here (see "Breakfast, Not Brunch," p. 206). If all you want is a burger, don't worry—it's a classic, too.

Despite the authentic fare, the diner is comfortable, modern, and appealing, with an artsy slant and delicious house-made desserts. Veselka surpasses its status as a popular after-hours hangout with clubbers and other night owls to be a favorite at any hour.

144 Second Ave. (at 9th St.). ⓒ 212/228-9682. Reservations not accepted. Main courses $5–$13. AE, DC, DISC, MC, V. Daily 24 hr. Subway: 6 to Astor Place.

7 Greenwich Village & the Meat-Packing District

EXPENSIVE

A.O.C. Bedford ⚅⚅ *(Finds)* MEDITERRANEAN   You'll find this brick-walled, cozy, romantic charmer tucked away on equally cozy and romantic Bedford Street in the West Village. Here the A.O.C. in the restaurant name stands for *appellation d'origine controlee*—the French designation for high-quality food products. But on the menu you'll not only find A.O.C. products from France, but also D.O.C, the Italian designation, and D.O, the Spanish. If the appetizer of octopus "carpaccio" is on the menu, which changes seasonally, order up; your octopus, pounded thin and tender, will be served with D.O. dry red pepper from Spain and A.O.C *fleur de sel* from France. The Caesar salad will have D.O.C-grade Parmesan cheese from Italy. But you won't need all those designations to know that what you are eating is of high quality—just a few bites will suffice. The paella marinera, a constant on the menu, is prepared for two, stuffed with jumbo shrimp (heads on, for more flavor), squid, scallops, mussels, and clams and cooked in Spanish Calasparra rice. Another standout is the duck, a crispy breast prepared best medium rare, and served with a Bosc pear. Finish with a selection of cheeses, A.O.C.-, D.O.C.-, and D.O.-quality only, of course. The restaurant has an impressive wine list, and bottles are decanted at your table.

14 Bedford St. (btwn Sixth Ave. and Downing St.). ⓒ 212/414-4764. www.aocbedford.com. Reservations recommended. Main courses $21–$32. AE, DC, MC, V. Sun–Thurs 5:30–11pm; Fri–Sat 5:30–11:30pm. Subway: 1 to Houston St.

Bar Blanc ⚅ CONTEMPORARY AMERICAN   I'm not sure the three owners who are all alumni of David Bouley restaurants, really mean to say that Bar Blanc is a bar before it is a restaurant. The narrow space and the whitewashed look lends itself perfectly to the name, and the *caipiroska*, the vodka version of the caipirinha, was as good as I've had in any bar, but still, there is no doubt that the food is foremost here. The menu is as sparse as the decor, and in neither case is that a bad thing. It's not about quantity, it's about quality. And at Bar Blanc there is no skimping on the latter. An appetizer of two pan-seared jumbo scallops wrapped in a fatty piece of smoked pork belly might not seem like much, but each bite was memorable. The entrees are not much more formidable than the appetizers, but just as delicious; especially the juicy, milk-fed porcelet (an elegant way of describing pork), flavored with chanterelles and roasted brussels sprouts, and the strip steak, grilled over Japanese charcoal (as opposed to New Jersey charcoal?) and accompanied by a bone marrow sauce.

Where to Dine in Greenwich Village & the Meat-Packing District

A.O.C. Bedford **11**
Bar Blanc **6**
El Faro **2**
Gray's Papaya **5**
Joe's Pizza **8**
John's Pizza **7**

Mas **10**
Murray's Bagels **3**
Paradou **1**
Rare Bar & Grill **9**
Strip House **4**

Maybe the modest portions encourage patrons to indulge in dessert, and that's smart because the Meyer lemon soufflé is not to be missed. If you can, ask for a table in the back, away from the bar where you might be able to have a quiet conversation.

142 W. 10th St (at Waverly Pl.). ✆ 212/255-2330. www.barblanc.com. Reservations recommended. Main courses: $29–$36; AE, DISC, MC, V. Tues–Sun 5:30pm–11pm. Subway: A, B, C, D, E, F, V to W. 4th St.

Mas ✿✿ (Finds) FRENCH   I've never had the pleasure of dining in a French country farmhouse, but if the experience at Mas is anything like it, I know now what I've been missing. This "farmhouse" is located in the West Village, and though there are nods to the rustic in the decor, with wood beams and a bar of sandstone with stools made from tree trunks from one of the owner's farms in Massachusetts, there is also an atmosphere of sophistication. A glass-enclosed wine cellar is visible from the small dining room, the restaurant stays open late, and you'll find hipsters in jeans and T-shirts as well as folks in power suits. And it's that combination, along with the creative menu, that makes Mas so special. The dishes are innovative and the ingredients are fresh, many supplied by upstate New York farms. The tender, perfectly prepared braised pork belly, from Flying Pig Farm, is served with polenta and a stew of escargot and lima beans; the duck breast, from Stone Church Farm, melds magically with apple puree, sautéed Brussels sprouts, and chestnuts; and the trout Piscator, rainbow trout from the Neversink River, is stuffed with watercress and smoked trout and topped with a tangy apple-and-horseradish dressing. Service is low-key but attentive; and the seating, though somewhat cramped, is not enough to dim the romantic aura.

39 Downing St. (btwn Bedford and Varick sts.). ✆ 212/255-1790. www.masfarmhouse.com. Reservations recommended. 4-course tasting menu $68; 6-course $95; main courses $32–$36. AE, DC, DISC, MC, V. Mon–Sat 6pm–4am (small-plate tasting menu after 11:30pm). Subway: 1 to Houston St.

Paradou ✿ (Finds) FRENCH   It's nice to find a restaurant in the overhyped hysteria of the Meat Packing District where you can actually have a conversation. Even better is that the food here, traditional Provencal cuisine, is as down-to-earth and genuine as the restaurant itself. Take your time with a glass of Chablis while grazing on the *assiette de la terre,* a French antipasto plate with artisanal hams, salami, pâté, asparagus and haricort vert. The menu changes seasonally, but you'll always find the *zaatar* chicken "under brick" with truffled mashed potatoes, and for good reason. It's hard to order anything else, it's that good. The staff is helpful, and the environment here is fun, with regular events such as "Dirty Bingo," live music, and frequent wine tastings. The restaurant also features a lovely garden, enclosed in the winter, for year round use.

8 Little W. 12th St (at Ninth Ave.). ✆ 212/463-8345. www.paradounyc.com. Entrees: $19–$25. AE, MC, V. Mon–Wed 6pm–midnight; Thurs–Fri 6pm–1am; Sat noon–1am; Sun noon–10pm. Subway: A, C, E to 14th St.

Strip House ✿✿ STEAKS   With a photo gallery of seminude burlesque performers decorating the red velvet walls, roomy burgundy banquettes, and a steady flow of lounge music, you may, as I once did, mistakenly refer to the Strip House as the Strip Club. But despite the faux-*Playboy* look, the only decadence here is in the titanic portions of perfectly charred and seasoned red meat, specifically, the strip steak. I had the strip on the bone that I still remember with fondness. The filet mignon is simply and impeccably prepared; and the porterhouse for two, carved at your table, is in the Peter Luger league. The sides here are innovative variations on the standards: creamed spinach with black truffles, french fries with herbs and garlic, and, best of all, the crisp

Value Foodies Love Restaurant Week

Restaurant "Week" is a bit of a misnomer: It's 10 days (twice a year, in January and July) when some of the best restaurants in town offer threecourse prixfixe meals at *almost* affordable prices. Restaurant Week began as a oneoff in 1992 to welcome delegates to the Democratic National Convention (with the price of a meal $19.92). A hit with New Yorkers as well as visitors, it's become a muchloved tradition, as foodies get a chance to eat at some of the higherend restaurants in town without breaking the bank. (It's a tradition that's caught on in other good restaurant cities, too, from Atlanta to San Diego). These days, at lunch, the deal is $24.07 (as in 24/7), while dinner is $35. More than 230 restaurants participated in the summer version of Restaurant Week in 2008, all over town and in all styles of cuisine, including star venues like Aquavit, Chanterelle, Gramercy Tavern and Molyvos (all reviewed in this chapter). Call ℭ 212/484-1222 for info, or visit www.nycvisit.com.

goose-fat potatoes. Is goose fat a good fat or a bad fat? Only your dietitian knows for sure; but if you have a dietitian, you're probably in the wrong restaurant. Desserts are monumental, especially the multilayered chocolate cake, so have your waiter bring extra forks for sharing. With the exception of those few banquettes, seating is tight, so don't expect intimacy—unless it is with your neighbor.

13 E. 12th St. (btwn University Place and Fifth Ave.). ℭ 212/328-0000. www.striphouse.net. Reservations recommended. Main courses $31–$50. AE, DC, DISC, MC, V. Sun–Thurs 5–11pm; Fri–Sat 5pm–midnight. Subway: L, N, R, Q, 4, 5, 6 to 14th St./Union Sq.

INEXPENSIVE

The downtown branch of **Gray's Papaya** is at 402 Sixth Ave., at 8th Street (ℭ **212/ 260-3532**). The original **John's Pizzeria** is at 278 Bleecker St., near Seventh Avenue (ℭ **212/243-1680;** see "Pizza, New York–Style," p. 186). For one of the best slices of pizza, go to **Joe's Pizza,** 7 Carmine St., at Bleecker Street (ℭ **212/255-3946**). Also, you'll find **Murray's Bagels** at 500 Sixth Ave., between 12th and 13th streets (ℭ **212/462-2830;** see "The Hole Truth: N.Y.'s Best Bagels," p. 177).

A great neighborhood hangout that serves vegetarian/vegan food, is 'sNice, 45 Eighth Ave., at W. 4th St. (ℭ **212/645-0310**). You don't have to be vegetarian to enjoy the hearty, homemade sandwiches, wraps, salads, desserts, and tea/coffee served. There are board games, Wi-Fi, shared tables, and an all-ages crowd that appreciates the ambience. It's open Sunday to Thursday 7:30am to 10pm and Friday to Saturday 8am to 10pm.

8 Chelsea

To locate the restaurants in this section, see the map on p. 168.

EXPENSIVE

Buddakan ℭ ASIAN   Is Buddakan a bus depot disguised as a nightclub with a restaurant inside, or is it a restaurant with a night club persona housed inside a garishly designed (Buddha icons along with Renaissance Bacchanal paintings) bus depot? My expectations were of a loud, dance club scene in a large, 16,000-square-feet

Where to Dine in Midtown, Chelsea, Flatiron District & Gramercy Park

CENTRAL

UPPER WEST SIDE

Lincoln Center

W. 64th St.
W. 63rd St.
W. 62nd St.
W. 61st St.
West Drive
W. 60th St.
W. 59th St.
W. 58th St.
Central Park S.
Columbus Circle

Amsterdam Ave.
Columbus Ave.
Central Park W.
West End Ave.
Ninth Ave.
Tenth Ave.

W. 57th St.
W. 56th St.
W. 55th St.
W. 54th St.
W. 53rd St.
W. 52nd St.
W. 51st St.
W. 50th St.

DeWitt Clinton Park

THEATER DISTRICT

W. 49th St.
W. 48th St.
W. 47th St.
W. 46th St.   Restaurant   Row
W. 45th St.

MIDTOWN WEST

W. 44th St.
W. 43rd St.
W. 42nd St.
W. 41st St.
W. 40th St.
W. 39th St.
W. 38th St.
W. 37th St.
W. 36th St.
W. 35th St.

TIMES SQUARE

Port Authority

Twelfth Ave.
Eleventh Ave.
Tenth Ave.
Broadway
Seventh Ave.
Eighth Ave.
Ninth Ave.

Lincoln Tunnel

Javits Convention Center

GARMENT DISTRICT

W. 33rd St.
W. 34th St.

W 32nd St.

Penn Station/ Madison Square Garden

Tunnel Entrance

W. 31st St.
W. 30th St.
W. 29th St.
W. 28th St.

Chelsea Park

W. 27th St.
W. 26th St.
W. 25th St.
W. 24th St.
W. 23rd St.
W. 22nd St.
W. 21st   St.
W. 20th St.
W. 19th St.
W. 18th St.
W. 17th St.
W. 16th St.
W. 15th St.
W. 14th St.

CHELSEA

West Side Hwy.
Hudson River
Chelsea Piers

MEAT-PACKING DISTRICT

Seventh Ave.

M Subway stop

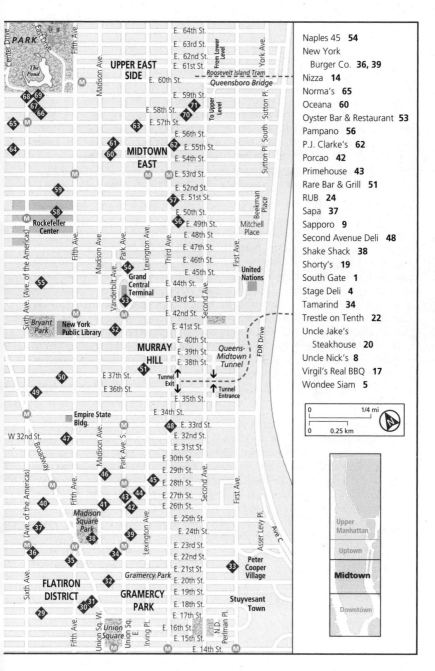

bi-level space where the food would be showy, but flavorless. I was right about the loud, dance-club scene, but I was wrong about the flavorless food. The "Brasserie" is the main dining room on the lower level, and the steps can seem steep after a few too many cocktails, such as the signature *Heat,* a combination of tequila, Cointreau, and chilled cucumbers, in the upstairs lounge; though they were not steep enough to deter a man from being carried down in his wheelchair the night I dined there. To fortify yourself after those cocktails don't hesitate to order some of Buddakan's superb appetizers such as the edamame dumplings, the crab and corn fritters, and most notably, the crispy calamari salad. In fact, you can make your meal out of sharing appetizers—the extensive menu at Buddakan works best for large parties and has the now obligatory "communal" table. But if you order one entree, make sure it's the sizzling short rib; tender and removed from the bone and sitting on top of a bed of mushroom chow fun.

75 Ninth Ave (at 16th St.). 🕾 212/989-6699. www.buddakannyc.com. Dim Sum–appetizers $9–$13; main courses $17–$35. AE, DC, MC, V. Hours: Sun–Wed 5:30pm–midnight; Thurs–Sat 5:30pm–1am. Subway: A, C, E to 14th St.

Cookshop 𝕽𝕽 AMERICAN   On far west Tenth Avenue, with a prime view of a parking garage across the street, Cookshop is brawny and boisterous with food to match. Seating can be tight, and you would hear your neighbor's conversation if it weren't so loud in the restaurant. But never mind: enjoy the chef's creations. A pizza with shaved king oyster mushrooms and *stracchino* cheese or the grilled Montauk squid in a *salsa verde* make good starters to complement the restaurant's innovative cocktails. Or combine a few of the snacks such as the addictive fried spiced hominy or the smoked pork tacos as starters for the table. Cookshop offers entree options in four categories: sauté, grill, wood oven, and rotisserie. The whole roasted porgy, head and all, cooked in the wood oven is moist and full of flavor, while the chili-braised beef short ribs, served over cheddar grits, from the sauté section are properly tender to the bone. Service is casually efficient and helpful. Maybe Cookshop's emergence to restaurant-barren Tenth Avenue will be the beginning of a new eating mecca.

156 Tenth Ave. (at 20th St.). 🕾 212/924-4440. www.cookshopny.com. Reservations recommended. Main courses $21–$36. AE, DC, MC, V. Mon–Sat 5:30pm–11:30; Sun 11:00am–3pm and 5:30–10pm. Subway: C, E to 23rd St.

Trestle On Tenth 𝕽   MODERN SWISS/FRENCH   There was a bar/restaurant on the corner of 24th and Tenth Avenue that, for many years, I used to frequent where the pints were good and cheap and the burgers satisfying. That place is gone, but in its location is Trestle on Tenth, where the ambience is still homey, but now mimics the burgeoning development of the West Chelsea neighborhood. The fireplace is no longer in use, but the garden is; and instead of burgers, chef/owner Ralf Kuettel has devised an innovative Alpine-based menu: Alpine meaning the food is drawn from influences of the northern regions of France and Kuettel's native Switzerland. Start with a selection of cured meats and aged Swiss cheeses to accompany a glass of wine or a pint of beer. The salad of butter lettuce, speckled with thick bits of smoked bacon in a buttermilk dressing, is a good prelude to one of the restaurant's many robust entree options such as the lamb saddle, layered on mustard greens with cippolini onions and the lamb bordered by a layer of fat purposely kept on to keep the meat tender and moist. For something less rich, opt for the seared wild sturgeon with baby bok choy and Hen-of-the-Wood mushrooms. Trestle on Tenth is the perfect place to unwind and ponder the art you might have experienced at some of the neighborhood's numerous galleries.

242 Tenth Ave. (at 24th St.). 🕾 212/645-5659. www.trestleontenth.com. Main Courses; $18–$24. AE, DC, MC, V. Mon 5:30–10pm; Tues–Thurs noon–10:30pm; Fri noon–11pm; Sat 11am–11pm; Sun 11am–10pm. Subway: C, E to 23rd St.

MODERATE

Bombay Talkie ✿ INDIAN   If it's in any way possible while dining in a stylish, modern restaurant in Chelsea, try to imagine you are on the streets of Bombay and you are hungry. There are inexpensive food options everywhere on those streets, and here at Bombay Talkie, with a Bollywood movie constantly playing behind the bar and a soundtrack on the speakers to match, some of those options are replicated for you in a much more comfortable environment. You can munch on a *dosa*, a thin, lightly fried bread stuffed with coconut and mustard-seed chicken or spiced potatoes. Or you might want to try the *Pau Bhaji*, grilled bread served with mixed, gingery vegetables. Whatever you choose, wash it down with one of the restaurant's innovative cocktails such as a passionfruit margarita or an Indian beer. The restaurant has two levels, a few booths on the lower level and a long communal table, which is fun for large groups. Bombay Talkie is the perfect spot for a respite from Chelsea gallery-hopping.

189 Ninth Ave. (btwn 21st and 22nd sts.). (✆ 212/242-1900. www.bombaytalkie.com. Reservations recommended. Street bites $6–$9; main courses $11–$16. AE, MC, V. Sun–Thurs 5–10:30pm; Fri–Sat 5–11:30pm. Subway: C, E to 23rd St.

La Nacional ✿✿ *Finds* SPANISH/TAPAS   It's not easy finding the oldest Spanish restaurant in New York; in fact, the search for this unmarked restaurant on West 14th Street might get you a bit frustrated. Once you find it, your perseverance will be rewarded. Founded in 1868 as a gathering spot for the Benevolent Spanish Society, La Nacional, a social club, is a hidden treat. At one time, food was secondary to the company of Spanish expatriates who congregated here, filling the room with smoke and talk of Spanish politics and football. It was here Gabriel Garcia Lorca spent countless hours documenting his New York City experience. The cigarette smoke has been replaced by the smoke of the grill, which turns out tasty tapas with sardines, octopus, and shrimp. There is a somewhat formal dining room in the front, while in the back, next to the open kitchen, there are a few tables and TVs usually tuned to soccer matches. Come and share a bottle of Spanish wine and make a meal out of the tapas— the *albondigas* (Spanish meatballs), *boquerones* (white anchovy filets), and aforementioned octopus are my favorites—or you can order the restaurant's excellent paella. Tapas range from $4 to $9, while no entree is more than $18. In a ballroom on the second level, the club sponsors flamenco performances and dance lessons.

239 W. 14th St. (btwn Seventh and Eighth aves.). (✆ 212/243-9308. www.lanacionaltapas.com. Tapas $7–$9; main courses $16–$18. AE, DC, DISC, MC, V. Sun–Wed noon–11pm; Thurs–Sat noon–11pm. Subway: A, C, E, 1, 2, 3 to 14th St.

RUB ✿✿ BARBECUE   Short for Righteous Urban Barbecue, RUB is a contradiction in terms if there ever was one. Since when was barbecue an urban thing—not to mention righteous? But I confess, the name is cool; and after tasting some of the BBQ that comes out of the restaurant's custom-made, New York City Health Department–approved smoker, righteous is an apt description. RUB is co-owned by Kansas City pit master Paul Kirk, who has won seven World Barbecue Championships and is a member of the Barbecue Hall of Fame, for those barbecue fanatics who are aware that there is a Barbecue Hall of Fame. The smoked turkey and barbecued chicken are the best I've had—moist inside with a distinctive smoked flavor—and the ribs, St. Louis–style, were delicate and crispy, yet tender and meaty. The "burnt ends," the fatty part of the brisket, however, were a bit tough. The best way to get a taste of all of RUB's barbecue is the humongous "Taste of the Baron," where a little of everything is piled high on a

The Prime Cut: Steaks! Steaks! Steaks!

The number of prime-cut palaces in New York continues to sprout like mushrooms. **Peter Luger Steakhouse** (p. 213) has been the steakhouse standard for years, but it gets a serious run for it's money from, stylishly ensconced in the TimeWarner Center, **Porter House New York** (p. 197) Beginning the steak-as-style trend a few years back was **BLT Steak** (p. 191), which proves there is substance with the style. Going overboard on the style side as well as pretty much everything else is **Kobe Club,** (p. 179) the nightclub posing as a steakhouse specializing in its namesake beef. The newest addition to the steakhouse galaxy was restaurateur Stephen Hanson's big (in many ways) venture **Primehouse** (p.175). Despite its bawdy name, **Strip House** (p. 166) steaks are no-nonsense. Wall Street traders and financial bigwigs often have carnivorous reputations, and at **Harry's Steak and Café** (p. 150) they don't have to go far to satisfy their cravings. Some of the city's oldest restaurants are steakhouses, and two of the oldest of those are **Frankie & Johnnie's** (p. 181) and **Keens Steakhouse** (p. 181) which was formerly known as a chophouse for their selection of such chops as their acclaimed mutton chop.

Don't expect an overpriced burger factory with waiters in Bulls jerseys and basketball-shaped plates from **Michael Jordan's—The Steak House**, on the mezzanine level overlooking the main concourse at Grand Central Terminal (© **212/655-2300;** www.theglaziergroup.com). Bursting with Beaux Arts–meets–Art Deco grandeur, Michael Jordan's is wholly for grownups. And with a perfect view of the legendary sky ceiling, this is more than just the city's best-looking steakhouse—it's an incredible "only-in–New York" dining experience.

One of the best of the traditional old-world steakhouses is the clubby, fun **Bull and Bear,** in the Waldorf=Astoria, 301 Park Ave., between 49th and 50th streets (© **212/872-1275**), which serves the best New York strip I've had

platter. The restaurant is cramped and loud and the prices urban (meaning high), but the food at RUB will provide all the comfort you need.

208 W. 23rd St. (btwn Seventh and Eighth aves.). © 212/524-4300. www.rubbbq.net. Sandwiches $9–$12; platters $15–$23; Taste of the Baron $46. AE, MC, V. Tues–Thurs noon–11pm; Fri–Sat noon–midnight. Subway: 1 to 23rd St.

INEXPENSIVE

Paradise Café, 141 Eighth Ave. (btwn 16th and 17th sts.; © **212/647-0066**) is a neighborhood gem in so-trendy-it's-exhausting Chelsea, where it's hard to find a good meal for under $10. A sign behind the counter reads "If you insist on ordering using Starbucks terms, we will be forced to charge you Starbucks prices." So don't order a "venti," but do order all kinds of free-trade tea and coffee, sandwiches, wraps, smoothies and homemade desserts. The narrow storefront has French doors that are left open in good weather, and you can sit on a bench out front or lounge at one of the indoor tables, reading the newspapers and magazines scattered about and enjoying the original art on the walls. It's open daily from 6am to 9pm.

in the city. You can also call the **Post House** ⟨⟨, (p. 207) where seats are claimed by VIPS; clubby, but that won't deter me from enjoying their Cajun-rubbed rib-eye.

There are better steaks to be had in New York, but there aren't many better steakhouses than **Ben Benson's Steakhouse,** 123 W. 52nd St., between Sixth and Seventh avenues (© **212/581-8888;** www.benbensons.com). Smack in the middle of Midtown, Ben Benson's is loud and large, and though it's definitely a man's world at Ben's, women are treated with respect here.

Like Ben Benson's, **Uncle Jack's Steakhouse** ⟨, 440 Ninth Ave., at 34th Street (© **212/244-0005;** www.unclejacks.com), is testosterone-fueled and the decor is plush and bawdy with huge banquettes. Portions are monstrous; the 48-ounce porterhouse, Uncle Jack's signature dish, is large enough for a big family.

Most entrees at these steakhouses tend to fall in the $22-to-$38 range. Always book ahead and inquire about dress codes, especially at the old-school spots.

There are steakhouses with claims to Peter Luger's all over the city, a few started by ex-Luger waiters. But the **Benjamin Steakhouse** ⟨, 52 E. 41st St., in the Dylan Hotel (© **212/297-9177;** www.benjaminsteakhouse.com), is the only one to feature an ex-chef, chef Arturo, from Luger's. The result is not quite Luger's-quality steaks, but it does have better service and a dramatic room highlighted by a huge walk-in fireplace.

Like the Benjamin, **Quality Meats** ⟨, 57 W. 58th St., between Fifth and Sixth avenues (© **212/371-7777;** www.qualitymeatsnyc.com), is set in a stunning bi-level space designed by the famous team of AvroKO (Sapa, p. 175). And the quality of the food matches the quality of the design, with some nontraditional steakhouse menu items such as pan-roasted lamb T-bones with figs and mint, and a flatiron steak with blackberries.

9 Union Square, the Flatiron District & Gramercy Park

To locate the restaurants in this section, see the map on p. 168.

EXPENSIVE

A Voce ⟨⟨ MODERN ITALIAN   The kind of food that is served at A Voce; rustic Italian for the most part with exceptional nods to innovation, seems somewhat out of place in the loud, postmodern dining room in a sleek high rise just off Madison Park. The restaurant would, I believe, be better suited in the Art Deco New York Life building next door. But that is a minor gripe considering the extraordinary tastes created by chef Andrew Carmellini, formerly of **Café Boulud** (p. 208). At A Voce you can start with something peasant-pleasing, such as Sardinian sheep's milk ricotta, and slather it on thick, crusty grilled bread, or you can sample the hip, wild *branzini tartara* (Mediterranean sea bass)—something no peasant would ever dare eat. The same can be said for the "secondi." Chef Carmellini offers "My Grandmother's meat ravioli," and though my grandmother never made meat ravioli—she thought meat ravioli was something you poured from a can—Carmellini's *nonna's* meat ravioli is so good it certainly was *not* from a can. Continuing on that rustic theme, the "country-style Tuscan tripe," with barlotti beans, tomato, fried duck egg, and grilled ciabatta bread, would have made my normally dour Calabrese grandfather happy (minus the duck egg for him). A Voce offers daily specials called "del mercato" which usually features the chef's more unique creations such as, on the day I visited, a "rabbit terrina" with salt-cured *foie gras.* You won't go wrong whether you try the rustic or the modern. The chef's palate-cleansing citrus tiramisu is the perfect conclusion.

41 Madison Avenue (at 26th St.). ℂ 212/545-8555. www.avocerestaurant.com. AE, DC, MC, V. Main courses: $18–$39. Mon–Fri 11:45am–2:30pm; 5:30–11pm; Sat–Sun 5:30–11pm. Subway: N, R, W to 23rd St.

BLT Fish 𝆑𝆑 SEAFOOD   The seafood branch of the **BLT** (Bistro Laurent Tourondel, BLT Steak, BLT Prime, BLT Market) empire, is actually two restaurants with two distinct kitchens. The downstairs is a moderately priced faux-seafood shack with a raw bar, fried fare, and the much-in-demand (deservedly so) lobster roll. Upstairs (you can walk the steps or take a glass elevator) is the elegant (with prices to match) dining room. Here you can sit under a skylight or near the open kitchen and watch an army of servers move from the kitchen with huge platters, where whole fish sit, dressed up beautifully, ready for consumption. One example is the crispy red snapper, Cantonese style, that is filleted tableside. Another is the sea-salt-crusted New Zealand pink snapper, for which you'll have to crack the hard salt shell to get to the tender, juicy flesh underneath. Of the smaller dishes, the Maine Day boat sea scallops stand out, along with the Alaskan black cod in a honey reduction sauce. For starters, the spicy tuna tartare and the grilled sardines are not to be missed. But with fish this fresh, you really won't go wrong with anything on the menu here. Like BLT Steak and BLT Prime, don't expect quiet conversation.

21 W. 17th St. (btwn Fifth and Sixth aves.). ℂ 212/691-8888. www.bltfish.com. Reservations recommended. Prices $25–$35. BLT Fish Mon–Thurs 5:30–11pm; Fri–Sat 5:30–11:30pm. BLT Fish Shack Mon–Fri 11:45am–2:30pm; Mon–Thurs 5:30–11pm; Fri–Sat 5:30–11:30pm; Sun 5–10pm. Subway: 4, 5, 6, L, N, R, Q, W to 14th St./Union Sq.

Dévi 𝆑𝆑 INDIAN   With the number of Indian restaurants in New York City, you would think another one would be redundant. But few of them are like this restaurant. Dévi offers $45 to $65 tasting menus (vegetarian and nonvegetarian), and that's really the way to go. The menu features small courses that will let you sample much of what the restaurant has to offer. Some of the highlights include tender tandoori chicken stuffed with spicy herbs, halibut coated in a cilantro rub accompanied with mint coconut chutney and lemon rice, *zimikand koftas,* delicate yam koftas in a creamy tomato-onion sauce, and the addictive, crispy okra, the Indian equivalent of french fries. With the tasting menus, you get a choice of desserts; I strongly recommend the fabulous *falooda,* an Indian sundae that's a refreshing combination of noodles with honey-soaked basil seeds, mango, and strawberry sorbet in lemongrass-infused coconut milk. Seating is comfortable and service is knowledgeable, though servers regrettably don bright orange uniforms that look a bit too much like prison garb.

8 E. 18th St. (btwn Fifth Ave. and Broadway). ℂ 212/691-1300. www.devinyc.com. Reservations recommended. AE, DISC, MC, V. Main courses $15–$30; tasting menus $65. Mon–Sat noon–2:30pm; and 5:30–11:00pm; Sun 5–10pm Subway: N, R, W, Q, 4, 5, 6 to 14th St./Union Sq.

Porcao ♙ BRAZILIAN   If you decide to dine at Porcao, make sure you not only bring a hefty appetite but also a serious craving for meat, red in particular. Porcao is a *rodizio,* a Rio-originated concept where waiters roam from table to table with skewers of hot, juice-dripping meat cooked *churrasco*-style, meaning cooked upright on a skewer over hot coals. There is no menu at Porcao: You pay one price for all you can eat, including 10 kinds of meats, a rolling tray of salmon, such sides as fried yucca and fried banana, and a full salad bar. Turn your pig chip to the green side and the waiters will arrive at your table and slice off a piece of meat that you will gracefully catch with the tongs provided. Before you have a chance to sample the meat, possibly the tender, juicy *picanha,* the noble part of the sirloin, or the equally delicious *alcatra,* top sirloin, there will be another to serve you. To slow the process, turn your chip to red, and the waiters will halt until you are ready for more. The room is sprawling with high ceilings; and if you get thirsty, your host, via his headphones, will summon a cart where *caipirinhas,* the lime-and-*cachaca* (sugar-cane liquor) Brazilian specialty drink, are made at your table. Desserts (and drinks) are not included in the all-you-can-eat price, but if there is any way, save some room for the fabulous coconut pudding. The bar here is a lively scene—off the bar there's also a Scotch club where regulars can store their own bottle(s).

360 Park Ave. S. (at 26th St.). ⓒ 212/252-7080. www.porcaous.com. Rodizio $51; executive lunch $23. AE, DC, MC, V. Mon–Thurs noon–11pm; Fri–Sat 2pm–midnight; Sun 1pm–10pm. Subway: 6 to 28th St.

Primehouse ♙ STEAKHOUSE   There are many meanings of the word "prime," and in the case of Primehouse, the newest (2007) from restaurateur Stephen Hanson (Fiamma, Dos Caminos, Ocean Grill, and so on), it means top-of-the-line meat, of which there are many cuts at Primehouse. Like other Hanson productions, Primehouse is far from subtle; and that, especially when it comes to red meat, is not a bad thing. The space is gargantuan; and, at times, when I dined at the restaurant, I felt service would have been a bit more prompt if the waiters could have used skateboards to traverse the long walk from kitchen to table. Once the food did arrive, however, all was forgiven. The combination of raw seafood and steak has traditionally been a natural one. At Primehouse, the oysters, from either the East or West Coast (or you can try a sampler of both coasts) were fresh and briny. The romaine, tomato, onion and Maytag blue cheese salad was crisp, even when smothered by the rich blue cheese dressing, but do not attempt to tackle it yourself—it will finish you before your steak arrives, and that would be a huge mistake, especially if you've splurged and ordered one of the special cuts aged in the restaurant's "Himalayan Salt Room." I sampled the 35-day aged Kansas City sirloin along with the 40-day aged rib-eye; and whatever they do in that "Salt Room" for all those days, it works. Even after all that you still might be tempted to reduce by a few layers the mountainous "Slice of Prime" seven-layer fudge cake. Good luck.

381 Park Ave. S. (at 27th St.). ⓒ 212/824-2600. www.brguestrestaurants.com. Reservations Recommended. Main courses: $24–$62. AE, DC, DISC, MC, V. Mon–Fri 11:30am–4pm; Sat–Sun 11am–4pm; Mon–Wed 5pm–11pm; Thurs–Sat 5pm–midnight; Sun 5pm–10pm. Subway: N,R,Q, W, 6 to 28th St.

Sapa ♙♙ FRENCH/VIETNAMESE   I am usually wary of fusion cuisine, but in Sapa's case, the combination of French and Vietnamese, based on the two countries' respective histories, is a natural one. It also helps that the food at Sapa is helmed by the talented Patricia Yeo. Begin your journey in the Mediterranean, with a spectacular salad of romaine hearts, endive, and Taleggio cheese with pear fritters in a pear vinaigrette. Move quickly to Vietnam and sample one or two rolls prepared at Sapa's "roll bar"; the spiced yellowfin tartare with avocado and green papaya sprouts was my favorite. When it comes to the main courses, there is a reason Yeo's ginger-crusted ahi tuna over braised oxtail is her signature dish; the unusual mix might seem too rich, but they mesh together perfectly. The restaurant is cavernous, with high ceilings and bright white walls, and service is extremely personable and knowledgeable. The dining experience at Sapa is exotic on every level—even the restroom area, with its candle-adorned bubbling pool, Chinese screens decorating the row of bathroom doors, and soft music, is worth the trip—even if you don't have to go.

43 W. 24th St. (btwn Broadway and Sixth Ave.). ℂ 212/929-1800. www.sapanyc.com. Reservations recommended. Roll bar $8–$12; main courses $22–$32. AE, DISC, MC, V. Mon–Fri 5:30–11:30pm; Sat 6pm–midnight; Sun 5:30–10:30pm; Sun brunch 10:30am–3:30pm. Subway: F, V to 23rd St.

Tamarind ⊛⊛ INDIAN   Like Dévi (p. 174) and Chola (p. 193), Tamarind offers innovative and flavorful variations on the old standards of Indian cuisine. The room is sleek and bleached white, giving it a gallerylike feel; in the middle of the restaurant, adjacent to the bar, is a glassed-in cubicle where you can watch the chefs work the tandoor ovens. And just about anything that comes out of those ovens is spectacular. Start with the *bhel poori,* assorted crisps and noodles with sweet-and-sour chutneys, and one of the soups. I love the she-crab soup with nutmeg, ginger juice, and saffron. Try not to fill up on the tandoor-baked breads—the nan is hard to resist. You can't go wrong with any of the tandoor-baked entrees; the *jhinga angarey,* jumbo prawns marinated in yogurt and chilies, is my favorite. If you venture from the tandoor, try the lamb *pasanda,* apricot-filled grilled lamb in a cashew-and-saffron sauce, or Tamarind swordfish marinated in tamarind chutney and fenugreek leaves. There are a number of vegetarian options; the Raji vegetarian *thali,* an assortment of tandoori salad, lentils, vegetables, chutneys, and relishes, is a treat. Desserts are special, too; try the *gujjia,* a samosa filled with semolina, raisins, cashews, and coconut. Service is efficient and friendly, and the owners will most likely stop by your table and greet you like a regular.

41–43 E. 22nd St. (btwn Broadway and Park Ave.). ℂ 212/674-7400. Reservations recommended. Main courses $11–$30. AE, DC, MC, V. Daily 11:30am–3pm and 5:30–11:30pm. Subway: N, R, 6 to 23rd St.

MODERATE

Hill Country ⊛ BARBECUE   In a competitive market, and the world of barbecue is *very* competitive, everyone needs an edge. Hill Country's edge is Texas-style barbecue, Austin in particular. And in Texas, beef reigns, so it's not surprising that the standouts are the barbecued beef items, specifically the brisket, served moist or lean (go for the moist) and especially the gargantuan beef ribs, coated with a spicy dry rub. If you can't go without your dose of the pig, the Kruez market sausage, shipped right from Texas, is the real deal. At Hill Country, once you are seated at one of the picnic tables in the Texas-sized, loud dining room, you are given a card. Then you proceed to the meat and/or sides counter where you order: by the pound for the meat or by the size container for the sides. Whatever you ordered, drinks and desserts included, are checked off, and on your way out, your card is tabbed up by a cashier. The system is a bit gimmicky and awkward, though maybe not for Austin, but all is forgiven once you dig in and the grease begins to spread on the brown butcher paper beneath your food. Hill Country is a mecca for meat lovers, but don't ignore those sides: the cheddar mac and cheese, beer braised cowboy pinto beans, and the white corn pudding are musts. Every Wednesday through Saturday, there is live country, rock, and blues in the restaurant's lower level.

30 W. 26th St (btwn Broadway–6th Ave.). ℂ 212/255-4544. www.hillcountryny.com. Meat $6.50–$20 per pound; sides $4.50–$16. AE, DISC, MC, V. Sun–Wed noon–10pm; Thurs–Sat noon–11pm. Subway: F, V to 23rd St.

The Hole Truth: N.Y.'s Best Bagels

Not many things are more New York than a bagel, and New Yorkers are loyal to their favorite bagel purveyors. In fact, discussions about who makes the best bagel can lead to heated arguments. Following are the top contenders:

Absolute Bagels, 2708 Broadway, between 107th and 108th streets (℘ 212/932-2052). A new player on the scene, their egg bagels, hot out of the oven, melt in your mouth, and their whitefish salad is perfectly smoky, not overpowering.

Ess-A-Bagel, 359 First Ave., at 21st Street (℘ 212/260-2252; www.ess-a-bagel.com). When it comes to size, Ess-a-Bagel's are the best of the biggest; plump, chewy, and oh so satisfying. Also at 831 Third Ave., between 50th and 51st streets (℘ **212/980-1010**).

H&H Bagels, 2239 Broadway, at 80th Street (℘ **212/595-8003**; www.handh bagel.com). Long reputed as the best bagel in New York, which may have resulted in the arrogant price hike to $1 a bagel. Some complain they are a bit too sweet, but I disagree. The bagels here are always fresh and warm, the bagel aficionado's prerequisite. Also at 639 W. 46th St., at Twelfth Avenue (℘ **212/595-8000**). Takeout only.

Kossar's Bialys, 367 Grand St, at Essex St. (℘ **877-4-BIALYS**; www.kossars bialys.com). We know about their bialys, but don't forget about their bagels. Also hand rolled, the result is a slightly crunchy exterior with a tender, moist middle. Sure you came for the bialys, but you will leave with both.

Murray's Bagels, 500 Sixth Ave., between 12th and 13th streets (℘ 212/462-2830), and 242 Eighth Ave., at 23rd Street (℘ **646/638-1335**; www.mbchelsea.com). There's nothing like a soft, warm bagel to begin your day, and Murray's does them beautifully. Their smoked fish goes perfectly on their bagels.

La Pizza Fresca Ristorante ★★ *Finds* PIZZA/ITALIAN When comparing the top pizzerias in New York, you rarely hear La Pizza Fresca Ristorante mentioned. And that's a mistake. Those who have sampled the genuine Neapolitan pizza (one of only two New York pizzerias certified for authenticity by the Italian organization, *Associazione Vera Pizza Napoletana*) swear by La Pizza Fresca's quality. To achieve certification there are a number of qualifications; wood burning oven, San Marzano tomatoes, bufala mozzarella, hand-pressed dough, and all the ingredients must be cooked with the pizza in the oven. The result is a pizza as good (almost) as you might find in Naples and as good as just about any other in New York. You can have your pizza many different ways, including the delicious *Quattro formaggi,* a combination of four cheeses and a hint of pancetta (Italian bacon); but for the unadulterated Neapolitan flavor, try the simple, tomato, bufala mozzarella, and basil pie. There are also a number of pastas and Italian entrees offered, but what, really, is the point when the pizza here is so good? Also impressive is La Pizza Fresca's 800-plus wine list. The restaurant is comfortable and cozy with low-lighting, exposed brick, and the constant glow from the pizza oven.

31 E. 20th St (btwn Park Ave and Broadway). (*C*) 212/598-0141. www.lapizzafresca.com. Reservations not accepted. Pizza $9–$19; main courses: $12–$28. AE, DC, DISC, MC, V. Mon–Sat noon–3:30pm; Mon–Sat 5:30pm–11pm; Sun 5pm–11pm. Subway: 6 to 23rd St.

INEXPENSIVE

Don't forget **Eisenberg's Coffee Shop,** 174 Fifth Ave., at 22nd Street ((*C*) 212/ 675-5096), for the New York diner experience. For more, see "Old Friends," on p. 162.

Also consider Danny Meyer's popular **Shake Shack** *⟨*, in Madison Square Park ((*C*) 212/889-6600). For healthy burgers, try either outlet of the **New York Burger Co.,** 303 Park Ave. S., between 23rd and 24th streets ((*C*) 212/254-2727), and 678 Sixth Ave., between 21st and 22nd streets ((*C*) 212/229-1404). For a burger with boutique quality meat, try **Brgr,** 287 Seventh Ave, at 26th St ((*C*) 212/488-7500) For more on all three, see the sidebar "Where to Find Your (Burger) Bliss," on p. 194.

City Bakery *⟨* *Kids* ORGANIC AMERICAN   City Bakery offers comfort food that manages to be delicious, nutritious, *and* ecofriendly. Its salad bar is unlike any other in the city, where the integrity of the ingredients is as important as the taste. This is health food, all right—roasted beets with walnuts, glistening sautéed greens, lavender eggplant tossed in miso—but with heart and soul, offering such favorites as French toast with artisanal bacon, flavorful mac 'n' cheese, tortilla pie, and smoked salmon with all the trimmings on Sunday. The "bakery" refers to the plethora of sinful desserts; kids love the spinning wheel of chocolate and the homemade marshmallows. *One caveat:* It's a bit pricey for a salad bar, but oh, what good eats!

3 W. 18th St. (btwn Fifth and Sixth aves.). (*C*) 212/366-1414. Salad bar $13 per lb.; soups $4–$7; sandwiches $5–$10. AE, MC, V. Mon–Fri 7:30am–7pm; Sat 7:30am–6:30pm; Sun 9am–6pm. Subway: N, R, Q, 4, 5, 6 to Union Sq.

10 Times Square & Midtown West

To locate the restaurants in this section, see the map on p. 168.

VERY EXPENSIVE

In addition to the choices below, consider the *New York Times,* four-star winner **Le Bernardin,** 155 W. 51st St., between Sixth and Seventh avenues ((*C*) 212/554-1515; www.le-bernardin.com). See the sidebar "Food Splurge," on p. 201.

Also consider the steakhouses in the box "The Prime Cut," on p. 172, **Uncle Jack's Steakhouse** *⟨*, 440 Ninth Ave., at 34th Street ((*C*) 212/244-0005; www.uncle jacks.com), **Ben Benson's Steakhouse,** 123 W. 52nd St., between Sixth and Seventh avenues ((*C*) 212/581-8888; www.benbensons.com), **Benjamin Steakhouse,** 52 E. 41st St., in the Dylan Hotel ((*C*) 212/297-9177; www.benjaminsteakhouse.com), and **Quality Meats** *⟨* 57 W. 58th St., between Fifth and Sixth avenues ((*C*) 212/371-7777).

Anthos *⟨⟨* INNOVATIVE GREEK   With a few tweaks, higher prices, and even more intriguing pairings, Anthos is Onera, the former Upper West Side restaurant helmed by chef/owner Michael Psilakis (Kefi, p. 203), transplanted to a new location across from legendary 21 Club and in the heart of the power crowd of Midtown. With hostess and co-owner Donatella Arpaia, of David Burke & Donatella, Psilakis has a grand, albeit slick stage in which to showcase his immense talents. The only nods here to Greek traditional cuisine are the grilled octopus, Greek salad, and the side order of moussaka that comes with the perfectly prepared lamb chop loin. Psilakis's signature Greek "crudo," or raw *mezes,* yellowtail, diver scallops, and tuna, that were so popular at Onera, thankfully are on Anthos's menu. The sardine escabeche, a row of properly briny, fresh from the sea, sardines, each on a sliver of cucumber along with the potato and garlic *skorkalia* soup, not really a soup at all, and the above-mentioned octopus are more than enough to make your meal. But a meal of only the mezes and you would miss out on such entrees as the whole, simply grilled, bursting with meat *loup de mer*, served boned but with the head included, or the tantalizing crispy turbot with eggplant puree. Desserts are irresistible; don't miss the sesame ice cream encased in a halvah shell. Service is first rate, and it better be considering the location and the price you are paying.

36 W. 52nd St. (btwn Fifth and Sixth aves.). © 212/582-6900. www.anthosnyc.com. Reservations recommended. Main course: $26–$45. AE, DC, DISC, MC, V. Mon–Fri noon–2:45pm; Mon–Thurs 5–10:30pm; Fri–Sat 5–11pm. Subway: B, D, F, V to 47, 50, Rockefeller Center.

BLT Market 𝒢𝒢 AMERICAN   The newest (in 2007) in the BLT (Bistro Laurent Tourondel) restaurant empire calls the Ritz-Carlton Central Park home. And it's the perfect setting, across from the greenery of Central Park, for the "market" cuisine served here. Other restaurants have chimed in on trendy market-fresh food, but few can do it as well as the people at BLT. The ingredients change seasonally, sometimes daily, depending on what's fresh at the market. Each month, the menu lists what is peak in that particular season. When I visited in November, sunchokes, pumpkin, black cod, bosc pear, chestnut, and a variety of mushrooms were just some of the fresh items used in the dishes prepared that day. Matsutake mushroom and sunchokes, for example could be found in the meaty roasted langoustine appetizer, while the amazingly flaky and moist entree of black cod sat atop a delicious celeriac puree. The bosc pear was used in a perfectly made tart tatin for dessert, while chestnuts were found in a floating island accompanied by orange blossom madeleines. Even my cocktail, a spin of the Brazilian *caipirinha* displayed seasonal ingredients with the addition of concord grapes. Service, as it is at all the BLT restaurants, is professional and helpful, and the room tries to recreate a rustic, farmhouselike ambience with water served in milk bottles and an old plow at the restaurant's entrance.

1430 Avenue of the Americas (at 59th St., in the Ritz-Carlton Central Park). © 212/521-6125. www.bltmarket.com. Reservations recommended. Main courses: $32–$45. AE, DC, DISC, MC, V. Daily 11:45am–2pm and 5:30–10pm. Subway: N, Q, R, W to 57th St.

Kobe Club 𝒢 STEAKHOUSE   There are many variations of the traditional steakhouse, but the Kobe Club takes the concept to the extreme. Glorying in excess, the Kobe Club is about fun—albeit wildly expensive fun. Here you are in what could be considered a combination night club/restaurant/theater. It's dark, with a relentless disco beat blaring; thousands of glimmering samurai swords dangle from the ceiling; a blazing forest fire flickers on a video screen; and private, leather-seated booths and big communal tables are scattered throughout the room. The show begins with a cocktail, the signature Kobe Punch: a mix of Grey Goose vodka with a choice of fresh squeezed juice served in a glass, carafe, or silver punch bowl ($150), is the best opening act, accompanied by the tantalizing American "kobe" beef cheek ravioli in a truffle sauce. Bring a pocket flashlight and hope that the cocktail will help you get through the overly complicated "mix-and-match mains" section of the menu where you can pair American, Australian, and Japanese kobe beef from bulls descended from Japanese Wagyu cattle. And then pick two sauces, butters, or toppings from the extensive list, along with the complimentary house steak sauce, and three types of salts. Or, just take a deep breath and go for the "Samurai's Flight," a combination of the three countries' (Australia, Japan, America) kobe and a 6-ounce American prime filet, a "bargain" at $190 for two people. Finally, try to enjoy the rich beef by not thinking about the enormous tab that will soon materialize on your table.

68 W. 58th St (btwn Fifth and Sixth aves.) ℂ 212/644-5623. www.chinagrillmanagement.com. AE, DC, MC, V. Main courses: $25–$39; Wagyu beef $35–$150. Mon–Fri 11:30am–2:30pm; Mon–Wed 5:30–11pm; Thurs–Sat 5:30–11:30pm. Subway: N, Q, R, W to 57th St.

EXPENSIVE

Abboccato ℛ ITALIAN   The Italian entry from the Livanos family, owners of **Molyvos** (p. 182) and **Oceana** (p. 192), and no ordinary Italian this! The menu is ambitious and hearty, with offerings that include such appetizers as the *affetati misti* (a platter of cured meats), *pesce crudo* (raw fish marinated in olive oil), and grilled tripe; unusual, rustic pastas such as spaghettini with razor clams and mullet roe and orecchiette with cuttlefish; plus such staples as tagliatelle Bolognese and spaghetti carbonara. Rich meat mains include braised (in chocolate and port wine) beef shortribs and crispy veal sweetbreads. Service is good, but not up to Oceana's levels. The room is a throwback; its round yellow booths are reminiscent of 1960s New York Italian.

136 W. 55th St. (btwn Sixth and Seventh aves.). ℂ 212/265-4000. www.abboccato.com. Reservations recommended. Pasta $23–$26; main courses $32–$42. AE, DC, MC, V. Breakfast Sat–Sun only 7:30–10:30am; Mon–Sat noon–3pm; Mon–Tues 5:00–11:00pm; Fri 5:00–11pm; Sat 5–11pm; Sun 4–10pm. Subway: N, R, Q, W to 57th St.

Barbetta ℛℛ ITALIAN   The debate over what is New York's oldest restaurant rages on, and Barbetta (est. 1906) is in the thick of that debate. But there is no debate over Barbetta's sustained excellence during that period. The first, and still one of the few, New York restaurants to serve cuisine from Piemonte (the Piedmont), Italy's northwestern-most region, Barbetta's food, like the restaurant's sumptuous decor, is richly elegant. This is far from your typical red-sauce joint. At Barbetta, if you dine in the autumn or winter, you just might have the pleasure of white truffles, flown in from Piemonte, and shaved over your already decadent *gnochetti ai formaggi*, freshly made, delicate gnocchi in an unforgettable cheese sauce, or the stunning creation of an edible quail's nest filled with *fonduta* cheese and surrounded by three tiny, speckled quail's eggs. On the menu you can choose from one of the restaurant's 1906 creations such as the *bolliti misti*, a Piemontesi specialty, a mix of boiled meats and broth served from an antique silver cart; but for a meal this unique, you must order 48 hours in advance. If you just can't go to an Italian restaurant without ordering something in tomato sauce, you won't go wrong with the 1906-creation *tajarin*, strands of homemade pasta in a simple but perfectly done tomato-basil sauce. Barbetta also features an impressive Italian wine list and, in the warmer months, one of the city's most romantic outdoor gardens. Though this is a Theater District restaurant, and many come for the pretheater prix-fixe, Barbetta is best experienced at a relaxed, leisurely pace.

321 W. 46th St. (btwn Eighth and Ninth aves.). ℂ 212/246-9171. www.barbettarestaurant.com. Reservations recommended. Prix-fixe dinner $49; main courses lunch $22–$29, dinner $28–$36. AE, DC, MC, V. Mon–Sat noon–2:30pm and 5pm–12am. Subway: C, E to 50th St.

db Bistro Moderne ℛ FRENCH BISTRO   Daniel Boulud of **Café Boulud** (p. 208) and **Daniel** (p. 201) fame opened db Bistro Moderne as a casual alternative to his other restaurants. Casual, in this case, means you get architect Jeffrey Beers to put a hip spin on the contemporary French bistro; the result immediately attracts a fashion-conscious crowd (meaning you can wear a T-shirt here—but make sure it's

Armani). To round out the "casual" experience, add a hamburger. But this is not your typical $5.95 burger deluxe; no, Boulud's creation comes in at $32 and is made with minced sirloin, *foie gras,* preserved black truffle, and braised short ribs, served on a Parmesan onion roll. If any hamburger is worth that much—and this point is debatable—this one is. Despite the silly burger excess, the food is, like all Boulud's ventures, outstanding—especially bistro favorites bouillabaisse, coq au vin, and frogs' legs.

55 W. 44th St. (btwn Fifth and Sixth aves.). (C) 212/391-2400. Reservations required. Lunch entrees $28–$32; pretheater 3-course prix-fixe $45; dinner entrees $29–$36. AE, DC, MC, V. Mon–Sat noon–2:30pm; daily 5–11pm; Sun–Mon til 10pm; Fri–Sat til 11:30pm. Subway: B, D, F, Q to 42nd St.

Frankie & Johnnie's (R)(R) STEAKHOUSE   When restaurants open other branches of their originals, red flags go up. Does that mean the restaurant has instantly become a chain and thus quality has eroded to chain-food status? In the case of Frankie & Johnnie's, the legendary Theater District former-speakeasy-turned-steakhouse, which opened another outlet in 2005 in the two-story town house owned once by actor John Barrymore, those fears were quickly allayed after one bite of their signature sirloin. It also helps that the dining room on the second floor of the town house is gorgeous, especially the Barrymore room, the actor's former study with stained-glass ceiling panels, dark wood walls, and a working fireplace. Not only are Frankie & Johnnie's steaks underrated in the competitive world of New York steakhouses, but the other nonsteak options are superb. The crabcake appetizer had an overwhelmingly high crab-to-cake ratio, while the sides of hash browns were the best I've ever had. Pastas and seafood are abundant on the menu and I'm sure they are excellent, but what's the point? Service is steakhouse old-school, and if you are staying in Midtown, the restaurant provides complimentary stretch limo service to and from the restaurant.

32 W. 37th St. (btwn Fifth and Sixth aves.). (C) 212/947-8940. www.frankieandjohnnies.com. Reservations recommended. Main courses $25–$36. Mon–Fri noon–2:30pm; Mon–Thurs 4–10:30pm; Fri–Sat 4–11pm. Subway: B, C, D, N, R, Q, W, V to 34th St./Herald Sq. Also at 269 W. 45th St. (at Eighth Ave.). (C) 212/997-9494. Subway: 1, 2, 3, 7, A, C, E, N, R, Q, S, W to 42nd St.

Keens Steakhouse (R)(R)(R) STEAKHOUSE   Until the latter part of the 20th century, Keens, which was established in the same location in 1885, referred to itself as a "chop house." They are now officially known as a steakhouse, but I wish they had remained true to their roots and hadn't submitted to modern-day marketing and made that change. To their credit, they are a steakhouse in name only. They serve the basics of a steakhouse—the porterhouse for two, aged T-Bone, and filet mignon with requisite sides such as creamed spinach and hash browns—but they still serve chops: lamb chops, prime rib, short ribs, and most notably, mutton chops. It is the mutton chop that has made Keens the true original that it is. The monstrous cut has two flaps of long, thick, rich, subtly gamy meat on either side of the bone that look kind of like mutton-chop sideburns. So which came first, the sideburns or the chop? Keens is no gussied-up remake of old New York: It's the real thing, from the thousands of ceramic pipes on the ceiling (regular diners were given their own personal pipes, including such celebrities as Babe Ruth, George M. Cohan, and Albert Einstein) to the series of rooms on two floors with wood paneling, leather banquettes, fireplaces (in some), a clubby bar with a three-page menu of single malts, and even the framed playbill Lincoln was reading at the Ford Theater that infamous evening in 1865. You might have a better porterhouse at **Peter Luger Steakhouse** (p. 213), but you'll have more fun at Keens.

72 W. 36th St. (at Sixth Ave.). (C) 212/947-3636. www.keens.com. Reservations recommended. Main courses $26–$45. AE, DC, DISC, MC, V. Mon–Fri 11:45am–10:30pm; Sat 5–10:30pm; Sun 5–9pm. Subway: B, D, F, N, R, W, Q, V to 34th St./Herald Sq.

Urban BBQ: The Best 'cue in New York City

New York is known for many things, but barbecue is not one of them. That is, finally changing. The hankering for slow-cooked, charred meat, so popular in the South and heartland, has made its way to the big city. And, really, what is more primal and satisfying than the sensation of tearing slow-smoked meat from bone, eating the meat with your fingers and then, of course, licking that sweet and savory sauce off your own natural utensils? New York is not Memphis or Kansas City, but every year new joints pop up, and we no longer embarrass ourselves when it comes to the fine art of smoking meats.

My current favorite is **RUB** *(p. 171)* helmed by a Kansas City pitmaster named Paul Kirk. The smoked turkey and chicken were as close to perfection as I've found. Close to the West Side Highway, **Dinosaur Bar-B-Que** (p. 210), a Syracuse transplant BBQ joint, is like a roadhouse in atmosphere, and the pulled pork is as good as it gets north of 125th Street. In the heart of tourist trap mecca Times Square, lies a kitschy, themed barbecue joint, **Virgil's Real BBQ** *(p. 185)*, which, especially for a theme restaurant, serves remarkably good 'cue.

French-trained and a former chef at Daniel, Adam Perry Lang, curiously, or maybe not so curiously, gave up the haute French cuisine to open his own joint called **Daisy May's BBQ**, 623 11th Ave., at 46th Street (*(C)* 212/977-1500; www.daisymaysbbq.com), with stellar results. Daisy May carts can be found in various locations around the city, but if you can't find a cart, squeeze into his cafeteria-style restaurant for Memphis-style dry-rub ribs, and you'll think that you are a block from the Mississippi River, not the Hudson.

Molyvos *GREEK*   When Molyvos opened in 1997, it was heralded as a trailblazer of upscale and innovative Greek cuisine. Now, over 10 years later, upscale and innovative Greek is the current "in vogue" cuisine in Manhattan. Molyvos's longterm success is based on its ability to please those who want simple, unpretentious traditional Greek food as well as exciting, original Greek-accented creations. For those who like their Greek unadulterated, you won't go wrong with cold *mezedes,* such as the spreads *tzatziki, melitzanosalata,* and *taramosalata,* and hot *mezedes* such as spinach pie or grilled octopus. For Greek food with an edge, there is ouzo cured salmon on a chickpea fritter or the terrific seafood Cretan bread salad. Just a sampling of the *mezedes* alone should be enough for anyone's hearty appetite, but with entrees as good as grilled *garides,* wild head-on prawns barbecued souvlaki-style, and the *chios* pork and *gigante* bean stew, not ordering one would be a mistake. The knowledgeable sommelier will pair your choices with a comparable Greek wine, of which there are many. Or, skip the wine and sample one or two of the dozens of ouzos available; but don't skip the desserts. Sure you've had baklava before, but have you ever had chocolate baklava? Yes, it's as good as it sounds.

871 Seventh Ave. (btwn 55th and 56th sts.). *(C)* 212/582-7500. www.molyvos.com. Reservations recommended. Main courses $17–$29 at lunch (most less than $20); $20–$36 at dinner (most less than $25); fixed-price lunch $24;

For Texas-style barbecue, visit **Hill Country** ⚜ (p. 176), for the amazing beef short ribs, and **Johnny Utah's** ⚜ (p. 184), where you can have your steak and watch silly white-collar workers get tossed from a mechanical bull.

Restaurateur Danny Meyer has made his name with such celebrated restaurants as the Gramercy Tavern, Eleven Madison Park, and the Union Square Café. A St. Louis native, Meyer wanted to replicate the barbecue he remembered growing up, so he opened **Blue Smoke**, 116 E. 27th St., between Lexington and Park avenues (© 212/447-7733; www.jazzstandard. net), as part of the jazz club, the **Jazz Standard** (see chapter 10). Blue Smoke offers the usual array of barbecue, made in Meyer's custom-built smoker, but with a few quirks such as a fried bologna sandwich.

Brooklyn is honing its 'cue skills with the recent addition of two joints, including the appropriately named **The Smoke Joint**, 87 S. Elliot Place (© 718/797-1011; www.thesmokejoint.com), in Fort Greene, where the "Baby Got Back" baby backs fall off the bone and are only outdone by the Joint's remarkable Black Angus hot dog. **Fette Sau** ⚜⚜ (Williamsburg, Brooklyn; p. 214) means "fat pig" in German, but though there is plenty of good fat in the pig served at Fette Sau, there is nothing German about that down-home smoky taste.

My favorite soul restaurant is **Charles' Southern-Style Kitchen** (see the box, "The Soul of Harlem," p. 212), so when Charles of said kitchen, Charles Gabriel, opened a barbecue joint called **Rack & Soul**, 2818 Broadway, at 109th Street (© 212/222-4800; www.rackandsoul.com), in my neighborhood, I was ecstatic. Rack & Soul not only offers his trademark fried chicken, but also barbecued baby back ribs that are so good you might have to pass on his chicken; or go for a combo platter where you can get a taste of both.

pretheater 3-course dinner $36 (5:30–6:45pm). AE, DC, DISC, MC, V. Mon–Thurs noon–11:30pm; Fri–Sat noon–midnight; Sun noon–11pm. Subway: N, R to 57th St.; B, D, E to Seventh Ave.

South Gate ⚜ CONTEMPORARY AMERICAN   After much anticipation, chef Kerry Heffernan's (formerly of 11 Madison Park) new restaurant, in the recently renovated Jumeirah Essex House, debuted in early 2008. Though the grandeur of the chef's former space has been replaced by a sleek, open dining room with bright mirrors, off-white banquettes, a huge walk in wine cellar, and a roaring fireplace, Heffernan's menu is, thankfully, less excessive. In fact, it's a rather small, uncomplicated menu, but what is on it, Heffernan does superbly. The flash-seared calamari with cauliflower custard in a lobster-coriander sauce is a unique, unfussy appetizer. The cannelloni of kabocha squash and ricotta entree is a keeper, while the spice-roasted cod layered on mustard greens is paired perfectly with a few slices of smoky linguica and Manila clams. For dessert, the choices in chocolate—the chocolate caramel tart or the chocolate Pot de Crème—make it hard to order anything else.

154 Central Park S. (btwn Sixth and Seventh aves.). © 212/484-5120. www.154southgate.com. Main courses: $26–$39. AE, DC, DISC, MC, V. Reservations Recommended. Sun–Thurs 5:30–10:00pm; Fri–Sat 5:30–10:30pm. Subway: A, B, C, D, 1 to 59th St.-Columbus Circle.

MODERATE

The family-style Italian restaurant **Carmine's** has a Times Square branch at 200 W. 44th St., between Broadway and Eighth Avenue (© **212/221-3800;** www.carmines nyc.com).

Becco ⓚ (Finds ITALIAN   If you're a fan of Lidia Bastianich's PBS cooking shows, you'll be happy to know you can sample her simple, hearty Italian cooking here. Becco, on Restaurant Row, is designed to serve her meals "at a different price point" (read: cheaper) than her East Side restaurant, Felidia. The prices are not rock-bottom, but in terms of service, portions, and quality, you get tremendous bang for your buck at Becco (which means to "peck, nibble, or savor something in a discriminating way"). The main courses can head north of the $20 mark, but take a look at the prix-fixe "Sinfonia de Pasta" menu ($17.95 at lunch, $22.95 at dinner), which includes a Caesar salad or an antipasto plate, followed by unlimited servings of the three fresh-made daily pastas. There's also an excellent selection of Italian wines at $25 a bottle. If you can't make up your mind about dessert, have them all: A tasting plate includes gelato, cheesecake, and whatever else the dessert chef has whipped up that day. Lidia herself does turn up at Becco and Felidia; you can even dine with her (see website for details).

355 W. 46th St. (btwn Eighth and Ninth aves.). © 212/397-7597. www.becconyc.com. Reservations recommended. Main courses lunch $13–$25; dinner $19–$35. AE, DC, DISC, MC, V. Mon noon–3pm and 5–10pm; Tues noon–3pm and 5pm–midnight; Wed 11:30am–2:30pm and 4pm–midnight; Thurs–Fri noon–3pm and 5pm–midnight; Sat 11:30am–2:30pm and 4pm–midnight; Sun noon–10pm. Subway: C, E to 50th St.

Johnny Utah's ⓚ BARBECUE   Any place in New York that has an actual mechanical bull, which Johnny Utah's does and is open for the public to ride, has to be labeled kitsch. But there is nothing kitschy about the barbecue at Johnny Utah's. Despite the hokey mechanical bull and the fact that you are right across from Rockefeller Center, this is the best Texas cowboy cuisine you will find in midtown Manhattan. Keep it simple when ordering; the smoked chorizo with pickled okra, served with plain saltine crackers makes a good accompaniment to a cold beer or spicy margarita. Since this is cowboy cuisine, it's hard to resist the Texas brisket. Here it's sliced thin, the meat perfectly tender, and served dry with a side of rice and red-eye gravy. If you prefer your barbecue from the pig, the mountain of smoked pork spareribs with a house BBQ sauce and coleslaw will keep you so occupied, you might not notice that someone just got tossed off the mechanical bull. If you can find room after all that, the banana pudding with Nilla wafers is a filling end to a substantial meal. Johnny Utah's is big and loud—exactly the way a cowboy place should be.

25 W. 51st St. (btwn Fifth and Sixth aves.). © 212/265-UTAH. www.johnnyutahs.com. Reservations recommended. Main courses: $14–$28. AE, DC, DISC, MC, V. Mon–Fri 11am–1am; Sat 4pm–2am. Subway: B, D, F, V to 47th–50th Rockefeller Center.

Marseille ⓚ FRENCH   Lively and casual with open, high ceilings and a tiled floor that creates a Casablancalike ambience, this restaurant, named after the infamous port city in France, features the food of that city, including its North African influences. That means you'll find such entrees as Moroccan chicken, couscous, and tangine on the menu along with Provençal specialties such as bouillabaisse, which comes in three varieties (chicken, vegetarian, and traditional, made with fish—stick with the traditional), short-rib daube, salad niçoise, and soup *au pistou*. You can make a meal of the *meze* (small plates), which feature a tangy grilled *merguez* sausage, anchovies, and roasted peppers; *brandade* (whipped salt cod); tapenade; and broiled sardines wrapped in *lardo* (thick bacon). Located in the Film Center building on Ninth Avenue, this is a good pre-theater choice, but even better when the pretheater rush is over.

630 Ninth Ave. (at 44th St.). © 212/333-2323. www.marseillenyc.com. Meze $4–$13; main courses $16–$28. AE, DC, MC, V. Mon–Fri 11:30–3pm; Sat–Sun 11am–3pm; Sun–Mon 5:15–11pm; Tues–Sat 5:15pm–midnight. Subway: A, C, E, 7 to 42nd St./Times Sq.

Metro Marché ⊘ FRENCH   Now, while scurrying through Port Authority, if you are hungry, or thirsty, you don't have to settle for soggy pizza or a trans-fat laden fast-food hamburger. You can stop at Metro Marché, the ambitious (for Port Authority) bistro located in that hub of transportation, for an authentic Belgian draft beer with a pot of *moules frites*. Inside the lively restaurant, you'll forget you are in a bus depot—and not a particularly attractive one—and whether waiting for a bus or for a nearby Broadway show to start, this is as good a place as any to spend an hour. Most of the bistro standards are on the menu, including a hearty onion soup overflowing with cheese, a rich pâté, and a watercress and frisée salad, the strong Roquefort cheese softened by a subtle citrus vinaigrette. You can get a decent hamburger here or the popular steak *frites*, but it's hard to pass up the aforementioned *moules frites*, prepared *mariniere, dijonaise*, or *diablo* (red-pepper) style. Save room for an aperitif; you'll need it once you leave Metro Marché for the harsh reality that lies outside its welcoming doors.

625 Eighth Ave. (at 41st St.). © 212/239-1010. www.metromarche.com. Main courses: $11–$20. AE, MC, V. Daily 6:30am–11pm. Subway: A, C, E, 7 to 42nd St.

Norma's ⊘⊘ CREATIVE AMERICAN BREAKFAST   Nowhere is breakfast treated with such reverence, and decadence, as at Norma's, a soaring, ultramodern ode to the ultimate comfort food. There's something for everyone on the huge menu. Classics come in styles both simple and haute: Blueberry pancakes come piled high with fresh Maine berries and Devonshire cream, while buttermilks are topped with fresh Georgia peaches and chopped walnuts. Even oatmeal is special: genuine Irish McCann's, dressed with sautéed green apples and red pears and brûléed for a flash of sugary sweetness. Don't pass on the applewood-smoked bacon, so good it's worth blowing any diet. Norma's can even win over breakfast foes with creative sandwiches, a generous Cobb salad with seared ahi, and a terrific chicken potpie. Not cheap for breakfast, but definitely worth the splurge.

At Le Parker Meridien Hotel, 118 W. 57th St. (btwn Sixth and Seventh aves.). © 212/708-7460. www.normas nyc.com. Reservations accepted. Main courses $8–$23 (most $13–$18). AE, DC, DISC, MC, V. Mon–Fri 6:30am–3pm; Sat–Sun 7am–3pm. Subway: B, N, Q, R, W to 57th St.

Virgil's Real BBQ ⊘⊘ (Kids BARBECUE/SOUTHERN   In the heart of the theme-restaurant wasteland known as Times Square is a theme restaurant that actually has good food. The theme is Southern barbecue, and the restaurant, sprawling over two levels, is made to look and feel like a Southern roadhouse with good-ol'-boy decorations on the walls and blues on the soundtrack. Virgil's does an admirable job in recreating that authentic flavor so hard to find north of the Mason-Dixon line. The spice-rubbed ribs are slow-cooked and meaty, but it's the Owensboro lamb (smoked slices of lamb) and the Texas beef brisket that are the standouts. Both are melt-in-your-mouth tender; the lamb is sprinkled with a flavorful mustard sauce, while the brisket is perfect with a few dabs of Virgil's homemade spicy barbecue sauce. For starters, the corn dogs with poblano mustard are something New Yorkers rarely have the pleasure of experiencing, while the BBQ nachos—tortilla chips slathered with

Pizza, New York–Style

Once the domain of countless first-rate pizzerias, Manhattan's pizza offerings have noticeably dropped in quality. The proliferation of Domino's Pizza, Pizza Hut, and other chains into the market have lowered pizza standards. Still, there is plenty of good pizza to be found. Don't be tempted by sad imitations; when it comes to pizza, search out the real deal. Here are some of the best:

DiFara Pizza ⍟, 1424 Avenue J, Brooklyn, at E. 15th Street (𝄐 718/258-1367; Subway: Q to Avenue J/16th St.). DiFara's is ballyhooed in all the local publications that claim it's the best pizza in the city. And though the exterior is nondescript—looking like your basic neighborhood pizzeria—and the interior is cramped, and to be kind, somewhat unkempt with bits of congealed cheese, olive oil, sauce, and crust from possibly a generation of diners still on the tables, DiFara's lives up to its reputation, thanks to the stubborn zeal of owner Dominic DeMarco, who, for over 40 years, makes every pizza himself. Stooped but determined, DeMarco, in his own deliberate way and using top ingredients, crafts each pizza finishing with hand-grated Parmesan cheese, a few dollops of extra-virgin olive oil, and then, using scissors, hand cutting fresh basil onto the pie. The result is a work of art, but one that might test your patience. Expect to wait an hour for a pie, maybe a bit less for a slice. But after one taste, you will know it was worth it.

Grimaldi's Pizzeria, 19 Old Fulton St., between Front and Water streets (𝄐 718/858-4300; www.grimaldis.com; Subway: 2, 3 to Clark St.; A, C to Clark St.; F to York St.). If you need incentive to walk across the Brooklyn Bridge, Grimaldi's, in Brooklyn Heights, easily provides it. In fact, the pizza is so good, made in a coal oven with a rich flavorful sauce and homemade mozzarella, you might run across the bridge to get to it. *Be warned:* It can get very crowded at dinnertime.

John's Pizzeria, 278 Bleecker St., near Seventh Avenue South (𝄐 212/243-1680). Since it has expanded from this original location—there are now three in the city—the once-gleaming luster of John's has faded slightly, but the pizza is still a cut above the rest. Thin-crusted and out of a coal oven with the proper ratio of tomato sauce to cheese, John's pizza has a loyal

melted cheese and barbecued pulled pork—are a meal in themselves. Desserts are what you would expect from a restaurant emulating a Southern theme: big and sweet. Try the homemade ice cream sandwich, made with the cookie of the day. Virgil's is a great place to bring the kids; if they're noisy, no one will notice.

152 W. 44th St. (btwn Sixth and Seventh aves.). 𝄐 212/921-9494. www.virgilsbbq.com. Reservations recommended. Sandwiches $10–$13; main courses and barbecue platters $15–$24 (most less than $19). AE, DC, DISC, MC, V. Sun–Mon 11:00am–11pm; Tues–Fri 11:30am–midnight; Sat 11am–midnight. Subway: 1, 2, 3, 7, N, R to 42nd St./Times Sq.

following. Though the quality at all of the locations is good, the original Bleecker Street location is the most old-world romantic and my favorite. Also at 260 W. 44th St., between Broadway and Eighth Avenue (© 212/391-7560), and 408 E. 64th St., between York and First avenues (© 212/935-2895).

Lombardi's, 32 Spring St., between Mulberry and Mott streets (© 212/941-7994; www.firstpizza.com; Subway: 6 to Spring St.). Claiming to be New York's first "licensed" pizzeria, Lombardi's opened in 1905 and still uses a generations-old Neapolitan family pizza recipe. The coal oven kicks out perfectly cooked pies, some topped with ingredients such as pancetta, homemade sausage, and even fresh-shucked clams. It's hard to go wrong here no matter what tops the pizza. A garden in the back makes it even more inviting during warm weather.

Patsy's Pizzeria &&, 2287 First Ave., between 117th and 118th streets (© 212/534-9783; www.patsyspizzeriany.com; Subway: 6 to 116th St.). My favorite, and also the favorite of Frank Sinatra, who liked it so much he had pies packed and flown out to Las Vegas. The coal oven here has been burning since 1932, and though the neighborhood in east Harlem where it is located has had its ups and downs, the quality of pizza at Patsy's has never wavered. Try the marinara pizza, a pie with fresh marinara sauce but no cheese that's so good you won't miss the mozzarella. Unlike the other pizzerias mentioned here, you can order by the slice at Patsy's. Don't be fooled by imitators using Patsy's name; this is the original and the best.

Totonno's Pizzeria Napolitano, 1524 Neptune Ave., between West 15th and West 16th streets, Coney Island, Brooklyn (© 718/372-8606; Subway: D to Stillwell Ave./Coney Island). This unassuming little pizzeria has been at the same spot since 1924, and it makes pizzas almost exactly as it did 80 years ago—thin crust, fresh sauce, and mozzarella, and that's about it. Don't even think about asking for an exotic topping on these pies (and why would you?). Enjoy it in all its simple unadorned glory. Totonno's second branch, on the Upper East Side, 1544 Second Ave., between 80th and 81st streets (© 212/327-2800), opened about 10 years ago—go ahead and order the exotic toppings there, but for the real deal, go to Coney Island.

INEXPENSIVE

If you're looking for the quintessential New York deli, you have a choice between the **Stage Deli,** 834 Seventh Ave., between 53rd and 54th streets (© 212/245-7850), known for its jaw-distending celebrity-named sandwiches, and the **Carnegie Deli,** 854 Seventh Ave., at 55th Street (© 800/334-5606), the place to go for the best pastrami, corned beef, and cheesecake in town. For more, see the sidebar "The New York Deli News," on p. 190.

There is a nice outlet of **John's Pizzeria** in Times Square, 260 W. 44th St., between Broadway and Eighth Avenue (© **212/391-7560;** subway: 1, 2, 3, 7, A, B, C, E, N, R, W, Q, S to 42nd St./Times Sq.; see the box "Pizza, New York–Style," p. 186). Also consider the aptly named **Burger Joint** *Value*, in the lobby of Le Parker Meridien Hotel, 118 W. 57th St. (© **212/708-7414**), for cheap yet excellent no-frills burgers (see the box "Where to Find Your [Burger] Bliss," p. 194).

For the New York version of the Philadelphia cheese steak, try **Shorty's** *Value*, at 576 Ninth Ave., between 41st and 42nd streets (© **212/967-3055**).

Afghan Kebab House *Value* MIDDLE EASTERN   You'll find Afghan Kebab Houses all over the city. Are they related? Who knows, but I like this one best for its heaping plates of first-rate Middle Eastern fare. Kebabs are the first order of business: All are pleasing, but my favorite is the *sultani,* chunks of ground lamb marinated in aromatic spices and broiled over wood coals with green peppers and tomatoes. The *tikka kebab,* in lamb or beef, is impressive, as is the chicken korma, slow-cooked with onions, tomatoes, peppers, and fresh herbs. All plates come with amazingly aromatic brown Indian basmati rice and flat Afghan bread. The room is simple and well worn but evocative, with Oriental carpets serving as table runners. Service is attentive.

764 Ninth Ave. (btwn 51st and 52nd sts.). © 212/307-1612 or 212/307-1629. Reservations accepted. Main courses $10–$16 (most under $12). AE, DC, DISC, MC, V. Daily 11am–11pm. Subway: C, E to 50th St.

Mandoo Bar *Finds* KOREAN   The heart of Manhattan's Koreatown is 32nd Street between Fifth and Sixth avenues—and the number of Korean restaurants on that 1 block is dizzying. You'll know you've found Mandoo Bar when you see the two women in the window rolling and stuffing fresh *mandoo* (Korean for dumpling). Because of the constant preparation, the dumplings, stuffed with a variety of ingredients, are incredibly fresh. There's the *mool mandoo* (basic white dumplings filled with pork and vegetables), the *kimchee mandoo* (steamed dumplings stuffed with potent kimchi [Korean spiced cabbage], tofu, pork, and vegetables), the green vegetable *mool mandoo* (boiled dumplings filled with mixed vegetables), and the *goon mandoo* (pan-fried dumplings filled with pork and vegetables). You really can't go wrong with any of these dumplings, so sample them all with a Combo Mandoo. Soups are also great here; try the beef noodle in a spicy, sinus-clearing broth. With seating that is nothing more than wooden benches, Mandoo Bar is better suited for quick eats rather than a lingering meal—a perfect lunch break from shopping in Herald Square or visiting the nearby Empire State Building.

2 W. 32nd St. (just west of Fifth Ave.). © 212/279-3075. Reservations not accepted. Main courses $7–$17. AE, MC, V. Daily 11:30am–10pm. Subway: B, D, F, N, Q, R, V, W to 34th St./Herald Sq.

Nizza *Value* FRENCH/ITALIAN   You won't do much better for pre- or post-theater dining than Nizza. New in 2007, Nizza offers the cuisine of the French Mediterranean, the city of Nice specifically, and its Ligurian-Italian influence. It's a restaurant where you can happily fill up on appetizers and salads, starting with the tangy tapenade of black olives served with light, freshly baked focaccia chips and *socca,* a chickpea pancake cooked in a brick oven and sprinkled with fresh herbs. Or savor a glass of wine with a plate of *salumi,* a selection of cured meats such as *coppa, mortadella,* prosciutto, and a variety of salamis, including duck. The romaine salad I had in a garlic vinaigrette with anchovies and shaved pecorino cheese made me swear off Caesar salad forever—well almost. From that same brick oven come pizzas, including a Provencal pie with ratatouille, goat cheese, and pesto; entrees such as the delicate *polpette* (meatballs), served on a bed of polenta and garnished with a hot green pepper; and wild boar lasagna that is much less ferocious than it sounds. The restaurant is loud and seating is on the tight side, but you easily forgive Nizza these faults once you sample the memorable food and, especially, the easy-on-your-wallet prices.

630 Ninth Ave (at 45th St.). *©* 212/956-1800. $8–$12. AE, MC, V. Tues–Sat 11:30am–2am; Sun–Mon 11:30am–midnight. Subway: A, C, E, 7 to 42nd Street.

Sapporo *℞ (Value* JAPANESE NOODLES Peruse the community bulletin board as you enter Sapporo and you might find yourself a deal on an apartment—that is, if you can read Japanese. Thankfully, the menu is in English in this longtime Theater District Japanese noodle shop. If the mostly Japanese clientele doesn't convince you of Sapporo's authenticity, the din of satisfied diners slurping huge bowls of steaming ramen (noodle soup with meat and vegetables) will. And though the ramen is Sapporo's specialty, the *gyoza* (Japanese dumplings) and the *donburi* (pork or chicken over rice with soy-flavored sauce) are also terrific. Best of all, nothing on the menu is over $10, and that's not easy to find in the oft-overpriced Theater District.

152 W. 49th St. (btwn Sixth and Seventh aves.). *©* 212/869-8972. Reservations not accepted. Main courses $6–$9. No credit cards. Mon–Sat 11am–11pm; Sun 11am–10pm. Subway: N, R to 49th St.

Uncle Nick's GREEK For stupendous portions of surprisingly good traditional Greek food at good prices, come to Uncle Nick's. Turn off your cellphone upon entering, not because you might disturb your neighbors, but because there is no way you will be able to have a phone conversation in this loud restaurant. But how can you talk if your mouth is filled with one or more of Nick's Greek dips such as *taramosalata* or *tzatziki,* or his perfectly tender, grilled baby octopus? If you haven't filled up on his appetizers, order one of Nick's grilled specialties: The grilled lamb kabob is an absolute winner and guaranteed for leftovers, while the gyro plate is a challenge for those with even the heartiest appetites. Seafood is also good, especially the swordfish kabobs. Desserts are standard; you won't have room for them anyway. Service is friendly and matches the rollicking atmosphere here. Next door is the slightly more intimate Uncle Nick's Ouzeria, specializing in *mezedes,* Greek small dishes like tapas.

747 Ninth Ave. (btwn 50th and 51st sts.). *©* 212/245-7992. Appetizers $8–$15; main courses $15–$25. Sun–Thurs noon–11:00pm; Fri–Sat noon–11:30pm. Nick's Ouzeria next door at 749 Ninth Ave. *©* 212/397-2892. Subway: C or E to 50th St.

Wondee Siam *℞ (Finds* THAI Hell's Kitchen offers countless ethnic culinary variations and one of the most prevalent is Thai—there are at least six Thai restaurants in a 5-block radius. My favorite among these is the tiny, zero-ambience Wondee Siam. I don't need colorful decorations or a fish tank to enjoy authentic, uncompromisingly spicy Thai food, and that's what I get at Wondee Siam. Here you don't have to worry that your waiter will assume you want a milder form of Thai. If there is a little red asterisk next to your item, you can be sure it is appropriately spicy. The soups are terrific, especially the sinus-clearing *tom yum.* In fact, there is an entire section of yum (chilies) dishes on the menu; my favorite being the *larb gai,* minced ground chicken with ground toasted rice. The curries are first-rate as are the noodles, including the mild pad Thai. This is BYOB and you'll want to do so to complement the spicy food. If you want a bit more comfort, try Wondee Siam II 1 block up. But make sure you ask your waiter not to dumb down the spice and serve up the food authentic Thai-style.

792 Ninth Ave. (btwn 52nd and 53rd sts.). *©* 212/459-9057. Reservations not accepted. Main courses $8.50–$18 (most under $10). No credit cards. Mon–Sat 11am–11pm; Sun 11am–10:30pm. Wondee Siam II, 813 Ninth Ave. (btwn 53rd and 54th sts.). *©* 917/286-1726. Subway: C, E to 50th St.

The New York Deli News

There's nothing more Noo Yawk than hunkering down over a mammoth pastrami on rye at an authentic Jewish deli, where anything you order comes with a bowl of lip-smacking sour dills and a side of attitude. Here are some of the best.

Artie's New York Delicatessen, 2290 Broadway, between 82nd and 83rd streets (© **212/579-5959**; www.arties.com). Compared to the legends below, Arties, which has been around since 1999, is the new kid on the deli block but can hold its own on the playground with the big boys, thank you very much (especially in the wiener department).

Barney Greengrass, the Sturgeon King, 541 Amsterdam Ave., between 86th and 87th streets on the Upper West Side (© **212/724-4707**). This unassuming, daytime-only deli has become legendary for its high-quality salmon (sable, gravlax, Nova Scotia, kippered, lox, pastrami—you choose), whitefish, and sturgeon (of course).

Carnegie Deli, 854 Seventh Ave., at 55th Street (© **800/334-5606** or 212/757-2245; www.carnegiedeli.com). It's worth subjecting yourself to surly service, tourist-targeted overpricing, and elbow-to-elbow seating for some of the best pastrami and corned beef in town. Even big eaters may be challenged by mammoth sandwiches with such names as "Fifty Ways to Love Your Liver" (chopped liver, hard-boiled egg, lettuce, tomato, and onion).

Katz's Delicatessen 愛愛, the city's best deli, remains fabulously old-world despite its hipster-hot Lower East Side location at 205 E. Houston St., at Ludlow Street (© **212/254-2246**). For more on Katz's, see p. 156.

2nd Avenue Deli 愛 162 E. 33rd St., between Lexington and Third avenues, (© **212/689-9000**; www.2ndavedeli.com). After a hiatus of more than 2 years, the Second Avenue Deli has returned, but now it's just off Third Avenue, about 20 blocks north of its former East Village location. That East Village feel is gone, but not the quality Kosher deli specialties. The standards: corned beef, pastrami and brisket are as good as you'll get, while such guilty pleasures as *gribenes*, (fried chicken skin) and chicken liver, despite their artery-clogging qualities, are almost impossible to resist. Unlike other delis, you might even get a smile from your waiter!

Stage Deli, 834 Seventh Ave., between 53rd and 54th streets (© **212/ 245-7850**; www.stagedeli.com). Noisy and crowded and packed with tourists, it's still as authentic as they come. The celebrity sandwiches, ostensibly created by the personalities themselves, are jaw-distending mountains of top-quality fixings: The Tom Hanks is roast beef, chopped liver, onion, and chicken fat, while the Dolly Parton is (drumroll, please) twin rolls of corned beef and pastrami.

11 Midtown East & Murray Hill

To locate the restaurants in this section, see the map on p. 168.

EXPENSIVE

Aquavit ✿✿✿ SCANDINAVIAN   The restaurant, located in the bottom of a glass tower on East 55th Street, is designed in sleek Scandinavian style with modernist furniture. In the front of the restaurant is an informal and less-expensive cafe, while past a long bar is the dining room. The smoked fish—all the fish—is prepared perfectly. I daydream about the herring plate: four types of herring accompanied by a tiny glass of *aquavit*, distilled liquor not unlike vodka flavored with fruit and spices, and a frosty Carlsberg beer. The hot smoked Arctic char on the main a la carte menu, served with clams and bean puree in a mustard green broth, is also a winner. Most fixed-price menus offer a well-chosen beverage accompaniment option.

65 E. 55th St. (btwn Park and Madison aves.). ✆ **212/307-7311.** www.aquavit.org. Reservations recommended. Cafe main courses $9–$32; 3-course fixed-price meal $24 at lunch, $35 at dinner; main dining room fixed-price meal $39 at lunch, $82 at dinner ($39 for vegetarians); 3-course pretheater dinner (5:30–6:15pm) $55; tasting menus $58 at lunch, $115 at dinner ($90 for vegetarians); supplement for paired wines $30 at lunch, $80 at dinner. AE, DC, MC, V. Mon–Fri noon–2:30pm; Sun–Thurs 5:30–10:30pm; Fri–Sat 5:15–10:45pm. Subway: E, F to Fifth Ave.

BLT Steak ✿✿✿ STEAKHOUSE/BISTRO   Steakhouses are often stereotyped as bastions of male bonding; testosterone-fueled with red meat and hearty drinks. But BLT (Bistro Laurent Tourendel) Steak breaks that mold in a big way; on the night I visited, I noticed more women—slinky and model-like—chomping on thick cuts of beef than men. That doesn't mean men can't also enjoy the beef here; served in cast-iron pots and finished in steak butter with a choice of sauces—béarnaise, red wine, horseradish, and bleu cheese, to name a few. The signature is the porterhouse for two (a whopping $70), but I recommend the New York strip or the short ribs braised in red wine. Both dishes can be shared, which may be a good idea, especially after devouring the airy complimentary popovers and sampling an appetizer such as the incredible tuna tartare or a side of onion rings, potato gratin, or creamy spinach. Even after sharing one of the meats, you might not have room for the chestnut-chocolate sundae or peanut-butter chocolate mousse, and that would be a shame. This is not a restaurant for intimate conversation; even the music was muffled by the din of the diners.

106 E. 57th St. (btwn Park and Lexington aves.). ✆ **212/752-7470.** www.bltsteak.com. Reservations highly recommended. Main courses $24–$39. AE, DC, MC, V. Mon–Fri 11:45am–2:30pm; Mon–Thurs 5:30–11pm; Fri–Sat 5:30–11:30pm. Subway: 4, 5, 6, N, R, W to 59th St.

Country ✿✿ FRENCH/AMERICAN   Supervised by chef Geoffrey Zakarian, the chef of the popular and acclaimed Town restaurant, it's hard to believe that this stunningly elegant, urbane restaurant in the recently renovated Hotel Carlton could be the "Country" in Zakarian's Town/Country duo. There's really nothing country about the place. And that's not a knock. Gorgeously designed by architect David Rockwell, the restaurant's magnificent centerpiece is the restored 200-square-foot Tiffany skylight dome that was hidden over the years by a dropped ceiling. Zakarian's prix-fixe menu changes every other week and matches the decor's sophisticated style. When I visited for an early spring dinner, warm asparagus in a light lemon vinaigrette was an outstanding first-course option while the lamb cannelloni (tender pieces of shredded lamb in a wonton-thin dumpling) made the perfect second-course accompaniment. Of the third-course options, the striped bass with crushed herbs, potatoes, and clams was the standout. A selection of cheeses is offered as a dessert option and it's hard to resist. Downstairs are the more countrified, darker, wood-paneled booths of Café at Country.

90 Madison Ave. (at 29th St.). ℂ 212/889-7100. www.countryinnnewyork.com. Reservations required. Prix-fixe $105; 5-course tasting menu $110; 4-course tasting menu $105; 6-course $135. AE, DC, DISC, MC, V. Sun–Thurs 5:30–10pm; Fri–Sat 5:30–11pm. Café at Country main courses $15–$27. Mon–Sat 11:30am–3pm and 5:30–11pm; Sun 10:30am–3pm. Subway: N/R to 28th St.; 6 to 28th St.

Mia Dona ✹✹ ITALIAN/GREEK   This newest (2008) venture by the team of chef Michael Psilakis and partner Donatella Arpaia (**Anthos**, p. 178) is a celebration of mostly rustic Italian dishes with a few nods to Greece along the way. The combination is a natural and best of all, at Mia Dona, easy on the wallet. The appetizer of grilled calamari and caponata salad (a combination of sweet [from currants] and sour from the pickled eggplant) works terrifically, the calamari grilled to tender perfection; while the crispy rabbit with salt and fingerling chips is a starter you most likely won't find anywhere else. Another original is the *gnudi*, gnocchilike pasta served with sheep's milk ricotta in a truffle butter sauce; it's the standout in a selection of very good pastas. Of the entrees, the olive oil poached cod with broccoli rabe in a sun-dried tomato pesto tasted as good as its description, while the hearty braised veal breast with escarole and cannellini beans is Italian comfort food at its best. The current trend in New York dining is high decibel and here it's no exception, making the noise-level the only negative to the Mia Dona experience.

206 E. 58th St. (btwn Second and Third aves.). ℂ 212/750-8170. www.miadona.com. Reservations recommended. Pastas $15–$16; entrees $17–$24. AE, DC, DISC, MC, V. Mon–Fri noon–2:30pm; Sat–Sun 11am–2pm; Mon–Thurs 5pm–10:30pm; Fri–Sun 5pm–11pm. Subway: 4, 5, 6, N, R, W to 59th St.-Lexington Ave.

Oceana ✹✹✹ SEAFOOD   When you enter Oceana, the nautical themes are obvious. But this is no seafood shack—it's more like a luxury ocean liner. Standouts include tartare of yellowfin tuna with daikon radish, black cardamom, and horseradish sorbet; striped bass wrapped in a ham croissant; and stuffed artichoke and Icelandic cod basted in butter and herbs. The dishes look so good on the plate you might not want to eat them, but that would be a big mistake. In this case the artwork is extremely edible. Oceana also features an excellent wine list and your waiter will help pair wines with your dishes if you desire. Though this is not your everyday restaurant—prices are too steep for that—the atmosphere is relaxed and the service is personable.

55 E. 54th St. (btwn Park and Madison aves.). ℂ 212/759-5941. www.oceanarestaurant.com. Reservations recommended. 3-course prix fixe $48 lunch, $78 dinner. AE, DISC, MC, V. Mon–Fri noon–2:30pm and 5:30–10:30pm; Sat 5–10:30pm. Subway: E, F to Fifth Ave.

Pampano ✹✹ MEXICAN SEAFOOD   I'm usually wary of overly presented and overpriced Mexican food, much preferring the working-stiff stuff I can buy from the taco trucks in east Harlem. Pampano, however, does things with Mexican ingredients, especially seafood, that no taco truck I know has ever done before—and the lovely, lush town house location is much more comfortable. You might want to venture from the fish on the menu, but I wouldn't recommend it. Start with the tasting of either three or four ceviches; they are all spectacular, especially the mahimahi bathed in lemon juice, cilantro, chilies, and avocado. For a rare and special treat, try a lobster taco—you won't find that at your local *taqueria*. Of the entrees, it would be difficult to order anything but the fantastic *pampano adobado,* sautéed pompano with creamy black rice, roasted garlic, and chile *guajillo* sauce, but you won't suffer too much if you settle for the memorable pan-fried baby red snapper in a *chile de arbol* sauce. Save room for chocolate flan for dessert and maybe a cleansing shot of one of the restaurant's many excellent tequilas. Pampano is a scene, but a festive one with a lively bar and a beautiful upstairs dining area.

209 E. 49th St. (at Third Ave.). *©* **212/751-4545.** Reservations recommended. Main courses $23–$30. AE, DC, MC, V. Mon–Fri 11:30am–2:30pm; Mon–Wed 5–10pm; Thurs–Sat 5–11:00pm; Sun 5–9:30pm. Subway: E, V to Lexington Ave./53rd St.; 6 to 51st St.

MODERATE

Also consider **P.J. Clarke's** *⌖*, 915 Third Ave., at 55th Street (*©* **212/317-1616;** www.pjclarkes.com), for their old-world charm and legendary hamburger. For a more innovative, experimental hamburger, try **Rare Bar & Grill,** 303 Lexington Ave., between 37th and 38th streets (*©* **212/481-1999**). For more information on both, see the box "Where to Find Your (Burger) Bliss," on p. 194.

Chola *⌖⌖ Finds* INDIAN   Don't let the nondescript, neighborhood Chinese restaurant look fool you. There is nothing nondescript or bland about the Indian cuisine served here, including a number of hard-to-find dishes from the Southern regions. The food of Chola is as good as you will find just about anywhere in Manhattan. The menu is extensive and features many vegetarian and vegan options. Of the vegetarian starters, the kurkuri bhindi (crispy okra and red onions flavored by a lime and chaat masala) is not to be missed, while the nonvegetarian cochin lamb chops, rubbed with southern spices and served with onions and garlic, is so good that it might tempt a vegetarian to cross over to the dark side. Long, crispy *dosas* (thin crepes stuffed with spiced potatoes and peas), are also available at Chola and, according to the menu, a favorite of Martha Stewart's. After a few bites, I concurred with Martha. Of the "Southern Specialties" listed on the menu *savitri amma's avail,* vegetables in a yogurt sauce, was unlike anything I had ever tasted in an Indian restaurant, but very much want to again. Chicken korma, seemingly a conventional Indian dish, was anything but at Chola, with the tender roasted chicken coated in a rich cashew sauce. Probably the best way to experience Chola and to sample a wide variety of its dishes is to visit the restaurant for its very popular weekend "maharaja" buffet, just don't expect to eat again for a long time.

225 E. 58th St. (btwn Second and Third aves.). *©* **212/688-4619.** wwwfineindiandining.com. Main courses: $14–$23; lunch buffet $14. AE, DC, DISC, MC, V. Mon–Fri noon–3pm; Sat–Sun 11am–3pm; nightly 5pm–11pm. Subway: 4, 5, 6, N, R, W to 59th St.

Naples 45 *⌖* ITALIAN/PIZZA   At times the bustle and noise in this expansive restaurant in the Met Life Building might remind you of the lobby of Grand Central Station, just down the escalators from it. But don't let the activity deter you from enjoying Naples 45's pizza, which is worthy of the city of its name. Made in a wood-burning brick oven, the pizzas are created with flour imported from Southern Italy, spring water, Fior de Latte mozzarella, and San Marzano tomatoes. Thankfully there are not too many varieties, and when the ingredients are this good, it's always best, in my opinion, to stick to the basics; in this case the Margherita D.O.C pizza with the San Marzano tomatoes and mozzarella is close to Neapolitan perfection. If you do choose to veer from the simple, try the Vesuvio, made with anchovies, olives and capers. If you want to try something on the menu while your pizzas are being prepared, the meatballs, made of veal and served in a sweet-and-sour tomato sauce, are good enough to risk slightly diminishing your appetite for the main event.

200 Park Ave. (at 45th St.). *©* **212/972-7001.** www.rapatina.com/naples45. Pizza $15–$35. AE, DC, MC, V. Mon–Fri 7:30am–10pm. Subway: 4, 5, 6, 7, S to 42nd St.-Grand Central.

Where to Find Your (Burger) Bliss in NYC

New York is hamburger happy. And that happiness has nothing to do with Mickey D's or BK. It's about real, solid, locally made burgers and there are plenty of places to find them without resorting to supersizing yourself. Here are some:

Brgr (★), 287 Seventh Ave., at 26th Street (© 212/488-7500; www.brgr.us). The hook here is top quality meats and homemade toppings. The beef is natural angus from Montana Legend beef, but just as good are the turkey burgers made from Plainville Farms all-natural turkeys. Some of the toppings include Roquefort cheese, sweet onion marmalade, and homemade burger sauce. Save room for a Brgr shake made with Ronnybrook farms milk and ice cream.

Burger Joint (★★), located discreetly behind a curtain in the lobby of Le Parker Meridien Hotel, 118 W. 57th St. (© **212/708-7414**), is like the burger joint you might remember in college—only the burgers are better. And for a place off the lobby of a fancy hotel, it's downright cheap.

New York Burger Co., 303 Park Ave. South, between 23rd and 24th streets (© **212/254-2727**), and 678 Sixth Ave., between 21st and 22nd streets (© **212/229-1404**). Here you won't feel guilty as you devour the burgers at this "healthy" fast-food alternative. The beef is all-natural Coleman beef, devoid of hormones or antibiotics and served on a fresh-baked brioche. What do they taste like? The burgers have plenty of flavor and come in a number of varieties.

P.J. Clarke's (★), 915 Third Ave., at 55th Street (© **212/317-1616**; www. pjclarkes.com). P.J. Clarke's has been a Midtown institution for over 50 years,

INEXPENSIVE

The lower concourse of **Grand Central Terminal** (★★), 42nd Street at Park Avenue, has developed into a quick-bite bonanza that is an ideal choice for lunch—and the setting is an architecture-lover's delight. Head downstairs and choose from among the many outlets, offering everything from bratwurst to sushi. Standouts include **Junior's,** an offshoot of the Brooklyn stalwart, serving deli sandwiches, terrific steak burgers, and their world-famous cheesecake in their own waiter-serviced dining area.

For a glorious meal, dining under an impressive curved and tiled ceiling, try the New York landmark **Oyster Bar & Restaurant** (★) (© **212/490-6650;** www.oyster barny.com). Excellent soups and sandwiches (most for under $10) fall into the inexpensive category, but you will head on up into moderate and expensive for full meals of the fresh, well-prepared seafood. For a complete list of vendors, check out **www. grandcentralterminal.com**.

In addition to the listings below, there's also **Ess-A-Bagel** (see "The Hole Truth: N.Y.'s Best Bagels," p. 177) at 831 Third Ave., at 51st Street (© **212/980-1010**).

Kalustyan's (★) MIDDLE EASTERN/INTERNATIONAL DELI The heady smell of spices and barrels full of nuts and other delicacies may have you lingering on and its hamburger, like the restaurant's old wood walls, broken telephone booth, and hidden dining nook for two, has been blessedly preserved. Nothing more than a slab of chopped meat cooked to order, on a bun; and for the curious price of $8.10, the hamburger is a simple masterpiece. There is a Clarke's in the Financial District downtown at 4 World Financial Center (© 212/285-1500) and a new location off Lincoln Center, 44 W. 63rd St. (© 212/957-9700).

Rare Bar & Grill ⭑, 303 Lexington Ave., between 37th and 38th streets (© 212/481-1999; www.rarebarandgrill.com). You might pay a little more for your burger at Rare Bar & Grill—they range from $9 to $20—but you are paying for 8 ounces of Grade A American chuck beef that is ground daily at the restaurant. Rare has a number of interesting varieties; my favorite is the "M&M" burger, with caramelized shallots, cheddar cheese, and apple-smoked bacon flambéed in whiskey. Rare is so popular, they recently opened another branch downtown, at 228 Bleecker St., between Carmine and Downing streets (© 212/691-7273).

Shake Shack, in Madison Square Park (© 212/889-6600; www.shakeshack. com). Open from the beginning of spring through most of November (and for phone orders and pickup in winter), Danny Meyer, of Gramercy Tavern, The Modern, and Eleven Madison Park fame, is behind this "shack" in the middle of Madison Square Park, where adoring fans line up early and often for takeout burgers, hot dogs, and milkshakes. Try to come during off-hours, if possible, to avoid the lines; the burgers are good, but we're just talking hamburgers here—not worth waiting interminably for.

the first floor, but before you start loading up with exotica, take the stairs up to the deli. A smiling little man in a white hat will likely be there to greet you. Magazine and newspaper articles plastered all over the place feature photographs of your new friend, the smiling little man with the white cap. Ask for the *mujadarra* (a traditional Arabian lentil-and-rice dish with caramelized onions, served as a salad or in pita bread), pay $4, and settle in at one of the little windowside tables.

123 Lexington Ave. (at 28th St.). © 212/685-3451. www.kalustyans.com. Soups, salads, sandwiches under $10. AE, MC, V. Mon–Sat 10am–8pm; Sun 11am–7pm. Subway: 6 to 28th St.

12 Upper West Side

To locate the restaurants in this section, see the map on p. 198.

VERY EXPENSIVE

Also consider the two four-star-rated restaurants on Columbus Circle: **Jean-Georges** ⭑⭑⭑, in the Trump International Hotel & Tower, 1 Central Park West, at 60th Street/Columbus Circle (© 212/299-3900; www.jean-georges.com), and **Masa,** in the Time Warner Center, 10 Columbus Circle (© 212/823-9800). See the sidebar "Food Splurge" on p. 201.

(Kids) Family-Friendly Restaurants

While it's always smart to call ahead to make sure a restaurant has kids' menus and highchairs, you can count on the following to be especially accommodating. And what kid doesn't love pizza? See the sidebar "Pizza, New York–Style," on p. 186, for suggestions.

Here are some other options for the entire family:

Big Nick's Burger and Pizza Joint ⍟ (p. 205) In the unlikely event that your kids can't find anything they like on the 27-page menu, they can just tune in to the nonstop *Three Stooges* marathon playing on the restaurant's TVs.

Bubby's Brooklyn ⍟ (p. 152) Larger than the TriBeCa branch, this Bubby's has a tremendous view of Manhattan and is across the street from a playground.

Carmine's ⍟ (p. 184 and 202) This rollicking family-style Italian restaurant was created with kids in mind. You won't have to worry about them making too much noise here.

City Bakery ⍟ (p. 178) What child wouldn't be taken with the chocolate spinning wheel and homemade marshmallows? As a bonus, the organic fare is nutritious *and* delicious.

Dinosaur Bar-B-Que (p. 210) Loud and casual, kids come away with dinosaur tattoos to go with the barbecue-sauce stains that they will undoubtedly wear on their clothes.

Good Enough to Eat ⍟ (p. 207) Comfort food for kids, such as macaroni and cheese, pizza, and great desserts.

Mickey Mantle's, 42 Central Park South (btw. Fifth & Sixth aves) (© 212/688-7777; www.mickeymantles.com). As a player, the Mick had a reputation for being testy with children, but he's made up for it in retirement when he opened his extremely kid-friendly restaurant located just across the street from Central Park.

Nick's Family-Style Restaurant and Pizzeria ⍟ (p. 209) With locations in both Queens and Manhattan, Nick's has been wowing families for over a decade with its praiseworthy pizza and Italian specialties.

Serendipity 3 (p. 210) Kids will love this whimsical restaurant and ice cream shop, which serves up a huge menu of American favorites, followed up by colossal ice cream treats.

Tavern on the Green (p. 197) Your kids will be wowed by the Central Park setting, and a children's menu makes feeding them easy and affordable. What's more, if the little ones get rambunctious, you just have to take them outdoors to blow off a little steam.

Virgil's Real BBQ ⍟⍟ (p. 185) This pleasing Times Square barbecue joint welcomes kids with open arms—and Junior will be more than happy, I'm sure, to be *expected* to eat with his hands.

Café des Artistes ☆ FRENCH   One of the oldest restaurants in Manhattan, Café des Artistes was established in 1917 as a haven for artists, many who lived in the surrounding area or upstairs at the Hotel des Artistes. One of those artists was Howard Chandler Christy, who painted the gorgeous "wood nymph" murals that still adorn the restaurant. Now, however, not many artists can afford the solid, country French food served at the Café. But this is a place to splurge—to soak in not only the history but the romantic aura emanating from those murals. You won't find any fancy twists on French cooking here and I recommend sticking with old favorites such as the starters—salmon five ways or snails (not escargots?)—or entrees such as Dover sole with brown butter sauce, roasted duck, or the challengingly hearty *pot-au-feu*, complete with marrow bone. For dessert, the chocolate bread pudding is a treat, while the hot-fudge Napoleon was truly, as described by my waiter, a "killer." The waiters here have been around the block a few times, so service is refreshingly old-school. The restaurant does a brisk, pre–Lincoln Center business, so if you want intimacy and romance, the main reason to come here, reserve before or after the crush.

1 W. 67th St. (at Central Park West). ℂ 212/877-3500. www.cafenyc.com. Reservations strongly recommended. Jackets preferred for men. Main courses $18–$29 for lunch; $29–$49 for dinner. AE, DC, DISC, MC, V. Mon–Fri noon–3pm; brunch Sat 11am–3pm; Sun 10am–3pm; Mon–Sat 5–11:45pm; Sun 5:30–11pm. Subway: 1 to 66th St.

Porter House New York ☆☆ STEAKHOUSE   Michael Lomonaco, the former chef of Windows on the World, the famed rooftop restaurant of the World Trade Center, experienced first hand the tragedy of September 11, 2001 when he lost not only his restaurant, but many of his friends and employees. He rebounded with a new-in 2006 restaurant featuring windows not looking out on the world, but almost as good—looking out on Central Park. The space, in the Time Warner Center on Columbus Circle, is sleek with large leather banquettes for groups along with smaller, white tableclothed tables by the floor-to-ceiling windows. But even if there was no view, this steakhouse satisfies the essentials of the best red meat emporiums, with a few inventive twists. I gambled by ordering the chili-rubbed rib-eye—would chili obscure the natural flavor of the meat? My gamble paid off; the chili was subtle and actually brought out the cut's essence. If you want your steak straight ahead, the dry-aged prime strip steak, cooked to perfection and bursting with flavor, won't let you down. Lomonaco tweaks some of the obligatory sides such as adding pieces of thick smoky bacon to the creamed spinach and offering porcini mushrooms on a bed of polenta as an alternative to mashed potatoes. But it's the meat—and that you are eating it overlooking Central Park—that makes Porter House New York so special.

10 Columbus Circle (4th Floor) in the Time Warner Center (at 60th St.) ℂ 212/823-9500. www.porterhouse newyork.com. Main courses: $24–$39. AE, DC, DISC, MC, V. Mon–Sun 11:30am–3pm; Mon–Thurs 5–10:30pm; Fri–Sat 5–11:30pm. Subway: A, B, C, D, 1 trains to 59th St.-Columbus Circle.

EXPENSIVE

Consider the legendary Central Park **Tavern on the Green,** at Central Park West and West 67th Street (ℂ **212/873-3200**). Here, food takes a back seat to dining in one of the city's prettiest settings. Views are wonderful; in good weather, try for a seat in the outdoor garden, with its whimsical topiary shrubs and Japanese lanterns. It's also a great place to visit during the holidays, and there's a menu just for kids.

'Cesca ☆☆ ITALIAN COUNTRY   It's not easy to describe the Italian food served in 'Cesca; it's like nothing many New Yorkers have experienced. Where else have you

Where to Dine Uptown

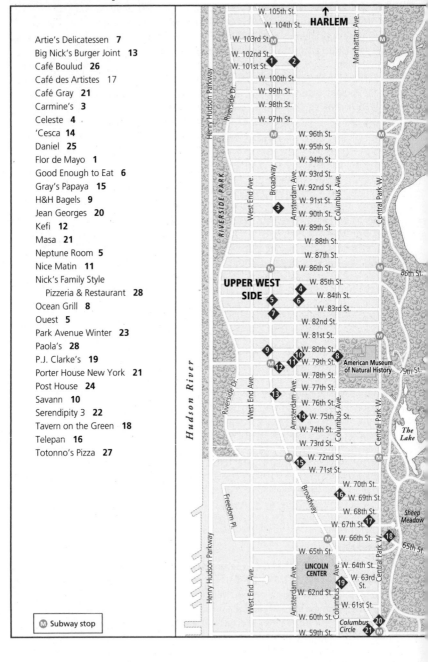

Ⓜ Subway stop

HARLEM

W. 105th St.
W. 104th St.
W. 103rd St.
W. 102nd St.
W. 101st St.
W. 100th St.
W. 99th St.
W. 98th St.
W. 97th St.
W. 96th St.
W. 95th St.
W. 94th St.
W. 93rd St.
W. 92nd St.
W. 91st St.
W. 90th St.
W. 89th St.
W. 88th St.
W. 87th St.
W. 86th St.
W. 85th St.
W. 84th St.
W. 83rd St.
W. 82nd St.
W. 81st St.
W. 80th St.
W. 79th St.
W. 78th St.
W. 77th St.
W. 76th St.
W. 75th St.
W. 74th St.
W. 73rd St.
W. 72nd St.
W. 71st St.
W. 70th St.
W. 69th St.
W. 68th St.
W. 67th St.
W. 66th St.
W. 65th St.
W. 64th St.
W. 63rd St.
W. 62nd St.
W. 61st St.
W. 60th St.
W. 59th St.

UPPER WEST SIDE

American Museum of Natural History

LINCOLN CENTER

Manhattan Ave.
Riverside Dr.
Henry Hudson Parkway
West End Ave.
Broadway
Amsterdam Ave.
Columbus Ave.
Central Park W.
RIVERSIDE PARK
Hudson River
Freedom Pl.
Freedom Pl.
Riverside Dr.
Amsterdam Ave.
Columbus Ave.
Central Park W.

The Lake
Sheep Meadow
Columbus Circle

86th St.
79th St.
65th St.

had roasted sardines paired with a soft egg? With a roaring wood-burning oven as its centerpiece—which is used to roast everything from oysters to peppers—this is as rustic as it gets. It's like you're in an Italian farmhouse where you are served such slow-cooked meats as pork shank, the fat cooked off and the meat falling from the bone, or a potato gnocchi with tender braised duck. The food is so intense here; a little goes a long way. But save room for the equally interesting desserts such as honey goat-milk gelato or fresh figs with fig gelato. Service is friendly and informal and the restaurant is spacious and comfortable, with a large bar area with long tables where you snack on marinated olives, *fritto misto,* or spicy parmigiana fritters, while sipping Italian wines from such regions as Sicily, Puglia, or Trentino. This is one of the most popular restaurants on the Upper West Side, so call well ahead for reservations.

164 W. 75th St. (at Amsterdam Ave.). ℂ 212/787-6300. www.cescany.com. Reservations strongly recommended. Main courses $31–$50. AE, DC, MC, V. Mon–Thurs 5–11pm; Fri–Sat 5–11:30pm; Sun noon–3:00, 5–10pm. Subway: 1, 2, 3 to 72nd St.

The Neptune Room ✿ SEAFOOD   With its aged yacht decor, the Neptune Room is a stylish, slightly formal version of the traditional seafood shack. Raw fresh oysters from both coasts, littleneck clams, shrimp cocktail, ceviches, cured anchovies, grilled octopus, and spicy, quickly steamed calamari come served on small plates over crushed ice and are delicious as part of the restaurant's "Bait Bar." The shack theme quickly fades when you move to the main courses and ponder Mediterranean-based items such as the wonderful cioppino (seafood stew), Parmesan-crusted skate, or the roasted, whole fish; the branzino (Mediterranean sea bass) I had was perfectly cooked and subtly seasoned in olive oil and herbs. In between shack mode and the Mediterranean seafood tour, cleanse your palate with one of the restaurant's excellent salads; the country salad made with frisée, apples, Gorgonzola, and candied almonds was a revelation. Service is knowledgeable and the wine list, all from the Mediterranean, is impressive.

511 Amsterdam Ave. (btwn 84th and 85th sts.). ℂ 212/496-4100. www.neptuneroom.com. Reservations recommended. Bait Bar $7; main courses $19–$29. AE, MC, V. Sun–Thurs 5:30–10pm; Fri–Sat 5:30–11pm; Sat–Sun brunch 11:30am–3pm. Subway: 1 to 86th St.

Ocean Grill ✿✿ SEAFOOD   The Stephen Hanson/BRGuest Restaurant empire (Primehouse, Blue Water Grill, Dos Caminos, and Fiamma to name a few) is vast, and sometimes the brawny restaurants in the group can be a wee bit impersonal. But Ocean Grill, despite its considerable size, defies that generalization. Maybe it's because the restaurant is across the street from the Museum of Natural History and feeds off that building's wondrous vibe? Or maybe because it is in the heart of the family-friendly Upper West Side that Ocean Grill feels more like an intimate neighborhood joint than part of an empire. And what makes Ocean Grill even more special is that the always fresh seafood, usually prepared without too many frills, complements that relaxed good feeling. Like other Hanson-run restaurants, there are numerous menu options, including a touch of Asian in the preparation of the seafood, specifically Japanese, with a generous selection of house made maki rolls—the creamy wasabi tuna is so good you will immediately forget any mercury warnings you've read about. But if raw tuna terrifies you, try one of the fish entrees such as the sublime Chilean sea bass in a violet mustard emulsion served with polenta fries, or any of the fish simply grilled with a choice of sauces, such as black olive tapenade or a soy-ginger vinaigrette, and sides such as bok choy or broccoli rabe. Most of the desserts change seasonally,

Food Splurge: Places to Empty Your Wallet

New York can often be silly with excess, especially when it comes to food. This is, after all, the city where a restaurant offers a seasonal double-truffle burger for $99, and a breakfast joint recently pushed a caviar-stuffed frittata (that's an omelet with salty fish eggs) for $1,000. But in this city, there is never a shortage of people who are willing to fork it over just for the pleasure of eating in a restaurant with a bunch of stars from some prestigious reviewer. The waiting lists for reservations at these places are sometimes months long. We, of course, would never waste our hard-earned money on such a frivolous thing as perfectly prepared and presented food in a memorable environment where the customer is really treated like royalty. Or *would* we?

Well, you only live once. So if you are going to go for it, here are five of New York's most expensive and best restaurants:

Daniel, 60 E. 65th St., between Madison and Park avenues (© **212/288-0033**; www.danielnyc.com). Neo-Renaissance features—rich mahogany doors, elegant Corinthian columns, and a soaring terra-cotta-tiled ceiling—make an ideal setting for acclaimed chef Daniel Boulud's faultless classic-goes-country French cooking. His eight-course tasting menu goes for $175, while you can get away relatively cheap here with a three-course prix-fixe for $96.

Jean-Georges ✰✰✰, in the Trump International Hotel & Tower, 1 Central Park West, at 60th Street/Columbus Circle (© **212/299-3900**; www.jean-georges.com). Another *New York Times* four-star winner, the signature restaurant of Jean-Georges Vongerichten is the ultimate special-occasion restaurant. And it better be a special occasion if you are going to shell out around $100 for his tasting menu, not including wine.

Le Bernardin, 155 W. 51st St., between Sixth and Seventh avenues (© **212/554-1515**; www.le-bernardin.com). Always one of the top New York restaurants in the *Zagat* guide, Le Bernardin also garnered four stars from the *New York Times.* So I guess it must be good. One of these days, when I save up enough money to pay for the $150 tasting menu, I hope to find out.

Masa, 10 Columbus Circle (© **212/823-9800**). This sushi joint in the Time Warner Center became a major conversation piece when the *Times* gave it four stars. The conversation was not so much about the undoubtedly exquisite sushi prepared by genius chef/owner Masayoshi Takayama, but more about the price, starting at $300 and sometimes climbing to $500 per person for the chef's *omakase* (chef's choice) lunch or dinner.

but, if you are lucky, the caramelized banana ice cream tower will be on the menu when you visit.

384 Columbus Ave (btwn 79th and 80th sts.). © **212/579-2300.** www.brguestrestaurants.com. Reservations recommended. Main courses: $20–$33. AE, DC, DISC, MC, V. Mon–Fri 11:30am–5pm; Sat 11:30am–4:30pm; Sun 10:30am–4:30pm; Mon–Tues 5pm–11pm; Wed–Thurs 5pm–11:30pm; Fri 5pm–midnight; Sat 4:30pm–midnight; Sun 4:30pm–11pm. Subway: B, C to 81st St.

Ouest *★★★* CONTEMPORARY AMERICAN   When chef/restaurateur Tom Valenti opened Ouest in 2002, it signaled a renaissance in the Upper West Side dining scene. With red banquettes and an intimate balcony area, Ouest is both cozy and clubby. Service is personable but also professional—so good you'll need to keep reminding yourself that you are on the Upper West Side. But what really draws the crowds is Valenti's mastery in the kitchen, especially with such meats as his signature braised lamb shank or his melt-in-your-mouth braised beef short ribs. The quality suffers not one iota when you switch to seafood. The sautéed skate is perfectly prepared, with a simple sauce of parsley and olive oil, while the baby calamari in a spicy tomato sopressata sauce appetizer was so good I actually smiled as I ate it.

2315 Broadway (at 84th St.). © 212/580-8700. www.ouestny.com. Reservations required well in advance. Main courses $23–$36. AE, DC, DISC, MC, V. Mon–Thurs 5:30–10:30pm; Fri–Sat 5:00–11:30pm; Sun 5–9:30pm. Subway: 1, 2 to 86th St.

Telepan *★★* AMERICAN   It's risky naming a restaurant after yourself, but also displays brash confidence in your abilities. Daniel Boulud has done it; Jean-Georges Vongrichten has done it; David Bouley has done it . . . all with positive results. And in 2006, Bill Telepan did it, opening his own restaurant under his name; and, like the aforementioned trio, his risk has paid off. The venue for Telepan is an Upper West Side town house with a dining room painted in soothing lime green. The cool design compliments the menu, which changes seasonally but always features farm-fresh products. I had the good fortune to dine in the spring and was greeted with fresh ramps, fiddleheads, and young peas in many of the dishes I sampled. There was no fresh produce, however, in the foie gras donuts listed as a "share." The "donuts" are dusted with cocoa and cinnamon and might work as well with a cup of java as with a cocktail. Of the appetizers, the standout was the wild green frittata which did indeed come with in-season ramps. Telepan offers "Mid Courses" and of them, the pea pancakes with pea agnolotti looked and, more importantly, tasted greenmarket fresh. Save room for an entree, specifically the haddock with a sweet lobster sauce. Whatever you choose to eat, you'll have no problem finding a complementary wine from the restaurant's long and impressive list. Telepan has become a pre–Lincoln Center favorite; so if you want to avoid the crush, make a reservation for after curtain.

72 W. 69th St. (at Columbus Ave.). © 212/580-4300. www.telepan-ny.com. Reservations recommended. Main courses: $29–$36; four-course tasting menu $59; five-course tasting menu $69. AE, DC, MC, V. Lunch Wed–Fri 11:30am–2:30pm; dinner Mon–Thurs 5–11pm, Fri–Sat 5–11:30pm, Sun 5–10:30pm; brunch Sat–Sun 11am–2:30pm. Subway: B, C to 72nd St.

MODERATE

Also consider **Rack & Soul,** 2818 Broadway, at 109th St. (© **212/222-4800**), for the unbeatable combination of barbecued ribs and pan-fried southern style fried chicken.

Carmine's *★* *Kids* FAMILY-STYLE SOUTHERN ITALIAN   Everything is B-I-G at this rollicking family-style mainstay with two locations, on the Upper West Side (the original) and in Times Square. In many cases big means bad, but not here. Carmine's, with a dining room vast enough to deserve its own zip code and massive portions, turns out better pasta and entrees than most 20-table Italian restaurants. I've never had pasta here that wasn't al dente, and the marinara sauce is as good as any I've had in Manhattan. The salads are always fresh and the fried calamari perfectly tender. Rigatoni marinara, linguini with white-clam sauce, and ziti with broccoli are pasta standouts, while the best meat entrees include veal parmigiana, broiled porterhouse steak, shrimp scampi, and the remarkable chicken *scarpariello* (chicken pan-broiled with a lemon-rosemary sauce). The tiramisu is pie-size, thick, creamy, and bathed in Kahlúa and Marsala. Order half of what you think you'll need. Don't expect intimate conversation; in fact, it's downright loud. Unless you come early, expect to wait.

2450 Broadway (btwn 90th and 91st sts.). © **212/362-2200**. www.carminesnyc.com. Reservations recommended before 6pm; accepted only for 6 or more after 6pm. Family-style main courses $19–$65 (most $23 or less). AE, DC, DISC, MC, V. Sun–Thurs 11:30am–11pm; Fri–Sat 11:30am–midnight. Subway: 1, 2, 3 to 96th St. Also at 200 W. 44th St. (btwn Broadway and Eighth Ave.). © **212/221-3800**. Subway: A, C, E, N, R, S, 1, 2, 3, 7 to 42nd St./Times Sq.

Kefi *Finds* GREEK   Kefi is like your Greek mother's (if you had a Greek mother) kitchen, and, in fact, the restaurant was inspired by chef Michael Psilakis's mother and her traditional recipes. Greek standards such as moussaka, spinach pie, Greek salad, and grilled fish are featured here. But oh what Psilakis does with the standards. The *mezes* (Greek appetizers) are good enough to make up a meal; it's hard to resist the selection of spreads accompanied by pita, the warm feta, tomatoes, capers and anchovies, and especially the sublime grilled octopus salad, as good as I've had anywhere. But something's gotta give if you want to save room for such entrees as the flat noodles with braised rabbit; the grilled whole branzino with potatoes, olives, tomatoes and feta; or the slow cooked, comforting lamb shank on a bed of orzo. If it is humanly possible after indulging in all of the above, don't miss out on the desserts, most notably the walnut cake with maple walnut ice cream. Service is casual and the space is a bit cramped, but not enough to deter you from the many pleasures of Kefi.

505 Columbus Ave. (at 84th St.). © **212/873-0200**. Reservations not taken. Main courses $10–$20. Cash only. Sun–Thurs 5–10pm; Fri–Sat 5–11pm. Subway: 1 to 79th St.

Nice Matin FRENCH PROVENÇAL   Named after Nice's major newspaper, appropriately you'll find such Provençal classics as *pistou, pissaladiere,* and *velouté* of mussels on the menu. You'll also find innovations such as the creamy, delicious fava-bean tortelloni, moist grilled sea bass with artichokes stewed in olive oil, and a rich daube of beef short ribs with chickpea fries. There are specials daily; and on Monday, normally not a great day to dine out, the *aioli monstre* is featured—salt cod, shrimp, meats, and vegetables accompanied by a tangy, fresh aioli. On any day you can order the five-napkin burger, also accompanied by that pleasingly persistent aioli. If cholesterol is no concern, opt for the decadently dense sweet-and-sour cream for dessert. Located in the Lucerne hotel, the restaurant, open for breakfast, lunch, and dinner, is loud and busy, so unless you can snare a comfortable booth, don't expect intimacy.

201 W. 79th St. (at Amsterdam Ave.). © **212/873-NICE**. www.nicematinnyc.com. Reservations recommended. Main courses $9.25–$20 at lunch, $16–$25 at dinner. AE, DC, MC, V. Breakfast Mon–Fri 7–11:30am, Sat–Sun 7–10:30am; lunch Mon–Sat 11:30am–3:30pm; dinner Mon–Sat 5:30pm–midnight, Sun 5–11pm; brunch Mon–Sat 7am–3:30pm, Sun 7am–2:30pm. Subway: 1 to 79th St.

Savann MEDITERRANEAN   The restaurant scene on Amsterdam Avenue in the low 80s is particularly volatile, but for over 9 years, Savann has survived on that difficult stretch of real estate thanks to consistently top-notch food, personable service, and a casual, low-key atmosphere. This is a neighborhood place with regulars who swear by the food. Some favorites include the home-cured gravlax, here served over a chickpea-scallion pancake in a flying-fish caviar and dill sauce; the grilled calamari; the Seafood Savann, a medley of seafood in a light tomato sauce served over linguine; the

Where the Editor Eats . . .

After a long day of shepherding Frommer's Travel Guides from manuscript to publication, this editor can use a good meal, a stiff drink, and a kind word. Here are some places where I can find them:

In the East Village, I've been going to **Christine's** (208 First Ave., between 12th and 13th sts.; ✆ 212/979-2810; Subway: L to First Ave.) for a couple of decades now, since I was a little typesetter correcting the spelling in gun and hairstyle magazines. The prices haven't gone up much, but it's a lot spiffier than it used to be. The waitresses are still the same bored, pretty eastern European women, the mushroom barley soup is still awesome, and you can still get a full dinner with entrees from kielbasa (like my Polish grandma used to make) to chicken livers with mushrooms to stuffed cabbage, all with two veggies for under $10, and pierogies of many varieties (a half-order of four will run you less than $4). (They don't serve alcohol, but there are plenty of bars in the neighborhood). It's open daily from 7am to 11pm.

Over in the West Village, I like to swing by **Cowgirl** (519 Hudson St., at W. 10th St.; ✆ 212/633-1133; www.cowgirlnyc.com; Subway: 1 to Christopher St.) for a blood-orange margarita or the "Bible Belt" (sort of a bourbon margarita), especially at happy hour, and enjoy some not-too-expensive Tex-Mex-style snacks or dinners (from chicken-fried chicken and chicken-fried steak, to Frito pie, and veggie options). It's a *very* mixed scene, with local families piling into the dining room, a gayish crowd at the bar, and people who want to hang out in the almost-hidden rec-room-style lounge toward the back, along with an additional dining room. The staff is friendly and sassy and part of the show.

Zuni (598 Ninth Ave., just below 43rd St.; ✆ 212/765-7626; www.zuni ny.com) is Off-Off-Broadway central; each evening waves of actors, directors, techies, and audiences flood the place from various theaters in the neighborhood. They make the bar a fun scene, with the booths in the back quiet enough to hear yourself talk, but with enough room to tablehop if you see friends. The menu is American/eclectic with a tilt toward Mexican (ask about the quesadilla of the day!). Also recommendable are the sandwiches (grilled salmon with wasabi aioli, an excellent burger) and solid entrees with daily specials and soups. The bar makes good, strong drinks. It's a bargain for the area, which means it'll cost more than a hole-in-the-wall, but a *lot* less than, say, Esca (which is directly across the street).

—Kathleen Warnock

mixed seafood phyllo purse; and the perfectly cooked filet mignon. For dessert don't miss the *tarte tatine*, a homemade apple tart served with cinnamon ice cream and warm honey. In warm weather, the sidewalk cafe is a great place for people-watching.

414 Amsterdam Ave. (btwn 79th and 80th sts.). ✆ 212/580-0202. www.savann.com. Reservations recommended. Main courses $12–$27 (most under $20). AE, MC, V. Mon–Fri noon–3:30pm; Sat–Sun 11am–3:30pm; daily 4–11pm. Subway: 1 to 79th St.

INEXPENSIVE

For breakfast or lunch, also consider **Artie's Delicatessen,** 2290 Broadway, between 82nd and 83rd streets (© **212/579-5959;** www.arties.com), and **Barney Greengrass, the Sturgeon King,** 541 Amsterdam Ave., between 86th and 87th streets (© **212/724-4707),** two of the best Jewish delis in town. See "The New York Deli News" sidebar on p. 190 for further details.

You'll find some of the best bagels in New York on the Upper West Side, including **H&H Bagels,** 2239 Broadway, at 80th Street (© **212/595-8003),** and **Absolute Bagels,** 2788 Broadway, between 106th and 107th streets (© **212/932-2052).** For more information, see the box "The Hole Truth: N.Y.'s Best Bagels," on p. 177.

For nonvegetarians and the non-health-minded, consider the cheapest, yet in some ways most comforting, indulgence: **Gray's Papaya,** 2090 Broadway, at 72nd Street (© **212/799-0243).** This 24-hour hot-dog stand is a New York institution. See the box "Food in a N.Y. Minute" for more.

Big Nick's Burger and Pizza Joint 🌟 *Kids* AMERICAN/PIZZA   A neighborhood landmark since 1962, Big Nick's has a menu that seems to have grown each year of its existence—it's now a whopping 27 pages long. Trying to decide if you want the Madrid burger, with olives, feta, and pimentos, with or without buffalo meat; a slice of Hawaiian pizza; or just an order of the spinach pie can be exhausting. If reading the menu is too much for you, peruse the numerous photos of celebrities who have supposedly chowed down at Big Nick's over the years, or just keep your eyes on the non-stop *Three Stooges* marathon playing on the restaurant's televisions. Whatever you do, you'll never forget your Big Nick's experience. With all those diversions, it's a great place to take the kids; they'll never be bored.

2175 Broadway (at 77th St.). © **212/362-9238.** www.bignicksnyc.com. Reservations not accepted. Main courses $3.50–$19 (most less than $10). Cash only. Daily 24 hrs. Subway: 1 to 79th St.

Celeste 🌟🌟 *Finds* ITALIAN   Tiny but charming Celeste features its own wood-burning pizza oven, which churns out thin-crusted, simple but delicious pizzas. But pizza is not the only attraction here; the *"fritti"* (fried) course is unique; the *fritto misto de pesce* (fried mixed seafood) is delectable, but the fried zucchini blossoms, usually available in the summer and fall, are amazing. The fresh pastas are better than the dried pasta; I never thought the fresh egg noodles with cabbage, shrimp, and sheep's cheese would work, but it was delicious. Not on the menu but usually available are plates of rare, artisanal Italian cheeses served with homemade jams. Though the main courses are also good, stick with the pizzas, antipasto, *frittis,* and pastas. For dessert, try the gelato; the pistachio was the best I've ever had in New York. The restaurant has been "discovered," so go early or late or expect a wait.

502 Amsterdam Ave. (btwn 84th and 85th sts.). © **212/874-4559.** Reservations not accepted. Pizza $10–$12; antipasto $7–$10; pasta $10; main courses $14–$16. No credit cards. Mon–Sat 5–11pm; Sun noon–10:30pm. Subway: 1 to 86th St.

Flor de Mayo *Finds* CUBAN/CHINESE   Cuban/Chinese cuisine is a New York phenomenon that started in the late 1950s when Cubans of Chinese heritage immigrated to New York after the revolution. Most of the immigrants took up residence on the Upper West Side, and Cuban/Chinese restaurants flourished. Many have disappeared, but the best one, Flor de Mayo, still remains and is so popular that a new branch opened farther south on Amsterdam Avenue. The kitchen excels at both sides

Breakfast, Not Brunch!

Brunch has always been a pet peeve of mine. I mean, what is it really but a slightly fancier version of breakfast at inflated prices? And it's not even served until midmorning—and only on weekends. I'll take breakfast any day over brunch—*especially* on weekends. Here are some of my favorite breakfast spots:

Big Wong King ⍟, 67 Mott St., between Canal and Bayard streets (℃ 212/964-0540). No eggs. No coffee. No pancakes. Can this be breakfast? You bet it is! Not much is more satisfying in the morning than a hot bowl of congee (rice porridge with either pork, beef, or shrimp) accompanied with a fried cruller and tea served in a glass. It might sound a little unusual, but you won't be alone; Big Wong is a favorite for breakfast among the residents of Chinatown. Opens daily at 8:30am. For more on Big Wong King, see p. 154.

Bubby's Pie Company ⍟, 120 Hudson St., at North Moore Street (℃ 212/ 219-0666; www.bubbys.com). I don't usually order grits north of the Mason-Dixon line, but I make an exception at Bubby's. They are the perfect complement to Bubby's Breakfast: two eggs, toast, bacon, and a cup of joe. Open at 8am Monday through Friday and 9am Saturday and Sunday. For more on Bubby's, see p. 152.

Clinton St. Baking Company ⍟, 4 Clinton St., at Houston Street (℃ 646/ 602-6263). The lines are long on weekend mornings, but you can get breakfast all day here. Meaning you can eat their unbelievable pancakes at 4 in the afternoon—if that's breakfast time for you.

Good Enough to Eat ⍟, 483 Amsterdam Ave., between 83rd and 84th streets (℃ 212/496-0163). The wait for breakfast at this Upper West Side institution on the weekends is ridiculous, so try to go during the week when you can gorge on pumpkin French toast; a "Wall Street" omelet, with honey-mustard-glazed ham with Vermont cheddar; or "Peter Paul" pancakes, filled with Belgian chocolate chips, coconut, and topped with coconut. I'm getting hungry writing this. Opens at 8am Monday through Friday and 9am Saturday and Sunday. See p. 207.

Norma's ⍟⍟, at Le Parker Meridien Hotel, 118 W. 57th St., between Sixth and Seventh avenues (℃ 212/708-7460). An ode to the ultimate comfort food. It's pricey, but worth it for classics done with style and creativity. See p. 185.

Veselka ⍟, 144 Second Ave., at 9th Street (℃ 212/228-9682). The Greek diner might be extinct in Manhattan, but this Ukrainian diner lives on. And we are all grateful because New York just would not be the same without Veselka's buckwheat pancakes and cheese blintzes. Open 24 hours. See p. 164.

of the massive menu, but the best dish is the *la brasa* half-chicken lunch special—beautifully spiced and slow-roasted until it's fork tender and falling off the bone, served with a giant pile of fried rice, bounteous with roast pork, shrimp, and veggies. Offered Monday through Saturday until 4:30pm, the entire meal is just $6.95, and it's enough to fortify you for the day. Service and atmosphere are reminiscent of

Chinatown: efficient and lightning-quick. My favorite combo: the hearty, noodles-, greens-, shrimp-, and pork-laden Chinese soup, with yellow rice and black beans.

2651 Broadway (btwn 100th and 101st sts.). © 212/663-5520 or 212/595-2525. Reservations not accepted. Main courses $4.50–$19 (most under $10); lunch specials $5–$7 (Mon–Sat to 4:30pm). AE, MC, V ($15 minimum). Daily noon–midnight. Subway: 1 to 103rd St. Also at 484 Amsterdam Ave. (btwn 83rd and 84th sts.). © 212/787-3388. Subway: 1 to 86th St.

Good Enough to Eat *Kids Finds* AMERICAN HOME COOKING For over 25 years the crowds have been lining up on weekends outside Good Enough to Eat to experience chef/owner Carrie Levin's incredible breakfasts (see "Breakfast, Not Brunch," p. 206). As a result, lunch and dinner have been somewhat overlooked. Too bad, because these meals can be just as great as the breakfasts. The restaurant's cow motif and farmhouse knickknacks imply hearty, home-cooked food, and that's what's done best here. Stick with the classics: meatloaf with gravy and mashed potatoes; turkey dinner with cranberry relish, gravy, and cornbread stuffing; macaroni and cheese; griddled corn bread; and the BBQ sandwich, roast chicken with barbecue sauce and homemade potato chips. And save room for the homemade desserts; though the selection is often overwhelming, I can never resist the coconut cake. This is food you loved as a kid, which is one reason why the kids will love it today. There are only 20 tables here, so expect a wait on weekends during the day or for dinner after 6pm.

483 Amsterdam Ave. (btwn 83rd and 84th sts.). © 212/496-0163. www.goodenoughtoeat.com. Breakfast $5.25–$12; lunch $8.50–$15; dinner $8.50–$23 (most under $18). AE, MC, V. Breakfast Mon–Fri 8:00am–4pm, Sat–Sun 9am–4pm; lunch Mon noon–4pm, Tues–Fri 11:30am–4pm; dinner Mon–Thurs 5:30–10:30pm, Fri–Sat 5:30–11pm, Sun 5:30–10pm. Subway: 1 to 86th St.

Noche Mexicana *Finds* MEXICAN This Mexican restaurant serves some of the best tamales in New York. Wrapped in cornhusks, as a good tamale should be, they come in two varieties: in a red mole sauce with shredded chicken or in a green tomatillo sauce with shredded pork. There are three tamales in each order, which costs only $6, making it a cheap and almost perfect lunch. The burritos are authentic and meals unto themselves. The *tinga* burrito, shredded chicken in a tomato-and-onion chipotle sauce, is my favorite. Each is stuffed with rice, beans, and guacamole. Don't get fancy here; stick with the tamales, burritos, and soft tacos, the best being the taco *al pastor,* a taco stuffed with pork marinated with pineapple and onions.

852 Amsterdam Ave. (btwn 101st and 102nd sts.). © 212/662-6900 or 212/662-7400. Burritos $6.50–$8.50; tacos $2; tamales $6; Mexican dishes $9.50–$11. AE, DISC, MC, V. Sun–Thurs 10am–11pm; Fri–Sat 10am–midnight. Subway: 1 to 103rd St.

13 Upper East Side

To locate the restaurants in this section, see the map on p. 198.

VERY EXPENSIVE

Also consider elegant **Daniel,** 60 E. 65th St., between Madison and Park avenues (© 212/288-0033; www.danielnyc.com). See the sidebar "Food Splurge," on p. 201.

The Post House STEAKHOUSE Yes, I know I've categorized the Post House as a steakhouse, and I know it is owned by the Smith & Wollensky group, the owners of that famous steakhouse along with Maloney & Porcelli and Quality Meats (see the box "The Prime Cut: Steaks! Steaks! Steaks!" on p. 172), and the windowless restaurant off the Lowell Hotel has a clubhouse (my seat was adorned with Ron

Pearlman's bronzed commemorative inscription) alpha male feel, but the Post House is not your traditional meat and potatoes steakhouse. There are as many non–red meat items on the menu as there are steak and chops. Most of the appetizers come from the sea and the cornmeal fried oysters layered on a potato chip with cole slaw is something I've never had in a steakhouse before. Dover Sole, lobster, and grilled chicken, are just a few of the non–red meat entree options you'll find at the Post House, but I've categorized the restaurant as a steakhouse because you need to forget those other options and order the Cajun rib eye steak, broiled in a subtle cayenne rub that perfectly melds with the richness of the meat. The starchy side dishes are traditional and served family-style (meaning large) so make sure you are eating with a family before ordering a platter of hash browns or onion rings. For dessert it will be worth your while to wait the extra ten minutes it takes to prepare the restaurant's classic chocolate soufflé.

28 E. 63rd St. (btwn Park and Madison aves.). ☎ **212/935-2888.** www.theposthouse.com. Reservations recommended. Main courses: $26–$70. AE, DC, DISC, MC, V. Mon–Fri noon–5pm; Mon–Thurs 5–11pm; Fri–Sun 5pm–midnight. Subway: 4, 5, 6, N, R, W at Lexington Ave-59th St.

EXPENSIVE

Café Boulud *(Value* FRENCH   Dying to try the stellar cuisine of Daniel Boulud, New York's best French chef, but can't quite afford **Daniel?** Then head to Café Boulud, Boulud's more casual playground for new ideas and culinary cross-pollinations. Daniel's high style has been pleasingly laid back and toned down here. With the food, Boulud has gone eclectic, offering four menus: *La Tradition,* featuring Boulud's signature French-country classics; *Le Potager,* a vegetarian menu; *La Saison,* seasonal dishes; and *Le Voyage,* a monthly globe-hopping menu highlighting Tuscany, Thailand, or somewhere in between. The experimental nature of the wide-ranging menu makes choosing a thrill, and even the most inventive dishes tend to dazzle the palate. But in true Boulud tradition, La Tradition and La Saison are where the kitchen really excels. The poached Dover sole with baby leeks and sauce *vin blanc* is truly memorable. All in all, a first-rate dining experience at more palatable prices than cuisine this memorable usually costs. Don't be in a rush, though, especially at lunch.

20 E. 76th St. (btwn Madison and Fifth aves.). ☎ **212/772-2600.** www.danielnyc.com. Reservations recommended. Main courses $25–$40 at lunch, $26–$43 at dinner; 2- or 3-course prix-fixe lunch $30–$38. AE, DC, DISC, MC, V. Daily 5:45–11pm; Tues–Sat noon–2:30pm (no lunch Sat July–Aug). Subway: 6 to 77th St.

Paola's *(* ITALIAN   There is no shortage of Italian restaurants on the Upper East Side, but strength is not always in numbers and many are mediocre at best. There is nothing, however, mediocre about Paola's, and having survived and thrived in the neighborhood for over 12 years is testament to the restaurant's quality and charms. The charm begins with Paola herself, almost always present and always the gracious host. The two dining rooms are comforting and inviting; the larger centered around a wood-burning oven used to cook many of the restaurant's meat dishes, the other the smaller, but cozy, wine room. Most appealing of all is the menu. Hope that Paola has found baby artichokes the day you visit because you will want to begin with the *carciofi alla Giudea,* artichokes prepared in the style of the Roman Jews—cooked twice and addictively crispy. The pastas are usually homemade; the pappardelle with a duck-meat ragu is a standout, while the hand-rolled *trofie* served with pesto is a Paola's specialty. The *stinco d'agnello,* slow-roasted lamb shank with sage and parmesan polenta, is a hearty main course that is roasted in the wood burning oven, as are the naturally raised, corn-fed poussins, served with potato gratin and sautéed greens. Fig ice cream topped with port-soaked figs is the decadent way to finish your meal.

245 E. 84th St. (btwn Second and Third aves.). (✆ **212/794-1890**. www.paolasrestaurant.com. Reservations recommended. Pasta $14–$17; main courses $22–$30. AE, MC, V. Sun–Fri 1–4pm; Sun–Wed 5–10pm; Thurs–Sat 5–11pm. Subway: 4, 5, 6 to 86th St.

Park Avenue Winter 🌀🌀 AMERICAN/MEDITERRANEAN   Not only might the name of this restaurant be different when you visit, but the look (created by award-winning design firm AvroKO) and the menu will be totally changed as well. The gimmick here is that the restaurant transforms itself each season. And though a restaurant with a gimmick is sometimes frowned upon, in this case, it's more than a gimmick: Park Avenue Winter (the season I happened to visit it) is first rate. For the winter look, the large, high-ceilinged dining room was a snowy, glacial white and the menu reflected the season. Starters included the hearty porcini ravioli with Swiss chard in a flavorful gorgonzola cream sauce, while you might not find a more comforting cold weather dish than the entree of filet mignon on a bed of shredded short ribs accompanied by root vegetables. But surprisingly, the winter fare here has a welcome light touch as evidenced in the delicate cornbread-crusted red snapper on a citrus salad. Even the side of potato latkes, notoriously leaden, here were actually light and airy. Light and airy are definitely not the words to describe the chocolate cube I had for dessert. Stuffed with chocolate bits and chocolate mousse, the cube was incredibly dense—and I would have it no other way. The only thing missing from the winter feel created in the restaurant was the quiet hush of newly-arrived snow; instead, like most restaurants these days, the decibel level is more like a violent summer thunderstorm.

100 E. 63rd St. (at Park Ave.). (✆ **212/644-1900**. www.parkavenuenyc.com. Reservations recommended. Main courses: $26–$48. AE, DC, DISC, MC, V. Mon–Fri 11:30am–3pm; Sat–Sun 11am–3pm; Mon–Thurs 5:30–11pm; Fri–Sat 5:30–11:30pm; Sun 5:30–10pm. Subway: F at Lexington Ave-63rd St.

INEXPENSIVE

For better-than-average pizza, head to **Totonno's Pizzeria Napolitano,** 1544 Second Ave., between 80th and 81st streets (✆ **212/327-2800**), the Manhattan branch of the famous Totonno's in Coney Island (see the box "Pizza, New York–Style," p. 186).

Nick's Family-Style Restaurant and Pizzeria 🌀 (Kids) ITALIAN   Since 1994, Nick Angelis has wowed them in Forest Hills, Queens, with his pizza. In 2003, he took his act to Manhattan, where the pizza is garnering equally high praise. The pizza here is thin-crusted, with the proper proportions of creamy, homemade mozzarella and fresh tomato sauce. But this is much more than a pizzeria: Try the light, lemony baked clams or "Josephine's" perfectly breaded eggplant parmigiana. If you dare combine pizza with a calzone, this is the place; Nick's calzone, stuffed with ricotta and mozzarella cheese, is spectacular. The orecchiette with broccoli rabe and sausage is the pasta winner, while the filet of sole oreganato Livornese with mussels is the standout main course. Save room for an extra-large cannoli for dessert; the shell is perfectly flaky and the filling ultracreamy. Full orders are enough to feed two or three and are a great bargain for a group, but half-orders are also available. The room is comfortable and far from fancy. Go early or be prepared to wait.

1814 Second Ave. (at 94th St.). (✆ **212/987-5700**. Pizza $12–$14; macaroni half-orders $6–$12, full orders $12–$24; entree half-orders $8.50–$12, full orders $17–$24. AE, DC, DISC, MC, V. Daily 11:30am–10pm. Subway: 6 to 96th St.

Serendipity 3 *(Kids)* AMERICAN   You'd never guess that this whimsical place was once a top stop on Andy Warhol's itinerary. Wonders never cease—and neither does the confection at this delightful restaurant and sweets shop. Tucked into a cozy brownstone a few steps from Bloomingdale's, happy people gather here at marble-topped ice-cream–parlor tables for burgers and foot-long hot dogs, country meatloaf with mashed potatoes and gravy, and salads and sandwiches with such cute names as "The Catcher in the Rye" (their own twist on the BLT, with chicken and Russian dressing—on rye, of course). The food isn't great, but the main courses aren't the point—they're just an excuse to get to the desserts. The restaurant's signature is frozen hot chocolate, a slushy version of everybody's cold-weather favorite, but other crowd-pleasers include dark double devil mousse, celestial carrot cake, lemon icebox pie, and anything with hot fudge. So cast that willpower aside and come on in—Serendipity is an irony-free charmer to be appreciated by adults and kids alike.

225 E. 60th St. (btwn Second and Third aves.). ⓒ 212/838-3531. www.serendipity3.com. Reservations accepted for lunch and dinner (not dessert only). Main courses $7.50–$20; sweets and sundaes $6–$20 (most under $10). AE, DC, DISC, MC, V. Sun–Thurs 11:30am–midnight; Fri 11:30am–1am; Sat 11:30am–2am. Subway: N, R to Lexington Ave.; 4, 5, 6 to 59th St.

14 Harlem

To locate these restaurants, see the map on p. 211.

INEXPENSIVE

Also consider **Patsy's Pizzeria** *(Kids)* (see "Pizza, New York–Style," p. 186); and see the box "The Soul of Harlem," on p. 212, for great soul-food restaurants.

Covo Trattoria & Pizzeria *(Finds)* ITALIAN   Covo means cave in Italian and coincidentally, the location of Covo, under the West Side Highway and down steep steps from Riverside Park, can be considered very cavelike. But this *covo* has a wood-burning pizza and bread oven manned by a trained Neapolitan pizza maker, along with a very affordable menu of rustic Italian dishes. If you want to put that Neapolitan to the test, try the *paesana* pizza, a pie made with tomato sauces, pecorino cheese, and black olives or an antipasti of bruschetta slathered with tomato and chick peas. Of the pastas, the homemade pappardelle with a honey braised short rib ragu is addictive, while the *rigatoni alla norma* (pasta with tomato sauce, eggplant, basil and fresh ricotta cheese) is the restaurant's signature dish. Try to save room for a "secondi" especially the earthy *coniglio*, braised, tender rabbit served simply with olive oil, rosemary, and black olives. The list of Italian wines is decent and easy on the wallet, but because you are in a *covo*, the sound level when the restaurant is busy can be deafening. Be prepared.

701 W. 135th St. (at 12th Ave.). ⓒ 212/234-9573. www.covony.com. Pizza $8–$13; main courses $10–$19. AE, DC, DISC, MC, V. Daily noon–midnight. Subway: 1 to 137th St.

Dinosaur Bar-B-Que *(Kids)* BARBECUE   It's one thing for a genuine Southern barbecue joint to infiltrate Manhattan, but it's quite another when the barbecue interloper is from up north. Now *that's* chutzpah! The popular Syracuse-based barbecue chain that built its reputation with bikers entered the New York City market with a roadhouselike restaurant on the outskirts of West Harlem. What can Syracuse know about barbecue, you ask? Well, they know pulled pork, which is slow-cooked till it's tender. And they know Texas brisket for the same reasons. The ribs I sampled didn't fare as well, but two out of three ain't bad—especially for a Yankee. Sides are standard: coleslaw, macaroni salad, collard greens, and standout barbecue beans. The restaurant is loud, but if you're lucky, you might be able to catch some of the good blues playing over the din. There's a lively bar and service is as

Where to Dine in Harlem

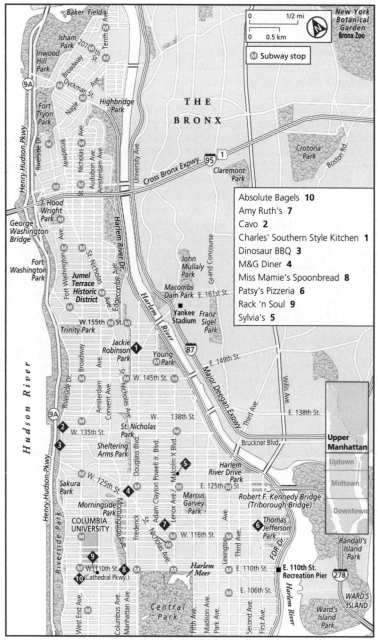

Absolute Bagels **10**
Amy Ruth's **7**
Cavo **2**
Charles' Southern Style Kitchen **1**
Dinosaur BBQ **3**
M&G Diner **4**
Miss Mamie's Spoonbread **8**
Patsy's Pizzeria **6**
Rack 'n Soul **9**
Sylvia's **5**

Ⓜ Subway stop

The Soul of Harlem

There is much soul in Manhattan, but Harlem seems to possess the mother lode when it comes to food. Here is one man's primer to Harlem's soul food:

Amy Ruth's, 113 W. 116th St., between Lenox and Seventh avenues (© 212/ 280-8779; www.amyruthsharlem.com). Claiming to be authentic soul, Amy Ruth's has become a mecca for Harlem celebs, with the kitschy gimmick of naming platters after some of them, such as the Rev. Al Sharpton (chicken and waffles) and the Rev. Calvin O. Butts III (chicken wings and waffles). Most of the celebrities gained their fame in Harlem, as did the chicken and waffles, or fried whiting and waffles, or steak and waffles. You can't go wrong with anything here as long as waffles are included.

Charles' Southern Style Kitchen ⟨ℛ, 2837 Eighth Ave., between 151st and 152nd streets (© 212/926-4313). Nothing fancy about this place, just a brightly lit, 25-seater on a not-very-attractive block in upper Harlem. But you don't come here for fancy, you come for soul food at its simplest and freshest. And come hungry. The $13 all-you-can-eat buffet features crunchy, moist, pan-fried chicken; ribs in a tangy sauce, with meat falling off the bone; smoky stewed oxtails in a thick brown onion gravy; macaroni and cheese; collard greens with bits of smoked turkey; black-eyed peas; and corn bread, warm and not overly sweet. Hours can be erratic, so call ahead before you make the trek.

M&G Diner, 383 W. 125th St., at St. Nicholas Avenue (© 212/864-7326). All the soul-food joints I've listed here serve top-notch fried chicken, but the best I've had is the perfectly pan-fried, supermoist bird at the M&G. This small, no-frills diner, open 8am to 11:30pm, is a treat any time of day. Start your day with a breakfast of eggs with salmon croquettes or eggs with grits or finish it with the chicken, chitterlings, or meatloaf. All the sides are freshly made, and the desserts, especially the sweet-potato pie, are phenomenal. There's also a great jukebox loaded with soul to complement the food.

Miss Mamie's Spoonbread Too, 366 W. 110th St., between Columbus and Manhattan avenues (© 212/865-6744; www.spoonbreadinc.com). Entering this strawberry-curtained charmer is like stepping into South Carolina. But you are in Harlem, or at least the southern fringe of Harlem, and you won't be paying South Carolina soul prices, or Harlem soul prices, either. Still, despite the prices, Miss Mamie's is the real deal, especially their barbecued ribs, falling off the bone in a sweet peppery sauce, and the smothered chicken, fried and then covered with thick pan gravy.

Sylvia's, 328 Lenox Ave., between 126th and 127th streets (© 212/996-0660; www.sylviassoulfood.com). Sylvia is the self-proclaimed queen of not only Harlem soul food but all soul food. In reality, Sylvia is queen of self-promotion. Sylvia's now has become a franchise, with canned food products, beauty and hair products, and fragrances and colognes. With all that attention to merchandising, the food at her original Harlem restaurant has suffered and now has regressed into a tourist trap. If you plan to go, however, make it on Sunday for the gospel brunch, which is an absolute joy.

down-home as an upstate restaurant can be. Though its location is seemingly remote—close to the West Side Highway—it's only a 3-block walk from the no. 1 train.

646 W. 131st St. (at Twelfth Ave.). © 212/694-1777. www.dinosaurbarbque.com. Main courses $13–$22. AE, MC, V. Tues–Thurs 11:30am–11pm; Fri–Sat 11:30am–midnight; Sun noon–10pm. Subway: 1 to 125th St.

15 The Outer Boroughs

THE BRONX

If you are looking for old-fashioned, Italian-American food—the kind you used to get before waiters began asking if you want your water tap or sparkling—look no farther than the Bronx. The best concentration of Italian-American "red sauce" restaurants can be found in the Little Italy of the Bronx, on and around **Arthur Avenue.** One of my favorites is **Mario's Restaurant,** 2342 Arthur Ave., between Crescent Avenue and East 187th Street (© 718/584-1188), where the Neapolitan pizza is magnificent and the ziti with broccoli unforgettable. Reservations are accepted, as are American Express, Discover, Diners Club, MasterCard, and Visa. Wonderful **Dominick's,** on the same block at 2335 Arthur Ave. (© 718/733-2807), is the inspiration behind family-style re-creations such as Carmine's. There's no menu here, but trust your waiter to ramble off what is on the day's menu, which almost always includes tender calamari marinara and luscious veal Francese. There's always a crowd, so go early or expect to wait for a communal table. Reservations are not accepted and please, cash only.

To get to Arthur Avenue, take the no. 4 or D train to Fordham Road and then the no. 12 bus east; the no. 2 or 5 train to Pelham Parkway, and the no. 12 bus west; or the Metro-North Harlem line to Fordham Road, and the shuttle bus to Belmont and the Bronx Zoo.

A few miles east of Arthur Avenue you'll find another classic Italian "red sauce" restaurant. This one, **Frankie and Johnnie's Pine Restaurant,** 1913 Bronxdale Ave., between Matthews and Muliner avenues (© 718/792-5956), has been around so long, I remember watching the Times Square ball drop on a black-and-white television in the dining room while devouring a bowl of *zuppa di pesce* one lonely New Year's Eve many years ago. I remember that New Year's, though lonely, very fondly mainly because of that *zuppa di pesce*. Now the Pine, as it's known, has become popular as a hangout for New York Yankees who crave pasta after their games at Yankee Stadium. As a result, you'll find plenty of baseball memorabilia on the walls. Reservations are not accepted, and it's cash only. Take the no. 2 or 5 train to Bronx Park East.

BROOKLYN

VERY EXPENSIVE

At the foot of the Brooklyn Bridge, with spectacular views of the New York skyline, **The River Café,** 1 Water St. (© 718/522-5200), could possibly be the most romantic special-occasion restaurant in New York. Service is good, prices are steep, and the contemporary Continental cuisine is more than adequate, but nothing can top that view.

EXPENSIVE

Peter Luger Steakhouse 🖘🖘 STEAKS   If you love steak, then book a table here and hop a cab to Williamsburg. Expect loads of attitude and nothing in the way of decor or atmosphere (beer hall is the theme)—but this 114-year-old institution is porterhouse heaven. The first-rate cuts—the only ones they serve—are dry-aged on the premises and come off the grill dripping with fat and butter, crusty on the outside and tender pink within. It's the best steak in the five boroughs. Nonbelievers can order sole or lamb chops, but don't bother if you're not coming for the cow. The $5.95 Peter Luger burger is a little-known treasure. As sides go, the German fried potatoes are crisp and delicious, and the creamed spinach is everything it should be. Bring wads of cash because this place is expensive but doesn't take credit cards (other than their own house account). And call far, far in advance, especially during the holiday seasons.

178 Broadway (at Driggs Ave.), Williamsburg, Brooklyn. ℭ 718/387-7400. www.peterluger.com. Reservations essential; call a month in advance for weekend bookings. Main courses $5–$20 at lunch; $20–$32 at dinner. No credit cards (Peter Luger accounts only). Mon–Thurs 11:45am–9:45pm; Fri–Sat 11:45am–10:45pm; Sun 12:45–9:45pm. Subway: J, M, Z to Marcy Ave. (Or take a cab.)

MODERATE

Consider **Bubby's Brooklyn,** 1 Main St., at Water Street (ℭ **718/222-0666**), the DUMBO outpost of the comforting, comfort-food **Bubby's** (p. 152).

Fette Sau ★★ *Finds* BARBECUE   I learn something new every day. Now I know that Fette Sau means "fat pig" in German. And could there be a more clever name for a barbecue joint? And would we expect fantastic barbecue from a place with a German name instead of something with a country honky tonk moniker? I don't think so, but Fette Sau is as good as any cutesy-named BBQ place you will find in the New York area. Housed in a former auto mechanic's garage in Williamsburg, Fette Sau is rustic; seating is wooden picnic tables—in the warmer months there are tables outside in the small driveway leading to the restaurant. Service is from a counter; you order your meats by the weight, making it tough to control your intake. The meats; pork and beef are organic and from local farms. Not all the cuts of meat are available daily. When I went, I was fortunate that barbecue pork belly (thicker, fattier bacon) was available. It was the first time that I ever experienced barbecue pork belly and it's one I want to repeat. The boneless beef ribs were perfectly smoked, charred on the outside and tender within, while the Berkshire rib chop, coated with fat to keep the thick, other white meat, moist was flavorful. The barbecue is so good here, don't bother with the sauces, but do try the burnt end baked beans; a meal in itself. Fette Sau also has a remarkable beer and bourbon list worth traveling for even if you are a vegetarian.

354 Metropolitan Avenue (btwn Havermeyer and Roebling sts.), Williamsburg. ℭ 718/963-3404. Main courses: $10–$25. MC, V. Sun–Thurs 5pm–2am; Fri–Sat 5pm–4am. Subway: L to Lorimer St.

INEXPENSIVE

The fabulous **Grimaldi's Pizza** is at 19 Old Fulton St., between Front and Water streets (ℭ **718/858-4300**). Out in Coney Island, the 1924-established and little-changed **Totonno's** is at 1524 Neptune Ave., between W.15th and W. 16th streets (ℭ **718/372-8606**). See "Pizza, New York–Style," on p. 186, for more information.

Also in Coney Island is the famous **Nathan's Famous,** 1310 Surf Ave., at Stillwell Avenue (ℭ **718/946-2202**), for hot dogs by the beach. See how many you can eat.

If you are traveling to BAM to see a show, you'll be tempted to have either your pre- or post-theater meal at **Junior's,** 386 Flatbush Ave., at DeKalb Avenue (ℭ **718/852-5257**). Everyone knows about Junior's world-famous cheesecake, the epitome of New York cheesecake, but don't miss the opportunity to experience the authentic Brooklyn atmosphere here, complete with old-school waiters you'll not soon forget. Don't expect anything fancy, but do expect great cheesecake.

The best ice cream in New York can be found right over the Brooklyn Bridge at the **Brooklyn Ice Cream Factory,** Fulton Ferry Landing Pier, Brooklyn (ℭ **718/246-3963**). Everything is freshly made, including the hot fudge for your sundae.

Finds **Restaurants Grow in Brooklyn**

It might seem like a stretch to leave Manhattan to experience fine, innovative dining. But a trend is developing in Brooklyn; top chefs are staking out claims all over the increasingly gentrified borough. There is one street in particular that has become a mecca for exciting restaurants. That street is Smith and it runs through the neighborhoods of Boerum Hill, Cobble Hill, and Carroll Gardens.

The Smith Street awakening began in 2005 when **The Grocery, 288 Smith St.** (© 718/596-3335; www.thegroceryrestaurant.com), cracked into the top food category with a rating of 26, if that means anything. But the awakening was only for those not familiar with the Grocery, because those in the neighborhood would often line up for a taste of the market fresh dishes prepared by chef/owners Charles Kiely and Sharon Pachter.

There are a number of Italian restaurants on Smith Street, but one I particularly like is at 116 Smith Street, **La Lunetta** (© **718/488-6269**), specializing in small plates and interesting pastas such as penne with homemade ricotta and lamb.

Representing a Gallic slant is **Café Luluc,** 214 Smith St. (© **718/625-3815**) with its high tin-ceilings and open, airy space giving it a bistro feel. But the bistro specialties aside, Café Luluc is open every day for breakfast, lunch, and dinner and is most popular for its eggs.

It's worth traveling to Smith Street to **Zaytoons,** 283 Smith St. (© **718/875-1880**; www.zaytoonsrestaurant.com) for Middle Eastern food as good, or arguably better, than you will find on the other side of the East River.

You can reach most of these restaurants fairly easily if you take the F train to Carroll St., which has an exit right onto Smith Street.

Ferdinando's Focacceria ✴ ITALIAN/SICILIAN   You might think that focaccia, that wonderful Italian bread coated with olive oil, herbs, and tomato sauce, is a recent culinary innovation. Think again. They've been making focaccia at Ferdinando's since 1904. But the focaccia they make at this Sicilian restaurant, in the increasingly trendy neighborhood of Carroll Gardens, is nothing like the focaccia you've tasted. Here the specialty focaccia is *panelle,* a deep-fried pancake made of chickpea flour. You can have your panelle plain or you can have it topped with ricotta and grated cheese. The restaurant also features Sicilian specials such as marinated octopus, stuffed calamari, tripe in tomato sauce, and a magnificent *caponatina* (eggplant salad).

151 Union St. (btwn Columbia and Hicks sts.), Cobble Hill. © **718/855-1545.** Panelle $4; main courses $15–$22. No credit cards. Mon–Thurs 11am–7pm; Fri–Sat 11am–10pm Subway: F, G to Carroll St.

QUEENS
EXPENSIVE
Water's Edge ✴✴ CONTEMPORARY AMERICAN   When it comes to dining with the best views of the Manhattan skyline, many consider the River Café tops. But the view from Water's Edge, where the lights of the Citicorp, Chrysler, United Nations, and Empire State buildings flicker right across the river, gives the River Café

Where the Editor Eats (Queens version)

Queens may not be the dining destination that Brooklyn is becoming, but there's lots of good, eclectic cuisine, usually much less expensive than across the East River. Combine a trip to one or more of the Western Queens attractions (see chapter 7) with a meal at one of my favorite spots off the N/W trains.

If you're headed to the American Museum of the Moving Image (p. 295), walk a few blocks down 36th Ave. for lunch or dinner at **Malagueta** at 25–35 36th Ave. (at 28th St.; © **718/937-4821**). Chef Herbert Gomes combines his Brazilian background with his training at the French Culinary Institute to create a menu that has made his corner storefront into a favorite. (It's regularly cited as one of the city's best in *Time Out New York's* "Cheap Eats" issue). It's small, but classy, with original art on the walls and Brazilian music playing in the background. Such appetizers as linguiça sausage with yucca fries and cilantro mayo lead up to a menu of main courses rarely topping $12 (except for seafood specials). My favorite is the *picanha* steak, served with rice and beans, and a delicate vinaigrette and farofa. There's wine by the glass and bottle, and some scrumptious desserts (we like the passionfruit mousse). It's open Tuesday to Thursday noon to 10pm; Friday noon to 11pm; Saturday 1 to 11pm; and Sunday 1 to 10pm. Subway: N/W to 36th/Washington Ave.

Combine a visit to the Noguchi Museum (p. 295) and Socrates Sculpture Garden (p. 297) with a stop at **Sanford's Restaurant,** just off the Broadway stop on the N/W line at 30–13 Broadway, in Astoria (© **718/935-9269**; www.sanfordsnyc.com), which has been serving the neighborhood since 1930. From a more traditional diner, the current generation of the Karalekas family, which owns the place, has kept such favorites as "build

a run for its money. Throw in free ferry service from Manhattan (a 10-min. ride) to the restaurant, the possibility of watching a family of swans frolicking in the river as you dine, and the succulent seasonal cuisine by chef Ari Nieminen, and the Water's Edge experience becomes memorable. It's rare when views this good are matched by magnificent food, but Nieminen is up to the task. In the spirit of autumn, the season I visited the restaurant, the hearty, tender pomegranate-marinated venison stew came served inside a minipumpkin served with figs, cranberries, and chestnuts, while the decadently rich seared duck *foie gras* was accompanied by delicious black-mission-fig chutney. For a real splurge, Water's Edge offers tasting menus and wine pairings with the course. But this is Queens and the splurge won't hit you quite as hard in the wallet as it would if you went to that other restaurant on the river in Brooklyn.

East River and 44th Dr., Long Island City, Queens. © 718/482-0033. www.watersedgenyc.com. Main courses $26–$36; 4-course tasting menu $75. AE, DC, DISC, MC, V. Mon–Fri noon–3pm and 5:30–11pm; Sat 5:30–11pm. Subway: E, V to 23rd St./Ely Ave.

EXPENSIVE/MODERATE
Jackson Avenue Steakhouse 🍴 (Finds) STEAKS   This is an old-style steakhouse with prices more manageable than the Manhattan superstars (and Brooklyn's Peter Luger), and it's one stop on the no. 7 train into Queens. On a recent occasion, two of

your own" omelets and a fantastic chicken orzo soup and buffed up the menu with entrees ranging from a three-mushroom truffle risotto to a penne with smoked salmon and applewood bacon in a cream sauce. There's also a well-chosen (and reasonable) beer and wine menu. We go for the panini, the focaccia, the weekend brunch (with a mimosa, wine, or fresh juice), the burgers, and everything in between. Burgers and omelets generally run well under $10, with dinner entrees (which include soup or salad) from $12 up, and popular prix-fixe brunch on weekends for $11. It's open 24/7/365, and you might spot locals lingering over meals at any hour with their laptops using the Wi-Fi. Note that it's cash only.

One of the few restaurants in the city serving pizza in a coal-fired oven (it cooks very quickly, and adds a crispness to the thin crust) is a couple blocks farther down Broadway at **Sac's Place** at 25–41 Broadway (© **718/204-5002**). Brothers Domenico and Anthony Sacramone have a full Italian menu, but it's the pizza, made with homemade mozzarella and San Marzano tomatoes imported from Italy, that gets the love from Astoria and beyond. You can get it to take out, but why not sit down and enjoy the homey ambience (and live music from a jazz trio a couple nights a week, and occasionally an Elvis impersonator)? Pizzas range from $8.95 to $16 for a cheese pizza, and there's a long list of toppings, ranging from homemade meatballs to sautéed portobello mushroom in white wine. Mmm. It's open Sunday to Thursday noon to 11pm; Friday to Saturday noon to midnight.

—Kathleen Warnock

us had drinks, appetizers, filet mignon with portobello mushroom in Madeira wine reduction, coffee, and dessert for around $150. The ambience is casual; the waitstaff will remember you after one visit as well as your drink of choice. The rooms are handsome and wood-paneled, with a fireplace in the back room and stained glass in some of the windows. The meats (steaks, chops, rack of lamb) range from $28 on up to $85 for the chateaubriand (for two). There are also seafood and chicken entrees. There's an affordable sandwich and pasta menu (until 5pm, or after if they know you) that runs from around $9 for burgers to $15-ish for the higher-end pastas. You can also make a good-value meal from the appetizers, salads and soups. Executive chef Francisco "Paco" Gonzalez often kibitzes at the bar, where a local crowd gathers.

12–23 Jackson Ave., Long Island City, Queens. © **718/784-1412**. www.jacksonsteakhouse.com. Main courses $15–$42; appetizers $5–$13. AE, DC, DISC, MC, V. Mon–Thurs 11:30am–10pm; Fri 11:30am–11pm; Sat 5–11pm; Sun 3–10pm. Subway: 7 to Vernon/Jackson.

INEXPENSIVE

The no. 7 train is sometimes known as the International Express (see chapter 8). Take it out of Manhattan and through the borough of Queens and you will pass one ethnic neighborhood after another. You could write a book on all the different restaurants located around the no. 7 train in Queens. Here are a few of my favorites:

Get off at the 69th Street stop in Woodside, walk 1 block north, and you might begin to detect the aroma of barbecued meats. That smell is coming from **Ihawan,** 40–06 70th St. (© **718/205-1480**), which claims to be home of the best barbecue in town. But unless you've been to the Philippines, Ihawan's country of origin, this is barbecue unlike any you've tasted before. Here you can sample barbecued pork on bamboo skewers, grilled marinated pork chops, and the local favorite, grilled marinated pork belly. The menu here also includes other Filipino specialties such as *dinuguan,* pork stewed in pork-blood gravy, and *lapu-lapu,* a whitefish, served in tamarind soup.

If you get off the train at the 82nd Street/Jackson Heights stop, a few steps from the elevated tracks, you'll find **Arunee Thai,** 37–68 79th St., off Roosevelt Avenue (© **718/205-5559**). Here, the Thai food is so authentic (and the clientele mostly Thai) that the menus are written in Thai and English. Everything is delicious, and the spice level is not toned down for delicate palates. The fish, served whole on the bone, with chili, garlic, and hot-and-sour sauce, will either take the chill off a cold winter's day or, if it's summer, the chilies will cool down your overheated body and soul.

Exit the last stop of the no. 7 train, Flushing-Main Street and you might think you're in downtown Beijing. Where you are is Flushing's Chinatown, bigger than Manhattan's and crammed with tea houses, noodle shops, banquet halls, bakeries and Asian supermarkets. The food choices are staggering and you won't go wrong at just about any of the countless restaurants. My favorite is a bare bones Szechuan restaurant called **Little Pepper,** 133–43 Roosevelt Avenue (© **718/939-7788**), where the food is as authentic as it gets, which means spicy. There are exotic items on the menu, such as bull frog, rabbit, eel, and a variety of offal, but if that is too challenging, you can't go wrong with such basics as the double-cooked pork or the family-style soups. For a Flushing Chinatown experience like no other, try **Minni's Shabu Shabu,** 136–17 38th Avenue (© **718/762-6277**), where in front of each setting at each table there is a built-in soup bowl with your own controls. You order what you want to cook in the broth including raw sliced beef or pork or a variety of seafood, add sauces, condiments and vegetables and let it cook right in front of you. It takes a bit of practice, but by the end of your meal, you'll have the procedure down for the perfect, and hearty, Chinese soup.

7

Exploring New York City

If this is your first trip to New York, face the facts: It will be impossible to take in the entire city—this time. Because New York is almost unfathomably big and constantly changing; you could live your whole life here and still make fascinating daily discoveries—we New Yorkers do. This chapter is designed to give you an overview of what's available in this multi-faceted place so you can narrow your choices to an itinerary that's digestible for the amount of time you'll be here—be it a day, a week, or something in between.

So don't try to tame New York—you can't. Decide on a few must-see attractions, then let the city take you on its own ride. See chapter 4, "New York City Neighborhoods & Suggested Itineraries," for my suggestions on what to see and how to cram it all into 1, 2, or 3 days. But inevitably, as you make your way around the city, you'll be blown off course by unplanned diversions that are just as much fun as what you meant to see.

After all, the true New York is in the details. As you dash from sight to sight, take time to admire a cornice on a prewar building, linger over a cup of coffee at a sidewalk cafe, or just idle away a few minutes on a bench watching New Yorkers parade through their daily lives.

1 Sights & Attractions by Neighborhood

MANHATTAN

CHELSEA

EAST VILLAGE & NOHO

THE FLATIRON DISTRICT/ UNION SQUARE

GREENWICH VILLAGE

HARLEM

LOWER EAST SIDE

Downtown Attractions

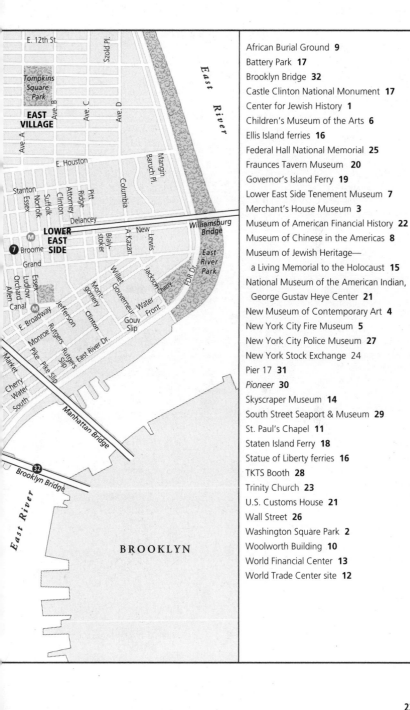

Midtown Attractions

UPPER WEST SIDE

CENTRAL

West Drive

Amsterdam Ave.
Columbus Ave.
Central Park W.

W. 64th St.
W. 63rd St.
W. 62nd St.
W. 61st St.
W. 60th St.
W. 59th St.
W. 58th St.
W. 57th St.
W. 56th St.
W. 55th St.
W. 54th St.
W. 53rd St.
W. 52nd St.
W. 51st St.
W. 50th St.
W. 49th St.
W. 48th St.
W. 47th St.
W. 46th St.
W. 45th St.
W. 44th St.
W. 43rd St.
W. 42nd St.
W. 41st St.
W. 40th St.
W. 39th St.
W. 38th St.
W. 37th St.
W. 36th St.
W. 35th St.
W. 34th St.
W. 33rd St.
W 32nd St.
W. 31st St.
W. 30th St.
W. 29th St.
W. 28th St.
W. 27th St.
W. 26th St.
W. 25th St.
W. 24th St.
W. 23rd St.
W. 22nd St.
W. 21st St.
W. 20th St.
W. 19th St.
W. 18th St.
W. 17th St.
W. 16th St.
W. 15th St.
W. 14th St.

Central Park S.

Columbus Circle

Broadway

THEATER DISTRICT

MIDTOWN WEST

TIMES SQUARE

Port Authority

GARMENT DISTRICT

Penn Station/ Madison Square Garden

Chelsea Park

CHELSEA

MEAT-PACKING DISTRICT

DeWitt Clinton Park

West End Ave.
Tenth Ave.
Ninth Ave.
Twelfth Ave.
Eleventh Ave.
Tenth Ave.
Eighth Ave.
Seventh Ave.
Ninth Ave.
Eighth Ave.
Seventh Ave.

Lincoln Tunnel

Javits Convention Center

West Side Hwy.

Eleventh Ave.
Tenth Ave.

Tunnel Entrance

Hudson River

Chelsea Piers

Uptown Attractions

224

Harlem Attractions

Abyssinian Baptist Church **8**
Astor Row Houses **11**
Cathedral of St. John
  the Divine **13**
The Cloisters **2**
Dyckman Farmhouse Museum **1**
Jumel Terrace Historic District **4**
The Little Red Schoolhouse **3**
Morris-Jumel Mansion **5**
Mother A.M.E. Zion Church **9**
Riverside Park **14**
Schomburg Center for
  Research in Black Culture **10**
Strivers' Row **7**
Studio Museum in Harlem **12**
Sugar Hill **6**
Sylvan Terrace **5**

Subway stop

Neue Galerie New York (p. 251)
Solomon R. Guggenheim Museum ₳
(p. 237)
Temple Emanu-El (p. 263)
Tisch Children's Zoo ₳ (p. 267)
Whitney Museum of American
Art ₳₳ (p. 240)

UPPER MANHATTAN
The Cloisters ₳₳ (p. 242)
Dyckman Farmhouse Museum (p. 259)
The Little Red Lighthouse (p. 273)

UPPER WEST SIDE
American Museum of Natural
History ₳₳₳ (p. 229)
The Ansonia (p. 256)
Cathedral of St. John the Divine ₳
(p. 261)
Central Park ₳₳₳ (p. 264)
Children's Museum of Manhattan ₳
(p. 283)
The Dakota (p. 256)
New-York Historical Society ₳
(p. 252)
Riverside Park ₳₳ (p. 271)
Rose Center for Earth and Space ₳
(p. 229)
Wollman Rink ₳ (p. 268)

OUTER BOROUGHS
THE BRONX
Bronx Museum of the Arts (p. 289)
Bronx Zoo Wildlife Conservation
Park ₳₳₳ (p. 284)
City Island (p. 288)
Edgar Allan Poe Cottage (p. 259)
New York Botanical Garden ₳
(p. 286)
Pelham Bay Park (p. 288)
Wave Hill ₳ (p. 287)

Woodlawn Cemetery (p. 289)
Yankee Stadium ₳₳ (p. 298)

BROOKLYN
Brooklyn Botanic Garden ₳ (p. 287)
Brooklyn Children's Museum (p. 283)
Brooklyn Heights Historic District
(p. 292)
Brooklyn Lyceum (p. 294)
Brooklyn Museum of Art ₳₳ (p. 241)
Brooklyn Tabernacle ₳ (p. 290)
Coney Island ₳₳ (p. 290)
Coney Island Museum (p. 290)
Dime Savings Bank (p. 294)
Grand Army Plaza (p. 292)
New York Aquarium (p. 291)
New York Transit Museum (p. 290)
Pratt Institute (p. 294)
Prison Ship Martyrs Monument
(p. 294)
Prospect Park ₳₳ (p. 292)
Williamsburg Art & Historical
Center (p. 294)

QUEENS
American Museum of the Moving
Image ₳ (closed until late 2009)
(p. 295)
Citi Field (p. 298)
Flushing Meadows–Corona Park
(p. 283)
Isamu Noguchi Garden Museum ₳
(p. 295)
Louis Armstrong House Museum ₳
(p. 295)
New York Hall of Science ₳ (p. 283)
P.S. 1 Contemporary Art Center
(p. 296)
Queens Museum of Art (p. 296)
Socrates Sculpture Park (p. 296)

Tips Subway Access Alert

On almost every weekend, and throughout the year, changes in normal subway service tend to occur. I *strongly* recommend you check with the **Metropolitan Transit Authority** at ℂ **718/330-1234** or **www.mta.info/nyct** before you plan your travel routes; your hotel concierge or any token-booth clerk should also be able to assist you.

---

2 The Top Attractions

In addition to the choices below, don't forget **Central Park** ⭑⭑⭑, the great green swath that is, just by virtue of its existence, New York City's greatest marvel. Central Park is so big and multifaceted that it earns its own section, starting on p. 264.

American Museum of Natural History ⭑⭑⭑ *Kids* This is one of the hottest museum tickets in town, thanks to the **Rose Center for Earth and Space** ⭑, whose four-story-tall planetarium sphere hosts the show, *Cosmic Collisions,* narrated by Robert Redford, about the violent beginnings of the universe. Prepare to be blown away by this astounding, literally earth-shaking short film.

Buy your tickets in advance for the Space Show in order to guarantee admission (they're available online); I also recommend buying tickets in advance for a specific IMAX film or special exhibition, such as the Butterfly Conservatory (see below), especially during peak seasons (summer, autumn, holiday time) and for weekend visits; otherwise, you might miss out.

Other must-sees include the Big Bang Theater, which re-creates the theoretical birth of the universe; the main Hall of the Universe, with its very own 16-ton meteorite; and the terrific Hall of Planet Earth, which focuses on the geologic processes of our home planet (great volcano display!). All in all, you'll need a minimum of 2 hours to fully explore the Rose Center. The rest of the 4-square-block museum is nothing to sneeze at, either. Founded in 1869, it houses the world's greatest natural-science collection in a group of buildings made of towers and turrets, pink granite, and red brick. The diversity of the holdings is astounding: some 36 million specimens, ranging from microscopic organisms to the world's largest cut gem, the Brazilian Princess Topaz (21,005 carats). Rose Center aside, it would take you all day to see the entire museum, and then you *still* wouldn't get to everything. If you don't have a lot of time, you can see the best of the best on free highlights tours offered daily every hour at 15 minutes after the hour from 10:15am to 3:15pm. Free daily spotlight tours, thematic tours that change monthly, are also offered; stop by an information desk for the day's schedule. Audio Expeditions, high-tech audio tours that allow you to access narration in the order you choose, are also available to help you make sense of it all.

If you only see one exhibit, see the **dinosaurs** ⭑, which take up the fourth floor.

The Hall of Biodiversity is an impressive multimedia exhibit, but its doom-and-gloom story about the future of rainforests and other natural habitats might be too much for the little ones. Kids 5 and up should head to the Discovery Room, with lots of hands-on exhibits and experiments. (*Parents, be prepared:* There seems to be a gift shop overflowing with stuffed animals at every turn.) The Spitzer Hall of Human Origins in the Anne and Bernard Spitzer Hall traces the evolution of man and even offers children's workshops where kids can compare skull casts of early humans.

The museum excels at special exhibitions, so check to see what will be on while you're in town in case any advance planning is required. The magical **Butterfly Conservatory** ⭑, a walk-in enclosure housing nearly 500 free-flying tropical butterflies, has developed into a can't-miss fixture from October through May; check to see if it's in the house while you're in town.

Central Park West (btwn 77th and 81st sts.). ☎ **212/769-5100** for information, or 212/769-5200 for tickets (tickets can also be ordered online for an additional $4 charge). www.amnh.org. Suggested admission $14 adults, $11 seniors and students, $8 children 2–12; Space Show and museum admission $22 adults, $17 seniors and students, $13 children under 12. Additional charges for IMAX movies and some special exhibitions. Daily 10am–5:45pm; Rose Center open 1st Fri of every month until 8:45pm. Subway: B, C to 81st St.; 1 to 79th St.

Value A Money & Time-Saving Tip

CityPass may be New York's best sightseeing deal. Pay one price ($65, or $49 for kids 12–17) for admission to six major attractions: The American Museum of Natural History (admission only; does not include Space Show), the Guggenheim Museum, the Empire State Building, the Museum of Modern Art, the Metropolitan Museum of Art and the Cloisters, and a 2-hour Circle Line harbor cruise. Individual tickets would cost more than twice as much (though I should point out that the Met is a "suggested" admission fee).

More important, CityPass is not a coupon book. It contains actual tickets, so you can bypass lengthy lines. This can save you hours, as sights such as the Empire State Building often have ticket lines of an hour or more.

CityPass is good for 9 days from the first time you use it. It's sold at all participating attractions and online at **http://citypass.com**. To avoid online service and shipping fees, you may buy the pass at your first attraction (start at an attraction that's likely to have the shortest admission line, such as the Guggenheim, or arrive before opening to avoid a wait at such spots as the Empire State Building). However, if you begin your sightseeing on a weekend or during holidays, when lines are longest, online purchase may be worthwhile.

For more information, call CityPass at © **888/330-5008** (note, however, that CityPass is not sold over the phone).

Brooklyn Bridge *🌟🌟* *Moments*   Its Gothic-inspired stone pylons and intricate steel-cable webs have moved poets such as Walt Whitman and Hart Crane to sing the praises of this great span, the first to cross the East River and connect Manhattan to Brooklyn. Begun in 1867 and ultimately completed in 1883, the Brooklyn Bridge is now the city's best-known symbol of the age of growth that seized the city during the late 19th century. Walk across the bridge and imagine the awe that New Yorkers of that age felt at seeing two boroughs joined by this span. It's still astounding.

Walking the bridge: Walking the Brooklyn Bridge is one of my all-time favorite New York activities, although there's no doubt that the Lower Manhattan views from the bridge now have a painful resonance as well as a joyous spirit. A wide wood-plank pedestrian walkway is elevated above the traffic, making it a relatively peaceful, and popular, walk. It's a great vantage point from which to contemplate the New York skyline and the East River.

There's a sidewalk entrance on Park Row, just across from City Hall Park (take the 4, 5, or 6 train to Brooklyn Bridge/City Hall). But why do this walk *away* from Manhattan, toward the far less impressive Brooklyn skyline? Instead, for Manhattan skyline views, take an A or C train to High Street, one stop into Brooklyn. From there, you'll be on the bridge in no time: Come above ground, then walk through the little park to Cadman Plaza East and head downslope (left) to the stairwell that will take you up to the footpath. (Following Prospect Place under the bridge, turning right onto Cadman Plaza East, will also take you directly to the stairwell.) It's a 20- to 40-minute stroll over the bridge to Manhattan, depending on your pace, the amount of foot traffic, and the number of stops you make to behold the spectacular views (there are benches along the way). The footpath will deposit you right at City Hall Park.

Tasty tips: The perfect complement to your stroll over the Brooklyn Bridge is a stop for pizza at **Grimaldi's** (p. 186), followed by homemade ice cream at the **Brooklyn Ice Cream Factory** (© 718/246-3963), at the Fulton Ferry Fire Boat House on the river and in the shadow of the bridge. The pizza and ice cream will fortify you for your stroll into Manhattan.

Subway: A, C to High St.; 4, 5, 6 to Brooklyn Bridge–City Hall.

Ellis Island 🏰🏰   One of New York's most moving sights, the restored Ellis Island opened in 1990, slightly north of Liberty Island. Roughly 40% of Americans (myself included) can trace their heritage back to an ancestor who came through here. For the 62 years when it was America's main entry point for immigrants (1892–1954), Ellis Island processed some 12 million people. The greeting was often brusque—especially in the early years of the century (until 1924), when as many as 12,000 came through in a single day. The statistics can be overwhelming, but the Immigration Museum skillfully relates the story of Ellis Island and immigration in America by placing the emphasis on personal experience.

It's difficult to leave the museum unmoved. Today you enter the Main Building's baggage room, just as the immigrants did, and then climb the stairs to the Registry Room, with its dramatic vaulted tiled ceiling, where millions waited anxiously for medical and legal processing. A step-by-step account of the immigrants' voyage is detailed in the exhibit, with haunting photos and touching oral histories. What might be the most poignant exhibit is "Treasures from Home," 1,000 objects and photos donated by descendants of immigrants, including family heirlooms, religious articles, and rare clothing and jewelry. Outside, the American Immigrant Wall of Honor commemorates the names of more than 500,000 immigrants and their families, from Myles Standish and George Washington's great-grandfather to the forefathers of John F. Kennedy, Jay Leno, and Barbra Streisand. You can even research your own family's history at the interactive American Family Immigration History Center. You might also make time to see the award-winning short film *Island of Hope, Island of Tears,* which plays on a continuous loop in two theaters. Short live theatrical performances depicting the immigrant experience are also often part of the day's events.

Touring tip: Ferries run daily to Ellis Island and Liberty Island from Battery Park and Liberty State Park at frequent intervals; see **Statue of Liberty** listing (p. 238) for details.

In New York Harbor. © 212/363-3200 (general info), or 212/269-5755 (ticket/ferry info). www.nps.gov/elis, www. ellisisland.org, or www.statuecruises.com. Free admission (ferry ticket charge). Daily 9:30am–5:15pm (last ferry departs around 3:30pm). For subway and ferry details, see the Statue of Liberty listing on p. 238 (ferry trip includes stops at both sights).

Empire State Building 🏰🏰🏰   It took 60,000 tons of steel, 10 million bricks, 2.5 million feet of electrical wire, 120 miles of pipe, and seven million man-hours to build. King Kong climbed it in 1933—and again in 2005. A plane slammed into it in

---

Impressions

"It's the nearest thing to heaven we have in New York."
—Deborah Kerr to Cary Grant in *An Affair to Remember,*
on the Empire State Building

Tips Empire State Building Ticket Buying

Lines can be horrible at the concourse-level ticket booth, so be prepared to wait—or consider purchasing advance tickets online using a credit card at **www.esbnyc.com**. Tickets to the ESB are also included in your **CityPass** (see box, p. 230). You'll pay slightly more—tickets were priced $2 higher on the website at press time—but it's well worth it, especially if you're visiting during busy seasons, when the line can be shockingly long. You're not required to choose a time or date for your tickets in advance; they can be used on any regular open day. However, order them well before you leave home, because only regular mail is free. Expect them to take 7 to 10 days to reach you (longer if you live outside of the U.S.). Overnight delivery adds $15 to your total order. With tickets in hand, you're allowed to proceed directly to the second floor—past everyone who didn't plan as well as you did!

Now you can call in advance to get an estimate of your wait in line along with the visibility from the observatory. Dial © **877/692-8439** for the service.

1945. The World Trade Center superseded it in 1970 as the island's tallest building. And in 1997, a gunman ascended it to stage a deadly shooting. On that horrific day of September 11, 2001, it once again regained its status as New York City's tallest building, after 31 years of taking second place. And through it all, the Empire State Building has remained one of the city's favorite landmarks and its signature high-rise. Completed in 1931, the limestone-and-stainless-steel Streamline Deco dazzler climbs 102 stories (1,454 ft.) and now harbors the offices of fashion firms, and, in its upper reaches, a jumble of high-tech broadcast equipment.

Always a conversation piece, the Empire State Building glows every night, bathed in colored floodlights to commemorate events of significance—red, white, and blue for Independence Day; green for St. Patrick's Day; red, black, and green for Martin Luther King Day; blue and white for Hanukkah; even blue for the New York Giants Super Bowl appearance in 2008 (you can find a complete lighting schedule online). The familiar silver spire can be seen from all over the city.

The best views, and what keeps the nearly three million visitors coming every year, are the ones from the 86th- and 102nd-floor observatories. The lower one is best—you can walk out on a windy deck and look through coin-operated viewers (bring quarters!) over what, on a clear day, can be as much as an 80-mile visible radius. The citywide panorama is magnificent. One surprise is the flurry of rooftop activity, an aspect of city life that thrives unnoticed from our everyday sidewalk vantage point. The higher observation deck is glass-enclosed and cramped.

Light fog can create an admirably moody effect, but it goes without saying that a clear day is best. Dusk brings the most remarkable views and the biggest crowds. Consider going in the morning, when the light is still low on the horizon, keeping glare to a minimum. Starry nights are pure magic.

In your haste to go up, don't rush through the three-story-high marble lobby without pausing to admire its features, which include a wonderful Streamline mural.

350 Fifth Ave. (at 34th St.). © **212/736-3100**. www.esbnyc.com. Observatory admission $19 adults, $17 seniors and children 12–17, $13 children 6–11, free for children under 6. Daily open 8am–2am, last elevator at 1:15am. Subway: B, D, F, N, R, Q, V, W to 34th St.; 6 to 33rd St.

Grand Central Terminal ⭑⭑ Even if you're not catching one of the subway lines or Metro-North commuter trains that rumble through Grand Central Terminal, come for a visit; it's one of the most magnificent public places in the country. And even if you arrive and leave by subway, be sure to exit the station, walking a couple of blocks south, to about 40th Street, before you turn around to admire Jules-Alexis Coutan's neoclassical sculpture *Transportation* hovering over the south entrance, with a majestic Mercury, the Roman god of commerce and travel, as its central figure.

The greatest visual impact comes when you enter the vast majestic main concourse. The high windows allow sunlight to penetrate the space, glinting off the half-acre Tennessee marble floor. The brass clock over the central kiosk gleams, as do the gold- and nickel-plated chandeliers piercing the side archways. The masterful sky ceiling, a brilliant greenish blue, depicts the constellations of the winter sky above New York. They're lit with 59 stars, surrounded by dazzling 24-carat gold and emitting light fed through fiber-optic cables, their intensities roughly replicating the magnitude of the actual stars as seen from Earth. Look carefully and you'll see a patch near one corner left unrestored as a reminder of the neglect once visited on this splendid overhead masterpiece. On the east end of the main concourse is a grand marble staircase.

This dramatic Beaux Arts splendor serves as a hub of social activity as well. Excellent-quality retail shops and restaurants have taken over the mezzanine and lower levels. The highlights of the West Mezzanine are **Michael Jordan's–The Steak House,** a gorgeous Art Deco space that allows you to dine within view of the sky ceiling (see "The Prime Cut: Steaks! Steaks! Steaks!" on p. 172) as well as the gorgeously restored **Campbell Apartment** (p. 379), which serves cocktails. Off the main concourse at street level, there's a nice mix of specialty shops and national retailers, as well as the truly grand **Grand Central Market** for gourmet

> **Impressions**
> *"If you're bored in New York, it's your own fault."*
> —Myrna Loy

foods. **The New York Transit Museum Store** (p. 333), in the shuttle passage, houses city transit-related exhibitions and a terrific gift shop that's worth a look for transit buffs. The lower **dining concourse** ⭑ houses a stellar food court and the famous **Oyster Bar & Restaurant** (see chapter 6 for details on both).

During the Christmas holidays, Grand Central Terminal is even more special with hourly laser shows on the ceiling of the main concourse, a toy train exhibit at the New York Transit Museum Store, and a crafts fair off the Main Concourse.

The **Municipal Art Society** (© 212/935-3960; www.mas.org) offers a walking tour of Grand Central Terminal on Wednesday at 12:30pm, which meets at the information booth on the Grand Concourse (for a $10 "suggested donation").

42nd St. at Park Ave. © 212/439-1049 (tour hot line). www.grandcentralterminal.com. Subway: S, 4, 5, 6, or 7 to 42nd St./Grand Central.

Metropolitan Museum of Art ⭑⭑⭑ Home of blockbuster after blockbuster, the Metropolitan Museum of Art attracts some five million people a year, more than any other spot in New York City. And it's no wonder—this place is magnificent. At 1.6 million square feet, this is the largest museum in the Western Hemisphere. Nearly all the world's cultures are on display through the ages—from Egyptian mummies to ancient Greek statuary to Islamic carvings to Renaissance paintings to Native American masks to 20th-century decorative arts—and masterpieces are the rule. You could go once a week for a lifetime and still find something new on each visit.

So unless you plan on spending your entire vacation in the museum (some people do), you cannot see the entire collection. My recommendation is to give it a good day—or better yet, 2 half-days so you don't burn out. One good way to get an overview is to take advantage of the little-known Museum Highlights Tour, offered every day at various times throughout the day (usually between 10:15am and 3:15pm; tours also offered in Spanish, Italian, German, and Korean). Even some New Yorkers who've spent many hours in the museum could profit from this once-over. Visit the museum's website for a schedule of this and subject-specific walking tours (Old Masters Paintings, American Period Rooms, Arts of China, Islamic Art, and so on); you can also get a schedule of the day's tours at the Visitor Services desk when you arrive. A daily schedule of Gallery Talks is available as well.

The least overwhelming way to see the Met on your own is to pick up a map at the round desk in the entry hall and choose to concentrate on what you like, whether it's 17th-century paintings, American furniture, or the art of the South Pacific. Highlights include the American Wing's Garden Court, with its 19th-century sculpture; the terrific ground-level Costume Hall; and the Frank Lloyd Wright room. The beautifully renovated Roman and Greek galleries are overwhelming, but in a marvelous way, as are the collections of Byzantine Art and later Chinese art. The highlight of the Egyptian collection is the Temple of Dendur, in a dramatic, purpose-built glass-walled gallery with Central Park views. The Greek Galleries, which at last fully realize McKim, Mead & White's grand neoclassical plans of 1917, and the Ancient Near East Galleries, are particularly of note. But it all depends on what your interests are. Special exhibitions can range from "Orazio and Artemisia Gentileschi: Father and Daughter Painters in Baroque Italy" to "Earthly Bodies: Irving Penn's Nudes, 1949–50."

The big news this season at the Met is that after 50 years of being used as a dining area, the Greek and Roman galleries reopened in the spring of 2007 after a $220 million renovation redesigned and expanded the galleries to 57,000 square feet. The galleries now exhibit ancient artifacts that had been in storage, including 30,000 feet of the square footage devoted to Roman collections.

The Met now opens on "holiday Mondays." On those Mondays, such as Memorial Day or Labor Day, the museum is open from 9:30am to 5:30pm.

To purchase **tickets** for concerts and lectures, call ⓒ **212/570-3949** (Mon–Sat 9:30am–5pm). The museum contains several dining facilities, including a full-service restaurant serving Continental cuisine (ⓒ **212/570-3964** for reservations). The roof garden is worth visiting if you're here from spring to autumn, offering peaceful views over Central Park and the city.

Moments Evenings at the Met

On Friday and Saturday evenings, the Met remains open late not only for art viewing but also for cocktails in the Great Hall Balcony Bar (5–8pm) and classical music from a string ensemble. A slate of after-hours programs (gallery talks, walking tours, family programs) changes by the week; call for the current schedule. The restaurant stays open until 10pm (last reservation at 8:30pm), and dinner is usually accompanied by piano music.

The Met's medieval collections are housed in upper Manhattan at **The Cloisters** ✪✪; see the full listing on p. 242.

Fifth Ave. at 82nd St. ⓒ **212/535-7710.** www.metmuseum.org. Suggested admission (includes same-day entrance to the Cloisters) $20 adults, $15 seniors and $10 students, free for children under 12 when accompanied by an adult. Sun, holiday Mon (Memorial Day, Labor Day, etc.), and Tues–Thurs 9:30am–5:30pm; Fri–Sat 9:30am–9pm. Strollers are permitted in most areas—inquire at Information Desks for gallery limitations. Oversized and jogging strollers are prohibited. Subway: 4, 5, 6 to 86th St.

Museum of Modern Art ✪✪
The newer, larger MoMA, after a 2-year renovation, is almost twice the space of the original. The renovation, designed by Yoshio Taniguchi, highlights space and light, with open rooms, high ceilings, and gardens— a beautiful work of architecture and a perfect complement to the art within. This is where you'll find van Gogh's *Starry Night,* Cezanne's *Bather,* Picasso's *Les Demoiselles d'Avignon,* and the great sculpture by Rodin, *Monument to Balzac.* Whenever I visit, I like to browse the fun "Architecture and Design" department, with examples of design for appliances, furniture, and even sports cars. MoMA also features edgy new exhibits and a celebrated film series that attracts serious cinephiles. But the heart of the museum remains the Abby Aldrich Rockefeller Sculpture Garden, which has been enlarged; the museum's new design affords additional views of this lovely space from other parts of the museum. And, as of Spring 2008, MoMA has installed a museum-wide Wi-Fi network so that visitors can access a mobile Web site on handheld devices with HTML browsers (which basically means Apple's iPhone and iPod Touch). They can then load up audio tours and commentary; content is available in eight languages as well as in specialized versions for children, teenagers, and the visually impaired. MoMA is one of the most expensive museums in New York, but does have a "free" day: on Fridays from 4 to 8pm.

11 W. 53rd St. (btwn Fifth and Sixth aves.). ⓒ **212/708-9400.** www.moma.org. Admission $20 adults, $16 seniors, $12 students, children under 16 free if accompanied by an adult. Sat–Mon and Wed–Thurs 10:30am–5:30pm; Fri 10:30am–8pm. Subway: E, V to Fifth Ave.; B, D, F to 47th–50th/Rockefeller Center.

Rockefeller Center ✪✪
A Streamline Moderne masterpiece, Rockefeller Center is one of New York's central gathering spots for visitors and New Yorkers alike. A prime example of the city's skyscraper spirit and historic sense of optimism, it was erected mainly in the 1930s, when the city was deep in the Depression as well as its most passionate Art Deco phase. Designated a National Historic Landmark in 1988, it's now the world's largest privately owned business-and-entertainment center, with 18 buildings on 21 acres.

For a dramatic approach to the entire complex, start at Fifth Avenue between 49th and 50th streets. The builders purposely created the gentle slope of the Promenade, known here as the Channel Gardens because it's flanked to the south by La Maison Française and to the north by the British Building (the Channel, get it?). You'll also find a number of attractive shops along here, including a big branch of the Metropolitan Museum of Art Store, a good stop for elegant gifts. The Promenade leads to the Lower Plaza, home to the famous ice-skating rink in winter (see next paragraph) and alfresco dining in summer in the shadow of Paul Manship's freshly gilded bronze statue *Prometheus.* All around, the flags of the United Nations' member countries flap in the breeze. Just behind *Prometheus,* in December and early January, towers the city's official and majestic Christmas tree.

The Rink at Rockefeller Center ✪ (ⓒ 212/332-7654; www.rockefellercenter.com) is tiny but positively romantic, especially during the holidays, when the giant Christmas

Moments   Heading for the Top of the Rock

Giving the Empire State Building some friendly competition when it comes to spectacular views is the observation deck of 30 Rockefeller Plaza, known as the **Top of the Rock** ⟨𝓡⟨𝓡. The deck, which comprises floors 67 to 70, which had been closed since 1986, reopened in 2005. The stately deck was constructed in 1933 to resemble the grandeur of a luxury ocean liner, and unlike the Empire State Building, the observation deck here is more spacious and the views, though not quite as high, just as stunning. You might have just as much fun getting up there as you will on the deck itself; the sky-shuttle elevators with glass ceilings project images from the 1930s through the present day as it zooms its way up. Reserved-time tickets help minimize the lines and are available online at **www.topoftherocknyc.com**. The observation deck is open daily from 8:30am to midnight; admission rates are $18 for adults, $16 for seniors, $11 for ages 6 to 12, and free for children under 6. For more information, call ℭ **877/NYC-ROCK (877/692-7625)** or 212/698-2000, or visit **www.topoftherocknyc.com**.

tree's multicolored lights twinkle from above. The rink is open from mid-October to mid-March, and you'll skate under the magnificent tree for the month of December. The focal point of this "city within a city" is the building at **30 Rockefeller Plaza** 𝓡, a 70-story showpiece towering over the plaza. It's still one of the city's most impressive buildings; walk through for a look at the granite-and-marble lobby, lined with monumental sepia-toned murals by José Maria Sert. You can pick up a walking-tour brochure on the center's art and architecture at the main information desk in this building. On the 65th floor, the legendary Rainbow Room is once again open to the public (p. 379).

NBC television maintains studios throughout the complex. *Saturday Night Live* and *Late Night with Conan O'Brien* originate at 30 Rock (see "Talk of the Town: TV Tapings," on p. 280, for tips on getting tickets). NBC's *Today* show is broadcast live on weekdays from 7 to 10am from the glass-enclosed studio on the southwest corner of 49th Street and Rockefeller Plaza; come early if you want a visible spot, and bring your HI MOM! sign.

The 70-minute **NBC Studio Tour** (ℭ **212/664-3700;** www.nbcuniversalstore.com) will take you behind the scenes at the Peacock network. The tour changes daily but might include the *Today* show, *NBC Nightly News, Dateline NBC,* and/or *Saturday Night Live* sets. Who knows? You may even run into Brian Williams or Meredith Viera. Tours run every 15 to 30 minutes Monday through Saturday from 8:30am to 5:30pm, Sunday from 9:30am to 4:30pm (later on certain summer days); of course, you'll have a better chance of encountering some real live action on a weekday. Tickets are $19 for adults, $16 for seniors and children 6 to 12. You can reserve your tickets in advance (reservations are recommended) or buy them right up to tour time at the NBC Experience store, on Rockefeller Plaza at 49th Street. They also offer a 60-minute Rockefeller Center Tour Monday to Saturday on the hour from 11am to 5pm , and –Sunday 11am to 3pm. Tickets are $12 for adults, $10 for seniors and children 6 to 12; two-tour combination packages are available for $23. Call ℭ **212/664-7174.**

Other notable buildings throughout the complex include the International Building, on Fifth Avenue between 50th and 51st streets, worth a look for its Atlas statue out front; and the McGraw-Hill Building on Sixth Avenue, between 48th and 49th streets, with its 50-foot sun triangle on the plaza.

Radio City Music Hall ⊛, 1260 Sixth Ave., at 50th Street (© **212/247-4777**; www.radiocity.com), is perhaps the most impressive architectural feat of the complex. Designed by Donald Deskey and opened in 1932, it's one of the largest indoor theaters, with 6,200 seats. But its true grandeur derives from its magnificent Art Deco appointments. The crowning touch is the stage's great proscenium arch, which from the distant seats evokes a faraway sun setting on the horizon of the sea. The men's and women's lounges are also splendid. The theater hosts the annual Christmas Spectacular, starring the Rockettes. The illuminating 1-hour **Stage Door Tour** is offered Monday through Saturday from 10am to 5pm, Sunday from 11am to 5pm; tickets are $17 for adults, $10 for children under 12.

Btwn 48th and 50th sts., from Fifth to Sixth aves. © **212/247-4777** (tour info). www.radiocity.com. Subway: B, D, F, V to 47th–50th sts./Rockefeller Center.

Solomon R. Guggenheim Museum ⊛

It's been called a bun, a snail, a concrete tornado, and even a giant wedding cake; bring your kids, and they'll probably see it as New York's coolest opportunity for skateboarding. Whatever description you choose to apply, Frank Lloyd Wright's only New York building, completed in 1959, is best summed up as a brilliant work of architecture—so consistently brilliant that it competes with the art for your attention. If you're looking for the city's best modern art, head to MoMA or the Whitney first; come to the Guggenheim to see the house. Though you might not see much except scaffolding; the exterior of the museum is undergoing a $29-million restoration with a completion date scheduled for mid-2008.

But the restoration has no effect on what's inside, and it's easy to see the bulk of what's on display in 2 to 4 hours. The museum's spiraling rotunda circles over a slowly inclined ramp that leads you past changing exhibits that, in the past, have ranged from "Matthew Barney: The Cremaster Cycle" to "Norman Rockwell: Pictures for the American People," said to be the most comprehensive exhibit ever of the beloved painter's works. Usually the progression is counterintuitive: from the first floor up, rather than from the sixth floor down. If you're not sure, ask a guard before you begin. Permanent exhibits of 19th- and 20th-century art, including strong holdings of Kandinsky, Klee, Picasso, and French Impressionists, occupy a stark annex called the Tower Galleries, an addition (accessible at every level) that some critics have claimed made the entire structure look like a toilet bowl backed by a water tank (judge for yourself—I think there may be something to that view).

The Guggenheim runs some special programs, including free docent tours daily, a limited schedule of lectures, free family films, avant-garde screenings for grown-ups, and curator-led guided gallery tours on select Friday afternoons.

1071 Fifth Ave. (at 89th St.). © **212/423-3500**. www.guggenheim.org. Admission $18 adults, $15 seniors and students, free for children under 12, pay what you wish Fri 5:45–7:15pm. Sat–Wed 10am–5:45pm; Fri 10am–7:45pm. Subway: 4, 5, 6 to 86th St.

Staten Island Ferry ⊛ _Value_

In 2006, the Staten Island Ferry celebrated its 100th anniversary. Over the years it has been one of New York's best bargains—sometimes costing a nickel and most of the time, like now, a free ride. It's New York's best freebie—especially if you just want to glimpse the Statue of Liberty and not climb her steps. You get an hour-long excursion (round-trip) into the world's biggest harbor.

This is not strictly a sightseeing ride but commuter transportation to and from Staten Island. As a result, during business hours, you'll share the boat with working stiffs reading papers and drinking coffee inside, blissfully unaware of the sights outside.

You, however, should go on deck and enjoy the harbor traffic. The old orange-and-green boats usually have open decks along the sides or at the bow and stern; try to catch one of these if you can, since the newer white boats don't have decks. Grab a seat on the right side of the boat for the best view. On the way out of Manhattan, you'll pass the Statue of Liberty (the boat comes closest to Lady Liberty on the way to Staten Island), Ellis Island, and from the left side of the boat, Governor's Island; you'll see the Verrazano Narrows Bridge spanning from Brooklyn to Staten Island in the distance.

When the boat arrives at St. George, Staten Island, if you are required to disembark, follow the boat-loading sign on your right as you get off; you'll circle around to the next loading dock, where there's usually another boat waiting to depart for Manhattan. The skyline views are simply awesome on the return trip. Well worth the time spent.

Departs from the Whitehall Ferry Terminal at the southern tip of Manhattan. ⓒ 718/727-2508. www.nyc.gov/html/dot/html/ferrybus/statferry.shtml. Free admission. 24 hr.; every 20–30 min. weekdays, less frequently during off-peak and weekend hours. Subway: R, W to Whitehall St.; 4, 5 to Bowling Green; 1 to South Ferry (ride in one of the 1st 5 cars).

Statue of Liberty ✯✯✯ *Kids*   For the millions who came by ship to America in the last century—either as privileged tourists or needy, hopeful immigrants—Lady Liberty, standing in the Upper Bay, was their first glimpse of America. No monument so embodies the nation's, and the world's, notion of political freedom and economic potential. Even if you don't make it out to Liberty Island, you can get a spine-tingling glimpse from Battery Park, from the New Jersey side of the bay, or during a ride on the Staten Island Ferry (see above). It's always reassuring to see her torch lighting the way.

Proposed by French statesman Edouard de Laboulaye as a gift from France to the United States, commemorating the two nations' friendship and joint notions of liberty, the statue was designed by sculptor Frédéric-Auguste Bartholdi with the engineering help of Alexandre-Gustave Eiffel (who was responsible for the famed Paris tower) and unveiled on October 28, 1886. *Touring tips:* Ferries leave daily every

---

Moments **Roosevelt Island Tram**

Want to take in a little-known but spectacular view of the New York skyline? Take them for a ride on the **Roosevelt Island Tram** (ⓒ **212/832-4543,** ext. 1; www.rioc.com.) This is the tram you have probably seen in countless movies, most recently *Spider-Man.* The tram originates at 59th Street and Second Avenue, costs $2 each way ($2 round-trip for seniors), and takes 4 minutes to traverse the East River to Roosevelt Island, where there are a series of apartment complexes and parks. During those 4 minutes you will be treated to a gorgeous view down the East River and the East Side skyline, with views of the United Nations and four bridges: the Queensboro, Williamsburg, Manhattan, and Brooklyn. On a clear day you might even spot Lady Liberty. And don't worry, despite what you've seen in the movies, the tram is safe, and your friendly neighborhood Spider-Man has everything under control. The tram operates daily from 6am until 2:30am and until 3:30am on weekends.

half-hour to 45 minutes from 9am to about 3:30pm, with more frequent ferries in the morning and extended hours in summer. Try to go early on a weekday to avoid the crowds that swarm in the afternoon, on weekends, and on holidays.

A stop at **Ellis Island** ⟨⟨ (p. 231) is included in the fare, but if you catch the last ferry, you can only visit the statue or Ellis Island, not both.

You can buy ferry tickets in advance via **www.statuereservations.com**, which will allow you to board without standing in the sometimes-long ticket line; however, there is an additional service charge of $1.75 per ticket. Even if you've already purchased tickets, arrive as much as 30 minutes before your desired ferry time to allow for increased security procedures prior to boarding. The ferry ride takes about 20 minutes.

Once on Liberty Island, you'll start to get an idea of the statue's immensity: She weighs 225 tons and measures 152 feet from foot to flame. Her nose alone is 4½ feet long, and her index finger is 8 feet long.

After September 11, 2001, access to the base of the statue was prohibited, but in recent years, access, while still somewhat limited (you can't climb to the statue's crown), was once again allowed. Now you can explore the Statue of Liberty Museum, peer into the inner structure through a glass ceiling near the base of the statue, and enjoy views from the observation deck on top of a 16-story pedestal.

On Liberty Island in New York Harbor. ⟨�C⟩ **212/363-3200** (general info), or 212/269-5755 (ticket/ferry info). www.nps.gov/stli or www.statuecruises.com. Free admission; ferry ticket to Statue of Liberty and Ellis Island $12 adults, $10 seniors, $5 children 3–17. Daily 9am–3:30pm (last ferry departs around 3:30pm); extended hours in summer. Subway: 4, 5 to Bowling Green; 1 to South Ferry. Walk south through Battery Park to Castle Clinton, the fort housing the ferry ticket booth.

Times Square *(Overrated* There's no doubting that Times Square has evolved into something much different than it was well over a decade ago, when it had a deservedly sleazy reputation. There is much debate among New Yorkers about which incarnation was better. For the natives, Times Square is a place we go out of our way to avoid. The crowds, even by New York standards, are stifling; the restaurants, mostly national chains, aren't very good; the shops, also mostly national chains, are unimaginative; and the attractions, such as Madame Tussaud's New York wax museum and Ripley's Believe it or Not, are kitschy. I suppose it's a little too Vegas for me. Still, you've come all this way; you've got to at least take a peek, if only for the amazing neon spectacle of it.

Most of the Broadway theaters are around Times Square, so plan your visit before or after the show you're going to see. For your pretheater meal, walk 2 blocks west to Ninth Avenue where you'll find a number of relatively inexpensive, good restaurants. If you are with the kids, the Ferris wheel in the Toys "R" Us store makes a visit to Times Square worthwhile.

Subway: 1, 2, 3, 7, S, N, Q, R, W to Times Sq.; A, C, E to 42nd St.–Port Authority.

Wall Street & the New York Stock Exchange   Wall Street—it's an iconic name, and the world's prime hub for bulls and bears everywhere. This narrow 18th-century lane (you'll be surprised at how little it is) is appropriately monumental, lined with neoclassical towers that reach as far skyward as the dreams and greed of investors who built it into the world's most famous financial market.

At the heart of the action is the New York Stock Exchange (NYSE), the world's largest securities trader, where billions change hands. The NYSE came into being in 1792, when merchants met daily under a nearby buttonwood tree to try to pass off to each other the U.S. bonds that had been sold to fund the Revolutionary War. By

World Trade Center Site (Ground Zero)

Do you call a place where over 3,000 people lost their lives an "attraction"? Or do you now call it a shrine? This is the quandary of the World Trade Center site. What had been a big hole for 5 years is a little more than that; construction began in early 2006 on the proposed "Freedom Tower" to be built at the site. But even though work is ongoing, there is still political bickering on what will rise from that hole. The new design retains essential elements of the original—soaring 1,776 feet into the sky, its illuminated mast evoking the Statue of Liberty's torch. From the square base, the Tower will taper into eight tall isosceles triangles, forming an octagon at its center. An observation deck will be located 1,362 feet above ground. Of course, all this could change by the time this book comes out.

For now, you can see the site through a viewing wall on the Church Street side of the site; on that "Wall of Heroes" are the names of those who lost their lives that day along with the history of the site, including photos of the construction of the World Trade Center in the late 1960s and how, after it opened in 1972, it changed the New York skyline and downtown. A walk along the Wall of Heroes remains a painfully moving experience.

The site is bounded by Church, Barclay, Liberty, and West streets. Call ℂ 212/484-1222, or go to www.nycvisit.com or www.southstseaport.org for viewing information; go to www.downtownny.com for lower-Manhattan area information and rebuilding updates. The Tribute Center gives guided tours of the site. Call ℂ 212/422-3520, or visit www.tributewtc.org for more information. Tours are given Monday to Friday at 11am and 1 and 3pm; Saturday and Sunday at noon, 1, 2, and 3pm. The fee is $10 for adults; under 12 free.

1903, they were trading stocks of publicly held companies in this Corinthian-columned Beaux Arts "temple" designed by George Post. About 3,000 companies are now listed on the exchange, trading nearly 314 billion shares valued at about $16 trillion. Unfortunately, the NYSE is no longer open to the public for tours.

11 Wall Street. ℂ 212/656-3000. www.nyse.com. Subway: J, M, Z to Broad St.; 2, 3, 4, 5 to Wall St.

Whitney Museum of American Art 𝕶𝕶   What is arguably the finest collection of 20th-century American art in the world belongs to the Whitney thanks to the efforts of Gertrude Vanderbilt Whitney. A sculptor herself, Whitney organized exhibitions by American artists shunned by traditional academies, assembled a sizable personal collection, and founded the museum in 1930 in Greenwich Village.

Today's museum is an imposing presence on Madison Avenue—an inverted three-tiered pyramid of concrete and gray granite with seven seemingly random windows designed by Marcel Breuer, a leader of the Bauhaus movement. The permanent collection consists of an intelligent selection of major works by Edward Hopper, George Bellows, Georgia O'Keeffe, Roy Lichtenstein, Jasper Johns, and other significant artists. A second-floor space is devoted exclusively to works from its permanent collection from 1900 to 1950, while the rest is dedicated to rotating exhibits.

Shows are usually well-curated and more edgy than what you'd see at MoMA or the Guggenheim (though not as left-of-mainstream as what you'll find at the New Museum). Topics range from topical surveys, such as "American Art in the Age of Technology" and "The Warhol Look: Glamour Style Fashion" to in-depth retrospectives of famous or lesser-known movements (such as Fluxus, the movement that spawned Yoko Ono, among others) and artists (Mark Rothko, Keith Haring, Duane Hanson, Bob Thompson). Free gallery tours are offered daily, and music, screenings, and lectures fill the calendar. The Whitney is notable for having the best museum restaurant in town: **Sarabeth's at the Whitney,** worth a visit in its own right.

945 Madison Ave. (at 75th St.). ⓒ 800/WHITNEY or 212/570-3676. www.whitney.org. Admission $15 adults, $10 seniors students free with valid IDs, free for children under 12, pay what you wish Fri 6–9pm. Wed–Thurs and Sat–Sun 11am–6pm; Fri 1–9pm. Subway: 6 to 77th St.

3 More Manhattan Museums

For the **Brooklyn Museum of Art** 𝕲𝕲, the **New York Transit Museum,** the **American Museum of the Moving Image** 𝕲, the **Queens Museum of Art,** the **Isamu Noguchi Garden Museum** 𝕲, the **P.S. 1 Contemporary Art Center,** and the **Louis Armstrong House Museum** 𝕲, see "Highlights of the Outer Boroughs," later in this chapter.

If you're traveling with the kids, also consider the museums listed under "Especially for Kids," on p. 282, which include the **Children's Museum of Manhattan** 𝕲, the **Sony Wonder Technology Lab,** and the **New York Hall of Science** 𝕲.

If you're interested in historic-house museums, see the box called "In Search of Historic Homes," on p. 259.

Also, don't forget to see what's on at the monumental **New York Public Library** 𝕲𝕲, which regularly holds excellent exhibitions. See p. 257.

American Folk Art Museum 𝕲𝕲   This gorgeous, ultramodern boutique museum is not only a stunning structure, but it also heralds American folk art's entry into the top echelon of museum-worthy art.

The modified open-plan interior features an extraordinary collection of traditional works from the 18th century to the self-taught artists and craftspeople of the present, reflecting the breadth and vitality of the American folk-art tradition. A splendid variety of quilts, in particular, makes the textiles collection the museum's most popular. The book-and-gift shop is outstanding, filled with one-of-a-kind objects.

45 W. 53rd St. (btwn Fifth and Sixth aves.). ⓒ 212/265-1040. www.folkartmuseum.org. Admission $9 adults, $7 seniors and students, free for children under 12, free to all Fri 5:30–8pm. Tues–Thurs and Sat–Sun 10:30am–5:30pm; Fri 10:30am–7:30pm. Subway: B, D, F, V 47th–50th/Rockefeller Center; E, V to Fifth Ave.

Asia Society   The Asia Society was founded in 1956 by John D. Rockefeller III with the goal of increasing understanding between Americans and Asians through art

---

Tips **Be an Early Bird**

New York is the city that never sleeps, and you shouldn't either—at least not too much. Get an early start on your day. Check opening times for museums and attractions and be there as soon as they open to avoid the crowds. It's no fun waiting on lines or peering over throngs of people to view exhibits. So remember the early bird gets the worm, and the uncrowded attraction!

exhibits, lectures, films, performances, and international conferences. The society is a leader in presenting contemporary Asian and Asian-American art. After a $30-million renovation that doubled the exhibition space, the society's headquarters is bigger, smarter, and better than ever. Never has so much of the core collection, which comprises Rockefeller's Pan-Asian acquisitions dating from 2000 B.C. to the 19th century, been on display before. Well-curated temporary exhibits run the gamut from "The New Way of Tea," exploring Japan's elaborate tea ceremony, to "Through Afghan Eyes: A Culture in Conflict, 1987–95," a study in photographs and video. Additionally, the mammoth calendar of events ranges from film screenings to arts lectures to discussion panels featuring experts in Pan-Asian and global politics, business, and more; call or check the website for a current schedule.

725 Park Ave. (at 70th St.). ✆ 212/288-6400. www.asiasociety.org. Gallery admission $10 adults, $7 seniors, $5 students with ID, free for children under 16, free to all Fri 6–9pm. Tues–Sun 11am–6pm (Fri to 9pm; except July 4–Labor Day). Subway: 6 to 68th St./Hunter College.

Center for Jewish History *Finds*   This 125,000-square-foot complex is the largest repository of Jewish history, art, and literature in the Diaspora. It unites five of America's leading institutions of Jewish scholarship: the American Jewish Historical Society (www.ajhs.org); the national archives of the Jewish people in the Americas; the Leo Baeck Institute (www.lbi.org), which documents the robust history of German-speaking Jewry from the 17th century until annihilation under the Nazis; the Yeshiva University Museum (www.yumuseum.org), with general-interest exhibits, plus a renowned collection of Judaica objects confiscated by the Nazis; the YIVO Institute for Jewish Research (www.yivoinstitute.org), which focuses on exhibits exploring the diversity of the Jewish experience; and the American Sephardi Federation (www.American SephardiFederation.org), representing the spiritual, cultural, and social traditions of the American Sephardic communities (Jews from southern Europe, North Africa, and the Middle East). Together, this union represents about 100 million archival documents, 500,000 books, and thousands of objects of art and ephemera, ranging from Thomas Jefferson's letter denouncing anti-Semitism to memorabilia of famous Jewish athletes.

The main gallery space is the **Yeshiva Museum,** which comprises four galleries, an outdoor sculpture garden, and a children's workshop; a range of exhibits also showcase various holdings belonging to the other institutions as well. A central feature is the **Reading Room,** home to open stacks accessible by serious researchers and lay historians alike, as well as the **Center Genealogy Institute,** which offers assistance in family-history research. Another huge component of the center is its 250-seat state-of-the-art auditorium, home to a packed schedule of lectures, music, and film presentations. If you get hungry, a kosher cafe is on-site.

15 W. 16th St. (btwn Fifth and Sixth aves.). ✆ 212/294-8301. www.cjh.org. Admission to Yeshiva University Museum $8 adults, $6 seniors and students; free admission to all other facilities. Yeshiva University Museum Sun and Tues–Thurs 11am–5pm. Reading Room and Genealogy Institute Mon–Thurs 9:30am–5pm; Fri by appt. All other exhibition galleries Mon–Thurs 9:30am–5pm; Fri 9am–3pm.; Sun 11am–5pm. Subway: L, N, R, 4, 5, 6 to 14th St./Union Sq.; F, V to 14th St.

The Cloisters *★★*   If it weren't for this branch of the Metropolitan Museum of Art, many New Yorkers would never get to this northernmost point in Manhattan. This remote yet lovely spot is devoted to the art and architecture of medieval Europe. Atop a cliff overlooking the Hudson River, you'll find a 12th-century chapter house, parts of five cloisters from medieval monasteries, a Romanesque chapel, and a 12th-century

Spanish apse brought intact from Europe. Surrounded by peaceful gardens, this is the one place on the island that can approximate the kind of solitude suitable to such a collection. Inside you'll find extraordinary works that include the Unicorn tapestries, sculpture, illuminated manuscripts, stained glass, ivory, and precious metal work.

Despite its remoteness, the Cloisters are quite popular, especially in fine weather, so try to schedule your visit during the week rather than on a crowded weekend afternoon. A free guided Highlights Tour is offered Tuesday through Friday at 3pm and Sunday at noon; gallery talks are also a regular feature. Additionally, Garden Tours are offered Tuesday through Sunday at 1pm in May, June, September, and October; lectures and other special programming are always on Sunday from noon to 2pm; and medieval music concerts are regularly held in the stunning 12th-century Spanish chapel. For an extra-special experience, you may want to plan your visit around one.

At the north end of Fort Tryon Park. © **212/923-3700.** www.metmuseum.org. Suggested admission (includes same-day entrance to the Metropolitan Museum of Art) $20 adults, $15 seniors, $10 students, free for children under 12. Nov–Feb Tues–Sun 9:30am–4:45pm; Mar–Oct Tues–Sun 9:30am–5:15pm. Subway: A to 190th St., then a 10-min. walk north along Margaret Corbin Dr., or pick up the M4 bus at the station (1 stop to Cloisters). Bus: M4 Madison Ave. (Fort Tryon Park–The Cloisters).

Cooper-Hewitt National Design Museum 🕭
Part of the Smithsonian Institution, the Cooper-Hewitt is housed in the Carnegie Mansion, built by steel magnate Andrew Carnegie in 1901, and undergoing a renovation of the Fox and Miller town houses and the Museum Mansion, which will create a third floor and expand gallery space by 80%. The renovation is scheduled to be completed in 2010. During the renovations, the museum remains open and galleries will continue to be devoted to changing exhibits that are invariably well conceived, engaging, and educational. Shows are both historic and contemporary in nature, and topics range from "The Work of Charles and Ray Eames: A Legacy of Invention" to "Russell Wright: Creating American Lifestyle" to "The Architecture of Reassurance: Designing the Disney Theme Parks." Many installations are drawn from the museum's own vast collection of industrial design, drawings, textiles, wall coverings, books, and prints.

On your way in, note the fabulous Art Nouveau–style copper-and-glass canopy above the entrance. And be sure to visit the garden, ringed with Central Park benches from various eras.

2 E. 91st St. (at Fifth Ave.). © **212/849-8400.** www.cooperhewitt.org. Admission $15 adults, $10 seniors and students, free for children under 12, free to all Fri 5–9pm. Mon–Thurs 10am–5pm; Fri 10am–9pm; Sat 10am–6pm; Sun noon–6pm. Subway: 4, 5, 6 to 86th St.

Dahesh Museum of Art
If you consider yourself a classicist, this small museum is for you. It's dedicated to 19th- and early-20th-century European academic art, a continuation of Renaissance, baroque, and rococo traditions that were overshadowed by the arrival of Impressionism on the art scene. (If you're not familiar with this academic school, expect lots of painstaking renditions of historical subjects and pastoral life.) Artists represented include Jean-Léon Gérôme, Lord Leighton, and Edwin Long, whose *Love's Labour Lost* is a cornerstone of the permanent collection.

580 Madison Ave. (btwn 56th and 57th sts.). © **212/759-0606.** www.daheshmuseum.org. Admission $10 adults, $8 seniors, $6 students, free for children under 12 and to all 1st Thurs of the month 6–9pm. Tues–Sun 11am–6pm; 1st Thurs of the month until 9pm. Subway: N, R, Q, W to 57th St.; 4, 5, 6 to 59th St.

El Museo del Barrio
What started in 1969 with a small display in a classroom in East Harlem is today the only museum in America dedicated to Puerto Rican,

Caribbean, and Latin American art. The northernmost Museum Mile institution has a permanent exhibit ranging from pre-Columbian artifacts to photographic art and video. The display of *santos de palo* (wood-carved religious figurines) is noteworthy, as is "Taíno, Ancient Voyagers of the Caribbean," dedicated to the highly developed cultures that Columbus encountered when he landed in the "New World." The well-curated exhibitions tend to focus on 20th-century artists and contemporary subjects.

1230 Fifth Ave. (at 104th St.). ℂ 212/831-7272. www.elmuseo.org. Suggested admission $6 adults, $4 seniors (free on Thurs) and students, free for children under 12. Wed–Sun 11am–5pm. Subway: 6 to 103rd St.

The Frick Collection 𝒦𝒦   Henry Clay Frick could afford to be an avid collector of European art after amassing a fortune as a pioneer in the coke and steel industries at the turn of the 20th century. To house his treasures and himself, he hired architects Carrère & Hastings to build this 18th-century French-style mansion (1914), one of the most beautiful remaining on Fifth Avenue.

Most appealing about the Frick is its intimate size and setting. This is a living testament to New York's vanished Gilded Age—the interior still feels like a private home (albeit a really, really rich guy's home) graced with beautiful paintings, rather than a museum. Come here to see the classics by some of the world's most famous painters: Titian, Bellini, Rembrandt, Turner, Vermeer, El Greco, and Goya, to name only a few. A highlight of the collection is the Fragonard Room, graced with the sensual rococo series "The Progress of Love." The portrait of Montesquieu by Whistler is also stunning. Included in the price of admission, the AcousticGuide audio tour is particularly useful because it allows you to follow your own path rather than a prescribed route. A free 22-minute video presentation is screened in the Music Room every half-hour from 10am to 4:30pm (from 1:30pm on Sun); starting with this helps to set the tone for what you'll see.

In addition, free chamber music concerts are held twice a month, generally every other Sunday at 5pm in fall and winter and select Thursdays at 5:45pm in warm weather; once-a-month lectures are offered select Wednesdays at 5:30pm. Call or visit the website for the current schedule and ticket information.

1 E. 70th St. (at Fifth Ave.). ℂ **212/288-0700**. www.frick.org. Admission $15 adults, $10 seniors, $5 students. Children under 10 not admitted; children under 16 must be accompanied by an adult. Tues–Sat 10am–6pm; Sun 11am–5pm. Closed all major holidays. Subway: 6 to 68th St./Hunter College.

International Center of Photography 𝒦 *(Finds)*   The ICP is one of the world's premier educators, collectors, and exhibitors of photographic art. The state-of-the-art gallery space is ideal for viewing rotating exhibitions of the museum's 50,000-plus prints as well as visiting shows. The emphasis is on contemporary photographic works, but historically important photographers aren't ignored. This is a "must see" on any photography buff's list.

1133 Sixth Ave. (at 43rd St.). ℂ 212/857-0000. www.icp.org. Admission $12 adults, $8 seniors and students, under 12 free. Tues–Thurs and Sat–Sun 10am–6pm; Fri 10am–8pm. Subway: B, D, F, V to 42nd St.

USS *Intrepid* Sea-Air-Space Museum 𝒦𝒦 *(Kids)*   After almost 2 years in drydock, the USS *Intrepid* is scheduled to return to its now refurbished home on Pier 86 in October, 2008; and the museum will reopen on Veteran's Day, November 11 2008. The most astonishing thing about the aircraft carrier USS *Intrepid* is how it can be simultaneously so big and so small. It's a few football fields long, weighs 40,000 tons, holds 40 aircraft, and sometimes doubles as a ballroom for society functions. But stand there and think about landing an A-12 jet on the deck and suddenly it's minuscule. Furthermore, in the narrow passageways below, you'll find it isn't quite the roomiest of vessels. Now a National Historic Landmark, the exhibit also includes the naval destroyer USS *Edson* and the submarine USS *Growler,* the only intact strategic missile submarine open to the public anywhere in the world, as well as a collection of vintage and modern aircraft, including the A-12 Blackbird, the world's fastest spy plane, and a retired British Airways Concorde jet.

Kids just love this place. They, and you, can climb inside a replica Revolutionary War submarine, sit in an A-6 Intruder cockpit, and follow the progress of America's astronauts as they work in space. There are even navy flight simulators—including a "Fly with the Blue Angels" program—for educational thrill rides in the Technologies Hall. Look for family-oriented activities and events at least 1 Saturday a month.

The program "All Hands on Deck" teaches children and adults how things work on ships, plus there's a AH-1 Cobra attack helicopter. The action-packed *Intrepid Wings* shows aircraft carrier take-offs and recoveries in the new Allison and Howard Lutnick Theater; the film runs continuously throughout the day. The exhibit "Remembering 9/11" recalls those lost, both civilians and rescuers. The grand visitor center makes for an impressive entrance, and the massive museum store is well stocked; goods include NYPD and FDNY logo gear. Dress warmly for a winter visit—it's almost impossible to heat an aircraft carrier.

Pier 86 (W. 46th St. at Twelfth Ave.). © 212/245-0072. www.intrepidmuseum.org. At press time, rate and hours were not announced. Call or check the website for the most up-to-date information, and to see if the museum reopening is still on schedule. Subway: A, C, E to 42nd St./Port Authority. Bus: M42 Crosstown.

The Jewish Museum   Housed in a Gothic-style mansion renovated in 1993 by AIA Gold Medal winner Kevin Roche, this wonderful museum now has the world-class space it deserves to showcase its remarkable collections, which chronicle 4,000 years of Jewish history. The two-floor permanent exhibit, "Culture and Continuity: The Jewish Journey," tells the story of the Jewish experience from ancient times through today, and is the museum's centerpiece. Artifacts include daily objects that might have served the authors of the books of Genesis, Psalms, and Job, and a great assemblage of intricate torahs. A wonderful collection of classic TV and radio programs is available for viewing through the Goodkind Resource Center (as any fan of television's golden age knows, its finest comic moments were Jewish comedy). The scope of the exhibit is phenomenal, and its story an enlightening—and intense—one. A random-access audio guide is geared to families (free with admission). In addition to the in-house shop, don't miss the Jewish Museum Design Shop, housed in the adjacent brownstone.

1109 Fifth Ave. (at 92nd St.). © 212/423-3200. www.thejewishmuseum.org. Admission $12 adults, $10 seniors $7.50 students, free for children under 12, pay what you wish on Sat. Check website for special online admission discounts ($2 off at press time). Sat–Wed 11am–5:45pm; Thurs 11am–8pm; Fri 11am–3pm. Subway: 4, 5, 6 to 86th St.; 6 to 96th St.

Lower East Side Tenement Museum 🎯 *Kids*   This museum is the first-ever National Trust for Historic Preservation site that was not the home of someone rich or famous. It's something quite different: a five-story tenement that 10,000 people from 25 countries called home between 1863 and 1935—people who had come to the United States looking for the American dream and made 97 Orchard St. their first stop. The tenement museum tells the story of the great immigration boom of the late 19th and early 20th centuries, when the Lower East Side was considered the "Gateway to

America." A visit here makes a good follow-up to an Ellis Island trip to see what happened to all the people who passed through that famous way station.

The only way to see the museum is by guided tour. Two primary tenement tours, held on all open days and lasting an hour, offer a satisfying exploration of the museum: "Piecing It Together: Immigrants in the Garment Industry," which focuses on the restored apartment and the lives of its turn-of-the-20th-century tenants, an immigrant Jewish family named Levine from Poland; and "Getting By: Weathering the Great Depressions of 1873 and 1929," featuring the homes of the German-Jewish Gumpertz family and the Sicilian-Catholic Baldizzi family, respectively. A knowledgeable guide leads you into each dingy urban time capsule, where several apartments have been restored to their lived-in condition, and recounts the real-life stories of the families who occupied them in fascinating detail. You can pair them for an in-depth look at the museum, since the apartments and stories are so different; however, one tour serves as an excellent introduction if you don't want to invest an entire afternoon here.

These tours are not really for kids, however, who won't enjoy the serious tone and "don't touch" policy. Much better for them is the 45-minute, weekends-only Confino Family Apartment tour, a living-history program geared to families, which allows kids to converse with an interpreter who plays teenage immigrant Victoria Confino (ca. 1916); kids can also handle whatever they like and try on period clothes.

The hour-long **Streets Where We Lived** neighborhood heritage walking tour is also offered on weekends from April through December. Small permanent and rotating exhibits, including photos, videos, and a model tenement, are housed in the visitor center and exhibition space in the tenement building at 97 Orchard St. Special tours and programs are sometimes on the schedule.

Tours are limited in number and sell out quickly, so it pays to buy tickets in advance, which you can do online or over the phone by calling **Ticketweb** at ℂ **800/965-4827.**

108 Orchard St. (btwn Delancey and Broome sts.). ℂ **212/431-0233.** www.tenement.org. Tenement and walking tours $15 adults, $11 seniors and students; Confino Apt. $17 adults, $13 seniors and students. Tenement tours depart Tues–Fri every 40 min. 1–4pm; Sat–Sun every half-hour 11am–4:45pm. Confino Apt. tour Sat–Sun hourly noon–3pm. Walking tour Apr–Dec Sat–Sun 1 and 3pm. Subway: F to Delancey St.; J, M, Z to Essex St.

Morgan Library 𝕶𝕶 𝓕𝓲𝓷𝓭𝓼   This New York treasure, boasting one of the world's most important collections of original manuscripts, rare books and bindings, master drawings, and personal writings has become newly popular since extensive renovations and an addition designed by architect Renzo Piano were completed in 2006. Those renovations include a welcoming entrance on Madison Avenue; new and renovated galleries, so that more of the library's holdings can be exhibited; a modern auditorium; and a new Reading Room with greater capacity and electronic resources and expanded space for collections storage. Some of the Library's recent exhibitions include one on the life of Bob Dylan through music, letters, and memorabilia and an exhibit on illustrator, Saul Steinberg. You can lunch in the intimate **Morgan Dining Room** as if you were dining in JP's own quarters.

225 Madison Ave. (between 36th and 37th sts.). ℂ **212/685-0008.** www.themorgan.org. $12 adults, $8 seniors and students, under 12 free. Tues–Thurs 10:30am–5pm, Fri 10:30am–9pm, Sat 10am–6pm, Sun 11am–6pm. Subway: 6 to 33rd St.

Museum of Arts and Design 𝕶 𝓕𝓲𝓷𝓭𝓼   Formerly called the American Craft Museum, this small but aesthetically pleasing museum is the nation's top showcase for contemporary crafts. The collection focuses on objects that are prime examples of form and function, ranging from jewelry to baskets to vessels to furniture. You'll see a strong emphasis on material as well as craft, whether it be fiber, ceramics, or metal. Special exhibitions can range from Expressionist clay sculpture to fine bookbinding, and can celebrate movements or single artisans. Stop into the gorgeous shop even if you don't make it into the museum. After closing its current home on W. 53rd St. at the end of April, 2008, the museum will move a little uptown and west, reopening in September 2008, in the quirky and controversial building designed by modernist architect Edward Durrell Stone in 1963 at 2 Columbus Circle. The Museum's exhibition space will more than double. Check with the Museum's website for any price or hour changes, and updates on the move.

2 Columbus Circle (as of Sept 2008). ✆ 212/956-3535. www.madmuseum.org. Admission $9 adults, $7 students and seniors, free for children under 12, pay what you wish Thurs 6–8pm. Fri–Wed 10am–6pm; Thurs 10am–8pm. Subway: 1, 2, 3, A, C, B, D to 59th St./Columbus Circle.

Museum of Chinese in the Americas   In the heart of Chinatown, on the second floor of a century-old school building, this museum is dedicated to "reclaiming, preserving, and interpreting the history and culture of Chinese and their descendants in the Western Hemisphere." Past exhibitions include "Have You Eaten Yet? The Chinese Restaurant in America" and "Fly to Freedom," a collection of 123 paper sculptures made by passengers of the ill-fated ship *Golden Venture* which ran aground in 1993 and most of whose passengers were detained by immigration officials for up to 4 years.

70 Mulberry St. (at Bayard St.) ✆ 212/619-4785. www.moca-nyc.org. Admission: $2 adults, $1 students and senior, free on Fridays and for children under 12. Open Tues–Sun noon–6pm. Subway: 6, N, R, Q, W, J, M, Z to Canal St.

Museum of Jewish Heritage—A Living Memorial to the Holocaust ♺   In the south end of Battery Park City, the Museum of Jewish Heritage occupies a strikingly spare six-sided building designed by award-winning architect Kevin Roche, with a six-tier roof alluding to the Star of David and the six million murdered in the Holocaust. The permanent exhibits—"Jewish Life a Century Ago," "The War Against the Jews," and "Jewish Renewal"—recount the daily prewar lives, the unforgettable horror that destroyed them, and the tenacious renewal experienced by European and immigrant Jews in the years from the late 19th century to the present. The museum's power derives from the way it tells that story: through the objects, photographs, documents, and, most poignantly, through the videotaped testimonies of Holocaust victims, survivors, and their families, all chronicled by Steven Spielberg's Survivors of the Shoah Visual History Foundation.

While advance tickets are not usually necessary, you may want to purchase them to guarantee admission; call ✆ **212/945-0039.** Audio tours narrated by Meryl Streep and Itzhak Perlman are available at the museum for an additional $5.

36 Battery Place (at 1st Place), Battery Park City. ✆ **646/437-4200.** www.mjhnyc.org. Admission $10 adults, $7 seniors, $5 students, free for children under 12 and for everyone Wed 4–8pm. Check website for $2-off admission coupon (available at press time). Sun–Tues and Thurs 10am–5:45pm; Wed 10am–8pm; Fri and eves of Jewish holidays 10am–3pm. Subway: 4, 5 to Bowling Green.

Museum of Sex *Finds*   How many cities can claim their own Museum of Sex? Not many in the U.S., that's for sure! This one, despite its provocative title, offers a studied, historical look at the history of sex in our culture. In 2008, the exhibit "Action: Sex and the Moving Image" and "Sex in Design" were featured. *Note:* Many of the displays are very graphic, so the museum may not be for everyone.

233 Fifth Ave. (at 27th St.). ✆ 212/689-6337. www.museumofsex.com. Admission adults $15 plus tax; students and seniors $14 plus tax. No one under 18 admitted. Sun–Fri 11am–6:30pm; Sat 11am–8pm. Last ticket sold 45 min. before museum closing. Subway: N, R, 6 to 28th St.

Art for Art's Sake: The Gallery Scene

Manhattan has more than 500 private art galleries, selling everything from old masters to tomorrow's news. Galleries are free to the public, generally Tuesday through Saturday from 10am to 6pm. Saturday afternoon gallery hopping, in particular, is a favorite pastime—nobody will expect you to buy, so don't worry.

The best way to winnow down your choices is by perusing the "Art Guide" in the Friday weekend section of the *New York Times,* or in the back of the Sunday "Arts & Leisure" section; the listings section at the back of the weekly *New York* magazine, which I find to be particularly descriptive and user-friendly; the Art section in the weekly *Time Out New York;* or the *New Yorker*'s weekly "Goings on About Town" section. You can also find the latest exhibition listings online at **www.nymetro.com**, whose "Arts" page gives you full access to *New York* magazine's listings, **www.artnet.com**, and **www.galleryguide.org**. An excellent source—more for practicals on the galleries and the artists and genres they represent rather than current shows—is **www.artincontext.org**. The *Gallery Guide* is available at most galleries around town.

I suggest picking a gallery or a show in a neighborhood that seems to suit your taste, and just start browsing from there. Be aware that my list below doesn't even begin to scratch the surface. There are many, many more galleries in each neighborhood, as well as smaller concentrations of galleries in areas like the East Village, TriBeCa, and Brooklyn (check the Art in Context site).

Keep in mind that uptown galleries tend to be more traditional and exclusive-feeling, downtown galleries more high-ticket contemporary, and far-west Chelsea galleries the most cutting-edge. Museum-quality works dominate uptown, while raw talent and emerging artists are most common in west Chelsea. But there are constant surprises in all neighborhoods.

UPTOWN   Uptown galleries are clustered in and around the glamorous crossroads of Fifth Avenue and 57th Street as well as on and off stylish Madison Avenue in the 60s, 70s, and 80s. Unlike their upstart Chelsea and SoHo counterparts, these blue-chip galleries maintain a quiet white-glove demeanor. They include art-world powerhouses **Gagosian Gallery,** 980 Madison Ave. (© 212/744-2313; www.gagosian.com), and **PaceWildenstein,** 32 E. 57th St. (© 212/421-3292; www.pacewildenstein.com), whose focus is on classic modernism, representing such artists as Jim Dine, Barbara Hepworth, and Claes Oldenburg; the **Richard Gray Gallery,** 1018 Madison Ave., fourth floor (© 212/472-8787; www.richardgraygallery.com), featuring American and European contemporary works, with artists ranging from Joan Miró to David Hockney; the **Margo Feiden Galleries,** 699 Madison Ave. (© 212/677-5330; www.alhirschfeld.com), the sole authorized representative of the works of the late master ink caricaturist Al Hirschfeld; the Mary Boone Gallery, 745 Fifth Ave. (© 212/752-2929; www.maryboonegallery.com), known for success with such artists as Ross Bleckner and Nancy Ellison; and **Wildenstein & Co, Inc.**, the classical big brother of PaceWildenstein, 19 E. 64th St. ((C) **212/879-0500**; www.wildenstein.com), both specializing in big-ticket works: old masters, Impressionism, and Renaissance paintings and drawings.

CHELSEA The area in the west 20s, between Tenth and Eleventh avenues, is home to the avant-garde of today's New York art scene, with west 26th serving as the unofficial "gallery row." Most galleries are not in storefronts but in the large spaces of multistory former garages and warehouses. Galleries worth seeking out include **Paula Cooper**, 534 W. 21st St. ((C) **212/255-1105**), a heavyweight in the modern-art world, specializing in conceptual and minimal art; one of Chelsea's biggest galleries, the **Matthew Marks Gallery**, 523 W. 24th St. ((C) **212/243-0200**); **the George Billis Gallery**, 511 W. 25th St. ((C) **212/645-2621**; www.georgebillis.com), which shows works by talented emerging artists; **Barbara Gladstone Gallery**, 515 W. 24th St. ((C) **212/206-9300**; www.gladstonegallery.com); uptown powerhouse **Gagosian Gallery**, 555 W. 24th St. ((C) **212/741-1111**; www.gagosian.com), which shows such major modern artists as Richard Serra and Julian Schnabel; **Kinz Tillou Feigen**, 529 W. 20th St., 11th Floor ((C) **212/929-0500**; www.ktfgallery.com), the modern counterpart to the uptown Old Masters gallery; **Cheim & Read**, 547 W. 25th St. ((C) **212/242-7727**; www.cheimread.com), which often shows works by such high-profile pop artists as Diane Arbus and Robert Mapplethorpe; **Alexander and Bonin**, 132 Tenth Ave. ((C) **212/367-7474**; www.alexanderandbonin.com), which mounts excellent solo exhibitions; **James Cohan Gallery**, 533 W. 26th St. ((C) **212/714-9500**; www.jamescohan.com), particularly strong in modern photography; and **Lehmann Maupin**, 540 W. 26th St. ((C) **212/255-2923**; www.lehmannmaupin.com), whose roster runs the gamut from young unknowns to such contemporary masters as Ross Bleckner. For a comprehensive listing of the Chelsea galleries, check the website **www.westchelseaarts.com**.

DOWNTOWN SoHo remains colorful, if less edgy than it used to be, with the action centered around West Broadway and encroaching onto the edge of Chinatown. **Peter Blum Gallery**, 99 Wooster St. ((C) **212/343-0441**), which showcased the divine Kim Sooja, a Korean artist who uses traditional Korean bedcovers to comment on the promise of wedded bliss; **O. K. Harris**, 383 W. Broadway ((C) **212/431-3600**; www.okharris.com), which shows a fascinating variety of contemporary painting, sculpture, and photography; and **Louis K. Meisel**, 141 Prince St. ((C) **212/677-1340**; www.meiselgallery.com), specializing in photo-realism and American pinup art (yep, Petty and Vargas girls). In TriBeCa, try **Cheryl Hazan Arts Gallery**, 35 N. Moore St. ((C) **212/343-8964**; www.cherylhazan.com), or **DFN Gallery**, 210 11th Ave. 6th Floor ((C) **212/334-3400**; www.dfngallery.com), which focus on fresh, distinctive contemporary art.

Nights at the Museum

No, the exhibits do not come alive once the sun goes down. But on certain nights the usually demure museum atmosphere changes into one of a slightly-less-demure party scene. Here are a few museums that offer a variety of nighttime revelry amongst the art.

Bronx Museum of the Arts (1040 Grand Concourse; ✆ **718/681-6000;** www. bronxmuseum.org): Party in the house! Or, in this case, the museum. On the first Friday every month, from 6 until 10pm, the museum features live music, poetry readings, video screenings and art performance. Admission is free.

Brooklyn Museum, (200 Eastern Parkway, ✆ **718/638-5000;** www.brooklyn-museum.org): **First Saturday** is the Brooklyn Museum of Art's ambitious and popular program that takes place on (you guessed it), the first Saturday of each month. It runs from 5 to 11pm and includes free admission and a slate of live music, films, dancing, curator talks, and other entertainment that can get pretty esoteric—think karaoke, lesbian poetry, silent film, experimental jazz, and disco.

The Rose Center for Earth and Space at the American Museum of Natural History (Central Park West, btwn 77th and 81st sts.; ✆ 212/769-5100 for information, or 212/769-5200): On the first Friday each month, the museum, open until 8:45pm features "Starry Nights," live jazz, and tapas and wine. The museum's suggested admission covers admission to Starry Nights, but seating is on a first come, first serve basis.

Solomon R. Guggenheim Museum (1071 Fifth Ave., at 89th St.; ✆ **212/ 423-3500.** www.guggenheim.org.): "Art After Dark: First Fridays at the Guggenheim." You can explore the Guggenheim on the first Friday of every month from 9pm until 1am while sipping cocktails and listening to DJs spin their magic. Admission is $25 or free to Guggenheim members.

Whitney Museum of Art (945 Madison Ave., at 75th St.; ✆ **800/944-8639;** www.whitney.org): Every Friday, between 6 and 9pm, it's "Whitney After Hours" featuring live music and artist appearances with a "pay-as-you-wish" admission.

Museum of the City of New York   A wide variety of objects—costumes, photographs, prints, maps, dioramas, and memorabilia—trace the history of New York City from its beginnings as a humble Dutch colony in the 16th century to its present-day prominence. Two outstanding permanent exhibits are the re-creation of John D. Rockefeller's master bedroom and dressing room, and the space devoted to "Broadway!," a history of New York theater. Kids will love "New York Toy Stories," a permanent exhibit showcasing toys and dolls owned and adored by centuries of New York children. The permanent "Painting the Town: Cityscapes of New York" explores the changing cityscape from 1809 to 1997, and carries new profundity in the wake of the September 11, 2001, terrorist attacks. In 2008, the exhibits, "Manhattan Noon: The photographs of Gus Powell" and "Catholics in New York" were featured.

1220 Fifth Ave. (at 103rd St.). 𝒞 **212/534-1672**. www.mcny.org. Suggested admission $9 adults, $5 seniors, students, and children, $20 families. Tues–Sun 10am–5pm. Admission free Sun 10am–noon. Subway: 6 to 103rd St.

National Museum of the American Indian, George Gustav Heye Center

This impressive collection represents the Smithsonian Institution. The collection spans more than 10,000 years of native heritage, gathered a century ago mainly by New York banking millionaire George Gustav Heye. About 70% of the collection is dedicated to the natives of North America and Hawaii; the rest represents the cultures of Mexico and Central and South America. There's a wealth of material here, but it's not as well organized as it could be. The museum also hosts temporary themed exhibitions and interpretive programs, plus free storytelling, music, and dance presentations.

The museum is in the beautiful 1907 Beaux Arts **U.S. Customs House** 𝒜, designed by Cass Gilbert, a National Historic Landmark worth a look in its own right.

1 Bowling Green (btwn State and Whitehall sts.). 𝒞 **212/514-3700**. www.nmai.si.edu. Free admission. Daily 10am–5pm (Thurs until 8pm). Subway: 4, 5 to Bowling Green; R, W to Whitehall; 1 to South Ferry.

Neue Galerie New York (Finds

This museum is dedicated to German and Austrian art and design, with a particular focus on the early 20th century. Displayed on two floors, the collection features painting, works on paper, decorative arts, and other media from such artists as Klimt, Kokoschka, Kandinsky, Klee, and leaders of the Wiener Werkstätte decorative arts and Bauhaus applied arts movements, such as Adolf Loos and Mies van der Rohe, respectively. The gallery made headlines in 2006 when it acquired Klimt's *Portrait of Adele Bloch-Bauer I*—dubbed the "Golden Adele"—for a record-setting $135 million. The museum floated the idea of adding a high premium (up to $50) to view its new masterpiece, but the outcry caused the management to reconsider. You can see the Golden Adele for the $15 admission fee, without extra charge. In Fall 2008 through early 2009, you can see the work of Alfred Kubin, and Spring 2009 brings the exhibition "The Birth Of Expressionism: Brücke In Dresden And Berlin, 1905–13" through the end of June. Once occupied by Mrs. Cornelius Vanderbilt III, the impeccably restored, landmark-designated 1914 Carrère & Hastings building (they built the New York Public Library as well) is worth a look itself. **Cafe Sabarsky** is modeled on a Viennese cafe, so museumgoers in need of a snack break can expect a fine Linzer torte.

1048 Fifth Ave. (at 86th St.). 𝒞 **212/628-6200**. www.neuegalerie.org. Admission $15 adults, $10 seniors and students, under 12 not admitted, under 16 must be accompanied by an adult. Fri 11am–9pm; Thurs and Sat–Mon 11am–6pm. Subway: 4, 5, 6 to 86th St.

New Museum of Contemporary Art 𝒜

Like boxes haphazardly piled upon one another, the seven-story New Museum of Contemporary Art, rising above the tenements of the Lower East Side, is New York's newest (2007) museum icon. But it's not only the exterior that catches the eye; the exhibits at the New Museum reflect the slightly offbeat, slanted look of the museum. The museum's debut exhibition, "Unmonumental," a four-part series displaying 21st-century sculptures, objects, video, and collages by 30 international artists, was a fitting beginning to what promises to be a bright future. On the first Saturday of each month, the museum offers programs for families with thematic tours, conversations with artists, and creative activities, all free of charge. Advance registration is required.

235 Bowery (at Prince St.) 𝒞 **212/219-1222**. www.newmuseum.org. Admission: $12 adult, $8 Senior, $6 student, 18 and under free; free for all Thurs 7–10pm. Wed noon–6pm; Thurs–Fri noon–10pm; Sat–Sun noon–6pm. Subway: 6 to Spring St; N, R to Prince St.

New York City Fire Museum *&* *(Kids*   Housed in a three-story 1904 firehouse, the former quarters of FDNY Engine Co. 30, this museum offers one of the country's most extensive collections of fire-service memorabilia from the 18th century to the present. It is also the best place to pay tribute to the 343 heroic firefighters who lost their lives blocks away in the World Trade Center disaster. Expect ongoing changing exhibits relating to the September 11, 2001, terrorist attacks. Other displays range from vintage fire marks to fire trucks (including the last-known example of a 1921 pumper) to the gear and tools of modern firefighters. Also look for leather hoses, fire-boats, and Currier & Ives prints, plus a new exhibit on fire safety and burn prevention especially geared toward families. Best of all, real firefighters are almost always on hand to share stories and fire-safety information with kids. The retail store sells authorized FDNY logo wear and souvenirs. Call ahead for details on scheduling a guided tour.

278 Spring St. (btwn Varick and Hudson sts.). *C* 212/691-1303. www.nycfiremuseum.org. Suggested admission $5 adults, $2 seniors and students, $1 children under 12. Tues–Sat 10am–5pm; Sun 10am–4pm. Subway: C, E to Spring St.;1 to Houston St.

New York City Police Museum   Located in the first precinct station house, built in 1901, the museum exhibits police equipment from throughout the years, such as pistols, uniforms, and vehicles, along with really fun stuff such as master burglar Willie Sutton's lock picks and a machine gun used by Al Capone. At press time, a permanent exhibit chronicling the role the NYPD played in the response to the September 11 terrorist attacks was under construction.

100 Old Slip (btwn Water and South sts.) *C* 212/480-3100. www.nycpolicemuseum.org. Admission: $5 adults, $3 seniors, $2 children 6–18, free for under 6. Mon–Sat 10am–5pm. Subway: 2, 3 to Wall St.

New-York Historical Society *&*   Launched in 1804, the New-York Historical Society is a major repository of American history, culture, and art, with a special focus on New York and its broader cultural significance. The grand neoclassical edifice near the Museum of Natural History has finally emerged from the renovation tent. Now open on the fourth floor is the **Henry Luce III Center for the Study of American Culture,** a state-of-the-art study facility and gallery of fine and decorative arts, which displays more than 40,000 objects amassed over 200 years—including paintings, sculpture, Tiffany lamps, textiles, furniture, even carriages—that had been in storage for decades. Also look for paintings from Hudson River School artists Thomas Cole, Asher Durand, and Frederic Church, including Cole's five-part masterpiece "The Course of Empire." Of interest to scholars and ephemera buffs are the extensive Library Collections, which include books, manuscripts, maps, newspapers, photographs, and documents chronicling the American experience. (An appointment may be necessary to view some or all of the Library Collections, so call ahead.)

An extensive, top-quality calendar of programs runs the gamut from story hours to Irving Berlin music nights to lectures by such luminaries as Ric Burns to expert-led walks through Manhattan neighborhoods and self-guided interactive tours such as the remarkable "Hidden Sites of Slavery and Freedom" tour; call or check the website for schedules.

170 Central Park West (at 77th St.). *C* 212/873-3400. www.nyhistory.org. Admission $10 adults, $7 seniors and educators, $6 students, free for children 12 and under; free Fri 6–8pm. Tues–Sun 10am–6pm (Fri until 8pm). Subway: B, C to 81st St.; 1 to 79th St.

The Paley Center for Media   Formerly known as the Museum of Television and Radio, if you can resist the allure of this museum, I'd wager you've spent the last 70

Moments Sacred Ground

In 1991, during the construction of a federal building on the corner of Duane Street and Broadway, workers unearthed human remains. Those remains, it turned out, were of enslaved and free African slaves, and the site where they were discovered was part of the largest Colonial-Era cemetery for blacks in the United States. Building on the site was halted and in 1993 declared a National Historic Landmark. In 2006, the site was designated a national monument and put under the jurisdiction of the National Parks Services. Finally, in late 2007, after almost 16 years, the **African Burial Ground Memorial** (between Duane and Elk sts.; ℂ **212/637-2019**; www.nps. gov/afbg) was constructed to honor the final resting place of an estimated 15,000 Africans.

The granite memorial sandwiched between towering glass-and-steel federal buildings has seven design elements, including a triangular structure that symbolizes the ship passage to the new world from Africa, and religious symbols from 20 countries of the African Diaspora on a spiral wall that leads down to a map of the world centered in West Africa. It's a moving memorial and well worth visiting while exploring downtown New York.

There is a small **visitor's center** in the IRS building at 290 Broadway, adjacent to the memorial, but because it is a federal building, you have to go through a security check to enter. The Memorial is open to the public, free of charge, from 9am until 5pm daily except Thanksgiving, Christmas, and New Year's Day.

years in a bubble. You can watch and hear all the great personalities of TV and radio—from Uncle Miltie to Johnny Carson to Jerry Seinfeld—at a private console (available for 2 hrs.). You can also conduct computer searches to pick out the great moments of history, viewing almost anything that made its way onto the airwaves, from the Beatles' first appearance on *The Ed Sullivan Show* to the crumbling of the Berlin Wall (the collection consists of 75,000 programs and commercials). Selected programs are also presented in two theaters and two screening rooms, which can range from "Barbra Streisand: The Television Performances" to little-seen Monty Python episodes.

25 W. 52nd St. (btwn Fifth and Sixth aves.). ℂ **212/621-6600**. www.mtr.org. Admission $10 adults, $8 seniors and students, $5 children under 14. Tues–Sun noon–6pm (Thurs until 8pm) Subway: B, D, F, V to 47th–50th sts./Rockefeller Center; E, V to 53rd St.

Scandinavia House: The Nordic Center in America *(Finds* Dedicated to both the shared and unique cultures of Denmark, Finland, Iceland, Norway, and Sweden, Scandinavia House features two floors of galleries and an outdoor sculpture terrace displaying rotating art and design exhibits that can range from "Scandia: Important Early Maps of the Northern Regions" to "Strictly Swedish: An Exhibition of Contemporary Design." The rest of the space, including the 168-seat Victor Borge Hall, is dedicated to a full calendar of lectures, films, music and drama performances, and scholarly presentations, all of a Nordic ilk. The exquisite modern building—designed to showcase Scandinavian materials and aesthetics—is worth a look in itself, especially if you're a modern-architecture buff. Guided tours are offered Tuesday and Thursday at 2pm and last a half-hour; they're free, but reservations are recommended.

The shop is a riot of fine Scandinavian design, and the excellent AQ Café—an off-shoot of the terrific Midtown restaurant Aquavit (p. 191)—serves up Swedish meat-balls and other Scandinavian delicacies.

58 Park Ave. (btwn 37th and 38th sts.). ℂ 212/879-9779. www.scandinaviahouse.org. Suggested admission to 3rd-and 4th-floor galleries $3, $2 seniors and students; free admission to other spaces. Exhibitions Tues–Sat noon–6pm; cafe Mon–Sat 10am–5pm; store Mon–Sat noon–6pm. Subway: 6 to 33rd St.; 4, 5, 6, 7, S to 42nd St./Grand Central.

Schomburg Center for Research in Black Culture   Arturo Alfonso Schomburg, a black Puerto Rican, set himself to accumulating materials about blacks in America, and his massive collection—one of the largest collections of African-American mate-rials in the world—is housed and preserved at this research branch of the New York Public Library. The Exhibition Hall, the Latimer/Edison Gallery, and the Reading Room host changing exhibits related to black culture, such as "Lest We Forget: The Triumph over Slavery" and "Masterpieces of African Motherhood." A rich calendar of talks and performing-arts events is also part of the program. Make an appointment for a guided tour so you can see the 1930s murals by Harlem Renaissance artist Aaron Douglas; it'll be worth your while. Academics and others interested in a more com-plete look at the center's holdings can preview what's available online. Call to inquire about current exhibitions and information on tours and public programs.

515 Malcolm X Blvd. (Lenox Ave., btwn 135th and 136th sts.). ℂ 212/491-2200. www.nypl.org. Free admission. Tues–Sat 10am–6pm; Sun 1–5pm. Subway: 2, 3 to 135th St.

Skyscraper Museum   Wowed by the sheer verticality in this town? Awed by the architectural marvel that is the high-rise? You're not alone. If you'd like to learn more about the technology, culture, and muscle behind it all, seek out this formerly itiner-ant museum, which moved into its first permanent home in 2004 in the 38-story Skidmore, Owings & Merrill tower that also houses the Ritz-Carlton New York, Bat-tery Park. The space comprises two galleries, one housing a permanent exhibition ded-icated to the evolution of Manhattan's commercial skyline, the other for changing shows. In 2008 the museum featured "Vertical Cities: Hong Kong/New York," an exhibition of the world's two major skyscraper cities.

39 Battery Place (Little West St. and 1st Place). ℂ 212/968-1961. www.skyscraper.org. Admission: $5 adults, $2.50 seniors and students. Wed–Sun noon–6pm. Subway: 4, 5 to Bowling Green.

South Street Seaport & Museum _Kids_   Dating back to the 17th century, this landmark historic district on the East River encompasses 11 square blocks of historic buildings, a maritime museum, several piers, shops, and restaurants.

You can explore most of the Seaport on your own. It's a beautiful but somewhat odd place. The mainly 18th- and 19th-century buildings lining the cobbled streets and alleyways are impeccably restored but nevertheless have a theme-park air about them, no doubt due to the mall-familiar shops housed within. The Seaport's biggest tourist attraction is Pier 17, a historic barge converted into a mall, complete with food court and cheap-jewelry kiosks.

Despite its rampant commercialism, the Seaport is well worth a look. There's a good amount of history to be discovered here, most of it around the South Street Sea-port Museum, a fitting tribute to the sea commerce that once thrived here. On week-ends the museum dedicates Saturday and Sunday afternoons to family fun with music, art, and other activities for children 4 and older.

In addition to the galleries—which house paintings and prints, ship models, scrimshaw, and nautical designs, as well as frequently changing exhibitions—there are a number of historic ships berthed at the pier to explore, including the 1911 four-masted *Peking* and the 1893 Gloucester fishing schooner *Lettie G. Howard.* A few of the boats are living museums and restoration works in progress; the 1885 cargo schooner *Pioneer* (© 212/748-8786) offers 2-hour public sails daily from early May through September. Tickets for the early and late voyages (1 and 9:30pm) are $25 for adults and $20 for students, seniors, and children 12 and under. Add $5 to the prices for the 4 and 7pm departures. If you'd rather keep those sea legs on dry land, the museum offers a number of guided walking tours; call or check **www.southstseaport. org** for details.

Even Pier 17 has its merits. Head up to the third-level deck overlooking the East River, where the long wooden chairs will have you thinking about what it was like to cross the Atlantic on the *Normandie.* From this level you can see south to the Statue of Liberty, north to the Gothic majesty of the Brooklyn Bridge, and Brooklyn Heights on the opposite shore.

At the gateway to the Seaport, at Fulton and Water streets, is the *Titanic* Memorial Lighthouse, a monument to those who lost their lives when the ocean liner sank on April 15, 1912. It was erected overlooking the East River in 1913 and moved to this spot in 1968, just after the historic district was so designated.

A variety of events take place year-round, ranging from street performers to concerts to fireworks. Check the website or dial © **212/SEA-PORT.**

At Water and South sts.; museum visitor center is at 12 Fulton St. © **212/748-8600** or 212/SEA-PORT. www.south stseaport.org. Museum admission $8 adults, $6 students and seniors, $4 children 5–12, free for children under 5. Museum Apr–Oct Tues–Sun 10am–6pm, Thurs 10am–8pm; Nov–Mar Fri–Mon 10am–5pm. Subway: 2, 3, 4, 5 to Fulton St. (walk east, or downslope, on Fulton St. to Water St.).

Studio Museum in Harlem   This small but lovely museum is devoted to presenting 19th- and 20th-century African-American art as well as 20th-century African and Caribbean art and traditional African art and artifacts. Rotating exhibitions are a big part of the museum's focus, such as "Smithsonian African-American Photography: The First 100 Years, 1842–1942"; the silk-screens and lithographs of Jacob Lawrence; and an annual exhibition of works by emerging artists as part of its Artists-in-Residence program. Through June 2008, the museum featured "The World of Charles Ethan Porter: 19th-Century African-American Artist." There's also a small sculpture garden, a good gift shop, and a full calendar of special events.

144 W. 125th St. (btwn Lenox Ave. and Adam Clayton Powell Blvd.). © **212/864-4500.** www.studiomuseum.org. Admission $7 adults, $3 seniors and students, free for children under 12; free to all 1st Sat of the month. Wed–Fri noon–6pm; Sat–10am–6pm; Sun noon–6. Subway: 2, 3 to 125th St.

4 Skyscrapers & Other Architectural Highlights

For details on the **Empire State Building** 𝒜𝒜𝒜, see p. 231; for **Grand Central Terminal** 𝒜𝒜, p. 233; for **Rockefeller Center** 𝒜𝒜, p. 235; for the **U.S. Customs House,** p. 260; and for the **Brooklyn Bridge** 𝒜𝒜, p. 230. You might also wish to check out "Places of Worship," later in this chapter, for such treasures as **St. Patrick's Cathedral, Temple Emanu-El,** and the **Cathedral of St. John the Divine** 𝒜. See also chapter 2, "History and Culture," for a look at the city's evolving architecture.

In addition to checking out the landmarks below, architecture buffs may also want to seek out these notable buildings: **The Lever House,** built in 1952 at 390 Park Ave.,

Harlem's Architectural Treasures

Originally conceived as a bucolic suburbia for 19th-century Manhattan's moneyed set, Harlem has always had more than its share of historic treasures. To find them, pay a call on the **Astor Row Houses,** 130th Street between Fifth and Lenox avenues, a fabulous series of 28 redbrick town houses built in the early 1880s by the Astor family and graced with wooden porches, generous yards, and ornamental ironwork.

Equally impressive is **Strivers' Row,** West 139th Street between Adam Clayton Powell, Jr., and Frederick Douglass boulevards, where hardly a brick has changed among the gorgeous McKim, Mead & White neo–Italian Renaissance town houses since they were built in 1890. Once the original white owners had moved out, these lovely houses attracted the cream of Harlem, such "strivers" as Eubie Blake and W. C. Handy.

Handsome brownstones, limestone town houses, and row houses are atop **Sugar Hill,** 145th to 155th streets, between St. Nicholas and Edgecombe avenues, named for the "sweet life" enjoyed by its residents. In the early 20th century, such prominent blacks as W. E. B. DuBois, Thurgood Marshall, and Roy Wilkins lived in the now–landmark building at 409 Edgecombe Ave.

And if you're venturing this far uptown, don't miss the **Jumel Terrace Historic District,** west of St. Nicholas Avenue between 160th and 162nd streets. Of particular note is Sylvan Terrace, which feels more like an upstate Hudson River town than a part of Harlem—well worth seeking out for architecture lovers. A walk along it will lead you directly to the grand **Morris-Jumel Mansion** ⟨⟩, which is open to the public for tours (see "In Search of Historic Homes," below).

---

between 53rd and 54th streets, and the neighboring **Seagram Building** (1958), at 375 Park Ave., are the city's best examples of the form-follows-function, glass-and-steel International style, with the latter designed by master architect Mies van der Rohe. Also in Midtown East is the **Sony Building,** at 550 Madison Ave., designed in 1984 by Philip Johnson, with a pretty rose-granite facade and a playful Chippendale-style top that puts it a cut above the rest on the block.

The Upper West Side is home to two of the city's prime examples of residential architecture. On Broadway, between 73rd and 74th streets, is the **Ansonia,** looking for all the world like a flamboyant architectural wedding cake. This splendid Beaux Arts building has been home to the likes of Stravinsky, Toscanini, and Caruso, thanks to its virtually soundproof apartments. (It was also the spot where members of the Chicago White Sox plotted to throw the 1919 World Series, a year before Babe Ruth moved in after donning the New York Yankees' pinstripes.) Even more notable is the **Dakota,** at 72nd Street and Central Park West. Legend has it that the angular 1884 apartment house—accented with gables, dormers, and oriel windows that give it a brooding appeal—earned its name when its developer, Edward S. Clark, was teased by friends that he was building so far north of the city that he might as well be building in the Dakotas. The building's most famous resident, John Lennon, was gunned down outside the 72nd Street entrance on December 8, 1980; Yoko Ono still lives inside.

Chrysler Building 🎔🎔   Built as Chrysler Corporation headquarters in 1930 (they moved out decades ago), this is perhaps the 20th century's most romantic architectural achievement, especially at night when the lights in its triangular openings play off its steely crown. As you admire its facade, be sure to note the gargoyles reaching out from the upper floors, looking for all the world like Streamline-Gothic hood ornaments.

There's a fascinating tale behind this building. While it was under construction, its architect, William Van Alen, hid his final plans for the spire that now tops it. Working at a furious pace in the last days of construction, the workers assembled in secrecy the elegant pointy top—and then they raised it right through what people had assumed was going to be the roof, and for a brief moment it was the world's tallest building (a distinction stolen by the Empire State Building a few months later). Its exterior chrome sculptures are magnificent and spooky. The observation deck closed long ago, but you can visit its lavish ground-floor interior, which is Art Deco to the max. The ceiling mural depicting airplanes and other marvels of the first decades of the 20th century evince the bright promise of technology. The elevators are works of art, masterfully covered in exotic woods (especially note the lotus-shaped marquetry on the doors).

405 Lexington Ave. (at 42nd St.). Subway: S, 4, 5, 6, 7 to 42nd St./Grand Central.

Flatiron Building   This triangular masterpiece was one of the first skyscrapers. Its wedge shape is the only way the building could fill the triangular property created by the intersection of Fifth Avenue and Broadway, and that happy coincidence created one of the city's most distinctive buildings. Built in 1902 and fronted with limestone and terra cotta (not iron), the Flatiron measures only 6 feet across at its narrow end. So called for its resemblance to the laundry appliance, it was originally named the Fuller Building, then later "Burnham's Folly" because folks were certain that architect Daniel Burnham's 21-story structure would fall down. It didn't. There's no observation deck, and the building mainly houses publishing offices, but there are a few shops on the ground floor. The building's existence has served to name the neighborhood around it—the Flatiron District, home to a bevy of smart restaurants and shops.

175 Fifth Ave. (at 23rd St.). Subway: N, R to 23rd St.

New York Public Library 🎔🎔   The New York Public Library, adjacent to Bryant Park 🎔 (p. 271) and designed by Carrère & Hastings (1911), is one of the country's finest examples of Beaux Arts architecture, a majestic structure of white Vermont marble with Corinthian columns and allegorical statues. Before climbing the broad flight of steps to the Fifth Avenue entrance, note the famous lion sculptures—*Fortitude* on the right, and *Patience* on the left—so dubbed by whip-smart former mayor Fiorello La Guardia. At Christmastime they don natty wreaths to keep warm.

This library is actually the Humanities and Social Sciences Library, only one of the research libraries in the New York Public Library system. The interior is one of the finest in the city and features Astor Hall, with high arched marble ceilings and grand staircases. Thanks to restoration and modernization, the stupendous Main Reading Rooms have been returned to their stately glory and moved into the computer age (goodbye, card catalogs!). After a $5-million restoration, what was once known only as Room 117, a Beaux Arts masterpiece with incredible views of Fifth Avenue and

42nd Street, is now known as the Lionel Pincus and Princess Firyal Map Division. Here you will find possibly the finest and most extensive collection of maps in the world. And in 2008, the Library's facade will begin a 3-year restoration, to be completed for the building's centennial in 2011.

Even if you don't stop in to peruse the periodicals, you may want to check out one of the excellent rotating exhibitions. Call or check the website to see what's on while you're in town. There's also a full calendar of lecture programs, with past speakers ranging from Tom Stoppard to Pico Iyer; popular speakers often sell out, so it's a good idea to purchase tickets in advance.

Fifth Ave. at 42nd St. ☎ **212/869-8089** (exhibits and events), 212/661-7220 (library hours), or 212/930-0800 (general number). www.nypl.org. Free admission to all exhibitions. Tues–Wed 11am–7:30pm; Thurs–Sat 10am–6pm; Sun 1–5pm. Subway: 1, 2, 3, to 42nd St./Broadway; B, D, F, V to 42nd St./6th Ave.; S, 4, 5, 6, to Grand Central/42nd St.; 7 to 5th Ave.

United Nations   In the midst of New York City is this working monument to world peace. The U.N. headquarters occupies 18 acres of international territory—neither the city nor the United States has jurisdiction here—along the East River from 42nd to 48th streets. Designed by an international team of architects (led by American Wallace K. Harrison and including Le Corbusier) and finished in 1952, the complex along the East River weds the 39-story glass slab Secretariat with the free-form General Assembly on beautifully landscaped grounds donated by John D. Rockefeller, Jr. The 180 member-nations use the facilities to arbitrate worldwide disputes.

Guided tours leave every half-hour or so and last 45 minutes to an hour. Your guide will take you to the General Assembly Hall and the Security Council Chamber and introduce the history and activities of the United Nations and its related organizations. Along the tour you'll see donated objects and artwork, including charred artifacts that survived the atomic bombs at Hiroshima and Nagasaki, stained-glass windows by Chagall, a replica of the first *Sputnik,* and a mosaic called *The Golden Rule,* based on a Norman Rockwell drawing, which was a gift from the United States in 1985.

If you take the time to wander the beautifully landscaped grounds, you'll be rewarded with lovely views and some surprises. The mammoth monument *Good Defeats Evil,* donated by the Soviet Union in 1990, fashioned a contemporary St. George slaying a dragon from parts of a Russian ballistic missile and an American Pershing missile.

For an unusual treat, try a multiethnic meal while visiting the U.N. at the **Delegates' Dining Room** (☎ **212/963-7625**). Lunch is served from 11:30am to 2pm. Diners must be 12 years or older.

At First Ave. and 46th St. ☎ **212/963-8687**. www.un.org/tours. Guided tours $14 adults, $9 seniors, high school, and college students, $7.50 children 5–14. Children under 5 not permitted. Daily tours every half-hour 9:30am–4:45pm; Jan–Feb Sat–Sun 10am–4:30pm; limited schedule may be in effect during the general debate (late Sept to mid-Oct). Subway: S, 4, 5, 6, 7 to 42nd St./Grand Central.

Woolworth Building ⟡   This soaring "Cathedral of Commerce" cost Frank W. Woolworth $14 million worth of nickels and dimes in 1913. Designed by Cass Gilbert, it was the world's tallest edifice until 1930, when it was surpassed by the Chrysler Building. At its opening, Pres. Woodrow Wilson pressed a button from the White House that illuminated the building's 80,000 electric light bulbs. The neo-Gothic

In Search of Historic Homes

The Historic House Trust of New York City preserves 19 houses, located in city parks in all five boroughs. Those particularly worth seeking out include the **Morris-Jumel Mansion** in Harlem at 65 Jumel Terrace, at 160th Street, east of St. Nicholas Avenue (© **212/923-8008;** www.morrisjumel.org; Wed–Sun 10am–4pm), a grand colonial mansion built in the Palladian style (in 1765) and now Manhattan's oldest surviving residential house.

Built around 1764, the **Dyckman Farmhouse Museum,** farther uptown at 4881 Broadway, at 204th Street (© **212/304-9422;** www.historichousetrust. org; Wed–Sat 11am–4pm; Sun noon–4pm), is the only Dutch colonial farmhouse remaining in Manhattan, stoically and stylishly surviving the urban development that grew up around it.

The **Edgar Allan Poe Cottage,** 2460 Grand Concourse, at East Kingsbridge Road in the Bronx (© **718/881-8900;** www.bronxhistoricalsociety.org; Sat 10am–4pm, Sun 1–5pm), was the last home (1846–49) of the brilliant but troubled poet and author, who moved his wife here because he thought the "country air" would be good for her tuberculosis. The house is outfitted as a memorial to the writer, with period furnishings and exhibits on his life and times.

The **Merchant's House Museum**, 29 E. 4th St., between Lafayette Street and Bowery in NoHo (© **212/777-1089;** www.merchantshouse.org; Thurs–Mon noon–5pm), is a rare jewel: a perfectly preserved 19th-century home, complete with intact interiors, whose last resident is said to be the inspiration for Catherine Sloper in Henry James's *Washington Square.*

Each of the 15 other houses also has a fascinating story to tell. A brochure listing the locations and touring details of all 19 of the historic homes is available by calling © **212/360-8282.** You'll also find information online at **www.historichousetrust.org.** Admission to each house is generally no more than $5 ($8 at Merchant's House).

architecture is rife with spires, gargoyles, flying buttresses, vaulted ceilings, 16th-century-style stone-as-lace traceries, castlelike turrets, and a churchlike interior. Housing financial institutions and high-tech companies, the grand tower is still dedicated to the almighty dollar.

Step into the lofty marble entrance arcade to view the gleaming mosaic Byzantine-style ceiling and gold-leafed neo-Gothic cornices. The corbels (carved figures under the crossbeams) in the lobby include whimsical portraits of the building's engineer Gunvald Aus measuring a girder (above the staircase to the left of the main door), Gilbert holding a model of the building, and Woolworth counting coins (both above the left-hand corridor of elevators). Stand near the security guard's podium and crane your neck for a glimpse at Paul Jennewein's murals *Commerce* and *Labor,* half hidden up on the mezzanine. Cross Broadway for the best overview of the exterior.

233 Broadway (at Park Place, near City Hall Park). Subway: 2, 3 to Park Place; R to City Hall.

Historic Downtown Structures

New York is neither Rome nor Athens, yet the city can boast a few old structures, at least New World old. To find a good sampling of "ancient" New York, head downtown, where it all began.

You might want to first stop at the southern tip of the island at Battery Park, where an old fort called **Castle Clinton National Monument** (ℂ 212/344-7220; www.nps.gov/cacl) still stands. The fort, or what remains of it, was built between 1808 and 1811 to defend New York Harbor against the British. In the mid–19th century the fort was the city's first immigration center. A small museum was added to the monument in 1986, with exhibits that follow the evolution of the fort.

Not far from Castle Clinton, at 1 Bowling Green, is the relatively modern 1907-built **U.S. Customs House** ⓡ, which houses the National Museum of the American Indian, George Gustav Heye Center (p. 251). Designed by Cass Gilbert and now a National Historic Landmark, the granite structure features giant statues carved by Daniel Chester French (of Lincoln Memorial fame) lining the front that personify Asia (pondering philosophically), America (bright-eyed and bushy-tailed), Europe (decadent and whose time has passed), and Africa (sleeping). Inside, the airy oval rotunda designed by Spanish engineer Raphael Guastavino was frescoed by Reginald Marsh to glorify the shipping industry (and, by extension, the Customs office once housed here).

One of Wall Street's most recognizable sights is the imposing, majestic **Federal Hall National Memorial,** 26 Wall St. (ℂ 212/825-6888; www.nps.gov/feha). Built in 1842, the memorial, with the 1883-built statue of George Washington on the steps directly across from the New York Stock Exchange, was erected on the site of New York's first City Hall. Inside, it's now a museum, with exhibits that elucidate the events surrounding the memorial and other aspects of American history. The infrastructure of the memorial suffered from the massive shock of the nearby attack on the World Trade Center; as a result, the memorial is undergoing a $16-million rehabilitation. Call to see if the museum's reopened in time for your visit.

George Washington was a visible presence in 18th-century New York and he worshiped at the still-standing **St. Paul's Chapel,** built in 1766 and part of the Trinity Church (p. 263) at 74 Trinity Place (ℂ 212/233-4164). The chapel now serves as a memorial to the victims of 9/11.

So now we know where Washington worshiped, but where did he eat? At **Fraunces Tavern,** the same place where he bade farewell to his officers at the end of the American Revolution. This 1907-built tavern is an exact replica of the original 1717 tavern. It's now a museum, at 54 Pearl St., near Broad Street (ℂ 212/425-1778; www.frauncestavernmuseum.org), and an actual restaurant.

5 Places of Worship

New York has an incredible range of renowned religious institutions, notable for their history, architecture, and/or inspirational music. I've listed two of Harlem's premier gospel institutions below; if you would rather go to one of these gospel services in the company of a knowledgeable guide, see "Organized Sightseeing Tours," on p. 274 of this chapter. Additionally, if you would like to hear the rousing gospel of the four-time Grammy Award–winning **Brooklyn Tabernacle Choir** ⊛, see p. 290.

If you do plan to attend a gospel service, be prepared to stay for the entire 1½- to 2-hour service. It is impolite to exit early. (Services are extremely popular, so you'll find it just plain difficult to leave before the end anyway.)

Abyssinian Baptist Church ⊛   The most famous of Harlem's more than 400 houses of worship is this Baptist church, founded downtown in 1808 by African-American and Ethiopian merchants. It was moved uptown to Harlem back in the 1920s by Adam Clayton Powell, Sr., who built it into the largest Protestant congregation—white or black—in America. His son, Adam Clayton Powell, Jr. (for whom the adjoining boulevard was named), carried on his tradition, and also became the first-ever black U.S. congressman. Abyssinian is now the domain of the fiery, activist-minded Rev. Calvin O. Butts, whom the chamber of commerce has declared a "living treasure." The Sunday morning services—at 9 and 11am—offer a wonderful opportunity to experience the Harlem gospel tradition.

132 Odell Clark Place (W. 138th St., btwn Adam Clayton Powell Blvd. and Lenox Ave.). ⓒ 212/862-7474. www.abyssinian.org. Subway: 2, 3, B, C to 135th St.

Cathedral of St. John the Divine ⊛   The world's largest Gothic cathedral, St. John the Divine has been a work in progress since 1892. Its sheer size is amazing enough—a nave that stretches two football fields and a seating capacity of 5,000—but keep in mind that there is no steel structural support. The church is being built using traditional Gothic engineering—blocks of granite and limestone are carved out by master masons and their apprentices—which may explain why construction is still ongoing, more than 100 years after it began, with no end in sight, In December 2001, fire destroyed the north transept, which housed the gift shop. But this phoenix rose from the ashes quickly; the cathedral was reopened to visitors within a month, even though the scent of charred wood was still in the air and restoration will not be complete for months to come. That's precisely what makes this place so wonderful: Finishing isn't necessarily the point. Though maybe it is; in late 2007 scaffolding was finally removed from the church's southwest tower exposing that magnificent structure for the first time in over 15 years. And in late 2008, after a $16.5 million cleaning and repair from the 2001 fire, the great nave is expected to open.

Though it's the seat of the Episcopal Diocese of New York, St. John's embraces an interfaith tradition. Internationalism is a theme found throughout the cathedral's iconography. Each chapel is dedicated to a different national, ethnic, or social group. The genocide memorial in the Missionary chapel—dedicated to the victims of the Ottoman Empire in Armenia (1915–23), of the Holocaust (1939–45), and in Bosnia-Herzegovina since 1992—moved me to tears, as did the FDNY memorial in the Labor chapel. Although it was originally conceived to honor 12 firefighters killed in 1966, hundreds of personal notecards and trinkets of remembrance have evolved it into a moving tribute to the 343 firefighting heroes killed on September 11, 2001.

You can explore the cathedral on your own, or on the Public Tour, offered 6 days a week; also inquire about the periodic (usually twice monthly) Vertical Tour, which takes you on a hike up the 11-flight circular staircase to the top, for spectacular views. At press time, these were still suspended due to the fire. Check the website for updates. St. John the Divine is also known for presenting outstanding workshops, musical events, and important speakers. The free New Year's Eve concert draws thousands of New Yorkers; so, too, does its annual Feast of St. Francis (Blessing of the Animals), held in early October (see the "New York City Calendar of Events," in chapter 3). Call for event information and tickets. To hear the incredible pipe organ in action, attend the weekly Choral Evensong and Organ Meditation service, which highlights one of the nation's most treasured pipe organs, Sunday at 6pm.

1047 Amsterdam Ave. (at 112th St.). ✆ **212/316-7490** or 212/932-7347 for tour information and reservations, 212/662-2133 for event information and tickets. www.stjohndivine.org. Suggested admission $2; tour $5. Mon–Sat 7am–6pm; Sun 7am–7pm. Tours offered Tues–Sat 11am; Sun 1pm. Worship services Mon–Sat 8 and 8:30am (morning prayer and holy Eucharist), 12:15 and 5:30pm (1st Thurs service 7:15am); Sun 8, 9, and 11am and 6pm; AIDS memorial service 4th Sat of the month at 12:15pm. Subway: B, C, 1 to Cathedral Pkwy.

The Church of the Transfiguration *Finds*

When you come upon this oddly beautiful historic structure amidst modern high-rise condos in the burgeoning Madison Square neighborhood, you will once again be awed at the diversity of New York. Also known as the Little Church Around the Corner, this Episcopalian house of worship, with its twists and turns, has been compared to a "holy cucumber vine." Built in 1849, the church was granted United States landmark status in 1973. Its history includes sheltering escaped slaves during the Civil War draft riots, being one of the first churches to hand out food for the poor at the start of the Depression, and, most significantly, for its close relationship to the theater. In 1923, the Episcopal Actor's Guild was formed at the church and some of the noted actors involved include Basil Rathbone, Mary Pickford, and Tallulah Bankhead, with Charlton Heston, Barnard Hughes, and, most recently Sam Waterston serving as presidents.

1 E. 29th St. (btwn Fifth and Madison aves.). ✆ **212/684-6770**. www.littlechurch.org. Subway: 6 to 28th St; R to 28th St.

Mother A.M.E. Zion Church

Another of Harlem's great gospel churches is this African Methodist Episcopal house of worship, the first black church to be founded in New York State. Established on John Street in Lower Manhattan in 1796, Mother A.M.E. was known as the "Freedom Church" for the central role it played in the Underground Railroad. Among the escaped slaves the church hid was Frederick Douglass; other famous congregants have included Sojourner Truth and Paul Robeson. Mother A.M.E. relocated to Harlem in 1914 and moved into this grand edifice in 1925. Rousing Sunday services are at 11am.

140–7 W. 137th St. (btwn Adam Clayton Powell Blvd. and Lenox Ave.). ✆ **212/234-1544**. Subway: 2, 3, B, C to 135th St.

St. Patrick's Cathedral

This incredible Gothic white-marble-and-stone structure is the largest Roman Catholic cathedral in the United States, as well as the seat of the Archdiocese of New York. Designed by James Renwick, begun in 1859, and consecrated in 1879, St. Patrick's wasn't completed until 1906. Strangely, Irish Catholics picked one of the city's WASPiest neighborhoods for St. Patrick's. After the death of the beloved John Cardinal O'Connor in 2000, Pope John Paul II installed Bishop Edward Egan, whom he elevated to cardinal in 2001. The vast cathedral seats a congregation of 2,200; if you don't want to come for Mass, you can pop in between services to get a look at the impressive interior. The St. Michael and St. Louis altar came from Tiffany & Co. (also located here on Fifth Ave.), while the St. Elizabeth altar—honoring Mother Elizabeth Ann Seton, the first American-born saint—was designed by Paolo Medici of Rome.

Fifth Ave. (btwn 50th and 51st sts.). ℂ 212/753-2261. www.ny-archdiocese.org. Free admission. Sun–Fri 7am–8:30pm; Sat 8am–8:30pm. Mass Mon–Fri 7, 7:30, and 8am, noon, and 12:30, 1, and 5:30pm; Sat 8am, noon, and 12:30 and 5:30pm; Sun 7, 8, 9, and 10:15am (Cardinal's mass), noon, and 1 and 5:30pm; holy days 7, 7:30, 8, 8:30, and 11:30am, noon, and 12:30, 1, and 5:30pm. Subway: B, D, F, V to 47th–50th sts./Rockefeller Center.

Temple Emanu-El   Many of New York's most prominent and wealthy families are members of this Reform congregation—the first to be established in New York City— housed in the city's most famous synagogue. The largest house of Jewish worship in the world is a majestic blend of Moorish and Romanesque styles, symbolizing the mingling of Eastern and Western cultures. The temple houses a small but remarkable collection of Judaica in the Herbert & Eileen Bernard Museum, including a collection of Hanukkah lamps with examples ranging from the 14th to the 20th centuries. Three galleries also tell the story of the congregation Emanu-El from 1845 to the present. Tours are given after morning services Saturday at noon. Inquire for a schedule of lectures, films, music, symposiums, and other events.

1 E. 65th St. (at Fifth Ave.). ℂ 212/744-1400. www.emanuelnyc.org. Free admission. Daily 10am–5pm. Services Sun–Thurs 5:30pm; Fri 5:15pm; Sat 10:30am. Subway: N, R to Fifth Ave.; 6 to 68th St.

Trinity Church   Serving God and mammon, this Wall Street house of worship—with neo-Gothic flying buttresses, beautiful stained-glass windows, and vaulted ceilings—was designed by Richard Upjohn and consecrated in 1846. At that time, its 280-foot spire dominated the skyline. Its main doors, embellished with biblical scenes, were inspired in part by Ghiberti's famed doors on Florence's Baptistery. The historic Episcopal church stood strong while office towers crumbled around it on September 11, 2001; however, an electronic organ has temporarily replaced the historic pipe organ, which was severely damaged by dust and debris. The gates to the historic church currently serve as an impromptu memorial to the victims of 9/11, with countless tokens of remembrance left by both locals and visitors alike.

The church runs a brief **tour** daily at 2pm (a second Sun tour follows the 11:15am Eucharist); groups of five or more should call ℂ **212/602-0872** to reserve. There's a small museum at the end of the left aisle displaying documents (including the 1697 church charter from King William III), photographs, replicas of the Hamilton-Burr duel pistols, and other items. Surrounding the church is a churchyard whose monuments read like an American history book: a tribute to martyrs of the American Revolution, Alexander Hamilton, Robert Fulton, and many more. Lined with benches, this makes a wonderful picnic spot on warm days.

Also part of Trinity Church is **St. Paul's Chapel,** at Broadway and Fulton Street, New York's only surviving pre-Revolutionary church, and a transition shelter for homeless men until it was transformed into a relief center after September 11, 2001; it returned to its former duties in mid-2002. Built by Thomas McBean, with a templelike portico and fluted Ionic columns supporting a massive pediment, the chapel resembles London's St. Martin-in-the-Fields. In the small graveyard, 18th- and early-19th-century notables rest in peace and modern businesspeople sit for lunch.

Trinity holds its renowned **Noonday Concert** series of chamber music and orchestral concerts Monday and Thursday at 1pm; call ✆ **212/602-0747** or visit the website for the schedule and to see if concert programming has resumed at St. Paul's.

At Broadway and Wall St. ✆ **212/602-0800** or 212/602-0872 for concert information. www.trinitywallstreet.org. Free admission and free tours; $2 suggested donation for noonday concerts. Museum Mon–Fri 9–11:45am; Sun–Fri 1–3:45pm; Sat 10am–3:45pm. Services Mon–Fri 8:15am, 12:05, and 5:15pm (additional Healing Service Thurs at 12:30pm); Sun 9 and 11:15am (also 8am Eucharist service at St. Paul's Chapel, btwn Vesey and Fulton sts.). Subway: 4, 5 to Wall St.

6 Central Park & Other Places to Play

CENTRAL PARK

Without the miracle of civic planning that is **Central Park** ✹✹✹, Manhattan would be a virtual unbroken block of buildings. Instead, smack in the middle of Gotham, an 843-acre natural retreat provides a daily escape valve and tranquilizer for millions of New Yorkers. (For a lovely color map of the park and its major attractions, you can turn to the insert at the front of this book.)

While you're in the city, be sure to take advantage of the park's many charms—not the least of which is its sublime layout. Frederick Law Olmsted and Calvert Vaux won a competition with a plan that marries flowing paths with sinewy bridges, integrating them into the natural rolling landscape with its rocky outcroppings, man-made lakes, and wooded pockets. Construction concluded in 1870 and designers predicted the hustle and bustle to come, and tactfully hid traffic from the eyes and ears of park-goers by building roads that are largely hidden from the bucolic view.

On just about any day, Central Park is crowded with New Yorkers and visitors alike. On nice days, especially weekend days, it's the city's party central. Families come to play in the snow or the sun, depending on the season; in-line skaters come to fly through the crisp air and twirl in front of the band shell; couples come to stroll or paddle the lake; dog owners come to hike and throw Frisbees to Bowser; and just about everybody comes to sunbathe at the first sign of summer. On beautiful days, the crowds are part of the appeal—folks come here to peel off their urban armor and relax, and the common goal puts a general feeling of camaraderie in the air. On these days, the people-watching is more compelling than anywhere else in the city. But even on the most crowded days, there's always somewhere to get away from it all, if you just want a little peace and quiet and a moment to commune with nature.

ORIENTATION & GETTING THERE   Look at your map of the city—that great green swath in the center of Manhattan is Central Park.

It runs from 59th Street (also known as Central Park South) at the south end to 110th Street at the north end, and from Fifth Avenue on the east side to Central Park West (the equivalent of Eighth Ave.) on the west side. A 6-mile rolling road, Central Park Drive, circles the park, and has a lane set aside for bikers, joggers, and in-line skaters. A number of transverse (cross-town) roads cross the park at major points—at 65th, 79th, 86th, and 97th streets—but they're built down a level, largely out of view, to minimize intrusion on the bucolic nature of the park.

A number of subway stops and lines serve the park, and which one you take depends on where you want to go. To reach the southernmost entrance on the west side, take an A, B, C, D, 1 to 59th Street/Columbus Circle. To reach the southeast corner entrance, take the N, R to Fifth Avenue; from this stop, it's an easy walk into the park to the **Information Center** in the Dairy (✆ **212/794-6564;** Tues–Sun

10am–5pm, to 4pm in winter), midpark at about 65th Street. Here you can ask questions, pick up park information, and purchase a good park map.

If your time for exploring is limited, I suggest entering the park at 72nd or 79th Street for maximum exposure (Subway: B, C to 72nd St. or 81st St./Museum of Natural History). From here, you can pick up park information at the visitor center at **Belvedere Castle** (© 212/772-0210; Tues–Sun 10am–5pm, to 4pm in winter), midpark at 79th Street. There's also a visitor center at the **Charles A. Dana Discovery Center** (© 212/860-1370; daily 10am–5pm, to 4pm in winter), at the northeast corner of the park at Harlem Meer, at 110th Street between Fifth and Lenox avenues (Subway: 2, 3 to Central Park North/110th St.). The Dana Center is also an environmental education center hosting workshops, exhibits, music, and park tours, and lends fishing poles for fishing in Harlem Meer (park policy is catch-and-release).

Food carts and vendors are set up at all of the park's main gathering points, so finding a bite to eat is never a problem. You'll also find a fixed food counter at the Conservatory, on the east side of the park north of the 72nd Street entrance, and both casual snacks and more sophisticated New American dining at the **Boat House,** on the lake near 72nd Street and Park Drive North (© 212/517-2233; www.thecentral parkboathouse.com).

GUIDED WALKS   The Central Park Conservancy offers a slate of free walking tours of the park; call © 212/360-2726 or check **www.centralparknyc.org** for the current schedule (click on the "Walking Tours" button on the left). The Dana Center hosts ranger-guided tours on occasion (call © 212/860-1370, or 311 for a schedule). Also consider a private walking tour; many of the companies listed in "Organized Sightseeing Tours," later in this chapter, offer guided tours of the park.

FOR FURTHER INFORMATION   Call the main number at © 212/310-6600 for recorded information, or 212/628-1036 to speak to a person. Call © **888/NY-PARKS** for events information. The park also has two comprehensive websites that are worth checking out: the city parks department's site at **www.centralpark.org**, and the **Central Park Conservancy's** site at **www.centralparknyc.org**, both of which feature excellent maps and a far more complete rundown of park attractions and activities than I have room to include here. If you have an emergency in the park, dial © **911,** or for a less pressing matter, call © **311,** and you will be connected to the park rangers.

SAFETY TIP   Even though the park has the lowest crime rate of any of the city's precincts, keep your wits about you, especially in the more remote northern end. It's a good idea to avoid the park entirely after dark, unless you're heading to one of the restaurants for dinner or to a SummerStage or Shakespeare in the Park event (see "Park It! Shakespeare, Music & Other Free Fun," p. 354), when you should stick with the crowds. For more safety tips, see "Playing It Safe," in chapter 2.

EXPLORING THE PARK

The best way to see Central Park is to wander along the park's 58 miles of winding pedestrian paths, keeping in mind the following highlights.

Before starting your stroll, stop by the **Information Center** in the Dairy (© 212/794-6564; Tues–Sun 10am–5pm), midpark in a 19th-century-style building overlooking Wollman Rink at about 65th Street, to get a good park map and other information on sights and events, and to peruse the kid-friendly exhibit on the park's history and design.

The southern part of Central Park is more formally designed and heavily visited than the relatively rugged and remote northern end. Not far from the Dairy is the **Carousel,** with 58 hand-carved horses (© 212/879-0244; daily, weather permitting, Apr–Nov 10am–6pm, to 4:30pm in winter; rides are $1.50); the zoo (see below); and the Wollman Rink for roller- or ice-skating (see "Activities," below).

The Mall, a long formal walkway lined with elms shading benches and sculptures of sometimes forgotten writers, leads to the focal point of Central Park, **Bethesda Fountain** ★ (along the 72nd St. transverse road). Bethesda Terrace and its grandly sculpted entryway border a large lake where dogs fetch sticks, rowboaters glide by, and dedicated early-morning anglers try their luck at catching carp, perch, catfish, and bass. You can rent a rowboat at or take a gondola ride from Loeb Boathouse, on the eastern end of the lake (see "Activities," below). Boats of another kind are at Conservatory Water (on the east side at 73rd St.), a stone-walled pond flanked by statues of both Hans Christian Andersen and Alice in Wonderland. On Saturday at 10am, diehard yachtsmen race remote-controlled sailboats in fierce competitions that follow Olympic regulations. (Sorry, model boats aren't for rent.)

If the action there is too intense, Sheep Meadow on the southwestern side of the park is a designated quiet zone, where Frisbee throwing and kite flying are as energetic as things get. Another respite is **Strawberry Fields** ★, at 72nd Street on the west side. This memorial to John Lennon, who was murdered across the street at the Dakota apartment building (72nd St. and Central Park West, northwest corner), is a gorgeous garden centered on an Italian mosaic bearing the title of the lead Beatle's most famous solo song and his lifelong message: IMAGINE. In keeping with its goal of promoting world peace, the garden has 161 varieties of plants, donated by each of the 161 nations in existence when it was designed in 1985. This is a wonderful place for peaceful contemplation.

Bow Bridge, a graceful lacework of cast iron designed by Calvert Vaux, crosses over the lake and leads to the most bucolic area of Central Park, the Ramble. This dense 38-acre woodland with spiraling paths, rocky outcroppings, and a stream is the best spot for bird-watching and feeling as if you've discovered an unimaginably leafy forest right in the middle of the city.

North of the Ramble, Belvedere Castle is home to the **Henry Luce Nature Observatory** (© 212/772-0210) Tues to Sun, 10am to 4:30pm, worth a visit if you're with children. From the castle, set on Vista Rock (the park's highest point at 135 ft.), you can look down on the Great Lawn, where softball players and sun worshipers compete for coveted greenery, and the Delacorte Theater, home to Shakespeare in the Park (see chapter 10). The small Shakespeare Garden, south of the theater, is scruffy, but it does have plants, herbs, trees, and other greenery mentioned by the Bard. Behind the Belvedere Castle is the **Swedish Cottage Marionette Theatre** ★ (© 212/988-9093), hosting marionette plays for children throughout the year; call to see what's on.

Continue north along the east side of the Great Lawn, parallel to East Drive. Near the glass-enclosed back of the **Metropolitan Museum of Art** ★★★ (p. 233) is Cleopatra's Needle, a 69-foot obelisk originally erected in Heliopolis around 1475 B.C. It was given to the city by the khedive of Egypt in 1880. (The khedive bestowed to the city of London a similar obelisk, which sits on the embankment of the Thames.)

North of the 86th Street Transverse Road is the Jacqueline Kennedy Onassis Reservoir, renamed for the beloved first lady, who lived nearby and often enjoyed a run along the 1½-mile jogging track that circles the reservoir.

North of the reservoir is my favorite part of the park. It's much less traversed and in some areas absolutely tranquil. The North Meadow (at 96th St.) features 12 baseball and softball fields. Sadly, the North Meadow is circled by a not-very-attractive fence, and 6 months of the year that fence is locked and the meadow closed. An unfortunate recent trend in Central Park has been the proliferation of fences. They have become so prevalent that at times you get the feeling you are not really in a park but a museum.

North of the North Meadow, at the northeast end of the park, is the **Conservatory Garden** *(at 105th St. and Fifth Ave.), Central Park's only formal garden, with a magnificent display of flowers and trees reflected in calm pools of water. (The gates to the garden once fronted the Fifth Ave. mansion of Cornelius Vanderbilt II.) The **Lasker Rink and Pool** (© 917/492-3857) is the only swimming pool in Central Park, and in the winter it's converted to a skating rink that offers a less hectic alternative to Wollman Rink (see "Activities," below). Harlem Meer and its boathouse were recently renovated and look beautiful. The boathouse now berths the **Charles A. Dana Discovery Center,** near 110th Street between Fifth and Lenox avenues (© 212/860-1370) open Tues–Sun, 10am to 5pm, where children learn about the environment and borrow fishing poles for catch-and-release at no charge. The Pool (at W. 100th St.), possibly the most idyllic spot in all of Central Park, was recently renovated and features willows, grassy banks, and a pond populated by some very well-fed ducks. You might even spot an egret and a hawk or two.

GOING TO THE ZOO
Central Park Zoo/Tisch Children's Zoo *(Kids*   Here is a pleasant refuge within a refuge, where lithe sea lions frolic in the central pool area with beguiling style, gigantic but graceful polar bears glide back and forth across a watery pool that has glass walls through which you can observe very large paws doing very smooth strokes, monkeys seem to regard those on the other side of the fence with knowing disdain, and in the hot and humid Tropic Zone, large colorful birds swoop around in freedom, sometimes landing next to nonplused visitors.

Because of its small size, the zoo is at its best with its displays of smaller animals. The indoor multilevel Tropic Zone is a real highlight, its steamy rainforest home to everything from black-and-white colobus monkeys to Emerald tree boa constrictors to a leaf-cutter ant farm; look for the new dart-poison-frog exhibit, which is very cool. So is the large penguin enclosure in the Polar Circle, which is better than the one at San Diego's SeaWorld. In the Temperate Territory, look for the Asian red pandas (cousins to the big black-and-white ones), which look like the world's most beautiful raccoons. Despite their pool and piles of ice, however, the polar bears still look sad.

The zoo is good for short attention spans; you can cover the entire thing in 1½ to 3 hours, depending on the size of the crowds and how long you like to linger. It's also very kid-friendly, with lots of well-written and -illustrated placards that older kids can understand. For the littlest ones, there's the $6-million **Tisch Children's Zoo** *. With goats, llamas, potbellied pigs, and more, this petting zoo and playground is a real blast for the 5-and-under set.

830 Fifth Ave. (at 64th St., just inside Central Park). © 212/439-6500. www.wcs.org/zoos. Admission $8 adults, $4 seniors, $3 children 3–12, free for children under 3. Apr–Oct Mon–Fri 10am–5pm, Sat–Sun 10am–5:30pm; Nov–Mar daily 10am–4:30pm. Last entrance 30 min. before closing. Subway: N, R to Fifth Ave; 6 to 68th St.

ACTIVITIES

The 6-mile rolling road circling the park, Central Park Drive, has a lane set aside for bikers, joggers, and in-line skaters. The best time to use it is when the park is closed to traffic: Monday to Friday 10am to 3pm (except Thanksgiving to New Year's) and 7 to 10pm. It's also closed from 7pm Friday to 6am Monday, but when the weather is nice, the crowds can be hellish.

BIKING Off-road mountain biking isn't permitted; stay on Central Park Drive or your bike may be confiscated by park police.

You can rent 3- and 10-speed bikes as well as tandems in Central Park at the **Loeb Boathouse,** midpark near 72nd Street and Park Drive North, just in from Fifth Avenue (© **212/517-2233**), for $9 to $15 an hour, with a complete selection of kids' bikes, cruisers, tandems, and the like ($200 deposit required); at **Metro Bicycles,** 1311 Lexington Ave., at 88th Street (© **212/427-4450;** www.metrobicyclescom), for about $7 an hour, or $35 a day; and at **Toga Bike Shop,** 110 West End Ave., at 64th Street (© **212/799-9625;** www.togabikes.com), for $30 a day. No matter where you rent, be prepared to leave a credit card deposit.

BOATING From March through November, gondola rides and rowboat rentals are available at the **Loeb Boathouse,** midpark near 74th Street and Park Drive North, just in from Fifth Avenue (© **212/517-2233;** www.thecentralparkboathouse.com). Rowboats cost $10 for the first hour, $5 for every half-hour thereafter, and a $30 (cash) deposit is required; reservations are accepted.

HORSE-DRAWN CARRIAGE RIDES At the entrance to the park at 59th Street and Central Park South, you'll see a line of horse-drawn carriages waiting to take passengers on a ride through the park or along certain of the city's streets. Horses belong on city streets as much as chamber pots belong in our homes. You won't need me to tell you how forlorn most of these horses look; if you insist, a ride is about $50 for two for a half-hour, but I suggest skipping it.

ICE-SKATING Central Park's **Wollman Rink** ⟨�⟩, on the east side of the park between 62nd and 63rd streets (© **212/439-6900;** www.wollmanskatingrink.com) is the city's best outdoor skating spot, more spacious than the tiny rink at Rockefeller Center. It's open for skating from mid-October to mid-April, depending on the weather. Rates are $9.50 for adults ($12 Sat–Sun), $4.75 for seniors and kids under 12 ($8.25 Sat–Sun), and skate rental is $5; lockers are available (locks are $3.75). **Lasker Rink** © **212/534-7639,** on the east side around 106th Street, is a less expensive alternative to the more crowded Wollman Rink. Open November through March. Rates are $4.50 for adults, $2.25 for kids under 12, and skate rental is $4.75.

IN-LINE SKATING Central Park is the city's most popular place for blading. See the beginning of this section for details on Central Park Drive, the main drag for skaters. On weekends, head to West Drive at 67th Street, behind Tavern on the Green, where you'll find trick skaters weaving through a New York Roller Skating Association (NYRSA) slalom course, or to the mall in front of the band shell (above Bethesda Fountain) for twirling to tunes. In summer **Wollman Rink** ⟨�⟩ converts to a hotshot roller rink, with half-pipes and lessons available (see "Ice-Skating," above).

You can rent skates for $20 a day from **Blades Board and Skate,** 156 W. 72nd St., between Broadway and Columbus Avenue (© **212/787-3911;** www.blades.com). Wollman Rink (see above) also rents in-line skates for park use at similar rates.

(*Finds*) **Frozen in Time: Governor's Island**

Stand at the edge of Battery Park and look southwest about 800 yards into New York Harbor and you will see an island. No, it's not Staten Island, but **Governor's Island,** one of the first settlements of the Dutch West India Company in 1624. Later it was used as a military fort during the pre- and post-Revolutionary War period and most recently was the site of the 1988 summit between Ronald Reagan and USSR President Mikhail Gorbachev. In 2003, Governor's Island was transferred to the State and City of New York and, with the exception of 22 acres designated as a National Monument, the remaining 150 acres belong to the city and state and are open to the public from June through August. The island is a place frozen in time—kind of a ghost town where you'll find abandoned mansions, forts, bus stops (but no buses) and parade grounds. The views of downtown Manhattan are spectacular and the lack of cars and traffic make it a serene antidote to the bustle of the Financial District. In 2007, a design plan for a 40-acre park on the southern half of the island was approved. Part of the plans include a 2-mile waterfront promenade, a new park where former Coast Guard buildings now stand and will be demolished, and an improved park on the island's northern historic district, where hills will be created from the detritus from the buildings that will be destroyed, offering majestic views of downtown Manhattan and the Statue of Liberty. The project is estimated to cost about $400 million and be completed by 2012. In the meantime, enjoy it as is. Ferries are free but have a limited 250-passenger capacity; they run from May 31 through Labor Day. (212/440-2202. www.govisland.com. Subway: 1 to South Ferry; R, W to Whitehall St.; 4, 5 to Bowling Green.

PLAYGROUNDS   Nineteen Adventure Playgrounds are scattered throughout the park, perfect for jumping, sliding, tottering, swinging, and digging. At Central Park West and 81st Street is the **Diana Ross Playground** (*, voted the city's best by *New York* magazine. Also on the west side is the Spector Playground, at 85th Street and Central Park West, and, a little farther north, the Wild West Playground, at 93rd Street. On the east side is the Rustic Playground, at 67th Street and Fifth Avenue, a delightfully landscaped space rife with islands, bridges, and big slides; and the Pat Hoffman Friedman Playground, right behind the Metropolitan Museum of Art at East 79th Street, is geared toward older toddlers.

RUNNING   Marathoners and wannabes regularly run in Central Park along the 6-mile Central Park Drive, which circles the park (please run toward traffic to avoid being mowed down by wayward cyclists and in-line skaters). The **New York Road Runners** ((212/860-4455; www.nyrr.org), organizers of the New York City Marathon, schedules group runs 7 days a week at 6am and 6pm, leaving from the entrance to the park at 90th Street and Fifth Avenue. (For the NYRRC's list of the suggested running routes, see the box titled "Running the City," below.)

SWIMMING   The only pool in Central Park, **Lasker Pool** (on the east side at around 106th St.; (212/534-7639), is open July 1 through Labor Day weekend. It's free. Bring a towel and other supplies, including a lock.

Tips   Running the City

Here are the New York Road Runners' top picks for routes in Manhattan.

- **Jacqueline Kennedy Onassis Reservoir:** Possibly the most famous running route in the world; presidential candidates have run this 1½-mile route as well as the famous former first lady for whom it is now named.

- **The Loop in Central Park:** I used to run past Madonna and her bodyguards when she was a frequenter of the 6-mile loop. Now I see Howard Stern jogging, no bodyguards in sight, but usually with a female companion or two.

- **East River:** Entering on 63rd Street and York Avenue and running up to 125th Street and back is a 6-mile jog where you will pass Gracie Mansion, high-rises overlooking the river, and fishermen testing the river waters.

- **Hudson River South:** Enter at Chelsea Piers at West 23rd Street and continue down to Battery Park City and back for this approximately 5-mile run. In the warm months it's a carnival downtown, with in-line skaters, kayakers, musicians, and cyclists crowding the slim downtown park.

- **Hudson River North:** This approximately 6-mile run starts at Riverbank State Park, at 145th Street on the Hudson River, and continues through lovely Riverside Park, passing the 79th Street Boat Basin, and ending at the *Intrepid* Sea-Air-Space Museum.

OTHER PARKS

For parks in Brooklyn and Queens, see "Highlights of the Outer Boroughs," later in this chapter. For more information on these and other city parks, go online to **www.nycgovparks.org**.

Battery Park 𝒢𝒢   As you traverse Manhattan's concrete canyons, it's sometimes easy to forget that you're actually on an island. But here, at Manhattan's southernmost tip, you get the very real sense that just out past Liberty, Ellis, and Staten islands is the vast Atlantic Ocean.

The 21-acre park is named for the cannons built to defend residents after the American Revolution. Castle Clinton National Monument (the place to purchase tickets for the Statue of Liberty and Ellis Island ferry; see listings earlier in this chapter) was built as a fort before the War of 1812, though it was never used as such.

Battery Park is a park of monuments and memorials, many paying tribute to tragedy and death. Here you will find the East Coast Memorial, dedicated to 4,601 servicemen who died in Atlantic coastal waters during World War II; the New York Korean War Veterans Memorial; the American Merchant Mariner's Memorial, dedicated to Merchant Mariner's lost at sea; the Salvation Army Memorial; the Hope Garden dedicated to those who live with HIV or have died from AIDS; the Irish Hunger Memorial, a tribute to those who died during the potato famine in Ireland; and the 22-ton bronze sphere by Fritz Koenig that was recovered from the rubble of the World Trade Center, where it stood on the plaza between the two Twin Towers as a symbol of global peace—severely damaged but still whole. Mingling throughout these memorials you will find the requisite T-shirt vendors, hot-dog carts, and Wall Streeters eating deli sandwiches on the many park benches. Pull up your own bench for a good view out across the harbor.

From State St. to New York Harbor. (C) 212/334-3491. www.thebattery.org. Subway: R, W to Whitehall St.; 1 to South Ferry; 4, 5 to Bowling Green.

Riverside Park *(Finds)* I spent much of my time in my early years in New York in Riverside Park ((C) **212/408-0264;** www.nycgovparks.org) staring at the New Jersey skyline, jogging along the wind-swept Hudson river, playing hoops at the courts on 77th Street (when I still could jump), taking strolls along the promenade on hot summer nights, and watching the comings or goings of the unusual community that lives in the boats at the 79th Street Boat Basin. This underrated beauty, designed by Frederick Law Olmsted, the same man who designed Central Park, stretches 4 miles from 72nd Street to 158th Street. The serpentine route along the Hudson River offers a variety of lovely river vistas, 14 playgrounds, two tennis courts, softball and soccer fields, a skate park, beach volleyball, the aforementioned Boat Basin, two cafes—the **Boat Basin Café,** at 79th Street ((C) **212/496-5542;** www.boatbasincafe.com), and **Hurley's Hudson Beach Café,** at 105th Street ((C) **917/370-3448**), open April through September only— and monuments such as the Eleanor Roosevelt statue at 72nd Street, the Soldiers and Sailors Monument at 90th Street, and Grant's Tomb at 122nd Street ((C) **212/ 666-1640**). Open daily 9am to 5pm. But here's the best part: On a hot summer day, when Central Park is teeming with joggers, sunbathers, and in-line skaters, Riverside Park, just a few blocks from Central Park's western fringe, is comparatively serene. The **Riverside Park Fund** ((C) **212/870-3070;** www.riversideparkfund.org) has an excellent website with a comprehensive list of events and gives history with illustrations of the parkland. They also sell a map of the park for $2 (see website).

Bryant Park *(Another)* success story in the push for urban redevelopment, Bryant Park is the latest incarnation of a 4-acre site that was, at various times in its history, a graveyard and a reservoir. Named for poet and *New York Evening Post* editor William Cullen Bryant (look for his statue on the east end), the park actually rests atop the New York Public Library's many miles of underground stacks. Another statue is also notable: a squat and evocative stone portrait of Gertrude Stein, one of the few outdoor sculptures of women in the city.

This simple green swath, just east of Times Square, is welcome relief from Midtown's concrete, taxi-choked jungle, and good weather attracts brown-baggers from neighboring office buildings. Just behind the library is **Bryant Park Grill** ((C) **212/ 840-6500**), a gorgeous, airy bistro with spectacular views but merely decent New American food. Still, brunch is a good bet, and the grill's two summer alfresco restaurants—**The Terrace,** on the Grill's roof, and the casual **Cafe,** with small tables beneath a canopy of trees—are extremely pleasant on a nice day.

Le Carrousel complements the park's French classical style. It's not as big as the Central Park Carousel but utterly charming nonetheless, with 14 different animals that revolve to the sounds of French cabaret music. Le Carrousel is open all year, weather permitting, Thursday to Sunday 11:30am to 6pm, and costs $2 per ride.

From mid-October until mid-January, you can skate (for free!) on a seasonal ice rink called **The Pond.** Additionally, the park plays host to New York's **Seventh on Sixth** fashion shows, set up in billowy tents (open to the trade only) in the spring and fall.

Behind the New York Public Library, at Sixth Ave. btwn 40th and 42nd sts. (C) 212/768-4242. www.bryantpark.org. Subway: B, D, F, Q to 42nd St.; 7 to Fifth Ave.

Tips **The Greening of New York**

Whenever I travel to a city anywhere around the world, I make it a priority to visit that city's greenmarket, or farmers' market. I've been to some great ones, and I might be a bit prejudiced, but I haven't been to many better than the **Union Square Greenmarket** ✿✿ in New York City. New York has greenmarkets throughout the city on different days of the week, but the biggest and best is at Union Square every Monday, Wednesday, Friday, and Saturday. You'll find pickings from upstate and New Jersey farms, fresh fish from Long Island, homemade cheese and other dairy products, baked goods, plants, and organic herbs and spices. It's a true New York scene with everyone from models to celebrated chefs poring over the bounty. The Union Square Greenmarket is open year-round but is at its peak August through October when the local harvest—tomatoes, corn, greens, grapes, peppers, and apples—flourishes. If you are lucky enough to be in the city during this period, don't miss the bonanza, and pick up some apples or grapes for your travels around the city—but check it out no matter what the season. For more information and locations and schedules, see the **Council on the Environment of New York City** website at **www.cenyc.org**, or call ✆ **212/788-7900**.

Union Square Park   Here's a delightful place to spend an afternoon. Reclaimed from drug dealers and abject ruin in the late 1980s, Union Square Park is now one of the city's best assets and home of the New York's most famous **greenmarket** (see box above). The seemingly endless subway work should no longer be disturbing the peace by the time you're here. This patch of green remains, with or without the construction, the focal point of the newly fashionable Flatiron and Gramercy Park neighborhoods. Don't miss the grand equestrian statue of George Washington at the south end or the bronze statue (by Bartholdi, the sculptor of the Statue of Liberty) of the Marquis de Lafayette at the east end, gracefully glancing toward France. A cafe is open at the north end of the park in warm weather.

From 14th to 17th sts. (btwn Park Ave. South and Broadway). www.nycgovparks.org/parks/unionsquarepark. Subway: 4, 5, 6, L, W, N, Q, R to 14th St./Union Sq.

Washington Square Park   You'll be hard-pressed to find much "park" in this mainly concrete square—a burial ground in the late 18th century—but it's undeniably the focal point of Greenwich Village. Chess players, skateboarders, street musicians, New York University students, gay and straight couples, the occasional film crew, and not a few homeless people compete for attention throughout the day and most of the night. (If anyone issues a friendly challenge to play you in the ancient and complex Chinese game of Go, don't take them up on it—you'll lose money.)

In the 1830s, elegant Greek Revival town houses on Washington Square North, known as "The Row" (note especially nos. 21–26), attracted the elite. Stanford White designed Washington Arch (1891–92) to commemorate the centenary of George Washington's inauguration as first president. The arch was refurbished in 2004 and now features exterior lighting. The park is currently undergoing a major renovation, so sections of it may be shut off during your visit, but there are still ongoing activities scheduled throughout the project, which is slated to be complete in Spring 2009.

At the southern end of Fifth Ave. (where it intersects Waverly Place, btwn MacDougal and Wooster sts.). Subway: A, C, E, F, V to W. 4th St. (use 3rd St. exit).

CHELSEA PIERS

One of the city's biggest—and most successful—private urban-development projects is the 30-acre **Chelsea Piers Sports & Entertainment Complex** (✆ **212/336-6666; www.chelseapiers.com**). Jutting out into the Hudson River on four huge piers between 17th and 23rd streets, it's a terrific multifunctional recreational facility.

The **Sports Center** (✆ **212/336-6000**), a three-football-fields-long megafacility, does health clubs one better. It offers not only the usual cardiovascular training, weights, and aerobics but also a four-lane quarter-mile indoor running track, a boxing ring, basketball courts, a sand volleyball court, a gorgeous 25-yard indoor pool with a whirlpool and sun deck, the world's most challenging rock-climbing wall plus a bouldering wall, and the Spa at Chelsea Piers, which offers massage, reflexology, facials, and the like. Day passes to the Sports Center are $50 for nonmembers; spa treatments are extra, of course.

The **Golf Club** (✆ **212/336-6400**) has 52 all-weather fully automated hitting stalls on four levels and a 200-yard, net-enclosed, artificial-turf fairway jutting out over the water, making it the best place in the city to hit a few. Prices start at $25 for 90 balls (147 balls during off-peak hours), and club rentals are available.

The **Sky Rink** (✆ **212/336-6100**) has twin around-the-clock indoor rinks for recreational skating and pickup hockey games with Hudson River views. General skating is $13 for adults, $10 for seniors and kids 12 and under; skate rental is $7 Due to organized skating activities, general skating is limited, so call ahead to find out schedules of availability.

The **Field House** (✆ **212/336-6500**) is mainly for team sports, but young rock climbers will enjoy the 30-foot indoor climbing wall, designed for kids as well as grown-ups. Open climbs are $20, with climbs limited to 2½ hours on weekdays, they start taking same-day climb reservations at 9am, and weekends can book up quickly. Children's lessons are available. Batting cages are $5 per 15 pitches.

Feeling like a little 10-pin tonight? State-of-the-art **AMF Chelsea Piers Lanes** (✆ **212/835-BOWL; www.amf.com**) offers 40 lanes of fun. Games are $8.75 per person, and shoe rental is $5.

Beyond its athletics, the complex is a destination in and of itself. The 1¼-mile esplanade has benches and picnic tables with terrific river views; they serve as the

---

Moments The Little Red Lighthouse

Also known as Jeffrey's Hook Lighthouse, this little red lighthouse located under the George Washington Bridge in Fort Washington Park on the Hudson River was the inspiration for the 1942-children's book classic, *The Little Red Lighthouse and The Great Gray Bridge*, by Hildegarde Swift and Lynd Ward. Built in New Jersey in 1880 and reconstructed and moved to its current spot in 1921, it was operational until 1947. The lighthouse was to be removed in 1951, but because of its popularity there was a public outcry and it was saved. It's now a New York City landmark and on the list of National Register of Historic Places. It's a fun place for the kids to explore and scenic picnic spot in nice weather. It's open to the public, with guided tours by the **New York City Urban Rangers** (✆ **212/304-2365**) from Spring through Fall.

perfect vantage point for watching a cruise ship head out to sea, or the navy and Coast Guard ships sailing in for Fleet Week each May.

Getting there: Chelsea Piers is accessible by taxi and the M23 or M14 crosstown buses. The nearest subway is the C and E at 23rd Street and Eighth Avenue, then pick up the M23 or walk 4 long blocks west. Another option is to take the A, C, E to 14th Street or the L train to Eighth Avenue, walk to the river, then follow the walking/riding/running path along the river north.

7 Organized Sightseeing Tours

Reservations are required for some of the tours listed below, but even if they're not, it's always best to call ahead to confirm prices, times, and meeting places.

HARBOR CRUISES

If you'd like to sail the New York Harbor aboard the 1885 cargo schooner *Pioneer,* see the listing for South Street Seaport & Museum on p. 254.

Note that some of the lines below may have limited schedules in winter, especially for evening cruises. Call ahead or check online for current offerings.

Bateaux New York   The most elegant and romantic of New York's evening dinner cruises. Cruises are aboard the *Celestial,* designed to accommodate 300 guests with two suites, one dance floor, two outdoor strolling decks, a state-of-the-art sound system, and windows galore. Dinner is a three-course sit-down affair, with jackets and ties suggested for men, evening dresses for women. The food isn't what you'd get at Jean-Georges, but Bateaux (sister to egalitarian Spirit Cruises; see below) offers a very nice supper-club-style night on the town, and the views are fabulous. A live quartet entertains with jazz standards and pop vocal tunes.

Departs from Pier 62, Chelsea Piers, W. 23rd St. and Twelfth Ave. ✆ **212/727-7735**. www.bateauxnewyork.com. 2-hr. lunch cruises $46; 3-hr. dinner cruises $88–$117. Subway: C, E to 23rd St.

Circle Line Sightseeing Cruises 🎯🎯   A New York institution, the Circle Line is famous for its 3-hour tour around the entire 35 miles of Manhattan. This Full Island cruise passes by the Statue of Liberty, Ellis Island, the Brooklyn Bridge, the United Nations, Yankee Stadium, the George Washington Bridge, and more, including Manhattan's wild northern tip. The panorama is riveting, and the commentary isn't bad. The big boats are basic but fine, with lots of deck room for everybody to enjoy the view. Snacks, soft drinks, coffee, and beer are available onboard for purchase.

If 3 hours is more than you or the kids can handle, go for either the 2-hour Semi-Circle or the Sunset/Harbor Lights cruise, both of which show you the highlights of the skyline. There's also a 1-hour Seaport Liberty version that sticks close to the south end of the island. But of all the tours, the kids might like the Beast best, a thrill-a-minute speedboat ride offered in summer only.

In addition, a number of adults-only live music and DJ cruises sail regularly from the seaport from May through September ($20–$40 per person). Depending on the night of the week, you can groove to the sounds of jazz, Latin, gospel, dance tunes, or blues as you sail along viewing the skyline.

Departing from Pier 83, at W. 42nd St. and Twelfth Ave. Also departing from Pier 16 at South St. Seaport, 207 Front St. ✆ **212/563-3200**. www.circleline42.com and www.seaportmusiccruises.com. Check the website or call for the most up to date schedule. Sightseeing cruises $12–$29 adults, $16–$24 seniors, $13–$16 children 12 and under. Subway to Pier 83: A, C, E to 42nd St. Subway to Pier 16: J, M, Z, 2, 3, 4, 5 to Fulton St.

The Attack of the Double-Decker Buses

They are everywhere. There is no escape. They clog up the already over-crowded streets, spewing exhaust, their red or blue exteriors splashed with a garish display of self-promotion and advertising, loudspeakers blaring as the people huddled on the upper deck (swathed in plastic ponchos when it rains) look down at the natives on the streets. I'm talking about double-decker buses. They run in the morning, they run at night, they run all day long. Can you tell I'm not a fan? I think New York is best appreciated on foot, or on public buses and subways. Sure these double-decker buses have guides but take the facts they dish out with a grain of salt; they aren't always accurate. If you insist, the top bus tour is **Gray Line New York Tours** (✆ **800/669-0051** or 212/445-0848; www.graylinenewyork.com). Tours depart from various locations. Hop-on, hop off bus tours start at $49 adults, $39 children 3to 11.

New York Waterway 🐟🐟   New York Waterway, the nation's largest privately held ferry service and cruise operator, like Circle Line, also does the 35-mile trip around Manhattan, but does it in 2 hours, taking in all the same sights. They also offer a staggering amount of different sightseeing options, including a very good 90-minute New York Harbor Cruise, a Romantic Twilight Cruise, a Friday Dance Party Cruise, and Baseball cruises to Yankee games.

Departing from 38th St. Ferry Terminal (at W. 38th St. and Twelfth Ave). ✆ 800/533-3779. www.nywaterway.com. Sightseeing cruises $22 adults, $18 seniors, $12 children. Free bus transportation from 57th, 49th, 42nd, and 34th sts. to 38th St. Terminal; you can flag down any of the big red buses labeled NY WATERWAY or wait at any of the bus stops along those streets.

Spirit Cruises   Spirit Cruises' modern ships are floating cabarets that combine sightseeing in New York Harbor with freshly prepared meals, musical revues, and dancing to live bands. The atmosphere is festive, fun, and relaxed. The buffet meals are nothing special, but they're fine.

Departing from Pier 61 at Chelsea Piers, W. 23rd St. and Twelfth Ave. ✆ 866/482-3866. www.spiritcruises.com. 2-hr. lunch cruises $36–$48; 3-hr. dinner cruises $73 per person. Inquire about children's rates. Subway: C, E to 23rd St.

AIR TOURS

Liberty Helicopters   How about a bird's-eye view of Manhattan? These flight-seeing trips offer a quick thrill—literally. Five-minute tours from Midtown take in the Midtown skyscrapers and Central Park, while longer tours last 10 or 15 minutes and take in a wider view that includes lower Manhattan and the Statue of Liberty. If you opt for the longest tour, you'll fly far enough uptown to take in the George Washington Bridge and Yankee Stadium. Flights leave every 15 minutes daily from 9am to 9pm, but note that at least a 24-hour advance reservation is required.

Departing 1 block north of VIP Heliport, W. 30th St. and Twelfth Ave. ✆ 212/967-6464 or 800/542-9933. www. libertyhelicopters.com. Pilot-narrated tours $69–$186. Subway: A, C, E to 34th St. Also at the Downtown Manhattan Heliport, Pier 6, 111 Wall St and the Downtown Heliport at 6 East River Drive.

SPECIALTY TOURS

In addition to the options below, for those interested in touring lower Manhattan, the **Downtown Alliance** (✆ 212/566-6700; www.downtownny.com) offers two free walking tours: a **Historic Downtown Tour** every Tuesday at noon and a **Wall Street**

Walking Tour (see below). Both are 90 minutes long and are free. The Municipal Art Society (see below) and the Grand Central Partnership offer free walking tours of Grand Central Terminal 🌟 Wednesday at 12:30pm and Friday at 12:30pm, respectively (though there is a "suggested donation" for those tours); see p. 233.

The free 90-minute **Wall Street Walking Tour** 🌟 departs every Thursday and Saturday at noon, rain or shine. This guided tour explores the vivid history and amazing architecture of the nation's first capital and the world center of finance. Stops include the New York Stock Exchange, Trinity Church, Federal Hall National Monument, and many other sites of historic and cultural importance. Tours meet on the steps of Cass Gilbert's gorgeous **U.S. Customs House** 🌟 (p. 260), at 1 Bowling Green (Subway: 4, 5 to Bowling Green). Reservations are not required (unless you're a group), but you can call © 212/606-4064 or visit www.downtownny.com to confirm the schedule.

CULTURAL ORGANIZATIONS

The Municipal Art Society 🌟 (© 212/439-1049 or 212/935-3960; www.mas.org) offers excellent historical and architectural walking tours aimed at intelligent, individualistic travelers. Each is led by a highly qualified guide who offers insights into the significance of buildings, neighborhoods, and history. Topics range from the urban history of Greenwich Village to "Williamsburg: Beyond the Bridge" to an examination of the "new" Times Square. Monday to Friday walking tours are $12; Saturday and Sunday tours are $15. Reservations may be required depending on the tour, so it's best to call ahead. The full schedule is available online.

The 92nd Street Y 🌟 (© 212/415-5500; www.92ndsty.org) offers a wonderful variety of walking and bus tours, many featuring funky themes or behind-the-scenes visits. Subjects can range from "Diplomat for a Day at the U.N." to "Secrets of the Chelsea Hotel," or from "Artists of the Meat-Packing District" to "Jewish Harlem." Prices range from $25 to $60 (sometimes more for bus tours), but many include ferry rides, afternoon tea, dinner, or whatever suits the program. Guides are well-chosen experts on their subjects, ranging from respected historians to an East Village poet, mystic, and art critic (for *"Allen Ginsberg's New York"* and *"East Village Night Spots"*), and many routes travel into the outer boroughs; some day trips even reach beyond the city. Advance registration is required for all walking and bus tours. Schedules are planned a few months in advance, so check the website for tours that might interest you.

INDEPENDENT OPERATORS

NYC Discovery Tours (© 212/465-3331) offers more than 70 tours of the Big Apple, divided into five categories: neighborhood (including "Central Park" and "Brooklyn Bridge and Heights"), theme (such as "Gotham City Ghost Tour" and "Art

---

Grabbing a (Pedi)cab

You really don't want to burden that nag with a carriage ride through Central Park in the middle of the summer, do you? Better you should hire a real beast of burden—a driver of a **pedicab** who probably really needs the money. Pedicabs are becoming very common sights on the streets of New York. The drivers are friendly, informative, and don't litter the streets. The **Manhattan Rickshaw Company** (© 212/604-4729; www.manhattanrickshaw.com), is one pedicab company, where fares range from $15 to $30 or more for a pickup to $50 for an hour-long ride.

Tips Take the M5: A City Bus That Hits the Highlights

If your feet are worn out from walking, but you still want to see some sights, I suggest hopping on the **M5 bus.** Its route runs from Washington Heights down to Greenwich Village. If you board uptown, around 125th Street and Riverside Drive, and take it downtown, you'll pass landmarks such as Grant's Tomb, Riverside Church, Lincoln Center, Columbus Circle, St. Patrick's Cathedral, Rockefeller Center, the New York Public Library, Empire State Building, Flatiron Building, and Washington Square. And all you need is $2 from your MetroCard (or exact coin change) and your trusty *Frommer's New York City* guide book with your maps in hand. The bus will move slowly enough where you will be able to consult your book and find the corresponding landmarks.

History NYC"), biography ("John Lennon's New York"), tavern/food tasting, and American history and literature ("The Charles Dickens Tours"). Tours are about 2 hours long and cost $15 per person ($20 for food tasting tours).

All tours from **Joyce Gold History Tours of New York** *AA* (✆ **212/242-5762;** www.nyctours.com) are offered by Joyce Gold herself, an instructor of Manhattan history at New York University and the New School for Social Research, who has been conducting history walks around New York since 1975. Her tours can really cut to the core of this town; Joyce is full of fascinating stories about Manhattan and its people. Tours are arranged around such themes as "The Colonial Settlers of Wall Street," "The Genius and Elegance of Gramercy Park," "Downtown Graveyards," "The Old Jewish Lower East Side," "Historic Harlem," and "TriBeCa: The Creative Explosion." Tours are offered most weekends March to December and last from 2 to 3 hours, and the price is $15 per person; reservations are not required. Private tours can be arranged year-round, either for individuals or groups.

Myra Alperson, founder and lead tour guide for **NoshWalks** (✆ **212/222-2243;** www.noshwalks.com), knows food in New York City and knows where to find it. For the past 6 years, Alperson has been leading adventurous, hungry walkers to some of the city's most delicious neighborhoods. From the Uzbek, Tadjik, and Russian markets of Rego Park, Queens, to the Dominican coffee shops of Washington Heights in upper Manhattan, Alperson has left no ethnic neighborhood unexplored. Tours are conducted on Saturday and Sunday, leaving around 11:30am and 2:30pm. The preferred means of transportation is subway and the tours generally last around 3 hours and cost about $33 (Bronx Bites tours higher; check website for updated prices), not including the food you will undoubtedly buy on the tour. Space is limited, so book well in advance.

On Location Tours (✆ **212/209-3370;** www.sceneontv.com) offers narrated minibus tours through TV history on their Manhattan TV Tour; tickets are $34 for adults. Or, if you want to see Carrie Bradshaw's Big Apple, cut right to the chase and take the company's 3½-hour *Sex and the City* Tour, which includes over 40 show-related sights; tickets are $40. Most tours are on Saturday and depart from the Times Square Visitors Center (see "Orientation," in chapter 5). There's also a 4-hour *Sopranos* Tour that will take you over to New Jersey for an afternoon of sights that range from Satriale's Pork Store to the Bada-Bing! club; this tour leaves from Bryant Park on Saturday and Sunday at 2pm and costs $42. Reservations are strongly suggested for all

---

Finds **Offbeat New York Tours**

So maybe you've taken a harbor cruise or the bus tour, but you don't feel you got a taste of the gritty, quirky, neurotic elements that make New York unique. You want to see those sights that even many native New Yorkers have never seen. Here are a few alternatives to the conventional tours that might satisfy that need:

East Village Walking Tours (© 917/215-2575; www.avenuea.org): Some of the quirky tours offered by East Village Walking Tours include the must do, "Gangsters, Murderers, and Weirdos" tour ($15 per person) where you traverse the stomping grounds of such criminal luminaries as Charles "Lucky" Luciano, Bugsy Siegal, Al Capone, subway vigilante Bernie Goetz, and Ethel and Julius Rosenberg, and the "Counter Culture Bar Crawl" ($50 per person including a drink at each stop or $20 without drinks), where you will drink where the Rolling Stones, Frank Sinatra, and Madonna drank and hung out during their New York years. For the latter, you must be 21 or older, with ID to prove it.

Soundwalk (© 347/249-1506; www.soundwalk.com): This innovative company behind the audio self-guided-tour CDs debuted in 2003, with audio tours offering insider's peeks at Chinatown, the Lower East Side, Times Square, DUMBO, and the Meat-Packing District. All of these are great fun and will take you places no tour bus will, but my favorite is the three-CD set "Bronx Soundwalk." The CD set includes *Baseball,* a tour of Yankee Stadium and environs, narrated by longtime employee Tony Morante; *Graffiti,* a tour of Hunts Point and the trail of some of the legendary graffiti artists, narrated by BG183 (aka Sotero Ortiz), founding member of the TATS Cru and Mural Kings of the Bronx; and *Hip Hop,* a Bronx River tour narrated by hip-hop DJ the Original Jazzy Jay, which takes you to the birthplace of hip-hop and the haunts of such rap pioneers as Afrika Bambataa and Cool Herc.

---

tours, as most sell out in advance; it also makes sense to confirm days and times and check for any additional offerings.

Harlem Spirituals (© 800/660-2166 or 212/391-0900; www.harlemspirituals.com) specializes in gospel and jazz tours of Harlem that can be combined with a traditional soul-food meal. A variety of options is available, including a tour of Harlem sights with gospel service, and a soul-food lunch or brunch as an optional add-on. The Harlem jazz tour includes a neighborhood tour, dinner at a family-style soul-food restaurant, and a visit to a local jazz club; there's also an Apollo Theater variation on this tour. Bronx and Brooklyn tours are also an option for those who want a taste of the outer boroughs. Prices start at $49, $39 for children, for a Harlem Gospel tour, and go up from there based on length and inclusions (tours that include food and entertainment are pay-one-price). All tours leave from Harlem Spirituals' Midtown office (690 Eighth Ave., between 43rd and 44th sts.), and transportation is included.

Active visitors with an adventurous spirit can hook up with **Bike the Big Apple** (also known as Tours by Bike) (© **201/837-1133** outside U.S.; 877/865-0078 inside

These tours are *very* authentic; on the Bronx tour you'll even visit the G&R Pastry Shop where Mr. Steinbrenner, we learn, is a big fan of the shop's cheese Danish. CDs are $20, or you can buy MP3s for $13; all you need is a portable CD player, map, MetroCard, walking shoes, and an adventurous spirit. You can purchase CDs on the website or at retailers listed on the site.

Wildman Steve Brill 🎈 (www.wildmanstevebrill.com): If you ever get stranded in Central Park, a tour with Wildman Steve Brill might help you survive. I've seen him in the park, raggedy beard, shorts, hiking boots, and pith helmet, leading groups of eager-eyed followers while instructing them on what flora and fauna they can forage—breaking off a stick of some edible tree and gnawing on it as an example. Brill's Central Park tours occur twice monthly and are not only hilarious, they are educational. If you're lucky, maybe he'll regale you with his tale of his arrest by a park ranger for eating a dandelion. Reservations must be made in advance; call ☎ 914/835-2153. Suggested donation is $15. Cash only, exact change.

Hidden Jazz Haunts (www.bigapplejazz.com): This tour, hosted by New York jazz expert Gordon Polatnick, is the real deal for jazz buffs. Polatnick's tours are small (2–10 people) and are tailor-made to the jazz interests of his clients. If you're into bebop, he'll show you Minton's Playhouse, the still-standing but now defunct jazz club that was the supposed birthplace of bop. From there he'll take you to other active Harlem clubs that he feels embody that Minton's bebop spirit. If you're into the 1960s bohemian Village scene, he'll take you to clubs that represent that golden era of Village jazz clubs. Big Apple Jazz has a store and performance space at 2236 Seventh Ave, between 131st and 132nd Streets. The tour fee is $75 per hour, with a 4 hour minimum for most tours, plus cost of entrance fees, drinks, et cetera. They described the tours as "customizable." For reservations, call ☎ 212/283-JAZZ.

U.S.; www.bikethebigapple.com). Tours by Bike offers guided half-day, full-day, and customized tours through a variety of city neighborhoods, including the fascinating but little-explored upper Manhattan and Harlem; an ethnic tour that takes you over the legendary Brooklyn Bridge, through Chinatown and Little Italy, to Ground Zero, and around Flushing, Queens, where you'll feel like you're biking around Hong Kong. You don't have to be an Ironman candidate to participate; tours are designed for the average rider, with an emphasis on safety and fun; shorter rides are available, but the rides generally last around 4 to 7 hours. Tours are offered year-round; prices run $80 and include all gear and a bike.

For a bit more whimsy on your tour, **Levy's Unique New York** (☎ 877/692-5869; www.levysuniqueny.com) offers a lighter look at the city's history and landmarks. The tours are all custom-planned, depending on the size and needs of the group; most are walking but some are conducted by bus. A few of their unique tours include the "Bohemians and Beats of Greenwich Village Literary Tours," and "Hey Ho! Let's Go! Punk Rock on the Bowery" tour, which contrasts the culture of the 1850s with the punk rockers of the 1970s. The group is Brooklyn-based, and they are extremely knowledgeable about their home borough; tours of Coney Island and another called "Edible Ethnic Brooklyn Eats" are just a few that feature Brooklyn. Tours range from $25 to $65 per person.

Take the 45-minute **Inside CNN** guided tour of the network's studios in the Time Warner Center, 10 Columbus Circle (© **866/4CNNYC;** www.cnn.com/insidecnn), and learn a little about the newsgathering process. The tour includes views of three of CNN's working studios, demonstrations, and hands-on use of television technology. The tour costs $15 for adults, $14 for seniors, $11 for children 4 to 18, and are free for children 3 and under.

8 Talk of the Town: TV Tapings

The trick to getting tickets for TV tapings in this city is to be from out of town. You visitors have a much better chance than we New Yorkers; producers are gun-shy about filling their audiences with obnoxious locals and see everybody who's not from New York as being from the heartland—and therefore their target TV audience.

If you're set on getting tickets to a show, request them as early as possible— 6 months ahead isn't too early, and earlier is better for the most popular shows. Most shows have "ticket request" areas on their websites, which will ask you the number of tickets you want, your preferred dates of attendance (be as flexible as you can), and your address *and* phone number. Tickets are always free. Even if you send in your request early, don't be surprised if tickets don't arrive at your house until shortly before the tape date.

If you come to town without any tickets, all is not lost. Because they know that every ticket holder won't make it, many studios give out a limited number of standby tickets on the day of taping. If you can just get up a little early and don't mind standing in line for a couple (or a few) hours, you have a good chance of getting one (note that the Letterman show no longer has standby lines, you have to call). Now, the bad news: Only one standby ticket per person is allowed, so *everybody* who wants to get in has to get up at the crack of dawn and stand in line. And even if you get your hands on a standby ticket, it doesn't guarantee admission; they usually only start seating standbys after the regular ticket holders are in. Still, chances are good.

For additional information on getting tickets to tapings, call the **NYCVB** at © **212/561-9000.** And remember—you don't need a ticket to be on the *Today* show.

If you do attend a taping, be sure to bring a sweater, even in summer. As anybody who watches Letterman knows, it's *cold* in those studios. And bring ID, as proof of age may be required.

The Colbert Report   Jon Stewart's star reporter Steve Colbert, of *The Daily Show,* became so popular he was given his own show on Comedy Central. Now he is giving Stewart a run for his money in the ratings. As of press time, tickets to *The Colbert Report* were only available on a standby basis. Arrive at the studio no later than 4pm to sign up: 513 W. 54th St., between Tenth and Eleventh avenues. Check the website, **www.comedycentral.com/shows/the_colbert_report**, for ticket information.

The Daily Show with Jon Stewart   Comedy Central's irreverent, often hilarious mock newscast tapes Monday through Thursday at 5:45pm, at 513 W. 54th St. *The Daily Show* no longer takes phone requests. For tickets, send an e-mail with your full name and daytime phone number to **requesttickets@thedailyshow.com**. Last-minute ticket requests *only* are allowed by telephone on the Friday prior to the desired show. Call ℭ **212/586-2477.**

Late Night with Conan O'Brien Conan's taking over the Tonight show in 2009, so if you want to see him on "Late Night," better do it soon. Tapings are Tuesday through Friday at 5:30pm (plan on arriving by 4:45pm if you have tickets), and you must be 16 or older to attend. You can reserve up to four tickets in advance by calling ℭ **212/664-3056.** Standby tickets are distributed on the day of taping at 9am outside 30 Rockefeller Plaza, on the 49th Street side of the building (under the NBC Studios awning), on a first-come, first-served basis (come *very* early to get one).

The Late Show with David Letterman Here's the most in-demand TV ticket in town. Submit ticket requests online at **www.cbs.com/lateshow**; or stop by the Ed Sullivan Theater Monday to Friday from 9:30am to 12:30pm or Saturday and Sunday from 10am to 6pm to submit an in-person request. Tapings are Monday through Thursday at 5:30pm (arrive by 4:15pm), with a second taping Thursday at 8pm (arrive by 6:45pm). You must be 18 or older to attend. On tape days, there are no standby lines anymore; call ℭ **212/247-6497** at 11am for up to two standby tickets; start dialing early, because the machine will kick in as soon as all standbys are gone. If you do get through, you may have to answer a question about the show to score tickets.

Live! with Regis and Kelly Tapings with Regis Philbin and Kelly Ripa are Monday through Friday at 9am at the ABC Studios at 7 Lincoln Sq. (Columbus Ave. and W. 67th St.) on the Upper West Side. You must be 10 or older to attend (children younger than 18 must be accompanied by a parent). Send an SASE (four tickets max) at least a *full year* in advance to *Live!* Tickets, Ansonia Station, P.O. Box 230777, New York, NY 10023-0777 (ℭ **212/456-3054**). Standby tickets are sometimes available. Arrive at the studio no later than 7am and request a standby number; standby tickets are handed out on a first-come, first-served basis, so earlier is better.

Rachael Ray Show You can apply to be featured on the show (if you fit one of the topics they are doing a segment on, like "Do you have a crush on a reality TV star?" or "Kids not turning out the way you expected?") or request tickets on the website (**www.rachaelrayshow.com**). Demand for the tickets is high, and you may be in for a long wait. When it's in production, the show tapes twice a day on Tuesdays, Wednesdays and Thursdays at Ray's studio at 222 East 44th Street (between 2nd and 3rd aves.). You must be over 16 years old to attend a taping, and bring a valid photo ID. There's a rather detailed dress code (no capris! no sequins!). You can also stop by on the day of taping to see if standby tickets are available.

Saturday Night Live *SNL* tapings are Saturday at 11:30pm (arrival time 10:45pm); there's also a full dress rehearsal at 8pm (arrival time 7:15pm). You must be 16 or older to attend. Here's the catch: Email requests (at snltickets@nbcuni.com) are taken only in August and the odds are always long. However, you can try for standby tickets on the day of the taping, which are distributed at 7am outside 30 Rockefeller Plaza, on the 49th Street side of the building (under the NBC Studios awning), on a first-come, first-served basis; only one ticket per person will be issued. If you want to try your luck with advance tickets, call ℭ **212/664-3056** *as far in advance of your arrival in New York as possible* to determine the current ticket-request procedure.

The *Today* Show Anybody can be on TV with Matt and cuddly weatherman Al Roker and Meredith Vieira. All you have to do is show up outside *Today's* glass-walled studio at Rockefeller Center, on the southwest corner of 49th Street and

---

⌒Tips Who Wants to Be on a Game Show?

The syndicated daily version of *Who Wants to Be a Millionaire,* hosted by Meredith Vieira, goes through a lot of contestants and is always on the lookout for smart cookies to sit in the Hot Seat. Check the website (http://millionairetv.com) to see if auditions are being held while you're in town (auditions are usually held Aug–Dec). You can sign up over the Net to attend a taping/take the test on a specific date; you will receive an e-mail confirmation. When the show is taping, you'll be expected to attend as an audience member for a couple of episodes in addition to taking the test (all the better to practice your skills on "Ask the Audience"). On your audition date, report to the ABC studios at 30 W. 67th St. (off Central Park West). Bring ID! You'll take a multiple-choice test and if you score in the top 10% or so, you'll have a brief interview with show staff. If you're selected for the contestant pool, you'll get a postcard telling you that you're in contention for a spot. If you're selected to go into the Hot Seat, you'll have to plan another trip to New York City, so remember where you put this book!

Rockefeller Plaza, with your HI, MOM! sign. Tapings are Monday through Friday from 7 to 10am, but come at the crack of dawn if your heart's set on being in front. Who knows? If it's a nice day, you may even get to chat with Meredith, Matt, or Al in a segment. Come extra early to attend a Friday Summer Concert Series show.

The View   ABC's hugely popular girl-power gabfest tapes live Monday through Friday at 11am (ticket holders must arrive by 9:30am). Requests, which should be made 12 to 16 weeks in advance, can be submitted online (www.abc.go.com/theview). Since exact-date requests are not usually accommodated, try standby: Arrive at the studio before 10am and put your name on the standby list; earlier is better, as tickets are handed out on a first-come, first-served basis. You must be 18 or older to attend.

9 Especially for Kids

Some of New York's sights and attractions are designed specifically with kids in mind, and I've listed those below. But many I've discussed in the rest of this chapter are terrific for kids as well as adults; so I've included cross-references to the best of them.

Probably the best place of all to entertain the kids is in **Central Park** 𝘼𝘼𝘼, which has kid-friendly diversions galore (see the section beginning on p. 264). For kid-friendly theatrical performances, see the "Kids Take the Stage: Family-Friendly Theater" box, on p. 342.

For general tips and additional resources, see "Family Travel" under "Specialized Travel Resources" in chapter 3.

MUSEUMS

In addition to the museums specifically for kids detailed below, consider the following, discussed elsewhere in this chapter: The **American Museum of Natural History** 𝘼𝘼𝘼 (p. 229), whose dinosaur displays are guaranteed to wow both you and the kids; the **New York City Fire Museum** 𝘼 (p. 252), in a real firehouse; the **American Museum of the Moving Image** 𝘼 (p. 295), where you and the kids can learn how movies are actually made (and play vintage video games); the **Lower East Side Tenement Museum** 𝘼 (p. 245), whose weekend living-history program intrigues school-age kids;

the **New York Transit Museum** (p. 290), where kids can explore vintage subway cars and other hands-on exhibits; the **South Street Seaport & Museum** (p. 254), which little ones will love for its theme-park-like atmosphere and old boats bobbing in the harbor, and at press time, after a 6-year $46-million renovation, the **Brooklyn Children's Museum** (145 Brooklyn Ave.; © **718/735-4400;** www.brooklynkids.org) was set to open.

Children's Museum of the Arts (Kids)

Interactive workshop programs for children ages 1 to 12 and their families are the attraction here. Kids dabble in puppet making and computer drawing or join in singalongs and live performances. Also look for rotating exhibitions of the museum's permanent collection featuring WPA work. Call or check the website for the current exhibition and activities schedule.

182 Lafayette St. (btwn Broome and Grand sts.). © **212/941-9198** or 212/274-0986. www.cmany.org. Admission $9 for everyone 65 and under, pay what you wish Thurs 4–6pm. Wed–Sun noon–5pm (Thurs to 6pm). Subway: 6 to Spring St.; R, W to Prince; N to Canal St.

Children's Museum of Manhattan (R) (Kids)

Here's a great place to take the kids when they're tired of being told not to touch. Designed for ages 2 to 12, this museum is strictly hands-on. Interactive exhibits and activity centers encourage self-discovery—and a recent expansion means that there's even more to keep the kids busy and learning. The Time Warner Media Center takes children through the world of animation and helps them produce their own videos. The Body Odyssey is a zany, scientific journey through the human body. This isn't just a museum for the 5-and-up set—there are exhibits designed for babies and toddlers, too. The schedule also includes art classes and storytellers, and a full slate of entertainment on weekends.

212 W. 83rd St. (btwn Broadway and Amsterdam Ave.). © **212/721-1234.** www.cmom.org. Admission $9 children and adults, $6 seniors. School season Wed–Sun and school holidays 10am–5pm; summer Tues–Sun 10am–5pm. Subway: 1 to 86th St.

New York Hall of Science (R) (Kids)

Children of all ages will love this huge hands-on museum in the borough of Queens, which bills itself as "New York's Only Science Playground." This place is amazing for school-age kids. Exhibits let them float on air in an antigravity mirror, compose music by dancing in front of light beams, and explore the more-than-miniature world of microbes. There are even video machines that kids can use to retrieve astronomical images, including pictures taken by the *Galileo* in orbit around Jupiter. There's a Preschool Discovery Place for the really little ones. But probably best of all is the summertime Outdoor Science Playground for kids 6 and older—ostensibly lessons in physics, but really just a great excuse to laugh, jump, and play on jungle gyms, slides, seesaws, spinners, and more.

The museum is in Flushing Meadows–Corona Park, where kids can enjoy even more fun beyond the Hall of Science. Not only are there more than 1,200 acres of park and playgrounds, but there's also a zoo, a carousel, an indoor ice-skating rink, an outdoor pool, and bike and boat rentals. The park is also home to the **Queens Museum of Art** (p. 296) as well as Shea Stadium and the U.S. Open Tennis Center.

47–01 111th St., in Flushing Meadows–Corona Park, Queens. © **718/699-0005.** www.nyscience.org. Admission $11 adults, $8 seniors and children 2–17, free on Fri from 2–5pm and on Sun from 10–11am. except for July–Aug. Additional $3 for Science Playground. Mon–Thurs 9:30am–2pm (till 5pm July–Aug); Fri 9:30am–5pm; Sat–Sun 10am–6pm. Subway: 7 to 111th St.

Sony Wonder Technology Lab (Kids)

This place is mot as much of an infomercial as you'd expect. Both kids and adults love this four-level high-tech science-and-technology center, which explores communications and information technology. You can experiment with robotics, explore the human body through medical imaging, edit a music video, mix a song, design a video game, and save the day at an environmental command center. The lab also features the first high-definition interactive theater in the United States. Admission is absolutely free; this place is extremely popular, however, so it's wise to make reservations in advance. Reservations can be made up to 3 months in advance by calling ℭ **212/833-5414,** Monday through Friday between 9am and 2pm. Otherwise, you may not get in, or you may get tickets that require you to return at a different time. At press time, the third and fourth floors were under renovation and closed. Check with the website for the most up-to-date status.

Sony Plaza, 550 Madison Ave. (at 56th St.). ℭ 212/833-8100, or 212/833-5414 for reservations. www.sonywonder techlab.com. Free admission. Sun noon–5pm; Tues–Sat 10am–5pm; last entrance 30 min. before closing. Subway: E, V to Fifth Ave.; 4, 5, 6, N, R to 59th St.; F to 57th St.

OTHER KID-FRIENDLY DIVERSIONS

SHOPPING   Everybody loves to shop in New York—even kids. Don't forget to take them to Books of Wonder; that temple of sneakerdom, NIKETOWN; the NBA Store; Dylan's Candy Bar, for a real Willy Wonka experience; and Toys "R" Us in Times Square, with its very own indoor Ferris wheel. See chapter 8 for details.

SKY-HIGH VIEWS   Kids of all ages can't help but turn dizzy with delight at views from atop the **Empire State Building** (p. 231). The Empire State Building also has the New York Skyride (ℭ **800/759-7433;** www.skyride.com), which is a short motion-flight-simulation sightseeing tour of New York, in case the real one isn't enough for your kids. Open daily 10am to 10pm; *when purchased online,* tickets are $26 for adults, $19 for seniors and kids 12 to 17, $18 for kids 6 to 11; tickets cost $4 more when purchased at the Empire State Building. Combination Empire State observation deck/New York Skyride tickets are available at a discount.

SPECIAL EVENTS   Children's eyes grow wide at the yearlong march of parades (especially Macy's Thanksgiving Day Parade), circuses (Big Apple and Ringling Bros. and Barnum & Bailey), and holiday shows (the Rockettes' Christmas and Easter performances). See the "New York City Calendar of Events," in chapter 3, for details.

ZOOS & AQUARIUMS   Bigger kids will love the legendary **Bronx Zoo** (p. 284), while the **Central Park Zoo**, with its **Tisch Children's Zoo** (p. 267), is particularly suitable for younger kids. At the **New York Aquarium** at Coney Island (p. 290), kids can touch starfish and sea urchins and watch bottle-nosed dolphins and California sea lions stunt-swim in the outdoor aqua theater. **Brooklyn's Prospect Park** (p. 292) also boasts a wonderful little zoo.

10 Highlights of the Outer Boroughs

IN THE BRONX

In addition to the options below, literary buffs might also want to visit the Edgar Allan Poe Cottage, the last home of the brilliant but troubled author of *The Raven, The Tell-Tale Heart,* and other masterworks. See the sidebar "In Search of Historic Homes," on p. 259.

Bronx Zoo Wildlife Conservation Park *(Kids*   Founded in 1899, the Bronx Zoo is the largest metropolitan animal park in the United States, with more than 4,000 animals living on 265 acres, and one of the city's best attractions.

Bronx Botanical Gardens	**3**
Bronx Museum of the Arts	**7**
Bronx Zoo	**4**
City Island	**6**
Pelham Bay Park	**5**
Wave Hill	**1**
Woodlawn Cemetery	**2**
Yankee Stadium	**8**

One of the most impressive exhibits is the Wild Asia Complex. This zoo-within-a-zoo comprises the Wild Asia Plaza education center; Jungle World, an indoor re-creation of Asian forests, with birds, lizards, gibbons, and leopards; and the Bengali Express Monorail (open May–Oct), which takes you on a narrated ride high above free-roaming Siberian tigers, Asian elephants, Indian rhinoceroses, and other non-native New Yorkers (keep your eyes peeled—the animals aren't as interested in seeing you). The Himalayan Highlands is home to 17 extremely rare snow leopards, as well as red pandas and white-naped cranes. The 6½-acre Congo Gorilla Forest is home to Western lowland gorillas, okapi, red river hogs, and other African rainforest animals.

The Children's Zoo (open Apr–Oct) allows young humans to learn about their wildlife counterparts. Kids can compare their leaps to those of a bullfrog, slide into a turtle shell, climb into a heron's nest, see with the eyes of an owl, and hear with the ears of a fox. There's also a petting zoo. Camel rides are another part of the summertime picture, as is the Butterfly Zone and the Skyfari aerial tram (each an extra $3 charge).

If the natural settings and breeding programs aren't enough to keep zoo residents entertained, they can always choose to ogle the two million annual visitors. But there are ways to beat the crowds. Try to visit on a weekday or on a nice winter's day. In summer, come early in the day, before the heat of the day sends the animals back into their enclosures. Expect to spend an entire day here—you'll need it.

(Value) A Trolley in the Bronx

Proving that the Bronx is not the bad-boy borough it has often been portrayed as in movies, the **Bronx Tourism Council** (© **718/590-2766;** www.llovethebronx. com) sponsors free tours in a quaint trolley-replica bus. The Bronx Trolley operates on weekends and holidays from April through October and nighttime during the Christmas holiday season and makes stops at Arthur Avenue, the **Bronx Zoo** (p. 284), and the **New York Botanical Garden** (p. 286). On the weekends, the trolley departs at 9:30am from the NYC Visitors Information Center, at Seventh Avenue and 53rd Street in Manhattan, and makes hop on/hop off stops throughout the day. On the first Wednesday of every month, the trolley is transformed into the Bronx Cultural Trolley and is sponsored by the **Bronx Council of the Arts** (© **718/931-9500;** www.bronxarts.org). The trolley takes you on a cultural tour of the lower Grand Concourse area of the South Bronx.

Getting there: Liberty Lines' BxM11 express bus, which makes stops on Madison Avenue, will take you directly to the zoo; call © **718/652-8400.** By subway, take the no. 2 train to Pelham Parkway and then walk west to the Bronxdale entrance.

Fordham Rd. and Bronx River Pkwy., the Bronx. © **718/367-1010.** www.bronxzoo.com. Admission $14 adults, $12 seniors, and $10 for children 2–12; discounted admission Nov–Mar; free Wed year-round. There may be nominal additional charges for some exhibits. Nov–Mar daily 10am–4:30pm (extended hours for Holiday Lights late Nov–early Jan); Apr–Oct Mon–Fri 10am–5pm, Sat–Sun 10am–5:30pm. Transportation: See "Getting there," above.

New York Botanical Garden ✿ A National Historic Landmark, the 250-acre New York Botanical Garden was founded in 1891 and today is one of America's foremost public gardens. The setting is spectacular—a natural terrain of rock outcroppings, a river with cascading waterfalls, hills, ponds, and wetlands.

Highlights of the Botanical Garden include the 27 specialty gardens, an exceptional orchid collection, and 40 acres of uncut forest, as close as New York gets to its virgin state before the arrival of Europeans. The Enid A. Haupt Conservatory, a stunning series of Victorian glass pavilions that recall London's former Crystal Palace, shelters a rich collection of tropical, subtropical, and desert plants as well as seasonal flower shows. There's also a Children's Adventure Garden. Natural exhibits are augmented by year-round educational programs, musical events, bird-watching excursions, lectures, special family programs, and many more activities. Best of all is the annual Holiday Train Show (late Nov–early Jan; call for exact dates), where railway trains and trolleys wind their way through more than 100 replicas of historic New York buildings and attractions—such as the Statue of Liberty, the Metropolitan Museum of Art, and the Garden's own Enid A. Haupt Conservatory—all made from plant parts and other natural materials. There are so many ways to see the garden—tram, golf cart, walking tours—that it's best to call or check the website for more information.

Getting there: Take Metro-North (© **800/METRO-INFO** or 212/532-4900; www.mta.nyc.ny.us/mnr) from Grand Central Terminal to the New York Botanical Garden station; the ride takes about 20 minutes. By subway, take the D or 4 train to Bedford Park, then take bus Bx26 or walk southeast on Bedford Park Boulevard for 8 long blocks.

200th St. and Kazimiroff Blvd., the Bronx. © **718/817-8700.** www.nybg.org. Admission $6 adults, $3 seniors, $2 students, $1 children 2–12. Extra charges for Everett Children's Adventure Garden, Enid A. Haupt Conservatory, T. H.

Everett Rock Garden, Native Plant Garden, and narrated tram tour; entire Garden Passport package $13 adults, $11 seniors and students, $5 children 2–12. Apr–Oct Tues–Sun and Mon holidays 10am–6pm; Nov–Mar Tues–Sun and Mon holidays 10am–5pm. Transportation: See "Getting there," above.

Wave Hill (*Finds*   Formerly a private estate with panoramic views of the Hudson River and the Palisades, Wave Hill has, at various times in its history, been home to a British U.N. ambassador as well as Mark Twain and Theodore Roosevelt. Set in a stunningly bucolic neighborhood that doesn't look anything like you'd expect from the Bronx, its 28 gorgeous acres were bequeathed to the city of New York for use as a public garden that is now one of the most beautiful spots in the city. It's a wonderful place to commune with nature, both along wooded paths and in beautifully manicured herb and flower gardens, where all of the plants are clearly labeled by careful horticulturists. Benches are positioned throughout the property for quiet contemplation and spectacular views. It's a great spot for taking in the Hudson River vibe without having to rent a car and travel to Westchester to visit the Rockefeller estate; in 2004, a 28-acre public garden and cultural center opened, making it even more attractive and accessible. Programs range from horticulture and environmental education to landscape history and forestry to dance performances and concerts.

Getting there: Take the no. 1 subway to 231st Street, then take the Bx7 or Bx10 bus to the 252nd Street stop; or take the A train to 207th Street and pick up the Bx7 to 252nd Street. From the 252nd Street stop, walk west across the parkway bridge and turn left; at 249th Street, turn right. Metro North trains (© **212/532-4900**) go from Grand Central to the Riverdale station; from there, it's a 5-block walk to Wave Hill.

675 W. 249th St. (at Independence Ave.), the Bronx. © 718/549-3200. www.wavehill.org. Admission $6 adults, $3 seniors and $2 students; free admission in winter, and Sat mornings and Tues in summer. Tues–Sun 9am–4:30pm; extended hours in summer (check ahead). Transportation: See "Getting there," above.

IN BROOKLYN

For details on walking the **Brooklyn Bridge** (**), see p. 230.

It's easy to link visits to the Brooklyn Botanic Garden, the Brooklyn Museum of Art, and Prospect Park, as they're all an easy walk from one another, just off Grand Army Plaza. Designed by Frederick Law Olmsted and Calvert Vaux as a suitably grand entrance to their Prospect Park, it boasts a Civil War memorial arch designed by John H. Duncan (1892–1901) and the main Brooklyn Public Library, an Art Deco masterpiece completed in 1941 (the garden and museum are on the other side of the library, down Eastern Pkwy.). The area is a half-hour subway ride from Midtown.

Brooklyn Botanic Garden (*   Down the street from the Brooklyn Museum of Art (see below) is the most popular botanic garden in the city. This 52-acre sanctuary is at its most spectacular in May, when the thousands of pink blossoms of cherry trees are abloom. Well worth seeing is the spectacular Cranford Rose Garden, one of the largest and finest in the country; the Shakespeare Garden, an English garden featuring plants mentioned in his writings; a Children's Garden; the Osborne Garden, a 3-acre formal garden; the Fragrance Garden, designed for the blind but appreciated by all noses; and the Japanese Hill-and-Pond Garden. The renowned C. V. Starr Bonsai Museum is home to the world's oldest and largest collection of bonsai, while the impressive $2.5-million Steinhardt Conservatory holds the garden's extensive indoor plant collection.

900 Washington Ave. (at Eastern Pkwy.), Brooklyn. © 718/623-7200. www.bbg.org. Admission $8 adults, $4 seniors and students, free for children under 16, free to all Tues and Sat 10am–noon year-round, plus Wed–Fri from mid-Nov through Feb. Apr–Sept Tues–Fri 8am–6pm, Sat–Sun 10am–6pm; Oct–Mar Tues–Fri 8am–4:30pm, Sat–Sun 10am–4:30pm. Subway: Q to Prospect Park; 2, 3 to Eastern Pkwy./Brooklyn Museum.

Finds **The Bronx You Never Knew Existed**

The Bronx is far more than just the home of a great zoo and baseball stadium. Here are a few under-the-radar highlights of that under appreciated
borough.

1. **The Point Community Development Corporation** (940 Garrison Ave.;
   © **718/542-4139;** www.thepoint.org; Subway: 6 to Hunts Point Ave.).
   The Point Community Development Corporation, or just "The Point" as
   the locals know it, is a community space to keep the young people of
   the neighborhood out of trouble. It has grown from its humble beginnings in the early 1990s into a cultural mecca. At the Point you can check
   out photographic exhibitions of works produced by talented young
   people under the tutelage of the International Center of Photography
   (ICP); the Edge Theater, where there's a menu of movies, plays, musical
   performances, and other art-related activities; performances and tutelage by the Rock Steady Crew, whose break-dance style grew out of the
   late-1970s movement; and graffiti art by none other than Tats Cru,
   whose work has been featured in movies, commercials and on the
   streets of NYC. At the Point you'll also find Angel Rodriguez, one of
   NYC's most important Puerto Ricans, with over 40 years' experience in
   performing salsa and mambo music, not to mention his legendary
   conga sessions, which you can catch at the Edge Theater.
2. **Pelham Bay Park.** Most tourists think the largest park in New York City
   is Central Park. Surprise! It's the Bronx's own Pelham Bay Park. In the
   northeast corner of the Bronx, Pelham Bay Park was created in 1888
   and covers over 2,700 acres. It is also the playground for residents of
   nearby Co-op City, the biggest private-housing development on the
   East Coast. The park boasts an equestrian center where you can take
   lessons or go on guided horseback tours, lagoons where you can canoe,
   and trails along which you can bike or hike. You are also only a short
   bus ride from the Bronx's only beach, Orchard Beach, created by New
   York City's infamous commissioner of parks, Robert Moses, in the early
   20th century. Subway: 6 to Pelham Bay Park.
3. **City Island** (www.cityisland.com). Take the no. 6 train to its last stop,
   Pelham Bay Park. Then transfer to City Bus Bx29 towards hidden-treas-
   ure City Island. During colonial times, City Island was known as Minneford Island, which reflected the area's connection to its traditional
   owners, the Sinawoy Minneford tribe. Today City Island is connected to

Brooklyn Museum of Art *★★*   One of the nation's premier art institutions, the
Brooklyn Museum of Art rocketed into public consciousness in 1999 with the controversial "Sensation: Young British Artists from the Saatchi Collection," which drew
international media attention and record crowds who came to see just what an artist—
and a few conservative politicians—could make out of a little elephant dung.

the mainland by a 600-foot-long bridge that takes you from parkland to fishing village. The island itself is a little over a mile long and a quarter of a mile wide and houses native Bronxites, whose heritage on the island can be traced back more than 150 years. On City Island, marinas dot the tiny coast. The marinas played an important part in the war effort during World Wars I and II, playing host to the construction of minesweepers and costal patrol craft. In more recent times, however, City Island has been involved in the construction of yachts that have won several America Cup titles. City Island offers an abundance of top-quality seafood restaurants, including the late great Salsa musician Tito Puente's own spot.

4. **The Bronx Museum of the Arts** (1040 Grand Concourse, at 165th St.; ✆ **718/681-6000**; www.bronxmuseum.org; Subway: B, D to 167th St./ Grand Concourse). The Bronx Museum of the Arts was founded in 1971 and specializes in contemporary art produced by talented New Yorkers of Latin, Asian, and African-American descent. The museum displays a number of works inspired by the Bronx itself with over 700 pieces in the permanent collection. The artwork was made public in 1986, and exhibitions over the years have included "One Planet Under a Groove Hip-Hop, Contemporary Art" and "Urban Mythologies: The Bronx Represented Since the 1960s." For those travelers on a budget, admission to the museum won't set you back much at $5 for adults and $3 for children; it's free Friday and for children under 12. The museum is a 15-minute walk from Yankee Stadium and a good complement to a day watching the Yankees play.

5. **Woodlawn Cemetery** (Webster Ave. and E. 233rd St.; ✆ **718/920-0500**; www.thewoodlawncemetery.org; Subway: 4 to Woodlawn Station). Woodlawn Cemetery is no ordinary cemetery. It was created in 1863 and is best known for its ornate and imaginative mausoleums and monuments. The grounds stretch over 400 acres and house the country's first community mausoleum, which opened in 1967. Woodlawn Cemetery is one of the city's most famous, and you'll find a number of notable people laid to rest here including salsa superstar Celia Cruz, jazz geniuses Miles Davis and Duke Ellington, former mayor of New York City Fiorello La Guardia, Joseph Pulitzer, songwriter George M. Cohan, and theater impresario Oscar Hammerstein. Weekend guided tours are available.

Indeed, the museum is known for its consistently remarkable temporary exhibitions as well as its excellent permanent collection. The museum's grand Beaux Arts building, designed by McKim, Mead & White (1897), befits its outstanding holdings, most notably the Egyptian, Classical, and Ancient Middle Eastern collection of sculpture, wall reliefs, and mummies. The decorative-arts collection includes 28 American period rooms from 1675 to 1928 (the extravagant Moorish-style smoking room from John D. Rockefeller's 54th St. mansion is my favorite). Other highlights are the African and Asian arts galleries, dozens of works by Rodin, a good costumes and textiles collection, and a diverse collection of both American and European painting and sculpture that includes works by Homer, O'Keeffe, Monet, Cézanne, and Degas.

Spring 2007 brought the opening of the Elizabeth A. Sackler Center for Feminist Art, which feature permanent and rotating exhibitions of art made by women. One of the prizes of the collection is Judy Chicago's famous "The Dinner Party."

200 Eastern Pkwy. (at Washington Ave.), Brooklyn. ℂ 718/638-5000. www.brooklynmuseum.org. Suggested admission $8 adults, $4 seniors and students, free for children under 12, free to all 1st Sat of the month 11am–11pm. Wed–Fri 10am–5pm; 1st Sat of the month 11am–11pm, each Sat thereafter 11am–6pm; Sun 11am–6pm. Subway: 2, 3 to Eastern Pkwy./Brooklyn Museum.

Brooklyn Tabernacle 𝒜   Under the direction of passionate orator Pastor Jim Cymbala and his choral-director wife, Carol, this nondenominational Christian revival church has grown into one of the largest—with a congregation of nearly 10,000 from all walks of city life—and most renowned inner-city churches in the nation. Folks come from all over the world to see the 275-voice, four-time Grammy Award–winning Brooklyn Tabernacle Choir, one of the nation's most celebrated gospel choirs.

The gloriously renovated 1918 building is the fourth-largest theatrical space in the five boroughs, and seats nearly 4,000 for each service. Still, come early for a prime seat, especially when the choir sings (at the noon and 4pm Sun services).

17 Smith St. (btwn Fulton and Livingston sts.), downtown Brooklyn. ℂ 718/290-2000. www.brooklyntabernacle.org. Services Sun 9am, noon, and 3:30pm; Tues 7pm. Subway: A, C, F to Jay St./Borough Hall; 2, 3 to Hoyt St.; 4, 5 to Borough Hall; M, R to Lawrence St.

Coney Island 𝒜𝒜 (Moments   Sure, Coney Island is just a shell of what it was in its heyday in the early 20th century. But it's that shell and what remains that make it such an intriguing attraction. The almost-mythical Parachute Jump, recently refurbished, though long inoperable, stands as a monument to Coney Island. But this is not a dead amusement park; Astroland, home of the famed Cyclone roller coaster, has some great rides for children and adults; though 2008 will be its last season. The new owners will keep the National Historic Landmark Cyclone, however; and the Wonder Wheel, next door at Deno's, will still be turning. The best amusement of all, however, is the people-watching. Maybe because it is at the extreme edge of New York City, but Coney Island attracts more than its share of the odd, freaky, and funky. It's here where Nathan's Famous Hot Dogs holds its annual hot-dog-eating contest on July 4 at noon; where the wholly entertaining **Mermaid Parade** 𝒜 spoofs the old bathing-beauty parades (late June); and where members of the Polar Bear Swim Club show their masochistic gusto by taking a plunge into the icy ocean on January 1. The best time to visit is between Memorial Day and mid-September, when the rides and amusement park are open. Bring your bathing suit and test the waters.

If you are here in the summer, or even if you are not, I recommend a visit to Coney Island just to see it; and you can always visit the nearby **Coney Island Museum,** 1208 Surf Ave. (ℂ 718/372-5159; www.coneyisland.com). Open Saturdays and Sundays year round, here you will find relics from Coney Island's heyday as the premier amusement park in the world. Check out an original "steeplechase horse," vintage bumper cars, or fun-house distortion mirrors. And for a mere 99¢, even if all you want to do is use the clean bathroom, the museum is a bargain.

Brooklyn. Subway: D, F, N, Q to Coney Island–Stillwell Ave..

Brooklyn Botanic Garden **9**
Brooklyn Lyceum **6**
Brooklyn Museum of Art **8**
Brooklyn Tabernacle **2**
Dime Savings Bank **5**
Grand Army Plaza **7**
New York Aquarium **10**
New York Transit Museum **3**
Pratt Institute **4**
Prison Ship Martyrs
  Monument **4**
Williamsburg Art
  & Historical Center **1**

New York Aquarium (Kids) Because of the long subway ride (about an hour from midtown Manhattan) and its proximity to Coney Island, it's best to combine the two attractions, preferably in the summer. This surprisingly good aquarium is home to hundreds of sea creatures. Taking center stage are Atlantic bottle-nosed dolphins and California sea lions that perform daily during summer at the Aquatheater. Also basking in the spotlight are gangly Pacific octopuses, sharks, and a brand-new sea-horse exhibit. Black-footed penguins, California sea otters, and a variety of seals live at the Sea Cliffs exhibit, a re-creation of a Pacific coastal habitat. But my absolute favorites are the beautiful white Beluga whales, which exude buckets of aquatic charm. Children love the hands-on exhibits at Discovery Cove. There's an indoor oceanview cafeteria and an outdoor snack bar, plus picnic tables.

502 Surf Ave. (at W. 8th St.), Coney Island, Brooklyn. (C) **718/265-FISH.** www.nyaquarium.com. Admission $12 adults, $8 seniors and children 2–12. Daily 10am–4:30pm. Subway: F, Q to West 8th St..

New York Transit Museum (C) (Kids) Housed in a real (decommissioned) subway station, this underground museum is a wonderful place to spend an hour or so. The museum is small but very well done, with good multimedia exhibits exploring the history of the subway from the first shovelful of dirt scooped up at groundbreaking (Mar 24, 1900) to the present. Kids and parents alike will enjoy the interactive elements and the vintage subway cars, old wooden turnstiles, and beautiful station mosaics of yesteryear. A recent exhibit dedicated to surface transportation called "On the Streets: New York's Trolleys and Buses," continues to be on display. It's a very worthy hands-on tribute to an important development in the city's history.

The smaller Gallery Annex & Store at Grand Central Station also houses rotating exhibitions and a terrific transit-themed gift shop (see "Museum Stores," in chapter 8).

Boerum Place and Schermerhorn St., Brooklyn. ☎ **718/694-1600**. http://mta.info/mta/museum/index.html. Admission $5 adults, $3 seniors and children 3–17, free for seniors Wed noon–4pm. Tues–Fri 10am–4pm; Sat–Sun noon–5pm. Subway: A, C, to Hoyt St.; F to Jay St.; M, R to Court St.; 2, 3, 4, 5 to Borough Hall. Gallery Annex: In Grand Central Terminal (on the main level, in the shuttle passage next to the Station Masters' office), 42nd St. and Lexington Ave. ☎ **212/878-0106**. Subway: 4, 5, 6, 7, S to 42nd St./Grand Central.

Prospect Park 🏮🏮 Designed by Frederick Law Olmsted and Calvert Vaux after their success with Central Park, this 562 acres of woodland, meadows and ponds is considered by many to be their masterpiece and the *pièce de résistance* of Brooklyn.

The best approach is from **Grand Army Plaza,** presided over by the monumental **Soldiers' and Sailors' Memorial Arch** (1892) honoring Union veterans. For the best view of the lush landscape, follow the path to Meadowport Arch, and proceed through to the Long Meadow, following the path that loops around it (it's about an hour's walk). Other park highlights include the 1857 Italianate mansion **Litchfield Villa** on Prospect Park West; the **Friends' Cemetery** Quaker burial ground (where Montgomery Clift is eternally prone—sorry, it's fenced off to browsers); the wonderful 1906 Beaux Arts **boathouse;** the 1912 **carousel,** with white wooden horses salvaged from a famous Coney Island merry-go-round (open Apr–Oct; rides 50¢); and **Lefferts Homestead Children's Historic House Museum** (☎ **718/789-2822**), a 1783 **Dutch farmhouse** with a museum of period furniture and exhibits geared toward kids (Apr–Nov Thurs–Sun noon–5pm; Dec–Mar Sat–Sun noon–4pm). There's a map at the park entrance that you can use to get your bearings.

On the east side is the **Prospect Park Zoo** (☎ **718/399-7339**), a modern children's zoo where kids can walk among wallabies, explore a prairie-dog town, and more. Admission is $6 for adults, $2.25 for seniors, $2 for children 3 to 12. From April through October, it's open Monday through Friday from 10am to 5pm (to 5:30pm weekends and holidays); November through March, open daily from 10am to 4:30pm.

At Grand Army Plaza, bounded by Prospect Park West, Parkside Ave., and Flatbush Ave., Brooklyn. ☎ **718/965-8999** for events information. www.prospectpark.org. Subway: 2, 3 to Grand Army Plaza (walk down Plaza St. West 3 blocks to Prospect Park West and the entrance) or Eastern Pkwy./Brooklyn Museum.

BROOKLYN HEIGHTS HISTORIC DISTRICT

Just across the Brooklyn Bridge is **Brooklyn Heights** 🏮, a peaceful neighborhood of tree-lined streets, more than 600 historic houses built before 1860, landmark churches, and restaurants. Even with its magnificent promenade providing sweeping views of lower Manhattan's ragged skyline, it feels more like its own village than part of the larger urban expanse.

This is where Walt Whitman lived and wrote *Leaves of Grass,* one of the great accomplishments in American literature. And in the 19th century, fiery abolitionist Henry Ward Beecher railed against slavery at Plymouth Church of the Pilgrims on Orange Street between Henry and Hicks streets (his sister wrote *Uncle Tom's Cabin*). If you walk down Willow Street between Clark and Pierrepont, you'll see three houses (nos. 108–112) in the Queen Anne style that was fashionable in the late 19th century, as well as an attractive trio of Federal-style houses (nos. 155–159) built before 1829.

Brooklyn Heights Highlights

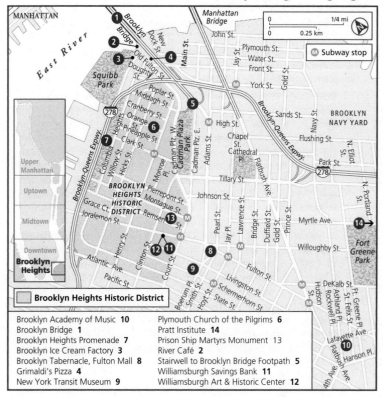

Brooklyn Academy of Music **10**
Brooklyn Bridge **1**
Brooklyn Heights Promenade **7**
Brooklyn Ice Cream Factory **3**
Brooklyn Tabernacle, Fulton Mall **8**
Grimaldi's Pizza **4**
New York Transit Museum **9**

Plymouth Church of the Pilgrims **6**
Pratt Institute **14**
Prison Ship Martyrs Monument **13**
River Café **2**
Stairwell to Brooklyn Bridge Footpath **5**
Williamsburgh Savings Bank **11**
Williamsburgh Art & Historic Center **12**

Also visit lively Montague Street, the main drag of Brooklyn Heights and full of cafes and shops. On Water Street, under the Brooklyn Bridge, is the **River Café** (✆ **718/ 522-5200;** www.rivercafe.com), where a drink or dinner at twilight, as the lights of Manhattan begin to flicker on, will offer an unforgettable view.

GETTING THERE   Bounded by the East River, Fulton Street, Court Street, and Atlantic Avenue, the Brooklyn Heights Historic District is one of the most outstanding and easily accessible NYC sights beyond Manhattan. The neighborhood is reachable via a number of subway trains: the A, C, F to Jay St.; the 2, 3, 4, 5 to Clark Street or Borough Hall; or the R to Court Street.

It's easy to link a walk around Brooklyn Heights and along its promenade with a walk over the **Brooklyn Bridge** ★★ (p. 230), a tour that makes for a lovely afternoon on a nice day. Take a no. 2 or 3 train to Clark Street (the first stop in Brooklyn). Turn right out of the station and walk toward the water, where you'll see the start of the Brooklyn Promenade. Stroll along the promenade admiring both the stellar views of lower Manhattan to the left and the gorgeous brownstones to the right, or park yourself on a bench for a while to contemplate the scene.

The promenade ends at Columbia Heights and Orange Street. To head to the bridge from here, turn left and walk toward the Watchtower Building. Before heading downslope, turn right immediately after the playground onto Middagh Street. After 4

How to See Brooklyn Like a Native

Here are five Brooklyn sights that, according to Norman Oder of the above-mentioned New York Like a Native tours, are often missed by guidebooks but much appreciated by Brooklyn natives.

1. **Downtown Brooklyn:** The 1907 Beaux Arts-style Dime Savings Bank, now operated by Washington Mutual, is a spectacular example of the financial cathedral. Check the Mercury dimes at the top of the interior Corinthian columns as well as the aphorisms about thrift carved into the marble benches. It's open 9am to 6pm Monday to Friday and 9am to 1pm on Saturday; no interior photos. Next door is the iconic restaurant Junior's, famous for its cheesecake (try the chocolate mousse variety). The bank is at 9 DeKalb Avenue, just west of Flatbush Avenue.

2. **Williamsburg Art & Historical Center:** Located in the 1867-built Kings County Savings Bank at 135 Broadway, this is the largest gallery space in Williamsburg (② **718/486-7372;** www.wahcenter.net). The shows here are funky and diverse. Not far from **Peter Luger Steakhouse** (p. 213), browsing the museum is a good way to work off one of Luger's porterhouses. Subway: L to Bedford Ave. or J/M/Z to Marcy Ave.

3. **Prison Ship Martyrs Monument:** In Fort Greene Park (www.fortgreenepark.org) this oft-overlooked monument, designed by the legendary architectural firm of McKim, Meade & White, was dedicated by President Taft in 1908 and commemorates the sacrifices of more than 11,000 patriots during the Revolutionary War. (Open for outside views during daylight hours.) Subway: R, Q, B to DeKalb Avenue or 2, 3, 4, 5 to Nevins Street.

4. **Pratt Institute** (200 Willoughby Ave., ② **718/636-3600;** www.pratt.edu): Before Brooklyn native Pete Hamill went on to a celebrated writing career, he studied art here. The campus has a terrific sculpture garden and a wide array of works, surrounded by buildings both modern and classic. Subway: G to Clinton/Washington.

5. **Brooklyn Lyceum** (227 Fourth Ave.; ② **866/GOWANUS;** www.brooklynlyceum.com): On the edge of the very residential neighborhood known as Park Slope, this quirky and cavernous performance space for music, theater, and more was once a public bathhouse. Subway: R to Union St.

or 5 blocks, you'll reach a busy thoroughfare, Cadman Plaza West. Cross the street and follow the walkway through little Cadman Plaza Park; veer left at the fork in the walkway. At Cadman Plaza East, turn left (downslope) toward the underpass, where you'll find the stairwell up to the Brooklyn Bridge footpath on your left.

BROOKLYN TOURS

A Slice of Brooklyn Pizza Tour ⊕ (② **212/209-3370;** www.bknypizza.com): What better way to experience history-rich Brooklyn than by a tour centered on pizza. And Brooklyn has no dearth of good pizza. Guided by affable and knowledgeable Brooklyn native and pizza aficionado, Tony Muia, the bus tour begins in Manhattan and heads over the Manhattan Bridge for a look at DUMBO, the Brooklyn Bridge, Fulton Ferry Landing, and then pizza at **Grimaldi's** (p. 186) for Neapolitan pizza. From Grimaldi's, the bus keeps to the south of the borough passing the Brooklyn Navy Yard, the neighborhood of Red Hook, and then into Bay Ridge and Bensonhurst where Tony will show you film locations for movies such as Saturday Night Fever, Goodfellas, and the French Connection. The bus stops at L&B Spumoni Gardens in Bensonhurst for authentic Brooklyn Sicilian pizza, and then on to Coney Island where, if it is summer, you can ride the famous Cyclone roller coaster and attempt to keep all the pizza you have just eaten in your stomach. The 4½-hour tour is $75, including two slices of pizza at both pizzerias and soft drinks.

There are New York natives and there are Brooklyn natives—please don't confuse the two. Norman Oder is the latter and proud of it. His **New York Like a Native Tours** (© 718/393-7537; www.nylikeanative.com) cover the borough, the fourth-largest city in America, as extensively as anyone, from his "Brooklyn 101," which takes visitors to the heart of Brooklyn, Grand Army Plaza, Prospect Park, Park Slope, and Brooklyn Heights, to the more neighborhood-specific tours like that of the Polish-populated Greenpoint and the Orthodox and Hasidic Jewish Borough Park. Tours run from 2 to 3 hours and prices range from $15 to $18, not including food.

IN QUEENS

For details on the **New York Hall of Science** ✪ and **Flushing Meadows–Corona Park** (also home to the Queens Museum of Art; see below), see p. 296.

American Museum of the Moving Image ✪ (Kids)   The museum is undergoing a $65-million reconstruction. It is scheduled to reopen in winter 2009–10. In the meantime, it is hosting some screenings and events at various venues in Manhattan and Queens (such a "evenings" with films and talks by filmmakers such as Michael Gondry, Stanley Tucci, and Jonathan Demme). Check the website for updates.

35th Ave. at 36th St., Astoria, Queens. © 718/784-0077. www.movingimage.us.

Isamu Noguchi Garden Museum ✪ (Finds)   No place in the city is more Zen than this marvelous indoor/outdoor garden museum showcasing the work of Japanese American sculptor Isamu Noguchi (1904–88). The museum showcases the beautifully curated collection of the artist's masterworks in stone, metal, wood, and clay; you'll even see theater sets, furniture, and models for gardens and playgrounds that Noguchi designed. A new gallery highlights the artist's work in interior design. A renovation that has shut off some areas of the museum to the public is expected to be completed in November, 2008.

9–01 33rd Rd. (at Vernon Blvd.), Long Island City, Queens. © 718/204-7088. www.noguchi.org. Suggested admission $10 adults, $5 seniors and students. Wed–Fri 10am–5pm; Sat–Sun 11am–6pm. Subway: N to Broadway. Walk west (toward Manhattan) on Broadway until Broadway ends at Vernon Blvd.; turn left on Vernon and go 2 blocks.

Louis Armstrong House Museum ✪ (Finds)   What is it about celebrities' homes that we find so fascinating? Is it that we get to see how they lived away from the glare of the cameras; how they functioned on a daily basis just like the rest of us? Armstrong was an international celebrity and could have lived anywhere, yet this unassuming, bi-level house in the working-class neighborhood of Corona, Queens, was the great Satchmo's home from 1943 until his death in 1971. It was bought and designed by his fourth wife, Lucille, who lived in it until her death in 1983. No one has lived in the house since, and in 2003 the house, a National Historic Landmark and a New York City landmark, opened its doors to the public as a museum. The 40-minute tour takes you through the small, impeccably preserved home and explains the significance

Moments The International Express

The **no. 7 train**—which originates in Manhattan at Times Square, makes three stops in that borough, and then snakes, mostly above ground, through the heart of ethnic Queens—is also popularly known as the International Express. Built by immigrants in the early 1900s, the no. 7 IRT (Interborough Rapid Transit) brought those same immigrants to homes on the outer fringes of New York City. That tradition has continued as immigrants from around the world have settled close by the no. 7's elevated tracks. Get off in Sunnyside and see Romanian grocery stores and restaurants; a few stops farther in Jackson Heights, you'll see Indians in saris and Sikhs in turbans; go all the way to Flushing and you'll think you are in Chinatown. You are—Flushing's Chinatown, as big or bigger than Manhattan's. In 1999, the Queens Council on the Arts nominated the International Express for designation as a National Millennium Trail, and that resulted in its selection as representative of the American immigrant experience by the White House Millennium Council, the United States Department of Transportation, and the Rails-to-Trails Conservancy. For more information and for tours, visit the **Queens Council on the Arts** website, at **www.queenscouncil arts.org** (© **718/647-3377**).

of each room to both Louis and Lucille. My favorite is Armstrong's den, where he kept his reel-to-reel tape recordings, cataloging everything he taped—music, conversations, and compositions, some of which are displayed on his desk. The house also includes a small exhibit with some of his memorabilia, including two of his trumpets, and a gift shop, where many of his CDs are for sale along with other Satchmo-centric items. If you have any interest in jazz and in Armstrong, this is a must-see.

34–56 107th St., Corona, Queens. © 718/478-8274. www.satchmo.net. $8 adults, $6 seniors, students, and children. Tues–Fri 10am–5pm; Sat–Sun noon–5pm; last tour at 4pm. Subway: 7 to 103rd St./Corona Plaza. Walk north on 103rd St., turn right on 37th Ave., turn left onto 107th St., and the house is a half-block north of 37th Ave.

P.S. 1 Contemporary Art Center   If you're interested in contemporary art that's too cutting-edge for most museums, don't miss this MoMA affiliate museum. Originally a public school (hence the name), this is the world's largest institution exhibiting contemporary art from America and abroad. You can expect to see a kaleidoscopic array of works from artists ranging from Jack Smith to Julian Schnabel; the museum is particularly well known for large-scale exhibitions by artists such as James Turrell. In 2005, the museum featured a well-received and popular exhibit entitled "Greater New York," featuring works by more than 160 New York–based artists who have come into prominence since the year 2000.

22–25 Jackson Ave. (at 46th Ave.), Long Island City, Queens. © 718/784-2084. www.ps1.org. Suggested admission $5 adults, $2 seniors and students. Thurs–Mon noon–6pm. Subway: E, V to 23rd St./Ely Ave. (walk 2 blocks south on Jackson Ave. to 46th Ave.); 7 to 45th Rd./Court House Sq. (walk 1 block south on Jackson Ave.).

Queens Museum of Art   One way to see New York in the shortest time (albeit without the street life) is to visit the Panorama, created for the 1939 World's Fair, an enormous building-for-building architectural model of New York City complete with an airplane that takes off from LaGuardia Airport. The 9,335-square-foot Gotham City is the largest model of its kind in the world, with 895,000 individual structures

American Museum of the Moving Image
  (closed through late 2009) **3**
Isamu Noguchi Garden Museum **2**
P.S. 1 Contemporary Art Center **4**
Socrates Sculpture Park **1**

built on a scale of 1 inch=100 feet. A red-white-and-blue ribbon is draped mournfully over the Twin Towers, which still stand in this "Big Apple."

Also on permanent display is a collection of Tiffany glass manufactured at Tiffany Studios in Queens between 1893 and 1938. The "Contemporary Currents" series features rotating exhibits focusing on the works of a single artist, often with an international theme (suitable to New York's most diverse borough). History buffs should take note of the museum's NYC Building, which housed the United Nation's General Assembly from 1946 to 1952. Art exhibitions, tours, lectures, films, and performances are part of the program, making this a very strong museum on all fronts.

Next to the Unisphere in Flushing Meadows–Corona Park, Queens. ☏ **718/592-9700.** www.queensmuseum.org. Suggested admission $5 adults, $2.50 seniors and students, free for children under 5. Wed–Fri 10am–5pm; Sat–Sun noon–5pm. Subway: 7 to Willets Point/Shea Stadium (follow the yellow signs for the 10-min. walk through the park to the museum, which sits next to the Unisphere).

Socrates Sculpture Park *Kids*   This former riverside landfill is now the best exhibition space for large-scale outdoor sculpture in the city. No velvet ropes and motion sensors here—interaction with the artwork is encouraged. It's well worth a look, especially on a lovely day, and has a spectacular view of Roosevelt Island and the East Side of Manhattan. Check the website for the current exhibition schedule—or just let

yourself be happily surprised. The park also offers outdoor movie screenings and free
tai chi and yoga classes in the summer.

32–01 Vernon, at Broadway, Long Island City, Queens. ℂ **718/956-1819.** www.socratessculpturepark.org. Free
admission. Daily 10am–sunset. Subway: N, W to Broadway; walk 8 blocks along Broadway toward the East River.

11 Spectator Sports

For details on the New York City Marathon and the U.S. Open tennis championships,
see the "New York City Calendar of Events," in chapter 3.

BASEBALL   In 2009, it will be goodbye Shea Stadium and hello Citi Field, the new
ballpark in Queens for the New York Mets. While in the Bronx, the Yankees will open
their new billion-dollar ballpark, to be called, as the old one was, Yankee Stadium.
And with two baseball teams in town, you can catch a game almost any day, from
opening day in April to the beginning of the playoffs in October. Though because
both teams will have new stadiums, tickets will be even more difficult to land.

Ticket prices for the 2008 season, which are priced at Gold, Silver, Bronze and Platinum levels (based on the team the Mets are playing and the day of the week: i.e., any
Yankees game is Platinum; certain early season games are "Value," with deeply discounted tickets), range from $5 to $37 for "Value" games, to $22 to $70 for Platinum
games, with many variations. Trust me, you *do* need a program . . . or to study the
seating chart on the team website. For information, call the **Mets Ticket Office** at
ℂ **718/507-TIXX,** or visit **www.mets.com**. Also keep in mind that you can buy
game tickets (as well as logo wear and souvenirs, if you want to dress appropriately for
the big game) at the **Mets Clubhouse Shop,** which has two midtown Manhattan
locations; see chapter 8.

New Yankee Stadium, will be across the street from the old one (Subway: C, D, 4
to 161st St./Yankee Stadium). **NY Waterway** (p. 275) offers baseball cruises to games;
call ℂ **800/533-3779,** or visit **www.nywaterway.com** for more info. For single game
tickets ($12–$63 in 2008), contact **Ticketmaster** (ℂ **212/307-1212** or 212/307-
7171; www.ticketmaster.com) or **Yankee Stadium** (ℂ **718/293-6000;** www.yankees.
com). Serious baseball fans check the schedule well in advance for Old Timers' Day,
usually held in July, when pinstriped stars of years past return to the stadium to take
a bow.

At current Yankee Stadium, upper-tier box seats (which run about $42), especially
those behind home plate, give you a great view of all the action. Upper tier reserve
seats are behind the box seats and significantly cheaper ($20). Bleacher seats are even
cheaper ($12), and the rowdy commentary from that section's roughneck bleacher
creatures is absolutely free. Most of the expensive seats (field boxes) are sold out in
advance to season-ticket holders. You can often purchase these same seats from
scalpers, but you'll pay a premium for them. Tickets can be purchased at the team's
clubhouse shop in Manhattan, at the stadium on the day of the game, online at
http://newyork.yankees.mlb.com, and on such online resale sites as **Stub Hub**
(www.stubhub.com), where you can also find Mets tickets. Expect prices for tickets at
both parks to go way up, especially for the higher end seats, in 2009.

Minor-league baseball ⊛ coexists with the show in the boroughs, with the **Brook-
lyn Cyclones,** the New York Mets' minor league farm team, and the **Staten Island
Yankees,** the Yanks' minor leaguers. Boasting their very own waterfront stadium, the
Cyclones have been a major factor in the revitalization of Coney Island; KeySpan Park

A Big Renovation for MSG

The owners of Madison Square Garden announced that the facility will undergo a $500-million renovation in 2009–10 The construction will be done during the summers of 2009 and 10 (the off-season for the Rangers and Knicks), which means that the WNBA's New York Liberty will be looking for new digs for all or part of those seasons.

sits right off the boardwalk (Subway: D, F, N, Q to Stillwell Ave./Coney Island). The SI Yanks also have their own playing field, the Richmond County Bank Ballpark, just a 5-minute walk from the Staten Island Ferry terminal (Subway: N, R to Whitehall St.; 4, 5 to Bowling Green; 1 to South Ferry). What's more, with bargain-basement ticket prices (which topped out at $15 for the Cyclones, $13 for the Yanks in the 2008 season), this is a great way to experience baseball in the city for a fraction of the major-league hassle and cost. Both teams have a rabidly loyal fan base, so it's a good idea to buy your tickets for the June through September season in advance. For the Cyclones, call ℂ **718/449-8497** or visit **www.brooklyncyclones.com**; to reach the SI Yanks, call ℂ **718/720-9200** or go online to **www.siyanks.com**.

BASKETBALL   Though the New Jersey Nets are supposed to be moving to Brooklyn (pending construction of a new arena), there are two pro hoops teams that already play in New York at **Madison Square Garden,** Seventh Avenue, between 31st and 33rd streets (ℂ **212/465-6741** or www.thegarden.com; 212/307-7171 or www.ticket master.com for tickets; Subway: A, C, E, 1, 2, 3 to 34th St.). The **New York Knicks** (ℂ **877/NYK-DUNK** or 212/465-JUMP; www.nyknicks.com) are the NBA team from NYC, and their tickets range from $35 to $335. The WNBA's **New York Liberty** (ℂ **212/465-6080;** www.wnba.com/liberty), who electrify fans with their tough defense and scrappy youngsters, occupy MSG from late May through September. Tickets for the Liberty (which celebrated its 12th season in 2008) start at $10 and go up to about $229 for courtside seats, with plenty of good seats available ranging from $10 to $30.

ICE HOCKEY   NHL hockey is represented in Manhattan by the **New York Rangers,** who play at Madison Square Garden, Seventh Avenue between 31st and 33rd streets (ℂ **212/465-6741;** www.newyorkrangers.com or www.thegarden.com; Subway: A, C, E, 1, 2, 3, to 34th St.). Rangers tickets are hard to get, so plan well ahead; call ℂ **212/307-7171,** or visit **www.ticketmaster.com** for online orders. Ticket prices range from $27 to $140 and *waaaaaaaaaaaaay* up (for VIP seats).

8

Shopping

For many, shopping is their *raison d'être*—an uncontrollable urge, almost an addiction. What more perfect place than New York to satisfy that urge? No city in the world has the breadth and variety of stores; it's a shopper's paradise.

In this chapter, I've done my best to point out the city's shopping highlights; it's certainly enough to get you started. For much, much more on the New York shopping scene, check out shopping guru Suzy Gershman's latest edition of ***Born to Shop New York*** (Wiley Publishing, Inc.).

1 The Top Shopping Streets & Neighborhoods

Here's a rundown of New York's most interesting shopping areas, with highlights of each to give you a feel for the neighborhood. If location is not given, refer to the store's expanded listing in the appropriate category in "Shopping A to Z," later this chapter.

DOWNTOWN

LOWER MANHATTAN & THE FINANCIAL DISTRICT

South Street Seaport (© 212/732-8257; Subway: 2, 3, 4, 5 J, Z, M to Fulton St.) carries the neighborhood's torch. Familiar names such as Abercrombie & Fitch, Ann Taylor, and the Sunglass Hut line Fulton Street, the Seaport's main cobbled drag; several tiers of largely nondescript shops and a large food court fill the levels at Pier 17, a waterfront barge–turned–shopping mall. There's nothing here you can't get anywhere else in Manhattan; come for the historic ambience and the wonderful harbor views. For a store list, visit **www.southstreetseaport.com**.

Century 21, the king of discount department stores, is across the street from the World Trade Center site. Electronics megamart **J&R** is still going strong, now occupying a full city block, with great prices on everything from cameras and computers to CDs and software. Purchase electronics here rather than at the "going-out-of-business" places in Midtown.

CHINATOWN

Don't expect to find the purchase of a lifetime on Chinatown's crowded streets, but there's some quality browsing. The fish and herbal markets along Canal, Mott, Mulberry, and Elizabeth streets are fun for their bustle and exotica. Dispersed among them (especially along Canal St.), you'll find a mind-boggling collection of knockoff sunglasses and watches, backpacks, leather goods, and exotic souvenirs. It's a fun browse, but don't expect quality—and be sure to bargain before you buy. (Also, skip the bootleg CDs, videos, and software—these are stolen goods, and you *will* be disappointed with the product.) Steer clear of such electronics as answering machines, radios, and the like, but if you find that you *must* buy, be sure to open the package before you buy.

Tips Sales Tax

New York City sales tax is 8.375%, but it is not added to **clothing and footwear items under $110.** If you're visiting from out of state, consider having your purchases shipped directly home to avoid paying sales tax. As with any shipped purchase, be sure to get proper documentation of the sale and keep those receipts handy until the merchandise arrives at your door.

It's a common scam for a sealed box to be offered for sale very cheap, and when you get home you find you've paid for . . . a bunch of newspaper or a brick.

Mott Street, between Pell Street and Chatham Square, boasts the most interesting of Chinatown's off-Canal shopping, with an antiques shop or two dispersed among the tiny storefronts selling blue-and-white Chinese dinnerware. Just around the corner, peek into **Ting's Gift Shop** (18 Doyer St.; © **212/962-1081**), one of the oldest operating businesses in Chinatown. Under a vintage pressed-tin ceiling, it sells good-quality Chinese toys, kits, and lanterns.

THE LOWER EAST SIDE

The bargains aren't what they used to be in the **Historic Orchard Street Shopping District**—which basically runs from Houston to Canal along Allen, Orchard, and Ludlow streets, spreading outward along both sides of Delancey Street—but prices on leather bags, shoes, luggage, linens, and fabrics on the bolt are still good. Be aware, though, that the hard sell on Orchard Street can be hard to take. Still, the district is a nice place to discover a part of New York that's disappearing. Come during the week; many stores are Jewish-owned and close Friday afternoon and all day Saturday. Sunday tends to be a madhouse.

The artists and other trendsetters who have been turning this neighborhood into a bastion of hip have also added a cutting edge to its shopping scene in recent years. You'll find a growing—and increasingly upscale—crop of alterna-shops south of Houston and north of Grand Street, between Allen and Clinton streets to the east and west, specializing in up-to-the-minute fashions and edgy club clothes for 20-somethings, plus funky retro furnishings, Japanese toys, and other offbeat items. Before you browse, stop in at the **Lower East Side Visitor Center,** 261 Broome St., between Orchard and Allen streets (© **866/224-0206** or 212/226-9010; Subway: F to Delancey St.), for a shopping guide that includes vendors both old-world and new. Or you can preview the list online at **www.lowereastsideny.com**.

SOHO

People love to complain about superfashionable SoHo—it's become too trendy, too tony, too "Mall of America." True, **J. Crew** is only one of many big names that have supplanted many of the artists' lofts that used to inhabit its historic buildings. But SoHo is still one of the best shopping 'hoods in the city—and few are more fun to browse. The elegant cast iron architecture, the cobblestone streets, and the distinct rich-artist vibe: SoHo has a look and feel unlike any other Manhattan neighborhood.

SoHo's shopping grid runs from Broadway west to Sixth Avenue, and Houston Street south to Canal Street. **Broadway** is the most commercial strip, with such recognizable names as **Pottery Barn, Banana Republic, Sephora,** and **A/X Armani**

Exchange. H&M, the Swedish department store with cutting-edge fashions sold at very low prices, has two stores that face one another on Broadway. **Bloomingdale's** has opened up a downtown branch on Broadway. **Prada**'s flagship store, also on Broadway, is worth visiting for its spacious, almost soothing design alone (by Dutch architect Rem Koolhaus). A definite highlight is the two-story **Pearl River** Chinese emporium (see "Gifts" in "Shopping A to Z," later in this chapter), which offers everything from silk cheongsam (traditional Chinese high-necked dresses) to teaware.

The big names in avant-garde fashion (see "Clothing" in "Shopping A to Z," later in this chapter) have landed in SoHo, but you'll also find one-of-a-kind boutiques, such as the **Hat Shop,** 120 Thompson St., between Prince and Spring streets (© 212/219-1445), a full-service milliner for women that also features plenty of off-the-rack toppers, plus shoe stores galore and high-end home design and housewares boutiques.

If you're still hungry for the ultramodern and cutting-edge, stop by the **Museum of Modern Art Design Store.** The Midtown museum has an enormous shop in SoHo and it offers the same wonderful chrome and asymmetrical goodies as the original, ranging from pencils to furniture from the museum's collection. There are several not-to-be-missed art galleries along West Broadway and peppered throughout the SoHo area. So if you're looking to expand your collection or just see the work of the next big thing in the art world, be sure to stop by. You can find a full listing of galleries and their hours (most are closed on Mon) at **www.artseensoho.com.**

NOLITA

Not so long ago, **Elizabeth Street** was a quiet adjunct to Little Italy. Today it's one of the hottest shopping strips in the neighborhood known as Nolita. Elizabeth and neighboring **Mott** and **Mulberry streets** are dotted with increasing numbers of shops between Houston Street and the Bowery. It's an easy walk from the Broadway/

Tips **Additional Sources for Serious Shoppers**

If you're looking for specific items, check the shopping listings at **www.new york.citysearch.com, www.timeoutny.com,** and **www.nymag.com** before you leave home.

For an online guide to sample sales/designer bargains, you can't do better than the free registration site **www.nysale.com,** which will let you in on unadvertised sales taking place throughout the city.

Hard information about current sales, new shops, sample and close-out sales, and special art, craft, and antiques shows is best found in the "Check Out" section of *Time Out New York* or the "Sales & Bargains," "Best Bets," and "Smart City" sections of *New York* magazine. *New York* also runs daily updates of sales at **www.nymag.com,** and *Time Out* publishes a twice-yearly shopping guide that's available on newsstands for about $6.

Other Web sources include **www.dailycandy.com,** a daily newsletter highlighting store openings and where to find the day's sales, and **www.girlshop. com,** dedicated to New York insider fashion news. Now Girlshop aficionados have more than just the website: To visit the online's own store, **Girlshop Boutique,** go to the Meat-Packing District (819 Washington St., between Little W. 12th and Gansevoort sts.; © 212/255-4985).

⌜Tips⌝ **Take a Shopping Tour**

If you want some help in your shopping and feel a bit intimidated by all the options Manhattan has to offer, you might want to consider taking a shopping tour. **Shop Gotham** (© 212/209-3370; www.shopgotham.com) offers walking tours of SoHo, Fifth Avenue, the Garment Center, and a Big Store tour, where you'll hit stores such as Macy's, Bloomingdale's, and Century 21 all in 4 hours. Tours range from 2 to 4 hours and from $25 to $85.

Lafayette stop on the F, V line to the neighborhood, as it starts just east of Lafayette Street; you can also take the no. 6 train to Spring Street, or the N, R to Prince Street, and walk east from there.

Nolita is the stepchild of SoHo—meaning don't expect cheap. Its wall-to-wall boutiques are largely the province of shopkeepers specializing in high-quality fashion-forward products. More and more, it's become a beacon of ethnic designs from around the world. **Indomix** (232 Mulberry St.; © 212/334-6356; www.indomix.com) offers beaded tunics and other colorful south-Asian styles by five top designers in India. Texan-born designer and skateboarder **Tracy Feith** (209 Mulberry St.; © 212/334-3097) creates irresistibly pretty slip dresses, skirts, and tops in eye-popping colors and light-as-air Indian silk in his eponymous store on Mulberry Street.

Nolita is also an accessories bonanza; stop in at **Sigerson Morrison** (28 Prince St.; © 212/219-3893) for great shoes, or **Push** (240 Mulberry St.; © 212/965-9699) for eye-catching jewelry. You'll find more standouts in the listings in "Shopping A to Z," later in this chapter, but just cruising the blocks will do the trick.

THE EAST VILLAGE

The East Village personifies bohemian hip, though many New Yorkers would argue that SoHo's gentrification has engulfed this refuge for alternative purists. The easiest subway access is the no. 6 train to Astor Place, which is just a couple blocks east to the prime hunting grounds.

East 9th Street, between Second Avenue and Avenue A, is lined with an increasingly smart collection of boutiques, proof that the East Village isn't just for kids anymore. Designers, including **Jill Anderson** (331 E. 9th St.; © 212/253-1747) and **Huminska** (315 E. 9th St.; © 212/677-3458), sell excellent-quality and original fashions for women along here.

If it's strange, possibly illegal, or funky, it's probably available on **St. Marks Place,** which takes over for 8th Street, running east from Third Avenue to Avenue A. This strip is a permanent street market, with countless T-shirt and boho jewelry stands and tattoo parlors. The height of the action is between Second and Third avenues, which is prime hunting grounds for used-record collectors (see "Music," in "Shopping A to Z," later this chapter). If you're in search of the harder-edge East Village and feeling a little brave, explore the side streets closer to Avenue A and southward toward the Bowery.

LAFAYETTE STREET FROM SOHO TO NOHO

Lafayette Street has a retail character all its own, distinct from the rest of SoHo. It has grown into something of an Antiques Row, especially strong in furniture. Prices are high, but so is quality. The stretch to stroll is between 8th Street to the north and Spring Street to the south. Take the no. 6 train to Astor Place and work your way south, or get off at Spring Street and walk north, or take the F or V to Broadway-Lafayette and you'll be in the heart of the action. Highlights include **Guéridon,** (37 W. 20th St.; ✆ **212/462-2149;** www.gueridon.com), for sophisticated 20th-century European pieces, mainly French, plus some original designs in the same vein.

GREENWICH VILLAGE

The West Village is great for browsing and gift shopping. Specialty bookstores and record stores, antiques and craft shops, and gourmet food markets dominate. On 8th Street—NYU territory between Broadway and Sixth Avenue—you can find trendy footwear and affordable fashions.

But the biggest shopping boom of late has happened on **Bleecker Street** west of Sixth Avenue. Between Carmine Street and Seventh Avenue, foodies will delight in the strip of boutique food shops, including **Amy's Bread, Wild Edibles,** and **Murray's Cheese.** In between are record stores, guitar shops, and a sprinkling of artsy boutiques. On **Christopher Street,** you'll find such wonders as **Aedes De Venutas,** a gorgeous little boutique selling fabulous perfumes and scented candles that are difficult to find in the States, and **The Porcelain Room,** 13 Christopher St. (✆ **212/367-8206**), which is located below street level and offers amazing antique and contemporary porcelains that have to be seen to be believed.

The Oscar Wilde Bookshop, the world's first gay bookstore has been on the sleepy eastern end of Christopher Street since 1967. Follow Christopher Street westward, where Bleecker becomes boutique alley, and one jewel box of a shop follows another. Among them: **Intermix, Olive & Bette, Ralph Lauren, Lulu Guinness,** and **Marc Jacobs.**

Those who really love to browse should also wander **west of Seventh Avenue** and along **Hudson Street,** where charming shops such as **House of Cards and Curiosities,** 23 Eighth Ave., between Jane and 12th streets (✆ **212/675-6178**), the Village's own funky take on an old-fashioned nickel-and-dime, are tucked among the brownstones.

CHELSEA/MEAT-PACKING DISTRICT

Almost overnight it seems, far west Chelsea has been transformed into the **Chelsea Art District,** where more than 200 galleries have sprouted up in a once-moribund enclave of repair shops and warehouses. The district unofficially stretches between 14th to 29th streets and the West Side Highway and Seventh Avenue, but the high-density area lies between 20th and 26th streets, between Tenth and Eleventh avenues.

The Meat-Packing District has also zoomed from quaint to hot (and some say over) in no time, with such big-name designers as **Stella McCartney** (429 W. 14th St.; ✆ **212/255-1556**), **Christian Louboutin** (59 Horatio St.; ✆ **212/255-1910**), and **Alexander McQueen** (417 W. 14th St.; ✆ **212/645-1797**) in residence. **Jeffrey New York,** an offshoot of the Atlanta department store, has pricey designer clothes, an amazing shoe collection, and the friendliest staff in New York.

UNION SQUARE/THE FLATIRON DISTRICT

The hottest shopping/eating/hanging-out neighborhood in the city may be Union Square. The long-forlorn south side of the square is now a mega–shopping area with **Whole Foods, Filene's Basement,** and **DSW (Designer Shoe Warehouse).** Just to the right is a **Virgin Megastore.** On the north side, **Barnes & Noble** is situated in a beautifully restored 1880 cast iron building. Of course, the beating heart of Union Square is the 4-days-a-week **Greenmarket,** the biggest farmers' market in the city.

On Broadway, just a few blocks north of Union Square, is the amazing shopping emporium **ABC Carpet & Home,** where the loft-size floors hold brilliantly decadent displays of furniture, housewares, linens (thread counts off the charts), and tchotchkes of all sizes and shapes.

Upscale retailers who have rediscovered the architectural majesty of **lower Fifth Avenue** include **Banana Republic, Victoria's Secret,** and **Kenneth Cole.** You won't find much that's new along here, but it's a pleasing stretch nonetheless.

When 23rd Street was the epitome of New York uptown fashion more than 100 years ago, the major department stores stretched along **Sixth Avenue** for about a mile from 14th Street up. These elegant stores stood in huge cast iron buildings that were long ago abandoned and left to rust. In the last several years, however, the area has become the city's discount shopping center, with superstores and off-pricers filling up the renovated spaces: **Filene's Basement, TJ Maxx,** and **Bed Bath & Beyond** are all at 620 Sixth Ave., while **Old Navy** is next door, and **Barnes & Noble** is just a couple of blocks away, at Sixth Avenue near 22nd Street.

MIDTOWN
HERALD SQUARE & THE GARMENT DISTRICT

Herald Square—where 34th Street, Sixth Avenue, and Broadway converge—is dominated by **Macy's,** the self-proclaimed world's biggest department store. At Sixth Avenue and 33rd Street is the **Manhattan Mall** (*©* 212/465-0500; www.manhattan mallny.com), home to such standards as LensCrafters and RadioShack.

A long block over on Seventh Avenue, not much goes on in the grimy, heavily industrial Garment District. This is, however, where you'll find that quintessential

---

Tips When Is It Open?

Open hours can vary significantly from store to store—even different branches of Gap can keep different schedules depending on location and management. Generally, stores open at 10 or 11am Monday through Saturday, and 7pm is the most common closing hour (although sometimes it's 6pm). Both opening and closing hours tend to get later as you move downtown; stores in the East Village often don't open until 1 or 2pm, and they stay open until 8pm or later.

All of the big department stores are open 7 days a week. However, unlike department stores in suburban malls, most of these stores don't keep a regular 10am-to-9pm schedule. The department stores and shops along major strips, such as Fifth Avenue, usually stay open later 1 night a week (often Thurs), although not all shops comply. Sunday hours are usually noon to 5 or 6pm. Most shops are open 7 days a week, but smaller boutiques may close 1 day a week; in addition, some neighborhoods virtually shut down on a particular day—namely the Lower East Side on Saturday, the East Village on Monday, and most of the Financial District for the weekend. But at holiday time, anything goes: Macy's often stays open until midnight for the last couple of weeks before Christmas!

Your best bet is to **call ahead** or print out the schedule from the store website if your heart's set on visiting a particular store.

New York experience, the **sample sale** (the box titled "Additional Sources for Serious Shoppers," above, explains how to find out about upcoming sample sales).

TIMES SQUARE & THE THEATER DISTRICT

You won't find much in the heart of Times Square to entice the serious shopper, because you can find most of the goods at superstores and malls back home. Among the best are Richard Branson's rollicking **Virgin Megastore** (though it's set to close in early 2009), and the fabulous **Toys "R" Us** flagship on Broadway and 44th Street, which even has its own full-scale Ferris wheel.

West 47th Street between Fifth and Sixth avenues is the city's famous **Diamond District;** see "Jewelry & Accessories" in "Shopping A to Z," later in this chapter.

You'll also notice a wealth of **electronics stores** throughout the neighborhood, many suspiciously trumpeting GOING OUT OF BUSINESS sales. These guys have been going out of business since the Stone Age. That's the bait-and-switch; pretty soon you've spent too much money for not enough MP3 player. If you want to check out what they have to offer, go in knowing the going price on that PDA or digital camera you're interested in. You can make a good deal if you know exactly what the market is, but these guys will be happy to suck you dry given half a chance. It's better to head downtown to J&R for *real* bargains.

Don't leave the neighborhood just yet. **Ninth Avenue,** aka Hell's Kitchen (Ninth Ave. to Tenth Ave., between 42nd and 57th sts.), has been undergoing a gentrification, and with it has come a wealth of little shops and charming restaurants. One of the more interesting is **Scent Elate** (313 W. 48th St., between Eighth and Ninth aves.; ✆ 212/258-3043). Scent Elate features scented candles, handmade soaps, specialty incenses, essential oils, an array of products produced by local artists, and the legendary Lampe Berger perfume lamps (one of the few places to find them in the city) all in a bright, cozy little shop. One of the things that places this trove above the scores of other scent emporiums in the city is that the owner, who is almost always on hand, actually selects and tries each product and lends his gregarious manner to helping customers find the scent that's just right. Prices are incredibly reasonable, and this little gem (set farther back from the sidewalk than the surrounding storefronts) should not be missed. The only thing yummier than the scents at Scent Elate are the cookies at **Ruby et Violette** (457 W. 50th St., between Ninth and Tenth aves.; ✆ 212/582-6720). Stop in and gorge on some of the over 55 utterly divine chocolate chunk flavors.

Mall with a View

The Shops at Columbus Circle mall, in the Time Warner Center, features not only some of the biggest (and most expensive) names in retail, it also offers shopping with a view of Central Park. Just off the southwest corner of Central Park, the mall is 2 city blocks long and four stories high. But does the picturesque view really matter to the shoppers who set their sights on the goods at such retailers as **Williams Sonoma, A/X Armani Exchange, Coach, Hugo Boss, Joseph Abboud, Eileen Fisher, Thomas Pink, Border's Books,** and the massive 59,000-square-foot **Whole Foods Market?** For more information and a complete list of stores, check the mall's website at **www.shopsatcolumbus.com**, or call ✆ 212/823-6300.

> ## Tips Take the L Train
>
> Sounds like a good jazzy song title. But really, taking the L train gets you to Williamsburg, Brooklyn, and if you want to see what shopping is like on the other side of the East River, this is the place to come. In fact, you may just want to do all your shopping here, the area is becoming that much of a shopping destination. Here are some of Williamsburg's shopping highlights, all reachable via the L Train, Bedford Avenue stop.
>
> **Beacon's Closet,** 88 N. 11th St (btwn Berry St. and Wythe Ave.; ✆ **718/486-0816;** www.beaconscloset.com). This converted warehouse is not only Brooklyn's best vintage clothing and music store, it just may be New York City's as well. You can find women's and men's clothing here, very slightly worn, for under $10; also used CDs and even some vinyl records as well.
>
> **Brooklyn Industries,** 162 Bedford Ave (at N. 8th St; ✆ **718/486-6464;** www.brooklynindustries.com). There are various outlets of this designer in Brooklyn and even a couple in Manhattan, but you are in Brooklyn, so come to the original source, and find Brooklyn hoodies and sweatshirts along with funky underwear. Here you will find the epitome of urban kitsch to bring back home to the 'burbs or anywhere else outside of Brooklyn.
>
> **Earwax,** 218 Bedford Ave (at N. 5th St.; ✆ **718/486-3771**). Tower Records might be gone and Virgin is a "megastore," so if you like to peruse your music in an intimate, eclectic setting, come to Earwax. They also have an impressive collection of used CDs and Vinyl.
>
> **Mini Mini Market,** 218 Bedford Ave (near N. 6th St.; ✆ **718/302-9337;** www.miniminimarket.com). The stock is geared toward girls, especially the inexpensive antique jewelry. The store also features beauty products, hats, bags, and throwback toys.
>
> **Noisette,** 54 N. 6th St (near Kent St.; ✆ **718/388-5188;** www.noisettenyc.com). Very feminine and *tres français* in style, but very Brooklyn in price. What more could a girl ask for? Don't answer that.

If you've still got room for a meal, you're in luck: You're a stone's throw from **Restaurant Row** (46th St. between Eighth and Ninth aves.), where you're sure to be sated, if a bit overwhelmed, by a city block of cuisine from over 11 countries. You might even stop for drinks and a show in one of the many cabaret bars on the street. Find out more at **www.restaurantrownyc.com**.

FIFTH AVENUE & 57TH STREET

The heart of Manhattan retail ranges up Fifth Avenue to 57th Street and across. **Tiffany & Co.,** which has long reigned supreme, sits a stone's throw from **NIKETOWN,** the **NBA Store,** and the huge **Louis Vuitton** flagship at the corner of 57th Street and Fifth Avenue. In addition, a good number of mainstream retailers, such as **Banana Republic,** have flagships along Fifth, shifting the breadth of higher-end shopping to Madison Avenue north of 59th Street. You will find a number of big-name, big-ticket

Shopping One-Two-Five Street

Maybe it was the arrival of Bill Clinton on the block. Or maybe it's just the latest wave of a Harlem renaissance. Whatever the reason, 125th Street is more vibrant than ever; a true shopping thoroughfare, especially on the blocks between St. Nicholas Avenue and Fifth Avenue. Big chains, such as **Old Navy, The Children's Store, H&M, The Body Shop, Starbucks,** and **Modell's,** have recently set up franchises on 125th. Not everyone is happy with this retail gentrification, believing that Harlem might be losing its identity. But sprinkled among the big names are plenty of stores that represent that unique Harlem character. Hip-hop boutiques such as **Jimmy Jazz,** 239 W. 125th St., near Frederick Douglass Boulevard (✆ **212/663-2827**), and **Jersey Man Cap USA,** 112 W. 125th St., between Lenox and Fifth avenues (✆ **212/222-7942**), where you can get anything from a Kangol cap to Girbaud Femme, are mainstays on the Street. Since 1979, the **125th St. Record Shack,** at 274 W. 125th St., between Lenox Avenue and Adam Clayton Powell Jr. Boulevard, has been selling jazz, gospel, R&B, doo-wop, and hip-hop, the music usually carrying well out into the already loud street.

At West African importer **African Paradise,** 27 W. 125th St., at Lenox Avenue (✆ **212/410-5294**), you'll find all the supplies you'll need for ancestral worship.

On your shopping tour, you might get hungry—and there is no shortage of places to eat. Skip the usual fast-food options and try the local grub at such places as the **M&G Diner,** 383 W. 125th St., at St. Nicholas Avenue (✆ **212/864-7326**), where you'll get some of the best fried chicken in the city (see chapter 6 for more). For coffee, some fine pie, and even a martini, don't miss **Wimp's Southern-Style Bakery, Skye Café and Martini Bar,** 29 W. 125th St., between Fifth and Lenox avenues (✆ **212/410-2296**). For a cultural diversion, stop in at the **Studio Museum in Harlem,** 144 W. 125 St., between Lenox Avenue and Adam Clayton Powell Jr. Boulevard (✆ **212/864-4500**), which also features an interesting gift shop (for more, see chapter 7).

designers radiating from the crossroads, including **Versace, Chanel, Dior,** and **Cartier.** You'll also find big-name jewelers here, as well as grand old department stores such as **Bergdorf Goodman, Henri Bendel,** and **Saks Fifth Avenue**—all Fifth Avenue mainstays that must at least be browsed, even if your budget won't allow for more than longing glances at the goods.

UPTOWN
MADISON AVENUE
Madison Avenue from 57th to 79th streets boasts the most expensive retail real estate in the world. Bring lots of plastic. This ultradeluxe strip—particularly in the high 60s—is home to *the* most luxurious designer boutiques, with **Barneys New York** as the anchor. For a sampling of local designers, see "Clothing" in "Shopping A to Z," later in this chapter.

Don't be intimidated by the glamour of this shopper's mile or any of the celebrities you're likely to bump into. There are affordable treasures to be had, such as the Ginger Flower room spray at **Shanghai Tang** (714 Madison Ave.; ✆ **212/888-0111**) or a pair of crystal cufflinks at the **Lalique** flagship boutique next door, at 712 Madison Ave. (✆ **212/355-6550**).

UPPER WEST SIDE

The Upper West Side's best shopping street is **Columbus Avenue.** Small shops catering to the neighborhood's white-collar mix of young hipsters and families line both sides of the pleasant avenue from 66th Street (where you'll find an excellent branch of **Barnes & Noble**) to about 86th Street. Highlights include **Maxilla & Mandible** for museum-quality natural-science-based gifts and **Harry's Shoes** (see "Museum Stores" and "Shoes," in "Shopping A to Z," later in this chapter), but you won't lack for good browsing along here. **The Shops at Columbus Circle** also offers a world of upscale choices for shopping (see the box "Mall with a View," below).

Boutiques also dot Amsterdam Avenue, but main-drag **Broadway** is most notable for its terrific gourmet edibles at **Zabar's** and **Fairway** markets (see "Edibles," in "Shopping A to Z," later in this chapter).

THE OUTER BOROUGHS

Brooklyn is a shopping destination in its own right, and some of the best and most interesting things can be found in **Williamsburg.** See the box "Take the L Train," for more on Willliamsburg.

The other burgeoning area in Brooklyn is **DUMBO** (that's **D**own **U**nder the **M**anhattan **B**ridge **O**verpass), and high-end stores are beginning to move in, including **Jacques Torres Chocolate** (see the sidebar "Chocolate City," later in this chapter).

There is not much fine shopping in any of the other boroughs, with the notable exception of the **Arthur Avenue Retail Market** (see "Edibles," in "Shopping A to Z," later in this chapter) in the Little Italy of the **Bronx.**

2 The Big Department Stores

ABC Carpet & Home ⭐⭐   Shopping ABC has often been compared to taking a fantasy tour of your very rich and very well-traveled ancestor's attic. This two-building emporium is legendary and deserves to be: It's the ultimate home-fashions-and-furnishings department store. On the west side of the street is the stunning 10-floor home emporium. The goods run the gamut from Moroccan mosaic-tile end tables to hand-painted Tuscan pottery to Tiffany-style lamps to distressed bed frames sporting meltingly soft Italian linens to much, much more, all exquisitely displayed. An entire floor of on-the-bolt upholstery fabrics is to die for. These are high-end goods, but sales can produce substantial bargains. The Parlor floor boasts an eclectic collection of beautiful gift items and housewares, and some of the smaller items are quite affordable. Across the street is the multifloor carpet store, which boasts a stunning collection of area rugs. 881 and 888 Broadway (at 19th St.). ✆ **212/473-3000.** www.abchome.com. Subway: L, N, R, 4, 5, 6 to 14th St./Union Sq.

Barneys New York ⭐   After financial woes forced the closure of the original Chelsea store a few years back, New York's self-made temple of chic is back on top. While the store focuses on hot-off-the-runway women's wear, its menswear runs the gamut from classic to cutting edge. The fragrance department works hard to offer offbeat and unusual scents as well as the classics. Bring your platinum card, because nothing comes cheap here, although house brands are solidly made and aren't off-the-chart expensive. Both the downtown (in two locations) and uptown **Barneys Co-Ops** have blossomed into real fashion hot spots, sisterly but separate from the chic Barneys New York Madison Avenue headquarters. At Barneys Co-Op, more downtown-casual fashions for men and women—from such designer names as Diane von Furstenberg, Juicy Couture, and Rebecca Taylor—set the tone. Prices are more reasonable than at the flagship but not cheap by any means.

Tip: Twice a year, Barneys hosts its famous warehouse sale in Chelsea. Prices are changed daily, but markdowns are 50% to 80% off the original retail prices on all clothing and gifts. So if you are planning a shopping trip to the city, keep your eyes open for when the sales will occur. 660 Madison Ave. (at 61st St.). ℂ 212/826-8900. www. barneys.com. Subway: N, R to Fifth Ave. Barneys Co-Op: 116 Wooster St. (btwn Prince and Spring sts.). ℂ 212/965-9964. Subway: N, R to Prince St. 236 W. 18th St. (btwn Seventh and Eighth aves.). ℂ 212/593-7800. Subway: 1 to 18th St. 2151 Broadway (btwn 75th and 76th sts.). ℂ 646/335-0978. Subway: 1 to 79th St. Barneys Warehouse: 255 W. 17th St. (btwn Seventh and Eighth aves.). No phone.

Bergdorf Goodman 🌂🌂 Bergdorf's is a sybarite's delight. The store is designed on an intimate scale and lacks the kicky nouveau-riche feel of Bendel's. Although the customer base is primarily composed of ladies who lunch and businesswomen with gobs of money but little time for nonsense, fashionistas in the know appreciate Bergdorf's little secret: Sales can garner fantastic bargains, with designer-clothing prices slashed to the bone. Finely tuned designer salons represent both couture powerhouses and downtown darlings. The fifth floor is an open space filled with fashions at more reasonable prices. The jewelry on the main floor and the unparalleled gift and tabletop floor are worth a browse alone. The store has two ladies'-shoe departments, one tops for one-stop designer shopping in the $300-and-up range, and the less-expensive fifth-floor salon. On the 7th floor is **BG Restaurant,** overlooking Central Park, where (for prices similar to the rest of the store) you can enjoy a full menu, including afternoon tea, and cocktails. Just across the street is **Bergdorf Goodman Man,** a palace of men's fine fashion. 754 Fifth Ave. (at 57th St.). ℂ 212/753-7300 or 800/558-1355. www.bergdorfgoodman. com. Subway: E, F to Fifth Ave.

Bloomingdale's 🌂 More accessible than Barneys and more affordable than Saks, Bloomingdale's has a certain New York pizazz. Taking up an entire city block, Bloomie's stocks just about anything you could want, from clothing (both designer and everyday basics) and fragrances to housewares and furniture—not necessarily a good thing, because sometimes it feels too stuffed full of merchandise for comfort. It pays to make a reconnaissance trip to get the overview, then move in for the kill. The main entrance is on Third Avenue, but pop up to street level from the 59th Street station and you'll be right at the Lexington Avenue entrance. A smaller, downtown branch opened on Prince Street, offering pricier and edgier items. 1000 Third Ave. (Lexington Ave. at 59th St.). ℂ 212/705-2000. www.bloomingdales.com. Subway: 4, 5, 6 to 59th St. 504 Broadway (at Broome St.). ℂ 212/729-5900. Subway: N, R to Prince St.

Century 21 *Value* Prices here on designer goods are 40% to 70% off what you would pay at a department store or designer boutique. Don't think that $250 Armani blazer is a bargain? Look again at the tag—the retail price is upward of $800. This is the place to find $5 Liz Claiborne tees, $20 Todd Oldham pants, or the $50 Bally loafers you've been dreaming of—not to mention underwear, hosiery, and ties so cheap that they're almost free. Kids' clothes, linens, and housewares are also part of the extensive stock.

Tips Sale Seasons

These may be obvious to the serious shopper, but for those of us/you that are less than serious, here are New York's prime sale seasons:

Thanksgiving: Black Friday, or the day after Thanksgiving, is the beginning of the Holiday shopping season. Many stores inaugurate the season with major sales. Stores open ridiculously early and the crowds become more like mobs. Proceed at your own risk.

Pre-Christmas: "Shoppers! Only three [insert hottest gift of the season] left at these amazingly low prices!" You might hear that spiel just before Christmas. Believe it . . . or don't.

Post-Christmas: With the Christmas returns, the day *after* Christmas, come the markdowns.

Whites: Usually in January, this is a sale of linens...and these days, rarely white.

January Clearance: You'll find the European boutiques advertising clearance around the third week of January.

Valentine's Day: Anything red, chocolaty, or with a heart shape will be advertised "on sale."

President's Day: Late February, usually around the long weekend celebrating Washington's (and Lincoln's) birthday. The sales will be mostly for winter clothing.

Memorial Day: Stores hold promotional sales on the last weekend in May.

Fourth of July: Blowout sales on bathing suits and summer attire centered on the long Fourth of July weekend.

Midsummer Clearance: If there is anything summer-related left on the racks after the Fourth of July, you'll find them up until the middle of August.

Back-to-School: Oh, how I hated those three words when I saw them in stores advertising sales for school supplies, furnishings, and clothing . . . while there were still a few weeks left in the summer. Usually in middle August.

Columbus Day: Coats and early fall clothing go on sale on this long weekend, usually the second weekend in October.

Election Day: Whatever fall merchandise is hanging around after the Columbus Day sales will be offered at even further reduced prices on Election Day.

Expect big crowds and avoid the weekday lunch hour and Saturday if you can help it. 22 Cortlandt St. (btwn Broadway and Church St.). © 212/227-9092. www.c21stores.com. Subway: 2, 3, 4, 5, J, M to Fulton St.; A, C to Broadway/Nassau St.; E to Chambers St.; R, W to Cortlandt St.

Henri Bendel *Finds* This gorgeous Fifth Avenue store is fun to browse. It feels like you're shopping in the townhouse of a slightly offbeat, moneyed lady who doesn't think twice about throwing on a little something by Anna Sui and an outrageously wide-brimmed hat to go out shopping—she's got the panache to pull it off. It's a super-stylish, high-ticket collection for ladies with a flair for the funky and frilly—but sales are good, and there are always some one-of-a-kind accessories that make afford-able souvenirs (and earn you one of the black-and-white-striped shopping bags, the best in town). The makeup department is always on the cutting edge. The **tearoom** looks out on Fifth Avenue through Lalique windows. 712 Fifth Ave. (btwn 55th and 56th sts.). © 212/247-1100. Subway: N, R to Fifth Ave. or the 4, 5, 6 to 59th. St.

Lord & Taylor   Okay, so maybe Lord & Taylor isn't the first place you'd go for a vinyl miniskirt, but this New York institution has an understated, elegant mien. It now operates under the May Company banner but maintains its own sensibility. Long known as an excellent source for women's dresses and coats, L&T stocks all the major labels for men and women, with an emphasis on American designers. Their house-brand clothes (khakis, blazers, turtlenecks, and summer sportswear) are well made and a bargain. Sales, especially around holidays, can be stellar. The store is big enough to have a good selection (especially for petites) but doesn't overwhelm. 424 Fifth Ave. (btwn 38th and 39th St.). © 212/391-3344. www.lordandtaylor.com. Subway: F, V to 42nd St.

Macy's *(Overrated*   A four-story sign on the side of the building trumpets MACY'S, THE WORLD'S LARGEST STORE—a hard fact to dispute, since the 10-story behemoth covers an entire city block, dwarfing even Bloomie's on the other side of town. Macy's is a hard place to shop: The size is unmanageable, the service is dreadful, and the incessant din from the crowds on the ground floor alone will kick your migraine into action. But they do sell *everything*. Massive renovation over the past few years has redesigned many departments into more manageable "ministores"—there's a Metropolitan Museum Gift Shop, a Swatch boutique, and cafes and makeup counters on several floors—but the store's one-of-a-kind flair is just a memory now. Still, sales run constantly, holiday or no (1-day sales are popular on Wed and Sat), so bargains are guaranteed. And because so many feel adrift in this retail sea, the store provides personal guides/shoppers at no charge. My advice: Get the floor plan and consult it often to avoid wandering off into the sportswear netherworld. At Christmastime, come as late as you can manage (the store is usually open until midnight in the final shopping days before the holiday). At Herald Sq., W. 34th St., and Broadway. © 212/695-4400 or 212/494-7300. www.macys.com. Subway: B, D, F, N, Q, R, 1, 2, 3 to 34th St.

Saks Fifth Avenue *∕𝄐∕𝄐*   There are branches of Saks all over the country now, but this is it: Saks *Fifth Avenue.* No other store better typifies the Big Apple these days than this legendary flagship store, which is well worth your time—and the smaller-than-most size makes it quite manageable. There's something for everyone here. Saks carries a wide range of clothing; departments err on the pricey designer side (stay out of the lingerie department if you're looking for affordable basics), but run the gamut to affordable house-brand basics. The men's department is the finest in the city. The cosmetics and fragrance departments on the main floor are justifiably noteworthy—they carry many hard-to-find and brand-new brands, including Laura Mercier, the Big Apple's own Kiehl's, and more—as are the extensive fine and costume jewelry counters. And the location, right across from Rockefeller Center, makes it a convenient stop for those on the sightseeing circuit. 611 Fifth Ave. (btwn 49th and 50th sts.). © 212/753-4000. www.saksfifthavenue.com. Subway: B, D, F, Q to 47th–50th sts./Rockefeller Center; E, F to Fifth Ave.

Takashimaya *∕𝄐∕𝄐* *(Finds*   This petite branch of Japan's most famous department-store chain exudes an appealingly austere, Japanese-tinged French-country charm. Come to see some of the city's most beautiful displays of tableware and boudoir fashions. Paris's most famous florist, Christian Tortu, has a main-floor boutique that's a work of art in its own right. The cosmetics department on the top floor is a must for fans of high-end designer brands looking for something special. The serenely elegant **Tea Box** specializes in delicate bento lunches and beautiful sweets. Aesthetes shouldn't miss this place; it's a wonderful spot for delicate, elegant gifts. 693 Fifth Ave. (btwn 54th and 55th sts.). ℭ 212/350-0100. Subway: E, F to Fifth Ave.

3 Shopping A to Z
ANTIQUES & COLLECTIBLES

Antiques hounds will be dazzled by the bounty that New York has to offer, from Louis XIV settees to vintage DeFranco Family lunchboxes. Be prepared, however—you will pay top dollar for everything.

Traditionalists will love the blocks off **Broadway near 10th** and **11th streets,** where the bounty includes Kentshire Galleries (see below); and **East 59th, 60th,** and **61st streets** around Second Avenue, not far from the **Manhattan Art and Antiques Center** (1050 Second Ave., btwn 55th and 56th sts.; ℭ 212/355-4400), where about two dozen high-end dealers line the street and spill over onto surrounding blocks. Fans of midcentury furniture and Americana with a twist should browse **Lafayette Street** in SoHo/NoHo. Just about any dealer you visit will have the current issue of the free *Greyrock Antiques Guide* and/or *Antiques New York,* which will lead you to specialty dealers around the city.

Most called it the 26th Street flea market: The famous **Annex Antiques Fair and Flea Market** (ℭ 212/243-5343; www.hellskitchenfleamarket.com) is an outdoor emporium of nostalgia; you might remember it as filling a few parking lots along Sixth Avenue between 24th and 27th streets on weekends for many years; gentrification in Chelsea has moved the whole shebang uptown, to the (gentrifying) Hell's Kitchen neighborhood, aka "Clinton." It's now on 39th Street, between 9th and 10th avenues on Saturday and Sunday. The assemblage is hit-or-miss—some days you'll find treasures galore, and others it seems like there's nothing but junk. A few quality vendors are almost always on hand, though. The truly dedicated arrive early on Saturday, but the browsing is still good as late as 4pm. Sunday is always best, as there's double the booty on hand. In addition, there's an indoor branch just for antiques on two floors of an indoor garage in Chelsea, at 112 W. 25th St., between 5th and 6th avenues. It's open Saturday & Sunday from 6:30am to 5pm.

Also check out "Jewelry & Accessories," below.

Alphaville This gallery specializes in 1940s, 1950s, and 1960s toys and movie posters, all in mint condition and beautifully displayed. Space toys are an emphasis. Well worth a look for nostalgic baby boomers, even if you have no intention of buying. 226 W. Houston St. (btwn Sixth Ave. and Varick St.). ℭ 212/675-6850. www.alphaville.com. Subway: 1 to Houston St.

Chelsea Antiques Building This 12-floor building houses more than 100 dealers and is open daily. The permanent stalls run the gamut from 18th-century antiques to rare books to early-20th-century radios, jewelry, and toys. Prices are so good that it's known as a dealers' source, and shoppers are the type who love to prowl, touch everything, and sniff out a bargain. 110 W. 25th St. (btwn Sixth and Seventh aves.). ℭ 212/929-0909. Subway: F to 23rd St.

Kentshire Galleries Still going strong after a half-century, this large and lovely gallery is the city's prime stop for 18th- and 19th-century English antiques, ranging from jewelry and tabletop items to formal furnishings. Furniture is displayed in richly appointed rooms that make for great browsing. 37 E. 12th St. (btwn University Place and Broadway). ✆ 212/673-6644. www.kentshire.com. Subway: N, R, L, 4, 5, 6 to 14th St./Union Sq.

Lost City Arts   Lost City features vintage modern furnishings and a quirky selection of accessories (station signs, 3-D photos, and the like), plus their own new mid-century-inspired furniture and accessories, including one inspired by the otherwise forbiddingly expensive custom designs of Machine Age genius Warren MacArthur. A real treat. 18 Cooper Sq. (Third Ave. at 5th St.). ✆ 212/375-0500. www.lostcityarts.com. Subway: N, R to 8th St.; 6 to Astor Place.

Mood Indigo   This dandy of a shop is the city's top dealer in glassware, dishware, and kitchen accessories from the 1930s through the 1950s. The charming shopkeepers also specialize in Bakelite jewelry and 1939 World's Fair memorabilia and boast a whopping collection of 1950s novelty salt and pepper shakers and even Stork Club cologne (now what could that smell like?). Everything is pristine, so expect to pay accordingly. 181 Prince St. (btwn Sullivan and Thompson sts.). ✆ 212/254-1176. www.moodindigonewyork.com. Subway: C, E to Spring St.; N, R to Prince St. Showplace Antique Center, 40 W. 25th St. gallery 112 #222.

ART
See the box titled "Art for Art's Sake: The Gallery Scene," on p. 248.

BEAUTY
In addition to the choices below, consider the French beauty superstore **Sephora,** 597 Fifth Ave. (btwn 48th and 49th sts.; ✆ **212/980-6534;** www.sephora.com). There are outlets all over the city, but this Midtown branch is a real beauty.

C. O. Bigelow   Who'd think that a 166-year-old apothecary would carry the city's most eclectic, enjoyable, and international collection of healthy-skin and personal-care products? The goodies run the gamut from Kusco-Murphy hair creams to French Elgydium toothpaste, a bestseller. And now, taking a page from Kiehl's (see below), Bigelow has beautifully packaged its own house-brand line of soaps, salves, essential oils, and beauty treatments. 414 Sixth Ave. (btwn 8th and 9th sts.). ✆ 212/533-2700. www.bigelowchemists.com. Subway: A, C, E, F, V to W. 4th St.

Kiehl's   Kiehl's is more than a store, it's a virtual cult. Models, stockbrokers, foreign visitors, and just about everyone else stop by this always packed, old-time apothecary for its simply packaged, wonderfully formulated products for women and men. Kiehl's now has counters in several department stores (evidence of how they've really moved up in the world), but stop into the original if you can. Love the free samples! 109 Third Ave. (btwn 13th and 14th sts.). ✆ 212/677-3171. www.kiehls.com. Subway: L, N, R, 4, 5, 6 to 14th St./Union Sq.

Ricky's 🎭   This chain of funky drugstores also features a wide range of beauty products. It's a haven for makeup mavens, with multicolored wigs, rainbow-colored lipstick, glitter galore, green nail polish, over 80 kinds of hairbrushes, and even edible undies. Try going into Ricky's and coming out with just a pack of gum. 44 E. 8th St. (at Greene St.). ✆ 212/254-5247. Subway: N, R to 8th St. Also at 466 Sixth Ave. (at 11th St.). ✆ 212/924-3401. Subway: A, C, E, B, D, F to W. 4th St. 112 W. 72nd St. (btwn Columbus Ave. and Broadway). ✆ 212/769-3678. Subway: 1, 2, 3 to 72nd St. 728 Ninth Ave. (btwn 49th and 50th sts.). ✆ 212/245-1265. Subway: C, E to 50th St.

Zitomer's 🎭🎭   This three-story drugstore is more a mini–department store than a pharmacy. You'll find everything from electronics to pet supplies. But the first floor is where you'll spend most of your time if you're looking for beauty products. They have their own very good line of cosmetics called **Z New York.** Big Apple lip gloss will make a great souvenir; you won't find it in your local Walgreens. 969 Madison Ave. (at 76th St.). ℂ 212/737-5560. www.zitomer.com. Subway: 6 to 77th St. Z Chemists at 40 W. 57th St. ℂ 212/956-6000.

BOOKS

In addition to the choices below, there are the chains: **Barnes & Noble,** with my favorite outlet opposite Union Square, 33 E. 17th St. (ℂ **212/253-0810;** www.bn.com); and **Borders,** with four stores in Manhattan, including one in the Time Warner Center, 10 Columbus Circle (ℂ **212/823-9775;** www.bordersstores.com).

Argosy Books   Antiquarian-book hounds should check out this stately 77-year-old store, with high ceilings, packed shelves, a quietly intellectual air, and an outstanding collection of rarities, including 18th- and 19th-century prints, maps, and autographs. 116 E. 59th St. (btwn Park and Lexington aves.). ℂ 212/753-4455. www.argosybooks.com. Subway: 4, 5, 6 to 59th St.

Bauman Rare Books   Dealing strictly in highly prized volumes with topics ranging from philosophy and science to children's classics, Bauman is one of the foremost resources for serious collectors willing to spend big money for pristine first editions, ranging from Milton's *Paradise Lost* (1669) to Harper Lee's *To Kill a Mockingbird* (1960), signed by the author. 535 Madison Ave. (btwn 54th and 55th sts.). ℂ **800/99-BAUMAN** or 212/751-0011. www.baumanrarebooks.com. Subway: 6 to 51st St.

Bluestockings *(Finds*   The self-proclaimed "radical bookstore, fair-trade cafe, and activist center in the Lower East Side of Manhattan" packs a lot of literature and activity into its Allen Street storefront (a block south of Houston St.). In addition to books on queer and gender studies, capitalism, feminism, democracy, and liberation, they also carry "good ol' smutty fiction," as well as a variety of independent magazines, journals, and alternative menstrual products (probably the only bookstore in Manhattan so equipped). There's a cafe, so you can buy a cup of tea or coffee before joining the Dyke Knitting Circle or stepping up with your latest poem at an open mic. 172 Allen St. (btwn Stanton and Rivington sts.). ℂ 212/777-6028. www.bluestockings.com. Subway: F to Second Ave.; J, M, Z to Essex/Delancey St.

Books of Wonder *(Kids*   You don't have to be a kid to fall in love with this charming bookstore, which served as the model for Meg Ryan's shop in *You've Got Mail.* (Meg even worked here for a spell to train for the role.) Kids will love BOW's story readings; call or check the website for the latest schedule. 18 W. 18th St. (btwn Fifth and Sixth aves.). ℂ **212/989-3270.** www.booksofwonder.net. Subway: L, N, R, 4, 5, 6 to 14th St./Union Sq.

Complete Traveller   Whether your destination is Texas or Tibet, you'll find what you need in this, possibly the world's best, travel bookstore. There are travel accessories as well, plus a rare collection of antiquarian travel books whose facts may be outdated but whose writers' perceptions continue to shine. The staff is attentive. 199 Madison Ave. (at 35th St.). ℂ 212/685-9007. www.ctrarebooks.com. Subway: 6 to 33rd St.

Drama Book Shop *⟳*   This performing-arts bookstores has an in-house performance space, where you can head for discussions, panels, staged readings, and book signings with members of the theater community. Offering thousands of plays, from translations of Greek classics to this season's biggest hits, the shop also sells books, magazines, and newspapers on the craft and business of the performing arts. 250 W. 40th St. (btwn Eighth and Ninth aves.). ℂ 212/944-0595. www.dramabookshop.com. Subway: A, C, E to 42nd St.

Manhattanjudiaca   *The* Jewish bookstore of New York City, covering everything from cookbooks to Kaballah. The Brooklyn outlet, called Eichler's, is even bigger and features all manner of Judaica, including silver items, garments, music, gifts, and more. 62 W. 45th St. (btwn Fifth and Sixth aves.). ℂ 212/719-1918. www.eichlers.com. Subway: B, D, F, V to 42nd St. Also at 1401 Coney Island Ave. (btwn Aves. J and K). ℂ 888/EICHLERS or 718/258-7643. Subway: D, Q to Ave. J. www.manhattanjudaica.com.

Forbidden Planet   Here is the city's largest collection of sci-fi, comic, and graphic-illustration books. The proudly geeky staff really knows what's what. Great sci-fi-themed toys, too. 840 Broadway (at 13th St.). ℂ 212/473-1576. www.fpnyc.com. Subway: L, N, R, 4, 5, 6 to 14th St./Union Sq.

Housing Works Used Books Cafe *Finds*   Here's a way to do something good for yourself and others at the same time: Buy your reading material at this spacious yet cozy used-book shop, sporting 45,000 books and records. It's part of Housing Works, a not-for-profit organization that provides housing, services, and advocacy for homeless people living with HIV and AIDS. The collection is terrific and well-organized, with lots of well-priced paperbacks, hardbacks, advance copies, and coffee-table books. There's a cafe in back that serves coffee and tea as well as sandwiches, sweets, and other light bites, plus beer and wine. The bookstore often hosts readings by well-known writers as well as occasional music performances on Wednesday and Thursday evenings; call or check the website for the current listings. 126 Crosby St. (south of Houston St.). ℂ 212/334-3324. www.housingworksubc.com. Subway: B, F, D to Broadway–Lafayette St.; W, R to Prince St.

Hue-Man Bookstore   One of the nation's largest black-owned bookstores, providing the area's largest selection of African-American literature and books. Lines snaked around the block in 2004, when Bill Clinton staged a signing of his memoir. 2319 Frederick Douglass Blvd. (btwn 124th and 125th St. at Eighth Ave.). ℂ 212/665-7400. www.huemanbookstore. com. Subway: A, B, C, D to 125th St.

Kitchen Arts & Letters   Foodies, take note: Here's the ultimate cook's and food-lover's bookstore. You'll be wowed by the depth of the selection, which includes rare, out-of-print, and foreign-language titles focusing on food and wine. The staff will conduct free searches for hard-to-find titles. The shop is an overstuffed jumble, but if this is your bag, you'll be browsing for hours. 1435 Lexington Ave. (btwn 93rd and 94th sts.). ℂ 212/876-5550. www.kitchenartsandletters.com. Subway: 6 to 96th St.

Morningside Bookshop   Right across the street from Columbia University, this is the Upper West Side's best independent bookstore. It's a great place to browse, not only inside, but outside in the remainders bins where you never know what treasures you might find. The store is a favorite with children (and their parents); every Wednesday afternoon there is a singalong by children's entertainer Danna Banana. For the adults, the store hosts a number of book signings by celebrated authors (many of whom live in the neighborhood). 2915 Broadway (at 14th St.). ℂ 212/222-3350. www. morningsidebookshop.com. Subway: 1 to 116th St.

Oscar Wilde Bookshop   The world's oldest gay and lesbian bookstore was on the brink of extinction a few years ago but has made a strong comeback under new ownership. The nice staff makes browsing in this landmark a pleasure. Recipient of a 2006 Leadership Award from the Publishing Triangle, it's where you'll find the latest literary and popular LGBT work. 15 Christopher St. (btwn Sixth and Seventh aves.). ✆ 212/255-8097. www.oscarwildebooks.com. Subway: 1 to Christopher St.

Rizzoli   This clubby Italian bookstore is the classiest—and most relaxing—spot in town to browse for visual-art and design books, plus quality fiction, gourmet cookbooks, and other upscale reading. There's a decent selection of foreign-language, music, and dance titles as well. 31 W. 57th St. (btwn Fifth and Sixth aves.). ✆ 212/759-2424. www.rizzoliusa.com. Subway: N, R to Fifth Ave.

The Scholastic Store *(Kids*   This mammoth store is located at the ground level of the headquarters for children's book publisher Scholastic (which introduced a boy named Harry Potter to America). The 6,200-foot retail space is a veritable interactive playground for kids. Books, toys, and software products feature Scholastic's top-selling brands, from Clifford the Big Red Dog to Captain Underpants. Needless to say, Hogwarts is well represented. A full slate of in-store events, from author signings to craft workshops, also keeps kids busy; check the website or call for the current schedule. 557 Broadway (btwn Prince and Spring sts.). ✆ 212/343-6166. www.scholastic.com/sohostore. Subway: N, R to Prince St.

Skyline Books *(Value*   A precious holdout from the recent literary shakeout to overtake the city, this wonderful Fourth Avenue book-lover's haven sells rare, used, and hard-to-find books of all types, specializing in art, photography, modern literature, scholarly subjects, beat literature, first editions, and African-American literature. If you're a devotee of all things literary, dive in and wade through its stacks. 13 W. 18th St. (at Fourth Ave.). ✆ 212/759-5463. www.skylinebooks.com. Subway: L, N, R, 4, 5, 6 to 14th St./Union Sq.

The Strand *(Value*   Something of a New York legend, The Strand is worth a visit for its staggering "8 miles of books" as well as its extensive inventory of review copies and bargain titles at up to 85% off list price. It's unquestionably the city's best book deal—there's almost nothing marked at list price—and the selection is phenomenal in all categories (there's even a rare-book department on the third floor). Still, you'll work for it: The narrow aisles mean you're always getting bumped; the books are only roughly alphabetized; and there's no air-conditioning in summer. Nevertheless, it's a used-book-lover's paradise. Note that the lower Manhattan location is significantly smaller. 828 Broadway (at 12th St.). ✆ 212/473-1452. www.strandbooks.com. Subway: Q, W, L, N, R, 4, 5, 6 to 14th St./Union Sq. Strand Annex: 95 Fulton St. (btwn William and Gold sts.). ✆ 212/732-6070. Subway: 4, 5, A, C, J, M, Z, 2, 3, to Fulton/Broadway-Nassau.

Twelfth Street Books *(Value*   Tucked away on West 12th Street between Fifth Avenue and University Place, this cozy little trove offers great used books at amazing prices. Don't miss their small but impressive collection of vinyl records (remember those?) for sale. 11 E. 12th St. ✆ 212/645-4340. Subway: L, N, R, 4, 5, 6, to 14th St./Union Sq.

Urban Center Books   Housed in an architectural landmark, McKim, Mead & White's 1882 Villard Houses, the Municipal Art Society's bookstore boasts a terrific selection of new books on architecture, urban planning, and landscape design. In the Villard Houses, 457 Madison Ave. (at 51st St.). ✆ 212/935-3595. www.urbancenterbooks.org. Subway: 6 to 51st St. E, F to 53rd St.

CLOTHING
RETAIL FASHIONS
The Top Designers

The legendary locale for the classic designer names has always been Fifth Avenue and 57th Street. There's been some exodus to Madison Avenue (see below), but the opening of the **Gianni Versace** shop at 647 Fifth Ave., between 51st and 52nd streets (📞 **212/ 317-0224;** www.versace.com), just before the designer's death, heralded a new era of respect for the avenue. Other deluxe designer tenants from Italy's haute couture world are **Prada** (see "For Men & Women," below); **Salvatore Ferragamo,** no. 655, between 52nd and 53rd streets (📞 **212/759-3822;** www.ferragamo.com). Tom Ford's stellar **Gucci** is at Fifth Avenue and 54th Street (📞 **212/826-2600;** www.gucci.com) as well as their Madison Avenue location at 840 Madison Ave. (📞 **212/717-2619**), while classic **Chanel** is at 15 E. 57th St., between Fifth and Madison avenues (📞 **212/355- 5050;** www.chanel.com), with the freshly hip tartans of **Burberry** just down the block at 9 E. 57th St. (📞 **212/407-7100;** www.burberry.com).

The Upper East Side's Madison Avenue is the heartland of haute couture these days. The biggest names in clean-lined modern design line up along the platinum-coated boulevard; between 59th and 80th streets, you'll find **Calvin Klein, Giorgio Armani, Valentino, Bottega Veneta, Dolce & Gabbana, Emanuel Ungaro, Givenchy, Hermès, Issey Miyake, Krizia, Max Mara, Prada** (see below), **Polo/Ralph Lauren** (see below), **Roberto Cavalli, Versace** (see above), and many more; the density is greatest in the high 60s.

Established avant-garde designers hang out in SoHo. Highlights include **Anna Sui,** 113 Greene St., just south of Prince Street (📞 **212/941-8406;** www.annasui.com), who specializes in boho fashions with a glam edge. **Marc Jacobs,** 163 Mercer St., between Houston and Prince (📞 **212/343-1490;** www.marcjacobs.com), excels at modern takes on classic cuts. Girlish designs are the specialty of **Cynthia Rowley,** 376 Bleecker St., at Perry Street (📞 **212/242-3803;** www.cynthiarowley.com). SoHo has become so designer hot that plenty of established names have moved in, including **Louis Vuitton,** 116 Greene St., between Prince and Spring streets (📞 **212/274-9090;** www.vuitton.com); always-avant **Helmut Lang,** 142 Greene St., near Spring Street (📞 **212/563-0586** or 212/334-2487); **Burberry,** 131 Spring St., between Greene and Wooster streets (📞 **212/925-9300;** www.burberry.com); and, in the same block, **Chanel,** 139 Spring St. (📞 **212/334-0055**).

Talented up-and-comers have set up shop on and around **Bond Street** in NoHo; on **Elizabeth, Mott, and Mulberry streets** in Nolita; along **East 9th Street** in the East Village (see "For Men & Women," below); and on the **Lower East Side,** in the blocks south of Houston Street.

Fashion Flagships

Some New York flagship stores of the major brands are an experience you won't catch in your nearest mall. These stores are display cases for the complete line of fashions, so you'll often find much more to choose from than in your at-home branch. You'll find other locations throughout the city, but these are meant to be the biggest and best. Check out **Ann Taylor** at 645 Madison Ave., at 60th Street (📞 **212/832-2010;** www.anntaylor.com); the **Banana Republic** flagship at Rockefeller Center, 626 Fifth Ave., at 50th Street (📞 **212/974-2350;** www.bananarepublic.com); **Liz Claiborne,** 650 Fifth Ave., at 52nd Street (📞 **212/581-1019;** www.lizclaiborne.com), which carries all of Liz's lines; and **DKNY,** 655 Madison Ave., at 60th Street (📞 **212/223- DKNY;** www.dkny.com). **J. Crew** has a big bi-level SoHo store at 99 Prince St., between Mercer and Greene streets (📞 **212/966-2739;** www.jcrew.com), as well as a large store on Rockefeller Plaza at 50th Street (📞 **212/765-4227**). **Old Navy** has a huge flagship featuring its affordable basics and signature sense of humor at 610 Sixth Ave., at 18th Street (📞 **212/645-0663;** www.oldnavy.com).

For Men & Women

Brooks Brothers   The perfect definition of all that is preppy lies behind this clubby storefront. The label is synonymous with quality, quiet taste, and classic tailoring. The cut of the man's suit is a tad boxy, making it great for the full American body. 346 Madison Ave. (at 44th St.). ℂ 212/682-8800. www.brooksbrothers.com. Subway: S, 4, 5, 6, 7 to 42nd St./Grand Central. Also at 666 Fifth Ave. (btwn 52nd and 53rd sts.). ℂ 212/261-9440. Subway: 6 to 51st St. 1 Liberty Plaza. ℂ 212/267-2400. Subway: A, C, E to Chambers St.

H&M *(Value*   The Swedish super-discounter Hennes & Mauritz has sprouted up all over New York the past 5 years. The loud, bustling stores are mammoth, but the departments are better organized than those at most full-retail department stores. The men's and women's clothing is ultrachic, and the prices are low, low, low. A real fave with teens, in particular. The main Herald Square store carries all lines, including babies, children's, and maternity wear. 1328 Broadway (at 34th St.). ℂ 646/473-1165. www. hm.com. Subway: B, D, F, N, R, V, W to 34th St./Herald Sq. Also at 640 Fifth Ave. (at 51st St.). ℂ 212/489-0390. Subway: E, F to Fifth Ave. Smaller location at 558 Broadway (btwn Prince and Spring sts.). ℂ 212/343-2722. Subway: N, R to Prince St.

Jeffrey New York ℛ   At the end of a deserted street, in the still-industrial Meat-Packing District, is this oasis of cutting-edge haute couture. Jeffrey New York caters to the Barneys crowd, but this outpost of the famed Atlanta megaboutique is much more accessible and user-friendly. Great accessories and shoes galore. The collection is mostly geared to women, but there's a notable men's department, too. A worthy schlep for style hounds. 449 W. 14th St. (near Tenth Ave.). ℂ 212/206-1272. Subway: A, C, E, L to 14th St.

Paul Stuart   Paul Stuart is a touch more hip and a touch more expensive than Brooks Brothers. Stuart is the classic New York haberdasher—gorgeous fabrics, impeccable tailoring, expensive price tags on everything from suits to weekend wear; there's women's wear, too, but Paul Stuart is more about men. This is a way-of-life store for those who subscribe. Madison Ave. at 45th St. ℂ 866/278-8278. www.paulstuart.com. Subway: 4, 5, 6, 7, S to 42nd St./Grand Central.

Polo/Ralph Lauren   Among all the high-ticket designers whose shops line Madison Avenue, Ralph Lauren deserves special mention for the stunning beauty of his flagship store, housed in a landmark Rhinelander mansion. One of New York's first important free-standing American designer shops, it has continued to wear as well as the classics Ralph churns out. Housewares and infants' clothing as well as women's and men's clothes are for sale. The active wear and sporty country looks are at Polo Sport. 867 and 888 Madison Ave. (at 72nd St.). ℂ 212/606-2100. www.ralphlauren.com. Subway: 6 to 68th St.

Prada   Few designer labels are more body-conscious, cachet-laden, and downright chic than this sleek Italian line, which reaches beyond clothing to embrace shoes, accessories, and the hippest handbags on the globe (yes, still). 841 Madison Ave. (at 70th St.). ℂ 212/327-4200. Subway: 6 to 68th St.

Sean John   P. Diddy has come a long way from his Harlem roots. In 2004, he opened a flagship on Fifth Avenue and 41st Street featuring his signature hip-hop duds. But the store looks more like a refined library (maybe inspired by the big one across the street—the New York Public Library) than any gangsta club, uptown *or* downtown. Still, if you don't feel like making your way up to 125th Street, you'll find similar street style here in the heart of corporate brand-name Midtown. 475 Fifth Ave. (at 41st St.). ℂ 212/220-2633. Subway: B, D, F, V, 4, 5, 6, 7 to 42nd St.

Seize sur Vingt *Finds*   This Nolita shop custom-tailors Egyptian cotton shirts in bright colors and bold patterns for men and women—perfect for adding a bit of individual flair to your corporate threads. They've also reinvented the bespoke suit in clean, slim, contemporary lines. 243 Elizabeth St. (btwn Houston and Prince sts.). (£ **212/343-0476.** www.16sur20.com. Subway: F, V to Broadway–Lafayette St.; 6 to Spring St.

Ted Baker London   This hip Brit import, housed in a store that feels like an old-school country club, is a more-than-welcome addition to the men's clothing options in Manhattan. I like their sloppy-chic button-down shirts, which bring back memories of the post-Beatles British invasion. 107 Grand St. (at Mercer St.). (£ **212/343-8989.** www.tedbaker.co.uk. Subway: J, M, N, R, Z, 6 to Canal St.

Uniqlo *Value*   They call this place "the Japanese Gap"; I see it more like the Asian version of Scandinavian retailer H&M. Here you'll find hip, "youthful" apparel for men and women at very affordable prices. After a series of "pop-up" stores around the city with Uniqlo's clothes, in late 2006, Uniqlo opened a 36,000-square-foot, tri-level global flagship store in SoHo. The towering rows of shelves are stocked with cashmere sweaters, brightly colored sweatpants, jeans, and painted t-shirts (some for as little as $6). With most of the shelve space vertical, it's easy to browse here and, at these prices, hard to leave the store empty handed. 546 Broadway (btwn Prince and Spring sts.). (£ **212/221-9037.** www.uniqlo.com. Subway: N,R, to Prince St.

Just Women

Anthropologie   Funky, slightly exotic, and affordable wearables and accessories mix with fun gifts, furniture, and home-decorating items. Geared to funky-chic post-collegiate young women who've outgrown Urban Outfitters. 375 W. Broadway (btwn Spring and Broome sts.). (£ **212/343-7070.** www.anthropologie.com. Subway: C, E to Spring St. Also at 85 Fifth Ave. (at 15th St.). (£ **212/627-5885.** Subway: L, N, R, 4, 5, 6 to 14th St./Union Sq.

Eileen Fisher *★★*   Making their way around the nation in her own shops and through such outlets as Saks and the Garnet Hill catalog, Eileen Fisher's separates are a dream come true for stylish women looking for easy-to-wear classic pieces that transcend the latest fads. She designs fluid clothes in a pleasing neutral palette and uses natural fibers that don't sacrifice comfort for chic. The A-line styles look a bit droopy on shorter women, but otherwise suit all figure types well. The superior quality, fabrics, and style make these clothes worth every penny. The beautifully austere SoHo location is Fisher's prime showcase. The semiannual consolidation sales, in March and August, are a bargain hunter's delight. Note that only the SoHo flagship sells the complete line, including both the petite and women's collections. The closet-size East 9th Street location basically functions as an outlet store, with lots of sale merchandise and seconds on hand. 395 W. Broadway (btwn Spring and Broome sts.). (£ **212/431-4567.** www.eileen fisher.com. Subway: C, E to Spring St. Also at 521 Madison Ave. (at 53rd St.). (£ **212/759-9888.** Subway: 6 to 51st St. 341 Columbus Ave. (near 76th St.). (£ **212/362-3000.** Subway: B, C to 81st St. 1039 Madison Ave. (btwn 79th and 80th sts.). (£ **212/879-7799.** Subway: 6 to 77th St. 314 E. 9th St. (btwn First and Second aves.). (£ **212/529-5715.** Subway: 6 to Astor Place. 166 Fifth Ave. (at 22nd St.). (£ **212/924-4777.** Subway: N, R to 23rd St.

Huminska   If you're addicted to colorful, flirty dresses and shapely swirl skirts, make a beeline for this shop. The offerings change with the whims of the designer, but the current collection of dresses seems to be inspired by the 1950s and the wonder that is polka dots. 315 E. 9th St. (btwn First and Second aves.). (£ **212/677-3458.** www.huminska.com. Subway: 6 to Astor Place.

Intermix   The place to dress and accessorize in style, at not-too-expensive prices. The Flatiron location is the original, and remains the best. 125 Fifth Ave. (btwn 19th and 20th sts.). ✆ 212/533-9720. www.intermixonline.com. Subway: N, R to 23rd St. Also at 210 Columbus Ave. (btwn 69th and 70th sts.). ✆ 212/769-9116. Subway: B, C to 72nd St. 365 Bleecker St. ✆ 212/929-7180. Subway: 1 to Christopher St.

Jill Anderson *(Finds*   Finally, a New York designer who designs affordable clothes for real women to wear for real life—not just for 22-year-old size 2s to match with a pair of Pradas and wear out club-hopping. This narrow, peaceful shop and studio is lined on both sides with Jill's simple, clean-lined designs, which drape beautifully and accentuate a woman's form without clinging. They're wearable for all ages and many figure types. (Her small sizes are small enough to fit petites, and her larges generally fit a full-figured size 14.) Her clothes are feminine without being frilly, retro-reminiscent but completely modern, understated, and utterly stylish. 331 E. 9th St. (btwn First and Second aves.). ✆ 212/253-1747. www.jillanderson.com. Subway: 6 to Astor Place.

Searle *(**   If you're looking for a winter coat or jacket, there aren't many better choices than Searle. But the stores are not only known for their jackets, they also feature great clothes in beautiful colors and fabrics. 156 Fifth Ave. (btwn 20th and 21st sts.). ✆ 212/924-4330. www.searlenyc.com. Subway: N, R to 23rd St. Also at 805 Madison Ave. btwn 67th St. and 68th. ✆ 212/628-6665. Subway: 6 to 68th St. 1035 Madison Ave. (at 79th St.). ✆ 212/717-4022. Subway: 6 to 77th St.

Vera Wang   The petite powerhouse is still the hottest name in bridal fashions. Vera dresses scads of top stars (particularly petite ones with great figures) on their big day or for the Oscars in her simple, elegant designs. Vera's studio is open by appointment only, so brides-to-be should call ahead. There's also a Vera Wang salon on the third floor at **Bergdorf's** (p. 310). Ask about the annual warehouse sale, usually held in September. 991 Madison Ave. (at 77th St.). ✆ 212/628-3400. www.verawang.com. Subway: 6 to 77th St. Bridesmaids' store at 980 Madison Ave., 3rd floor (btwn 76th and 77th sts.). ✆ 212/628-9898. Subway: 6 to 77th St.

Just Men
Frank Stella   This refined shop sells casually elegant clothes for the well-dressed 21st-century man, including clean-lined blazers, quality knits, and beautifully cut trousers. 440 Columbus Ave. (at 81st St.). ✆ 212/877-5566. Subway: B, C to 81st St. Also at 921 Seventh Ave. (at 58th St.). ✆ 212/957-1600. Subway: A, B, C, D, 1 to 59th St./Columbus Circle.

Paul Smith   This temple of new English fashion is a can't-miss. When it comes to menswear that's at once fashion-forward and undisputedly classic, Paul Smith wins the prize, with jackets, suits, pants, shoes, sportswear, and accessories that are super-pricey but worth every cent. 108 Fifth Ave. (at 16th St.). ✆ 212/627-9770. www.paulsmith.co.uk. Subway: F to 14th St. Also at 142 Greene St., (betw Houston & Prince sts.). ✆ 212/254-3530. Subway: N/R to Prince St.; B, D, F to Broadway/Lafatette.

Saint Laurie Merchant Tailors *(Finds*   Family-owned since 1913, this custom tailor offers a huge selection of fabrics, from Scottish worsted wools to Italian silks, and offers you a selection of styles to choose from. The custom job is about $1,000 for a suit (less when sales are going on), substantially less for a blazer. 22 W. 32nd St. (at Fifth Ave.). ✆ 212/643-1916. www.saintlaurie.com. Subway: B, D, F, N, Q, R, V to 34th St.

Just Kids

If you need the basics, you'll find branches of **Gap Kids, Baby Gap,** and **The Children's Place** all over town—it's harder to avoid one than to find one. The department stores are also great sources, of course.

Bu & the Duck *Finds*   This divine shop sells its own unique vintage-inspired clothing and shoes that your kids can really wear. Delightful sock puppets and other vintage-inspired toys are also in the mix. 106 Franklin St. (btwn Church St. and W. Broadway). ℂ 212/431-9226. www.buandtheduck.com. Subway: 1 to Franklin St.

Shoofly   Top-quality clothing, footwear, and accessories for kids from newborns through teens. You'll find lots of distinctive stuff here, including imported lines. The shoe selection, in particular, is terrific, and not too pricey. The downtown store also sells toys and infant gifts. 42 Hudson St. (btwn Duane and Thomas sts.). ℂ 212/406-3270. www. shooflynyc.com. Subway: 1, 2, 3 to Chambers St.

Space Kiddets *Finds*   This sleeper in the Flatiron District has been around for 23 years and features children's clothing in refreshing styles—a cut above such chains as the Children's Place. But the prices are also a cut above. Sales are frequent. 46 E. 21st St. (at Broadway). ℂ 212/420-9878. www.spacekiddets.com. Subway: N, R to 23rd St.

Vintage & Consignment Clothing

Allan & Suzi *Finds*   Make it past the freaky windows and inside you'll find one of the best consignment shops in the city. Allan and Suzi have specialized in gently-worn 20th-century designer wear for over a decade, and their selection is marvelous. Their extensive vintage and contemporary couture collection, which ranges from conservative Chanel to over-the-top Halston, Mackie, and Versace, is so well priced that it's well within reach of the average shopper looking for something extra-glamorous. 416 Amsterdam Ave. (at 80th St.). ℂ 212/724-7445. Subway: 1 to 79th St.

Michael's *Value*   This consignment boutique boasts top-drawer designer wear for women, including such names as Chanel, YSL, Prada, Gucci, Richard Tyler, and Escada, at a fraction of the original cost. The bridal salon is an unbeatable find for engaged gals looking for a top-quality dress at an off-the-rack price. 1041 Madison Ave., 2nd floor (btwn 79th and 80th sts.). ℂ 212/737-7273. www.michaelsconsignment.com. Subway: 6 to 77th St.

Screaming Mimi's *Value*   Think you hate vintage shopping? Think again: Screaming Mimi's is as neat and well organized as any high-priced boutique, yet prices are surprisingly reasonable, especially given the pricey vintage shops that have popped up around the city in recent years. The vintage-housewares department is a wonderful cornucopia of kitsch and includes a selection of New York memorabilia; prices start under $10. 382 Lafayette St. (btwn E. 4th and Great Jones sts.). ℂ 212/677-6464. www.screaming mimis.com. Subway: 6 to Astor Place.

EDIBLES

Arthur Avenue Retail Market *★★*   This colorful, enclosed market opened in the heart of the Bronx's Little Italy in 1940 and is my absolute favorite. The market, like the Bronx, has had its ups and downs but now is thriving. You'll find fresh-produce purveyors, such as **Biano** fruits and vegetables, and **Joe Liberatore's Garden of Plenty,** where I buy the best tomato plants for my terrace. There is **Peter's Market,** for homemade sausages and braciole; **Mike's Deli,** for freshly made mozzarella and sandwiches; **Café al Mercato,** for their amazing broccoli rabe pizza and pasta *fagioli;*

the **Arthur Avenue Baking Company,** for loaves of *pane di casa* and Parmesan bread-sticks; and even **La Casa Grande Tobacco Company,** where they roll their own cigars. 2344 Arthur Ave., the Bronx. No phone. Subway: B, D to Fordham Rd.

Chelsea Market   Located in an old Nabisco factory, this big, dazzling food mall is the city's largest. Come for both raw and ready-to-eat foods, including divinely inspired baked goods and cappuccino from **Amy's Bread;** yummy soups from **Hale and Hearty;** Manhattan's best brownie at **Fat Witch Bakery;** and much more, including the wonderful **Chelsea Wine Vault. Chelsea Market Baskets** is a great place to pick up gifts for home. 75 Ninth Ave. (btwn 15th and 16th sts.). www.chelseamarket.com. Subway: A, C, E to 14th St.; L to Eighth Ave.

Dean & DeLuca   This, the original location, is a bright, clean-lined store that offers premier quality across the board: In addition to the excellent butcher, fish, cheese, and dessert counters (check out the stunning cakes and the character cookies) and beautiful fruits and veggies, you'll find a dried-fruit-and-nut bar, a huge coffee-bean selection, a gorgeous cut-flower selection, lots of imported waters and beers in the refrigerator case, and a limited but quality selection of kitchenware in back. A small cafe up front makes a great stop for a cappuccino break from SoHo shopping. 560 Broadway (at Prince St.). ✆ 212/226-6800. www.dean-deluca.com. Subway: N, R to Prince St.

DiPalo's Dairy ✪   Before there was Mario Batali, before Danny Meyer, or Daniel Boulud, there was Louie DiPalo, a true New York food celebrity if there ever was one. But thankfully, Louie won't be hosting any food shows anytime soon. He's too busy behind the counter of his 1910-originated, family-run store, putting together packages of the best and hardest to find Italian cheeses around for some of the city's most acclaimed restaurants and chefs. But you don't have to be a chef to enjoy DiPalo's; you just need a little patience—lines can get long and Louie and his staff will take their time with your order. The tiny store is one of the last authentic Italian vestiges in the now tacky and overly gentrified neighborhood of Little Italy. 200 Grand St. (at Mott St.) ✆ 212/226-1033. Subway: B, D to Grand St.

Fairway ✪✪ *Value*   There is no better all-in-one market in Manhattan than Fairway. Here you will find the best and most modestly priced vegetables in the city. Cheeses are top-of-the-line and well organized. The fish counter is excellent and, again, very modestly priced. The second floor of the Broadway store features hard-to-find health foods and a wide array of organic fruits and vegetables. Fairway also carries the gourmet items you might find at Dean & Deluca but at a fraction of the cost. The Harlem store is huge and features a walk-in freezer, complete with down jackets provided for customers' use. 2127 Broadway (btwn 74th and 75th sts.). ✆ 212/595-1888. www.fairwaymarket.com. Subway: 1, 2, 3 to 72nd St. Also at 2328 Twelfth Ave. (at 132nd St.). ✆ 212/234-3883. Subway: 1 to 125th St.

Zabar's ✪   More than any other of New York's gourmet food stores, Zabar's is an institution. This giant deli sells prepared foods, packaged goods from around the world, coffee beans, excellent fresh breads, and much more (no fresh veggies, though). This is the place for lox, and the rice pudding is the best I've ever tasted. You'll also find an excellent—and well-priced—collection of housewares and restaurant-quality cookware on the second floor. Prepare yourself for serious crowds. The attached cafe serves terrific sandwiches and takeout—ideal for a Central Park picnic. 2245 Broadway (at 80th St.). ✆ 212/496-1234. www.zabars.com. Subway: 1 to 79th St.

Chocolate City

The Big Apple is fast becoming a city consumed by a near-feverish craving for chocolate. Many sweets shops around the city now are turning out homemade chocolates in every variety that are so good, the stores, like four-star restaurants, are destinations in their own right. The best of these can be found just over the Brooklyn Bridge in DUMBO at **Jacques Torres Chocolate** 🎯🎯, 66 Water St., Brooklyn (📞 **718/875-9772**; www.mrchocolate. com). Torres, the former celebrated pastry chef at Le Cirque, ventured out on his own a few years ago and opened this mecca to chocolate, where your mouth will water as you watch chocolate being made. The variations here are staggering and include chocolate peanut brittle, chocolate-covered corn flakes, champagne truffles, and some of the best hot chocolate you've ever tasted. Take home a tin of the "wicked" hot chocolate, which features all-spice, cinnamon, sweet ancho chile peppers, and hot chipotle peppers. Also, the **Jacques Torres Chocolate** chocolate-manufacturing facility, open to the public, is at 350 Hudson St., at King Street, in TriBeCa (📞 **212/414-2462**).

In Manhattan, steps from the Metropolitan Museum of Art, is the Madison Avenue incarnation of the Paris import **La Maison du Chocolat,** 1018 Madison Ave., at 78th Street (📞 **212/744-7117**; www.lamaisonduchocolat. com). This boutique takes its chocolate very seriously. Here you will find possibly the best pure chocolate you've ever tasted. They abhor any bitterness in their chocolate and make it a point to claim that they use nothing stronger than 65% cocoa. Now that's serious chocolate.

One of the oldest chocolate shops in the city is the 1923-established **Li-Lac Chocolates,** 40 Eighth Ave. (at Jane St.; 📞 **212/370-4866** or 212/924-2280; www.li-lacchocolates.com), formerly on Christopher Street, which, after 81 years, has moved to new digs and now boasts a satellite store in Grand Central Terminal. This West Village shop makes their sweets by hand and whips up its chocolate fudge daily. In fact, they do chocolate fudge like no one else in the city.

Also in the Village is **The Chocolate Bar,** 127 E. 7th Street (at Ave. A). (📞 **212/366-1541**; www.chocolatebarnyc.com). Their homemade chocolate bars are worthy of their name. I love the mocha, with its flecks of coffee. For those who worship the cocoa gods, go for the super-dark 72%, so dark and rich you might speak in tongues after a few bites.

For the unconventional chocolate, head to **Kee's Chocolates,** 80 Thompson St, near Spring Street (📞 **212/334-3287**; www.keeschocolates.com), where owner Kee Ling Tong makes her own unique creations 6 days a week, including such flavors as balsamic, mango green tea, and Thai chili.

COFFEE & TEA

Ito En *Finds*   You want green tea? You want black tea? Herbal tea? White tea? No problem. There are so many varieties of teas here you need a catalog to peruse the selections. Located in a Madison Avenue town house, Ito En is like an art gallery of teas; everything is neatly displayed and there is a calming, serene feel to the store. There is a *sencha* bar (tea bar), where you can sample some of their teas and get tea advice from the experts working there. They also sell green-tea-dusted chocolate-covered almonds that are an addictive, and very expensive, munchie. 822 Madison Ave. (at 69th St.). ⓒ 212/988-7111. www.itoen.com. Subway: 6 to 68th St.

McNulty's Tea & Coffee Company ⍟   McNulty's has been around since 1895, making it one of the oldest coffee purveyors in the country. And it still has that old-time feel, with overflowing sacks of coffees and rare teas cluttering the quaint West Village store—and they roast their own coffees right there. The Colombia Supremo is as perfect as it gets, and I can't leave the store without my monthly fix of Italian roast espresso. 109 Christopher St. (btwn Bleecker and Hudson sts.). ⓒ 212/242-5351. www.mcnultys.com. Subway: 1 to Christopher St.

SWEETS

Dylan's Candy Bar ⍟   Dylan (daughter of Ralph) Lauren is one of the co-owners of this bazaar for sugar addicts. Located across the street from Bloomingdale's, you'll find all the candy classics, such as Necco Wafers, Charleston Chews, and both of my favorite childhood chewing gums, Black Jack and Gold Mine. Dylan's also makes signature chocolates; candy creations; candy spa products, such as hot-chocolate bath beads; and custom-made ice cream flavors. 1011 Third Ave. (at 60th St.). ⓒ 646/735-0078. www.dylanscandybar.com. Subway: 4, 5, 6, N, R , W to 59th St.

A Taste of New York

Do you want to bring back a *real* New York souvenir—something that evokes the genuine flavor of New York more than an I ♥ NEW YORK T-shirt or an Empire State Building figurine? Give your friends and family some real New York edibles. Possibly the best place to pick up food souvenirs is the Lower East Side. This neighborhood, home to so many immigrants over the years, is where a number of traditional New York foods originated. Do you have a friend who craves pickles, pregnant or not? Then venture to **Guss Pickles** at 85 Orchard St. (ⓒ 917/701-4000). Bring home a gallon of half or full sour, a mix of both, or pickled green tomatoes. If you can't lug it back home, have them ship it for you for about $49 a gallon.

If anyone can really explain what a bialy is exactly, I'm all ears. But whatever it really is doesn't matter as long as it tastes good. You'll find the oldest (over 65 years) bialy makers and the best in New York at **Kossar's Bialys**, 367 Grand St., between Norfolk and Essex streets (ⓒ 877-4BIALYS). A dozen go for around $9 and come in different flavors such as sesame, poppy, and garlic.

East Houston Street features two New York food-souvenir choices worth bringing home. Start with knishes from the 1910-established **Yonah Schimmel Knishes** at 137 E. Houston St., between First and Second avenues (ⓒ 212/477-2858). The choices range from potato to spinach to mushroom; a box of 12 goes for about $34. At 179 E. Houston St., between Allen and Orchard streets, the remarkable **Russ & Daughters** (ⓒ 212/475-4880; www.russanddaughters.com) has incomparable smoked fish and nova. A medley of smoked salmon goes for about $70 and, in my humble opinion, is worth every penny.

Economy Candy Store While Dylan's is the new generation of candy store, Economy Candy, which has been selling its sweet wares since 1937, in the gentrified Lower East Side, across the street from the Hotel on Rivington, is a blast from the past. Here, if you are somewhat aged (like your author), you will recognize such treats from your childhood as Hot Tamales, Bit O'Honey, Kosher rock candy, Atomic Fireballs, and Necco Wafers. You'll also find a fine selection of dried fruits and nuts and gourmet chocolate here. A trip to Economy Candy is definitely a trip back in time and worth taking. 108 Rivington St. (btwn Delancey and Norfolk sts.). ℂ 800/352-4544. www.economycandy.com. Subway: F to Delancey St.

Fauchon 🌟🌟 *Finds* This Parisian chocolatier operates a large, elegant boutique featuring an ultracharming tea salon and sparkling glass cases display a gorgeous array of chocolates and sweet treats flown in daily; the candied fruits are among the most gorgeous foods I've ever seen. Afternoon tea is served daily from noon to 6pm (to 5pm on Sun); you can choose between a two-course tea ($30) or a lovely array of salads, quiches, and so forth. Beautifully packaged candies, biscuits, preserves, and the like make elegant and pretty take-home treats. 442 Park Ave. (at 56th St.). ℂ 212/308-5919. www.fauchon.com. Subway: 4, 5, 6 to 59th St.

ELECTRONICS

The Apple Store 🌟 The largest Apple Store opened in early 2006, and hasn't closed yet (it's open 24/7). This glass edifice on Fifth Avenue and 59th Street features 18,000-square-feet. Descend a glass staircase or elevator to the store below ground where there is a 46-seat theater and 14 Internet-connected computers fully loaded with games; a geek's paradise. It's almost impossible to walk by without popping in to see what the fuss is all about. I'm not sure anyone actually buys all the Apple gadgets sold here, but it sure is fun to try out the floor samples. 767 Fifth Ave (at 59th St.). ℂ 212/336-1440. www.apple.com. Subway N, R to Fifth Avenue. Also at 103 Prince St. (at Greene St.). ℂ 212/226-3126. Subway: R to Prince St. And 401 W. 14th St. ℂ 212/444-3400. Subway: L to 8th Ave.

B&H Photo & Video 🌟🌟 *Value* Looking for a digital camera at a good price? You won't do any better than B&H, the largest camera store in the country. This camera superstore has everything from lenses to darkroom equipment. If you are a B&H virgin, the store can be somewhat intimidating, but service is helpful. Just follow the signs and they will direct you to whatever you are seeking. (**Note:** B&H is closed Sat.) 420 Ninth Ave. (at 34th St.). ℂ 800/606-6969 or 212/444-6615. www.bhphotovideo.com. Subway: A, C, E to 34th St.

J&R Music & Computer World 🌟 This block-long Financial District emporium is the city's top discount computer, electronics, small appliance, and office-equipment retailer. The sales staff is knowledgeable but can get pushy if you don't buy at once or know exactly what you want. Don't succumb—take your time and find what you need. Or better yet, peruse the store's copious catalog or extensive website, both of which make advance research, mail order, and comparison-shopping easy. 23 Park Row (at Ann St., opposite City Hall Park). ℂ 800/806-1115 or 212/238-9000. www.jandr.com. Subway: 2, 3 to Park Place; 4, 5, 6 to Brooklyn Bridge/City Hall.

GIFTS

For first-rate Fifth Avenue gifts, don't forget **Tiffany & Co.,** whose upper level boasts wonderful small gifts, all crafted in signature Tiffany silver or crystal and wrapped in the unmistakable blue box (see "Jewelry & Accessories," below).

For additional suggestions, see "Antiques & Collectibles," earlier in this chapter, and "Home Design & Housewares," below.

auto.   If a Lucite tic-tac-toe set sounds like a good idea to you, don't miss this witty Meat-Packing District boutique. The mod and minimalist home accessories and gift items—mostly original designs by Brooklyn-based artists—are well conceived and good-humored. 805 Washington St. (btwn Gansevoort and Horatio sts.). ℭ 212/229-2292. www. thisisauto.com. Subway: A, C, E, 1, 2, 3 to 14th St.; L to Eighth Ave.

Jack Spade   Looking for a gift for the man who has everything? Then head to Jack Spade, which specializes in vintage and new "guy toys." The inventory changes constantly, but expect goodies along the lines of vintage phonographs and microscopes, old maps and globes, cool desk accessories, and the like. This shop was launched by the husband of Kate Spade (she of chic handbags and paper-goods fame), so you can expect a smart, upmarket collection. 56 Greene St. (btwn Spring and Broome sts.). ℭ 212/625-1820. www.jackspade.com. Subway: C, E to Spring St.; N, R to Prince St.

Pearl River *(Value*   After moving from tight quarters on Canal Street to a more spacious location, this Chinese mall still overflows with affordable Asian exotica. You need vials of ginseng? They got it. How about a pair of Mandarin-collared silk pajamas or a mah-jongg set? They got it. While you're perusing the goods, enjoy a cup of tea at the cafe and meditate to the sound of the store's bubbling waterfall. 477 Broadway (at Grand St.). ℭ 212/431-4770. www.pearlriver.com. Subway: R, W to Prince; 6 to Spring.

Steuben Glass   This is the flagship store for America's premier manufacturer of fine glass and crystal, said to be the world's purest. The store is gorgeous, and the pieces—which run the gamut from fruit bowls to sculptures—are spectacularly crafted and refract light beautifully. Prices start around $200 for a "hand cooler" (a small collectible, often animal-shaped, that fits in your palm) and run into the five figures. The Corning Gallery, on the lower level, hosts rotating art exhibits. 667 Madison Ave. (at 61st St.). ℭ 800/STEUBEN. www.steuben.com. Subway: N, R to Fifth Ave.

HANDBAGS & LEATHER GOODS

Jutta Neumann *(Finds*   If you stop into this studiolike shop, you're likely to find the artist herself behind the counter, cutting and stitching her geometric, bold-hued leather goods—bags, wallets, boots, and more. Her mules and strappy sandals are also popular. 158 Allen St. (btwn Stanton and Rivington sts.). ℭ 212/982-7048. www.juttaneumann-new york.com. Subway: F to Delancey/Essex sts.

kate spade   Kate Spade revolutionized the high-end handbag market with her practical yet chic rectangular handbags, which have seemingly taken over the planet. They come in a wide range of fabrics and sizes, from pretty seersuckers to groovy prints to fashionable flannel to basic black, plus a wide range of solids. The daintier evening line is charming, particularly the grosgrain silks. The line has expanded to include chic baby bags, luggage, sexy shoes, and comfy pajamas. You can also find the signature bags at Saks, Barneys, Bergdorf Goodman, and Bloomingdale's. 454 Broome St. (at Mercer St.). ℭ 212/274-1991. www.katespade.com. Subway: N, R to Prince St. kate spade baby: 59 Thompson St. (btwn Spring and Broome sts.). ℭ 212/965-8654. Subway: C, E to Spring St.

Manhattan Portage Ltd. Store   Come here for the hippest nylon and canvas carryalls in town. True to its name, Manhattan Portage manufactures all its bags right in the city, and they're made from hard-wearing materials that can stand up to an urban lifestyle. Popular styles include all-purpose messenger bags, DJ bags, and backpacks (in both standard and nouveau one-shoulder styles) in a range of colors from irides-cent yellow to camouflage. Manhattan Portage bags are also sold through other out-lets, but you'll find the most complete selection here. 333 E. 9th St. (btwn First and Second aves.). © **212/995-5490.** Subway: 6 to Astor Place. Also at 301 W. Broadway. © **212/226-4557.** Sub-way: N, R to Prince St.

HOME DESIGN & HOUSEWARES

Attention, Oriental rug and cilium fans: Dealers line **Broadway** around the queen of home-furnishings department stores, **ABC Carpet & Home** (see "The Big Depart-ment Stores," earlier in this chapter). The second floor of **Zabar's** (see "Edibles," ear-lier in this chapter) is another excellent source for high-end kitchenware.

Broadway Panhandler If you're looking for restaurant-quality cookware and kitchen tools, you've found your place. The best combination of selection, prices, and service in town. 65 E. 8th St. (btwn Broadway and University Place). © **866/266-5927.** www. broadwaypanhandler.com. Subway: N,R, to 8th St.

Fishs Eddy ★★ *Value* What a great idea: selling remainders of kitschy, custom-designed china left over from yesteryear. Ever wanted a dish that *really* says "Blue Plate Special"? Or how about a mug with the terse logo "Cup o' Joe to Go"? The store is Browse Heaven, and prices on its American industrial china are low enough. The store's own designs are equally wonderful, especially its series with the New York sky-line. Other items for sale include basic vintage and retro-inspired flatware, heavy crockery bowls, and classic restaurant-supply glassware, such as soda-fountain and pint glasses, that can be hard to find in regular stores. 889 Broadway (at 19th St.). © **212/420-9020.** www.fishseddy.com. Subway: L, N, R, 4, 5, 6 to 14th St./Union Sq. St.

Frette This Italian linen maker has taken the hotel world by storm with its silky cotton sheets and plush terry towels and robes. If you've slept on some and now you want your own, head to this dedicated boutique or ABC Carpet & Home (p. 309) for the best selections. Also at Saks, Bloomingdale's, and Bergdorf's. 799 Madison Ave. (btwn 67th and 68th sts.). © **212/988-5221.** www.frette.it. Subway: 6 to 68th St.

Jonathan Adler Anybody who has been reading shelter magazines over the last couple of years will recognize this hot potter's bold vases and lamps instantly. His style merges organic shapes, geometric patterns, natural hues, and mod ideas into a one-of-a-kind style that works in almost any decor—really. Good throw pillows, too. 47 Green St. (at Broome St.). © **212/941-8950.** www.jonathanadler.com. Subway: N, R to Canal St. Also at 1097 Madison Ave. (btwn 83rd and 84th sts.). © **212/772-2410.** Subway: 6 to 86th St.

Character *Finds* New York's biggest collection of sleek and playful Alessi housewares from Italy (including Michael Graves's iconic teakettle with bird whistle), as well as European animation cells and toys starring Tintin, Babar, and Asterix. 19 Prince St. (btwn Elizabeth and Mott sts.). © **212/274-1966.** www.characternyc.com Subway: 6 to Spring St.

Leader Restaurant Equipment & Supplies *Value* The Bowery is the place to find restaurant-supply-quality kitchenware, and Leader is the best dealer on the block. This big, bustling, friendly shop is a good source for Chinese and Japanese wares—chopsticks, rice and noodle bowls, sushi plates, sake cups, and the like. You'll see a lot of the same styles you'd find at the high-end home stores in SoHo or the Village but at a fraction of the prices (this is where they buy, too). 134 Bowery (btwn Broome and Grand sts.). © **800/666-6888** or 212/677-1982. Subway: 6 to Spring St.

Moss If you have any interest in modern industrial design, don't miss this sleek, brightly lit store. All kinds of everyday objects are reinvented by cutting-edge European designers, from staplers to flatware to shelving units. The products were designed with 21st-century homes in mind, so they're surprisingly utilitarian and space-efficient—not to mention pricey. 150 Greene St. (btwn Houston and Prince sts.). ✆ 866/888-6677. www.mossonline.com. Subway: N, R to Prince St.

Terence Conran Shop Sir Terence Conran rules the London design and restaurant world, and now he's looking to make inroads in America with this bold sleek home shop. It's like an upscale—and, frankly, overpriced—version of IKEA, with lots of sleek contemporary lines, lightweight materials (chrome, blond woods, colorful plastic), and fun twists on standard household goods. Still, he set the tone for affordable contemporary design, and that alone makes this bright, browsable multilevel shop well worth a look. 407 E. 59th St. (at First Ave.). ✆ 212/755-9079. www.conran.com. Subway: 4, 5, 6 to 59th St.

Waterworks The place to give that most sacred of rooms, the bathroom, an entirely new, luxurious look. Half the store displays top-quality, hard-to-find designer hardware and fixtures, while the other half is dedicated to thick Egyptian terry towels, robes, and bathmats, plus stylish accessories for easy reinvention. 469 Broome St. (at Greene St.). ✆ 212/966-0605. www.waterworks.com. Subway: 6 to Canal St.; N, R to Prince St. Also at 225 E. 57th St. (btwn Second and Third aves.). ✆ 212/371-9266. Subway: 4, 5, 6 to 59th St.

JEWELRY & ACCESSORIES

Every big-name international jewelry merchant has a shop on Fifth Avenue in the 50s: glam Italian jeweler **Bulgari**, 730 Fifth Ave., at 57th Street (✆ 212/315-9000; www. bulgari.com); royal jeweler **Asprey & Garrard**, no. 725, at 56th Street (✆ 212/688-1811); ultraglamorous **Harry Winston**, no. 718, also at 56th Street (✆ 212/245-2000; www.harrywinston.com); **Cartier**, housed in a stunningly restored mansion at 653 Fifth Ave., at 52nd Street (✆ 212/446-3400; www.cartier.com); and, best of all, **Van Cleef & Arpels**, 744 Fifth Ave., at 57th Street (✆ 212/644-9500; www.van cleef.com), which also has a boutique at Bergdorf's.

⟮Value⟯ The Diamond District

West 47th Street between Fifth and Sixth avenues is the city's famous Diamond District. Apparently more than 90% of the diamonds sold in the United States come through this neighborhood first, so there are some great deals to be had if you're in the market for a nice rock or a piece of fine jewelry. The street is lined with showrooms; and you'll be wheeling and dealing with the largely Hasidic dealers, who offer quite a juxtaposition to the crowds. For a complete introduction to the district, including smart buying tips, point your Web browser to **www.diamonddistrict.org**. If you're in the market for wedding rings, there's only one place to go: Herman Rotenberg's **1,873 Unusual Wedding Rings**, 4 W. 47th St., booth 86 (✆ 800/877-3874 or 212/944-1713; www. unusualweddingrings.com). For semiprecious stones, head 1 block over to the **New York Jewelry Mart**, 26 W. 46th St. (✆ 212/575-9701). Virtually all of these dealers are open Monday through Friday only.

Some of the smaller boutique names are on Madison Avenue in the 60s. **Fred Leighton,** 773 Madison Ave., at 66th Street (© **212/288-1872;** www.fredleighton. com), specializes in magnificent estate jewelry.

Boucher *(Finds* This jewel box of a store sparkles on a gentrifying corner of the Meat-Packing District. Designer Laura Mady and her staff handcraft feminine, nature-inspired necklaces, earrings, and other jewelry using unusual gemstones in organic shapes and freshwater pearls in soft ice cream hues. Affordable, and ideal for dressing up or everyday. 9 Ninth Ave. (near Little W. 12th St., next to Pastis). © 212/206-3775. www.boucher jewelry.com. Subway: A, C, E to 14th St.; L to Eighth Ave.

Doyle & Doyle *(Finds* Elizabeth Doyle's lovely antiques boutique offers further evidence of the transformation of the Lower East Side from old-world cheap to exceptionally chic. Doyle & Doyle specializes in fine antique and estate jewelry, from the Georgian period to contemporary items. Pieces are all carefully chosen and beautifully displayed. 189 Orchard St. (btwn Houston and Stanton sts.). © 212/677-9991. www.doyledoyle.com. Subway: F to Second Ave. (exit at the front of the train and walk 1 block east).

Fortunoff *(Value* Despite the high-ticket facade, Fortunoff is a good resource for Swatch watches and a nice place to start pricing classic pieces: gold earrings, necklaces, bracelets, and the like. The styles aren't innovative, but the store tries to keep up an image as a discounter, and prices are low. It's great for silver and wedding gifts, too. 3 West 57th St. © 212/292-8800. www.fortunoff.com. Subway: R, N to Fifth Ave.

Jill Platner *(Finds* Platner's Aboriginal- and nature-inspired silver pieces are bold enough to look great on both men and women. Many are strung on brightly colored Tenara (a Gore-Tex-like thread) for a prehistoric-meets-21st-century feel. Prices are quite reasonable; it's easy to find a cool pair of earrings or a groovy ring for just a little more than $100. 113 Crosby St. (btwn Houston and Prince sts.). © 212/324-1298. www.jillplatner.com. Subway: N, R to Prince St.

Karen Karch Often featuring rough-hewn finishes and asymmetrical gems and stones, Karen Karch's eye-catching jewelry has attracted an A-list clientele to her Nolita shop. Six degrees of separation moment: If you buy one of her pieces, you'll take home a work of art from the designer who worked with Ethan Hawke to design Uma Thurman's wedding ring. Wonder whatever became of that ring? 240 Mulberry St. (btwn Prince and Spring sts.). © 212/965-9699. Subway: 6 to Spring St.

Tiffany & Co. The most famous jewelry store in New York—and maybe the world—deserves all the kudos. This wonderful multilevel store offers a breathtaking selection of jewelry, signature watches, tableware and stemware, and a handful of surprisingly affordable gift items. The store is so full of tourists that it's easy to browse without having any intention of buying. Believe it or not, it's not hard to find a lovely wearable piece in silver (Tiffany's best color, in my opinion) for around $200. If you do indulge, anything you buy—even a $50 silver bookmark or key chain—comes wrapped in that unmistakable blue box with a white ribbon tied just so. 727 Fifth Ave. (at 57th St.). © 212/755-8000. www.tiffany.com. Subway: N, R to Fifth Ave.

Tourneau Time Machine The snazzy three-floor emporium on East 57th Street is the world's largest watch store, carrying more than 90 brands and 8,000 different styles. The mind-boggling selection runs the gamut from Swatch to Rolex; Swiss Army knives, too. 12 E. 57th St. (btwn Fifth and Madison aves.). © 212/758-7300. www.tourneau.com. Subway: N, R to Fifth Ave. Also at 500 Madison Ave. (at 52nd St.). © 212/758-6098. Subway: 6 to 51st

St. 200 W. 34th St. (at Seventh Ave.). ℂ **212/563-6880.** Subway: 1, 2, 3 to 34th St. 10 Columbus Circle (The Shops at Columbus Circle). ℂ **212/823-9425.** Subway: A, B, C, D, 1 to Columbus Circle.

LOGO STORES

Firestore *Finds*   What better way to spend your souvenir budget than by saluting New York's bravest and finest? Here's the place to purchase FDNY logo wear, including T-shirts, sweatshirts, hats, and more. The goods are all top-quality, and a portion of the profits support the widows and children of the 343 firefighter victims lost in the September 11, 2001, terrorist attacks, and to NYPD-related charities.. The store, which moved to the West Village from Lafayette Street last year, along with its next-door neighbor, formerly known as **New York 911,** and now it's a one-stop for all things FDNY, NYPD, EMS, FBI, and NYC-coroner gear. The bounty includes shirts, caps, badge pins, patches, logo toys, and much more. (Not all of the products are licensed by the city, however; I suggest trying to stick with those that are.) The store is well-stocked and fun to browse, making it a great place to buy souvenirs and gifts for the folks back home. 17 Greenwich Avenue (west of 8th St. and Sixth Ave.). ℂ **212/226-3142.** www.nyfirestore.com. Subway: 1 to Christopher St.

Mets Clubhouse Shop   Stop in for goods galore—baseball caps, T-shirts, posters, Piazza jerseys, '69 Miracle Mets memorabilia, and much more amazin' merchandise. You can buy regular-season game tix here, too. 11 W. 42nd St. (btwn Fifth and Sixth aves.). ℂ **212/768-9534.** Subway: B, D, F, V to 42nd St.

The MTV Store   This petite boutique sits streetside, below the MTV studio. There's not much here—but your kids will surely find something they want. *Celebrity Death-match* T-shirt, anyone? Flyers advertising for audience members for MTV shows are sometimes on hand at the register—yet another reason for your teen to drag you in. 1515 Broadway (at 44th St.). ℂ **212/846-5655.** Subway: 1, 2, 3, 7, N, R, S to 42nd St./Times Sq.

NBA Store 🅖   For all things NBA and WNBA, head to this three-level megastore, a multimedia celebration of pro hoops, complete with a bleacher-seated arena for player appearances and signings. 666 Fifth Ave. (at 52nd St.). ℂ **212/515-6221.** www.nbastore. com. Subway: B, D, F, V to 47th–50th sts./Rockefeller Center.

NBC Experience   This mammoth, neon-lit store sits directly across from the *Today* show studio and sells all manner of NBC-themed merchandise, from Matt and Al's favorite mugs to a "You're Fired" T-shirt to "The Office" bobbleheads. And yes, there is a clearance department with merch from canceled shows . . . Your kids will enjoy the silly interactive features, such as the virtual-reality "Conan O'Brien's Wild Desk Ride," as well as the second-level candy shop. NBC Studio Tours also leave from here; call for details. 30 Rockefeller Plaza (at 49th St.). ℂ **212/664-3700.** www.nbcuniversalstore.com. Subway: B, D, F, N, V, W, R to 47th–50th sts./Rockefeller Center.

NIKETOWN   More multimedia advertorial than sportswear store, NIKETOWN is surprisingly low-key and attractive, with five floors of shoes and athletic wear displayed in Lucite and polished-metal surroundings. "Museum" cases display Sneakers of the Rich and Famous, and you're assailed by images of celebrity pitchmen and women. No sales or bargains here—plan on paying top dollar for the high-style athletic wear. Somebody's gotta pay for this place! 6 E. 57th St. (btwn Fifth and Madison aves.). ℂ **212/891-6453.** www.niketown.com. Subway: N, R to Fifth Ave.

Yankees Clubhouse Shop   For all your Bronx Bombers needs—hats, jerseys, jackets, and so on. Tickets for regular-season home games are also for sale, and there's a limited selection of other New York team jerseys. 245 W. 42nd St. (btwn Seventh and Eighth aves.). ℂ 212/768-9555. Subway: A, C, E to 42nd St./Port Authority. Also at 393 Fifth Ave. (btwn 36th and 37th sts.). ℂ 212/685-4693. Subway: 6 to 33rd St. 110 E. 59th St. (btwn Park and Lexington aves.). ℂ 212/758-7844. Subway: 4, 5, 6 to 59th St. 8 Fulton St. (in the South St. Seaport). ℂ 212/514-7182. Subway: 2, 3, 4, 5 to Fulton St.

MUSEUM STORES

Maxilla & Mandible *(Finds*   This shop is not affiliated with the American Museum of Natural History, but a visit here makes a good adjunct to your trip to the museum (which is around the corner). It may look like a freak shop at first glance, but it's really a fascinating natural-history emporium. Inside you'll find unusual rocks and shells from around the world, luminescent butterflies in display boxes, even surprisingly affordable real fossils containing prehistoric fish and insects that come with details on their history and where they were excavated. There's also a good variety of natural-history-themed

Shop the Museum

Besides the Museum stores listed above, here are some that are worthy of separate shopping trips. And many of the museums will allow you into their shops without having to pay the museum admission charge. For information about the museums listed here, see chapter 7.

Brooklyn Museum of Art, 200 Eastern Parkway, Brooklyn (ℂ **718/399-8440;** www.brooklynmuseum.org). You are in Brooklyn, so where better to find a genuine "Brooklyn" dish towel. For the children back home, Spanish Bingo might be a fun challenge while Global Feminism coffee mugs will enrich your feelings of sisterhood.

Cooper Hewitt National Design Museum, 2 E. 91st St, at Fifth Avenue (ℂ **212/849-8355;** www.cooperhewitt.org/shop). Here you will find ribbons for gift wrapping like none you've seen before or, even better, buy a pack of "Stop Talking" cards for that someone you love, but never shuts up.

Lower East Side Tenement Museum, 108 Orchard St, between Delancey and Grand Streets (ℂ **212/982-8420;** www.tenement.org). You've searched everywhere, but only at the Lower East Side Tenement can you find those "Heroes of the Torah" glass set you've always wanted. There is also an impressive collection of Irish, Italian and Jewish themed books here.

Morgan Library & Museum, 225 Madison Ave, at 36th Street (ℂ **212/685-0008** ext 524; www.morganlibrary.org). There are always new and interesting gifts at this charming museum gift shop. If you are lucky, they will have a Morgan Library letter opener in stock when you visit or, even better, paint tube doorstops. No home should be without them.

Museum of Sex, 233 Fifth Ave., at 27th Street (ℂ **212/681-6337;** www. museumofsex.com). If you can't shop for your erotica and toys guilt free here, you can't anywhere. "Faux Fur" handcuffs would be welcomed in almost any relationship while your own computer "body" mouse will make Internet surfing that much more pleasant.

toys for the kids. 451 Columbus Ave. (btwn 81st and 82nd sts.). ℂ 212/724-6173. www.maxillaand mandible.com. Subway: B, C to 81st St.

Metropolitan Museum of Art Store   Given the scope of the museum itself, it's no wonder that the gift shop is outstanding. Many treasures from the museum's collection have been reproduced as jewelry, china, and other *objets d'art.* The range of art books is dizzying, and upstairs is an equally comprehensive selection of posters and inventive children's toys. 1000 Fifth Ave. (at 82nd St.). ℂ 212/570-3894. www.metmuseum.org/store. Subway: 4, 5, 6 to 86th St. Also at Rockefeller Center, 15 W. 49th St. ℂ 212/332-1360. Subway: B, D, F, V to 47th–50th sts./Rockefeller Center. On the mezzanine level at Macy's, 34th St. and Sixth Ave. ℂ 212/268-7266. Subway: B, D, F, N, R, Q to 34th St./Herald Sq.

MoMA Design Store   Across the street from the Museum of Modern Art is this terrific shop, whose stock ranges from museum posters and clever toys for kids to fully licensed reproductions of many of the classics of modern design, including free-form Alvar Aalto vases, Frank Lloyd Wright chairs, and Eames recliners. If these high-design items are out of your reach, choose from plenty of more affordable outré home accessories. The SoHo store is equally fabulous. 44 W. 53rd St. (btwn Fifth and Sixth aves.). ℂ 212/767-1050. www.momastore.org. Subway: E, F to Fifth Ave.; B, D, F, Q to 47th–50th sts./Rockefeller Center. Also at 81 Spring St. (at Crosby St.). ℂ 646/613-1367. Subway: 6 to Spring St.

New York Transit Museum Store   Lots of nifty transportation-themed gifts—the cufflinks made out of subway tokens are just great. With all this train stuff, my 4-year-old son could spend hours here. Grand Central Terminal (on the main level, in the shuttle passage next to the Station Masters' office), 42nd St. and Lexington Ave. ℂ 212/878-0106. Subway: 4, 5, 6, 7, S to 42nd St./Grand Central. Also at Boerum Place (at Schermerhorn St.), Brooklyn. ℂ 718/694-1600. Subway: 4, 5 to Borough Hall.

MUSIC

Academy Records & CDs   This Flatiron District shop has a cool intellectual air that's more reminiscent of a good used-book store than your average used-record store. Academy is always filled with classical, opera, and jazz junkies perusing the extensive and well-priced collection of used CDs and vinyl. In addition to the extensive classical and jazz collection is a variety of other audiophile favorites, from rare '60s pop songsters to spoken word. 12 W. 18th St. (btwn Fifth and Sixth aves.). ℂ 212/242-3000. www.academy-records.com. Subway: L, N, R, 4, 5, 6 to 14th St./Union Sq.

Colony Music Center ♬   This long-lived Theater District shop ("since 1948") is housed in the legendary Brill Building, the Tin Pan Alley of 1950s and 1960s pop, where such songwriters as Leiber and Stoller and producers such as Don Kirshner and Phil Spector crafted the soundtrack for a generation. It's the perfect home for Colony, a nostalgia emporium filled with a pricey but excellent collection of vintage vinyl and new CDs. You'll find a great collection of Broadway scores and cast recordings; decades worth of recordings by pop song stylists both legendary and obscure; the city's best collection of sheet music (including some hard-to-find international stuff); and a great selection of original theater and movie posters. 1619 Broadway (at 49th St.). ℂ 212/265-2050. www.colonymusic.com. Subway: N, R to 49th St.; 1 to 50th St.

Generation Records *Value*   This tidy little store sells mostly CDs and is an excellent source for "import" live recordings. Originally specializing in hard-core, punk, and heavy metal, the new collection upstairs still has a heavy edge but has since diversified appreciably. Downstairs is a well-organized and well-priced used-CD selection that's not as picked over as most and runs the genre gamut; there's also a good selection of used LPs. Despite the help's tough look, they're actually quite friendly and helpful. 210 Thompson St. (btwn Bleecker and 3rd sts.). © 212/254-1100. Subway: A, B, C, D, E, F, V to W. 4th St.

House of Oldies ⟨⟩   I skipped many a high school class to spend time in this old store searching for doo-wop. I think it was here that I bought a mint "Woo Woo Train," by the Valentines, on Rama Records, for less than $5. That same record now probably costs over $60 and you can probably still find it at the House of Oldies. The store has over one million vinyl records in stock, in everything from R&B to surf music. If vinyl oldies are your thing, there's no better place. 35 Carmine St. (at Bleecker St.). © 212/243-0500. www.houseofoldies.com. Subway: A, B, C, D, F, V to W. 4th St.

Jazz Record Center   I have a friend from Paris who lives for jazz and this is the first place he hits whenever he visits New York. It's *the* place to find rare and out-of-print jazz records. In addition to the extensive selection of CDs and vinyl (including 78s), videos, books, posters, magazines, photos, and other memorabilia are available. Prices start at $5 for vinyl, $10 for CDs, and soar from there, befitting the rarity of the stock. Owner Frederick Cohen is extremely knowledgeable, so come here if you're trying to track down something obscure. (Cohen does mail-order business as well.) 236 W. 26th St., 8th floor (btwn Seventh and Eighth aves.). © 212/675-4480. www.jazzrecordcenter.com. Subway: 1 to 28th St.

Other Music ⟨Finds⟩   Head to Other Music for the wildest sounds in town. You won't find a major label here. This shop focuses exclusively on small international labels, especially those on the cutting edge. The bizarro runs the gamut from underground Japanese spin doctors to obscure Irish folk; needless to say, the world-music selection is terrific—fascinating and bound to be filled with music you've never heard of. The sales staff really know their stuff, so ask away. 15 E. 4th St. (btwn Broadway and Lafayette St.). © 212/477-8150. www.othermusic.com. Subway: F, V to Broadway–Lafayette St.; 6 to Astor Place.

Virgin Megastore   In the heart of Times Square, this superstore bustles day and night. For the size of it, the selection isn't as wide as you'd think; still, you're likely to find what you're looking for among the two levels of domestic and import CDs. Other pluses are an extensive singles department, a phenomenal number of listening posts, plus a huge video department. There's also a bookstore, a cafe, and a multiplex movie theater, and you can even arrange airfare on Virgin Atlantic with the on-site travel agent. Look for a busy schedule of in-store appearances at both locations...for a few more months. The stores' latest owners have announced plans to shut down the Times Square store in 2009, and there's talk of Union Square closing as well. 1540 Broadway (at 45th St.). © 212/921-1020. www.virginmega.com. Subway: N, R, 1, 2, 3, 7 to Times Sq./42nd St. Also at 52 E. 14th St. (at Broadway). © 212/598-4666. Subway: 4, 5, 6, N, R, L to 14th St./Union Sq.

PAPER & STATIONERY

Kate's Paperie ⟨⟩   Three cheers to Kate's for keeping the art of letter writing alive in our computer age. You could browse for hours among this delightful shop's hand-made stationery and wrap, innovative invitations and thank-yous, imported notebooks, writing tools, and other creative paper products, including cool paper lampshades. Lovely art cards, too—perfect for writing the folks back home—a joy! The SoHo location is best. 72 Spring Street (btwn Crosby and Lafayette sts.). © 212/941-9816. www.katespaperie.com. Subway: N, R to Prince St. Also at 8 W. 13th St. (btwn Fifth and Sixth aves.). © 212/633-0570. Subway: F to 14th St. 1282 Third Ave. (btwn 73rd and 74th sts.). © 212/396-3670.

Subway: 6 to 77th St. 140 W. 57th St. (btwn Sixth and Seventh aves.). ℂ **212/459-0700.** Subway: 1, 2, 3 to 34th St.

SHOES

Designer shoe shops start on **East 57th Street** and amble up **Madison Avenue,** becoming pricier as you move uptown. **SoHo** is an excellent place to search for the latest styles; the streets are overrun with terrific shoe stores. Cheaper copies of the trendiest styles are sold along **8th Street** between Broadway and Sixth Avenue in the Village, which some people call "Shoe Row."

Most department stores have two shoe departments—one for designer stuff and one for daily wearables. See "The Top Shopping Streets & Neighborhoods" and "The Big Department Stores," earlier in this chapter. For **Prada** and **Polo/Ralph Laren,** see "Clothing," and for **NIKETOWN,** see "Logo Stores," both earlier in this section.

Camper This Big Apple outpost features the full line of made-in-Spain Camper footwear for men and women. These are the hippest walking shoes and boots on the planet, hands down—ideal for those with an eye for style and a craving for comfort. 125 Prince St. (at Wooster St.). ℂ **212/358-1842.** www.camper.com. Subway: N, R to Prince St.; C, E to Spring St.

Giraudon New York This French designer offers fashionable, well-made street shoes for hip men and women who want something clean-lined and stylish but not too chunky or trendy. Not cheap, but not overpriced—these shoes last forever. Prices run $115 to $200, and sales are excellent. 152 Eighth Ave. (btwn 17th and 18th sts.). ℂ **212/ 633-0999.** www.giraudonnewyork.com. Subway: A, C, E to 14th St.; L to Eighth Ave.

Harry's Shoes 𝄞 This shoe store was an Upper West Side institution even before gentrification hit the neighborhood over 20 years ago. They were one of the first shoe stores to carry New Balance in the city, and now their selection of brands range from Bruno Magli to retro Keds. With a huge selection of children's brands, Harry's is the place for kids' shoes, which is why you might want to stay away, unless you don't mind parental hysteria during the back-to-school frenzy of late August as well as the presummer camp throngs that descend in late June. 2299 Broadway (at 83rd St.). ℂ **866/4-HARRYS.** www.harrys-shoes.com. Subway: 1 to 86th St.

Jimmy Choo *The* boutique for *sexy* stilettos. The shoe display is gorgeous at this sophisticated three-floor emporium. 645 Fifth Ave. (at 51st St.). ℂ **212/593-0800.** www.jimmy choo.com. Subway: E, F to Fifth Ave. Also at 716 Madison Ave. (at 63rd St.). ℂ **212/759-7078.** Subway: F, V to Lexington Ave.

Manolo Blahnik These wildly sexy women's shoes are notorious for their cut and sway and the way they shape the leg. Most famous are the catch-me-if-you-can high heels, but there are plenty of flats and low heels, too. Custom shoes in your own fabric are also a possibility. 31 W. 54th St. (btwn Fifth and Sixth aves.). ℂ **212/582-3007.** Subway: E, F to Fifth Ave.

Sacco These mostly Italian-made women's shoes and wonderful boots combine style with supreme comfort. Good prices and sales, too. 94 Seventh Ave. (btwn 15th and 16th sts.). ℂ **212/675-5180.** www.saccoshoes.com. Subway: 1 to 18th St. Also at 14 E. 17th St. (btwn Fifth Ave. and Broadway). ℂ **212/243-2070.** Subway: L, N, R, S, 4, 5, 6 to 14th St./Union Sq. 111 Thompson St. (btwn Prince and Spring sts.). ℂ **212/925-8010.** Subway: C, E to Spring St. 324 Columbus Ave. (btwn 75th and 76th sts.). ℂ **212/799-5229.** Subway: B, C to 81st St.

Sigerson Morrison *(Finds* Women who love shoes and are willing to pay in the neighborhood of $200 to $300 for something really special should make a beeline for this Nolita shop. These fashion-forward originals wow with their immaculate details, bright color palette, and sexy, strappy retro appeal—worth every penny. You'll also find some of their styles at Bergdorf Goodman and Saks if you don't want to go downtown. Attention, bargain hunters: Check out the January winter and August summer sales; prices drop to less than half of retail as the sales wind down. 28 Prince St. (btwn Mott and Elizabeth sts.). C 212/219-3893. www.sigersonmorrison.com. Subway: B, D, F, Q to Broadway–Lafayette St.; N, R to Prince St.; 6 to Spring St.

SPORTING GOODS

Modell's *(*ⓚ* I confess, like the annoying ad, I often "gotta go to Mo's." And I have my reasons. The best is the very reasonable prices, especially for sneakers and other footwear. Another is the excellent selection of team apparel; I can get my retro New York Giant football cap at half the price that they sell it at Giants' Stadium. And there are stores in practically every neighborhood, making it very convenient to "go to Mo's." 1293 Broadway (at 33rd St.). C 212/244-4544. www.modells.com. Subway: B, D, F, N, R, V to 34th St. Also at 300 W. 125th St. (at Frederick Douglass Blvd.). C 212/280-9100. Subway: A, B, C, D to 125th St. 51 E. 42nd St. (at Vanderbilt Ave.). C 212/661-4242. Subway: 4, 5, 6, 7, S to Grand Central. 55 Chambers St. (at Broadway). C 212/732-8484. Subway: E to Chambers St.

Paragon Sporting Goods The emphasis at this excellent all-purpose sporting-goods store—New York's best—is on equipment and athletic wear for virtually every sport, from tennis to biking to mountain climbing. End-of-the-season sales, especially on sneakers and outdoor clothing, bring serious discounts. 867 Broadway (at 18th St.). C 800/961-3030 or 212/255-8036. www.paragonsports.com. Subway: L, N, R, 4, 5, 6 to 14th St./Union Sq.

Patagonia Expensive though it may be, Patagonia deserves kudos for its commitment to producing efficient and ecofriendly sports and adventure wear—fleece pullovers made from recycled plastic soda bottles, shell jackets in ultralight weatherproof materials, and organic cotton T-shirts. 101 Wooster St. (btwn Prince and Spring sts.). C 212/343-1776. www.patagonia.com. Subway: N, R to Prince St.; C, E to Spring St. Also at 426 Columbus Ave. (btwn 80th and 81st sts.). C 917/441-0011. Subway: B, C to 81st St.

TOYS

If your kids love to read, don't miss **Books of Wonder** (p. 315). For vintage toys, check out **Alphaville** (p. 313).

American Girl Place *(*ⓚ* Your princess will never forgive you if you don't take her to this 43,000-square-foot emporium for little girls featuring a cafe, bookstore, and theater. If you come, don't forget to bring her favorite doll so it can get a makeover at the store's own doll salon. Birthday parties at the store are extremely popular, so if you want to plan one for your visit to New York, make sure to book well in advance. 609 Fifth Ave. (at 49th St.). C 800/845-0005 (for reservations) or 212/371-2220. www.americangirl.com. Subway: B, D, F, V to 47th–50th sts./Rockefeller Center.

FAO Schwarz After eliminating products carried by the big discounters, FAO Schwarz now carries those hard-to-find and oh-so-expensive items such as Vespa scooters for older children, mini–luxury cars such as Hummers and Jaguars, and serious karaoke machines. There's also a soda fountain where the kids can load up on sugar to fuel their romp through the magical store. The giant piano keys made famous in the movie *Big* thankfully still remain. 767 Fifth Ave. (at 58th St.). ℂ 212/644-9400. www.faos.com. Subway: N, R to Fifth Ave. or 4, 5, 6 to 59th St.

Kidding Around   This boutique stocks pricey, high-quality toys, many imported from Europe. The emphasis is on the old-fashioned—low-tech goodies such as puzzles, rocking horses, and tops. One wall is devoted exclusively to tub toys, windups, and other stocking stuffers. 60 W. 15th St. (btwn Fifth and Sixth aves.). ℂ 212/645-6337. www.kiddingaroundnyc.com. Subway: F to 14th St.

Toys "R" Us   Geoffrey the Giraffe must be mighty pleased with this multilevel, high-tech home. It occupies almost an entire city block in the heart of Times Square, and even boasts its own full-scale Ferris wheel, which kids can ride for free. The huge collection is very well organized, and the store's "ambassadors" are abundant and very helpful; they'll even point you to restaurants and kid-friendly attractions in the neighborhood. Don't miss it if you're traveling with kids. 1514 Broadway (at 44th St.). ℂ 800/869-7787. Subway: 1, 2, 3, 7 to 42nd St.

WINE & SPIRITS

Acker Merrall & Condit Co.   In business since 1820—which makes Acker America's oldest wine shop—this attractive little store is the Upper West Side's best wine source. There are no bad bottles here. The careful selection is well displayed, with authoritative cards attached to each bin to help you choose. A supremely knowledgeable staff is on hand for additional assistance. 160 W. 72nd St. (btwn Broadway and Columbus Ave.). ℂ 212/787-1700. www.ackerwines.com. Subway: 1, 2, 3, 9 to 72nd St.

Astor Wines & Spirits *Value*   This large store is the source for excellent values on liquor and wine; their stock is deep and diverse. The staff is always willing to recommend a vintage. Astor hosts excellent wine tastings 2 to 3 afternoons a week, often paired with edibles from local restaurants and gourmet shops; call or check the website for the schedule. 399 Lafayette St. (at 4th St). ℂ 212/674-7500. www.astoruncorked.com. Subway: 6 to Astor Place.

Morrell & Company   One of the leading retailers in America boasts a friendly, helpful staff and has a Fine Wine Division that hosts high-profile auctions. Adjacent is the **Morrell Wine Bar & Cafe** (ℂ 212/262-7700; www.morrellwinebar.com), an ideal place to sample the goods. 1 Rockefeller Plaza (at 49th St.). ℂ 212/688-9370. www.morrellwine.com. Subway: B, D, F, V to 47th–50th sts./Rockefeller Center.

Sherry-Lehmann *Finds*   Zagat's has called Sherry-Lehmann the "Rolls-Royce of wine shops," and the readers of *Decanter* magazine just named it Best Wine Merchant in the United States. Their vast inventory is mind-boggling and includes ritzy gift baskets that make luxurious gifts. Service is excellent and free wine tastings are often offered. Although expensive, this is the place to come if you're looking for a special bottle. 505 Park Avenue. (btwn 59th and 60th sts.). ℂ 212/838-7500. www.sherry-lehmann.com. Subway: N, R to Lexington Ave.; 4, 5, 6 to 59th St.

Union Square Wines and Spirits *Finds*   This small, cozy wine store squeezes in over 4,000 varieties of wines. There are numerous wine tastings throughout the week and recommendations by sommeliers from local restaurants. The store is well located across from the Union Square Greenmarket. If you have loaded up with fresh produce for a picnic, have the very personable clerks pair a wine with your food. 140 Fourth Ave. (at 13th St.). ℂ 212/675-8100. www.unionsquarewines.com. Subway: L, N, R, 4, 5, 6 to 14th St./Union Sq.

9

New York City After Dark

New York's nightlife scene is an embarrassment of riches. There's so much to see and do in this city after the sun goes down that your biggest problem is probably going to be choosing among the many temptations.

There's no way that I can tell you in these pages what's going to be on the calendar while you're in town. For the latest, most comprehensive nightlife listings, from theater and performing arts to live music, and dance-club coverage, *Time Out New York* (www.timeoutny.com) is my favorite weekly source; a new issue hits newsstands every Thursday. The free weekly *Village Voice* (www.villagevoice. com), the city's legendary alterna-paper, is available late Tuesday downtown and early Wednesday in the rest of the city, with even more listings than in the paper copy online at their web site. The arts and entertainment coverage couldn't be more extensive, and just about every live-music venue advertises its shows here.

The *New York Times* (www.nytoday. com) features terrific entertainment coverage, particularly in the two-part Friday "Weekend" section. The cabaret, classical-music, and theater guides are particularly

useful. Other great weekly sources are the *New Yorker* (www.newyorker.com), in its "Goings on About Town" section; and *New York* magazine (www.nymag.com, an excellent online source) features the latest happenings in its "The Week" section.

Bar-hoppers should get a hold of the comprehensive ***Shecky's New York Bar, Club & Lounge Guide,*** printed annually. The website (www.sheckys.com) is even more current and offers updated nightlife news at the click of a button.

Another good online bar source is **www.murphguide.com**. This website has all the latest happy-hour information and is a particularly good source if you are seeking out an Irish pub, of which there are many in New York.

NYC/Onstage (© **212/768-1818;** www.tdf.org) is a recorded service providing schedules, descriptions, and other details on theater and the performing arts. The bias is toward plays, but NYC/Onstage is a good source for chamber and orchestral music (including all Lincoln Center events), dance, opera, cabaret, and family entertainment.

1 All the City's a Stage: The Theater Scene

Nobody does theater better than New York. No other city—not even London—has a theater scene with so much breadth and depth, with so many wide-open alternatives. Broadway, of course, gets the most ink and the most airplay, and deservedly so. It's where you'll find the big stage productions, from crowd-pleasing warhorses like *The Lion King* to more recent hits like *Jersey Boys*. But today's scene is thriving beyond the bounds of just Broadway—smaller, "alternative" theater has taken hold of the popular imagination, too. With bankable stars onstage, crowds lining up for hot tickets,

Theater District Theaters

Al Hirschfeld **19**	Ethel Barrymore **26**	New Amsterdam **42**
Ambassador **11**	Eugene O'Neill **12**	New Victory **41**
American Airlines **45**	Gerald Schoenfeld **29**	New World Stages **46**
American Place **34**	Gershwin **7**	Palace **32**
August Wilson **5**	Helen Hayes **40**	Playwright's Horizons **49**
Belasco **36**	Hilton Theatre **44**	Radio City Music Hall **27**
Bernard B. Jacobs **24**	Imperial **18**	Richard Rodgers **17**
Biltmore **14**	John Golden **20**	Samuel Beckett **48**
Booth **30**	Longacre **15**	Shubert **39**
Broadhurst **23**	Lunt-Fontanne **28**	Signature Theatre **51**
Broadway **4**	Lyceum **35**	Snapple Theater
Brooks Atkinson **16**	Majestic **21**	Center **8**
Cadillac Winter	Marquis **31**	St. James **22**
Garden **9**	Minskoff **38**	Studio 54 **3**
Circle in the Square **10**	Mitzi E. Newhouse **1**	Town Hall **37**
City Center Stage **2**	Music Box **25**	Vivian Beaumont **1**
Cort **33**	Nederlander **43**	Walter Kerr **13**
Douglas Fairbanks **50**	Neil Simon **6**	WestSide **47**

and hits popular enough to generate major-label cast albums, Off-Broadway isn't just for culture vultures anymore. (And Off-Off-Broadway is the cheapest theater in town, usually less than $20 a ticket.)

I can't tell you precisely what will be on while you're in town, so check the publications listed at the start of this chapter or the websites listed in "Online Sources for Theatergoers & Performing-Arts Fans," below, to get an idea of what you might like to see. Another useful source is the **Broadway Line** (© **888/BROADWAY;** www.live broadway.com), where you can get details and descriptions on current Broadway shows, hear about special offers and discounts, and choose to be transferred to Telecharge or Ticketmaster to buy tickets. The recorded service **NYC/Onstage** (© **212/768-1818;** www.tdf.org) provides the same kind of service for both Broadway and Off-Broadway productions.

Helping to ensure the recent success of the New York theater scene has been the presence of Hollywood stars such as Julia Roberts, Harry Connick, Jr., Julianne Moore, Antonio Banderas, Brooke Shields, Kevin Bacon, Liam Neeson, and Dame Judi Dench. But keep in mind that stars' runs are often limited, and tickets tend to sell out fast. If you hear that there's a celeb you'd like to see coming to the New York stage, don't put off your travel and ticket-buying plans. (The box office can tell you how long a star is contracted for a role.)

THE BASICS

The terms **Broadway, Off-Broadway,** and **Off-Off-Broadway** refer to theater size, pay scales, and other arcane details, not location—or, these days, even star wattage. Most of the Broadway theaters are in Times Square, huddled around the thoroughfare the scene is named for, but not directly on it: Instead, you'll find them dotting the side streets that intersect Broadway, mostly in the mid-40s between Sixth and Eighth avenues (44th and 45th sts. in particular) but running north as far as 53rd Street. There's even a Broadway theater outside Times Square: the Vivian Beaumont in Lincoln Center, on the Upper West Side at Broadway and 65th Street.

Off-Broadway, on the other hand, is not so much about location (it has to do with the contract the production has with Actors Equity). Off-Off-Broadway shows tend to be more avant-garde, experimental, and/or nomadic, in smaller theaters, usually with fewer than 100 seats, with fewer performances per week and overall. Off-Broadway productions usually run longer and on the usual 8-a-week performance schedule in slightly larger theaters. These productions are all over town, but there are mini–theater Districts within Midtown and on the Upper West Side, as well as downtown.

Broadway shows tend to keep pretty regular **schedules.** There are usually eight performances a week: evening shows Tuesday through Saturday, plus matinees on Wednesday, Saturday, and Sunday. Evening shows are usually at 8pm, while matinees are usually at 2pm on Wednesday and Saturday, and 3pm on Sunday, but schedules can vary, especially Off and Off-Off-Broadway. In recent years, especially with shows that are popular with a younger audience, shows sometimes offer more matinees, or earlier curtain times for evening performances. Broadway shows usually start on the dot, or within a few minutes of starting time; if you arrive late, you may have to wait until after the first act to take your seat (and with the plethora of shows without intermission, you may have to watch the whole thing on a monitor in the lobby!)

Ticket prices for Broadway shows vary dramatically. Expect to pay a *lot* for good seats; the high end for any given show is likely to be between $60 and $100 or more (though some shows have recently started charging premium prices for the very best seats, competing with the licensed ticket brokers). The cheapest end of the price range can be as low as $20 or as high as $50, depending on the theater configuration (or if they offer standing-room or rush tickets). If you're buying tickets at the low end of a wide available range, be aware that you may be buying obstructed-view seats. If all tickets are the same price or the range is small, you can pretty much count on all of the seats being pretty good. Otherwise, price is your barometer. Note that legroom can be tight in these old theaters, and you'll usually get more in the orchestra seats.

Off-Broadway and Off-Off-Broadway shows tend to be cheaper, with tickets often as low as $10 or $15. However, seats for the most established shows and those with star power can command prices as high as $50 to $75.

Don't let price be a deterrent to enjoying the theater. There are ways to pay less if you're willing to make the effort and be flexible, with a few choices at hand as to what you'd like to see. Read on.

TOP TICKET-BUYING TIPS
BEFORE YOU LEAVE HOME

Phone ahead or go online for tickets to the most successful or popular shows as far in advance as you can—in the case of such shows as *The Lion King* (yes, even after all these years), it's never too early.

Buying tickets can be simple if the show you want to see isn't sold out. You need only call **Telecharge** (© 212/239-6200; www.telecharge.com), which handles most Broadway and Off-Broadway shows and some concerts, or **Ticketmaster** (© 212/ 307-4100; www.ticketmaster.com), which also handles Broadway and Off-Broadway shows and most concerts.

Theatre Direct International (TDI) is a ticket broker that sells tickets for select Broadway and Off-Broadway shows, including some of the most popular crowd-pleasers, such as *Jersey Boys* and *Wicked!,* directly to individuals and travel agents. Check to see if they have seats to the shows you're interested in by calling © 800/ **BROADWAY** or 212/541-8457; you can also order tickets through TDI via their commercial website, **www.broadway.com**. (Disregard the discounted prices, unless you're buying for a group of 20 or more.) Because there's a minimum service charge of $15 per ticket, you'll definitely do better by trying Ticketmaster or Telecharge first; but because they act as a consolidator, TDI may have tickets left for a specific show even if the major outlets don't.

Another reputable ticket broker is **Keith Prowse & Co.** (© 800/669-8687; www. keithprowse.com). For a list of other licensed ticket brokers recommended by the New York Convention & Visitors Bureau (NYCVB), get a copy of the Official NYC Visitor Kit (see "Visitor Information," in chapter 3, for details). All kinds of ticket brokers list ads in the Sunday *New York Times* and other publications, but don't take the risk. Stick with a licensed broker recommended by the NYCVB.

You may have heard about a new development on the Broadway ticket scene: **Broadway Inner Circle** (© 866/847-8587; www.broadwayinnercircle.com), the ticket agency that, in a supposed effort to circumvent scalpers, has arranged with select in-demand shows to sell select premium seats for prices close to $500 a ticket. If price is no object, you might want to try this service.

If you don't want to pay a service charge, try calling or visiting the **box office** directly. Broadway theaters don't sell tickets over the telephone—the one major exception, the **Roundabout Theatre Company** (© 212/719-1300; www.roundabouttheatre.org),

Kids Take the Stage: Family-Friendly Theater

The family-friendly theater scene is flourishing these days. There's so much going on that it's best to check *New York* magazine, *Time Out New York,* or the Friday *New York Times* for current listings. Besides larger-than-life general-audience Broadway shows, the following offer some dependable kid-targeted entertainment options.

The stunningly renovated **New Victory Theater**, 229 W. 42nd St., 10th Floor, between Seventh and Eighth avenues (✆ **646/223-3020;** www.new victory.org), is a full-time family-oriented performing-arts center, and has hosted companies ranging from the Trinity Irish Dance Company to the astounding Flaming Idiots, who juggle everything from fire and swords to beanbag chairs.

The **Paper Bag Players** (✆ **212/663-0390;** www.paperbagplayers.org), called "the best children's theater in the country" by *Newsweek,* perform funny tales for children ages 4 to 9 in a set made from bags and boxes, in winter only, at Hunter College's Sylvia and Danny Kaye Playhouse, 68th Street between Park and Lexington avenues (✆ **212/772-4448**). If you can't make it to the Kaye, call the Players to inquire whether they'll be staging other performances about town.

TADA! Youth Theater, 15 W. 28th St., between Fifth Avenue and Broadway, 3rd Floor (✆ **212/252-1619;** www.tadatheater.com), is a terrific youth ensemble that performs musicals and plays with a multiethnic perspective for kids, including teens, and their families.

The **Swedish Cottage Marionette Theatre** (✆ **212/988-9093;** www.central park.org) puts on marionette shows for kids at its 19th-century Central Park theater throughout the year. Reservations are a must.

The "World Voices Club" of the **New Perspectives Theatre**, 456 W. 37th St. at Tenth Avenue (✆ **212/630-9945;** www.newperspectivestheatre.org),

charges a $5-per-ticket "convenience" fee—but a good number of Off-Broadway theaters do.

Also, before you call a broker to snag tickets to a hot show, consider calling the **concierge** at the hotel where you'll be staying. If you've chosen a hotel with a well-connected concierge, he or she may be able to have tickets waiting for you when you check in—for a premium, of course. For more on this, see "When You Arrive," below.

For details on how to obtain advance-purchase theater tickets at a discount, see "Reduced-Price Ticket Deals," below.

ONLINE SOURCES FOR THEATERGOERS & PERFORMING-ARTS FANS

Some of your best, most comprehensive, and up-to-date information sources for what's going on about town are in cyberspace.

Three competing commercial sites—**Broadway.com** (www.broadway.com), **Playbill Online** (www.playbill.com or www.playbillclub.com), and **TheaterMania** (www.theatermania.com)—offer complete information on Broadway and Off-Broadway has a different puppet show each month based on fables from different world cultures.

While David Mamet hardly seems like a playwright for the kiddies, the "Atlantic for Kids" series is making a go of it at the **Atlantic Theater Company,** 336 W. 20th St., between Eighth and Ninth avenues (𝒞 **212/645-8015;** www.atlantictheater.org), which Mamet co-founded with Academy Award–nominated actor William H. Macy.

Another excellent troupe that excels at children's theater is the **Vital Theatre Company,** 2162 Broadway, between 76th and 77th streets (𝒞 **212/579-0528;** www.vitaltheatre.org); it's well worth seeing what's on.

If you want to introduce your kids to the magic of live opera, check out the "Opera in Brief" program, which runs most Saturdays at 11:30am, at **Amato Opera Theatre** (p. 347). For kid-friendly classical music, see what's on at **Bargemusic** (p. 348), which presents kid-friendly chamber-music concerts throughout their regular season. Look for Young People's Concerts and Kid-zone Live!, in which kids get to interact with orchestra members prior to curtain time, at the **New York Philharmonic** (p. 348). Also check to see what's on for the entire family at **Carnegie Hall** (p. 352), which offers family concerts for a bargain-basement ticket price of just $8, plus the CarnegieKids program, which introduces kids ages 3 to 6 to basic musical concepts through a 45-minute music-and-storytelling performance. And don't forget "Jazz for Young People," Wynton Marsalis's stellar family concert series at **Jazz at Lincoln Center** (p. 353) and the new "Jazz for Kids" program at the **Jazz Standard** (p. 363), 116 E. 27th St., between Park and Lexington avenues (𝒞 **212/576-2232;** www.jazzstandard.net), which takes place every Sunday afternoon.

shows, with links to the ticket-buying agencies once you've selected your show. Each offers an **online theater club** that's free to join and can yield substantial savings—as much as 50%—on advance-purchase theater tickets for select Broadway and Off-Broadway shows. All you have to do is register, and you'll have access to discounts that can range from a few dollars to as much as 50% off regular ticket prices. You can sign up to be notified by e-mail as offers change. By far, I like the *Playbill Club* best; it was the first of the bunch, and its discount offers tend to be the most wide-ranging, often including the best Broadway and Off-Broadway shows. TheaterMania's **TM Insider** is the runner-up; the Broadway.com site wants a bit too much personal information for my taste. Nothing prevents you from signing up with all of them and taking advantage of the best deals.

As an information source for Broadway shows, you can't beat **LiveBroadway.com** (www.livebroadway.com), the official website of Broadway, sponsored by the League of American Theatres and Producers. Theater buffs will also enjoy perusing the **Internet Broadway Database** (www.ibdb.com), the official archival database for Broadway theater information, past and present.

Tips More Dramatic Venues Worth Seeking Out

When you want a spectacle, there's no place like Broadway: For jukebox musicals, singing green witches and collapsing chandeliers, Broadway is your ticket (and a high-priced one it is, too!). But you can see some amazing work at prices ranging from just-below-Broadway to less than $20 if you know where to look. For Off-Broadway, expect to pay $20 to $65 or so for tickets; Off-Off-Broadway rarely charges more than $20, and you can sometimes get in for $12 or less (so you don't feel as bad leaving at intermission if the show's a stinker!). There are even some theaters that let you see the show for free if you volunteer to usher. (See each company's website for information about how far ahead you should call or email).

Where do you find the hidden gems? The *Village Voice* (which sponsors the annual Obies, or Off-Broadway Awards) is a good source. *Timeout New York* has excellent listings and capsule descriptions for major Off-Broadway productions, as well as a decent listing of Off-Off shows. For more offerings Off-Off-Broadway, check the reviews on **Theatermania.com** (which also lets you purchase tickets and offers regular discounts) and **NYTheatre.com**.

Three resident theaters in New York—**Lincoln Center Theater** (p. 352), the **Roundabout Theatre** (p. 341), and **Manhattan Theatre Club** (www.mtc-nyc. org)—present work in Broadway houses, as well as in smaller venues Off-Broadway. You'll pay Broadway prices (or whatever discount you can get) for the best seats in the big houses, but you can also usually find special, lower prices for students or seniors; or last-minute rush tickets. In their smaller spaces (MTC's Stage II; the Roundabout's Laura Pels Theatre; Lincoln Center's Mitzi Newhouse) you can find good seats for less than $50 to see new plays and revivals by the likes of Terrence McNally and John Patrick Shanley. These theaters often offer extra events like "talkbacks" with the cast and production team, and so on—sometimes free, sometimes for a small charge. Following are a few other notable Off- and Off-Off-Broadway venues, but these are just the tip of the iceberg; check out the sources listed above for many, many more options.

• **Joseph Papp Public Theater** ⚘, 425 Lafayette St. (✆ **212/539-8500;** www. publictheater.org). Legendary among Off-Broadway theaters, this is the legacy of the late visionary theater producer Joseph Papp. The Public draws

WHEN YOU ARRIVE

Once you arrive in the city, getting your hands on tickets can take some street smarts—and failing those, cold hard cash. Even if it seems unlikely that seats are available, always **call or visit the box office** before attempting any other route. Single seats are often easiest to obtain, so people willing to sit apart from their companions may find themselves in luck.

You should also try the **Broadway Ticket Center,** run by the League of American Theatres and Producers (the same people behind LiveBroadway.com, above) at the Times Square Information Center, 1560 Broadway, between 46th and 47th streets (open Mon–Sat 9am–7pm; Sun 10am–6pm; hours subject to seasonal changes). They top talent to the stage with its groundbreaking stagings of Shakespeare's plays as well as new plays, classical dramas, and solo performances. The Public also hosts New York's best annual alfresco event, **Shakespeare in the Park,** each summer (see the box "Park It! Shakespeare, Music & Other Free Fun," on p. 354). If that's not enough, it's also home to **Joe's Pub** (p. 365).

- **Atlantic Theater Company,** 336 W. 20th St. (btwn Eighth and Ninth aves.). (ⓒ **212/645-8015;** www.atlantictheater.org), "produces great plays simply and truthfully, utilizing an artistic ensemble," according to its mission statement. It has recently presented new work by David Mamet, and the musical *Spring Awakening* transferred to Broadway in the spring of 2007, where it won the Tony award for Best Musical. The Atlantic also accepts volunteer ushers.

- **Signature Theatre Company,** 555 W. 42nd St. (ⓒ **212/244-PLAY;** www.signaturetheatre.org), presents season-long explorations of a playwright's work. You can also volunteer usher here. A corporate grant guaranteed that every seat in the 2008–09 Negro Ensemble Company season is available for $20.

- **New York Theater Workshop (NYTW),** 79 E. 4th St. (ⓒ **212/460-5475;** www.nytw.org), has been around since 1979, but it was *Rent* that put it on the map. Since the great success of the long-running musical (which finally closed on Broadway in 2008), several other plays developed by NYTW have gone on to award-winning commercial runs. NYTW specializes in new work, rethought revivals, and collaborations. All Sunday evening performances are $20; there are discounts for students and opportunities to usher.

- **Emerging Artists Theatre (EAT),** 464 W.25th St. #4 (ⓒ **212/247-2429;** www.eatheatre.org), has been producing new plays Off-Off-Broadway for 15 years and always seems to have something on offer: its fall and spring EATFests of short plays, its award-winning Off-Broadway premieres, and an annual month-long developmental series, which includes such programs as One Woman Standing and One Man Talking (solo shows), Laugh Out Loud (comedy), Notes on a Page (musicals), and Catch a Cabaret, with ticket prices in the $10 range.

often have tickets available for otherwise sold-out shows, both for advance and same-day purchase, and only charge about $5 extra per ticket.

Even if saving money isn't an issue for you, check the boards at the **TKTS Booth** in Times Square; more on that can be found under "Reduced-Price Ticket Deals," below.

In addition, your **hotel concierge** may be able to arrange tickets for you. These are usually purchased through a broker and a premium will be attached, but they're usually good seats and you can count on them being legitimate. (A $20 tip to the concierge for this service is reasonable—perhaps even more if the tickets are for an extremely hot show. By the time you've paid this tip, you might come out better by contacting a broker or ticket agency yourself.) If you want to deal with a licensed broker directly, **Keith Prowse & Co.** has a local office that accommodates drop-ins at 234 W. 44th St., between Seventh and Eighth avenues, Suite 1000 (✆ **800/669-8687;** Mon–Sat 9am–8pm; Sun noon–7pm).

If you buy from one of the **scalpers** selling tickets in front of the theater doors, you're taking a risk. They may be perfectly legitimate—a couple from the 'burbs whose companions couldn't make it for the evening, say—but they could be swindlers passing off fakes for big money. It's a risk that's not worth taking.

One preferred **insiders' trick** is to make the rounds of Broadway theaters at about 6pm, when unclaimed house seats are made available to the public. These tickets—reserved for VIPs, friends of the cast, the press, or other hangers-on—offer great locations and are sold at face value.

Also, note that **Monday** is often a good day to cop big-name show tickets. Though most theaters are dark on that day, some of the most sought-after choices aren't. Locals are at home on the first night of the workweek, so all the odds are in your favor. Your chances will always be better on weeknights, or for Wednesday matinees, rather than weekends. *Note:* If you're in town especially to see a big star in a show, check to see that said big star is playing all eight shows a week. While most producers' contracts with visiting Hollywood stars (think Julia Roberts or Denzel Washington) require them to play every performance, if it's a vocally demanding role, they may hand the matinees off to their understudies.

REDUCED-PRICE TICKET DEALS

Your best bet is to try before you go. You may be able to purchase **reduced-price theater tickets** in advance over the phone (or in person at the box office) by joining one or more of the online theater clubs. Membership is free and can garner you discounts of up to 50% on select Broadway and Off-Broadway shows. For further details, see "Online Sources for Theatergoers & Performing-Arts Fans," above.

Broadway shows—even blockbusters—sometimes have a limited number of cheaper tickets set aside for students and seniors, and they may even be available at the last minute; call the box office directly to inquire. *Rent* offered all kinds of bargains to keep younger theatergoers coming.

The best deal in town on same-day tickets for both Broadway and Off-Broadway shows is at the **Times Square Theatre Centre,** better known as the **TKTS** booth run by the nonprofit Theatre Development Fund in the heart of the Theater District. At press time its long time home at Duffy Square, 47th Street and Broadway was undergoing renovation, and the TKTS booth is temporarily housed across the street outside the New York Marriott Marquis between Broadway and Eighth avenues. The new booth is set to open by late 2008. The booth is open from 3 to 8pm for evening performances, 10am to 2pm for Wednesday and Saturday matinees, from 11am–8pm on Sunday for all performances.

Tickets for that day's performances are usually offered at half price, with a few reduced only 25%, plus a $2.50-per-ticket service charge. Boards outside the ticket windows list available shows; you're unlikely to find the biggest hits, but most other shows turn up. Only cash and traveler's checks are accepted (no credit cards). There's often a huge line, so show up early for the best availability and be prepared to wait—but frankly, the crowd is all part of the fun. If you don't care much what you see and you'd just like to go to a show, you can walk right up to the window later in the day and something's always available.

You can also get same-day tickets to evening shows at the **TKTS Lower Manhattan Theatre Centre,** at South Street Seaport, located at the corner of Front and John streets at 199 Water St. (Mon–Fri 11am–6pm, Sat 11am–7pm; Subway: 2, 3, 4, 5 to Fulton St.). All the same policies apply. The advantages to coming down here are that the lines are generally shorter, and matinee tickets are available the day before, so you can plan ahead. Visit **www.tdf.org** or call **NYC/Onstage** at ✆ **212/768-1818** and press "8" for the latest TKTS information.

2 Opera, Classical Music & Dance

While Broadway is the Big Apple's greatest hit, many other performing arts also flourish in this culturally rich and entertainment-hungry town.

In addition to the listings below, see what's happening at **Carnegie Hall** and the **Brooklyn Academy of Music,** two of the most respected—and enjoyable—multifunctional performing-arts venues in the city. The marvelous **92nd Street Y** also regularly hosts events that are worth considering. I've listed the operatic and symphonic companies housed at **Lincoln Center** below; also check the center's full calendar for all offerings. See "Major Concert Halls & Landmark Venues," below.

OPERA

New York has grown into one of the world's major opera centers. The season generally runs September through May, but there's usually something going on at any time of year.

Amato Opera Theatre *(Finds* This cozy, off-the-beaten-track venue functions as a showcase for young American singers. The intimate 100-plus-seat house celebrated its 60th season in 2007 amid a rising reputation and increasing ticket sales. The staple is full productions of Italian classics—Verdi's *La Traviata,* Puccini's *Madame Butterfly,* Bizet's *Carmen,* with an occasional Mozart tossed in—at great prices for regular performances ($30, $25 for seniors and kids). Performances, usually held on Saturday and Sunday, regularly sell out, so it's a good idea to reserve 3 weeks in advance.

Note for adults: On one Saturday a month, "Opera in Brief" offers fully costumed, kid-length versions of the classics interwoven with narration so chaperones have a palatable forum in which to introduce the little ones to opera. At $15 or so per ticket, these matinee performances are wallet-friendly, too. 319 Bowery (at 2nd St.). ✆ 212/228-8200. www.amato.org. Subway: B, D, F, V to Broadway-Lafayette.

Metropolitan Opera Tickets can cost a fortune—anywhere from $25 to $295. But for its full productions of the classic repertory and a schedule packed with world-class grand sopranos and tenors, the Metropolitan Opera ranks first in the world. Millions are spent on fabulous stagings, and the venue itself is a wonder of acoustics. Whatever is on the schedule, the quality will be second to none.

To guarantee that its audience understands the words, the Met has outfitted the back of each row of seats with screens for subtitles—translation help for those who want it, minimum intrusion for those who don't. James Levine continues his role as the brilliant and popular conductor of the orchestra. At the Metropolitan Opera House, Lincoln Center, Broadway and 64th St. ✆ 212/362-6000. www.metopera.org. Subway: 1 to 66th St.

New York City Opera The New York City Opera is a superb company, with a delightful duality to its approach: It not only attempts to reach a wider audience than the Met with its more "human" scale and significantly lower prices ($32–$115), but it's also committed to adventurous premieres, new operas, the occasional avant-garde work, American musicals *(Porgy and Bess)* and novels *(Of Mice and Men)* presented as fresh, innovative operettas, and even obscure works by mainstream or lesser-known composers. Its mix stretches from the "easy" works of Puccini, Verdi, and Gilbert and Sullivan to the more challenging oeuvres of the likes of Arnold Schönberg and Philip Glass. Because of renovations at the New York State Theater, where the New York City Opera will perform its 2008/09 season was still up in the air as of press time. At the New York State Theater, Lincoln Center, Broadway and 64th St. © 212/870-5570 (information or box office), or 212/307-4100 for Ticketmaster. www.nycopera.com or www.ticketmaster.com. Subway: 1 to 66th St.

New York Gilbert and Sullivan Players If you're in the mood for lighthearted operetta, try this lively company, which specializes in Gilbert and Sullivan's 19th-century English comic works. Tickets are affordable, usually in the $40-to-$95 range (exact prices for the 2008–09 season were not yet determined at press time). The annual calendar generally runs from October through April and includes four shows a year, with some performances held at **City Center** (p. 350). At Symphony Space, Broadway and 95th St. © 212/864-1414 or 212/769-1000. www.nygasp.org. Subway: 1, 2, 3 to 96th St.

CLASSICAL MUSIC

Bargemusic ☪ *(Finds)* Many thought Olga Bloom peculiar, if not deranged, when she transformed a 40-year-old barge into a chamber-music concert hall. More than 20 years later, Bargemusic is an internationally renowned recital room boasting more than 100 first-rate chamber-music performances a year. Visiting musicians love the chance to play in such an intimate setting, so the roster regularly includes highly respected international musicians as well as local stars such as violinist Cynthia Phelps.

There are three shows per week, on Thursday and Friday evenings at 7:30pm and Sunday afternoon at 4pm. The musicians perform on a small stage in a cherry-paneled, fireplace-lit room accommodating 130. The barge may creak a bit and an occasional boat may speed by, but the music rivals what you'll find in almost any other New York concert hall—and the panoramic view through the glass wall behind the stage can't be beat. Neither can the price: Tickets are just $35 ($25 for students), or $40 for performances by larger ensembles. Reserve well in advance. At Fulton Ferry Landing (just south of the Brooklyn Bridge), Brooklyn. © 718/624-2083 or 718/624-4061. www.bargemusic.org. Subway: 2, 3 to Clark St.; A to High St.; F to York St.

The Juilliard School *(Value)* During its school year, the nation's premier music-education institution sponsors about 550 performances of the highest quality—at the lowest prices. With most concerts free and $20 as a maximum ticket price, Juilliard is one of New York's greatest cultural bargains. Though most would assume that the school presents only classical-music concerts, Juilliard also offers other music as well as drama, dance, opera, and interdisciplinary works. The best way to find out about the wide array of productions is to call, visit the school's website (click on "Complete Calendar of Events"), or consult the bulletin board in the building's lobby. Note that tickets are sometimes required even for free performances. Watch for master classes and discussions open to the public featuring celebrity guest teachers. 60 Lincoln Center Plaza (Broadway at 65th St.). © 212/799-5000, or 212/721-0965 to charge tickets. www.juilliard.edu. Subway: 1 to 66th St.

New York Philharmonic Symphony-wise, you'd be hard-pressed to do better than the New York Philharmonic. The country's oldest orchestra is under the guidance of distinguished conductor Lorin Maazel for one last season (2008–09). His protégée the

Tips Last-Minute Ticket Buying

Most seats at New York Philharmonic performances are sold to subscribers, with just a few left for the rest of us. But there are still ways to get tickets. Periodically, a number of same-day orchestra tickets are made available at the Philharmonic and sold first thing in the morning for $25 a pop (two-ticket maximum). They usually go on sale at 10am weekdays, 1pm Saturday (noon if there's a matinee). And when subscribers can't attend, they may turn their tickets back to the theaters, which then resell them at the last moment. These can be in the most coveted rows of the orchestra. Ticket holders can donate unwanted tickets until curtain time, so tickets that are not available first thing in the morning may become available later in the day. The hopeful form "cancellation lines" 2 hours or more before curtain time for a crack at returned tickets on a first-come, first-served basis. Senior/student/disability rush tickets may be available for $12 (two-ticket max) on concert day, but never at Friday matinees or Saturday evening performances. To check availability for any of these programs at all performances, call Audience Services at ℰ 212/875-5656 before you head to the box office.

Note that Lincoln Center's **Alice Tully Hall** (where the Chamber Music Society performs and other concerts are held), the **Metropolitan Opera,** the **New York City Opera,** and **Carnegie Hall** offer similar last-minute and discount programs (the **New York City Ballet** offers Student Rush tickets only). It makes sense to call the box office first to check on same-day availability before heading to the theater—or, if you're willing to risk coming away empty-handed, be there at opening time for first crack.

following season will be 40-year-old Alan Gilbert. But don't expect quality to falter one bit. There's a summer season in July, when themed classics brighten the hall, as well as free summer concerts in Central Park that are worth checking into.

Tickets range from $28 to $94; opt for a rush-hour concert or a matinee for the lowest across-the-board prices. If you can afford it—and if the tickets are available—it's well worth it to pay for prime seats. The acoustics of the hall are such that, at the midrange price points, I prefer the second tier (especially the boxes) over the more expensive rear orchestra seats. Go cheap if you have to; you're sure to enjoy the program from any vantage point. At Avery Fisher Hall, 10 Lincoln Center Plaza, Broadway at 65th St. ℰ 212/875-5656 for audience services, 212/875-5030 for box office information, or Center Charge at 212/875-5656, same number for tickets. www.newyorkphilharmonic.org. Subway: 1 to 66th St.

DANCE

In general, dance seasons run September through February and then March through June, but there's almost always something going on. In addition to the major venues and troupes discussed below, some other names to keep in mind are the **Brooklyn Academy of Music,** the **92nd Street Y, Radio City Music Hall,** and **Town Hall** (see "Major Concert Halls & Landmark Venues," below). For particularly innovative works, see what's on at the **Dance Theater Workshop,** in the Bessie Schönberg Theater, 219 W. 19th St., between Seventh and Eighth avenues (ℰ **212/691-6500** or 212/924-0077; www.dtw.org), a first-rate launching pad for nearly a quarter century.

In addition to regular appearances at City Center (below), the **American Ballet Theatre** (www.abt.org) takes up residence at Lincoln Center's Metropolitan Opera House (© 212/477-3030) for 8 weeks each spring. The same venue also hosts such visiting companies as the Kirov, Royal, and Paris Opéra ballets.

The weekly *Time Out New York,* available on newsstands around town, maintains a section dedicated to dance events around town that's an invaluable resource to fans.

City Center   Modern dance usually takes center stage in this Moorish dome-topped performing-arts palace. The companies of Merce Cunningham, Martha Graham, Paul Taylor, Alvin Ailey, Twyla Tharp, the Dance Theatre of Harlem, and the American Ballet Theatre are often on the calendar. Don't expect cutting edge—but do expect excellence. Sightlines are terrific from all corners, and a new acoustical shell means the sound is pitch-perfect. Ticket prices range from $15 to $100. 131 W. 55th St. (btwn Sixth and Seventh aves.). © 212/247-0430 or 212/581-1212. www.citycenter.org. Subway: F, N, Q, R, W to 57th St.; B, D, E to Seventh Ave.

Joyce Theater   Housed in an old Art Deco movie house, the Joyce has grown into one of the world's greatest modern-dance institutions. You can see everything from Native American ceremonial dance to Maria Benites Teatro Flamenco to the innovative works of Pilobolus to the Martha Graham Dance Company. In residence annually is Eliot Feld's ballet company, Ballet Tech, which WQXR radio's Francis Mason called "better than a whole month of namby-pamby classical ballets." The Joyce has a second space, **Joyce SoHo,** where you can see rising young dancers and experimental works in the intimacy of a 70-seat performance space. In either space, seats go for $35 to $45. 175 Eighth Ave. (at 19th St.). © 212/242-0800 for tickets; © 212/691-9740 for theatre. www.joyce.org. Subway: A, C, E to 14rd St.; 1 to 18th St. **Joyce SoHo** at 155 Mercer St. (btwn Houston and Prince sts.). © 212/431-9233. Subway: R to Prince St.; 6 to Bleecker B, D, F, V to Broadway/Lafayette.

New York City Ballet   Highly regarded for its unsurpassed technique, the New York City Ballet is the world's best. The company renders with happy regularity the works of two of America's most important choreographers: George Balanchine, its founder, and Jerome Robbins. Under the direction of Ballet Master in Chief Peter Martins, the troupe continues to expand its repertoire and performs to a wide variety of classical and modern music. The cornerstone of the annual season is the Christmastime production of *The Nutcracker,* for which tickets usually become available in early October. Ticket prices for most events run $28 to $66. Because of renovation at the New York State Theater, the 2008–09 season will be altered somewhat. Check the website for schedule changes. At the New York State Theater at 20 Lincoln Center Plaza, Broadway at 64th St. © 212/870-5570. www.nycballet.com. Subway: 1 to 66th St.

3 Major Concert Halls & Landmark Venues

Apollo Theater ⚘ *Moments*   Built in 1914, this legendary Harlem theater launched or abetted the careers of countless musical icons—including Bessie Smith, Billie Holiday, Dinah Washington, Duke Ellington, Ella Fitzgerald, Sarah Vaughan, Count Basie, and Aretha Franklin. And thousands lined the streets in December of 2006 to pay their last respects to the Godfather of Soul on the Apollo stage, the place where he performed some of the greatest shows of all time. This historic venue is in large part responsible for the development and worldwide popularization of black music in America. By the 1970s, it had fallen on hard times, but a 1986 restoration breathed new life into the landmark. In 1992, a major $65-million restoration project was inaugurated and should be completed by 2009. The first phase of that project—refurbishing the terra-cotta facade, a new box office, and a high-tech marquee retaining the original 1940s style and features—was unveiled in late 2005. The theater remains open during the renovations and is still internationally renowned for its African-American acts of all musical genres, from hip-hop acts to Wynton Marsalis's "Jazz for Young People" events. Since 1934, Wednesday at the Apollo meant "Amateur Night." Forget American Idol, this loud, fun-filled night draws in young talents from all over the country with high hopes of making it big is the real deal. 253 W. 125th St. (btwn Adam Clayton Powell and Frederick Douglass boulevards). ✆ **212/531-5300** or 212/531-5301. www.apollo theater.com. Subway: 1 to 125th St.

Brooklyn Academy of Music *Finds* BAM is the city's most renowned contemporary-arts institution, presenting cutting-edge theater, opera, dance, and music. Offerings have included historically informed presentations of baroque opera by William Christie and Les Arts Florissants; pop opera from Lou Reed; Marianne Faithfull singing the music of Kurt Weill; dance by Mark Morris and Mikhail Baryshnikov; the Philip Glass ensemble accompanying screenings of *Koyaanisqatsi* and Lugosi's original *Dracula;* the Royal Dramatic Theater of Sweden directed by Ingmar Bergman; and many more experimental works by both renowned and lesser-known international artists as well as visiting companies from all over the world.

Of particular note is the **Next Wave Festival,** September through December, this country's foremost showcase for new experimental works (see the "New York City Calendar of Events," in chapter 3). The **BAM Rose Cinemas** show first-run independent films, and there's free live music every Thursday, Friday, and Saturday night at **BAMcafé,** which can range from atmospheric electronica by cornetist Graham Haynes to radical jazz from the Harold Rubin Trio to the rhythm and blues from Angela Johnson. 30 Lafayette Ave. (off Flatbush Ave.), Brooklyn. ✆ 718/636-4100. www.bam.org. Subway: 2, 3, 4, 5, M, N, Q, R, W to Pacific St./Atlantic Ave.

Carnegie Hall ✸✸   Perhaps the world's most famous performance space (*How* do you get there?), Carnegie Hall offers everything from grand classics to the music of Ravi Shankar. The **Isaac Stern Auditorium,** the 2,804-seat main hall, welcomes visiting orchestras from across the country and the world. Many of the world's premier soloists and ensembles give recitals. The legendary hall is visually and acoustically brilliant; don't miss an opportunity to experience it if there's something on that interests you.

Within the hall, there's also the intimate 268-seat **Weill Recital Hall,** usually used to showcase chamber music and vocal and instrumental recitals. Carnegie Hall has also, after being occupied by a movie theater for 38 years, reclaimed the ornate underground 650-seat **Zankel Concert Hall.** For last-minute ticket-buying tips, see the box on p. 349. 881 Seventh Ave. (at 57th St.). ✆ 212/247-7800. www.carnegiehall.org. Subway: N, Q, R, W to 57th St.

Lincoln Center for the Performing Arts   New York is the world's premier performing-arts city, and Lincoln Center is its premier institution. Whenever you're planning an evening's entertainment, check the offerings here, which can include opera, dance, symphonies, jazz, theater, film, and more—from the classics to the contemporary. Lincoln Center's many buildings serve as permanent homes to their own companies as well as major stops for world-class performance troupes from around the globe.

Resident companies include the following: The **Chamber Music Society of Lincoln Center** (✆ 212/875-5788; www.chambermusicsociety.org) performs at Alice Tully Hall or the Daniel and Joanna S. Rose Rehearsal Studio, often in the company

---

Lincoln Center Renovates for its 50th

The massive performing arts complex is turning 50 in 2009, and marking the anniversary with renovations that will add new performing spaces, a restaurant, visitor center, and redesign the open spaces within the "campus." **Alice Tully Hall** is closed for an 18-month renovation (it will reopen in 2009). Construction has also blocked off some of the entrances and public spaces in the venues, and may displace some of the companies for all or part of their 2008–09 seasons. For a detailed description of the entire project, complete with videos, timelines and illustrations of what it will all look like at the end, visit **www. lincolncenter.org/load_screen.asp?screen=transforming**. You can also call ✆ **212/LINCOLN** for current prerecorded information and speak to a live person by calling Customer Service at ✆ **212/875-5456,** Monday through Friday from 9am to 8pm.

Jazz at Lincoln Center: Not Actually at Lincoln Center

I'm usually a stickler for accuracy, but I'll make an exception for **Jazz at Lincoln Center,** which is not actually in Lincoln Center, but resides a few blocks south in the Time Warner Center at Broadway and 60th Street on Columbus Circle (℗ **212/258-9800;** www.jalc.org). Though the move was downtown, it was definitely a move up. Its complex on the fourth floor of Time Warner's northern tower features two amazing performance spaces, a jazz club, a mini jazz Hall of Fame, and a 7,000-square-foot atrium with views of Central Park.

The largest of the three venues is the **Rose Theater,** where you might see the Lincoln Center Jazz Orchestra, led by Wynton Marsalis, performing the swing music of Thad Jones. Acoustics are perfect and seating is spacious. The jewel of the Center is the **Allen Room** with its 4,500-square-foot glass backdrop behind the main stage offering glittering views of Central Park and the Manhattan night sky. Hard to believe that what was once played in smoky basements is now presented in venues as spectacular and opulent as these.

Also at Jazz at Lincoln Center is **Dizzy's Club Coca-Cola** (℗ **212/258-9595;** p. 362), a stylish, intimate jazz club that's open every day.

---

of such high-caliber guests as Anne Sofie von Otter and Midori. The **Film Society of Lincoln Center** (℗ **212/875-5600** for automated schedule; ℗ **212/875-5601** for box office; www.filmlinc.com) screens a daily schedule of movies at the Walter Reade Theater, and hosts a number of important annual film and video festivals as well as the Reel to Real program for kids, pairing silent screen classics with live performance. **Lincoln Center Theater** (℗ **212/362-7600;** www.lct.org) consists of the Vivian Beaumont Theater, a modern, comfortable venue with great sightlines that has been home to much good Broadway drama, and the Mitzi E. Newhouse Theater, a well-respected Off-Broadway house that has also boasted numerous theatrical triumphs. Past seasons have included excellent productions of Tom Stoppard's *Arcadia, Carousel* in revival, and the Tony Award–winning *Light in the Piazza.*

For details on the **Metropolitan Opera,** the **New York City Opera,** the **New York City Ballet, The Juilliard School,** the phenomenal **New York Philharmonic,** and the **American Ballet Theatre,** which takes up residence here every spring, see "Opera, Classical Music & Dance," earlier in this chapter.

Most of the companies' **major seasons** run from about September or October to April, May, or June. **Special series** such as Great Performers and the new American Songbook, showcasing classic American show tunes, help round out the calendar. Indoor and outdoor events are held in warmer months: Summer kicks off with the **JVC Jazz Festival** in June; July sees **Midsummer Night's Swing,** with partner dancing, lessons, and music on the plaza; August's **Mostly Mozart** attracts such talents as Alicia de Larrocha and André Watts; **Lincoln Center Festival** celebrates the best of the performing arts; **Lincoln Center Out-of-Doors** is a series of free alfresco music and dance performances; there's also the **New York Film Festival,** and more. Check the "New York City Calendar of Events" section, in chapter 3, or Lincoln Center's website to see what special events will be on while you're in town.

Tickets for performances at Avery Fisher and Alice Tully halls can be purchased through **CenterCharge** (℗ **212/721-6500**) or online at **www.lincolncenter.org** (click on "Event Calendar"). Tickets for all Lincoln Center Theater performances can

Park It! Shakespeare, Music & Other Free Fun

As the weather warms, New York culture comes outdoors to play.

Shakespeare in the Park, a New York institution since 1957, is as much a part of a New York summer as fireworks on the Fourth of July. The outdoor free event at the open-air Delacorte Theater in Central Park was the brainchild of the late Joseph Papp, former director of the Public Theater. Each summer usually features a revival of a Shakespeare play featuring a large company, including at least one or more "names" from film or television. The 2008 slate was set to feature *Hamlet* and that other Shakspearean classic rock musical (I'm kidding) *Hair.* The productions run from June to early September. Depending on the star power, tickets can be quite scarce.

The Delacorte Theater itself, next to Belvedere Castle near 79th Street and West Drive, is a dream—on a starry night, there's no better stage in town. Tickets are distributed at the theater free on a first-come, first-served basis (two per person) at 1pm on the day of the performance. The Delacorte might have 1,881 seats, but each is a hot commodity; whatever the show, people line up next to the theater 2 to 3 hours in advance (even earlier if a big name is involved). You can also pick up same-day tickets between 1 and 3pm at the Public Theater, at 425 Lafayette St. For more information, call the Public Theater at (C) **212/539-8500** or the Delacorte at (C) **212/535-4284,** or visit **www.publictheater.org**.

Free concerts by the **New York Philharmonic** and the **Metropolitan Opera** are held beneath the stars on Central Park's Great Lawn and in parks throughout the five boroughs. For schedules, call the Philharmonic at (C) **212/875-5656**

be purchased thorough **Telecharge** ((C) **212/239-6200;** www.telecharge.com). Tickets for New York State Theater productions (New York City Opera and Ballet companies) are available through **Ticketmaster** ((C) **212/307-4100;** www.ticketmaster.com), while tickets for films showing at the Walter Reade Theater can be bought up to 7 days in advance by calling (C) **212/496-3809.** For last-minute ticket-buying tips, see the box on p. 349.

Lincoln Center is also home to the **New York Public Library for the Performing Arts** ((C) **212/870-1630;** www.nypl.org), which is now reopened after a major renovation.

Offered daily, 1-hour **guided tours** of Lincoln Center tell the story of the great performing-arts complex, and even offer glimpses of rehearsals; call (C) **212/875-5350.** 70 Lincoln Center Plaza (at Broadway and 64th St.). (C) **212/546-2656.** www.lincolncenter.org. Subway: 1 to 66th St.

Madison Square Garden   U2, Springsteen, the Stones, Santana, and other monsters of rock and pop regularly fill this 20,000-seat arena, which is also home to pro sports teamssuch as the Knicks, the Rangers, and the Liberty. A cavernous concrete hulk, it's better suited to sports than to concerts, or in-the-round events such as the Ice Capades, Ringling Bros. and Barnum & Bailey Circus, or the International Cat Show. If you end up with seats in the back, you'd better have binoculars.

or the Metropolitan Opera at © **212/362-6000.** The Philharmonic maintains a list of their upcoming gigs at **www.newyorkphilharmonic.org**; look under "Attend Concerts."

The most active music stage in Central Park, however, is **SummerStage,** at Rumsey Playfield, midpark around 72nd Street. SummerStage has featured everyone from Chaka Khan to Patti Smith; recent offerings have included concerts by Hugh Masekela, the Jon Spencer Blues Explosion, and Marianne Faithfull; "Viva, Verdi!" festival performances by the New York Grand Opera; cabaret nights; and more. The season usually lasts from mid-June to August. While some big-name shows charge admission, tickets aren't usually required but donations are always accepted. Call the hot line at © **212/ 360-2777,** or visit **www.summerstage.org**.

Beyond Central Park, more free outdoor fun includes the **Bryant Park Summer Film Festival,** held in Bryant Park, just behind the main branch of the New York Public Library, at Sixth Avenue between 41st and 42nd streets. Every Monday night a classic film—think *Dr. Zhivago* or *Viva Las Vegas*—is shown on a large screen under the stars. The lawn is open at 5pm for blankets and picnicking; the movie starts at dusk (about 8 or 9pm). Rain dates are Tuesdays. For the schedule and more information, call © **212/512-5700.**

The calendar of free events heats up throughout the city's parks in summertime. You can find out what's happening by calling the **Parks and Recreation Special Events Hot Line** at © **888/NY-PARKS** or 212/360-3456 or pointing your browser to **www.nycgovparks.org**.

You'll find far better sightlines at the **Theater at Madison Square Garden,** an amphitheater-style auditorium with 5,600 seats that has also played host to some major pop stars, from the Rolling Stones to Bob Dylan. Watch for annual stagings of *The Wizard of Oz, A Christmas Carol,* and family shows such as *Sesame Street Live.* Newest at MSG is the Wamu Theater, for events such as comedy shows, the NFL and NBA Drafts and family programming.

Note that MSG's owners have announced a massive renovation project which will take place in the summers of 2009-10. For information on the changes, visit **http://msg.com/renovation.**

The box office is located at Seventh Avenue and 32nd Street. Or you can purchase tickets through **Ticketmaster** (© **212/307-7171;** www.ticketmaster.com). On Seventh Ave. from 31st to 33rd sts. © 212/465-MSG1. www.thegarden.com. Subway: A, C, E, 1, 2, 3 to 34th St.

92nd Street Y Tisch Center for the Arts (Value   This generously endowed community center offers a phenomenal slate of top-rated cultural happenings, from classical to folk to jazz to world music to cabaret to lyric theater and literary readings. Just because it's the Y, don't think this place is small potatoes: Great classical performers— Isaac Stern, Janos Starker, Nadja Salerno-Sonnenberg—give recitals here. In addition, the full concert calendar often includes luminaries such as Max Roach, John Williams, and Judy Collins; Jazz at the Y from Dick Hyman and guests; the long-standing

Moments Music Under New York

The noise of honking horns, car alarms, and sirens are not the only sounds you will hear in your travels around Manhattan. Music is everywhere. In the warm weather, a trumpet player or violinist will set up at a busy corner and play for hours. In the winter musicians head into subway stations, where, legally, they are not allowed to play, but I've rarely seen the law enforced. Many are very good, while others, well, are just trying to make a few bucks. Some of the good ones, who actually audition for the opportunity, perform under a program sponsored by the New York Metropolitan Transit Authority (MTA) called "Music Under New York." If selected, they can perform legally at designated subway stations, including Times Square/42nd Street, 34th Street/Sixth Avenue, 14th Street/Union Square, and 59th Street/Columbus Circle. In the summer there is a Music Under New York festival at Grand Central Station and Bowling Green Park. The variety of music is amazing and the quality is as good as you might see at some of New York's clubs. In subway stations I've heard gospel, blues, Cajun, Dixieland jazz, Andean, Brazilian drumming, rumba, and my favorite, doo-wop, the original sound of the New York subways. So take a few moments before boarding your train and listen to the music. For more information, visit the MTA website (**www.mta.info/mta/aft/muny**).

Chamber Music at the Y series; the classical Music from the Jewish Spirit series; and regular cabaret programs. The lectures-and-literary-readings calendar is unparalleled, with featured speakers ranging from James Carville to Ralph Nader to Katie Couric to Erica Jong to Ken Burns to Elie Wiesel to Alan Dershowitz to A. S. Byatt to . . . the list goes on and on. There's a regular schedule of modern dance, too, through the Harkness Dance Project. Best of all, readings and lectures are usually priced between $20 and $40 for nonmembers, dance is usually $20, and concert tickets generally go for $15 to $50—half or a third of what you'd pay at comparable venues. Additionally, a full calendar of entertainment targeted to the culturally aware in their 20s and 30s— from poetry readings to film screenings to live music, including the debut of a very young Norah Jones—is offered at the Upper West Side community center **Makor.** 1395 Lexington Ave. (at 92nd St.). ✆ 212/415-5500. www.92ndsty.org. Subway: 4, 5, 6 to 86th St.; 6 to 96th St. **Makor:** 35 W. 67th St. ✆ 212/601-1000. www.makor.org. Subway: 1 to 66th St.

Radio City Music Hall   This stunning 6,200-seat Art Deco theater, with interior design by Donald Deskey, opened in 1932, and legendary Radio City continues to be a choice venue, where the theater alone adds a dash of panache to any performance. Star of the Christmas season is the **Radio City Music Hall Christmas Spectacular,** starring the legendary Rockettes. Visiting pop-chart toppers, from Neil Young to the Gipsy Kings, also perform here. Thanks to perfect acoustics and uninterrupted sight-lines, there's hardly a bad seat in the house. The theater also hosts dance performances; family entertainment; a number of annual awards shows, such as the Essence Awards, the GQ Man of the Year Awards, and anything MTV is holding in town. 1260 Sixth Ave. (at 50th St.). ✆ 212/307-7171 for Ticketmaster. www.radiocity.com or www.ticketmaster.com. Subway: B, D, F, to 49th–50th sts./Rockefeller Center.

Symphony Space ⚛ *Finds*   An eclectic mix of culture can be found at this Upper West Side institution. The variety of shows at the **Peter Jay Sharp Theater** includes music, with series by the World Music Institute as well as classical, rock, and blues; dance, with marathon tributes to such choreographers as George Balanchine to original creations of Israeli Zvi Gotheiner; literature, such as the selected shorts series introduced by writers such as Jonathan Lethem, Edwidge Danticat, and Walter Mosely; and family, with performances by folk singer Tom Chapin and the Putuyamo Kids. Adjacent to the Sharp Theater is the **Leonard Nimoy Thalia Theater.** The film-revival house that was known for its quirky sightlines was rescued by none other than Mr. Spock and has now been totally renovated. Though I'm sure it is much more comfortable now, I'll miss having to peer around a pole to watch a movie such as *Plan Nine from Outer Space.* 2537 Broadway (at 95th St.). ✆ 212/864-1414. www.symphonyspace.org. Subway: 1, 2, 3 to 96th St.

Town Hall   This intimate landmark theater—a National Historic Site designed by McKim, Mead & White—is blessed with outstanding acoustics, making it an ideal place to enjoy many kinds of performances, including theater, dance, lectures, drama, comedy, film, and pop and world music. The calendar regularly includes such offerings as American tap and Brazilian tango exhibitions; doo-wop and global rhythms; live tapings of *A Prairie Home Companion* with Garrison Keillor or spoken word from Al Franken; lectures by luminaries such as Marianne Williamson and Frank Gehry; concerts by the likes of David Sanborn or They Might Be Giants; symphony, opera, and ballet companies from around the world; and much more. The grade is extremely steep, so unless Yao Ming sits in front of you, fellow audience members shouldn't block your view. 123 W. 43rd St. (btwn Sixth and Seventh aves.). ✆ 212/840-2824, or 212/307-4100 for Ticketmaster. www.the-townhall-nyc.org or www.ticketmaster.com. Subway: N, Q, R, S, W, 1, 2, 3, 7 to 42nd St./Times Sq.; B, D, F, V to 42nd St.

4 Live Rock, Jazz, Blues & More

I discuss the top venues, both large and small, below. But there are many more than these, and new ones are popping up all the time. For the latest, be sure to check the publications discussed in the introduction to this chapter as well as the online sources outlined in "Online Sources for Live-Music Fans," below.

LARGER VENUES

For coverage of **Madison Square Garden,** the **Theater at MSG,** and **Town Hall,** see "Major Concert Halls & Landmark Venues," earlier in this chapter.

Beacon Theatre   This pleasing midsize Upper West Side venue—a 1928 Art Deco movie palace with an impressive lobby, stairway, and auditorium seating about 2,700—hosts mainly pop-music performances, usually for the over-30 crowd. Featured acts have ranged from street-smart pop diva Sheryl Crow to a Hall & Oates reunion to a befuddled Beach Boy Brian Wilson to Band alumnus Levon Helm, to not-yet-dead Allman Brothers (who play an always-sold-out 2- or 3-week gig each spring giving more than a dozen performances). You'll also find such special events as the bodybuilding "Night of Champions" on the mix-and-match calendar. 2124 Broadway (at 74th St.). Event hotline/general number ✆ 212/465-6500. www.beacontheatre.com. Subway: 1, 2, 3 to 72nd St.

Tips **Ticket-Buying Tips**

Tickets for events at all larger theaters as well as at Hammerstein Ballroom, Roseland, Irving Plaza, B.B. King's, and S.O.B.'s can be purchased through **Ticketmaster** (℃ **212/307-7171**; www.ticketmaster.com).

Advance tickets for an increasing number of shows at smaller venues—including Bowery Ballroom and Mercury Lounge—can be purchased through **Ticketweb** (℃ **866/468-7619**; www.ticketweb.com). Do note, however, that Ticketweb can sell out in advance of actual ticket availability. Just because Ticketweb doesn't have tickets left for an event doesn't mean it's completely sold out, so be sure to check with the venue directly.

Even a sold-out show doesn't mean you're out of luck. There are usually a number of people hanging around at showtime trying to get rid of extra tickets for friends who didn't show, and they're usually happy to pass them off for face value. You'll also see professional scalpers, who often peddle forgeries and are best avoided—it doesn't take a rocket scientist to tell the difference. Be aware, of course, that all forms of resale onsite are illegal.

Roseland   This old warhorse of a venue, a 1919 ballroom gone to seed, has been under threat of the wrecking ball for years now. Everybody has played at this too-huge-for-its-own-good 2,500-capacity general-admission hall, from Marc Anthony to Fiona Apple to Busta Rhymes to Smashmouth to Rage Against the Machine to Jeff Beck. Recent bands-of-the-moment who have played here include New York's own Yeah Yeah Yeahs and the next-big-Brit-thing Arctic Monkeys. Thankfully, there's lots of room to steer clear of the pit and enjoy the show. Advance tickets can be purchased at the **Fillmore New York at Irving Plaza** box office (p. 359) without the Ticketmaster service fee. Take a moment on your way through the lobby to check out the display cases memorializing Roseland's postwar heyday as the city's premier dance hall. Ballroom dancing still takes place Sunday from 2:30 to 10pm; admission is $10. 239 W. 52nd St. (btwn Broadway and Eighth Ave.). ℃ **212/247-0200**, or 212/307-7171 for Ticketmaster. www.roselandballroom.com. Subway: C, E, 1 to 50th St.

MIDSIZE & MULTIGENRE VENUES

Also see what's on at the stellar **Joe's Pub** (p. 365), a top-flight cabaret that hosts intimate shows by pop acts. Another fairly new venue on the far West Side is the **Highline Ballroom,** at 431 W. 16th St, between 9th and 10th aves., ℃ **212/414-5994;** www.highlineballroom.com. It opened with a series of sold-out shows (it has a capacity of about 700) from acts ranging from Lou Reed to Amy Winehouse and Disco Biscuits.

B.B. King Blues Club & Grill   This 550-seat venue is one of the prime anchors of Times Square's "new" 42nd Street. Despite its name, B.B. King's seldom sticks to the blues; what you're likely to find instead is a bill full of pop, funk, and rock names, mainly from the past. The big-ticket talent runs the gamut from George Clinton and the P. Funk All Stars and John Mayall and the Bluesbreakers to Tower of Power to Jimmy Cliff and Delbert McClinton. A few more (relatively) esoteric acts such as surf guitarist Dick Dale take the stage on occasion. Tourist-targeted pricing makes for an expensive night on the town, word is that the food isn't as good as it was in the beginning, and seating policies can be convoluted, but there's no arguing with the quality of the talent. The Sunday gospel lunch is a genuine slice of joy. 237 W. 42nd St. (btwn Seventh and Eighth aves.). ℭ 212/997-4144, or 212/307-7171 for tickets. www.bbkingblues.com. Subway: A, C, E, Q, W, 1, 2, 3, 7 to 42nd St.

Bowery Ballroom   Run by the same people behind the **Mercury Lounge** (see below), the Bowery space is bigger, accommodating a crowd of 500 or so, and even better. The stage is big and raised to allow good sightlines from every corner. The sound couldn't be better, and Art Deco details give the place a sophistication that doesn't come easy to general-admission halls. The balcony has its own bar and seating alcoves. This place is a favorite with such alt-rockers as Vic Chesnutt, Travis, Steve Earle, Rinocerose, The Delgados, and Toshi Reagon, as well as more established acts (Neil Finn, Patti Smith, Joan Jett & the Blackhearts), who thrive in an intimate setting. Save on the service charge by buying advance tickets at Mercury's box office. 6 Delancey St. (at Bowery). ℭ 212/533-2111. www.boweryballroom.com. Subway: F to Delancey St.; J, M, Z to Bowery.

The Fillmore New York at Irving Plaza   This high-profile midsize music hall is the prime stop for national name rock bands that aren't quite big enough yet (or anymore) to sell out Hammerstein, Roseland, or the Beacon. Think Five for Fighting, the Eels, Jars of Clay, Badly Drawn Boy, the Reverend Horton Heat, the resurrected Television, Kenny Wayne Shepherd, Cowboy Junkies, and Cheap Trick. From time to time, big-name artists also perform—Bob Dylan, Prince, Patti Smith, and A. J. McLean of the Backstreet Boys have all played "secret" shows here. All in all, it's a very nice place to see a show, with a well-elevated stage and lots of open space even on sold-out nights. There's an upstairs balcony that offers unparalleled views, but come early for a spot. 17 Irving Place (1 block west of Third Ave. at 15th St.). ℭ 212/777-1224 or 212/777-6800. www.irvingplaza.com. Subway: L, N, Q, R, W, 4, 5, 6 to 14th St./Union Sq.

The Knitting Factory   New York's premier avant-garde music venue has four separate spaces, each showcasing performances ranging from experimental jazz and acoustic folk to spoken-word and poetry readings to out-there multimedia works. Regulars who use the Knitting Factory as their lab of choice include former Lounge Lizard John Lurie; around-the-bend experimentalist John Zorn; guitar gods Vernon Reid, Eliot Sharp, and David Torn; innovative sideman (to Tom Waits and Elvis Costello, among others) Marc Ribot; and Television's Richard Lloyd. (If these names mean nothing to you, chances are good that The Knitting Factory is not for you.) The schedule is peppered with edgy star turns from the likes of Yoko Ono, Taj Mahal, Faith No More's Mike Patton, and Lou Reed. There are often two showtimes a night in the remarkably pleasing main performance space, so it's easy to work a show around other

---

Online Sources for Live-Music Fans

These websites are your top online sources for live-music schedules:

- Clear Channel Entertainment: www.cc.com
- Ticketmaster: www.ticketmaster.com

    Additionally, Web sources **Citysearch (www.citysearch.com)**, *Time Out New York* **(www.timeoutny.com)**, and all of the hard-copy resources (and their corresponding websites) listed at the start of this chapter offer a wealth of live-music listings.

activities. The Old Office Lounge offers an extensive list of microbrews and free live entertainment. 74 Leonard St. (btwn Broadway and Church St.). © 212/219-3132. www.knitting factory.com. Subway: 1 to Franklin St.

Music Hall of Williamsburg   Brought to you by Bowery Presents, the concert promoters for the Bowery Ballroom, Mercury Lounge and Terminal 5 (see below), this new-in 2007 Brooklyn venue holds 550 people and recreates the style and substance of the Bowery Ballroom . . . in Brooklyn. Patti Smith was the debut concert this mid-size venue showcases such midsize bands as the Weakerthans, Pelican, and Tigercity. 66 North Sixth St, Williamsburg, Brooklyn (btwn Kent and Wythe aves). © 212/260-4700. www.music hallofwilliamsburg.com. Subway: L to Bedford Avenue.

Terminal 5   Located where the club Exit formerly existed, the name is in tribute to the famous T.W.A. terminal at JFK designed in 1962 by Eero Saarinen. The JFK terminal no longer exists, but this new-in 2007, a 40,000 square-foot rectangular box with two upper level balconies on three sides, unobstructed sightlines, and state of the art sound system, attempts to carry on the spirit of that terminal with groups such as the National, Beastie Boys, and The Hives, though I'm not sure I get the connection. 610 W. 56th St (btwn 11th and 12th aves.). © 212/260-4700. www.terminal4nyc.com. Subway: A, B, C, D, 1 to 59th St.-Columbus Circle.

(MOSTLY) ROCK CLUBS

Live music at rock clubs usually begins around 9pm, but check the sources listed at the beginning of this chapter for up-to-date starting times and prices.

In addition to the choices below, rock fans on the hunt for diamonds in the rough might also want to see what's on at folk's legendary **Bitter End,** 147 Bleecker St., between Thompson and LaGuardia streets in the heart of the Village (© 212/673-7030; www.bitterend.com).

Arlene's Grocery   This casual Lower East Side club boasts a friendly bar and a good sound system; unfortunately, music isn't always free anymore, but the quality of the artists is usually pretty high, and the cover usually tops out at $7. Arlene's Grocery primarily serves as a showcase for hot bands looking for a deal or promoting their self-pressed record. The crowd is an easygoing mix of club-hoppers, rock fans looking for a new fix, and industry scouts looking for new blood. Monday nights host the extremely popular "Hard Rock Karaoke," which is exactly what it sounds like. 95 Stanton St. (btwn Ludlow and Orchard sts.). © 212/995-1652. www.arlenesgrocery.net. Subway: F to Second Ave.

The Baggot Inn *(Value)*   This easygoing pub has become one of the best showcases in the city for unknown acts, especially if you like quality acoustic and folk-rock music. Blues, Irish music, poetry, acoustic jams, and open-mic nights also regularly pop up on the calendar. The cover is always bargain-priced; happy hour until 7pm and nightly drink specials round out the entertainment value. 82 W. 3rd St. (btwn Thompson and Sullivan sts., below the Boston Comedy Club). © 212/477-0622. www.thebaggotinn.com. Cover free–$5. Subway: A, C, E, F, V to W. 4th St.; 6 to Bleecker.

Mercury Lounge   The Merc is everything a top-notch live-music venue should be: unpretentious, extremely civilized, and outfitted with a killer sound system. The rooms themselves are nothing special: a front bar and an intimate back-room performance space with a low stage and a few tables along the wall. The calendar is filled with a mix of accomplished local rockers and such national acts as Fat Possum, the Mekons, and Sleepy Jackson. The crowd is grown-up and easygoing. The only downside is that it's consistently packed thanks to the high quality of the entertainment and all-around pleasing nature of the experience. 217 E. Houston St. (at Essex St./Ave. A). (ℓ 212/260-4700. www.mercuryloungenyc.com. Subway: F to Second Ave.

Rodeo Bar *Value*   Here's New York's oldest—and finest—honky-tonk. Hike up your Wranglers and head those Fryes inside, where you'll find longhorns on the walls, peanut shells underfoot, first-class margaritas at the bar, and Tex-Mex on the menu. But this place is really about the music: urban-tinged country, foot-stompin' bluegrass, swinging rockabilly, Southern-flavored rock. Bigger names, such as Brian Setzer, and up-and-comers on the tour circuit, such as Hank Williams III, occasionally grace the stage, but regular acts such as the Dixieland Swingers, the Flying Neutrinos, cowpunk goddess Rosie Flores, and the good-time BBQ Bob and the Spareribs usually supply free music, keeping the urban cowboys plenty happy. A 10-gallon hat full o' fun. It's happy hour until 7pm; the music starts around 10pm nightly and goes till at least 3am. 375 Third Ave. (at 27th St.). (ℓ 212/683-6500. www.rodeobar.com. Subway: 6 to 28th St.

JAZZ, BLUES, LATIN & WORLD MUSIC

Be aware that a night at a top-flight jazz club can be expensive. Cover charges can vary dramatically—from as little as $10 to as high as $65, depending on who's taking the stage—and there is likely to be an additional two-drink minimum (or a dinner requirement if you choose an early show). Call ahead so you know what you're getting into; reservations are also an excellent idea at top spots.

For those of you who like your jazz with an edge, see what's on at the **Knitting Factory** (p. 359). Swingsters should consider **Swing 46** (p. 384). Weekends at **Carnegie Club** (p. 377) are ideal for Sinatra fans looking to relive the moment.

Despite its name, **B.B. King Blues Club & Grill** extends well beyond the blues genre to embrace over-the-hill acts of just about any ilk, from Morris Day and the Time to Blue Oyster Cult. Still, the venerable bluesman does take the stage from time to time, so you might want to see what's on; turn to p. 358.

You might also consider **Jazz at the Kitano,** in the mezzanine of the Kitano Hotel, 66 Park Ave., at 38th Street (ℓ 800/548-2666 or 212/885-7119; www.kitano.com), for some first-rate jazz in a casual, comfortable setting. **The Kitchen,** 512 W. 19th St., between Tenth and Eleventh avenues (ℓ 212/255-5793; www.thekitchen.org), has a full slate of live music and performance art. In association with the 92nd Street Y, **Makor** (p. 355) offers a similarly eclectic mix, as does **Joe's Pub** (p. 365), which adds a cabaret spin.

There's also world-beat jazz every Friday and Saturday from 5 to 8pm in the rotunda at the **Guggenheim Museum;** see chapter 8. And don't forget **Jazz at Lincoln Center,** the nation's premier forum for the traditional and developing jazz canon; see p. 353.

Some of the bars mentioned later in this chapter also have occasional live music. For an eclectic mix of jazz, Latin, and R&B, **Creole** (p. 380) in East Harlem offers a full schedule.

Bill's Place ★★ *Moments*   Imagine hearing great live jazz in your living room. That's about as close as what you will experience at the intimate and special Bill's Place. Bill is Bill Saxton, a jazz saxophonist extraordinaire and a Harlem legend. Saxton was a Friday night regular for many years at **St. Nick's Pub** (p. 363) and has played at clubs all over Harlem and downtown. In late 2005 he opened his own club in the parlor level of a brownstone on West 133rd Street. In the 1920s, 133rd Street between Lenox and

Seventh Avenue, with a number of speakeasies and jazz joints up and down the block, was the original "swing street"; a 17-year-old Billie Holliday was discovered singing in a club on 133rd Street, and the block was the model that West 52nd emulated and tried to imitate in the 1940s and 1950s. So it's appropriate that Saxton's place is on this historic block—the jazz here is the real deal. There are no frills at Bill's Place: Come into the parlor, find a seat—there aren't many, so reservations are a must—and groove to Saxton's pure bop sound. Alcohol is not served, but soft drinks are available and you can bring your own bottle. Open on Friday and Saturday only. On Friday Saxton and his quartet perform while Saturday is reserved for legends and emerging talent. 148 W. 133rd St. (btwn Lenox and Seventh aves.). ℂ 212/281-0777; www.webbmmpr.com/Bills Place.html. Reservations essential. Admission: $15. Subway: 3 to 135th St.

Birdland This legendary club abandoned its distant uptown roost in 1996 for a more convenient Midtown nest, where it has established itself once again as one of the city's premier jazz spots. While the legend of Parker, Monk, Gillespie, and other bebop pioneers still holds sway, this isn't a crowded, smoky joint of yesteryear. The big room is spacious, comfy, and classy, with an excellent sound system and a top-notch talent roster any night of the week. Expect lots of accomplished big bands and jazz trios, plus occasional appearances by such stars as Oscar Peterson and Dave Brubeck. You can't go wrong with the regular Sunday night show, starring Chico O'Farrell's smokin' Afro-Cuban Jazz Big Band. At press time, Tuesday was the domain of the Duke Ellington Orchestra, led by Duke's grandson Paul Ellington every other week. 315 W. 44th St. (btwn Eighth and Ninth aves.). ℂ 212/581-3080. www.birdlandjazz.com. Subway: A, C, E to 42nd St.

Blue Note The Blue Note has attracted some of the biggest names in jazz to its intimate setting. Those who've played here include just about everyone of note: Dave Brubeck, Ray Charles, B. B. King, Manhattan Transfer, Dr. John, George Duke, Chick Corea, David Sanborn, Arturo Sandoval, Gato Barbieri, and the superb Ahmad Jamal. The sound system is excellent, and every seat in the house has a sightline to the stage. However, in recent years, the hard edge that once was the Blue Note has faded. Softer, smoother jazz is the domain now, so if that's your thing, enjoy. *But be warned:* Prices are astronomical. There are two shows per night, and dinner is served. 131 W. 3rd St. (at Sixth Ave.). ℂ 212/475-8592. www.bluenote.net. Subway: A, B, C, D, E, F, to 4th St.

Dizzy's Club Coca-Cola ℝ This beautiful, cozy new jazz club is part of the Jazz at Lincoln Center complex in the Time Warner Center on Columbus Circle. Acoustics and sightlines are excellent and, though not nearly as dramatic as the window in the complex's Allen Room, there is a window behind the stage with views of Central Park and the city. The club attracts an interesting mix of both up-and-coming and established bands. Every Monday the club features the Upstarts, a student showcase from local schools including Juilliard and the Manhattan School of Music. My only complaint is the high $30 to $35 cover every day of the week—even for the Upstarts. Time Warner Center, 60th St. and Broadway. ℂ 212/258-9595. www.jalc.org. Subway: A, B, C, D, 1 to Columbus Circle.

Iridium This well-respected and snazzily designed jazz club has relocated from its longtime perch across from Lincoln Center to an even better heart-of-the-Theater-District location. Everything else remains the same, including the accomplished talent and big-name acts that always take the stage. Like the Energizer bunny, Les Paul keeps on going, still playing every Monday night, while the very popular Mingus Big Band makes Iridium their home each Tuesday. Other top-notch performers who often appear include Jackie McLean, Mose Allison, McCoy Tyner, and saxophonist Houston Person.

Jazz in the Afternoon

I personally like my jazz in the evenings or the wee, wee hours, if I'm ever awake for them. But I like jazz enough to dig it in the afternoon as well. And in Harlem, you can get your jazz pretty much all day and night thanks to the emergence in 2006 of **Ez's Woodshed,** 2236 Adam Clayton Powell Blvd., between 131st and 132nd streets (✆ **212/283-5299;** www.bigapple jazz.com/ezswoodshed.html). At Ez's the gigs begin every day at 2 and go until 5pm, then again from 5:30 until 8pm. Thursday through Saturday, Ez's has nighttime sets from 8:30 until 11pm. Ez's features up and coming talent, but if you are lucky you just might be there when local talents such as Bill Saxton or Eric Reed stop by and sit in a set or two. There is never a cover or minimum, but there is a "suggested donation" of $10 to $15 dollars to keep the music flowing.

A full, rather sophisticated dinner menu is served. 1650 Broadway (at 51st St.). ✆ **212/582-2121.** www.iridiumjazzclub.com. Subway: 1 to 50th St.

Jazz at the Cajun   This cozy, rather casual New Orleans themed supper club is the best venue in town for genuine prewar big band and Dixieland jazz—think Jelly Roll Morton, Scott Joplin, early Duke. The fanatical crowd comes from all walks of life, united in their love of the old-school. The place jumps no matter what top-notch crew takes the stage. The food is affordable and just fine; be sure to reserve in advance. 129 Eighth Ave. (btwn 16th and 17th sts.). ✆ **212/691-6174.** www.cajonjazz.com. Subway: A, C, E to 14th St.; L to Eighth Ave.

Jazz Standard   Boasting a sophisticated retro-speakeasy vibe, the Jazz Standard is one of the city's largest jazz clubs, with well-spaced tables seating 150 and a reasonable $15 to $25 cover. The rule is straightforward, mainstream jazz by new and established musicians, including such stars as Branford Marsalis. On Sunday afternoons the club features a Jazz for Kids program. A limited menu from Danny Meyer's barbecue joint, **Blue Smoke** (p. 183), upstairs, is available. Jazz, blues, and barbecue—hard to go wrong with that. 116 E. 27th St. (btwn Park Ave. South and Lexington Ave.). ✆ **212/576-2232.** www. jazzstandard.net. Subway: 6 to 28th St.

Lenox Lounge   This beautifully renovated classic is a symbol of Harlem's current renaissance. The intimate, Art Deco–cool back room—complete with zebra stripes on the walls and built-in banquettes—hosts top-flight live jazz vocalists, trios, and quartets for a crowd that comes to listen and be wowed. Blues and R&B are the province of Thursday. The cover never goes higher than $15, which makes Lenox Lounge a good value to boot. There's a warm, cozy, and immensely popular bar up front. Good soul food is served. Well worth the trip uptown for those who want a genuine Harlem jazz experience. 288 Malcolm X Blvd. (Lenox Ave.; btwn 124th and 125th sts.). ✆ **212/427-0253.** www.lenoxlounge.com. Subway: 2, 3 to 125th St.

St. Nick's Pub ☆ *Finds*   As unpretentious a club as you'll find, St. Nick's in Harlem's Sugar Hill district is the real deal, with live entertainment every night and never a cover. On Tuesday, it's Oldies but Goodies provided by Sexy Charles and Poetry on the Hill, hosted by Chance & Lilah; on other nights the music mix features jazz and African music. 773 St. Nicholas Ave. (at 149th St.). ☎ 212/283-9728. Subway: A, B, C, D to 145th St.

Smoke ⚘⚘ *Value* A superstar in the New York jazz scene and the best place to hear it on the Upper West Side, Smoke is a welcome throwback to the informal, intimate clubs of the past—the kind of place that on most nights you can just walk in and experience solid jazz. And though it seats only 65, for no more than a $30 cover, Smoke still manages to attract such big names as the Steve Turre Quartet, Ron Carter, Eddie Henderson, and John Hicks. Sunday through Thursday there is no cover. On Sundays, the club features Latin jazz; every Tuesday it's B3 grooves and soul jazz, and Wednesdays features world jazz. There are three sets nightly, an affordable menu, and a very popular happy hour. 2751 Broadway (btwn 105th and 106th sts.). ☎ 212/864-6662. www.smokejazz.com. Subway: 1 to 103rd St.

S.O.B.'s If you like your music hot, hot, hot, visit S.O.B.'s, the city's top world-music venue, specializing in Brazilian, Caribbean, and Latin sounds. The packed house dances and sings along nightly to calypso, samba, mambo, African drums, reggae, or other global grooves, united in the high-energy, feel-good vibe. Bookings include top-flight performers from around the globe; Astrud Gilberto, Mighty Sparrow, King Sunny Ade, Eddie Palmieri, Buckwheat Zydeco, Beausoleil, and Baaba Maal are only a few of the names who have graced this lively stage. The room's Tropicana Club style has island pizazz that carries through to the Caribbean-influenced cooking and extensive tropical-drinks menu. This place is so popular that it's an excellent idea to book in advance, especially if you'd like table seating. Monday is dedicated to Latin sounds, Tuesday to reggae, Friday features a late-night French Caribbean dance party, while Saturday is reserved for samba. 204 Varick St. (at Houston St.). ☎ 212/243-4940. www.sobs.com. Subway: 1 to Houston St.

Uptown Jazz Lounge at Minton's Playhouse ⚘ *Finds* The big neon sign on 118th Street remains intact and is a cultural landmark. The 1948-mural behind the stage of a woman sleeping off a drunk while four musicians jam by her side looks as fresh as it ever did even after a 30-year hiatus while Minton's Playhouse was shuttered. In 2006, the club where Miles Davis, Charlie Christian, Dizzy Gillespie, Coleman Hawkins, and house pianist, Thelonius Monk once reigned reopened. The look is sparse; a few archive photos cover the burnt orange walls and hard-backed chairs and formica-topped tables are scattered around the small room. But who cares? The music is straight ahead jazz and the clientele is old school Harlem along with curious European and Japanese tourists. At press time, Patience Higgins and the Sugar Hill Quartet hold court every Wednesday, while Thursday headlines vocalist Gerald Hayes and the Qualified Gents. No cover Monday through Thursday. 208 W. 118th St (between St. Nicholas Ave. and Adam Clayton Powell Blvd.) ☎ 212/864-8346. www.uptownatmintons.com. Subway: B, C to 116th St.

The Village Vanguard ⚘⚘ What CBGB was to punk rock, the Village Vanguard is to jazz. One look at the photos on the walls will show you who's been through since 1935, from Coltrane, Miles, and Monk to recent appearances by Bill Charlap and Roy Hargrove. Expect a mix of established names and high-quality local talent, including the Vanguard's own jazz orchestra on Monday nights. The sound is great, but sightlines aren't, so come early for a front table. If you are looking for serious jazz, this is the place. 178 Seventh Ave. S. (just below 11th St.). ☎ 212/255-4037. www.villagevanguard.net. Subway: 1, 2, 3 to 14th St.

5 Cabaret

An evening spent at a sophisticated cabaret just might be the quintessential New York night on the town. It isn't cheap: Covers can range from $10 to $60, depending on the showroom and the act, and also require two-drink or dinner-check minimums. Always reserve ahead, and get the complete lowdown when you do.

Cafe Carlyle ✦ Cabaret doesn't get any better than this. This is where the late, great Bobby Short, held court for over 35 years. The club still attracts rarefied talents such as Betty Buckley and Barbara Cook. The room is intimate and as swanky as they come. Expect a high tab—admission is $65 to $75 with a $30 per-person minimum; with dinner, two people could easily spend $300—but if you're looking for the best of the best, look no further. Value-minded cabaret fans can save by reserving standing room (which usually results in a spot at the bar) for just $35. On most Mondays, Woody Allen joins the Eddy Davis New Orleans Jazz Band on clarinet to swing Dixie-style ($85 cover). At the Carlyle Hotel, 35 East 76th St. (at Madison Ave.). ✆ 212/744-1600. Closed July–Aug. Subway: 6 to 77th St.

Feinstein's at The Regency *(Finds)* This intimate and elegant cabaret-style night-club is the first from Grammy-winning impresario Michael Feinstein. Cover charges can soar, but you can count on a memorable night of first-quality dining and song, and no other cabaret merges old-school cool and hipster appeal so well. Recent high-wattage talent has included Keely Smith, Patti LuPone, and the man himself. Call ahead to reserve; you can also purchase tickets through Ticketmaster. At the Regency Hotel, 540 Park Ave. (at 61st St.). ✆ 212/339-4095, or 212/307-4100 for Ticketmaster. www.feinsteins attheregency.com or www.ticketmaster.com. Subway: 4, 5, 6 to 59th St.

Joe's Pub Joe's Pub isn't exactly your daddy's cabaret. Still, this beautiful—and hugely popular—cabaret and supper club, named for the legendary New York Shakespeare Festival founder Joseph Papp, is everything a New York cabaret should be. The multilevel space serves up an American menu and top-notch entertainment from a more eclectic mix of talent than you'll find on any other cabaret calendar. The sophisticated crowd comes for music and spoken word that ranges from operatic diva Diamanda Galas to solo shows from such Broadway stars as Daphne Rubin-Vega *(Les Miserables)* and Tom Wopat *(Annie Get Your Gun)* to first-class pop from husband-and-wife singer/songwriters Michael Penn and Aimee Mann to modern rumba masters Los Munequitos de Matanzas. There's always jazz on the calendar, and don't be surprised if Broadway actors show up on off nights to exercise their substantial chops. DJs take over during the late-night hours. At the Joseph Papp Public Theater, 425 Lafayette St. (btwn Astor Place and 4th St.). ✆ 212/539-8778, or 212/239-6200 for Telecharge (for advance tickets). www.joespub.com. Subway: 6 to Astor Place.

The Oak Room Recently refurbished to recall its glory days, the Oak Room is one of the city's most intimate, elegant, and sophisticated spots for cabaret. Headliners include such first-rate talents as Andrea Marcovicci, Steve Ross, Dave Frishberg, the marvelous Julie Wilson, and cool-cat jazz guitarist John Pizzarelli, plus occasional lesser names that are destined for greatness. At the Algonquin Hotel, 59 W. 44th St. (btwn Fifth and Sixth aves.). ✆ 212/419-9331. Closed July–Aug. Subway: B, D, F, V to 42nd St.

6 Stand-Up Comedy

Cover charges are generally in the $8-to-$20 range, with all-star Carolines going as high as $30 on occasion. Many clubs also have a two-drink minimum. Be sure to ask

Author! Author! Where to Hear Spoken Word

Readings can be some of the most inexpensive and entertaining events in New York City. There are several venues dedicated to presenting spoken word, and popular series are presented in venues ranging from bars to bookstores. Many readings are free; others charge a small cover; and except for the top names, you'll rarely see a charge over $10.

The best sources for finding out who's reading include the "Books" section of *Time Out New York,* which spotlights top readings in its "Don't Miss" section.

To find out which author (or celebrity who's had a book ghost-written) is reading at a NYC Barnes & Noble (there's *always* a major author in town), go to www.bn.com and click on "Meet the Writers."

Who are you likely to see at these venues? Everyone from bestselling authors (Candace Bushnell, Tom Wolfe, Augusten Burroughs), to spoken-word artists (Reg E. Gaines, Alix Olson) to whoever's just scribbled a poem on the back of an envelope at an open-mic event.

Below are some of the top venues/series in town:

• **The Unterberg Poetry Center** at the 92nd Street YMHA (92nd St. at Lexington Ave.; ✆ **212/415-5740;** www.92y.org; Subway: 4, 5, 6 to 96th St.). The 92nd Street Y has had all the heavy hitters in its lineup since 1939. In addition to talks and readings by the world's top poets, novelists, playwrights, and critics, the Y also offers "Biographers & Brunch" and "Critics & Brunch." Tickets are usually in the $20 range. The readings are in a 917-seat auditorium, which does on occasion sell out (for, say, a Nobel Prize winner or ex-president).

• **Nuyorican Poets Café** (236 E. 3rd St., btwn B and C aves.; ✆ **212/505-8183;** www.nuyorican.org; Subway: F or V to Second Ave.). For over 30 years, the Nuyorican, brainchild of Miguel Algarin, who still runs it, has presented poetry, drama, music, and film. The raucous, popular **Poetry Slams** (the cafe fields a championship Slam Team) present poetry as a sport: Aspiring stars show up and throw down their work in front of an audience and panel of judges, who score them on the quality of the work and presentation. The Friday slams begin around 10pm (cover charge $7) and feature an invited slam poet. Slam Opens are held most Wednesdays (also a $7 cover). The storefront bar gets crowded quickly, so get there early on Slam nights.

• **Bowery Poetry Club,** 308 Bowery (at 1st St., btwn Houston and Bleeker sts.). (✆ **212/614-0505;** www.bowerypoetry.com; Subway: F or V to Second Ave.). "Poetry Czar" (as anointed by the *Village Voice*) Bob Holman opened his "Home for Poetry" in an 1850 building on (you guessed it) the Bowery. It's open all day for snacks, coffee, and that writer essential, hanging out; a two-for-one happy hour at the bar precedes each evening's festivities. Poetry and fiction readings, open mics, monologues, words with music, and all manner of other spoken word is presented from about 5:30pm each night, with covers ranging from free to $6. National and rising stars on the poetry/spoken-word scene show up here. The space can hold up to 200 people.

- **KGB,** 85 E. 4th St. (btwn Second and Third aves.). (($\mathcal{C}$) **212/505-3360;** www. kgbbar.com; Subway: F or V to Second Ave.; 6 to Astor Place). This second-floor bar (it's not wheelchair-accessible) in an old East Village brownstone was once a Ukrainian social club and is decorated with vintage Communist memorabilia. There's never a cover (but you are urged to refresh your drink often) for the readings held almost every night of the week (check the website) starting at around 7pm. It's a tiny bar, holding perhaps 40 to 50 comfortably, and double that or more for a "hot" reader (think Aoibheann Sweeney, Eileen Myles, A. M. Homes), with "nights" curated by individual writers for poetry, science fiction, and other genres.

FESTIVALS & EVENTS

- **The *New Yorker*** magazine (http://festival.newyorker.com) has gone into the readings business with its "New Yorker Festival" in early October. You'll pay dearly (up to $30) for the privilege of seeing, say Sherman Alexie or R. Crumb read from or talk about their work at one of several venues, but the events almost always sell out. There are also free events and book signings scheduled throughout the festival.

- Every New Year's Day, the **Poetry Project at St. Mark's Church,** 131 E. 10th St. (($\mathcal{C}$) **212/674-0910;** www.poetryproject.com; Subway: N, R, W to Union Sq.; 6 to Astor Place), presents a marathon poetry reading starting around 2pm, and running till . . . whenever. Poets and performers ranging from Patti Smith to Eric Bogosian, Maggie Estep, Tuli Kupferberg, and many (many) more read to welcome in the new year and raise money for the Poetry Projects' readings, workshops, and other programs. Tickets run about $20.

- **Symphony Space,** 2537 Broadway, at 95th St. (($\mathcal{C}$) **212/864-5400;** www. symphonyspace.org; Subway: 1, 2, 3, to 96th St.; B, C to 96th St.), is the home of both **Selected Shorts** (Oct–Dec) and **Bloomsday on Broadway.** In Selected Shorts, modern and classic short stories are read by professional actors, ranging from the likes of Blair Brown, Cynthia Nixon, Eli Wallach, and John Shea, in the Peter Jay Sharpe Theater (which seats 760). Authors whose work you might hear include John Cheever, Truman Capote, and Woody Allen. Tickets range from $21 to $25, with discounts for students and seniors. And each June 16 (the day Leopold Bloom took his stroll around Dublin in 1904 in James Joyce's *Ulysses*) an ensemble cast of actors and avid Joyceans do a marathon reading from the masterwork. Its tickets ($20 adults, $17 students and seniors) are usually sold out well in advance.

about the night's cover when you make reservations, which are strongly recommended, *especially* on weekends.

With the addition of **Comix,** 353 W. 14th St (at Ninth Ave; ℂ **212/524-2500;** www.comixny.com), the hip Meat-Packing district got its own comedy club, which mixes headlinerssuch as Caroline Rhea and Alex Borstein (from "The Family Guy" and "MadTV") with "Fresh Meat" shows introducing up-and-coming talent, and regular nights such as the Wendy Williams Comedy Experience every Wednesday.

Ars Nova   You won't find traditional standup at this 99-seat Hell's Kitchen theater. But nothing is traditional about Ars Nova, and that's the point of the place. It's a venue for emerging artists from playwrights to cabaret acts and the comedy you'll find here, such as Viva La Diva, is of the alternative kind. 511 W. 54th St (at 10th Ave.) ℂ 212/ 481-9800. www.arsnovanyc.com. Subway: B, D, E to Seventh Avenue-53rd St.

Carolines on Broadway   Caroline Hirsch presents today's hottest headliners in her upscale Theater District showroom, which doesn't have a bad seat in the house. You're bound to recognize at least one or two of the names and hot up-and-comers on the bill in any given week, such as Dave Chapelle, Janeane Garofalo, Colin Quinn, Bill Bellamy, Kathy Griffin, Robert Wuhl, Jimmie Walker ("Dyn-o-mite!"), Pauly Shore, or Jay Mohr. Monday is usually New Talent Night, while HOT97 radio hosts up-and-coming black comedians on select Tuesdays. 1626 Broadway (btwn 49th and 50th sts.). ℂ 212/757-4100. www.carolines.com. Subway: N, R, W to 49th St.; 1 to 50th St.

Comedy Cellar *Finds*   This intimate subterranean club is the venue of choice for stand-up fans in the know, thanks to the best, most consistently impressive lineups in the business. I'll always love the Comedy Cellar for introducing an uproariously funny unknown comic named Ray Romano to me some years back. 117 MacDougal St. (btwn Bleecker and W. 3rd sts.). ℂ **212/254-3480.** www.comedycellar.com. Subway: A, B, C, D, E, F, V to W. 4th St. (use 3rd St. exit).

Dangerfield's   Dangerfield's is the nightclub version of the comedy club, with a mature crowd and a straight-outta-Vegas atmosphere. The comedians are all veterans of the comedy-club and late-night talk-show circuit. 1118 First Ave. (btwn 61st and 62nd sts.). ℂ **212/593-1650.** www.dangerfieldscomedyclub.com. Subway: N, R to Lexington Ave.; 4, 5, 6 to 59th St.

Gotham Comedy Club *Finds*   Here's the city's trendiest, most comfortable, and most sophisticated comedy club. The young talent—Tom Rhodes, Sue Costello, Mitch Fatel, Lewis Black of the *Daily Show*—is red hot. Jerry Seinfeld has also been exercising his chops here of late. Look for such theme nights as "Comedy Salsa" and "A Very Jewish Christmas." Tuesday is set aside for new talent. 208 W. 23rd St. (btwn Seventh and Eighth aves.). ℂ **212/367-9000.** www.gothamcomedyclub.com. Subway: F, N, R to 23rd St.

Stand-Up New York   The Upper West Side's premier stand-up comedy club hosts some of the brightest young comics in the business, plus frequent drop-ins such as Dennis Leary, Caroline Rhea, Robin Williams, and Mr. Upper West Side himself, Jerry Seinfeld. 236 W. 78th St. (at Broadway). ℂ **212/595-0850.** www.standupny.com. Subway: 1 to 79th St.

Upright Citizens Brigade Theatre *Value*   You've seen their twisted, highly original sketch comedy on Comedy Central—now you can see the Upright Citizens Brigade, New York's premier alternative comedy troupe, live. The best of the nonstop hilarity is *ASSSSCAT 3000,* the troupe's extremely popular long-form improv show, which often sells out in advance. The company has supplied a few members of the Not-Ready-for-Prime-Time Players in recent years, including Amy Poehler. Reservations are

a must and tickets are a cheap $8 or less. 307 W. 26th St. (btwn Eighth and Ninth aves.). © 212/
366-9176. www.ucbtheatre.com. Tickets $8 or less. Subway: 1 to 23rd St.

7 Bars & Cocktail Lounges

Remember: Smoking is prohibited in bars but allowed in outdoor spaces.

TRIBECA

Bubble Lounge   From the first cork that popped, this wine bar dedicated to the
bubbly was an effervescent hit. More than 300 champagnes and sparkling wines are
served in this glamorous living-room setting, more than 30 of them by the glass, to
pair with caviar, foie gras, cheese, and sweets. No jeans, sneakers, or baseball caps.
There's live bluesy jazz on Monday and Tuesday. 228 W. Broadway (btwn Franklin and White
sts.). © 212/431-3433. www.bubblelounge.com. Subway: 1 to Franklin St.

Church Lounge   The big, super stylish Larry Bogdanow–designed atrium-lobby bar
and restaurant at the **Tribeca Grand Hotel** (p. 102) is a great place to enjoy a top-
flight cocktail and rub elbows with the neighborhood's chic locals (which include just
about anybody who has business with Miramax). Dress well and call ahead to see
what's on tap that evening if you want to experience the height of the action—around
11pm. 2 Sixth Ave. (at White and Church sts.). © 212/519-6600. Subway: 1 to Franklin St.; A, C, E to
Canal St.

Walker's *Finds*   Walker's is an old holdout from prefabulous TriBeCa. It's got some
charm, with a tin ceiling, a long wooden bar, oldies on the sound system, and cozy
tables where you can dine on good, affordable meat-and-potatoes fare. Don't get fancy
with your drink orders; stick with Guinness or one of the other drafts. 16 N. Moore St.
(at Varick St.). © 212/941-0142. Subway: 1 to Franklin St.

CHINATOWN

Winnie's   I usually abhor karaoke bars, but I make an exception for Winnie's.
Maybe it's because I'm a sucker for Asian pop tunes or perhaps it's the "Hawaiian
Punch," a sickly sweet drink that, after a couple, will have you crooning in Cantonese.
Even if you don't partake in the Chinatown version of *American Idol,* you will enjoy
others as they drunkenly embarrass themselves in the spotlight. 104 Bayard St. (btwn Bax-
ter and Mulberry sts.). © 212/732-2384. Subway: J, M, N, Q, R, Z, 6 to Canal St.

THE LOWER EAST SIDE

Barramundi   This lounge has a friendly staff, and a settled-in feel in a neighborhood overrun by hipster copycats. Come on a weeknight to snare a table in the little
corner of heaven out back. A fireplace makes Barramundi almost as appealing on cool
nights. 67 Clinton St. (btwn Stanton and Rivington sts.). © 212/529-6900. Subway: F to Delancey St.

SOHO

Ear Inn *Value*   There are many debates about which is the oldest bar in New York,
and with its 1870s origins, Ear Inn is a serious contender for that crown. In superchic
SoHo, this pub is a welcome cranky relief. They pull an excellent draft of Guinness
and make a surprisingly good margarita. On Saturday afternoon the poetry readings
just might make you cry into your beer. In warm weather, tables are set up outside
within exhaust distance of the nearby UPS depot. *Note:* Respect the no-cellphone policy or suffer the consequences. 326 Spring St. (btwn Greenwich and Washington sts.). © 212/226-
9060. Subway: C, E to Spring St.; 1 to Houston.

Drinking with Ghosts

The ghosts are everywhere in New York. You might find them in the silent halls of some of the city's greatest structures. Or maybe wandering through narrow downtown streets. But for me, the best place to find the ghosts is in a few of the city's more aged drinking establishments.

Three of the oldest bars in town are a good place to start when seeking out the ghosts. **Pete's Tavern** (129 E. 18th St., at Irving Place; ℰ 212/473-7676) claims to be the city's oldest continuing operating establishment. Warm up at Pete's on a cold winter night and after a few frothy Guinesses, you might think you see writer O. Henry, a regular at Pete's over a hundred years ago, sitting alone and unkempt in a booth, sipping his beer in between paragraphs of his famous 1906-written Christmas tale *Gift of the Magi*.

From Pete's you might want to venture to the West Village and the **White Horse Tavern** (567 Hudson St., at 11th St.; ℰ 212/243-9260). At this 1880s pub, through the maze of frat boys chugging pints, you might see a desolate figure, head on table snoring, empty shot glasses in front of him. Could that be the ghost of Dylan Thomas, author of *A Child's Christmas in Wales* and White Horse regular who took his last sip at the legendary tavern in 1953? Or is it just another drunken yuppie?

McSorley's Old Ale House (15 E. 7th St., between Second and Third aves.; ℰ 212/474-9148) is over 140 years old and, while Pete's is the oldest tavern in New York, McSorley's claims to be the oldest "saloon." Could someone please explain the difference? Not that it matters to a ghost. Here, if you can avoid the busloads of Greeks (not from Greece) who come to pay respects to their shrine, and visit on, say, a quiet, hot afternoon, you might think you see a tall, well-dressed man sitting at the bar taking notes, nursing an 8-ounce mug of ale. Could that be the ghost of *New Yorker* magazine writer Joseph Mitchell, author of *Joe Gould's Secret?* And are those notes for his 1943 book, *McSorley's Wonderful Saloon?* Well go up and ask him—before he disappears.

A bit farther uptown, just a few blocks north of Union Square, is the 1892-established **Old Town Bar & Restaurant** (45 E. 18th St., between Broadway and Park Ave. South; ℰ 212/529-6732). You might recognize the tin ceiling from the *Late Night with David Letterman* opening; the Old Town has been the set for many movies and television shows, but it's never been gussied up for the cameras—the Old Town is the real deal. There are no celebrity ghosts to speak of at the Old Town, but whenever I come here, I see one. This ghost is familiar only to me. He is cramped into a table with a group of friends, a pint and one of the Old Town's very good hamburgers in front of him. He is talking animatedly—a young man with big dreams. He looks confident and happy—as happy as a ghost could possibly look. But then I look in the mirror at my own reflection and the ghost disappears. He always does.

MercBar Notable for its long tenure in the fickle world of beautiful-people bars, the upscale MercBar has mellowed nicely. The decor bespeaks civilized rusticity with warm woods, a canoe over the bar, copper-top tables, and butter-leather banquettes— think SoHo goes to Yosemite. The European martini (Stoli raspberry and Chambord) is divine. Look carefully, because there's no sign. 151 Mercer St. (btwn Prince and Houston sts.). ℭ 212/966-2727. www.mercbar.com. Subway: N, R to Prince St.

Pegu Club 🐀🐀 Mixologist and owner Audrey Saunders, formerly of Bemelman's Bar in the Carlyle Hotel, makes magic with cocktails. In 2005 she opened her own little downtown gathering spot where she can even better showcase her immense talents. The cocktails here change seasonally and will astound you with their creativity. It helps that the staff uses fresh squeezed juices, homemade ginger beer and the largest assortment of bitters you will find anywhere. You know you are in serious cocktail heaven when your drinks are served with liquid condiments; your Pisco Punch needs a bit more sugar, you can squeeze a dropperful in. Or your Gin-Gin Mule just doesn't pack the citrus tang you would like, add a dash of lime. Unless it's salty peanuts or pretzels, I usually disdain bar food, but for the Pegu Club's amazing Diver scallop miniburgers and addictive smoked trout deviled eggs, I will happily make an exception. 77 W. Houston St., 2nd Floor (at W. Broadway). ℭ 212/473-PEGU. www.peguclub.com. Subway: A, B, C, D, E, F, V to W. 4th St.

Puck Fair *Finds* This gleaming pub looks as if it could have been lifted wholesale out of an equally stylish corner of London and plunked down on this side of the pond. It's genuine through and through, but a young crowd and a hip soundtrack make it feel fresh rather than old-man-neighborhoody (like Fanelli's). Twenty beers are on tap (including Guinness, of course). If you can snare a table, the petite mezzanine makes a great spot to sit down and dig into the surprisingly good pub grub. 298 Lafayette St. (just south of Houston St.). ℭ 212/431-1200. Subway: F to Broadway–Lafayette St.

THE EAST VILLAGE & NOHO

Don't forget to visit **McSorley's Old Ale House** (see p. 370, "Drinking with Ghosts").

dba *Finds* dba has completely bucked the loungey trend that has taken over the city, instead remaining firmly and resolutely an unpretentious neighborhood bar. It's a beer- and scotch-lover's paradise, with a massive drink menu on giant chalkboards. Owner Ray Deter specializes in British-style cask-conditioned ales (the kind that you pump by hand) and stocks a phenomenal collection of single-malt scotches. Ray has enclosed the back garden, transforming it into a cozy East Village beer garden. Excellent jukebox, too. During the 2006 World Cup, they had a big sign out front "Footy on the Telly All Day!" Look for such daily specials as Sunday Bloody Marys with free lox and bagels from Russ & Daughters. 41 First Ave. (btwn 2nd and 3rd sts.). ℭ 212/475-5097. www.drinkgoodstuff.com. Subway: F to Second Ave.

KGB Bar This former Ukrainian social club still boasts its Soviet-themed decor, but it now draws creative types who like the low-key boho vibe. There's also free entertainment almost every night, thanks to KGB's excellent, eclectic reading series, where a talented pack of up-and-coming and established writers read their prose in various genres (fiction, science fiction, poetry, and so on) to a receptive crowd starting at 7pm. (The readings are usually over by 9pm, if you don't like literature with your beer). Past readers have included playwright Tina Howe *(Pride's Crossing),* Janice Erlbaum *(Girlbomb),* and Dave King *(The Ha-Ha).* 85 E. 4th St. (btwn Second and Third aves.). ℭ 212/505-3360. www.kgbbar.com. Subway: 6 to Astor Place.

Cocktails Alfresco (Who's Al Fresco?)

One of my favorite moments in the movie *The Producers* is when Max Bialystock (played by Zero Mostel) tries to woo Leo Bloom (Gene Wilder) into helping him carry out his theater scam. Bialystock tells Bloom that he will treat him to dinner and they will dine "alfresco." The next shot is Bialystock buying a hot dog for Bloom from a street vendor near Central Park.

But food and drink always *do* taste better alfresco. Here are some of my favorite places for cocktails out of doors.

The outdoor space at rowdy **Jeremy's Ale House,** 228 Front St. (② 212/964-3537; www.jeremysalehouse.com), near the South Street Seaport, is no fairy tale, but it does have one of the best views of the Brooklyn Bridge. Maybe that's because the bar is practically under the bridge (on the Manhattan side). Jeremy's is so close to the river you may think you smell the sea, but what you really smell is an endless supply of calamari and clams sizzling in the deep fryers and gallons of Coors beer, which are served in 32-ounce Styrofoam cups.

Some of the best outdoor drinking can be found at a few select hotels. The best of the best, way downtown at the southern tip of Manhattan, is the **Rise Bar** 🐼 at the Ritz-Carlton New York, Battery Park, 2 West St., just north of Battery Place (② 212/344-0800). Located on the 14th floor of the hotel, the bar boasts incomparable views of Lady Liberty and busy New York Harbor from the massive waterfront terrace.

For the more trendy set, where the eye candy is not just the spectacular views, take the elevator up to the top of the Hotel Gansevoort, 18 Ninth Ave., at 13th Street (② 212/206-6700) to **Plunge,** where the you can gaze out at New Jersey, inhale the chlorine fumes from the hotel's pool (which only guests can use), all the while sipping pricey cocktails. A few blocks north at the Maritime Hotel, 363 W. 16th St., at Ninth Avenue, the scene on the roof at **Cabanas** (② 212/242-4300) is like something out of Hollywood. In fact, you'll probably recognize a few Hollywood denizens sunning themselves with colorful drinks, umbrella stirrers and all, balanced on their abnormally firm abs. Uptown, in the heart of Midtown, the **Pen-Top Bar** at the classic grande dame the Peninsula Hotel, 700 Fifth Ave., at 55th Street (② 212/956-2888), offers views of the glittering neighboring spires and the bustle of Fifth Avenue below that are not only calming but romantic, if that is actually possible.

One of my favorite parks is Riverside Park (see chapter 8), and two of the reasons why I love this park are the **79th Street Boat Basin Café,** 79th Street at the Hudson River (② 212/496-5542; www.boatbasincafe.com), where you can sip a drink and watch the boats bob on the river as the sun sets, and **Hurley's Hudson Beach Café,** Riverside Park and 103rd Street (② 917/370-3448), where beach volleyball games and stunning sunsets are the entertainment, marred only by the constant automobile buzz of the nearby West Side Highway.

Marion's Continental   Formerly a gathering place for artists and musicians hosted by former model, Marion Nagy in the 50s and 60s, the bar was resurrected by her son in the 1990s where it now stands as a tribute to his mother. It still serves perfect martinis and offers a campy yet comfy alternative to the overwrought East Village scene. The retro décor, with plush colorful seats, "mood" lighting, and kitschy knick knacks on the walls adds to the allure. On Thursdays, it's "Girls Night Out" at Marion's while Sunday's, it's fondue for everyone; now that's a blast from the past. 354 Bowery (btwn Great Jones and East 4th sts.). ☎ 212/475-7621. www.marionsnyc.com. Subway: B, D, F, V to Broadway-Lafayette.

Temple Bar   One of the first comers to New York's lounge scene, Temple Bar is still a gorgeous Deco hangout, with a long L-shaped bar leading to a lovely seating area with velvet drapes, backlighting, and Sinatra crooning in the background. Cocktails don't get any better than the classic martini (with just a kiss of vermouth) or the smooth-as-peignoir-silk Manhattan (Johnnie Walker Black, sweet vermouth, bitters). Bring a date—and feel free to invite me along. Look for the petroglyphlike lizards on the otherwise-unmarked facade. 332 Lafayette St. (just north of Houston St., on the west side of the street). ☎ 212/925-4242. Subway: 6 to Bleecker St.

Tom & Jerry's (288 Bar)   Here's an extremely pleasing neighborhood bar minus the grunge factor that usually plagues such joints. The place has an authentic local vibe, and the youngish, artsy crowd is unpretentious and chatty. The beer selection is very good and the mixed drinks are better than average. Flea-market hounds will enjoy the vintage collection of "Tom & Jerry" punchbowl sets behind the bar, and creative types will enjoy the rotating collection of works from local artists, which changes monthly. There's no sign, but you'll spy the action through the plate-glass window on the east side of Elizabeth Street just north of Houston. 288 Elizabeth St. ☎ 212/260-5045. Subway: 6 to Bleecker St.

Zum Schneider *Finds*   You know New York has just about everything when you can find an authentic indoor German beer garden in Alphabet City. With long tables and bench seating, this is a fun place for a group. There are more than a dozen varieties of German beer on tap here, and all are served in sturdy steins. To complement those hearty beers, you can sample equally hearty German fare such as Bavarian blood sausage and rolled beef filled with pickle, bacon, and mustard. If that seems a bit much, you can just munch on the homemade pretzels. 107 Ave. C (at 7th St.). ☎ 212/598-1098. www.zumschneider.com. Subway: F to Second Ave.; L to First Ave.

GREENWICH VILLAGE & THE MEAT-PACKING DISTRICT

While in the West Village, visit the historic **White Horse Tavern** (see the sidebar, "Drinking with Ghosts," on p. 370).

Tips Whiling Away the Happy Hours

Many of the city's best bars suddenly become more affordable from 4 to 8pm or thereabouts, when it's definitely a happy hour if you can snag one of those signature cocktails ($10 martinis, anyone?) at half-price or two-for-one; or maybe there's some free bar food, or another value-saving offer. Happy hour is a great time to experience those pricey places you've heard so much about. For information on happy hour at many of the city's watering holes, check online at **www.sheckys.com** or **Murph's NYC Bar Guide** at **www.murphguide.com**, which is updated daily.

Late-Night Bites

I have fond, but now distant, memories of barhopping until the early hours, rounded off by a meal in one of Chinatown's 24-hour restaurants only to emerge as the sun was rising the next day. Throughout the city, but especially downtown, are some great late-night eats. Here's a sampling:

Open until 4am nightly, **Blue Ribbon,** 97 Sullivan St., between Prince and Spring streets in SoHo (© 212/274-0404), is where the city's top chefs come to unwind after they close their own kitchens. Thanks to a top-drawer oyster bar and excellent comfort food, this cozy bistro is always packed, so expect a wait.

Other great choices for after-hours eats include TriBeCa stalwart **The Odeon** (p. 153), an attractive and affordable Art Deco bistro that's one of the top after-hours eateries in town. In the East Village, head to **Veselka** (p. 164), a comfortable and appealing diner offering eastern European fare at rock-bottom prices; **Katz's Delicatessen** (p. 190) for first-class Jewish deli eats Friday and Saturday until 2:45am. In Chinatown, many restaurants are open late or all night, but don't miss **Wo Hop** (p. 162), open 24 hours, for really, really late-night dining.

In the Theater District feast on first-class pastrami and cheesecake until 3:45am at **Carnegie Deli** (p. 190), until 2am at the **Stage Deli** (p. 190).

Bowlmor/Pressure ✿ Supercool Bowlmor isn't your daddy's bowling alley: DJs spin, martinis flow, candy-colored balls knock down Day-Glo pins, and strikes and spares are automatically tallied into the wee hours. Bowlmor is a blast. Once you're finished with your 10-pin—or while you're waiting for your lane—head upstairs to the rooftop lounge, **Pressure,** housed in a 16,000-square-foot inflated bubble and boasting designer-mod furnishings, a cocktail menu that includes a luscious chocolate martini (infused with Godiva chocolate liqueur), a fleet of pool tables, and always-on movie screens adding an arty-party flair. 110 University Place (btwn 12th and 13th sts.). © 212/255-8188 (Bowlmor) or 212/352-1161 (Pressure). www.bowlmor.com or www.pressurenyc.com. Subway: 4, 5, 6, L, N, R to 14th St./Union Sq.

Chumley's Many bars in New York date their beginnings to Prohibition, but Chumley's still has that speakeasy feel. The crowd doesn't date back nearly as far, however. Come to warm yourself by the fire and indulge in a once-forbidden pleasure: beer. There is a good selection of on-taps and microbrews. The door is unmarked, with a metal grille on the small window; another entrance is at 58 Barrow St., which takes you in through a back courtyard. After a construction accident closed the place in the spring of 2007, the tough old legend announced that it would be reopening in the fall. 86 Bedford St. (at Barrow St.). © 212/675-4449. Subway: 1 to Christopher St.

Employee's Only ✿ Don't let the palm reader in the doorway of the non-descript exterior of this bar fool you; though if she reads your palm, I can guarantee she will predict that you will very soon savor a tantalizing beverage. Employees Only goes to great lengths to recreate a 1920's speakeasy with a tin ceiling and bartenders in period costume. But who needs gimmicks when the cocktails are as good as they are here?

The employees here have been well trained and drinks are done painstakingly and made with the freshest ingredients and top label liquors. The daiquiri I tried was so good, Hemingway would be proud. In fact, it's called the Hemingway Daiquiri. The Ginger Smash, a concoction of muddled ginger root, fresh cranberries, Beefeater Wet and Apple Liquor sounds like a disaster, but the disparate ingredients surprisingly form a classic cocktail. There is a full menu available, but skip the entrees and order a few of the very good appetizers to accompany your drinks, the best being the very ample Serbian charcuterie platter. 510 Hudson St. (btwn Christopher and W. 10th sts.) ℭ 212/ 242-3021. www.employeesonlynyc.com. Subway: 1 to Christopher St.

Hudson Bar & Books   This former gentlemen's club maintains a similar appeal as an elegant bar. Among the draws are cool jazz, a copper-topped marble bar, good lighting, comfortable seating, and an extensive—and expensive—champagne, cocktails, cognacs, and malts menu. Pleasantly, the crowd comprises more at-home locals than preening tourists. A great date place. 636 Hudson St. (btwn Horatio and Jane sts.). ℭ 212/ 229-2642. Subway: A, C, E to 14th St.; L to Eighth Ave.

CHELSEA

Bongo ⟨Value⟩   This casual, comfortable mid-(20th)century-modern lounge is the place to come for cocktails that are well made and a great value considering their bathtub size. Don't miss the French martini, made with Vox vodka and Lillet—yum! Even better: Bongo boasts a full raw bar—a half-dozen varieties of oysters, cherrystones, and littlenecks, even lobster and caviar—and an excellent lobster roll. The crowd is hip but, not too trendy. Come early if you want to have space to sit and eat. 299 Tenth Ave. (btwn 27th and 28th sts.). ℭ 212/947-3654. Subway: A, C, E to 23rd St.

Kanvas   Apropos to its location, just a stone's throw from west Chelsea's clutch of cutting-edge art galleries, this sleek Chelsea lounge doubles as an art gallery, so it makes a great place to commune with an artsy crowd. It's a plush designer space, with a classic, long wood bar up front, cozy banquettes in back, and artwork that rotates monthly. The martini menu boasts two dozen, including a mint chocolate-chip version. Monday through Wednesday, $20 pitchers of mojitos and sangria are the draw. 219 Ninth Ave. (btwn 23rd and 24th sts.). ℭ 212/727-2616. www.kanvasnyc.com. Subway: C, E to 23rd St.

THE FLATIRON DISTRICT, UNION SQUARE & GRAMERCY PARK

Two of the city's oldest bars are in the Flatiron District, **Old Town Bar & Restaurant** and **Pete's Tavern.** See the sidebar "Drinking with Ghosts," on p. 370, for more.

Aspen   My favorite part of a ski vacation was always sipping a soothing cocktail in the warmth of the lodge while those silly skiers took tumbles in the cold snow. Now I don't have to head to the mountains to get that warming feeling, I can snow plow downtown to Aspen where the drinks are hot, but the atmosphere; mounted Lucite deer heads, a snow white dining room, Aspen birch and original barn wood and a bar around a blazing cooper-hooded fire, even hotter. While nursing your toddy, you can munch on a variety of inventive western-inspired small plates. And who knows, maybe a dose of Aspen, along with a cold drink, in the dog days of August will give you cool thoughts. 30 W. 22nd St. (btwn Fifth and Sixth Aves.). ℭ 212/645-5040. www.aspen-nyc.com. Subway: F, V to 23rd St.

Dusk ⟨Finds⟩   This casual, artsy lounge is a great choice for a cocktail. There's a fab mirrored mosaic wall, cozy banquettes, a friendly bar serving affordable drinks, a pool table, and mostly U.K. tunes—from drum-and-bass to Super Furry Animals to Blur

The New York Dive Experience

Not all of New York nightlife means bars and clubs with cover charges, expensive cocktails, elegant finger food, beautiful people, and velvet ropes to keep you waiting in the cold. There are places that you should be rewarded for braving; old dark places where the drinks are cheap and the characters colorful. These are the dive bars and they are just as New York as their hot, trendy counterparts. Here are some of my favorites; swing by one of them for a real New York experience.

Jimmy's Corner, 140 W. 44th St., between Broadway and Sixth Avenue (℡ 212/221-9510). Owned by a former boxing trainer, Jimmy's is a tough-guy's joint that has been around for more than 30 years and survived the Disneyfication of Times Square. Pictures of boxers adorn the walls, and the jukebox plays lots of R&B and '70's disco. In the pre–smoking ban days, the smoke would get so thick in Jimmy's you needed night goggles to see through the haze. Beer is cheap and drinks aren't fancy. Skip the theme bars and restaurants in the area and go for an after-theater pop at Jimmy's instead.

Rudy's Bar & Grill, 627 Ninth Ave., between 44th and 45th streets (℡ 212/974-9169). This Hell's Kitchen establishment is no secret; its happy hour is legendary, and the small place is usually packed with slackers sucking up cheap beer, including the house brand, Rudy's Red, a weak brew served in a huge plastic cup for $3. My advice is to get here before happy hour, grab a seat on one of the few broken banquettes, and keep your eyes open for the hot-dog guy who gives out free hot dogs. You'll need one to balance out a bucket of Rudy's Red. In the summer, Rudy's opens its cement garden for drinks alfresco.

to Enya—on the sound system. Expect an easygoing, youngish crowd that stays relaxed and unpretentious into the evening. No sign, but look for the three blue lights attached to a dark storefront. 147 W. 24th St. (btwn Sixth and Seventh aves.). ℡ 212/924-4490. Subway: F to 23rd St.

Rose Bar ⊛   I usually abhor bars that are "scenes;" where you need to be on a list to gain entry. But what Ian Schrager and artist Julian Schabel have created in the Gramercy Park Hotel makes going through the various humiliations it might take to get in almost worth it. The space is spectacular with rose-colored velvet chairs, original Warhols and Schnabels on the walls, a wood-burning fireplace, a red and white tile floor, and a billiards table you will be very intimidated to even approach. But sit on one of those plush chairs, sip your $20 cocktail, enjoy the flawless sound system commandeered by various top name DJs and for a few moments you might forget that you really don't belong in this swanky, celebrity-laden environment. Reservations (and they are hard to get) are mandatory after 10pm and security is tight. 2 Lexington Ave. (btwn 20th and 21st sts.). ℡ 212/920-3300. Subway: 6 to 23rd St.

TIMES SQUARE & MIDTOWN WEST

Don't forget those dives—you can find **Jimmy's Corner** and **Rudy's Bar & Grill** in the neighborhood (see the box "The New York Dive Experience," above).

Subway Inn, 143 E. 60th St., at Lexington Avenue (© 212/223-8929). My all-time favorite dive, the Subway has been around for over 60 years and I believe some of the regulars have been on their stools the entire time. The red neon sign beckons from outside while inside, no matter what time of day, it's midnight dark. The bartender is ancient and until recently served Schaefer on tap. The demise of Schaefer was troubling, but thankfully, not much else has changed. The booths are still wobbly and the models of Godzilla and E.T. along with assorted other dusty junk continue to decorate the shelves behind the bar. The last time I visited, I was barred from entering the men's room by police who were shaking down one of the regulars during a drug bust. You might find workers from the upscale stores in the neighborhood and writers searching for "material" slumming at the subway, but this joint remains the pinnacle of divedom.

Tap a Keg, 2731 Broadway, between 103rd and 104th streets (© 212/749-1734). This dog-friendly establishment earned itself permanent Hall-of-Fame dive status when, on a recent visit, one of man's best friend found the middle of the bar's floor as the perfect spot to leave a hearty mound of affection that remained untouched by both the dog's clueless owner and the bar's unconcerned bartender. Tap a Keg claims to be a "Hell of a Joint," and now there is no doubt of that. If allowing free reign to dogs doesn't bother you, then you'll certainly enjoy the 7-hour happy hour with pints for about $3 and the regular gathering of wizened, disheveled characters.

Carnegie Club *Finds* Like sister lounge **The Campbell Apartment** (p. 379), this swellegant lounge is another architecturally magnificent space, with soaring ceilings and an intimate mezzanine, plus a grand stone fireplace—a Gothic mood warmed up with plush, contemporary furnishings and a romantic vibe. "Weekends with Sinatra" stars Cary Hoffman and the Stan Rubin Orchestra in a wonderfully evocative—and surprisingly exact—cabaret show featuring the music of Frank Sinatra (two shows nightly on Sat; cover $30, plus $15 minimum). There's also live swing on Friday. Reservations are recommended on live-music nights. 156 W. 56th St. (btwn Sixth and Seventh aves.). © 212/957-9676. Subway: F, Q to 57th St.

Hudson Bar Outfitted like a futuristic canteen, Hudson Bar, in the Hudson Hotel, glows from below with an underlit floor, while the low ceiling wears a Crayola-like fresco by Francesco Clemente. In between you'll find a tony, older-than-you'd-expect crowd. The one-of-a-kind cocktail menu is terrific. Enter at street level, on the Ninth Avenue side of the hotel's main entrance; dress well to avoid attitude. 356 W. 58th St. (btwn Eighth and Ninth aves.). © 212/554-6000. Subway: A, B, C, D, 1 to 59th St./Columbus Circle.

Mickey Mantle's *Kids* Before Mickey Mantle's opened years ago, I was walking past the restaurant, peered into the window, and there was my boyhood idol, the Mick, sitting at the bar by himself. Through the window I waved—and he waved

Checking into Hotel Bars

A hotel bar should provide comfort and hospitality to the out-of-town visitor. It should be the kind of place where you can unwind after a day of seeing the sights, have a leisurely drink before heading out to dinner or a show, or enjoy a quiet nightcap before retiring. When the bar becomes a nighttime destination unto itself, and hotel guests have to fight their way through a throng of locals just to get a drink, well, I'd say that hotel bar has defeated its purpose. Thankfully, New York has plenty of hotel bars that draw outsiders but keep their own guests happy, too. Here are my top picks:

Bemelmans Bar, in the Carlyle Hotel, 35 E. 76th St., at Madison Avenue (ⓒ 212/744-1600). This is my choice as New York's best hotel bar. It has everything you want in a hotel bar: white-coated service; lush seating with many dark romantic corners to sink into; a nice mix of locals and guests; and incredible cocktails, such as the Old Cuban, a *mojito* topped with champagne. The bar is named after children's-book illustrator Ludwig Bemelmans, who created the *Madeline* books after he painted the whimsical mural here.

Bull and Bear, in the Waldorf=Astoria, 301 Park Ave., between 49th and 50th streets (ⓒ 212/872-1275). The Bull and Bear is like a gentlemen's pub, with brass-studded red leather chairs, a waistcoated staff, and a grand troika-shaped mahogany bar polished to a high sheen at the center of the room. Still, it's plenty comfy for casual drinkers. Ask Oscar—who's been here for more than 30 years—or one of the other accomplished bartenders to blend you a classic cocktail such as The Bronx, a combination of gin, orange juice, and fresh pineapple juice. An ideal place to kick back after a hard day of sightseeing.

King Cole Bar, in the St. Regis, 2 E. 55th St., at Fifth Avenue (ⓒ 212/753-4500). The birthplace of the Bloody Mary, this theatrical spot may just be New York's most historic hotel bar. The Maxfield Parrish mural alone is worth the price of a classic cocktail (ask the bartender to tell you about the "hidden" meaning of the painting). The one drawback is the bar's small size; after-work hours and holiday times, the bar is jammed.

Oak Room at the Algonquin, in the Algonquin Hotel, 59 W. 44th St., between Fifth and Sixth avenues (ⓒ 212/840-6800). The splendid oak-paneled lobby of this venerable literati-favored hotel is the comfiest and most welcoming in the city, made to linger over pre- or post-theater cocktails. You'll feel the spirit of Dorothy Parker and the Algonquin Round Table that pervades the room. Try the Matilda, a light, refreshing blend of orange juice, Absolut Mandarin, triple sec, and champagne, named after the Algonquin's legendary feline in residence.

back. It made my day. And though the food's not very good and the drinks are over-priced, I still have a soft spot for Mickey Mantle's and always will. With plenty of Yankee memorabilia on the walls and sports on all the televisions, it's an ideal place to watch a game, but stick with the basics: beer and burgers. 42 Central Park South (btwn Fifth and Sixth aves.). ⓒ 212/688-7777. www.mickeymantles.com Subway: F to 57th St.

Morrell Wine Bar & Cafe   One of the leading wine purveyors in America (p. 337) has created the ideal place to sample the first-rate collection of vintages in comfort. Situated at the heart of Rockefeller Center, just across the alley from the plaza, the bi-level space is contemporary and comfortable and attended by an extremely knowledgeable waitstaff. In addition to the extensive bar and lounge space, a nice New American menu is also served. Make reservations for dinner. 1 Rockefeller Plaza (at 49th St.). ☎ 212/262-7700. www.morrellwinebar.com. Subway: B, D, F, V to 47th–50th sts./Rockefeller Center.

Rainbow Room   Skip eating here, but come to this legendary bar, sip a too-expensive cocktail, and soak in the ambience, views, and live piano music. No jeans or sneakers, please. There's a cover for drinks and dancing on select Fridays and Saturdays, but you can stop by to have a drink (in appropriate attire) without a cover other times. 30 Rockefeller Plaza (entrance on 49th St., btwn Fifth and Sixth aves., 65th floor). ☎ 212/632-5100. www.rainbowroom.com. Subway: B, D, F, V to 47th–50th sts./Rockefeller Center.

Russian Samovar ✿   Yes it's a restaurant with Russian food, but the main attraction of this Theater District legend is the vodka. There are over 20 flavors of house-infused vodkas including dill, garlic, ginger, tarragon and, host and impresario Roman Kaplan's favorite, cranberry-lemon. Despite what it might do to you and how it will affect the plans you might have the next 24 hours, it's difficult to resist sampling many of them while listening to standards played by the house pianist. You might want to soften the bite of the vodka with a few appetizers such as the Royal Fish Platter, a selection of smoked fish and a little caviar. Do not make this a pre-theater stop—you'll never make it to your show. 256 W. 52nd St. (btwn Eighth Ave. and Broadway). ☎ 212/757-0168. www.russiansamovar.com. Subway: 1 to 50th St.

MIDTOWN EAST & MURRAY HILL

The Campbell Apartment   This swank lounge on the mezzanine level at Grand Central Terminal has been created out of the former business office of prewar businessman John W. Campbell, who transformed the space into a pre-Renaissance palace worthy of a Medici. The high-ceilinged room has been restored to its full Florentine glory, and serves wines and champagnes by the glass, single-malt scotches, and haute noshies to a well-heeled commuting crowd. Try to snag a seat in the little-used upstairs room if you want some quiet. Call ahead before heading over, as the space tends to be closed for private parties on a rather frequent basis. No sneakers, baseball caps, athletic wear, or ripped jeans. In Grand Central Terminal, 15 Vanderbilt Ave. ☎ 212/953-0409. Subway: S, 4, 5, 6, 7 to 42nd St./Grand Central.

The Ginger Man   The big bait at this upscale beer bar is the 66 gleaming tap handles lining the wood-and-brass bar, dispensing everything from Sierra Nevada and Hoegaarden to cask-conditioned ales. The cavernous space has a clubby feel. The Cohiba fumes were ripe here before the smoking ban but the new nonsmoking laws have not stopped the crowds from coming to this popular Murray Hill hangout. 11 E. 36th St. (btwn Fifth and Madison aves.). ☎ 212/532-3740. Subway: 6 to 33rd St.

Monkey Bar   This legendary bar and restaurant has experienced quite a resurgence since Carrie and Mr. Big hooked up here on *Sex and the City.* It definitely deserved the attention: The swanky space is dolled up like a Hollywood supper club from the 1930s, the drinks are faultless, and the legendary monkey murals alone are worth a look. Skip the dining room and head directly to the piano bar for the ultimate Monkey Bar experience. At the Hotel Elysée, 60 E. 54th St. (btwn Madison and Park aves.). ☎ 212/838-2600. Subway: 6 to 51st St.

Under the Volcano *(Finds* If you've been shopping crowded Macy's or braving the lines at the Empire State Building and want (need?) a drink, one of the few choices in the area, but a good one, is this Mexican-themed tequila bar. The decor is Mexican folk with Frida Kahlo undertones throughout, but the main attractions are the 16 varieties of tequila and the very smooth, subtly potent margaritas. The bar also features an excellent selection of aged rums. 12 E. 36th St. (btwn Fifth and Madison aves.). © 212/ 213-0093. Subway: B, D, F, N, R to 34th St.

UPPER WEST SIDE

Dublin House For years, like a welcoming beacon, the Dublin House's neon harp has blinked invitingly. This very old pub is a no-frills Irish saloon and the perfect spot for a drink after visiting the nearby Museum of Natural History or Central Park. There's a long, narrow barroom up front and a bigger room in the back that's good for groups. Original wood veneer detail remains, adding to the pub's charm. The Guinness is cheap and drawn perfectly by the very able and sometimes crusty bartenders. Best enjoyed in the late afternoon or early evening when the regulars populate the bar. Stay away on weekend nights and St. Patrick's Day when the place is overrun with amateurs: frat boys and sorority girls on pub crawls. 225 W. 79th St. (btwn Broadway and Amsterdam Ave.). © 212/874-9528. Subway: 1 to 79th St.

UPPER EAST SIDE

Elaine's *The Big Chill* claimed that Elaine's was over and done with way back when. They were dreaming. Glittering literati still come here for dinner and book parties. Look for regulars such as Woody Allen and other A-list types. If you can't get a table, you can always scan the room from the bar up front. 1703 Second Ave. (btwn 88th and 89th sts.). © 212/534-8103. Subway: 4, 5, 6 to 86th St.

Great Hall Balcony Bar *(Moments* One of Manhattan's best cocktail bars is only open on Friday and Saturday—and only from 4 to 8:30pm. The Metropolitan Museum of Art transforms the lobby's mezzanine into a cocktail-and-classical-music lounge twice weekly, offering a marvelous only-in–New York experience. The music is usually provided by a piano and string quartet. You'll have to pay the $10 admission, but the galleries are open until 9pm. At the Metropolitan Museum of Art, Fifth Ave. at 82nd St. © 212/535-7710. www.metmuseum.org. Subway: 4, 5, 6 to 86th St.

HARLEM

Creole Tucked away in El Barrio (also known as east Harlem) is a relatively new and welcome addition to the uptown music scene. Creole is an intimate bar/restaurant that features top-notch jazz, Latin, R&B, and on Sunday, gospel. Sit at the bar or enjoy the music while chowing down on very good Southern/Cajun specialties—the gumbo might be the best in the city. Entertainment begins at 8:30pm, but you might want to venture in a little early for Creole's fun happy hour from 5 to 7pm. 2167 Third Ave. (at 118th St.). © 212/876-8838. www.creolenyc.com. Subway: 6 to 116th St.

The Den *(Finds* For not only the most creative cocktails north of 96th Street, but also the most imaginative drink names in all of Manhattan, come uptown to the fun, funky Den. Here you can sip such concoctions as the "Pimp Slap," "Sex in the Inner City," "Bahama Baby Mama Drama," and the "Harlem Ice Tea," while watching a blaxploitation flick off the bar/restaurant's brick wall. Don't ask me what's in the drinks, just know that they are colorful, sweet, and very potent. On Saturday, the brick wall is the screen for kung fu movies, while on Wednesday it's live old- and new-school R&B. To fortify yourself from those drinks, sample the Den's kitchen creations such as the "Not ya mama's chicken and waffles," "Bruce LeeRoy's popcorn shrimp," "Mississippi Burnin' wings," or a "soul roll," the Den's take on sushi stuffed with, not raw fish, but BBQ pulled pork. 2150 Fifth Ave. (btwn 131st and 132nd sts.). ☎ 212/234-3045. www.theden harlem.com. Subway: 3 to 135th St.

OUTER BOROUGHS

Bohemian Beer Hall & Garden ⭐ (Finds)   At one time there were over 800 outdoor German beer gardens in New York. All are now gone except this lone Astoria survivor. A number of European, in particular, excellent Czech beers are available to drink under the stars on a balmy night from late spring to autumn. If you are hungry, there are Eastern European specialties such as pork schnitzel and Hungarian goulash to accompany your beer. The Garden features live jazz every Thursday and if you are a member of the Bohemian Benevolent Society of Astoria, you get ten percent off on food. Just something to think about. And even when the garden isn't open, you can still get the hearty Bohemian food (and beer) indoors year-round. 29–19 24th Avenue, Astoria, Queens (btwn 29th and 31st sts.). ☎ 718/274-4925. www.bohemianhall.com. Subway: N to Astoria Blvd.

Pete's Candy Store   This former candy store is Williamsburg's best place for live entertainment and games. The bar up front features the famous bi-weekly "spelling bee" held every other Monday, bingo on Tuesdays, a Quizz-Off on Wednesdays, and Scrabble on Saturdays. If games are not your thing, there is live music every night featuring some of New York's most promising up-and-coming rock bands. 709 Lorimer St (btwn Richardson and Frost sts.), Williamsburg, Brooklyn. ☎ 718/302-3770. www.petescandystore.com. Subway: L to Lorimer St.

Spuyten Dyvil ⭐   Hard core beer aficionados need to take the L train to the Williamsburg, Brooklyn to find the city's best and most interesting selection. But you need to know your stuff otherwise the vast offerings; from Smuttynose Portsmouth Lager on tap to Achel Blonde in bottle will have your head spinning even before your first sip. While you savor that obscure beer from some microbrewery in Idaho, you can listen to an equally eclectic selection of songs from Spuyten Dyvil's fantastic juke box ranging from Lee Scratch Perry to the Earl Hines Trio. If you insist, wine is also served along with cheese and meat platters to go with the beer. But, even better, cross Metropolitan Avenue and take out some of Spuyten Dyvil's sister establishment, Fette Sau's (p. 214) barbecue to go with your beer. 359 Metropolitan Ave., (at Havemeyer St.) ☎ 718/963-4140. www.spuytendyvilnyc.com. Subway: L to Lorimer St.

8 Dance Clubs & Party Scenes

Nothing in New York nightlife is as mutable as the club scene. In this world, hot spots don't even get 15 minutes of fame—their time in the limelight is usually more like a commercial break.

First things first: Finding and going to the latest hot spot is not worth agonizing over. Clubbers spend their lives obsessing over the scene. My rule of thumb is that if I know about a place, it must not be hip anymore. Even if I could tell you where the hippest club kids hang out today, they'll have moved on by the time you arrive in town.

"Clubs" as actual, physical spaces don't mean much anymore. The hungry-for-nightlife crowd now follows events of certain party "producers" who switch venues

---

Tips　Getting Beyond the Velvet Rope

If you are somewhat masochistic, enjoy humiliation and ridicule, and are determined to get into that oh-so-trendy club you heard about back home, here are a few pointers that may help tip the scale in your favor:

- **Dress well and fashionably.** Like it or not, the doorman is sizing you up to decide if you're hip enough to make the scene. If you want to get in, you have to play along.

- **Arrive early.** Frankly, the bouncers are just not as vigilant at 9pm, when the place is half empty, as they are at 11pm—and once you're inside, you're in for the night. Weeknights are also a better bet. Clubbers may tell you that eager beavers are disdained for arriving too early, but I find earlier to almost always be more successful than later.

- **Be polite.** No matter how obnoxious the doorman may be, giving attitude back won't help. And who knows? You might just charm him with your winning personality.

- **Don't try to talk your way in.** Don't drop names or make up some story to get in the door. These guys have heard it all. If you're not wanted, why bother? Take your business to a friendlier establishment, where you'll be happier in the long run.

---

and times each week. A number of bars and lounges listed in the previous section host "club" scenes on various nights of the week.

The tracking game is best left to the perennial party crowd who knows the guy at the door (who lets them in for free) and someone at the bar (who comps them drinks). You're not likely to get that well connected in your weeklong vacation. Just find someplace you like, and enjoy the crowd that enjoys it with you.

I've concentrated on a wide variety of club scenes below, from performance-artsy to perennially popular discos, most of which are generally easy to make your way into. You can find listings for the most current hot spots and movable parties in the **publications and online sources** listed at the start of this chapter. Additional online sources that might score you discount admissions to select clubs include **www. promony.com**. You can also check **www.sheckys.com** for VIP guest list access.

No matter what, **always call ahead,** because schedules change constantly and can do so at the last minute. Even better: You also may be able to put your name on a guest list that will save you a few bucks at the door.

New York nightlife starts late. With the exception of places that have scheduled performances, clubs stay almost empty until about 11pm. Don't depend on plastic— bring cash, and plan on dropping a wad at most places. Cover charges run anywhere from $7 to $30, and often get more expensive as the night wears on.

Avalon　In the former church where dance-club legend Limelight once reigned, the interior has been updated with VIP balconies that overlook the dance floor. Off the dance floor are many small rooms for commingling, if you are tired of dancing. 47 W. 20th St. (at Sixth Ave.). ℂ 212/807-7780. Subway: F to 23rd St.

Bungalow 8　This is the ultimate in dance-club extravagance. Here drinks might cost as much as a week at your hotel. All the cutthroat tactics learned on *The Apprentice* or

Survivor might not help to gain entry to this palace. 515 W. 27th St. (btwn Tenth and Eleventh aves.). © 212/629-3333. Subway: C, E to 23rd St.

Cafe Wha? You'll find a carefree crowd dancing in the aisles of this casual basement club just about any night of the week. From Wednesday through Sunday, the stage features the house's own Wha Band, which does an excellent job of cranking out crowd-pleasing covers of familiar rock-'n'-roll hits from the '70s, '80s, and '90s. Monday night is the hugely popular Brazilian Dance Party, while Tuesday night is Classic Funk Night. Expect to be surrounded by lots of Jersey kids and out-of-towners on the weekends, but so what? Reservations are a good idea. The cover runs from free to $10. 115 MacDougal St. (btwn Bleecker and W. 3rd sts.). © 212/254-3706. www.cafewha.com. Subway: A, B, C, D, E, F, V to W. 4th St.

Cain At Cain the theme is Africa—South Africa to be specific. The front door, if you gain entry, has elephant-trunk handles, there are zebra hides everywhere, and the big game is celebrity-spotting. The DJ's spin energetic house music to keep the hordes moving, but you might be better off sampling one of the club's excellent cocktails in the "premium seating lounge." God knows what it takes to get a seat there. 544 W. 27th St. (btwn 10th and 11th aves.). © 212/947-8000. Subway: C, E to 23rd St.

Cielo At Cielo you'll find the best sound system of any small club in New York. House is big here and they regularly bring in some of the best DJs from around the globe. The renowned Louis Vega is the DJ on Wednesday. There's a sunken dance floor and an authentic, glittering disco ball rotating above. What more could you want? 18 Little W. 12th St. (btwn Ninth Ave. and Washington St.). © 212/645-5700. www.cieloclub. com. Subway: A, C, E, to 14th St.; L to 8th Ave.

Club Shelter House-heads flock to this old-school disco. The big draw is the "Saturday Night Shelter Party," when late 1980s house music takes over. The crowd is racially and sexually diverse and dress is not fancy; wear whatever is comfortable for doing some heavy sweating on the dance floor. 150 Varick St. corner of Van Dam © 646/862-6117. www.clubshelter.com. Subway: 1 Houston; C, E to Spring.

Don Hill's This long-lived, eccentric, divey club draws a heavily integrated gay-lesbian/straight crowd that comes for rock, glam, and punk some nights, campy parties on others. There's a regular "Panty Party" late on Fridays, and regular Saturday night event called "Glamdammit." Drinks are affordable. 511 Greenwich St. (at Spring St.). © 212/219-2850. www.donhills.com. Subway: 1 to Canal St.

Mansion Located in the old Crobar space and after a million-dollar renovation, this club, with a sister in Miami, opened in early 2008. The dance floor is small (i.e. intimate) and the music booms with a Euro beat until 4 a.m. At press time the buzz was white hot but we know the dance crowd is fickle and that heat could fade fast. 530 W. 28th St (btwn 10th and 11th aves.). © 212/629-9000. www.mansionnewyork.com. Subway: C, E to 23rd St.

Pacha No, you are not on exotic Ibiza, but in Hell's Kitchen, New York. But enter Pacha and wade through the club's four levels, marvel at the palm trees, ogle discreetly the bikini-clad go-go girls dancing in the red-lit showers and you'll for a few hours be transported somewhere a little less hellish than Hell's Kitchen. 618 W. 46th St (btwn 11th Ave and the West Side Hwy.). © 212/209-7500. www.pachanyc.com. Subway: A, C, E, 7 to 42nd St.

Socialista With such investors as Harvey Weinstein, Sting, and Giuseppe Cipriani, and opened by a former doorman at Bungalow 8 (see above), Socialista is the furthest thing from a hangout for the common working man as its name implies. But who really wants to be considered common when sipping Cuban-inspired cocktails on fine leather furniture while ogling people much less ordinary and more beautiful than you? There is an exclusive upstairs lounge, but you need a secret telephone number to get in. 505 West St, (at Jane St.) ☏ 212/929-4303. www.socialist.us. Subway: A, C, E, L to 14th St-Eighth Ave.

Swing 46 *(Finds*   Swing is a nightly affair at this Theater District jazz and supper club (supper not required). Music is live nightly except Monday, when a DJ takes over, and runs the gamut from big band to boogie-woogie to jump blues. Do not miss Vince Giordano and His Nighthawks if they're on the bill, especially if sharp-dressed Casey McGill is singing and strumming his ukulele, too. The Harlem Renaissance Orchestra is another great choice. Even first-timers can join in the fun, as free swing lessons are offered Wednesday through Saturday at 9:15pm. No jeans or sneakers. 349 W. 46th St. (btwn Eighth and Ninth aves.). ☏ 212/262-9554. www.swing46.com. Subway: C, E to 50th St.

13 *(Value*   This little lounge is a great place to dance the night away. It's stylish but unpretentious, with a steady roster of fun weekly parties. Sunday night's Britpop fest Shout! lives on, as popular as ever—and with no cover, to boot. The rest of the week runs the gamut from '70s and '80s New Wave and glam nights to progressive house and trance to poetry slams and performance art. If there's a cover, it's usually $5, occasionally $7 or $10. Happy hour offers two-for-one drinks (and no cover) from 4 to 8pm. 35 E. 13th St. (btwn Broadway and University Place), 2nd floor. ☏ 212/979-6677. www.bar13. com. Subway: 4, 5, 6, L, N, R, Q, W to 14th St./Union Sq.

9 The Gay & Lesbian Scene

To get a thorough, up-to-date take on what's happening in gay and lesbian nightlife, pick up copies of *HX* (www.hx.com), *Gay City News* (www.gaycitynews.com), the *New York Blade* (www.nyblade.com), *GONYC* (www.gomag.com) or *Next.* They're available for free in bars and clubs all around town or at the **Lesbian and Gay Community Center**, at 208 W. 13th St., between Seventh and Eighth avenues (☏ 212/ 620-7310; www.gaycenter.org). *Time Out New York* boasts a terrific gay and lesbian section for events, meetings and parties; another great source is the free weekly *Village Voice.* Or try **Metro Source NY** (www.metrosource.com) a bi-monthly magazine which features an extensive entertainment section. Always remember that asking people in one bar can lead you to discover another that fits your tastes.

These days, many bars, clubs, cabarets, and cocktail lounges are neither gay nor straight but a bit of both, either catering to a mixed crowd or to varying orientations on different nights. In addition to the choices below, most of the clubs listed in "Dance Clubs & Party Scenes," above, cater to a gay crowd, some predominantly so.

Barracuda   Chelsea is central to gay life—and gay bars. This trendy, loungey place is a continuing favorite, regularly voted "Best Bar" by *HX* readers, while *Paper* singles out the hunky bartenders. There's a sexy bar for cruising out front and a comfy lounge in back. Look for the regular drag shows. 275 W. 22nd St. (btwn Seventh and Eighth aves.). ☏ 212/645-8613. Subway: C, E, 1 to 23rd St.

Boiler Room   This down-to-earth East Village bar is everybody's favorite gay dive. Despite the mixed guy-girl crowd, it's a serious cruising scene for well-sculpted beautiful boys and a perfectly fine hangout for those who'd rather play pool. 86 E. 4th St. (btwn First and Second aves.). ☏ 212/254-7536. Subway: F to Second Ave.

Brandy's Piano Bar   Though gay, this intimate, old-school piano bar attracts a mixed crowd for the friendly atmosphere and nightly entertainment. The talented

Cattyshack is a little ol' place where we can get together...

Head over to Park Slope (aka "Dyke Slope") NYC's favorite lesbian bar, **Cattyshack** ⓕ (249 Fourth Ave., between Carroll and President sts.; ℭ **718/230-5740**; www.cattyshackbklyn.com; Subway: R to Union St.; F to Fourth Ave./9th St.).

Brooke Webster, proprietor of the late, legendary Meow Mix, which succumbed to the rising rents and gentrification of the Lower East Side, took her party across the Manhattan Bridge to a much larger space that has quickly become a favorite hangout for NYC lesbians and their friends. The two-level club offers several kinds of ambience, ranging from casual pool playing, beer sipping, TV watching downstairs to upstairs dance parties where DJs play all genres of music, frequently featuring go-go girls.

Theme nights are popular, with regularly scheduled trivia contests, country nights, Guitar Hero competitions, and (of course) *The L Word* viewing parties and events.

On Sunday there's all-you-can-eat pizza and beer during football season (and after). And in good weather, everyone heads for the back patio, where a weekly barbecue/beer bust (with vegetarian selections!) draws crowds all summer long.

waitstaff does most of the singing while waiting for their big break, but enthusiastic patrons regularly join in. 235 E. 84th St. (btwn Second and Third aves.). ℭ **212/744-4949**. www.brandysnyc.com. Subway: 4, 5, 6 to 86th St.

The Cubby Hole   They call it a fusion bar, but chicks know it as a longtime lesbian hangout/watering hole. It's small, but rather than detract from its appeal, it's size only adds to it. In some cases intimacy breeds rancor, but not so the Cubby Hole where the faces always seem to be smiling. They must be doing something right. Look for drink specials every night, from Bloody Marys to Pomegranate Martinis. 281 W. 12th St (at W. 4th St) ℭ **212/243-9041**. www.cubbyholebar.com. Subway: A, C, E, L to 14th St.

Duplex Cabaret   The heart of the gay cabaret and piano-bar scene. Expect a high camp factor and lots of good-natured fun that runs the gamut from minimusicals to drag revues to stand-up comedy. 61 Christopher St. (at Seventh Ave.). ℭ **212/255-5438**. www.theduplex.com. Subway: 1 to Christopher St.

G Bar   Open daily until 4am, G Bar, (G is for gorgeous, what else?) in the heart of Chelsea, was one of the first gay lounges when it opened in 1997. There have been many since, but G Bar remains one of the best. On Sundays, there's DJ Xavier spinning, while DJ Jimmy brings his soul collection to the G on Wednesdays. And every night, no matter who is spinning, you can sip a perfectly made Cosmo. 225 W. 19th St (btwn 7th and 8th aves.). ℭ **212/929-1085**. www.glounge.com. Subway: 1 to 18th St.

The Gym   New York's best (only?) gay sports bar. With nine flatscreen televisions, a pool table, video games and other jock paraphernalia, the Gym could pass for any Upper East Side sports bar. But this one is in Chelsea and a comfortable, unpretentious place to watch a game, shoot some pool, and down a few shots of Energy Bombs.

167 8th Ave., (btwn 18th and 19th sts.). ℂ 212/337-2439. www.gymsportsbar.com. Subway: A, C, E, L to 14th St.

Henrietta Hudson This friendly and popular women's bar/lounge is known for drawing in an attractive, upmarket lipstick lesbian crowd that comes for the great jukebox and videos as well as the pleasingly low-key atmosphere. There's a $5-to-$7 cover when DJs spin tunes on Friday and Saturday and when live bands are in the house on Sunday. 438–444 Hudson St. (at Morton St.). ℂ 212/924-3347. www.henriettahudsons. com. Subway: 1 to Houston St.

Splash/SBNY Beautiful bartenders, video screens playing campy scenes, New York's best drag queens—Splash has it all. Theme nights are a big deal. The best is Musical Mondays, dedicated to Broadway video clips and music. Musical Mondays' singalongs are such a blast that they draw a crossover gay/straight crowd as well as such Broadway faves as Nathan Lane and the cast of *Mamma Mia!* 50 W. 17th St. (btwn Fifth and Sixth aves.). ℂ 212/691-0073. www.splashbar.com. Subway: F, V to 14th St.; 4, 5, 6, L, N, Q, R, W to 14th St./Union Sq.

Stonewall Bar The spot where it all started. A mixed gay and lesbian crowd—old and young, beautiful, and great personalities—makes this an easy place to begin. At least pop in to relive a defining moment in queer history. 53 Christopher St. (east of Seventh Ave.). ℂ 212/463-0950. Subway: 1 to Christopher St.

View Bar *(Finds* Up front is a very attractive and comfortable lounge, in back is a pool room with the name-worthy view, and throughout you'll find friendly bartenders, affordable drinks, and Kenneth Cole–dressed boys who could pass on either side of bi. A welcome addition to the scene. 232 Eighth Ave. (btwn 21st and 22nd sts.). ℂ 212/929-2243. Subway: C, E to 23rd St.

Appendix: Fast Facts, Toll-Free Numbers & Websites

AMERICAN EXPRESS Travel-service offices are at many Manhattan locations, including 295 Park Avenue South at 23rd Street (℃ **212/691-9797**); at the New York Marriott Marquis, 1535 Broadway, in the eighth-floor lobby (℃ **212/575-6580**); on the mezzanine level at Macy's Herald Square, 34th Street and Broadway (℃ **212/695-8075**); and 374 Park Ave., at 53rd Street (℃ **212/421-8240**). Call ℃ **800/AXP-TRIP,** or check **www.americanexpress.com** for other locations or general information.

AREA CODES There are four area codes in the city: two in Manhattan, the original **212** and the new **646;** and two in the outer boroughs, the original **718** and the new **347.** Also common is the **917** area code, which is assigned to cellphones, pagers, and the like. All calls between these area codes are local calls, but you'll have to dial 1 + the area code + the seven digits for all calls, even ones made within your area code.

ATM NETWORKS/CASHPOINTS See "Money & Costs," p. 56.

BUSINESS HOURS In general, **retail stores** are open Monday through Saturday from 10am to 6 or 7pm, Thursday from 10am to 8:30 or 9pm, and Sunday from noon to 5pm (see chapter 8). **Banks** tend to be open Monday through Friday from 9am to 5pm, with many open Saturday mornings, and some now even open on Sundays.

CAR RENTALS See "Toll-Free Numbers & Websites," p. 394.

DOCTORS For medical emergencies requiring immediate attention, head to the nearest emergency room (see "Hospitals," below). For less urgent health problems, New York has several walk-in medical centers, such as **DOCS at New York Healthcare,** 55 E. 34th St., between Park and Madison avenues (℃ **212/252-6001**), for non-emergency illnesses, and 202 W. 23rd, at Seventh Avenue ℃ **212/352-2600.** The clinic, affiliated with Beth Israel Medical Center, is open Monday through Friday from 8am to 7pm, Saturday from 9am to 1pm, and Sunday from 9am to 1pm. The **NYU Downtown Hospital** offers physician referrals at ℃ **212/312-5800.**

DRINKING LAWS The minimum legal age to purchase and consume alcoholic beverages in New York is 21. Liquor and wine are sold only in licensed stores, which are open 6 days a week, with some choosing to close on Sunday, others on an early or midweek day. (You can usually find an open liquor store on Sundays). Liquor stores are closed on holidays and election days while the polls are open. Beer can be purchased in grocery stores and delis 24 hours a day, except Sunday before noon. Last call in bars is at 4am, though many close earlier.

ELECTRICITY Like Canada, the United States uses 110 to 120 volts AC (60 cycles), compared to 220 to 240 volts AC (50 cycles) in most of Europe, Australia, and New Zealand. Downward converters that change 220 to 240 volts to 110 to

120 volts are difficult to find in the United States, so bring one with you if you are coming from overseas.

EMBASSIES & CONSULATES All embassies are in Washington, D.C. Some consulates are in New York and most nations have a mission to the United Nations. If your country isn't listed, call for directory information in Washington, D.C. (© **202/555-1212**) or log on to **www.embassy.org/embassies**.

The embassy of **Australia** is at 1601 Massachusetts Ave. NW, Washington, DC 20036 (© **202/797-3000;** www. austemb.org). There is a consulate in New York City.

The embassy of **Canada** is at 501 Pennsylvania Ave. NW, Washington, DC 20001 (© **202/682-1740;** www.canadian embassy.org). There is a consulate in New York City.

The embassy of **Ireland** is at 2234 Massachusetts Ave. NW, Washington, DC 20008 (© **202/462-3939;** www.ireland emb.org). Consulates are in Boston, Chicago, New York, and San Francisco. See website for complete listing.

The embassy of the **United Kingdom** is at 3100 Massachusetts Ave. NW, Washington, DC 20008 (© **202/588-6500;** www.britainusa.com). There is a consulate in New York City.

EMERGENCIES Dial © **911** for fire, police, and ambulance. The **Poison Control Center** can be reached at © **800/222-1222** toll-free from any phone.

HOLIDAYS Banks, government offices, post offices, and many stores, restaurants, and museums are closed on the following legal national holidays: January 1 (New Year's Day), the third Monday in January (Martin Luther King, Jr., Day), the third Monday in February (Presidents' Day), the last Monday in May (Memorial Day), July 4 (Independence Day), the first Monday in September (Labor Day), the second Monday in October (Columbus Day), November 11 (Veterans' Day/Armistice Day), the fourth Thursday in November (Thanksgiving Day), and December 25 (Christmas). The Tuesday after the first Monday in November is Election Day, a federal government holiday in presidential-election years (held every 4 years, and next in 2008).

For more information on holidays see "New York City Calendar of Events," in chapter 3.

HOSPITALS The following hospitals have 24-hour emergency rooms. Don't forget your insurance card.

Downtown: New York University Downtown Hospital, 170 William St., between Beekman and Spruce streets (© 212/312-5063 or 212/312-5000); **St. Vincent's Hospital and Medical Center,** 153 W. 11th St., at Seventh Avenue (© 212/604-7000); and **Beth Israel Medical Center,** First Avenue and 16th Street (© 212/420-2000).

Midtown: Bellevue Hospital Center, 462 First Ave., at 27th Street (© 212/562-4141; **New York University Medical Center,** 550 First Ave., at 33rd Street (© 212/263-7300); and **St. Luke's/Roosevelt Hospital,** 425 W. 59th St., between Ninth and Tenth avenues (© 212/523-4000).

Upper West Side: St. Luke's Hospital Center, 1111 Amsterdam Avenue at 114th Street (© 212/523-4000); and **Columbia Presbyterian Medical Center,** 622 W. 168th St., between Broadway and Fort Washington Avenue (© 212/305-2500).

Upper East Side: New York Presbyterian Hospital, 525 E. 68th St., at York Avenue (© 212/472-5454); **Lenox Hill Hospital,** 100 E. 77th St., between Park and Lexington avenues (© 212/434-2000); and **Mount Sinai Medical Center,** 1190 Fifth Avenue at 100th Street (© 212/241-6500).

HOT LINES Department of Consumer Affairs ℂ 212/487-4444; and **taxi complaints** at ℂ 212/NYC-TAXI. If you suspect your car may have been towed, call the **Department of Transportation TOWAWAY Help Line** at ℂ 311. You can also call 311 for any non-emergency city matters or questions pertaining to New York City.

INSURANCE Medical Insurance Although it's not required of travelers, health insurance is highly recommended. Most health insurance policies cover you if you get sick away from home—but check your coverage before you leave.

International visitors to the U.S. should note that unlike many European countries, the United States does not usually offer free or low-cost medical care to its citizens or visitors. Doctors and hospitals are expensive, and in most cases will require advance payment or proof of coverage before they render their services. Good policies will cover the costs of an accident, repatriation, or death. Packages such as **Europ Assistance's "Worldwide Healthcare Plan"** are sold by European automobile clubs and travel agencies at attractive rates. **Worldwide Assistance Services, Inc.** (ℂ 800/777-8710; www.worldwideassistance.com) is the agent for Europ Assistance in the United States. Though lack of health insurance may prevent you from being admitted to a hospital in non-emergencies, don't worry about being left on a street corner to die: The American way is to fix you now and bill you later.

If you're ever hospitalized more than 150 miles from home, **MedjetAssist** (ℂ 800/527-7478; www.medjetassistance.com) will pick you up and fly you to the hospital of your choice in a medically equipped and staffed aircraft 24 hours day, 7 days a week. Annual memberships are $225 individual, $350 family; you can also purchase short-term memberships.

Canadians should check with their provincial health plan offices or call **Health Canada** (ℂ 866/225-0709; www.hc-sc.gc.ca) to find out the extent of their coverage and what documentation and receipts they must take home in case they are treated in the United States.

Travelers from the U.K. should carry their **European Health Insurance Card** (EHIC), which replaced the E111 form as proof of entitlement to free/reduced cost medical treatment abroad (ℂ 0845/606-2030; www.ehic.org.uk). Note, however, that the EHIC only covers "necessary medical treatment," and for repatriation costs, lost money, baggage, or cancellation, travel insurance from a reputable company should always be sought (www.travelinsuranceweb.com).

TRAVEL INSURANCE The cost of travel insurance varies widely, depending on the destination, the cost and length of your trip, your age and health, and the type of trip you're taking, but expect to pay between 5% and 8% of the vacation itself. You can get estimates from various providers through **InsureMyTrip.com**. Enter your trip cost and dates, your age, and other information, for prices from more than a dozen companies.

U.K. citizens and their families who make more than one trip abroad per year may find an annual travel insurance policy works out cheaper. Check **www.money supermarket.com**, which compares prices from providers for single- and multitrip policies.

Most big travel agencies offer their own insurance and will probably try to sell you their package when you book a holiday. Think before you sign. **Britain's Consumers' Association** recommends that you insist on seeing the policy and reading the fine print before buying travel insurance. **The Association of British Insurers** (ℂ 020/7600-3333; www.abi.org.uk) gives advice by phone and publishes Holiday Insurance, a free guide to policy provisions and prices. You might also shop around for better deals: Try **Columbus Direct** (© **0870/033-9988;** www.columbusdirect.net).

TRIP CANCELLATION INSURANCE

Trip-cancellation insurance will help retrieve your money if you have to back out of a trip or depart early, or if your travel supplier goes bankrupt. Trip cancellation traditionally covers such events as sickness, natural disasters, and Department of State advisories. The latest news in trip-cancellation insurance is the availability of **expanded hurricane coverage** and the **"any-reason"** cancellation coverage—which costs more but covers cancellations made for any reason. You won't get back 100% of your prepaid trip cost, but you'll be refunded a substantial portion. **Travel-Safe** (© **888/885-7233;** www.travelsafe.com) offers both types of coverage. Expedia also offers any-reason cancellation coverage for its air-hotel packages. For details, contact one of the following recommended insurers: **Access America**(© **866/807-3982;** www.accessamerica.com); **Travel Guard International** (© **800/826-4919;** www.travelguard.com); **Travel Insured International** (© **800/243-3174;** www.travelinsured.com); and **Travelex Insurance Services** (© **888/457-4602;** www.travelex-insurance.com).

INTERNET CENTERS
See the box "Where to Check Your E-Mail in the City that Never Sleeps," in chapter 3.

LEGAL AID
If you are "pulled over" for a minor infraction (such as speeding), or return to your car to find a parking violation, never attempt to pay the fine directly to a police officer; this could be construed as attempted bribery, a very serious crime. Pay fines by mail, or directly into the hands of the clerk of the court. If accused of a more serious offense, say and do nothing before consulting a lawyer. Here the burden is on the state to prove a person's guilt beyond a reasonable doubt, and everyone has the right to remain silent, whether he or she is suspected of a crime or actually arrested. Once arrested, a person can make one telephone call to a party of his or her choice. International visitors should call your embassy or consulate.

LIBRARIES
The **New York Public Library** is on Fifth Avenue at 42nd Street (© **212/930-0800**). This Beaux Arts beauty houses more than 38 million volumes, and the beautiful reading rooms have been restored to their former glory. More efficient and modern, if less charming, is the mid-Manhattan branch at 455 Fifth Ave., at 40th Street, across the street from the main library (© **212/340-0833**). There are other branches in almost every neighborhood; most provide public computer terminals and are equipped with Wi-Fi. You can find a list online at **www.nypl.org**.

LOST & FOUND
Be sure to tell all of your credit card companies the minute you discover your wallet has been lost or stolen and file a report at the nearest police precinct. Your credit card company or insurer may require a police report number or record of the loss. Most credit card companies have an emergency toll-free number to call if your card is lost or stolen; they may be able to wire you a cash advance immediately or deliver an emergency credit card in a day or two. Visa's U.S. emergency number is © **800/847-2911** or 410/581-9994. American Express cardholders and traveler's check holders should call © **800/221-7282.** MasterCard holders should call © **800/307-7309** or 636/722-7111. For other credit cards, call the toll-free number directory at © **800/555-1212.**

If you need emergency cash when banks and American Express offices are closed on weekends or holidays, you can have money wired to you via **Western Union** (© **800/325-6000;** www.westernunion.com).

MAIL   At press time, domestic postage rates were 27¢ for a postcard and 42¢ for a letter. For international mail, a first-class letter of up to 1 ounce costs from 72¢ (69¢ to Canada and Mexico), depending on size and destination; a first-class postcard costs the same as a letter. For more information go to **www.usps.com** and click on "Calculate Postage."

If you aren't sure what your address will be in the U.S., mail can be sent to you, in your name, c/o General Delivery at the main post office of the city or region where you expect to be. (Call ℭ **800/275-8777** for information on the nearest post office.) The addressee must pick up mail in person and must produce proof of identity (driver's license, passport, etc.). Most post offices will hold your mail for up to 1 month, and are open Monday to Friday from 8am to 6pm, and Saturday from 9am to 3pm.

Always include zip codes when mailing items in the U.S. If you don't know your zip code, visit www.usps.com/zip4.

MEDICAL CONDITIONS   If you have a medical condition that requires **syringe-administered medications,** carry a valid signed prescription from your physician; syringes in carry-on baggage will be inspected. Insulin in any form should have the proper pharmaceutical documentation. If you have a disease that requires treatment with **narcotics,** you should also carry documented proof with you—smuggling narcotics aboard a plane carries severe penalties in the U.S.

For **HIV-positive visitors,** requirements for entering the United States are somewhat vague and change frequently. For up-to-the-minute information, contact **AIDSinfo** (ℭ **800/448-0440** or 301/519-6616 outside the U.S.; www.aidsinfo.nih.gov) or the **Gay Men's Health Crisis** (ℭ **212/367-1000;** www.gmhc.org).

NEWSPAPERS & MAGAZINES   There are three major daily newspapers: the *New York Times,* the *Daily News,* and the *New York Post.* There are also two free daily papers, *AM-New York* and *Metro,* usually distributed in the morning near subway stations and in self-serve boxes around town.

If you want to find your hometown paper, visit **Universal News & Magazines,** at 234 W. 42nd St., between Seventh and Eighth avenues (ℭ **212/221-1809**), and 977 Eighth Ave., between 57th and 58th streets (ℭ **212/459-0932**); or **Hotalings News Agency,** 624 W. 52nd St., between Eleventh and Twelfth avenues (ℭ 212/974-9419). Other good bets include the **Hudson** news dealers, located in Grand Central Terminal, at 42nd Street and Lexington Avenue, and Penn Station, at 34th Street and Seventh Avenue.

PASSPORTS   The websites listed provide downloadable passport applications as well as the current fees for processing applications. For an up-to-date, country-by-country listing of passport requirements around the world, go to the "International Travel" tab of the U.S. Department of State at **http://travel.state.gov**.

International visitors to the U.S. can obtain a visa application at the same website. *Note:* Children are required to present a passport when entering the United States at airports. More information on obtaining a passport for a minor can be found at **http://travel.state.gov**. Allow plenty of time before your trip to apply for a passport; processing normally takes 4 to 6 weeks (3 weeks for expedited service) but can take longer during busy periods (especially spring). And keep in mind that if you need a passport in a hurry, you'll pay a higher processing fee.

For Residents of Australia   You can pick up an application from your local post office or any branch of Passports Australia, but you must schedule an interview at the passport office to present your application materials. Call the **Australian Passport**

Information Service at ✆ **131-232,** or visit the government website at **www.passports.gov.au.**

For Residents of Canada Passport applications are available at travel agencies throughout Canada or from the central **Passport Office,** Department of Foreign Affairs and International Trade, Ottawa, ON K1A 0G3 (✆ **800/567-6868;** www.ppt.gc.ca). *Note:* Canadian children who travel must have their own passport. However, if you hold a valid Canadian passport issued before December 11, 2001, that bears the name of your child, the passport remains valid for you and your child until it expires.

For Residents of Ireland You can apply for a 10-year passport at the **Passport Office,** Setanta Centre, Molesworth Street, Dublin 2 (✆ **01/671-1633;** www.irlgov.ie/iveagh). Those under age 18 and over 65 must apply for a 3-year passport. You can also apply at 1A South Mall, Cork (✆ **21/494-4700**), or at most post offices.

For Residents of New Zealand You can pick up a passport application at any New Zealand Passports Office or download it from their website. Contact the **Passports Office** at ✆ **0800/225-050** in New Zealand or 04/474-8100, or log on to **www.passports.govt.nz.**

For Residents of the United Kingdom To pick up an application for a standard 10-year passport (5-yr. passport for children under 16), visit your nearest passport office, major post office, or travel agency or contact the **United Kingdom Passport Service** at ✆ **0870/521-0410,** or search its website at **www.ukpa.gov.uk.**

PHARMACIES There are a number of 24-hour pharmacies in Manhattan. Downtown, try **Walgreen's** at 145 Fourth Avenue (at 14th Street), ✆ **212/677-0054.** Midtown on the East Side, head for **CVS** at 630 Lexington Ave. (at 53rd St.), ✆ **917/369-8688.** Midtown on the

West Side, try **Duane Reade,** 224 W. 57th St. at Broadway, ✆ **212/541-9708. Duane Reade** has a 24-hour pharmacy on the Upper East Side at 1279 Third Ave. (at 74th St.) (✆ **212/744-2668**). On the Upper West Side there's another 24-hour pharmacy at the **Duane Reade,** 2522 Broadway (at 94th St.) ✆ **212/663-1580.**

POLICE Dial ✆ **911** in an emergency; otherwise, call ✆ **646/610-5000** or 718/610-5000 (NYPD headquarters) for the number of the nearest precinct. For non-emergency matters, call ✆ **311.**

SMOKING Smoking is prohibited on all public transportation, in the lobbies of hotels and office buildings, in taxis, bars, restaurants, and in most shops.

TAXES **Sales tax** is 8.375% on meals, most goods, and some services, but it is not charged on clothing and footwear items under $110. **Hotel tax** is 13.25% plus $2 per room per night (including sales tax). **Parking garage tax** is 18.375%.

The United States has no value-added tax (VAT) or other indirect tax at the national level. Every state, county, and city may levy its own local tax on all purchases, including hotel and restaurant checks and airline tickets. These taxes will not appear on price tags.

TIME For the correct local time, dial ✆ **212/976-1616.** New York City is on Eastern Time (GMT -5 hours).

Daylight saving time is in effect from 1am on the second Sunday in March to 1am on the first Sunday in November. Daylight saving time moves the clock 1 hour ahead of standard time.

TIPPING Tips are a very important part of certain workers' income, and gratuities are the standard way of showing appreciation for services provided. (Tipping is not compulsory if the service is poor!) In hotels, tip **bellhops** at least $1 per bag ($2–$3 if you have a lot of luggage) and tip the **chamber staff** $1 to $2 per day (more if you've left a disaster area to clean up). Tip the **doorman** or **concierge** only if he or she has provided you with some specific service (for example, calling a cab for you or obtaining difficult-to-get theater tickets). In restaurants, bars, and nightclubs, tip **service staff** 15% to 20% of the check, tip **bartenders** 10% to 15%, tip **checkroom attendants** $1 per garment, and tip **valet-parking attendants** $1 per vehicle.

As for other service personnel, tip **cab drivers** 15% of the fare; tip **skycaps** at airports at least $1 per bag ($2–$3 if you have a lot of luggage); and tip **hairdressers** and **barbers** 15% to 20%.

TOILETS You won't find public toilets or restrooms on the streets in New York City, but they can be found in hotel lobbies, bars, restaurants, museums, department stores, railway and bus stations. Large hotels and fast-food restaurants are often the best bet for clean facilities.

Public restrooms are available at the visitor centers in Midtown (1560 Broadway, between 46th and 47th sts.; and 810 Seventh Ave., between 52nd and 53rd sts.). Grand Central Terminal, at 42nd Street between Park and Lexington avenues, also has clean restrooms. There are staffed bathrooms open from early in the morning until fairly late at night in the Times Square subway station (closer to 7th Ave.) Your best bet on the street is Starbucks or another city java chain—you can't walk more than a few blocks without seeing one. The big chain bookstores are good for this, too. You can also head to hotel lobbies (especially the big Midtown ones) and department stores such as Macy's and Bloomingdale's. On the Lower East Side, stop into the Lower East Side BID Visitor Center, 261 Broome St., between Orchard and Allen streets (daily 10am–4pm, sometimes later).

TRANSIT INFORMATION For information on getting to and from the airport, see "Getting There," in chapter 3, or call **Air-Ride** at © **800/247-7433.** For information on subways and buses, call the **MTA** at © **718/330-1234;** go online to **www.mta.info**, or see "Getting Around," in chapter 3.

TRAVELER'S ASSISTANCE Travelers Aid (www.travelersaid.org) helps distressed travelers with all kinds of problems, including accidents, sickness, and lost or stolen luggage. There is an office on the first floor of Terminal 6 (JetBlue terminal) at JFK Airport (© **718/656-4870**), and one in Newark Airport's Terminal B (© **973/623-5052**).

VISAS For information about U.S. Visas go to **http://travel.state.gov** and click on "Visas." Or go to one of the following websites:

Australian citizens can obtain up-to-date visa information from the **U.S. Embassy Canberra,** Moonah Place, Yarralumla, ACT 2600 (© **02/6214-5600**) or by checking the U.S. Diplomatic Mission's website at **http://usembassyaustralia.state.gov/consular**.

British subjects can obtain up-to-date visa information by calling the **U.S. Embassy Visa Information Line** (© **0891/200-290**) or by visiting the "Visas to the U.S." section of the American Embassy London's website at **www.usembassy.org.uk**.

Irish citizens can obtain up-to-date visa information through the **Embassy of the USA Dublin,** 42 Elgin Rd., Dublin 4, Ireland (© **353/1-668-8777;** or by checking the "Consular Services" section of the website at **http://dublin.usembassy.gov**.

Citizens of **New Zealand** can obtain up-to-date visa information by contacting the **U.S. Embassy New Zealand,** 29 Fitzherbert Terrace, Thorndon, Wellington (© **644/472-2068**), or get the information directly from the website at **http://wellington.usembassy.gov**.

2 Toll-Free Numbers & Websites

MAJOR U.S. AIRLINES
(*flies internationally as well)

Alaska Airlines/ Horizon Air
© 800/252-7522
www.alaskaair.com

American Airlines*
© 800/433-7300 (in U.S. or Canada)
© 020/7365-0777 (in U.K.)
www.aa.com

Continental Airlines*
© 800/523-3273 (in U.S. or Canada)
© 084/5607-6760 (in U.K.)
www.continental.com

Delta Air Lines*
© 800/221-1212 (in U.S. or Canada)
© 084/5600-0950 (in U.K.)
www.delta.com

Frontier Airlines
© 800/432-1359
www.frontierairlines.com

JetBlue Airways
© 800/538-2583 (in U.S.)
© 080/1365-2525 (in U.K. or Canada)
www.jetblue.com

Midwest Airlines
© 800/452-2022
www.midwestairlines.com

North American Airlines*
© 800/371-6297
www.flynaa.com

Northwest Airlines
© 800/225-2525 (in U.S.)
© 870/0507-4074 (in U.K.)
www.flynaa.com

United Airlines*
© 800/864-8331 (in U.S. and Canada)
© 084/5844-4777 in U.K.
www.united.com

US Airways*
© 800/428-4322 (in U.S. and Canada)
© 084/5600-3300 (in U.K.)
www.usairways.com

Virgin America*
© 877/359-8474
www.virginamerica.com

MAJOR INTERNATIONAL AIRLINES

Aeroméxico
© 800/237-6639 (in U.S.)
© 020/7801-6234 (in U.K., information only)
www.aeromexico.com

Air France
© 800/237-2747 (in U.S.)
© 800/375-8723 (U.S. and Canada)
© 087/0142-4343 (in U.K.)
www.airfrance.com

Air India
© 212/407-1371 (in U.S.)
© 91-22/2279-6666 (in India)
© 020/8745-1000 (in U.K.)
www.airindia.com

Air Jamaica
© 800/523-5585 (in U.S. or Canada)
© 208/570-7999 (in Jamaica)
www.airjamaica.com

Air New Zealand
© 800/262-1234 (in U.S.)
© 800/663-5494 (in Canada)
© 0800/028-4149 (in U.K.)
www.airnewzealand.com

Air Tahiti Nui
© 877/824-4846 (in U.S. and Canada)
www.airtahitinui-usa.com

Alitalia
© 800/223-5730 (in U.S.)
© 800/361-8336 (in Canada)
© 087/0608-6003 (in U.K.)
www.alitalia.com

Bahamasair
✆ 800/222-4262 (in U.S.)
✆ 242/300-8359 (in Family Islands)
✆ 242/377-5505 (in Nassau)
www.bahamasair.com

British Airways
✆ 800/247-9297 (in U.S. and Canada)
✆ 087/0850-9850 (in U.K.)
www.british-airways.com

Aer Lingus
✆ 800/474-7424 (in U.S. & Canada)
✆ 087/0876-5000 (in U.K.)
www.aerlingus.com

Caribbean Airlines (formerly BWIA)
✆ 800/920-4225 (in U.S. and Canada)
✆ 084/5362 4225 (in U.K.)
www.caribbean-airlines.com

China Airlines
✆ 800/227-5118 (in U.S.)
✆ 022/715-1212 (in Taiwan)
www.china-airlines.com

EgyptAir
✆ 212/581-5600 (in U.S.)
✆ 020/7734-2343 (in U.K.)
✆ 09/007-0000 (in Egypt)
www.egyptair.com

El Al Airlines
✆ 972/3977-1111 (outside Israel)
✆ *2250 (from any phone in Israel)
www.el.co.il

Emirates Airlines
✆ 800/777-3999 (in U.S.)
✆ 087/0243-2222 (in U.K.)
www.emirates.com

Finnair
✆ 800/950-5000 (in U.S. and Canada)
✆ 087/0241-4411 (in U.K.)
www.finnair.com

Iberia Airlines
✆ 800/722-4642 (in U.S. and Canada)
✆ 087/0609-0500 (in U.K.)
www.iberia.com

Icelandair
✆ 800/223-5500 ext 2 prompt 1 (in U.S. and Canada)

✆ 084/5758-1111 (in U.K.)
www.icelandair.com
www.icelandair.co.uk (in U.K.)

Israir Airlines
✆ 877/477-2471 (in U.S. and Canada)
✆ 700/505-777 (in Israel)
www.israirairlines.com

Japan Airlines
✆ 012/025-5931 (international)
www.jal.co.jp

Korean Air
✆ 800/438-5000 (in U.S. and Canada)
✆ 0800/413-000 (in U.K.)
www.koreanair.com

Lan Airlines
✆ 866/435-9526 (in U.S.)
✆ 305/670-9999 (in other countries)
www.lanchile.com

Lufthansa
✆ 800/399-5838 (in U.S.)
✆ 800/563-5954 (in Canada)
✆ 087/0837-7747 (in U.K.)
www.lufthansa.com

Olympic Airlines
✆ 800/223-1226 (in U.S.)
✆ 514/878-9691 (in Canada)
✆ 087/0606-0460 (in U.K.)
www.olympicairlines.com

Quantas Airways
✆ 800/227-4500 (in U.S.)
✆ 084/5774-7767 (in U.K. or Canada)
✆ 13-13-13 (in Australia)
www.quantas.com

South African Airways
✆ 271/1978-5313 (international)
✆ 0861/FLYSAA (086/135-9122) (in South Africa)
www.flysaa.com

Swiss Air
✆ 877/359-7947 (in U.S. and Canada)
✆ 084/5601-0956 (in U.K.)
www.swiss.com

TACA
✆ 800/535-8780 (in U.S.)
✆ 800/722-TACA (8222) (in Canada)

© 087/0241-0340 (in U.K.)
© 503/2267-8222 (in El Salvador)
www.taca.com

Thai Airways International
© 212/949-8424 (in U.S.)
© 020/7491-7953 (in U.K.)
www.thaiair.com

Turkish Airlines
© 90 212 444 0 849
www.thy.com

Virgin Atlantic Airways
© 800/821-5438 (in U.S. and Canada)
© 087/0574-7747 (in U.K.)
www.virgin-atlantic.com

BUDGET AIRLINES

AirTran Airways
© 800/247-8726
www.airtran.com

Frontier Airlines
© 800/432-1359
www.frontierairlines.com

JetBlue Airways
© 800/538-2583 (in U.S.)
© 801/365-2525 (in U.K. or Canada)
www.jetblue.com

Southwest Airlines
© 800/435-9792 (in U.S., U.K. and Canada)
www.southwest.com

Spirit Airlines
© 800/772-7117
www.spiritair.com

WestJet
© 800/538-5696 (in U.S. and Canada)
www.westjet.com

Index

See also Accommodations and Restaurant indexes, below.

ACCOMMODATIONS